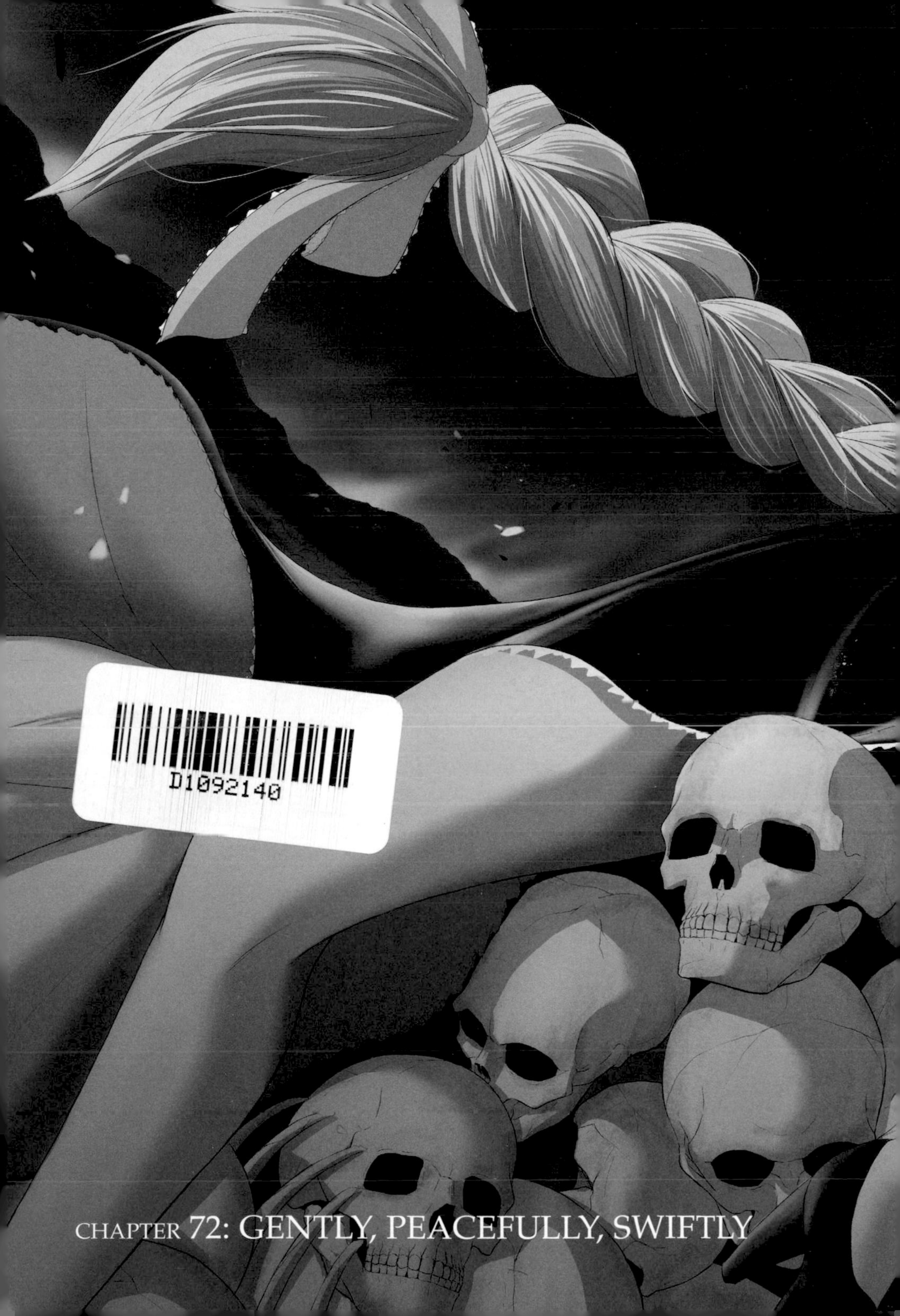

CHAPTER 72: GENTLY, PEACEFULLY, SWIFTLY

PLUNDERER 10

CONTENTS

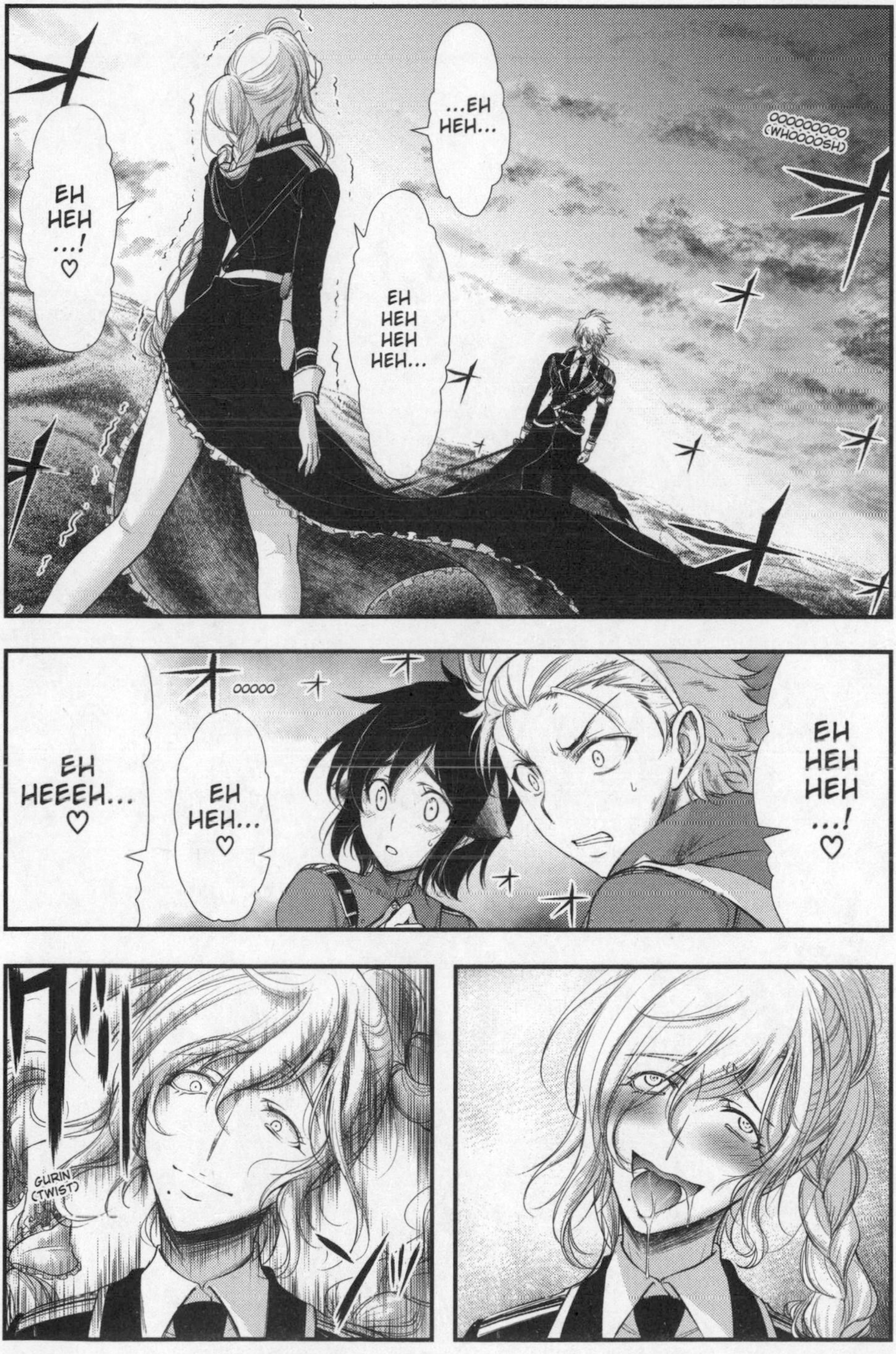
OOOOOOOOO (WHOOOOSH)
...EH HEH...
EH HEH HEH HEH...
EH HEH ...! ♡
EH HEH HEH ...! ♡
OOOOO
EH HEH... ♡
EH HEEEH... ♡
GURIN (TWIST)

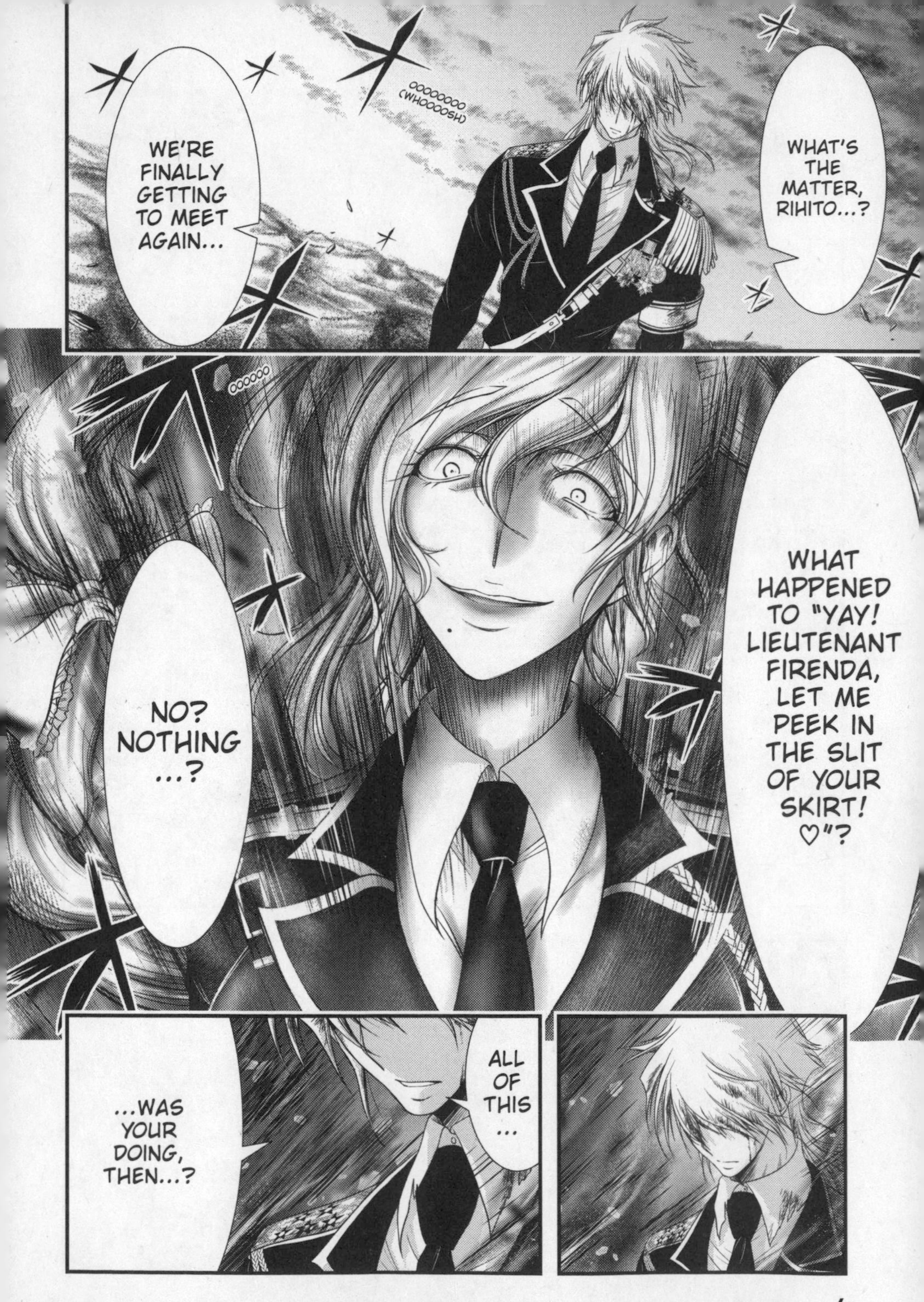
WHAT'S THE MATTER, RIHITO...?
OOOOOOOO (WHOOOOSH)
WE'RE FINALLY GETTING TO MEET AGAIN...
WHAT HAPPENED TO "YAY! LIEUTENANT FIRENDA, LET ME PEEK IN THE SLIT OF YOUR SKIRT! ♡"?
OOOOOO
NO? NOTHING ...?
ALL OF THIS ...
...WAS YOUR DOING, THEN...?

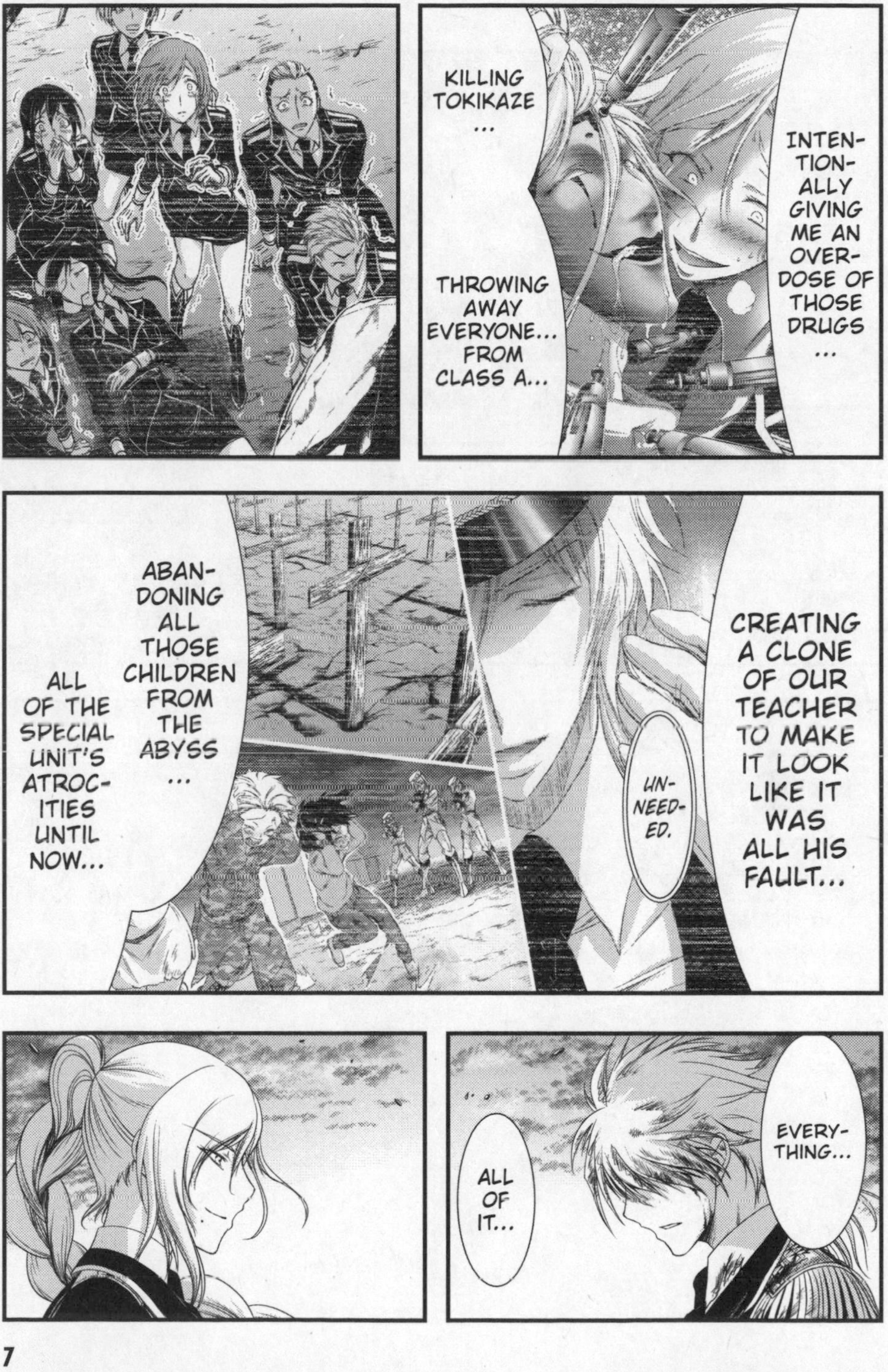
INTENTIONALLY GIVING ME AN OVERDOSE OF THOSE DRUGS...
KILLING TOKIKAZE...
THROWING AWAY EVERYONE... FROM CLASS A...
CREATING A CLONE OF OUR TEACHER TO MAKE IT LOOK LIKE IT WAS ALL HIS FAULT...
UNNEEDED.
ABANDONING ALL THOSE CHILDREN FROM THE ABYSS...
ALL OF THE SPECIAL UNIT'S ATROCITIES UNTIL NOW...
EVERYTHING...
ALL OF IT...
...

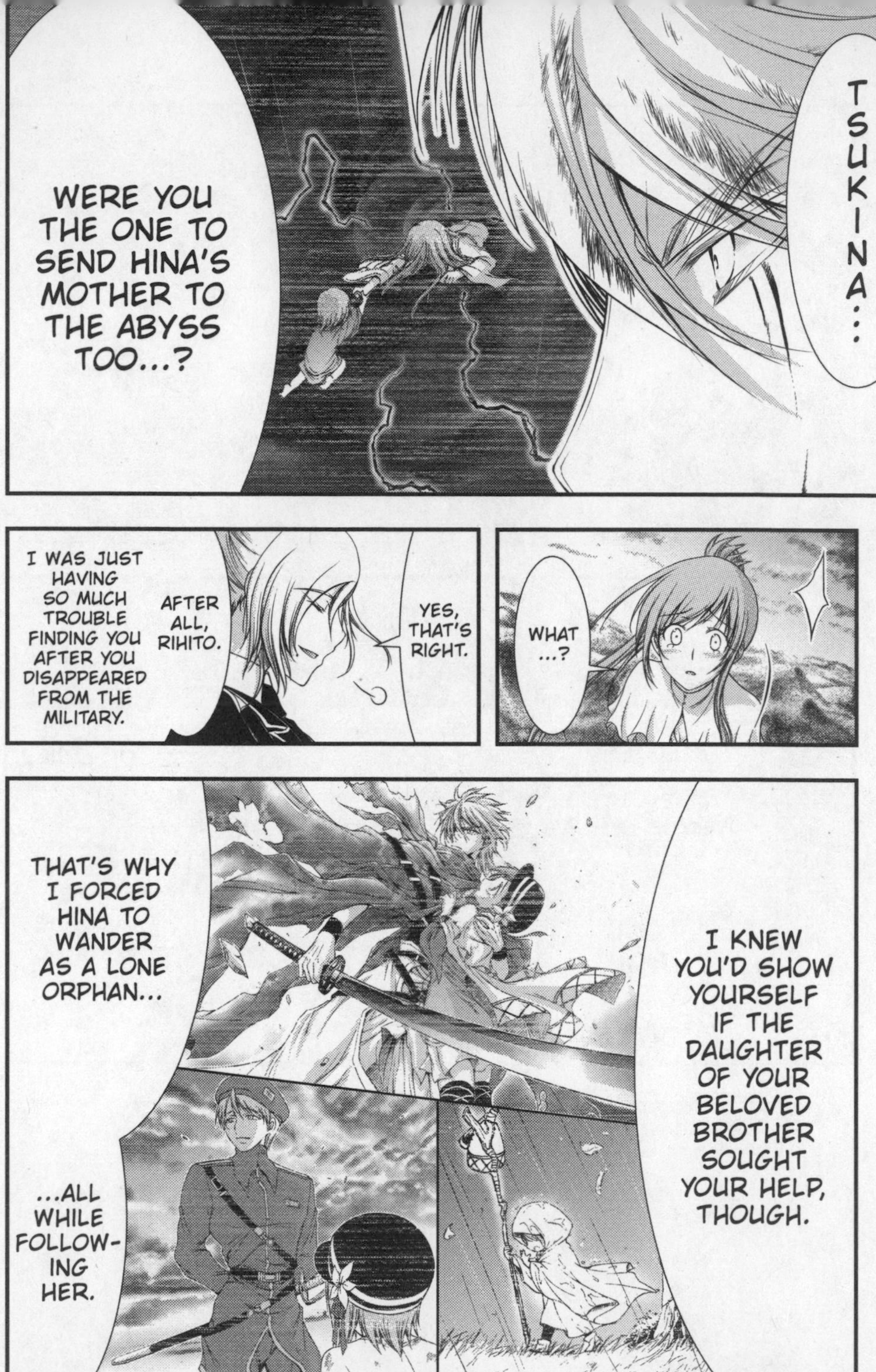
TSUKINA...
WERE YOU THE ONE TO SEND HINA'S MOTHER TO THE ABYSS TOO...?
WHAT ...?
YES, THAT'S RIGHT.
AFTER ALL, RIHITO.
I WAS JUST HAVING SO MUCH TROUBLE FINDING YOU AFTER YOU DISAPPEARED FROM THE MILITARY.
I KNEW YOU'D SHOW YOURSELF IF THE DAUGHTER OF YOUR BELOVED BROTHER SOUGHT YOUR HELP, THOUGH.
THAT'S WHY I FORCED HINA TO WANDER AS A LONE ORPHAN...
...ALL WHILE FOLLOWING-ING HER.

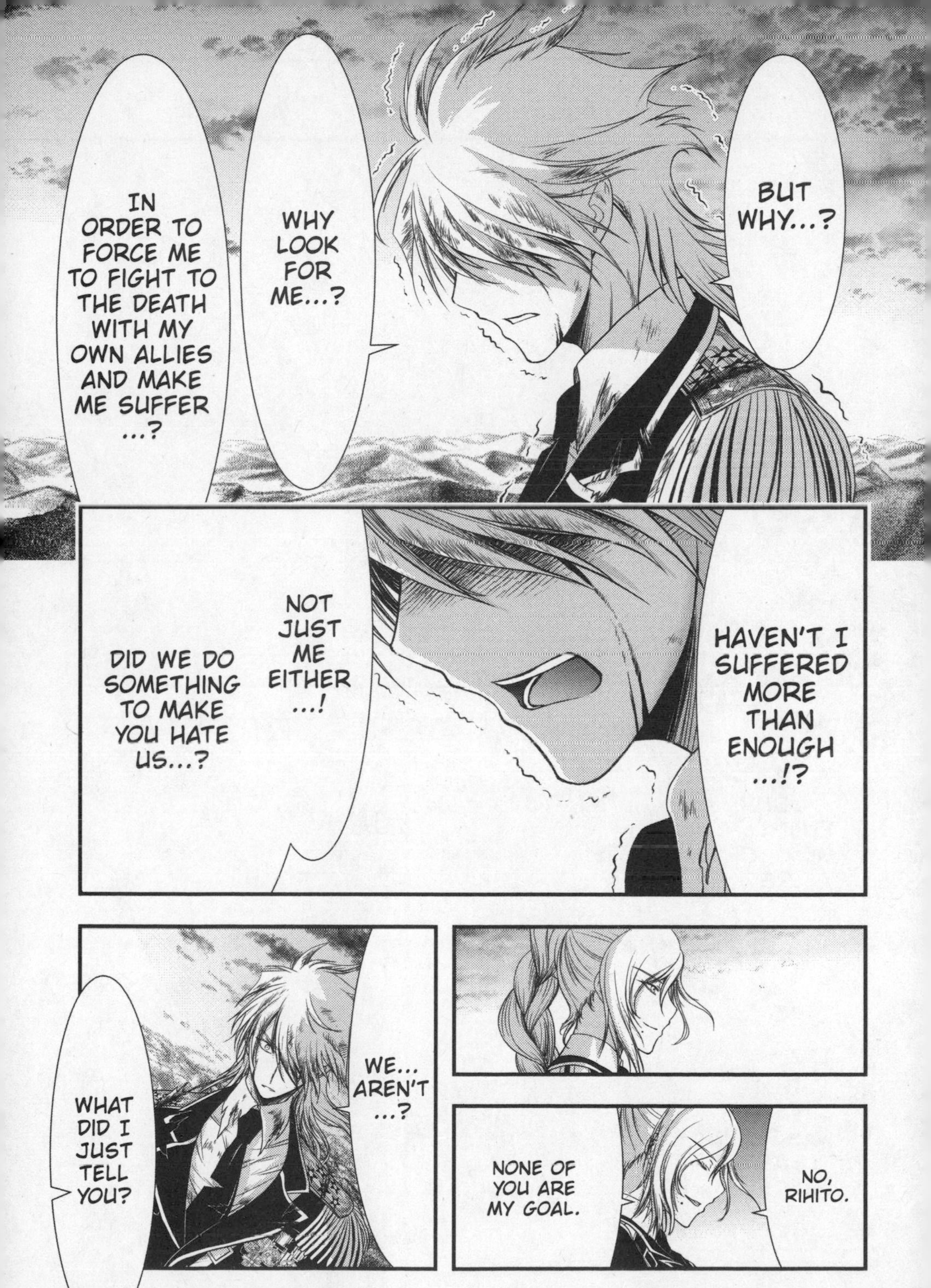
BUT WHY...?
WHY LOOK FOR ME...?
IN ORDER TO FORCE ME TO FIGHT TO THE DEATH WITH MY OWN ALLIES AND MAKE ME SUFFER ...?
HAVEN'T I SUFFERED MORE THAN ENOUGH ...!?
NOT JUST ME EITHER ...!
DID WE DO SOMETHING TO MAKE YOU HATE US...?
NO, RIHITO.
NONE OF YOU ARE MY GOAL.
WE... AREN'T ...?
WHAT DID I JUST TELL YOU?

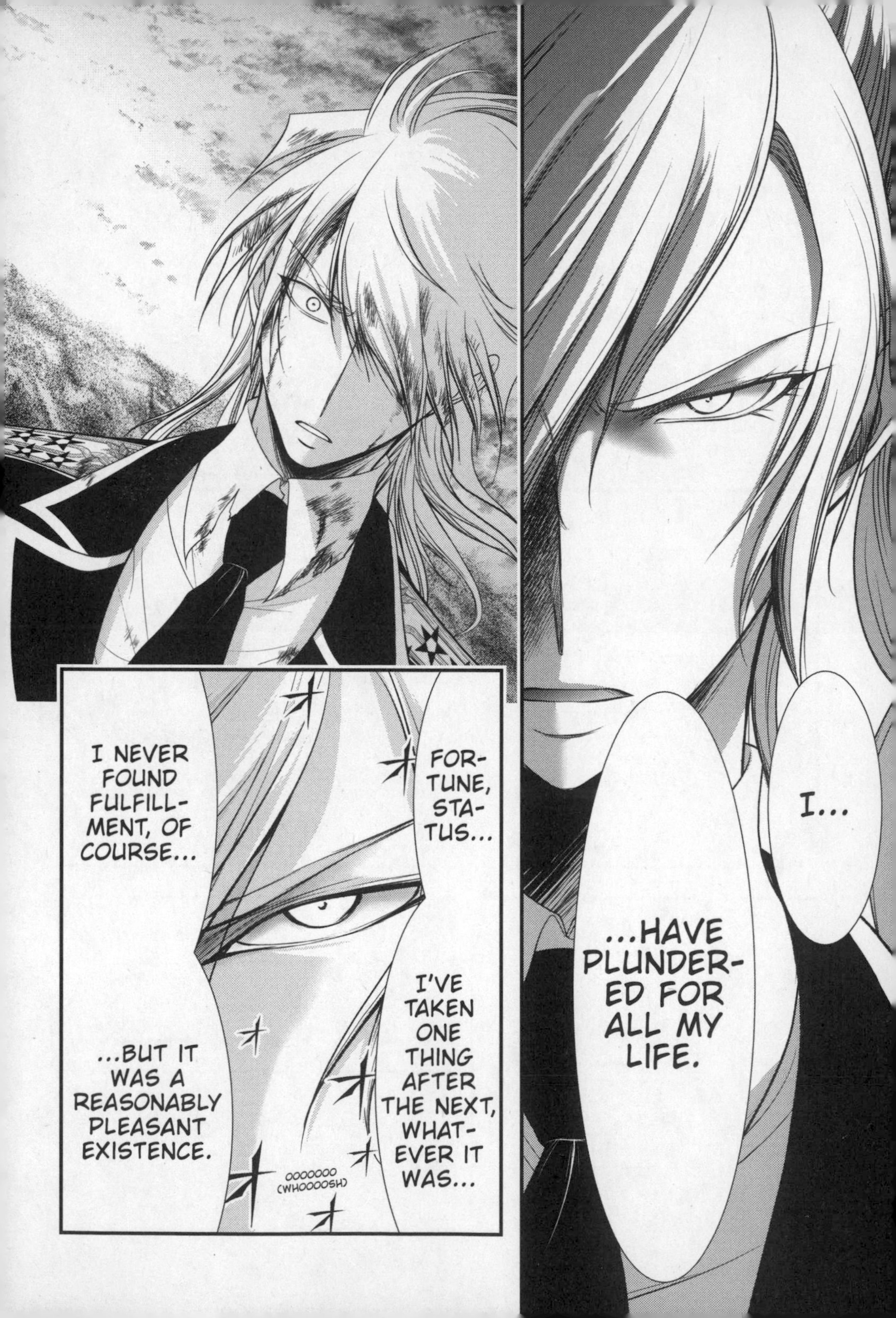
I...
...HAVE PLUNDERED FOR ALL MY LIFE.
FORTUNE, STATUS...
I NEVER FOUND FULFILLMENT, OF COURSE...
I'VE TAKEN ONE THING AFTER THE NEXT, WHATEVER IT WAS...
OOOOOOO (WHOOOOSH)
...BUT IT WAS A REASONABLY PLEASANT EXISTENCE.

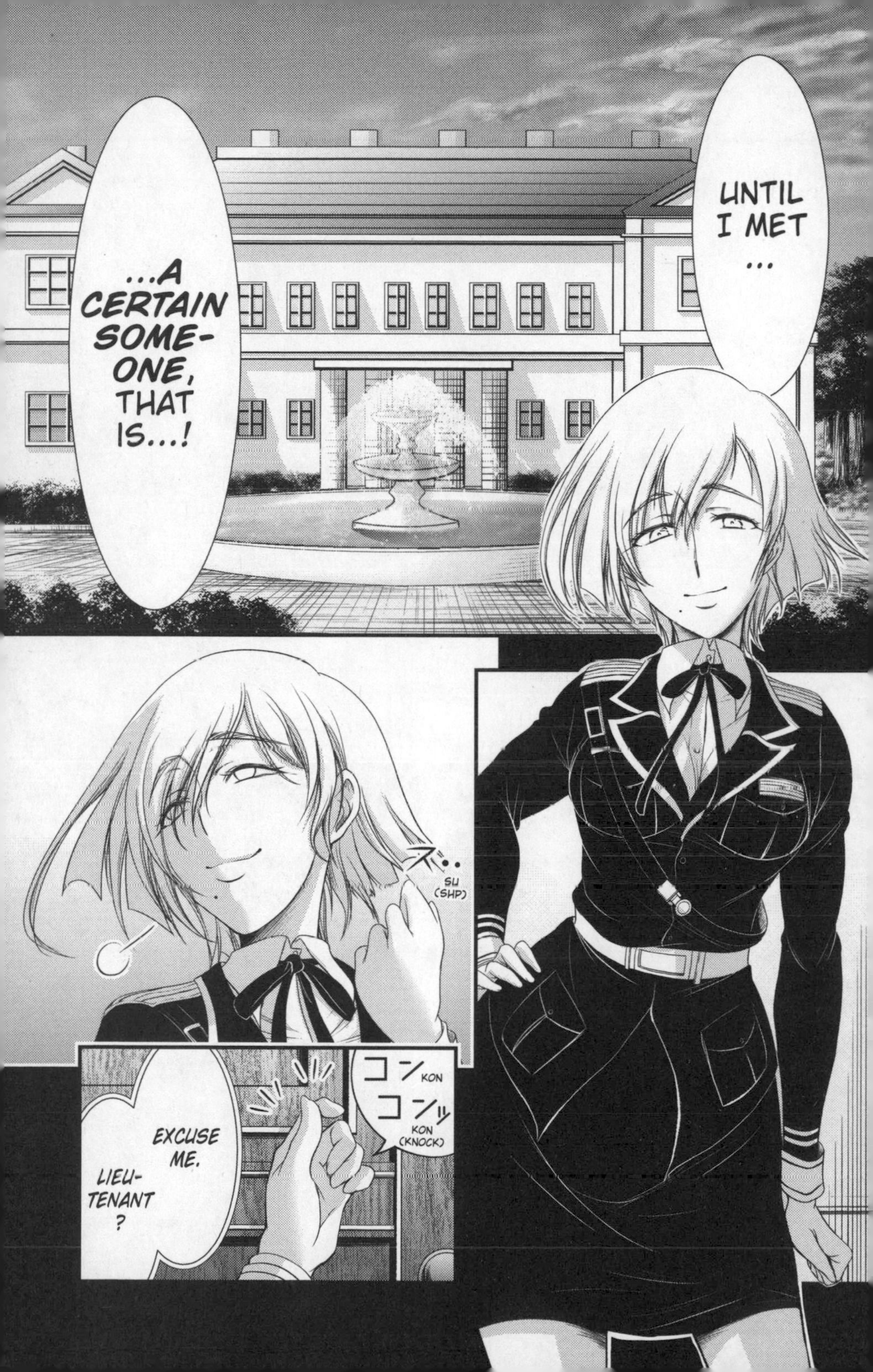
UNTIL I MET ...
...A CERTAIN SOME-ONE, THAT IS...!
ズ・・ SU (SHP)
コン KON
コンッ KON (KNOCK)
EXCUSE ME.
LIEU-TENANT ?

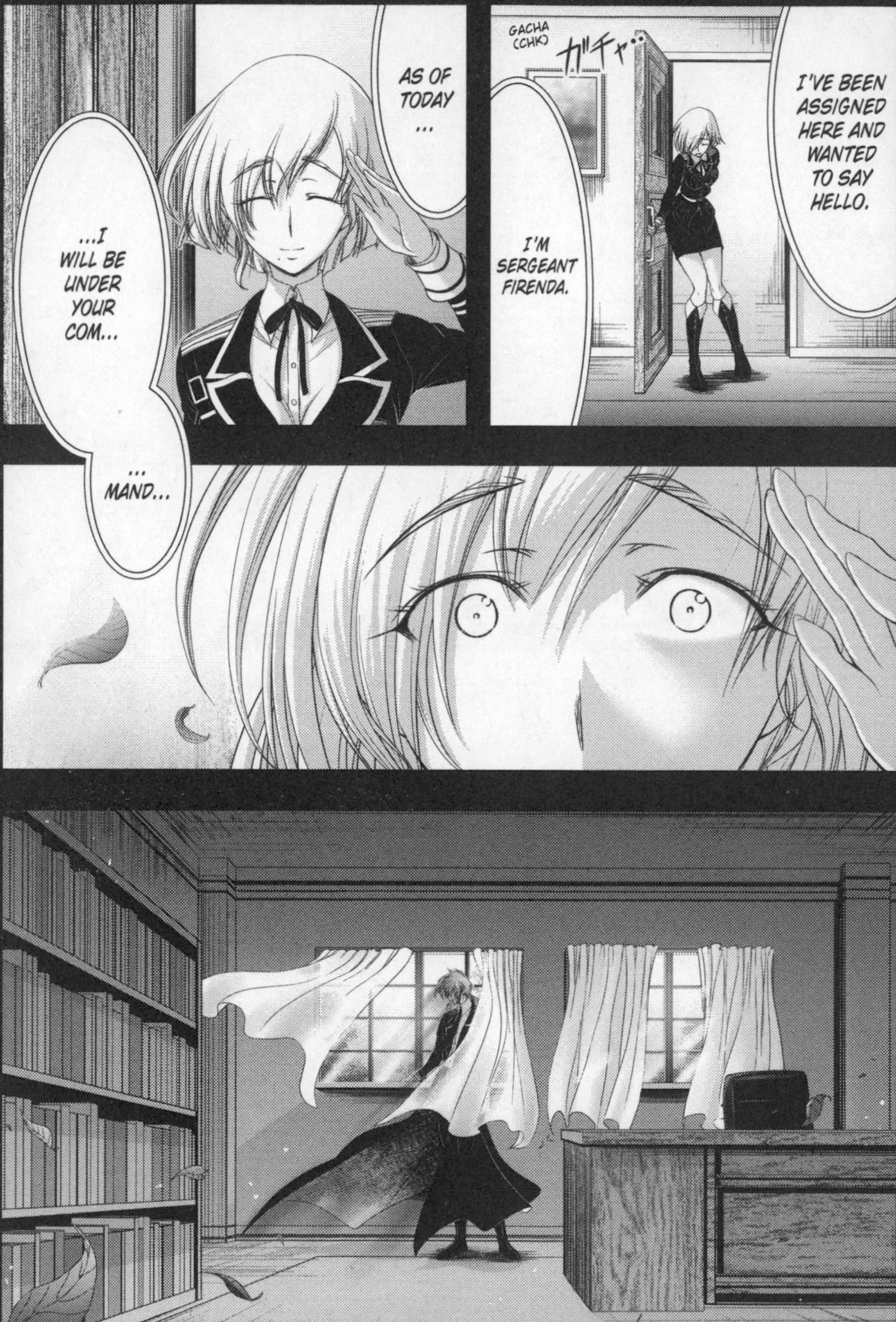
I'VE BEEN ASSIGNED HERE AND WANTED TO SAY HELLO.
GACHA (CHK)
ガチャ
I'M SERGEANT FIRENDA.
AS OF TODAY ...
...I WILL BE UNDER YOUR COM...
... MAND...

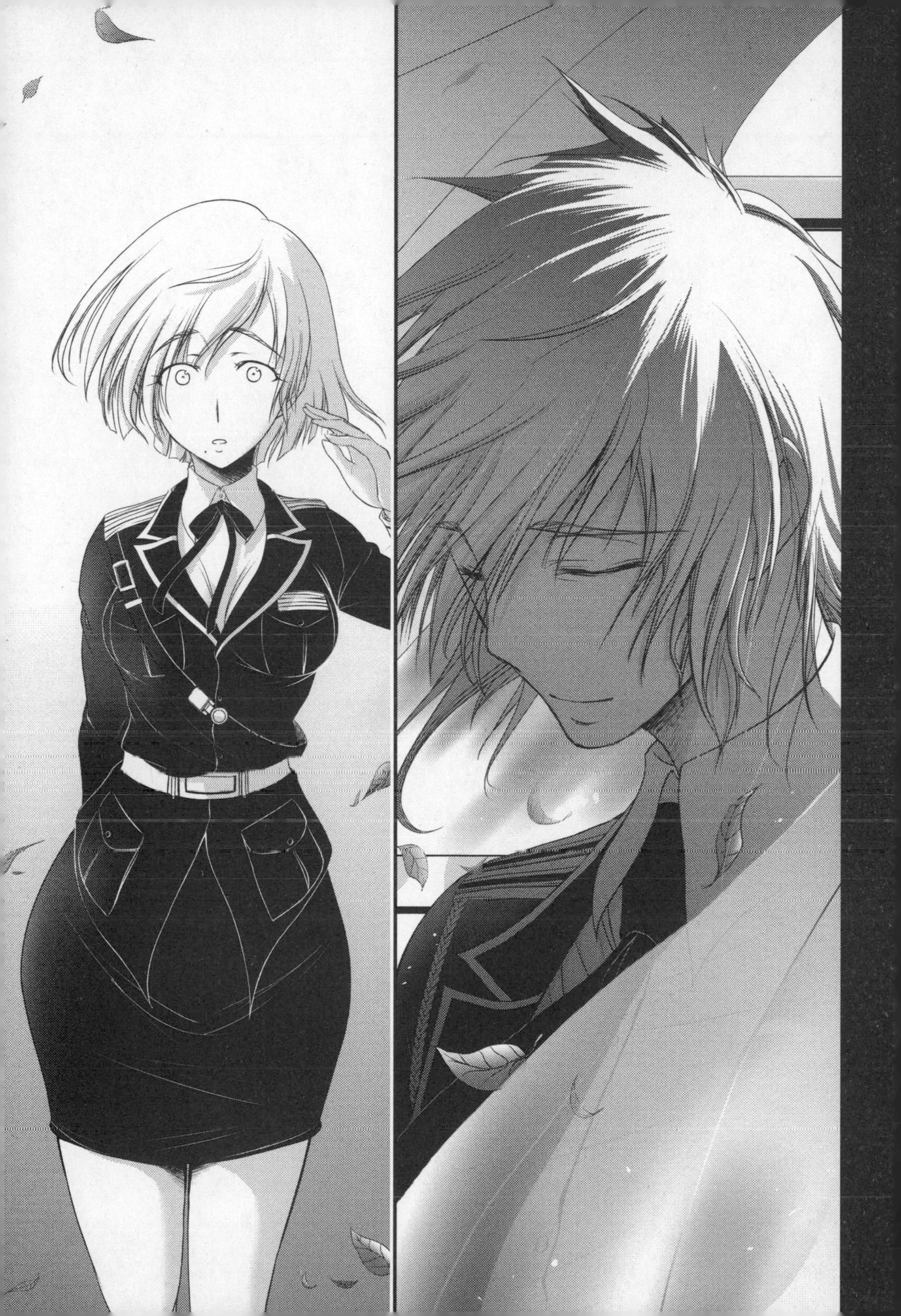

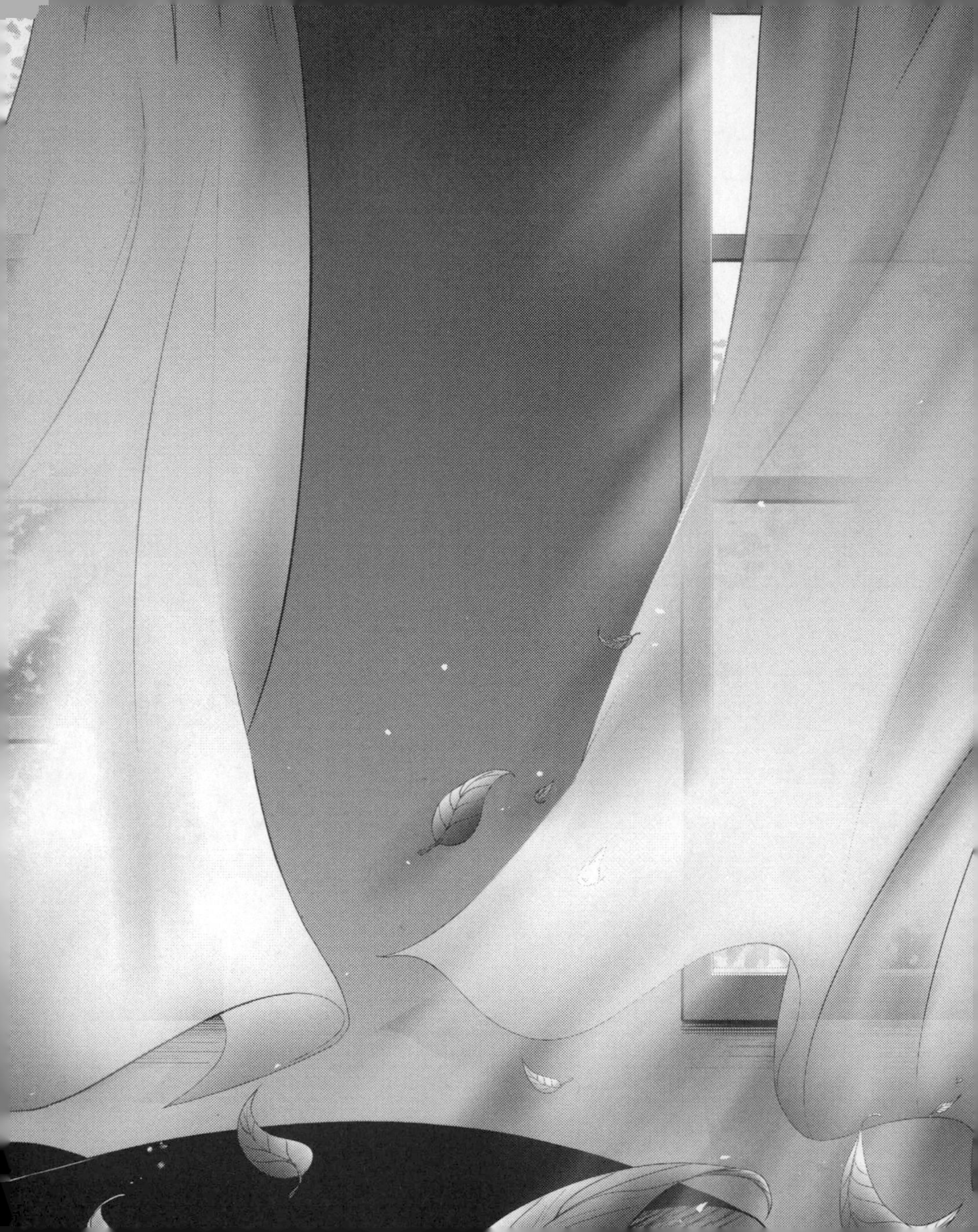

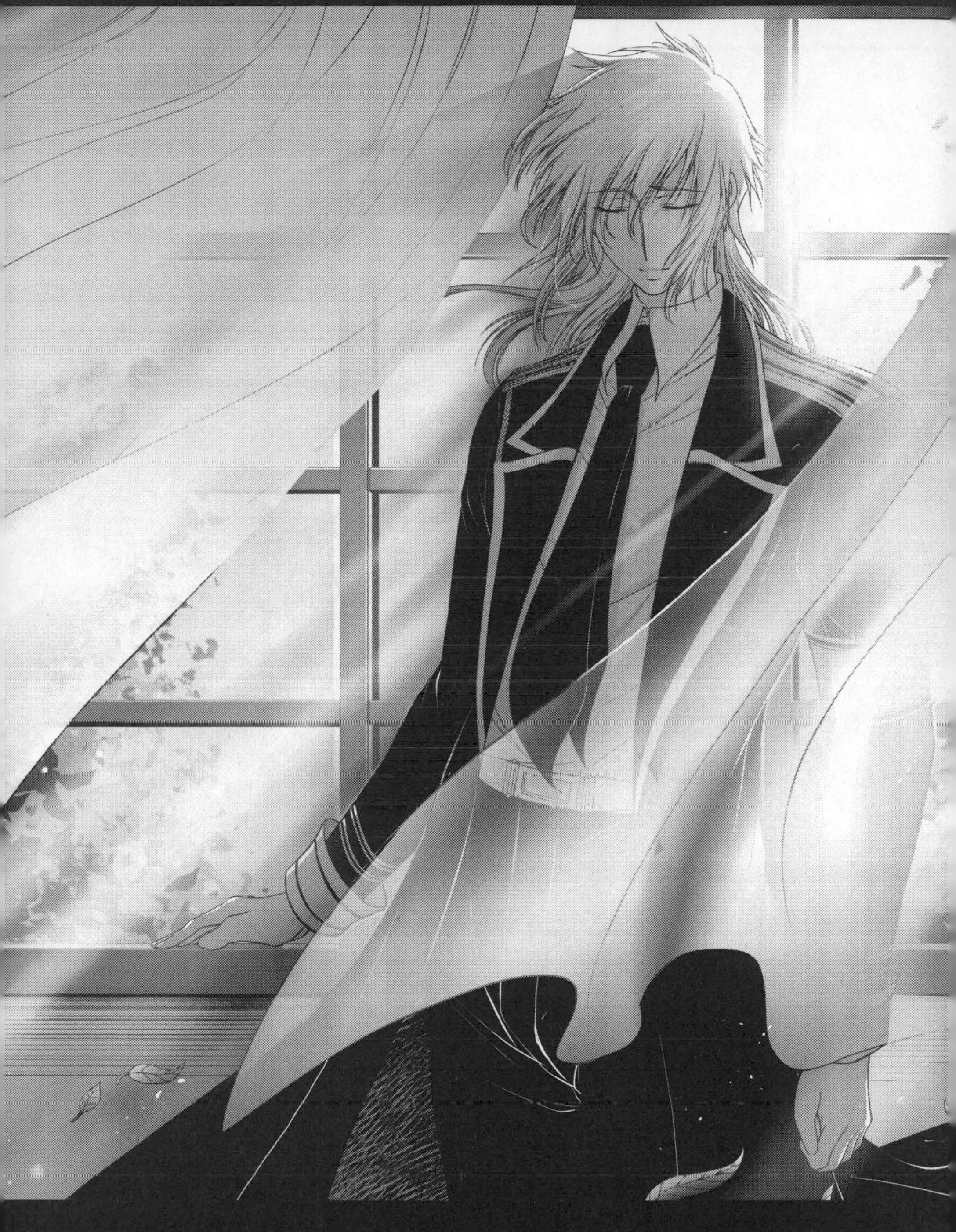

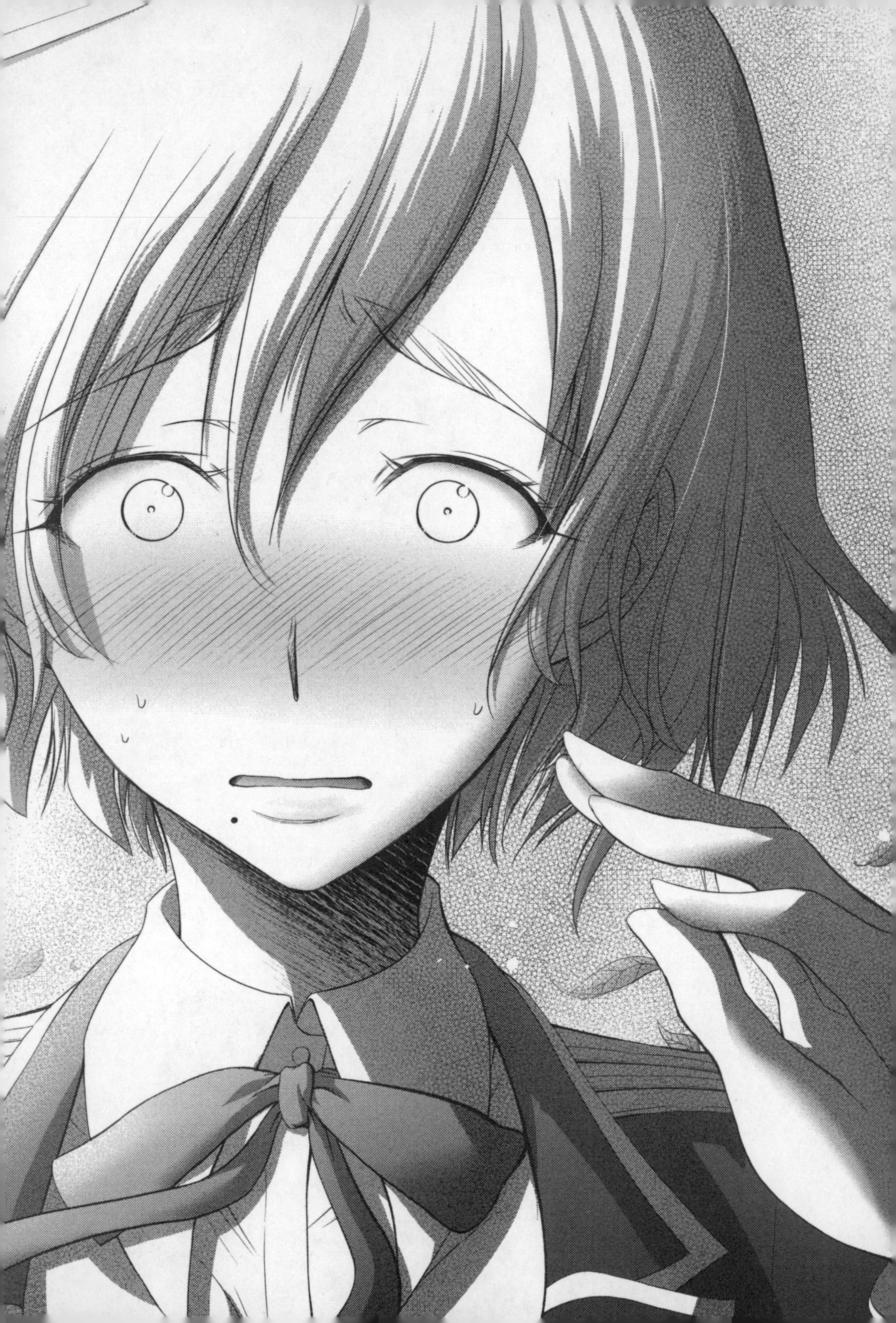

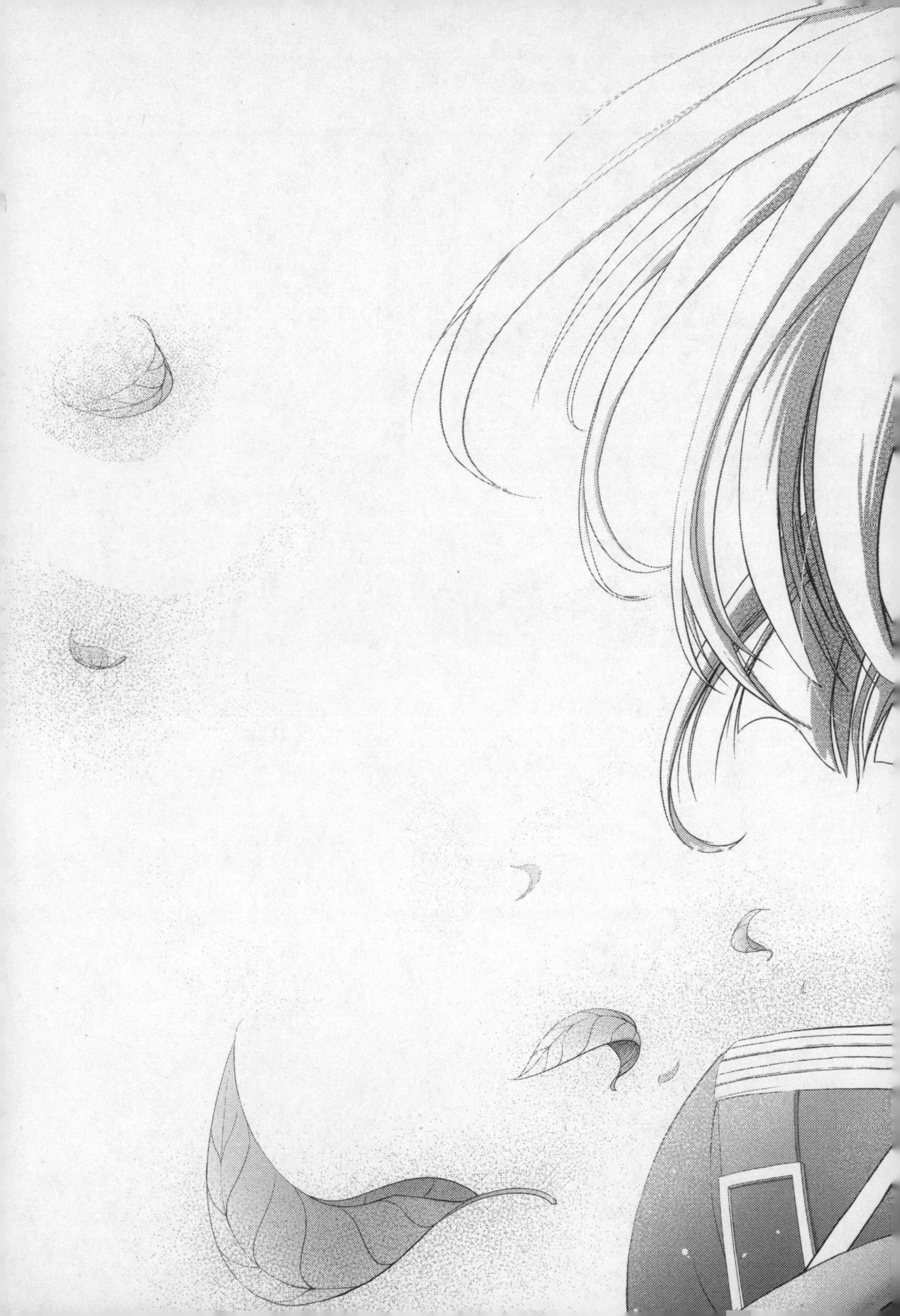

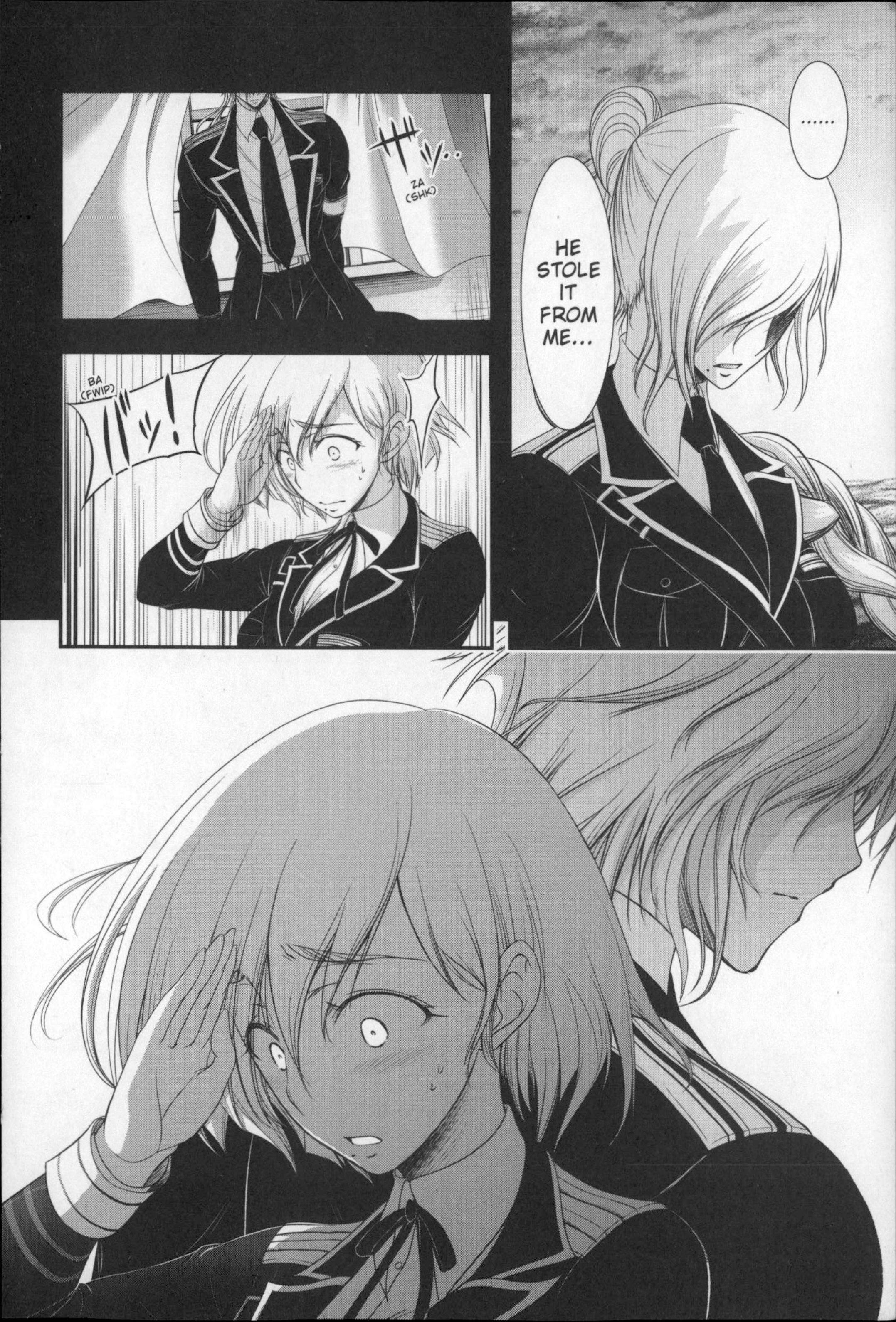
......
HE STOLE IT FROM ME...
ザッ..
ZA (SHK)
バッ!
BA (FWIP)

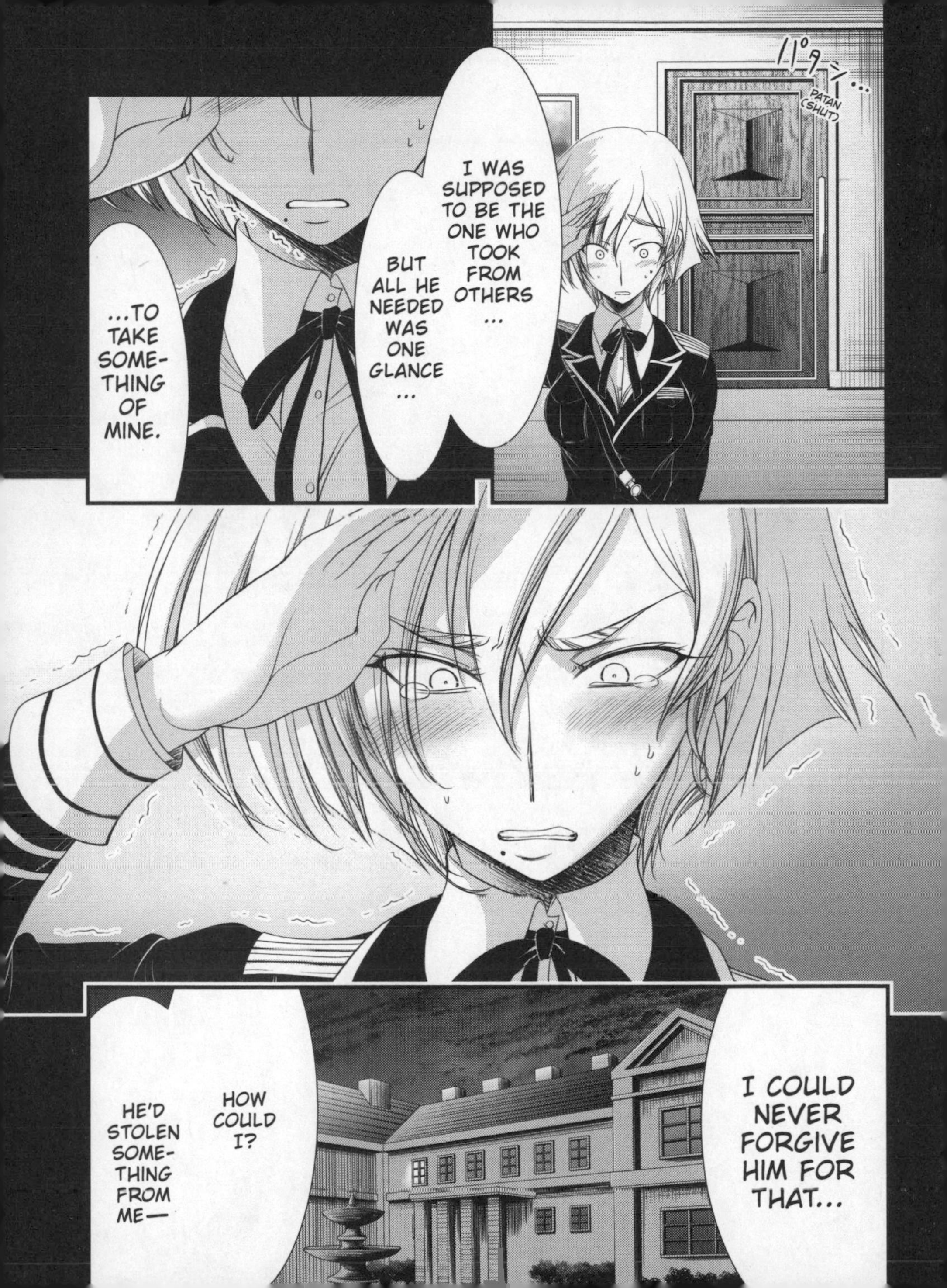
パタン…
PATAN (SHUT)
I WAS SUPPOSED TO BE THE ONE WHO TOOK FROM OTHERS...
BUT ALL HE NEEDED WAS ONE GLANCE...
...TO TAKE SOME-THING OF MINE.
I COULD NEVER FORGIVE HIM FOR THAT...
HOW COULD I?
HE'D STOLEN SOME-THING FROM ME—

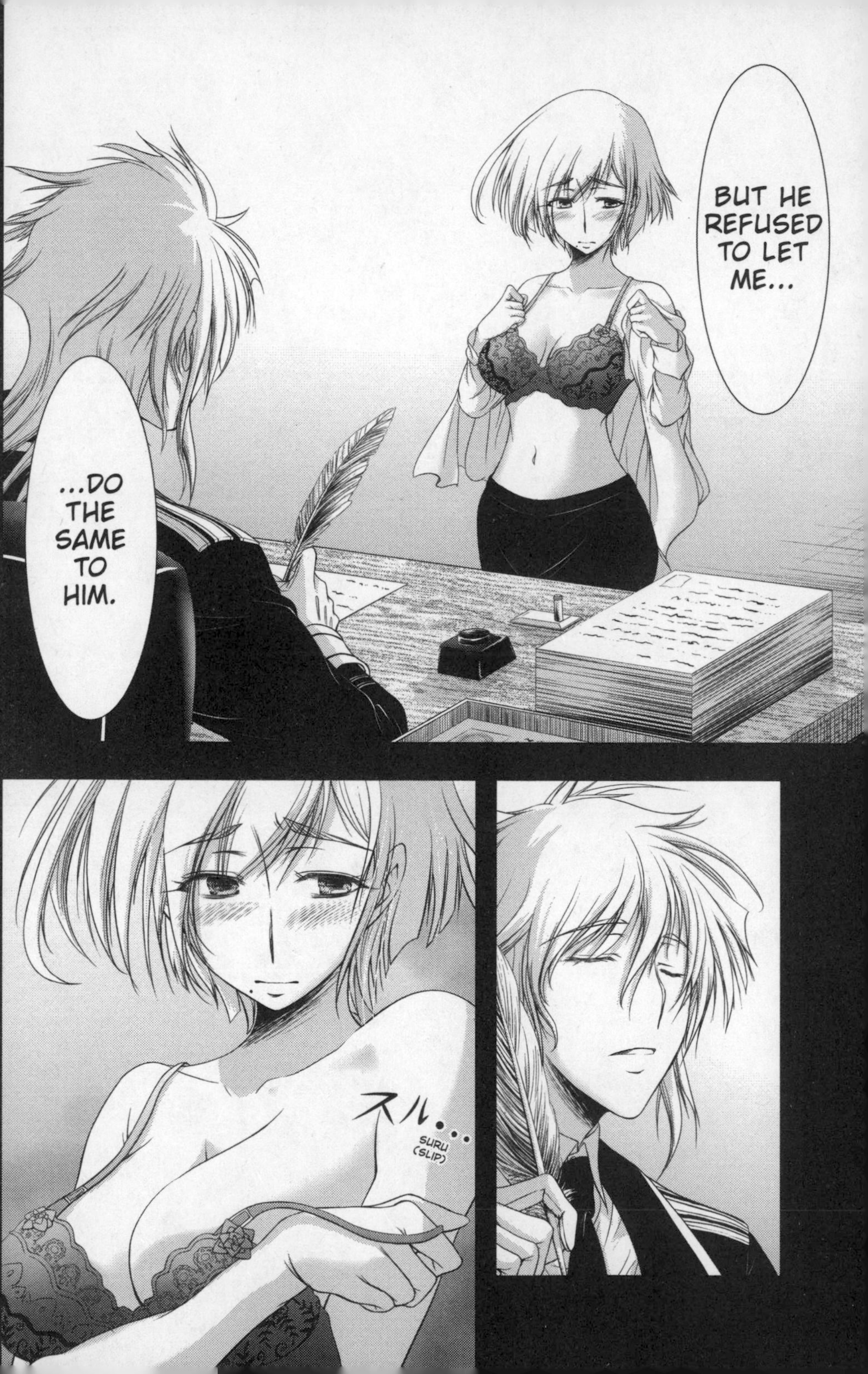
BUT HE REFUSED TO LET ME...
...DO THE SAME TO HIM.
スル...
SURU (SLIP)

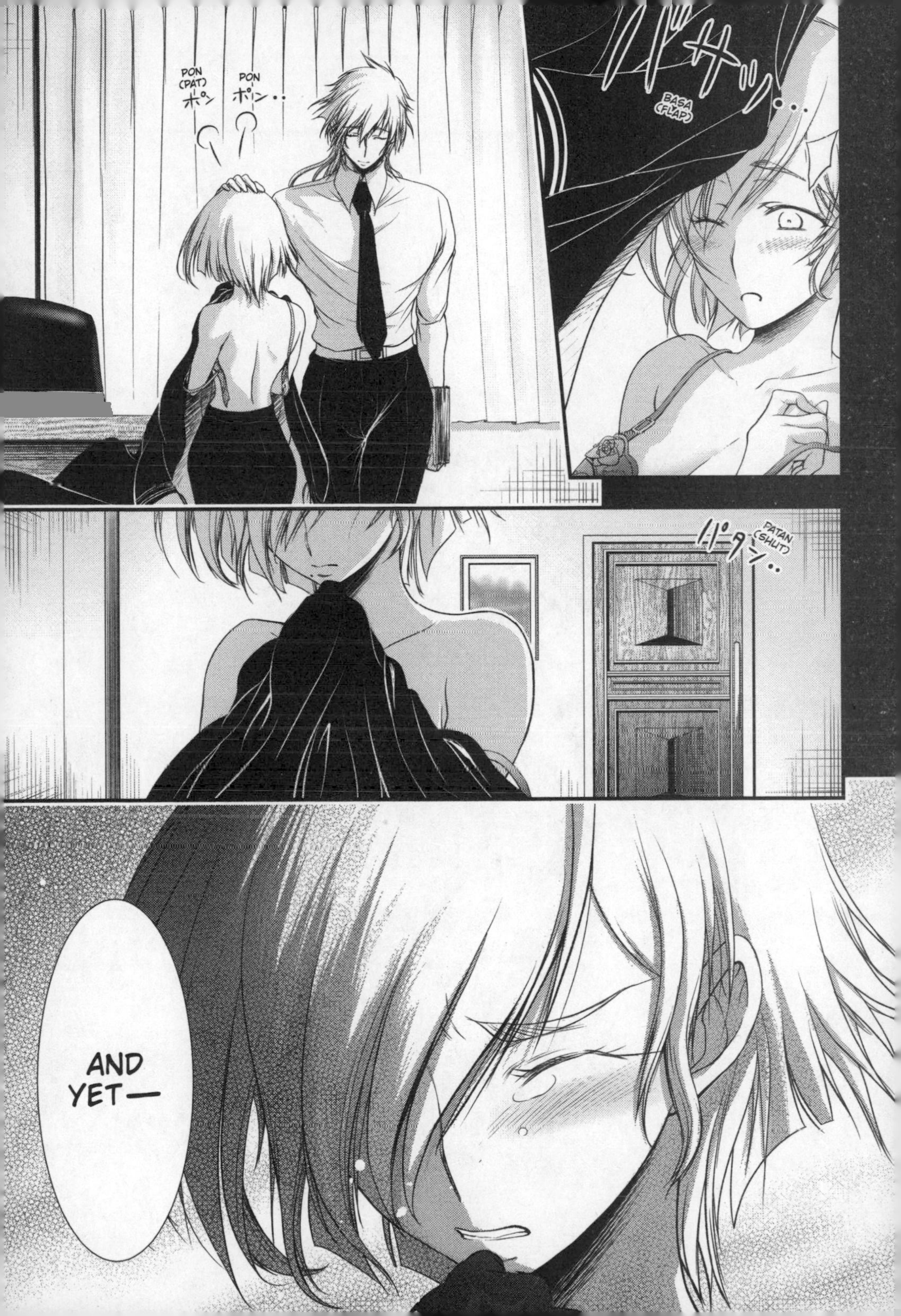

バサッ・・・
BASA (FLAP)
PON (PAT)
ポン
PON
ポン・・
PATAN (SHUT)
パタン・・
AND YET—

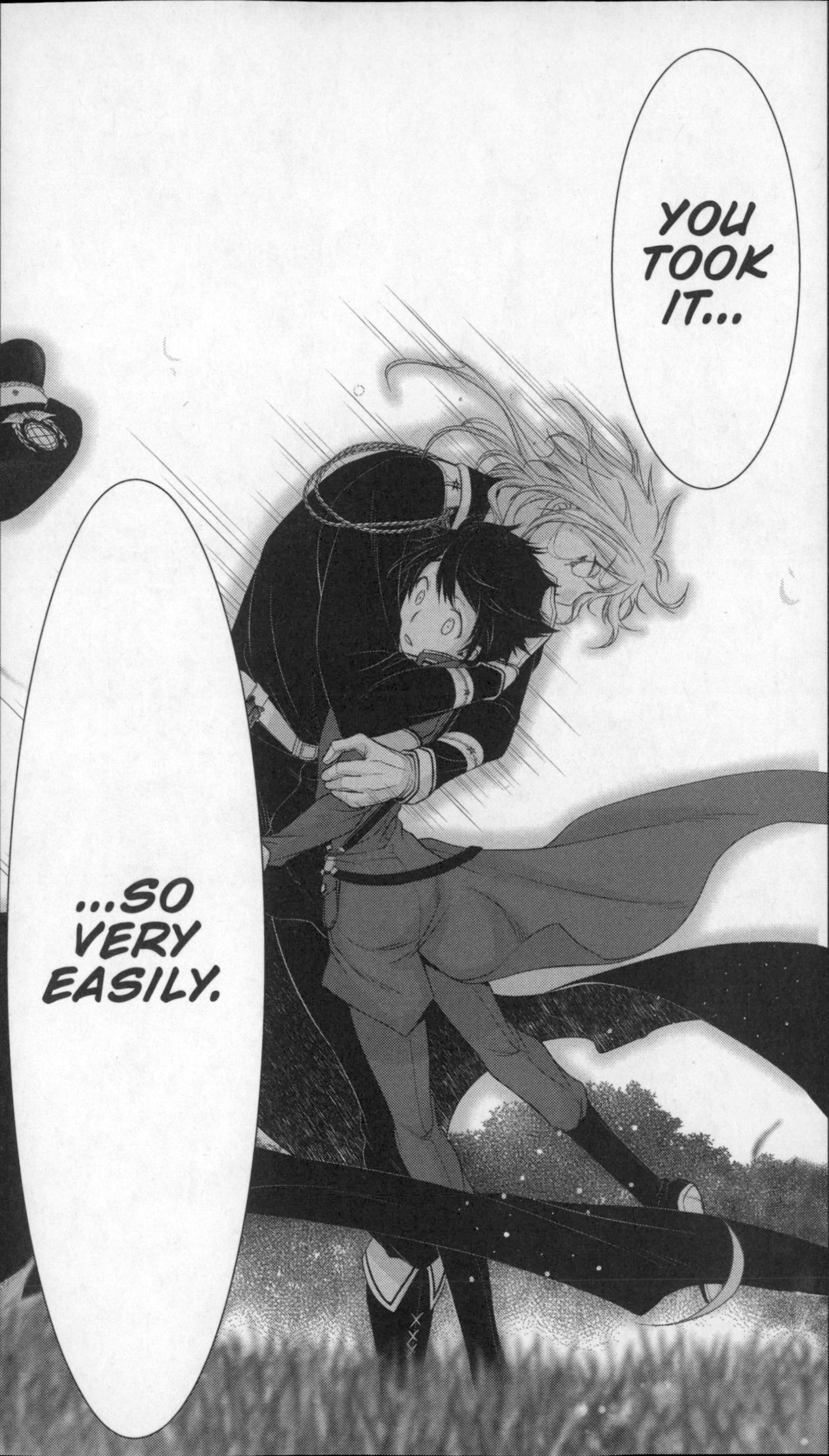
YOU TOOK IT...
...SO VERY EASILY.

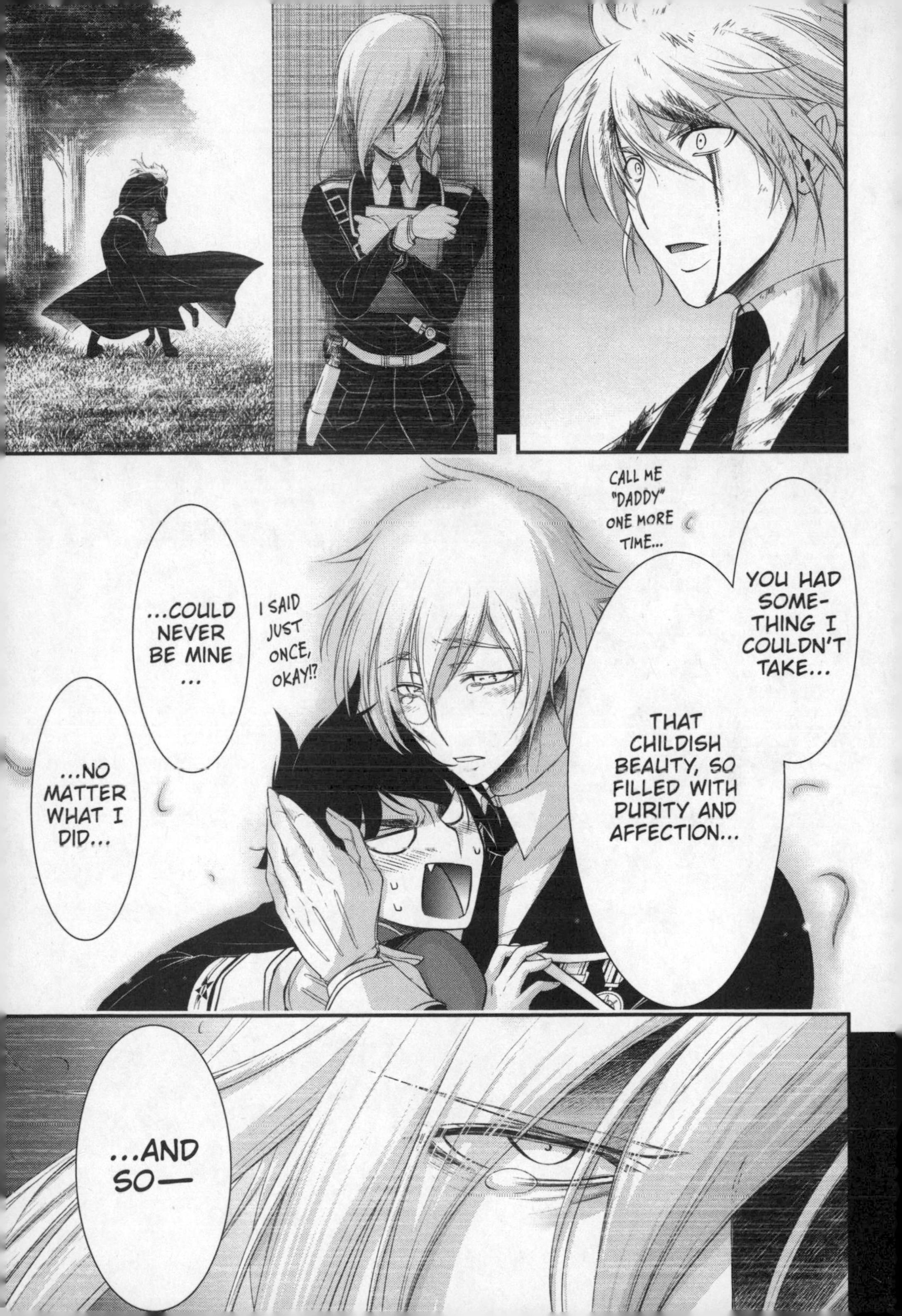
CALL ME "DADDY" ONE MORE TIME...
YOU HAD SOME-THING I COULDN'T TAKE...
THAT CHILDISH BEAUTY, SO FILLED WITH PURITY AND AFFECTION...
I SAID JUST ONCE, OKAY!?
...COULD NEVER BE MINE...
...NO MATTER WHAT I DID...
...AND SO—

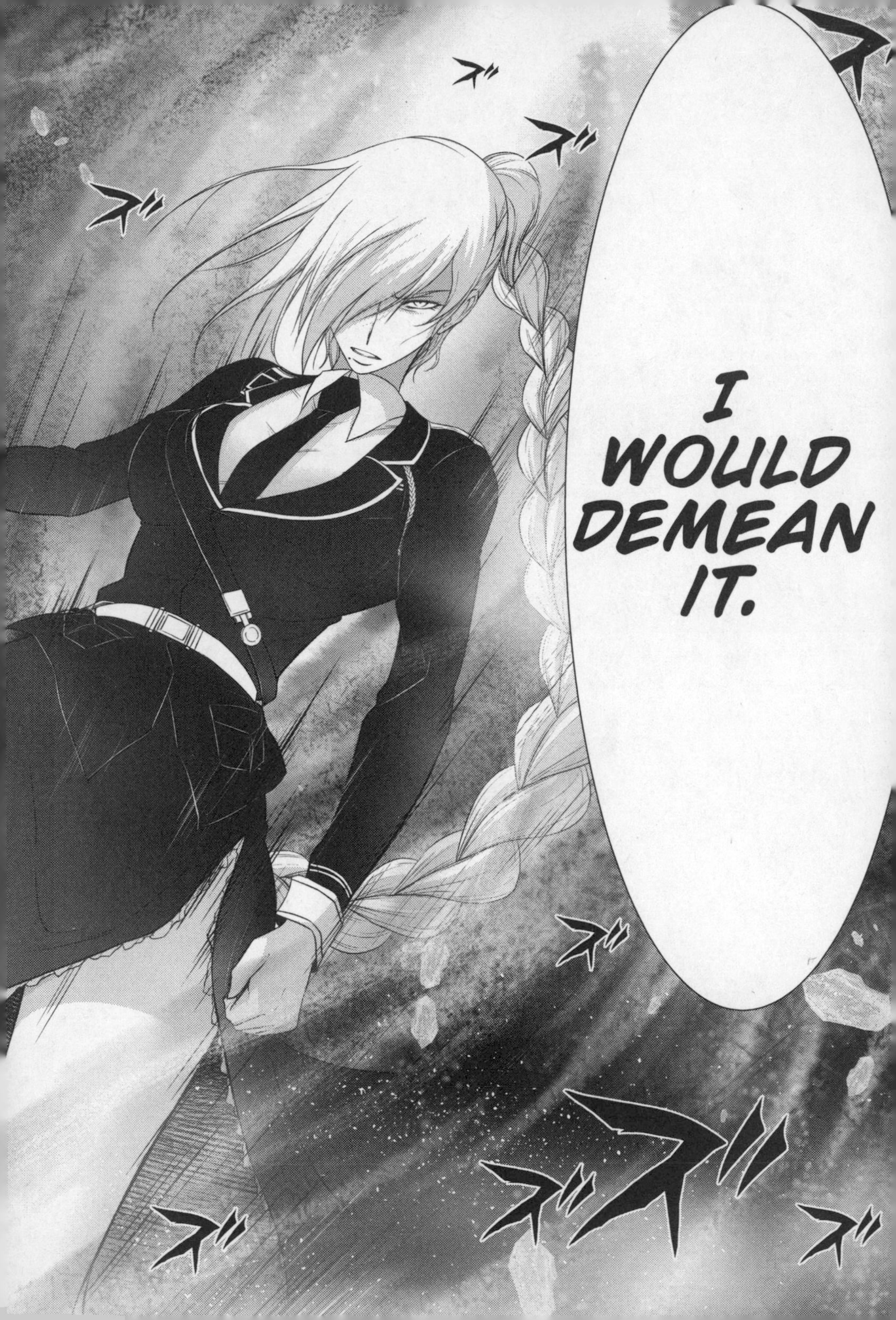
I WOULD DEMEAN IT.
ズズ!!

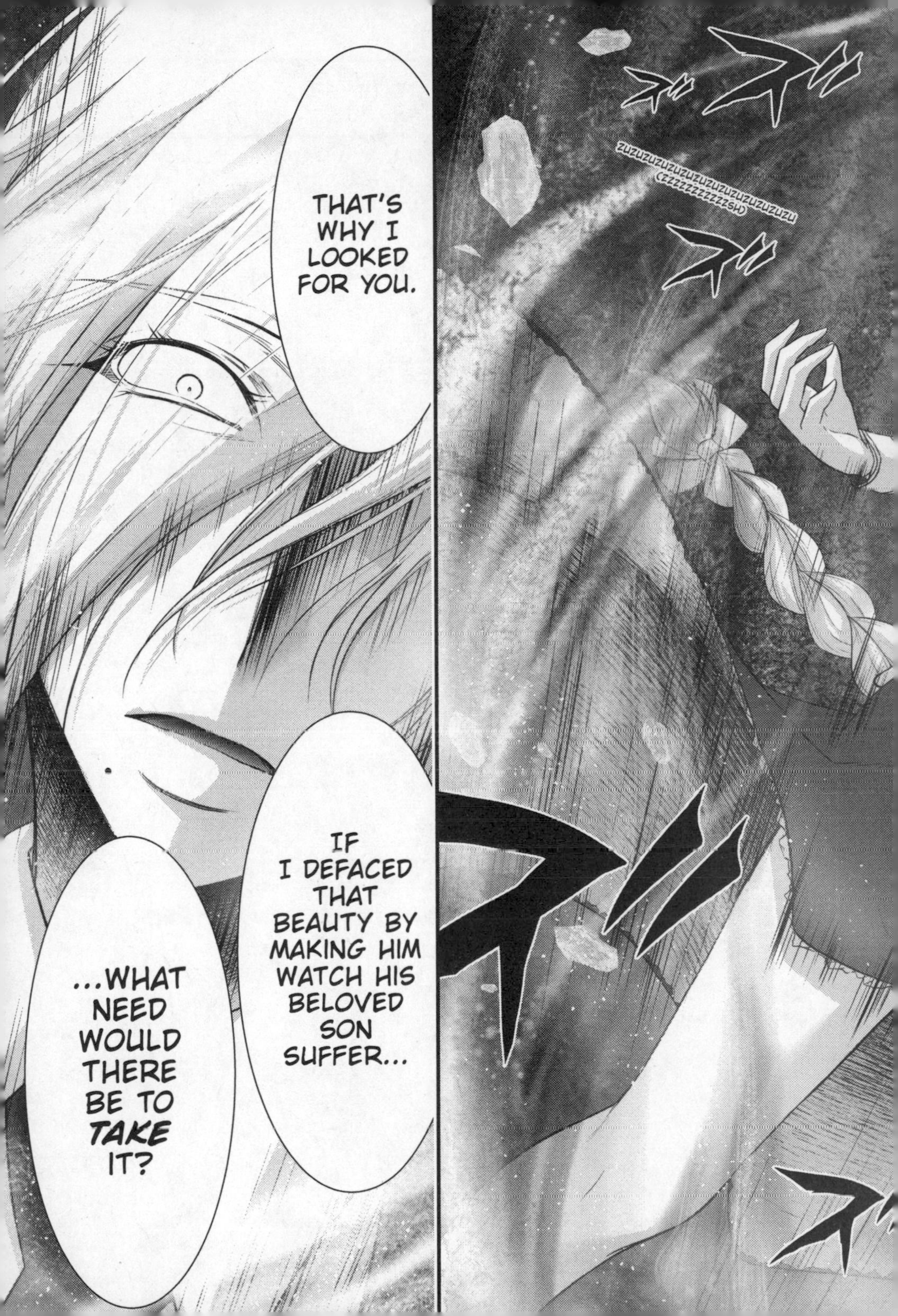
ZUZUZUZUZUZUZUZUZUZUZUZUZUZUZU
(ZZZZZZZZZZZZSH)
THAT'S WHY I LOOKED FOR YOU.
IF I DEFACED THAT BEAUTY BY MAKING HIM WATCH HIS BELOVED SON SUFFER...
...WHAT NEED WOULD THERE BE TO *TAKE* IT?

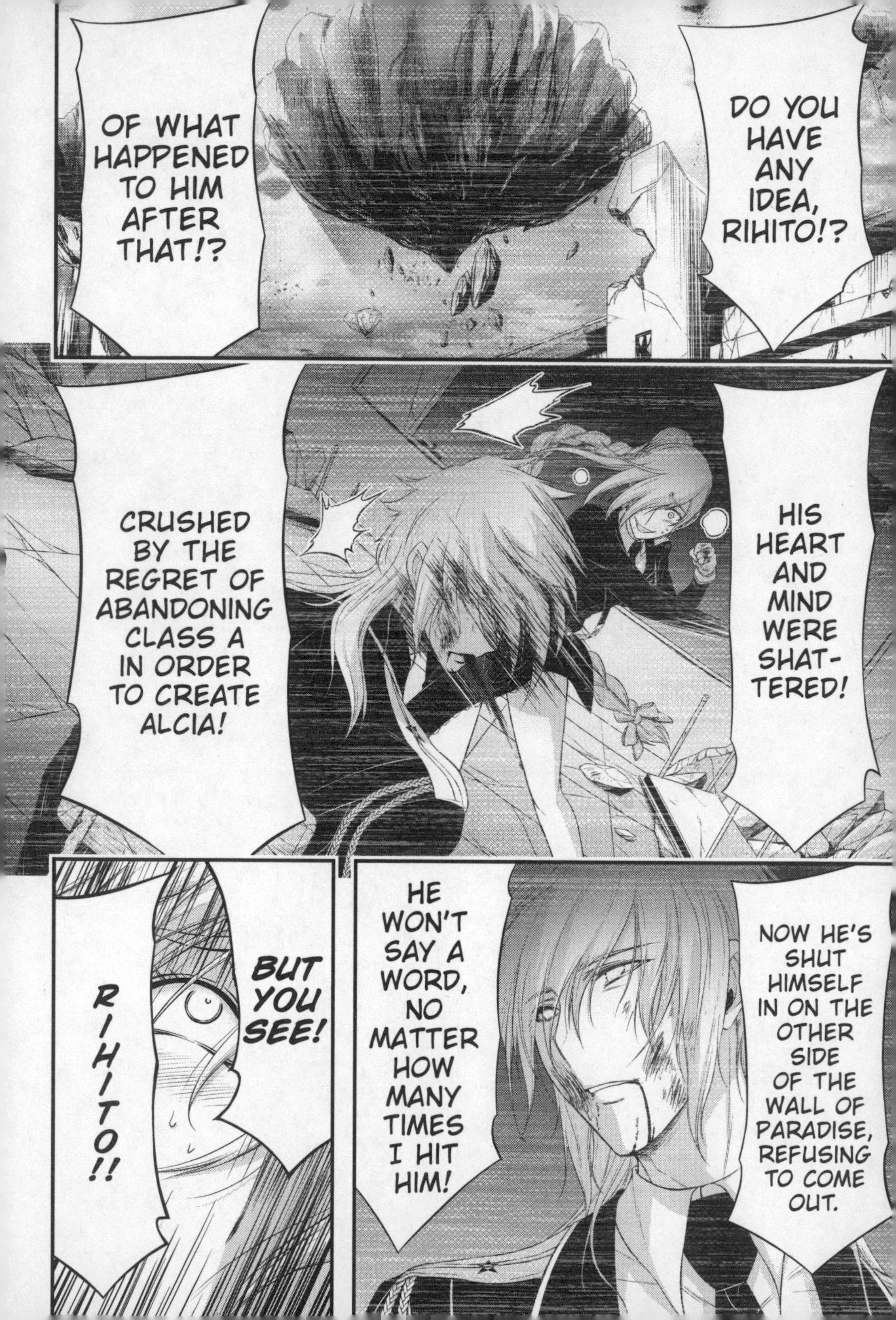
DO YOU HAVE ANY IDEA, RIHITO!?
OF WHAT HAPPENED TO HIM AFTER THAT!?
HIS HEART AND MIND WERE SHAT-TERED!
CRUSHED BY THE REGRET OF ABANDONING CLASS A IN ORDER TO CREATE ALCIA!
NOW HE'S SHUT HIMSELF IN ON THE OTHER SIDE OF THE WALL OF PARADISE, REFUSING TO COME OUT.
HE WON'T SAY A WORD, NO MATTER HOW MANY TIMES I HIT HIM!
BUT YOU SEE!
RIHITO!!

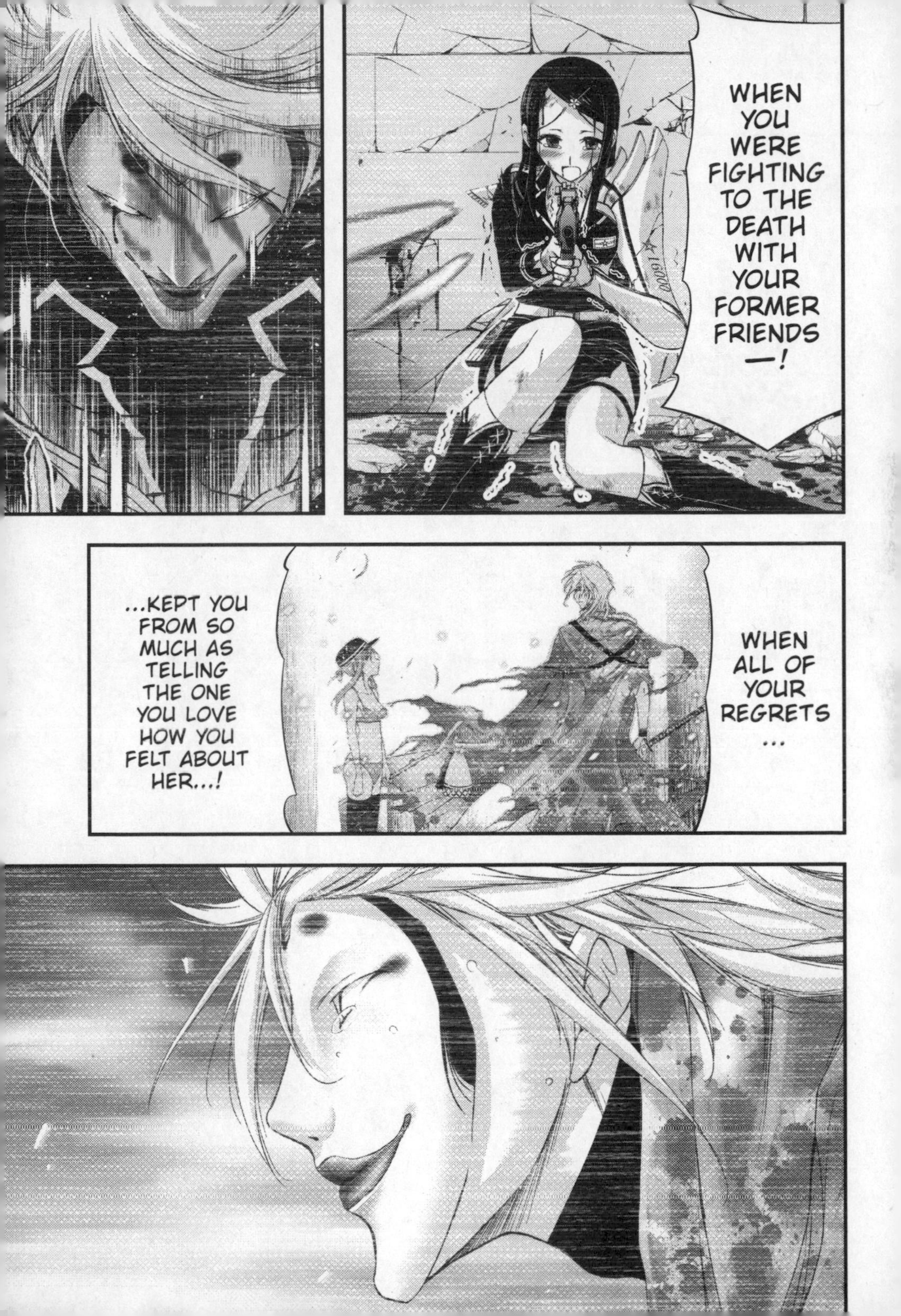
WHEN YOU WERE FIGHTING TO THE DEATH WITH YOUR FORMER FRIENDS—!
WHEN ALL OF YOUR REGRETS...
...KEPT YOU FROM SO MUCH AS TELLING THE ONE YOU LOVE HOW YOU FELT ABOUT HER...!

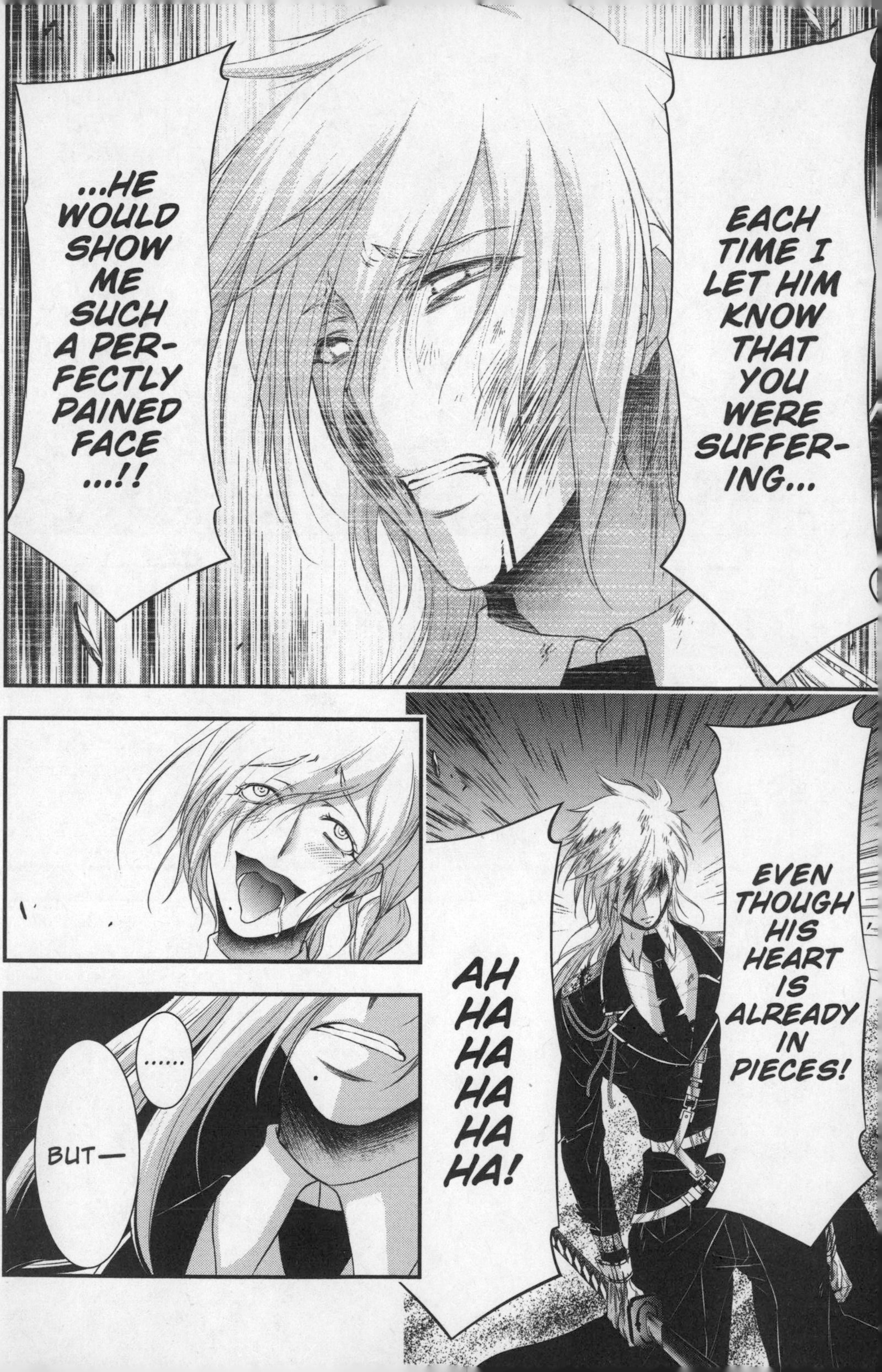
EACH TIME I LET HIM KNOW THAT YOU WERE SUFFERING...
...HE WOULD SHOW ME SUCH A PERFECTLY PAINED FACE...!!
EVEN THOUGH HIS HEART IS ALREADY IN PIECES!
AH HA HA HA HA HA HA!
......
BUT—

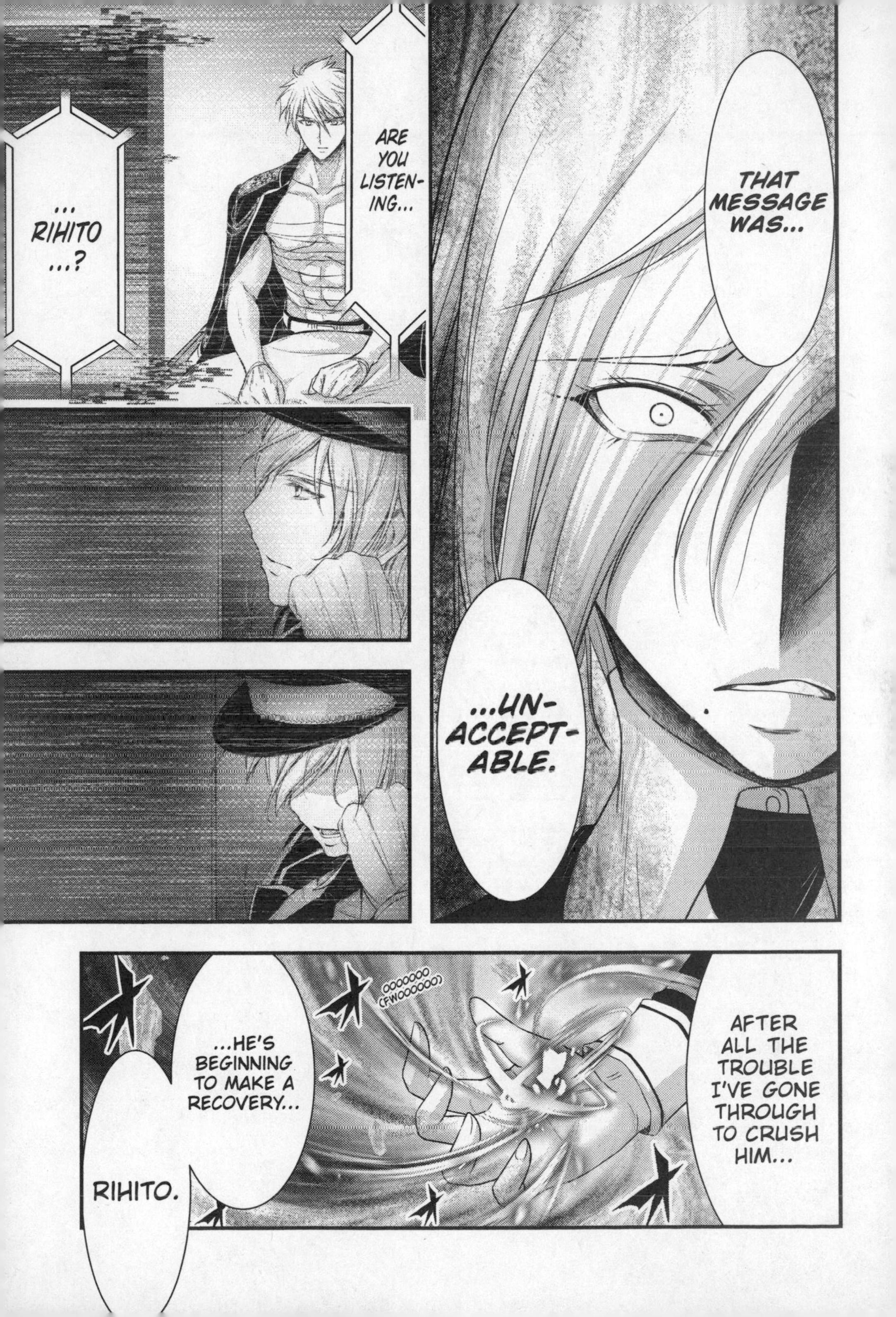
THAT MESSAGE WAS...
...UN-ACCEPT-ABLE.
ARE YOU LISTEN-ING...
...RIHITO...?
AFTER ALL THE TROUBLE I'VE GONE THROUGH TO CRUSH HIM...
OOOOOOO (FWOOOOOO)
...HE'S BEGINNING TO MAKE A RECOVERY...
RIHITO.

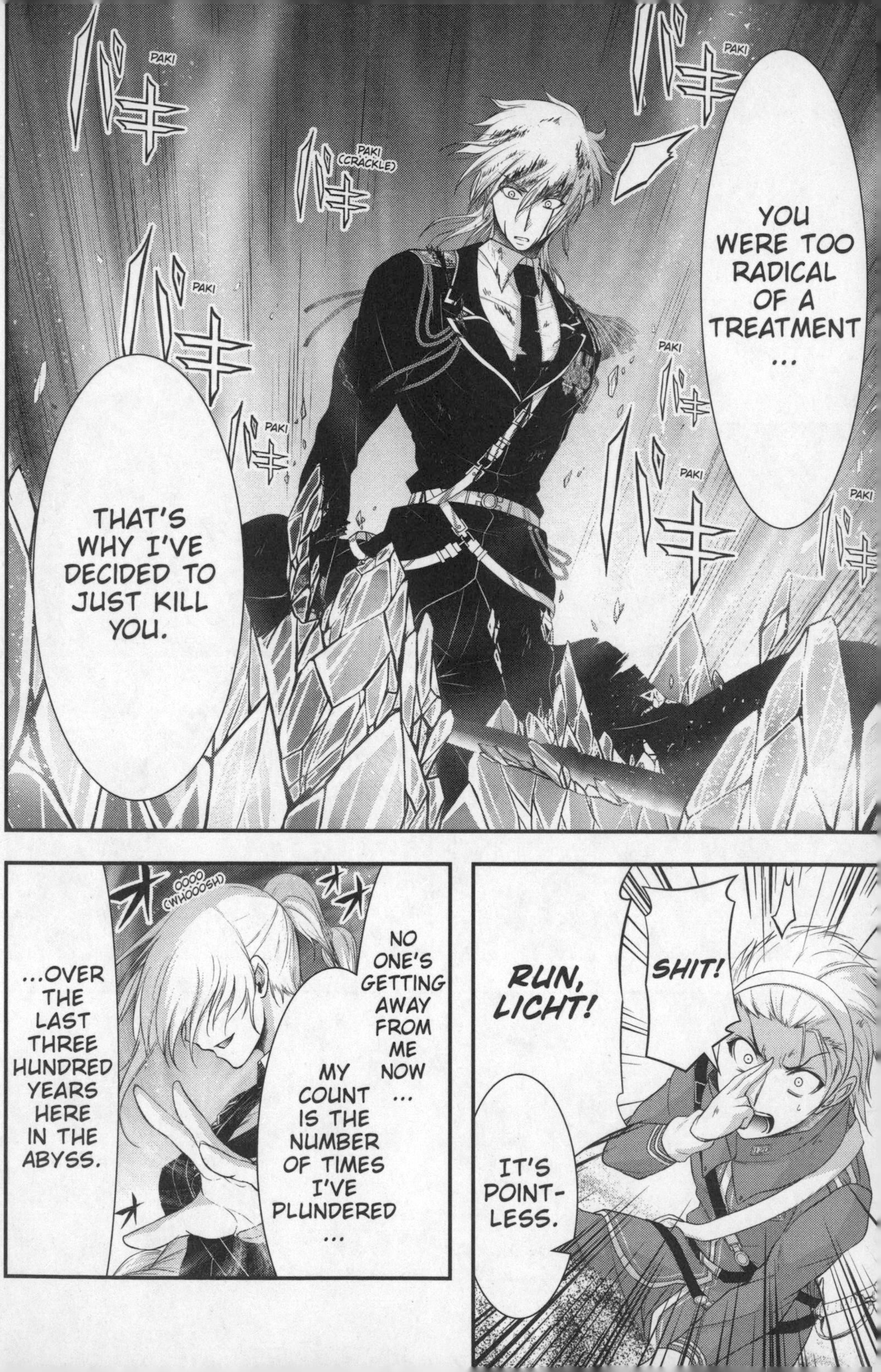
PAKI
PAKI
PAKI (CRACKLE)
YOU WERE TOO RADICAL OF A TREATMENT...
PAKI
PAKI
PAKI
PAKI
PAKI
THAT'S WHY I'VE DECIDED TO JUST KILL YOU.
SHIT!
RUN, LICHT!
IT'S POINT-LESS.
OOOO (WHOOOSH)
NO ONE'S GETTING AWAY FROM ME NOW...
MY COUNT IS THE NUMBER OF TIMES I'VE PLUNDERED...
...OVER THE LAST THREE HUNDRED YEARS HERE IN THE ABYSS.

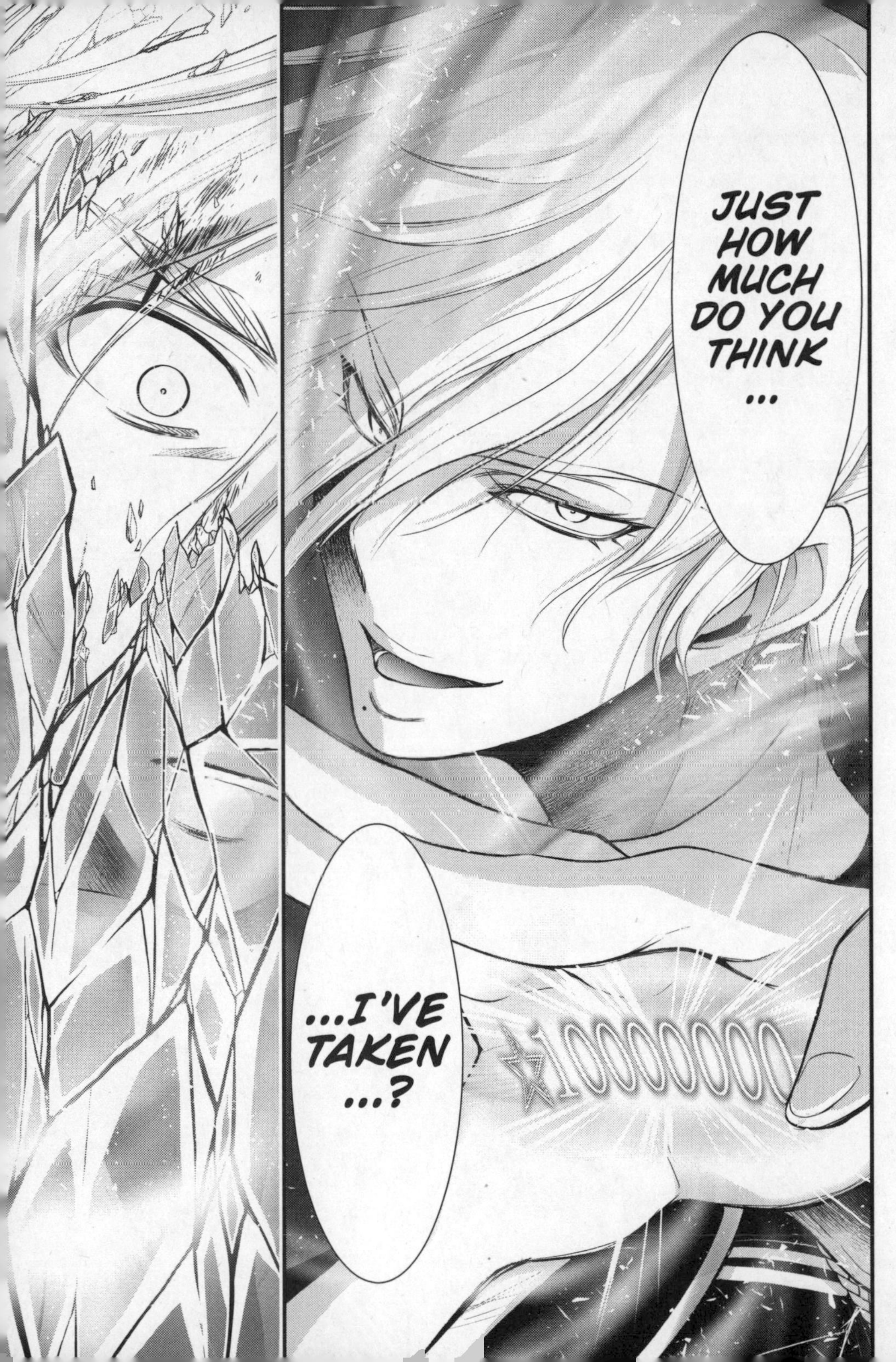
JUST HOW MUCH DO YOU THINK ...
...I'VE TAKEN ...?
☆10000000

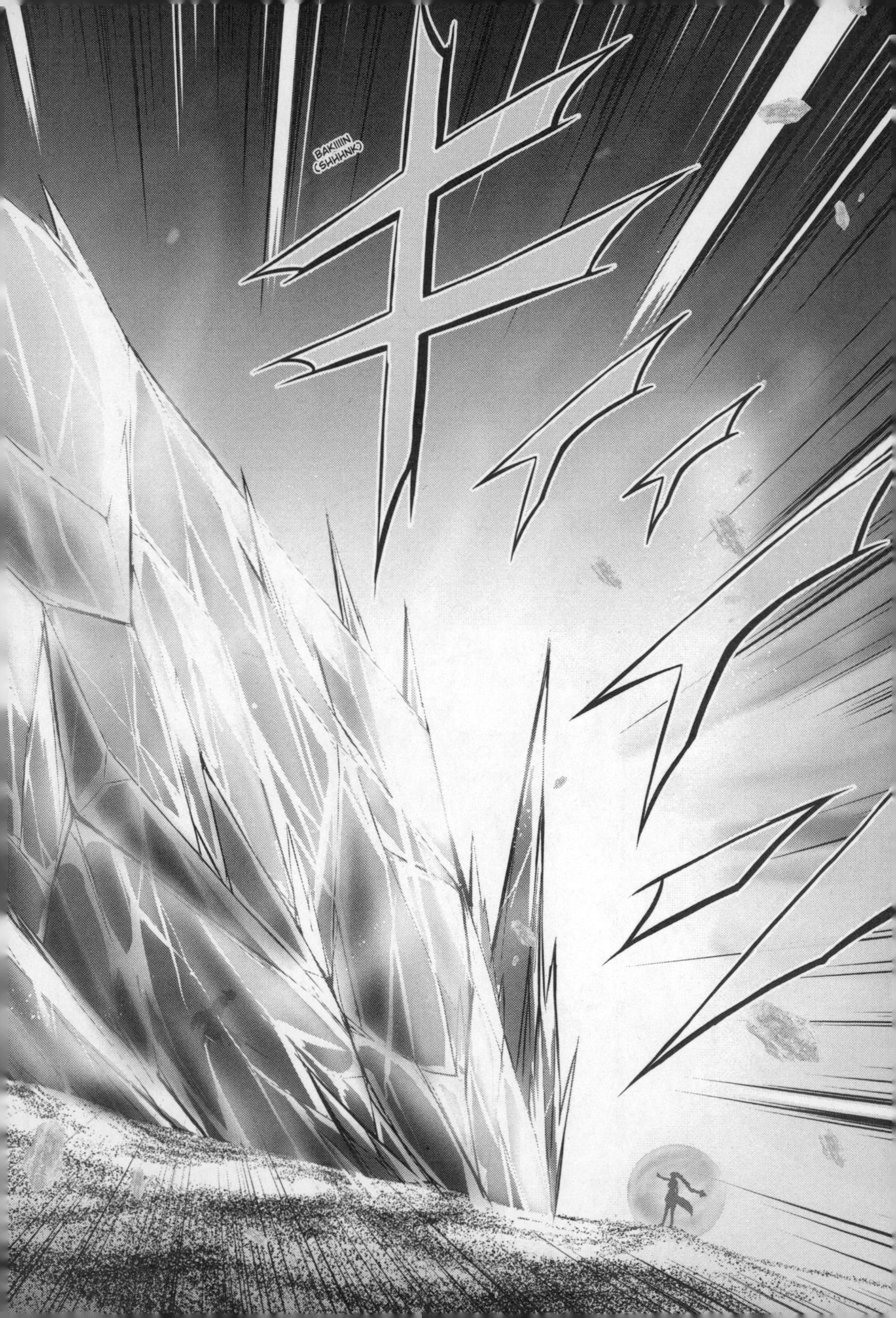
BAKIIIN (SHHHNK)

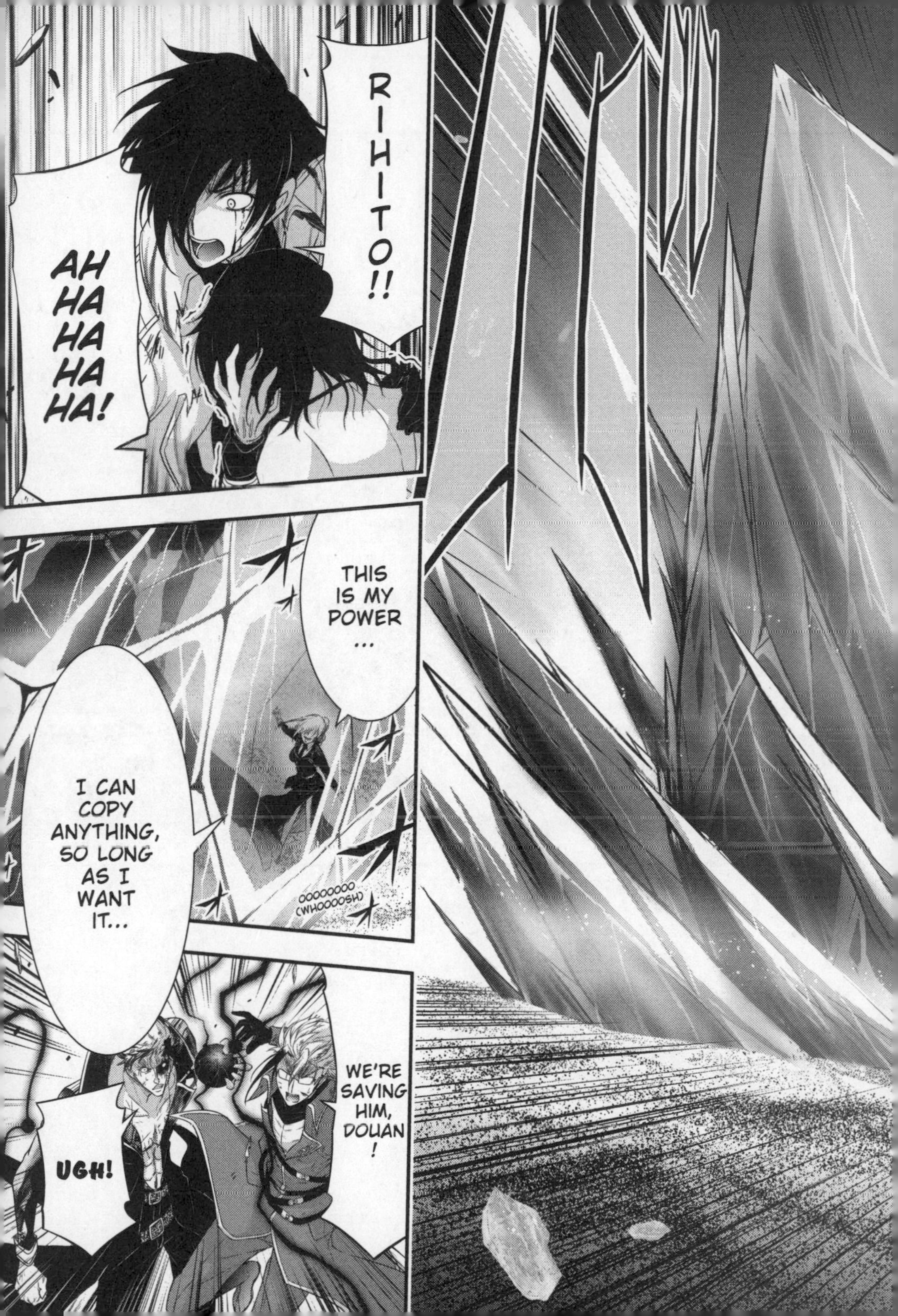
RIHITO!!
AH HA HA HA HA!
THIS IS MY POWER...
I CAN COPY ANYTHING, SO LONG AS I WANT IT...
OOOOOOOO (WHOOOOSH)
WE'RE SAVING HIM, DOUAN!
UGH!

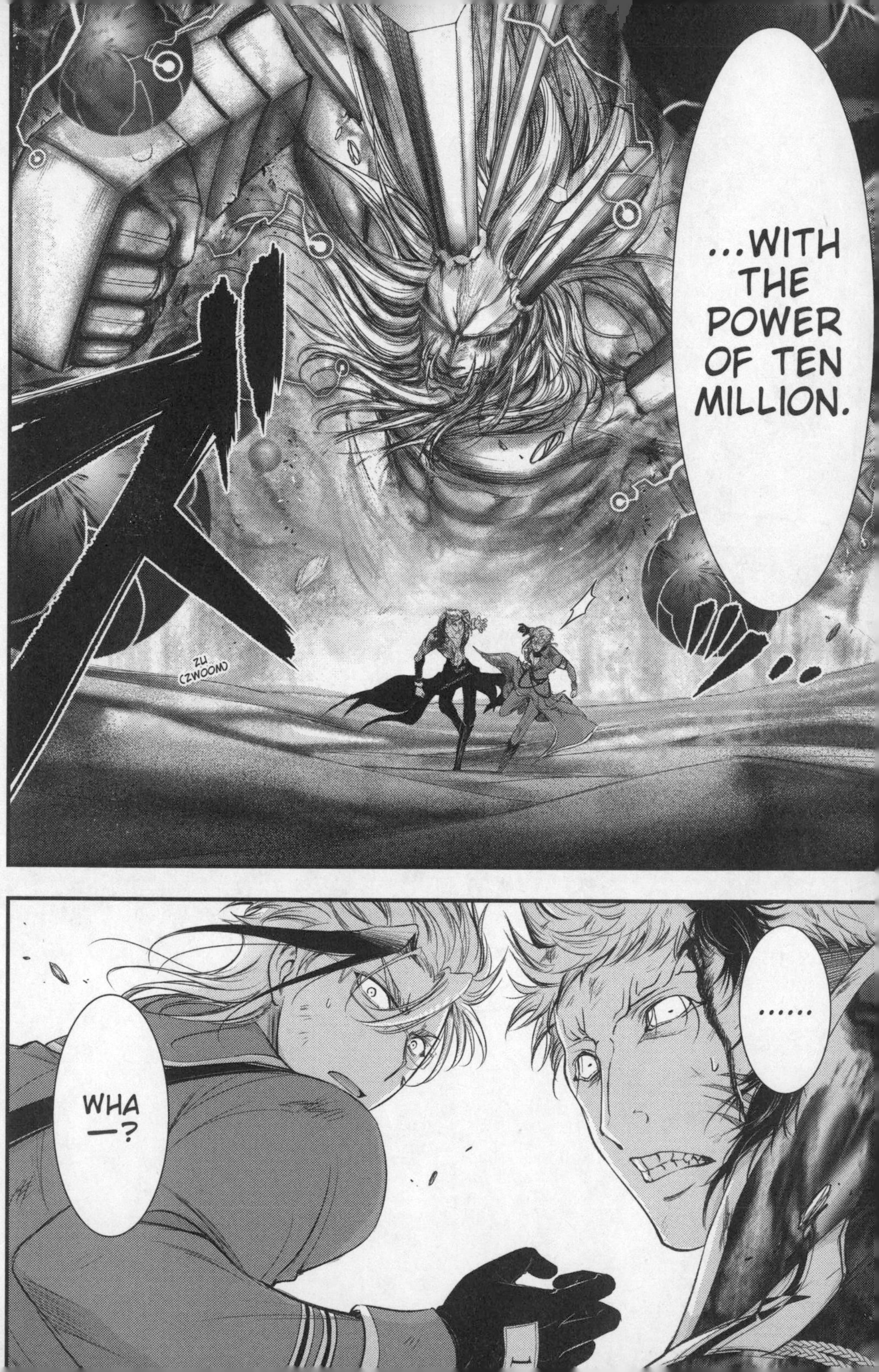
...WITH THE POWER OF TEN MILLION.
...
ZU (ZWOOM)
......
WHA—?

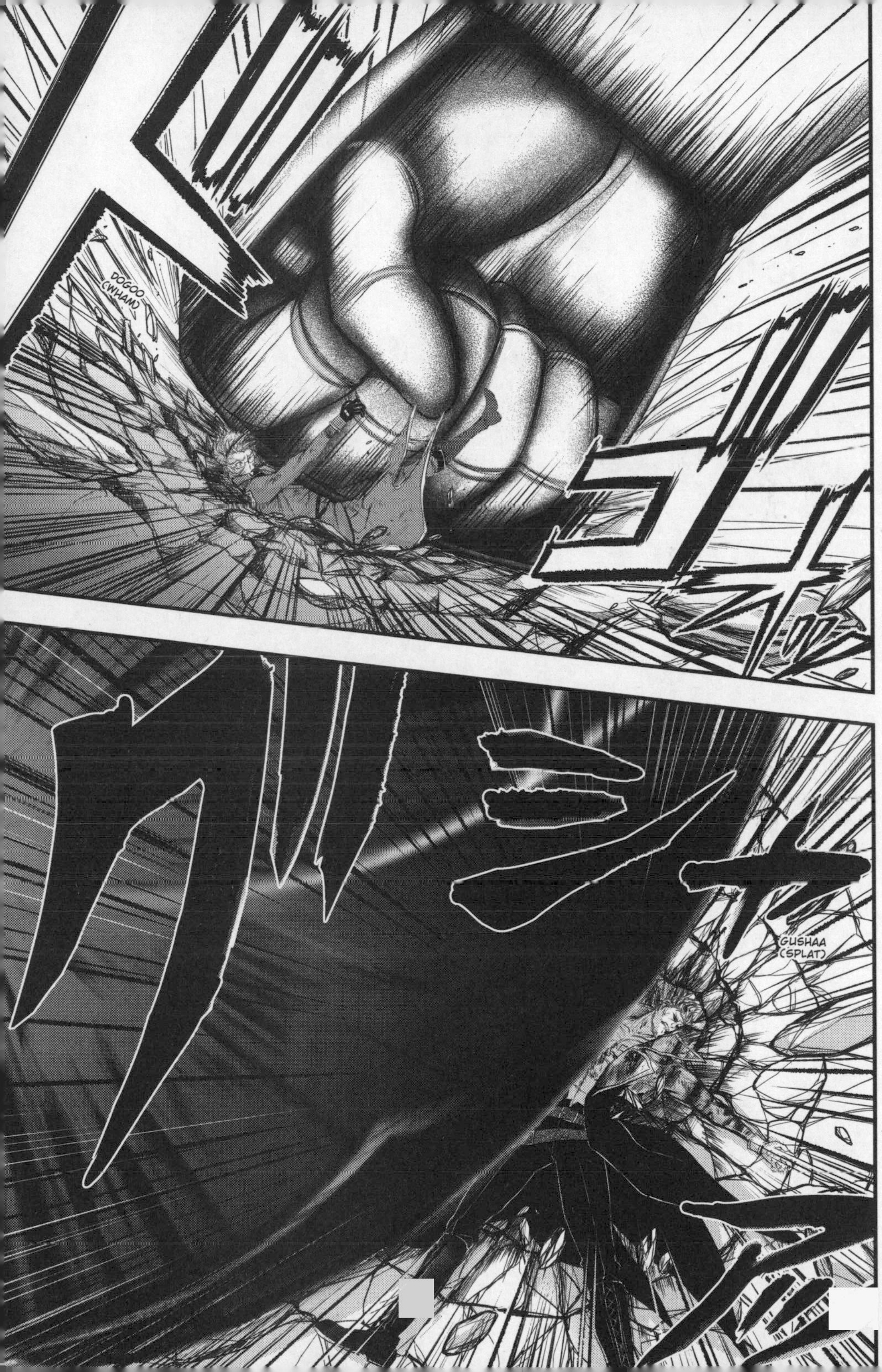
DOGOO (WHAM)
GUSHAA (SPLAT)

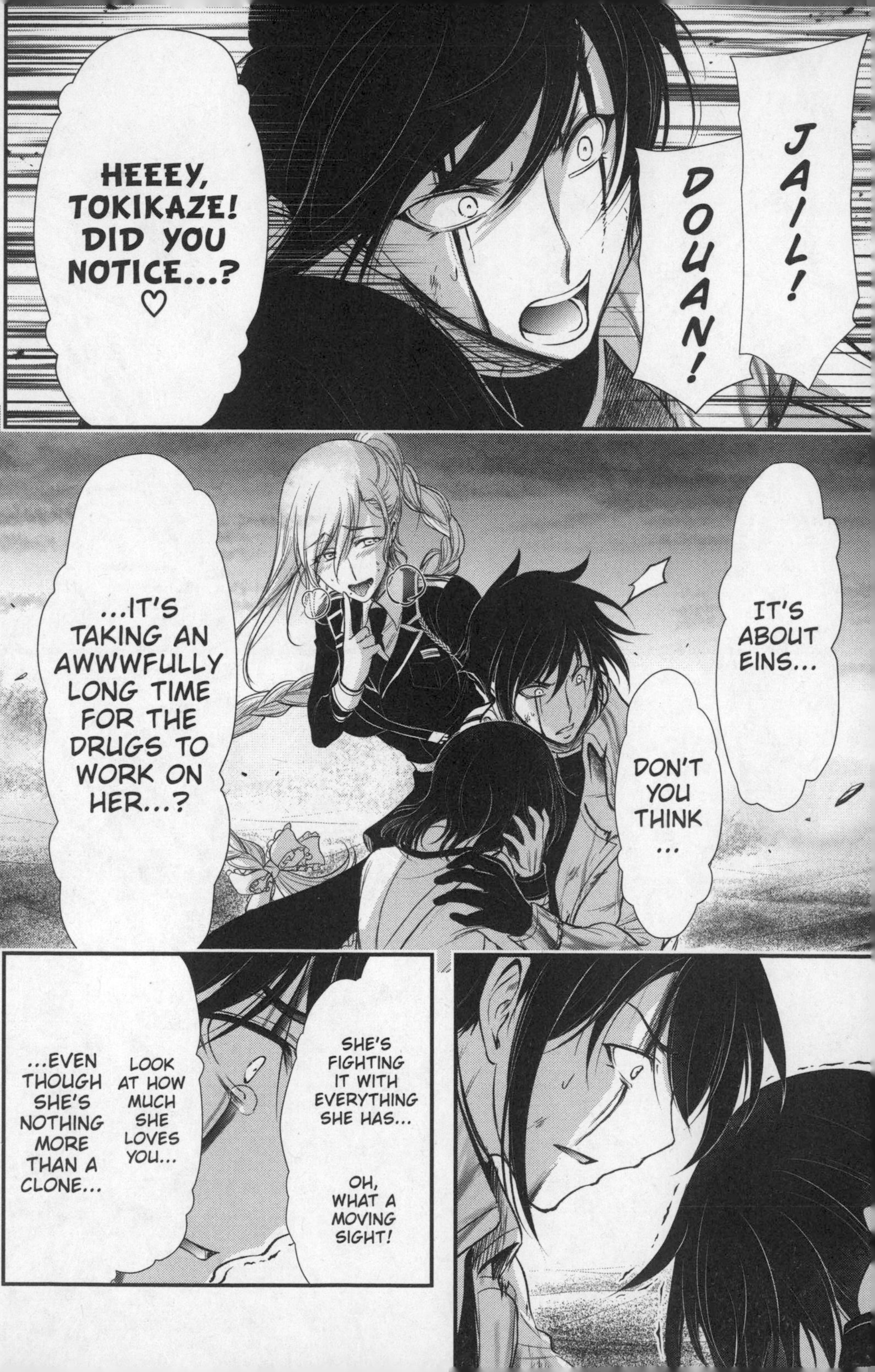
JAIL!
DOUAN!
HEEEY, TOKIKAZE! DID YOU NOTICE...? ♡
IT'S ABOUT EINS...
DON'T YOU THINK ...
...IT'S TAKING AN AWWWFULLY LONG TIME FOR THE DRUGS TO WORK ON HER...?
SHE'S FIGHTING IT WITH EVERYTHING SHE HAS...
OH, WHAT A MOVING SIGHT!
LOOK AT HOW MUCH SHE LOVES YOU...
...EVEN THOUGH SHE'S NOTHING MORE THAN A CLONE...

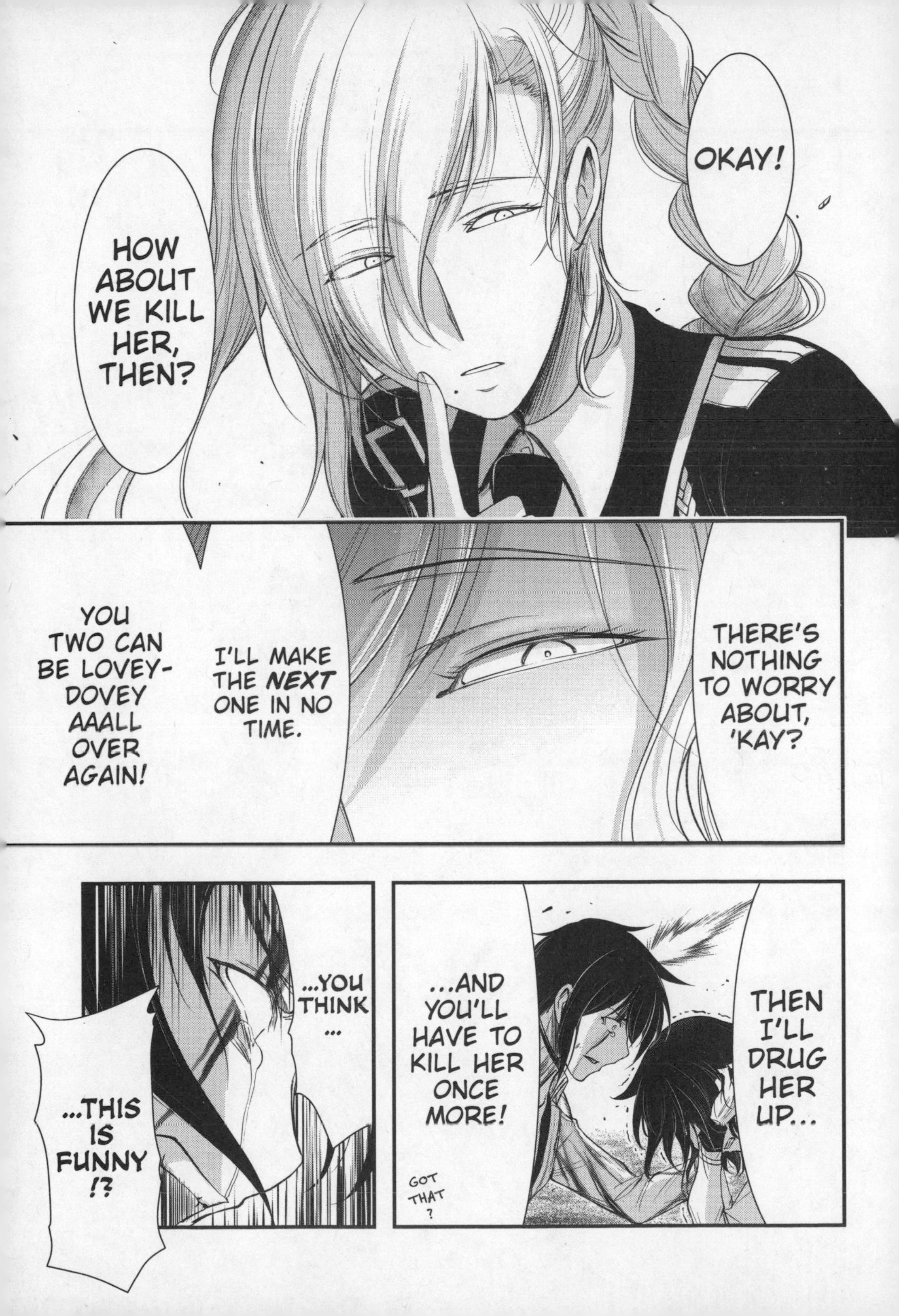
OKAY!
HOW ABOUT WE KILL HER, THEN?
THERE'S NOTHING TO WORRY ABOUT, 'KAY?
I'LL MAKE THE *NEXT* ONE IN NO TIME.
YOU TWO CAN BE LOVEY-DOVEY AAALL OVER AGAIN!
THEN I'LL DRUG HER UP...
...AND YOU'LL HAVE TO KILL HER ONCE MORE!
GOT THAT?
...YOU THINK...
...THIS IS FUNNY!?

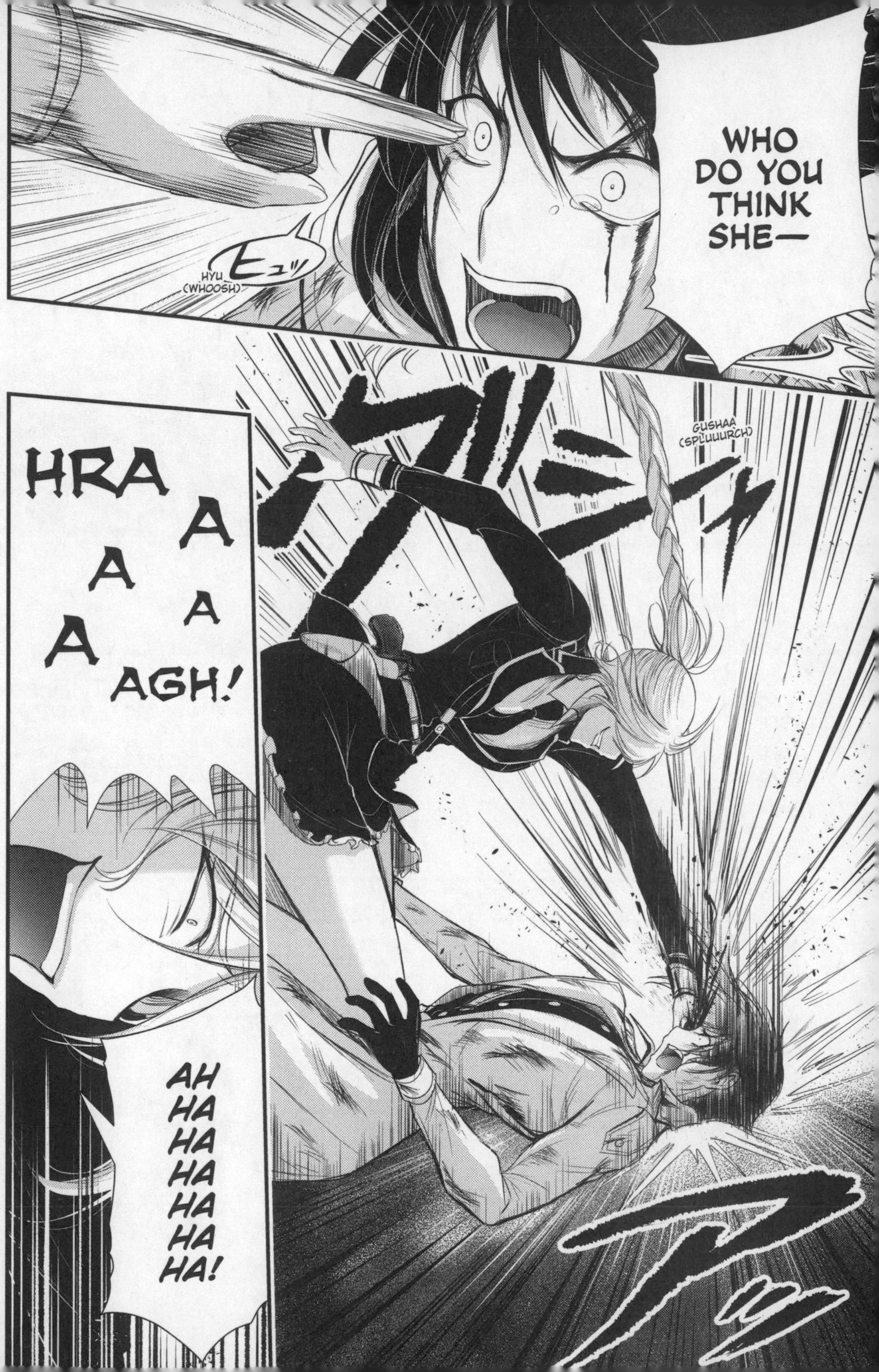
WHO DO YOU THINK SHE—
HYU (WHOOSH)
GUSHAA (SPLUUURCH)
HRAAAAAAGH!
AHHAHAHAHAHAHAHA!

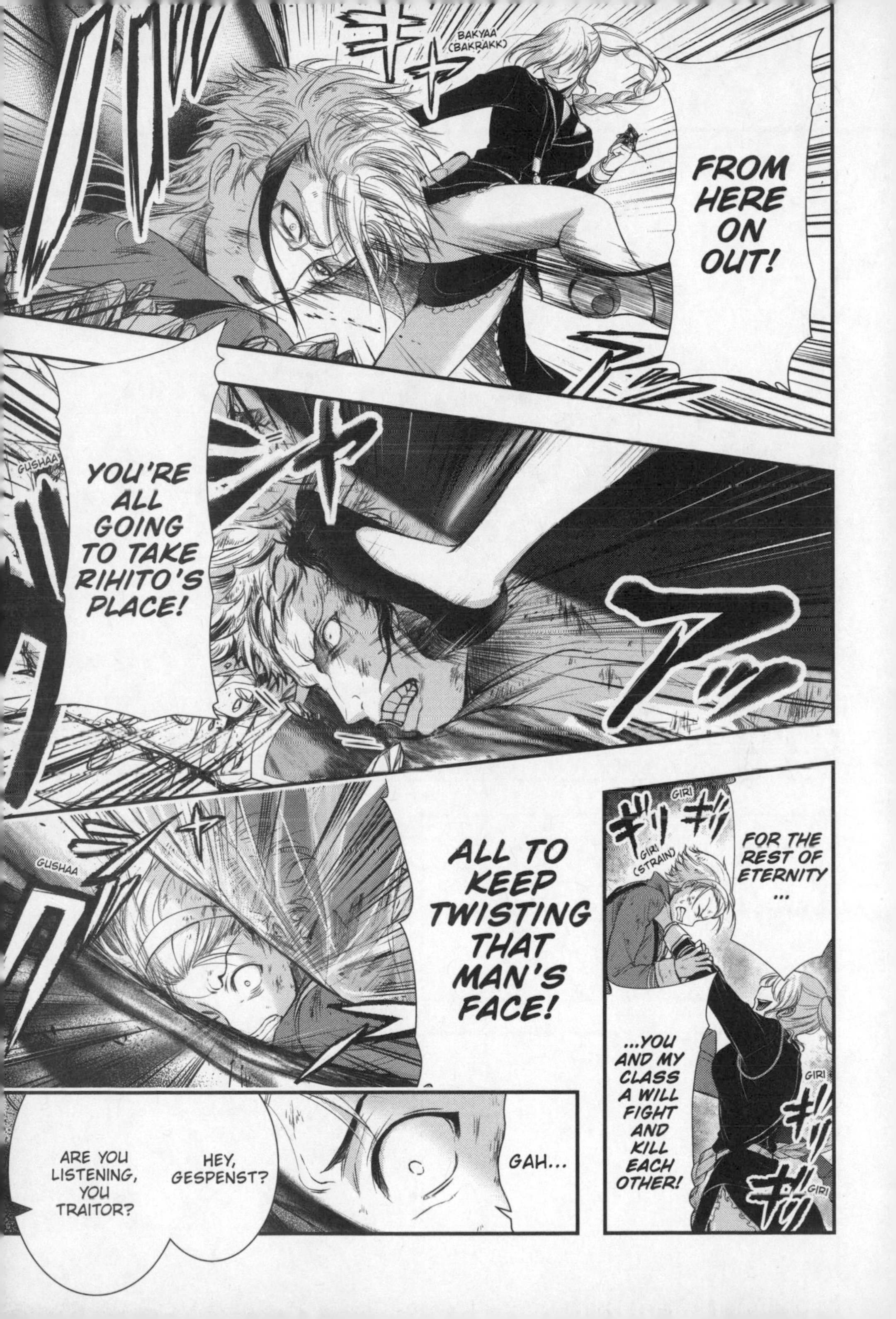
BAKYAA (BAKRAKK)
FROM HERE ON OUT!
GUSHAA
YOU'RE ALL GOING TO TAKE RIHITO'S PLACE!
GIRI
GIRI (STRAIN)
FOR THE REST OF ETERNITY...
...YOU AND MY CLASS A WILL FIGHT AND KILL EACH OTHER!
GIRI
GIRI
ALL TO KEEP TWISTING THAT MAN'S FACE!
GUSHAA
GAH...
HEY, GESPENST?
ARE YOU LISTENING, YOU TRAITOR?

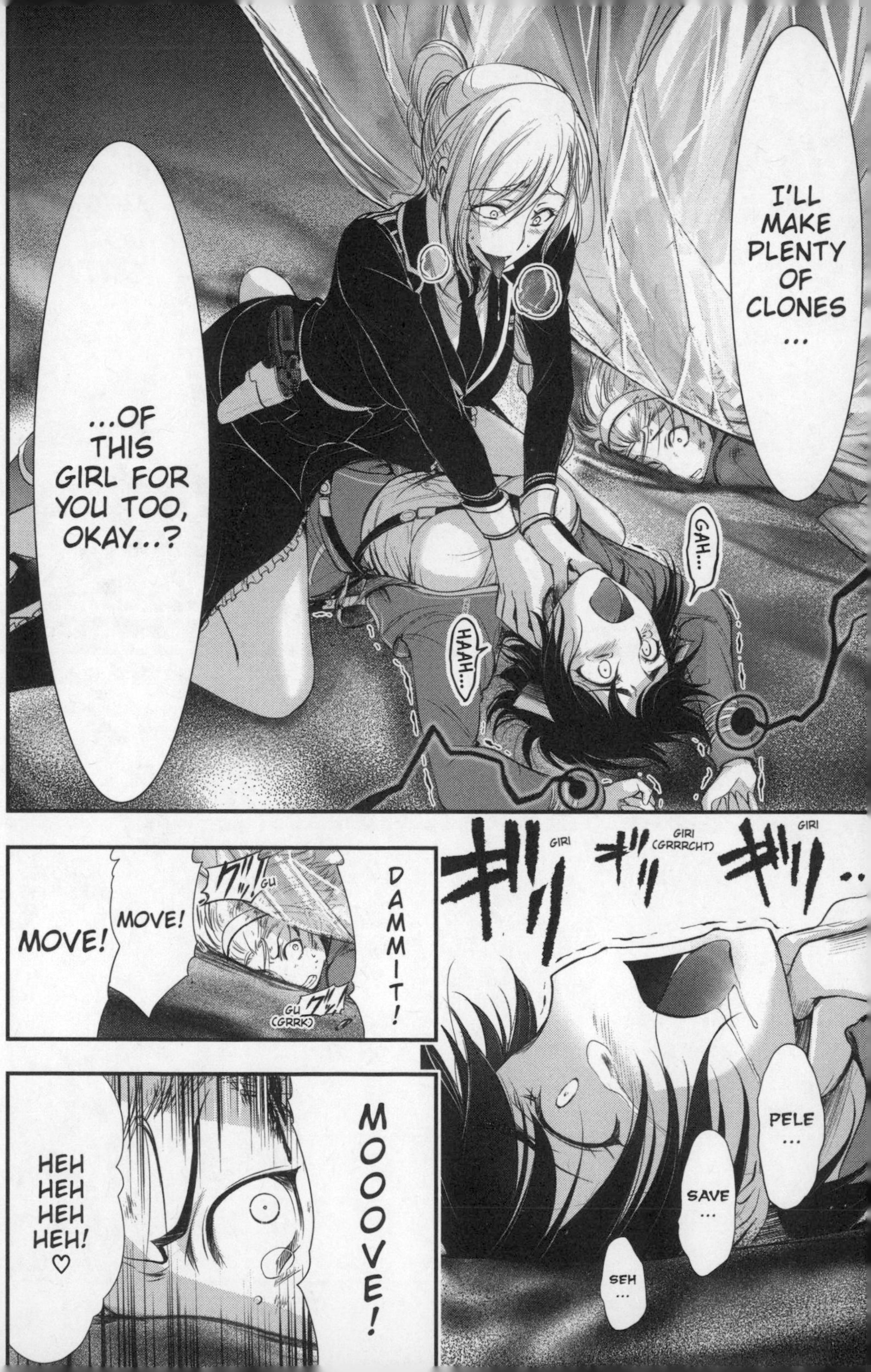
I'LL MAKE PLENTY OF CLONES...
GAH...
HAAH...
...OF THIS GIRL FOR YOU TOO, OKAY...?
ギリ GIRI
ギリ GIRI (GRRRCHT)
ギリ GIRI
PELE...
SAVE...
SEH...
DAMMIT!
グッ GU
MOVE!
MOVE!
グッ GU (GRRK)
MOOOVE!
HEH HEH HEH HEH! ♡

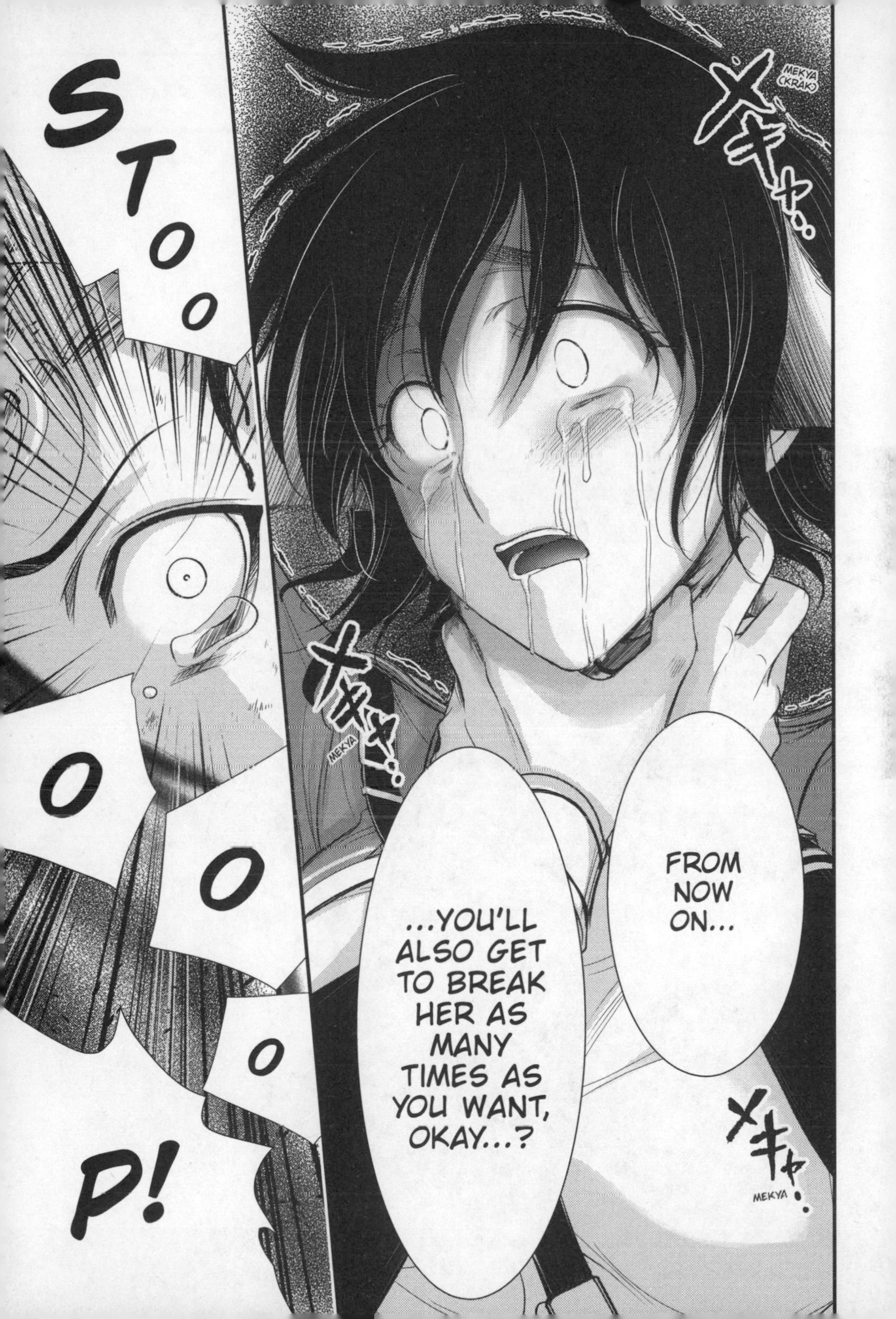
MEKYA (KRAK)
FROM NOW ON...
...YOU'LL ALSO GET TO BREAK HER AS MANY TIMES AS YOU WANT, OKAY...?
MEKYA
MEKYA
STOOOOOP!

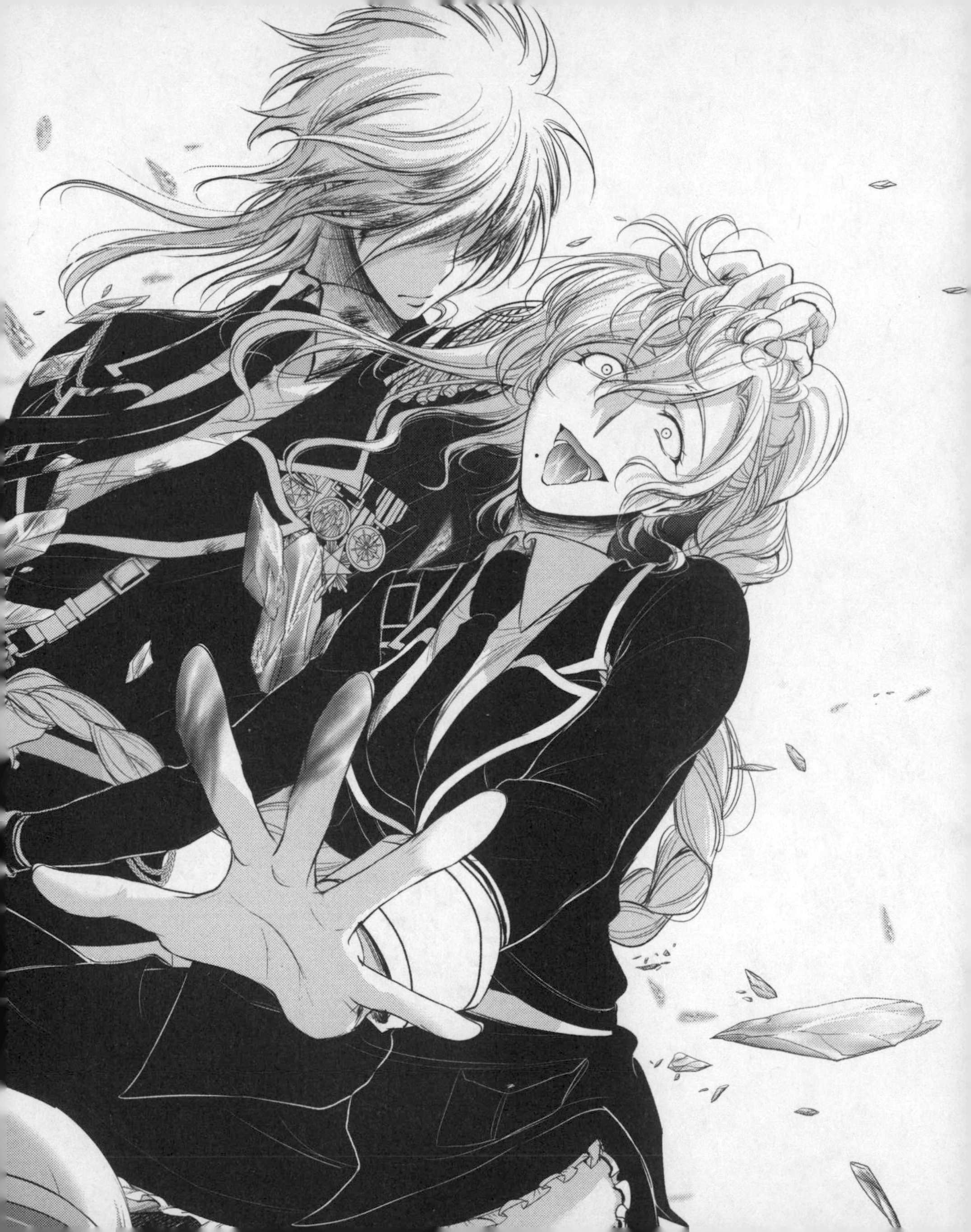

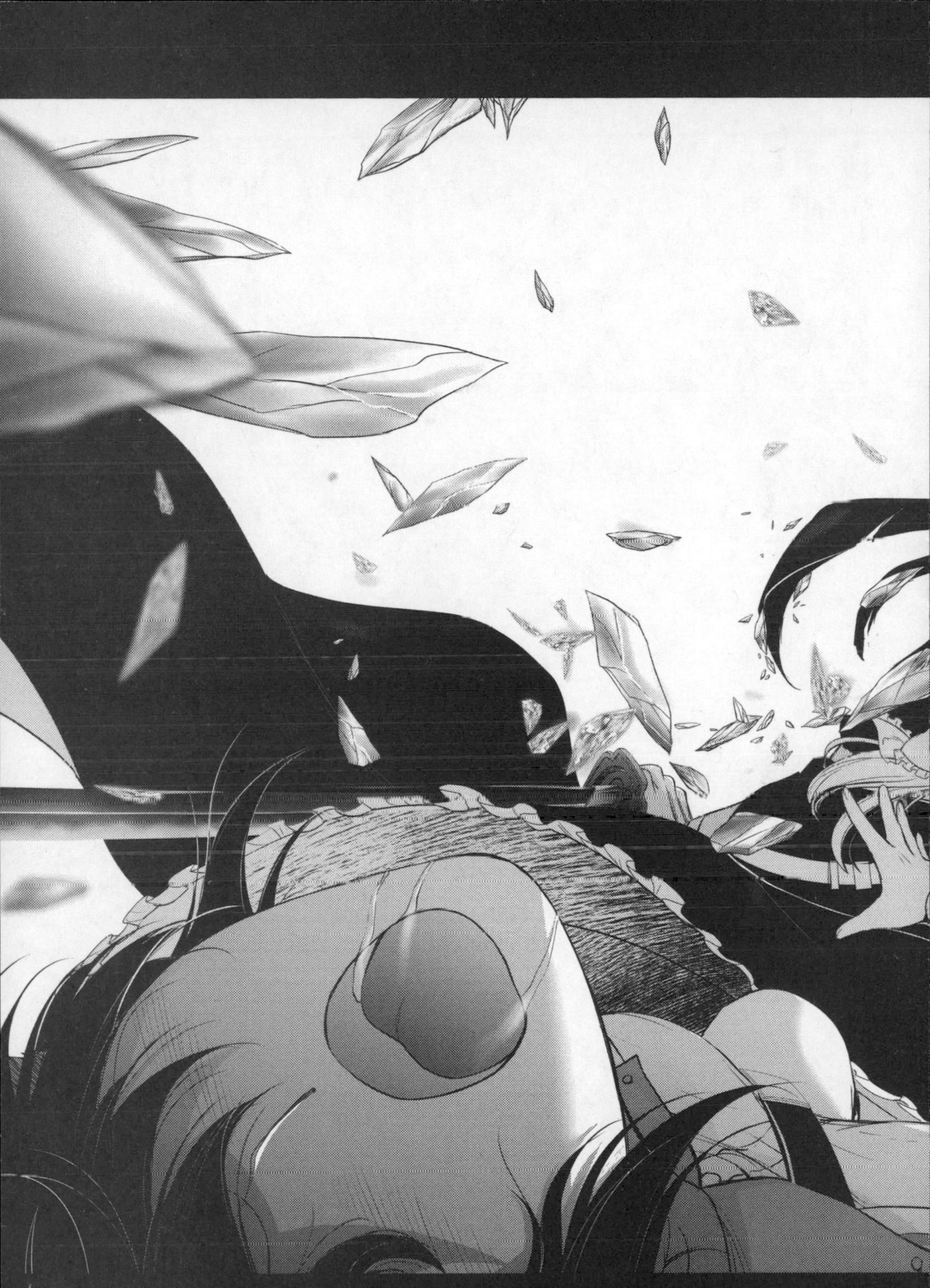

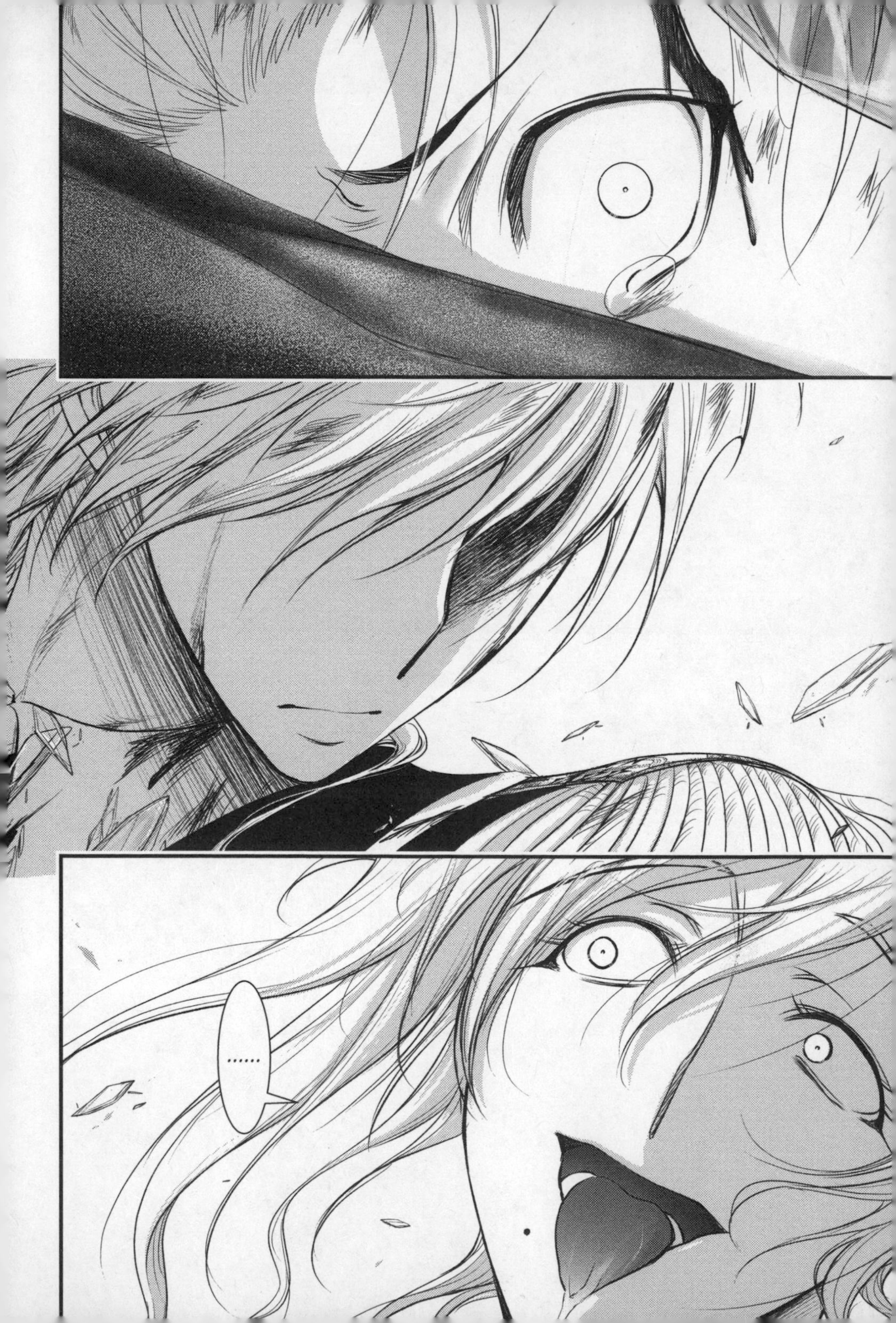
……

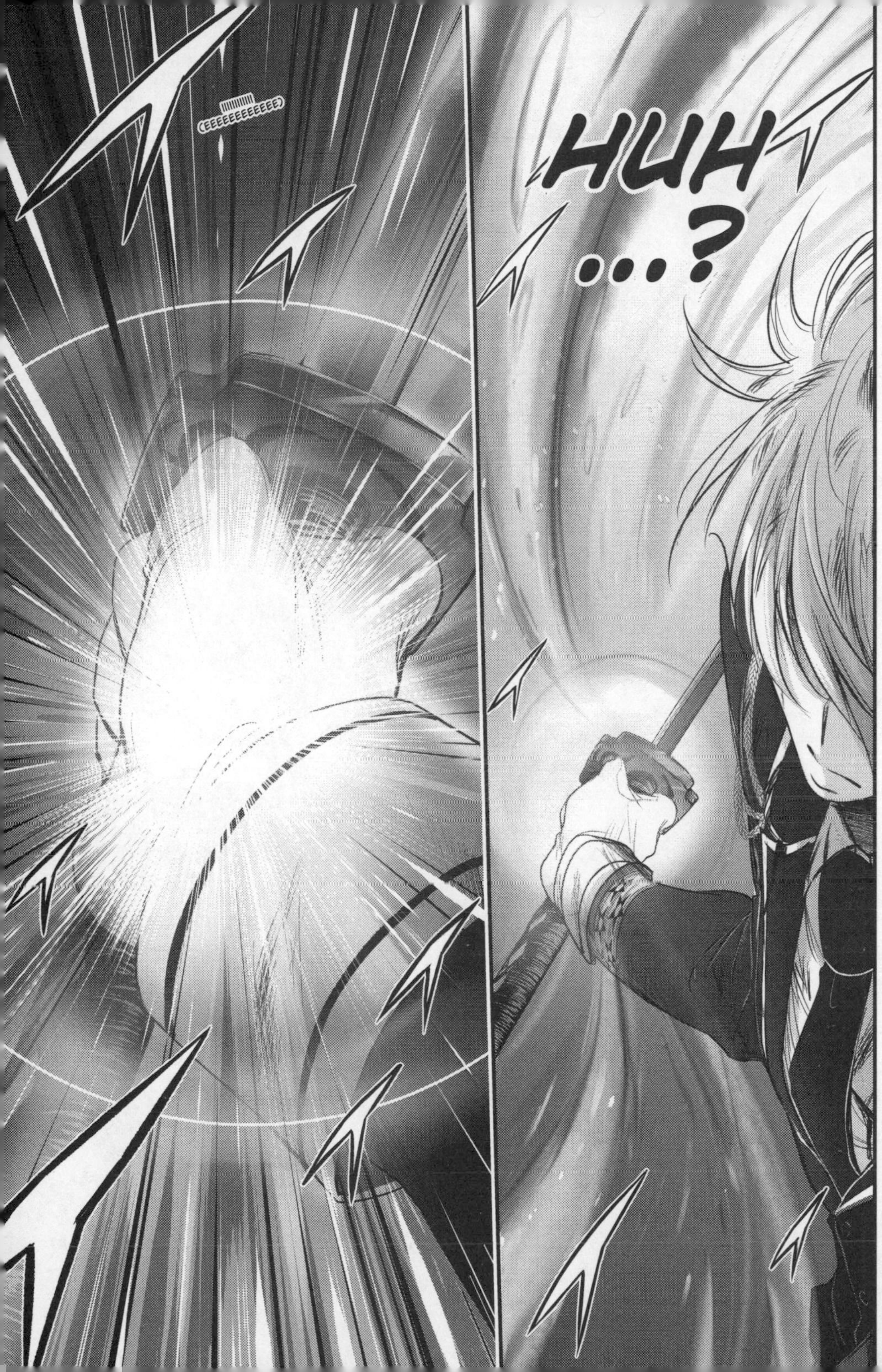
HUH...?
(EEEEEEEEEEEEE)

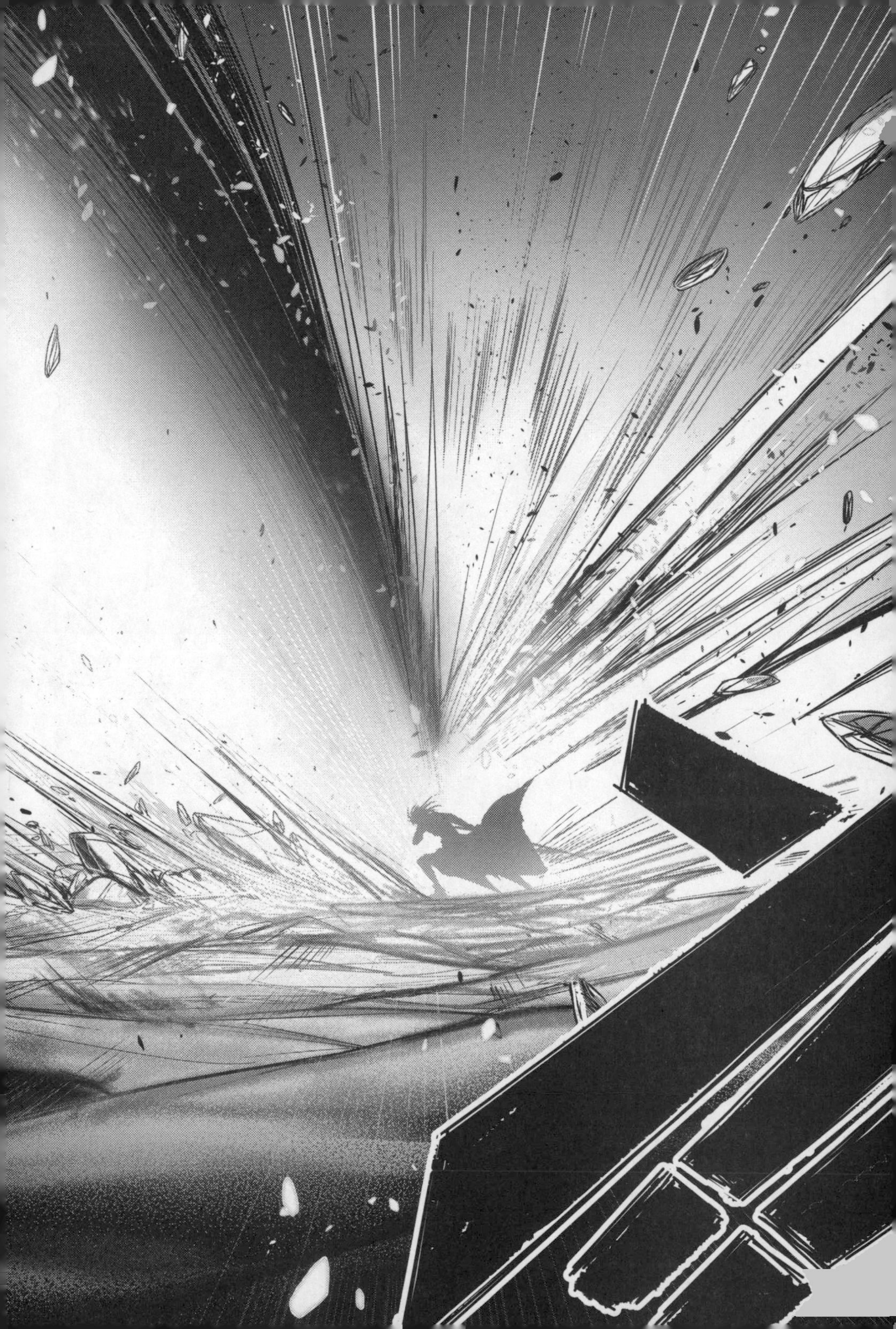

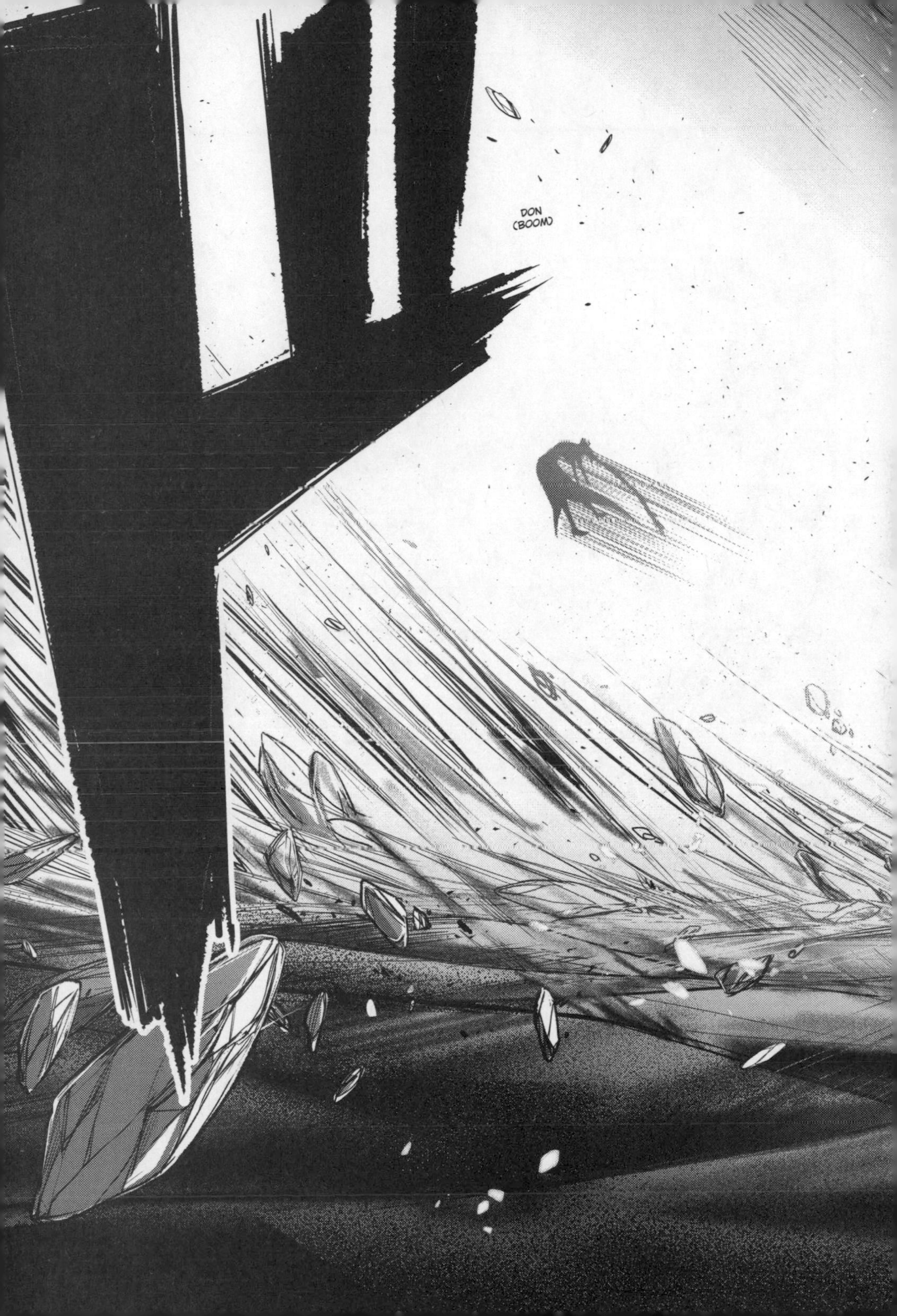
DON
(BOOM)

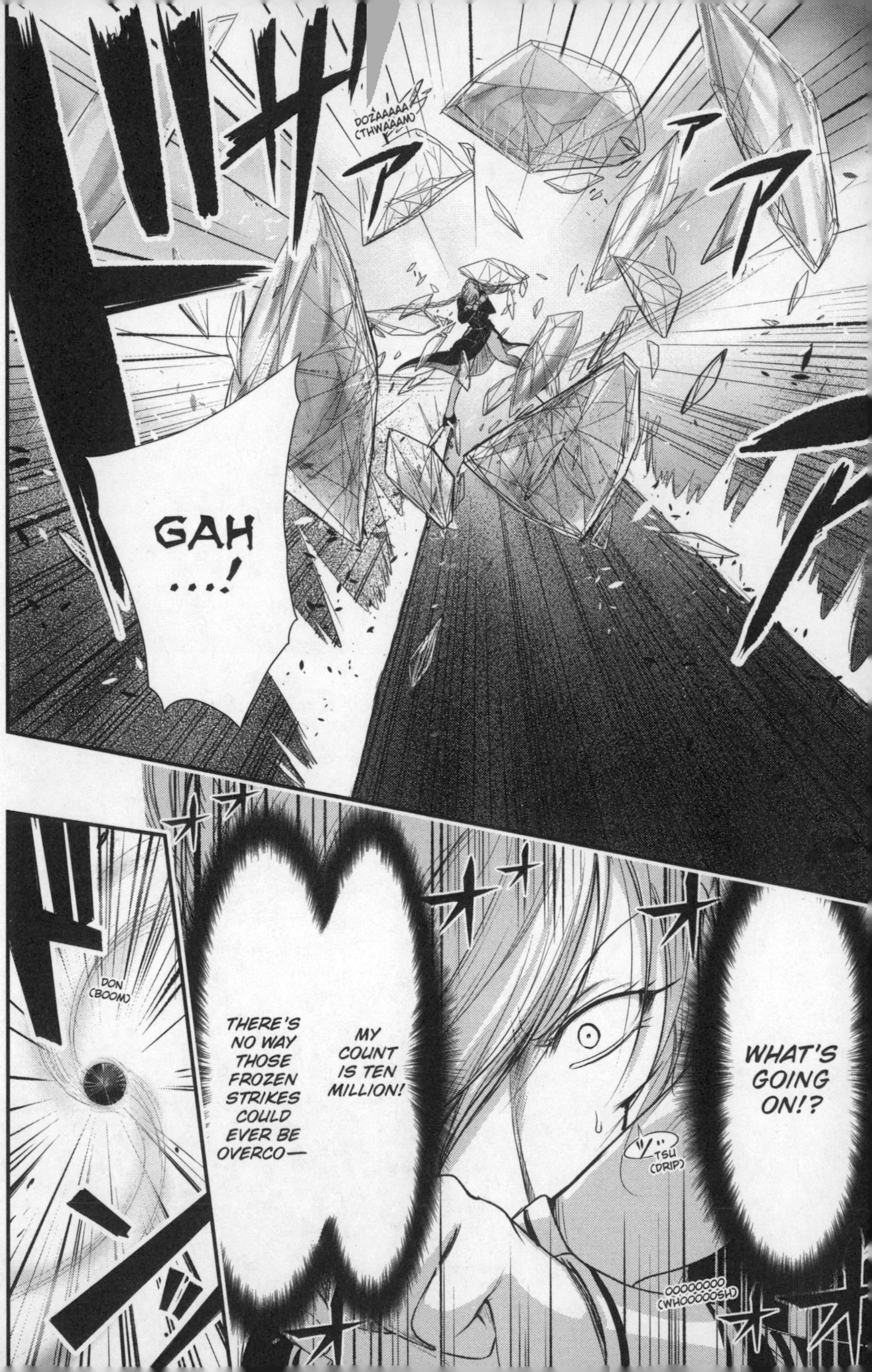
DOZAAAAA
(THWAAAM)
GAH ...!
WHAT'S GOING ON!?
TSU
(DRIP)
OOOOOOOO
(WHOOOOOSH)
MY COUNT IS TEN MILLION!
THERE'S NO WAY THOSE FROZEN STRIKES COULD EVER BE OVERCO—
DON
(BOOM)

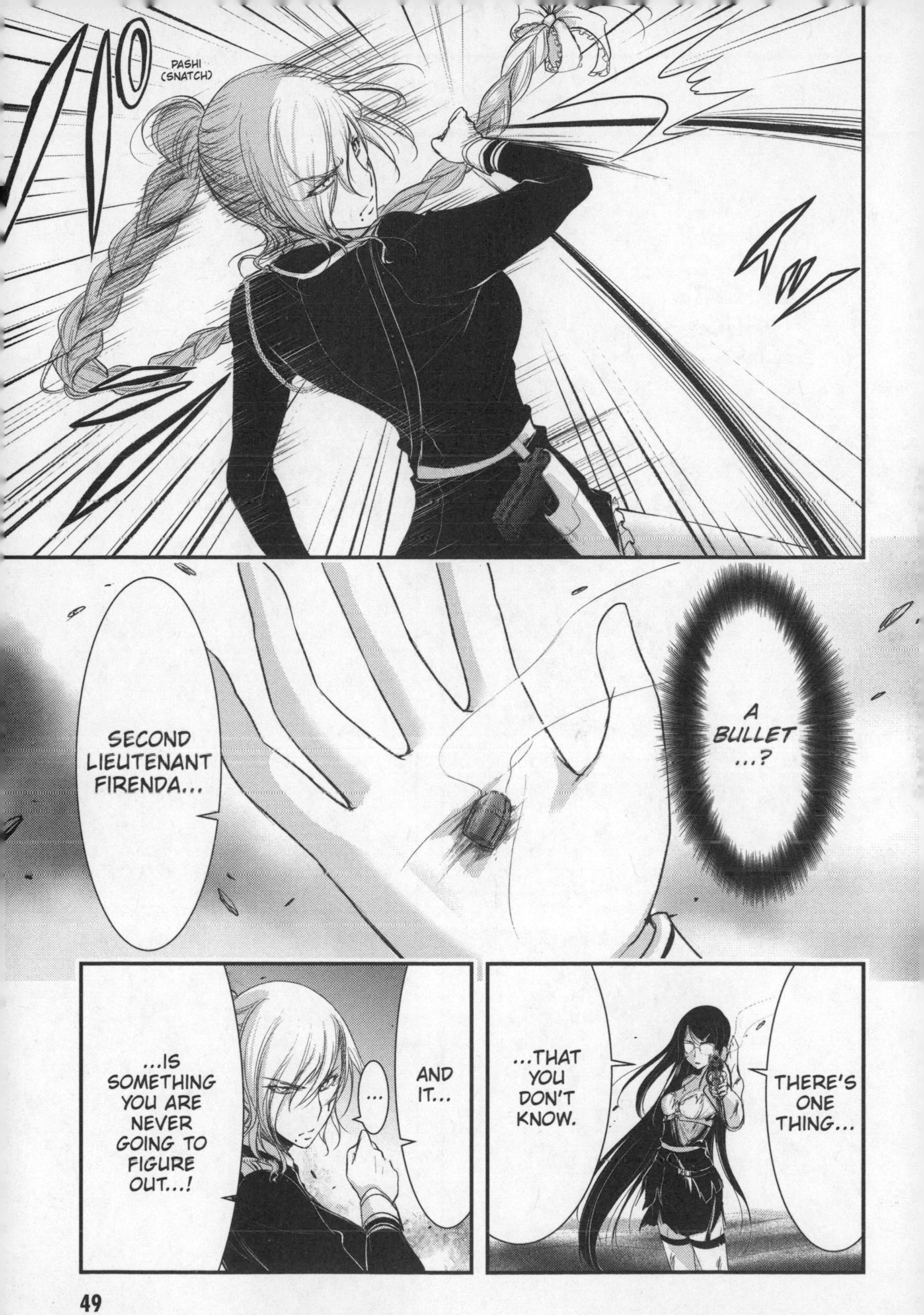
PASHI (SNATCH)
A BULLET ...?
SECOND LIEUTENANT FIRENDA...
THERE'S ONE THING...
...THAT YOU DON'T KNOW.
AND IT...
...
...IS SOMETHING YOU ARE NEVER GOING TO FIGURE OUT...!

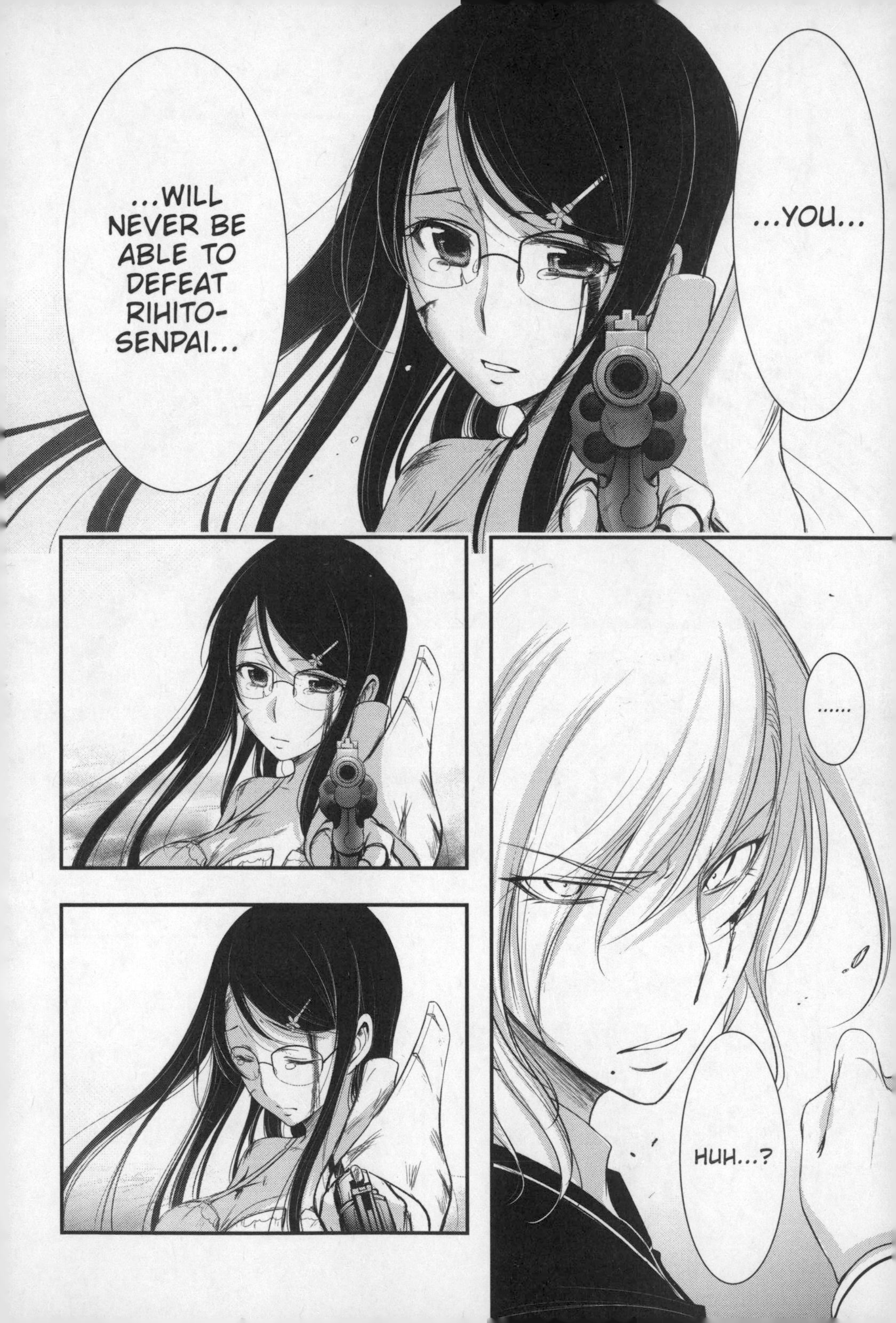
...YOU...
...WILL NEVER BE ABLE TO DEFEAT RIHITO-SENPAI...
......
HUH...?

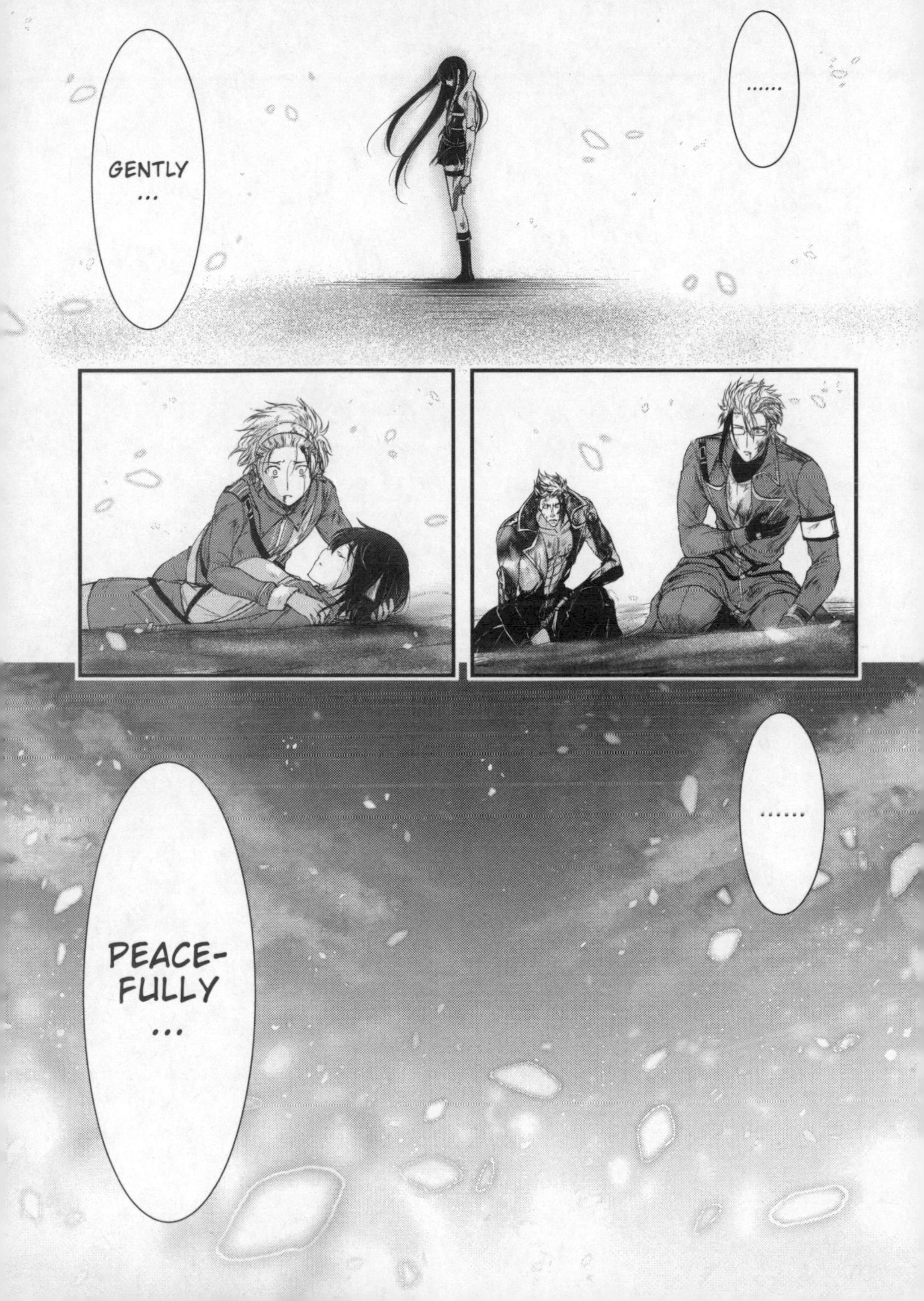
......
GENTLY ...
......
PEACE-FULLY ...

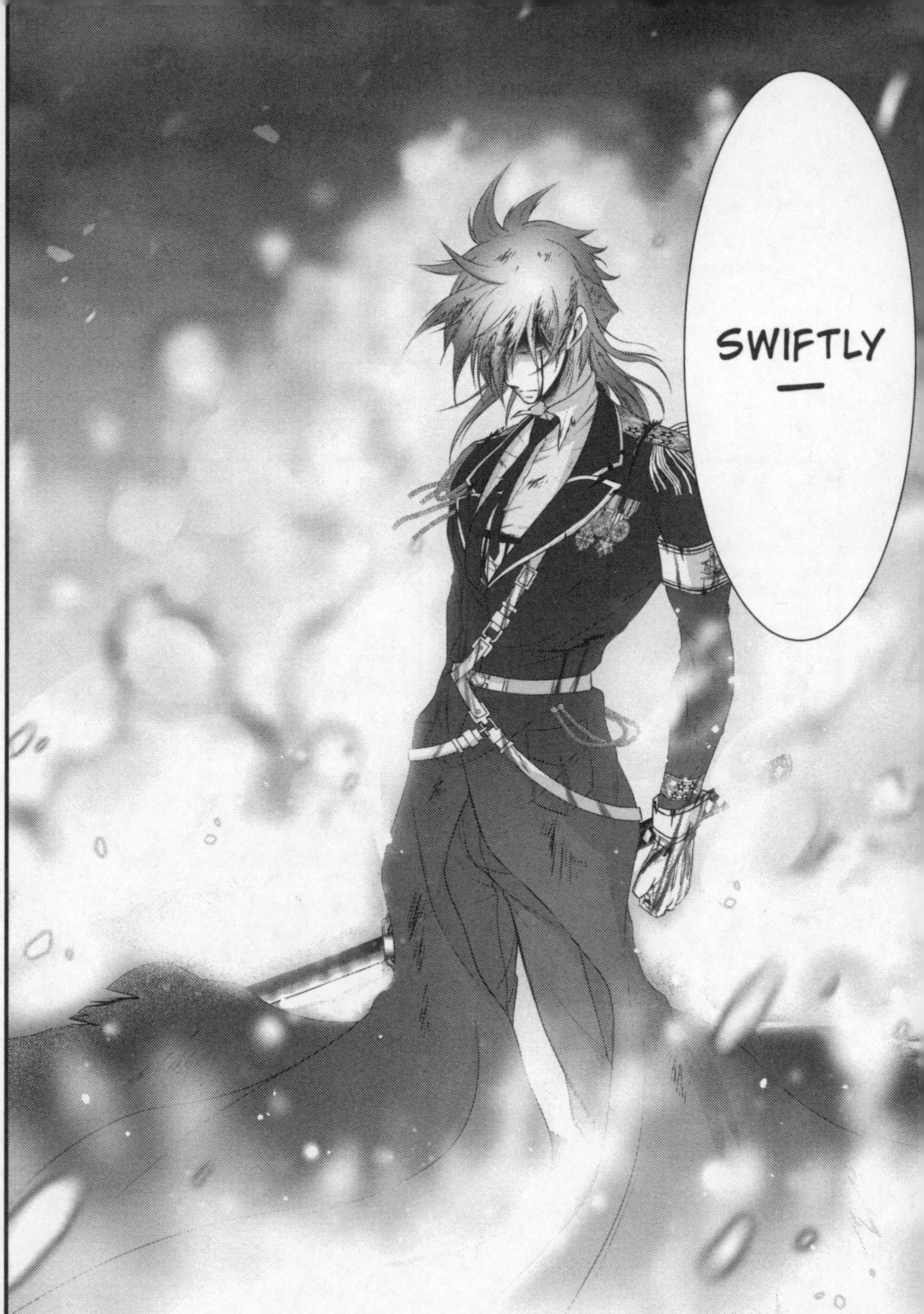
SWIFTLY —

CHAPTER 72: END

CHAPTER 73

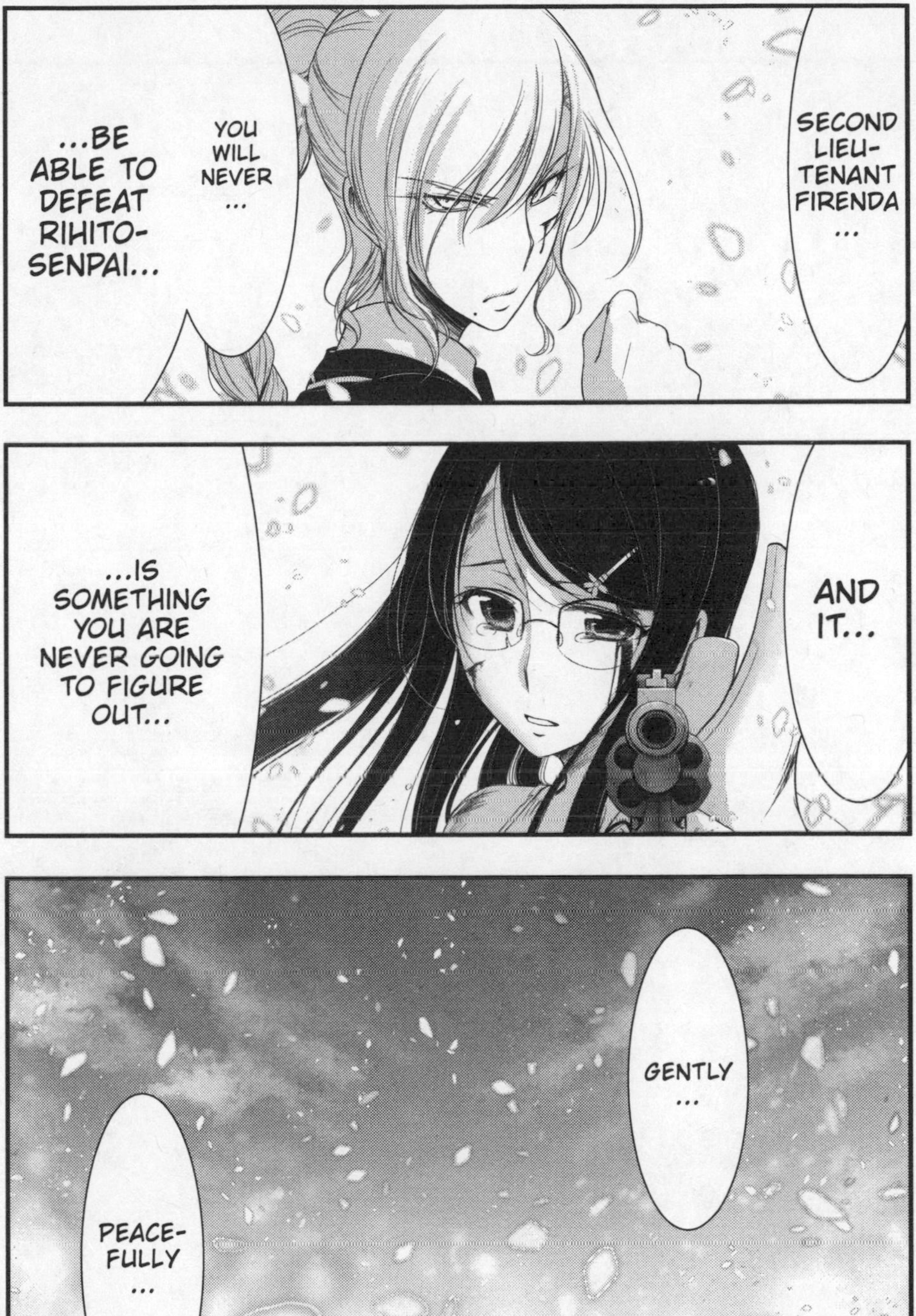
SECOND LIEU-TENANT FIRENDA...
YOU WILL NEVER...
...BE ABLE TO DEFEAT RIHITO-SENPAI...
AND IT...
...IS SOMETHING YOU ARE NEVER GOING TO FIGURE OUT...
GENTLY...
PEACE-FULLY...

Chapter 73: Hesitation

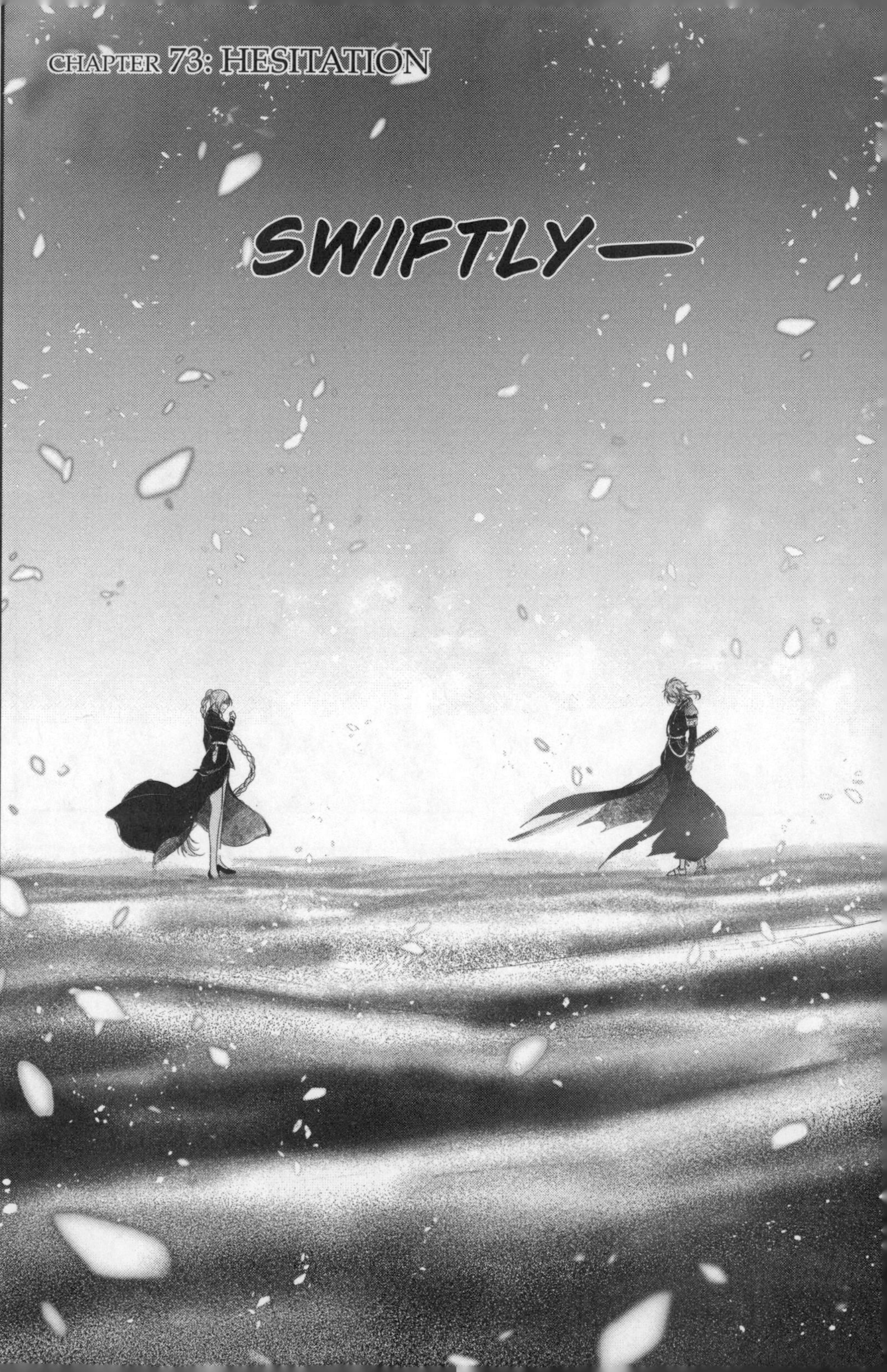
SWIFTLY—

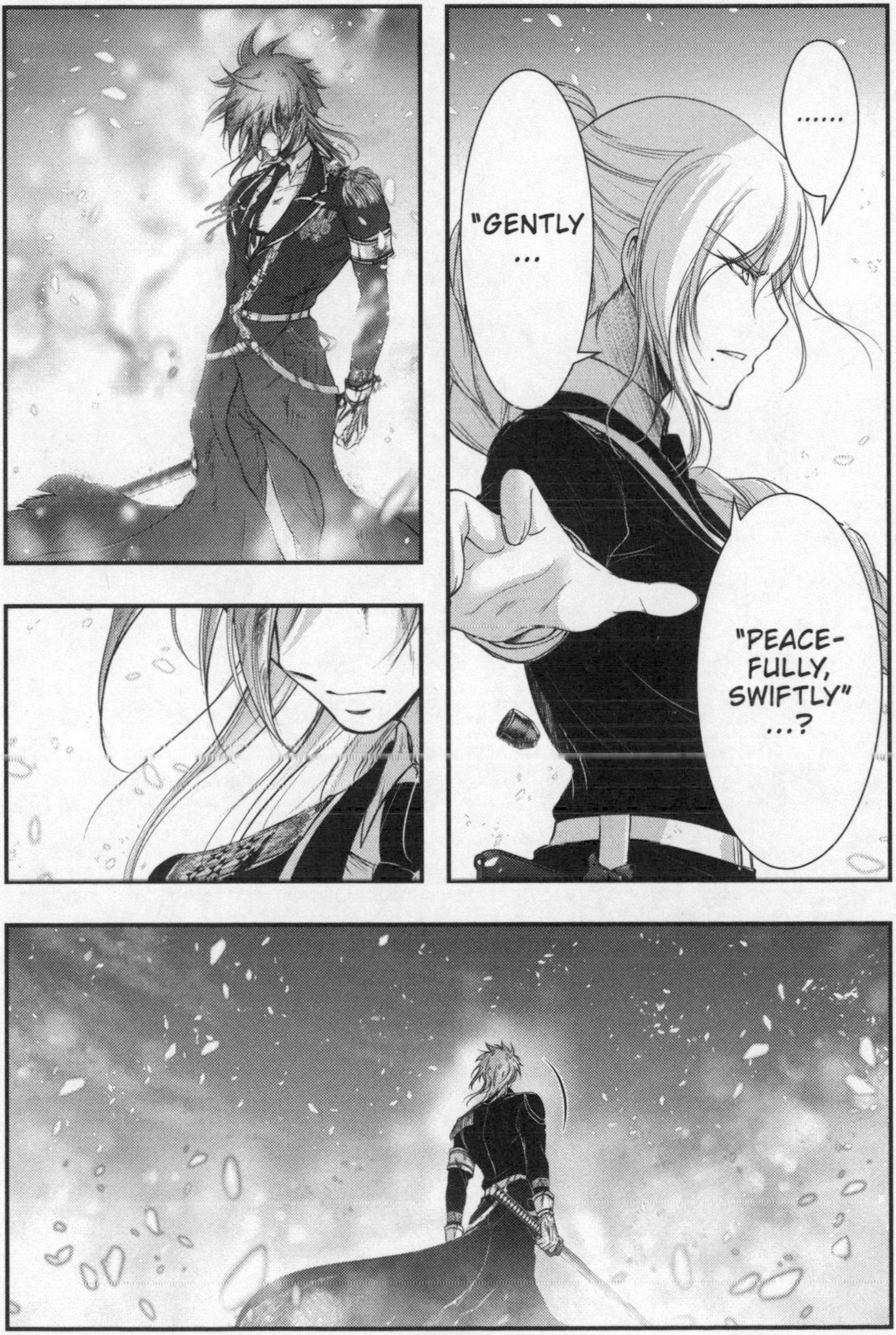
......
"GENTLY ...
"PEACE-FULLY, SWIFTLY" ...?

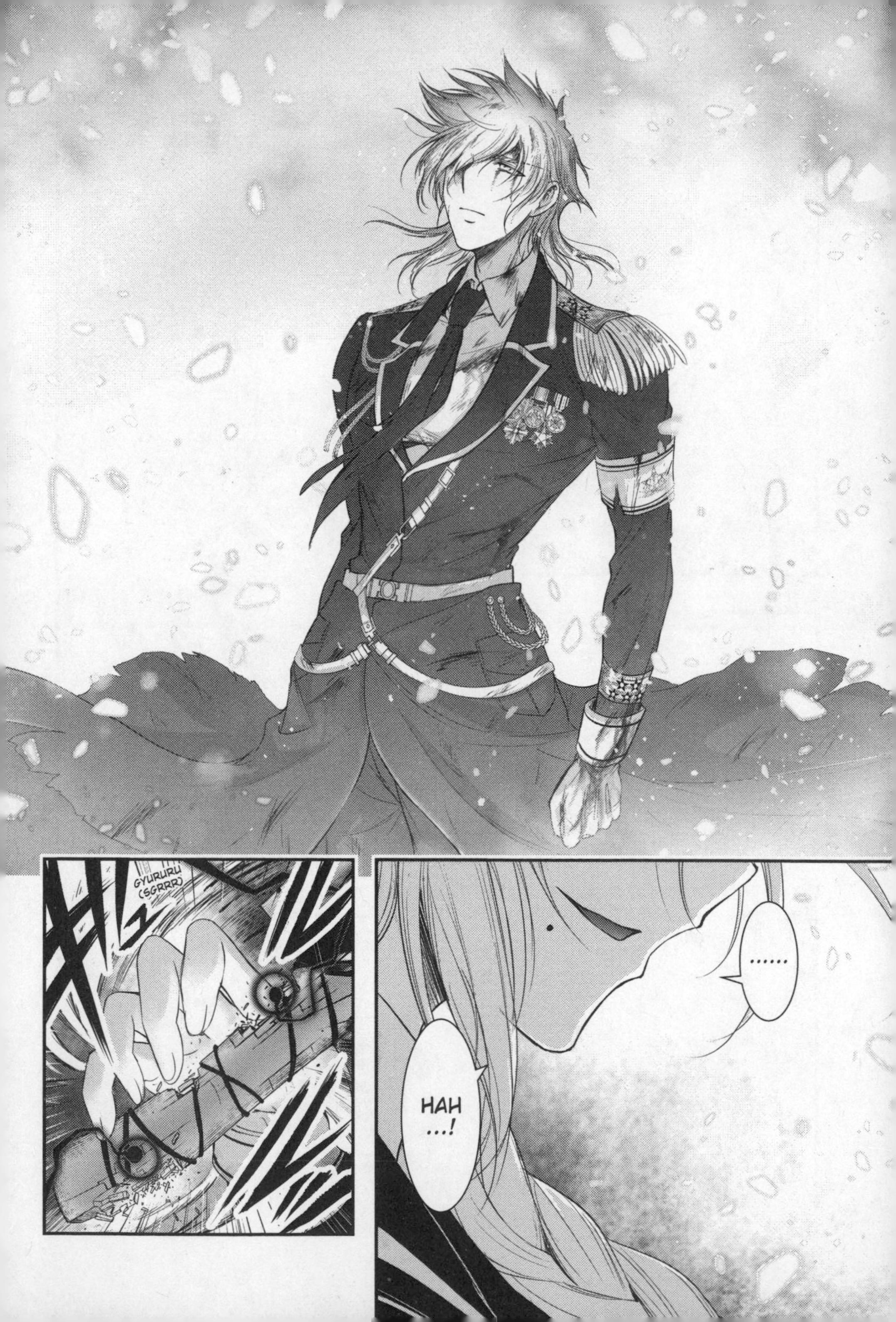
......
HAH ...!
GYURURU (SGRRR)

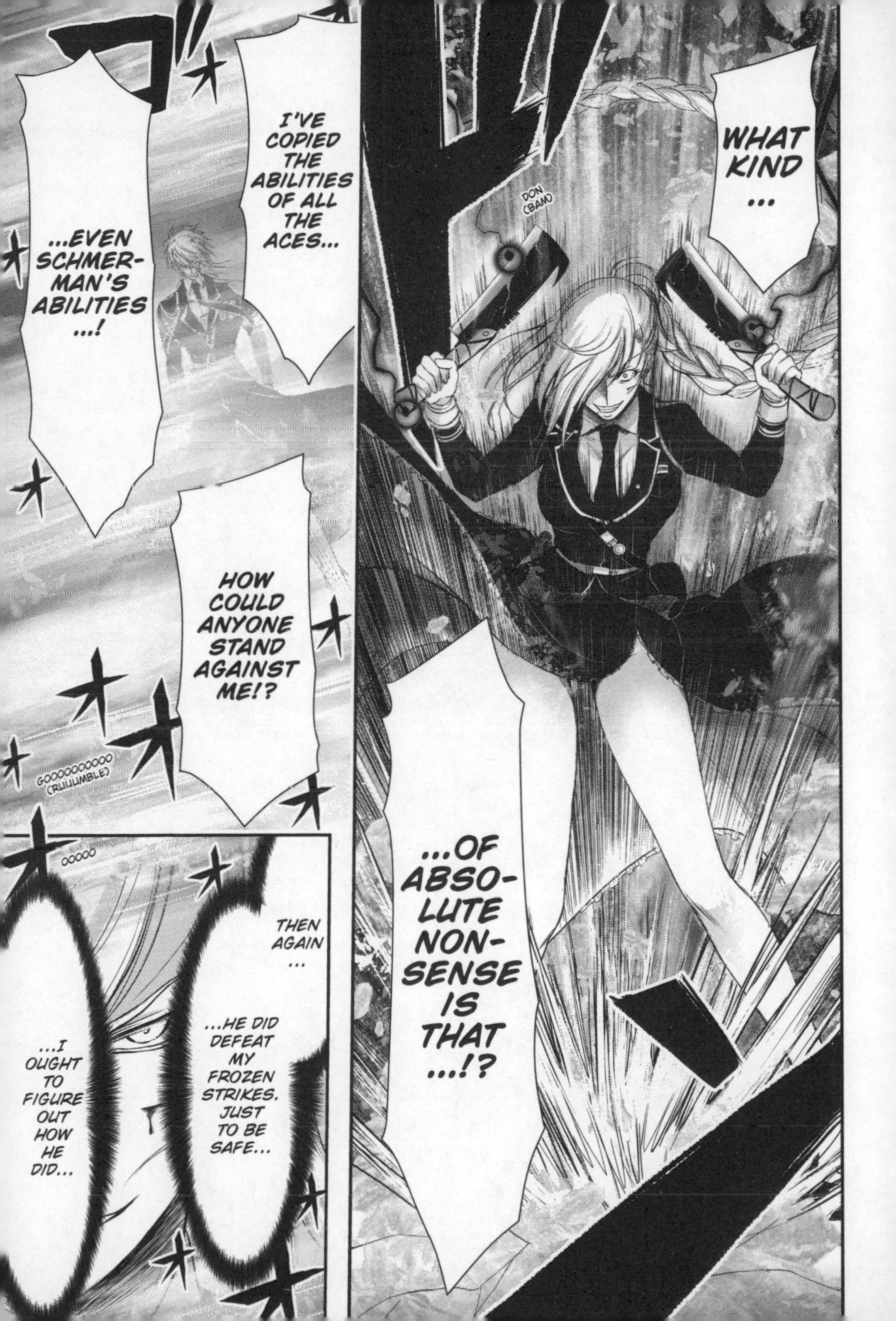
WHAT KIND...
DON (BAM)
...OF ABSOLUTE NONSENSE IS THAT...!?
I'VE COPIED THE ABILITIES OF ALL THE ACES...
...EVEN SCHMERMAN'S ABILITIES...!
HOW COULD ANYONE STAND AGAINST ME!?
GOOOOOOOOOO (RUUUMBLE)
OOOOO
THEN AGAIN...
...HE DID DEFEAT MY FROZEN STRIKES. JUST TO BE SAFE...
...I OUGHT TO FIGURE OUT HOW HE DID...

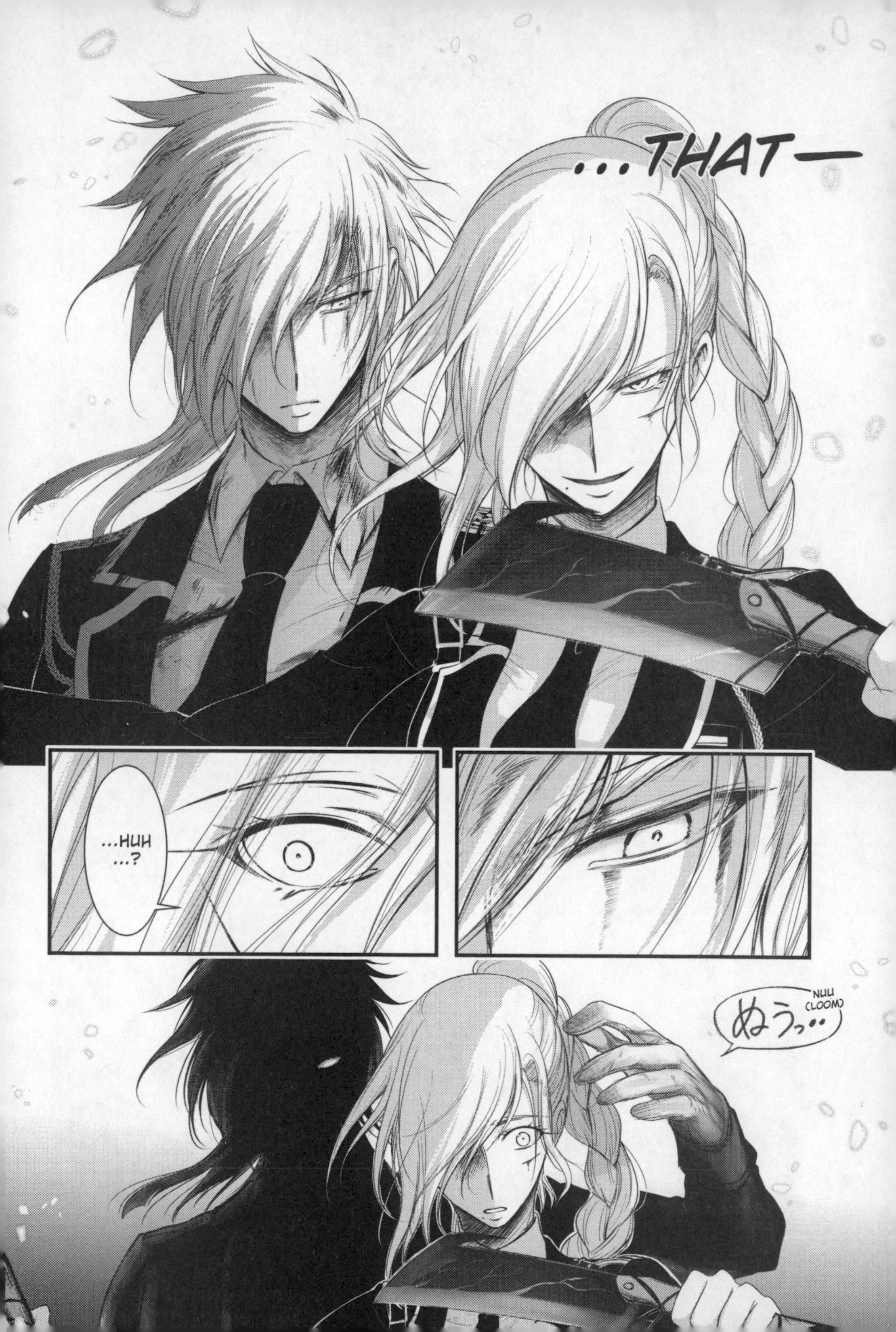
...THAT—
...HUH ...?
ぬうっ・・
NUU (LOOM)

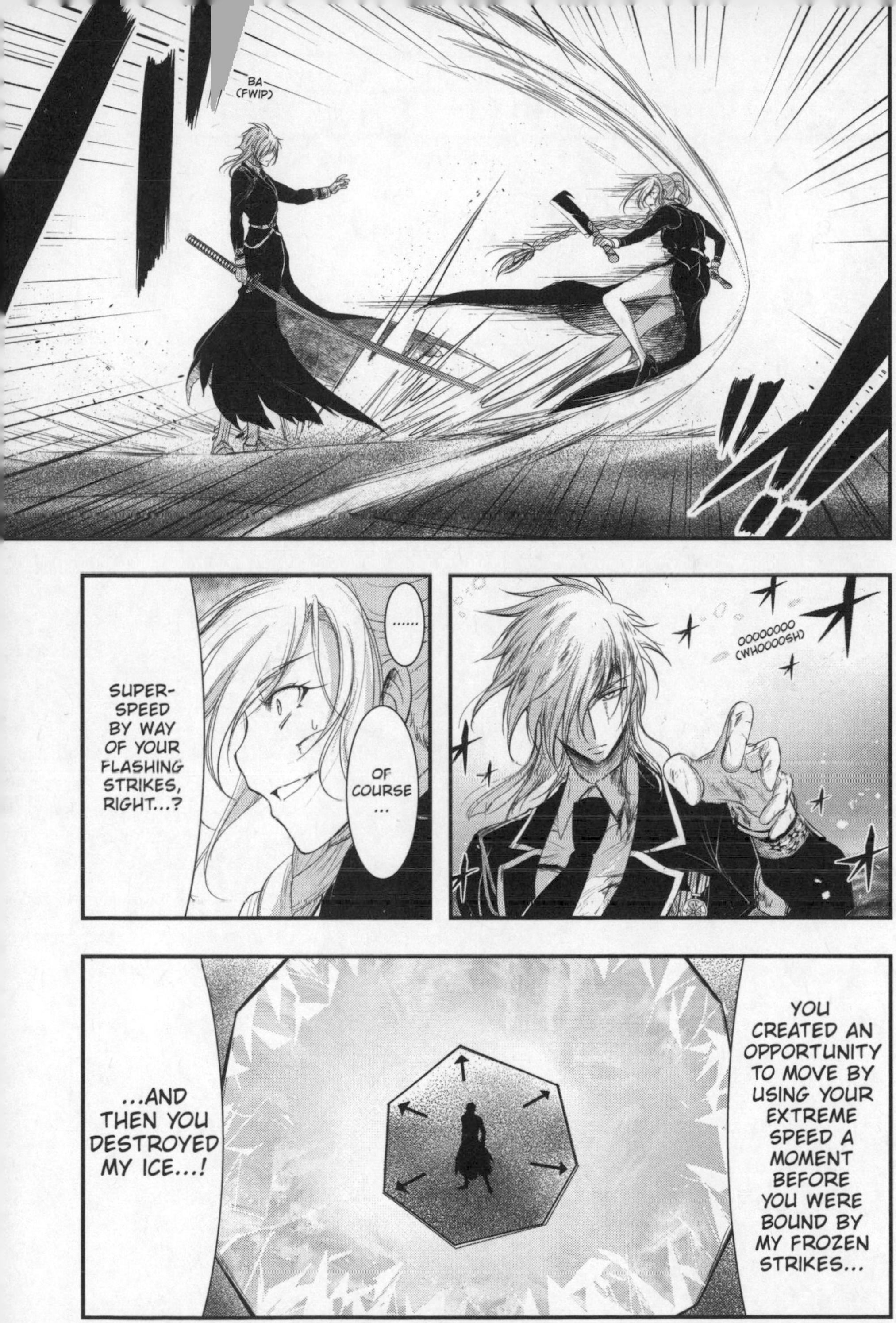
BA-
(FWIP)
OOOOOOOO
(WHOOOOSH)
......
OF COURSE ...
SUPER-SPEED BY WAY OF YOUR FLASHING STRIKES, RIGHT...?
YOU CREATED AN OPPORTUNITY TO MOVE BY USING YOUR EXTREME SPEED A MOMENT BEFORE YOU WERE BOUND BY MY FROZEN STRIKES...
...AND THEN YOU DESTROYED MY ICE...!

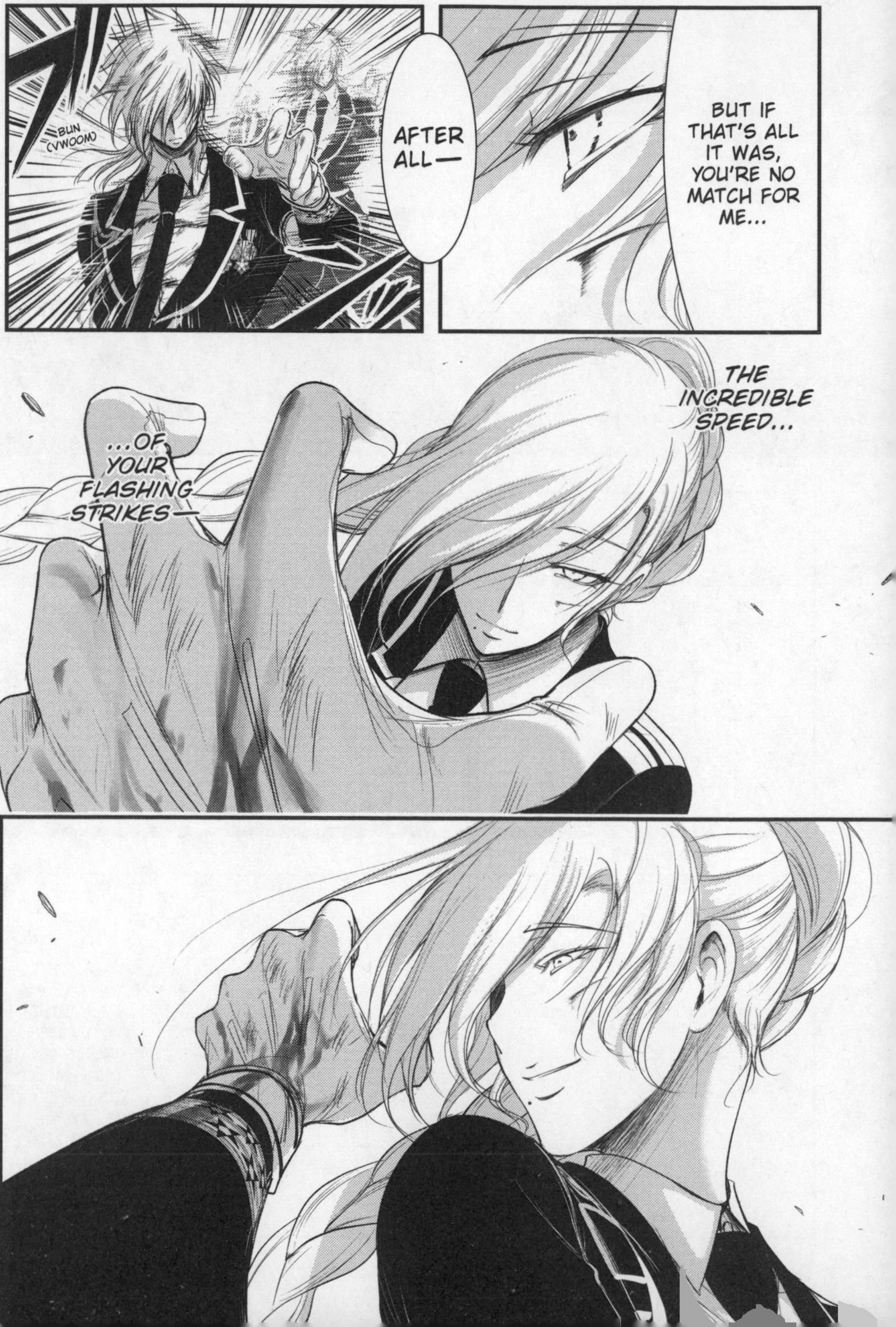
BUT IF THAT'S ALL IT WAS, YOU'RE NO MATCH FOR ME...
AFTER ALL—
BUN (VWOOM)
THE INCREDIBLE SPEED...
...OF YOUR FLASHING STRIKES—

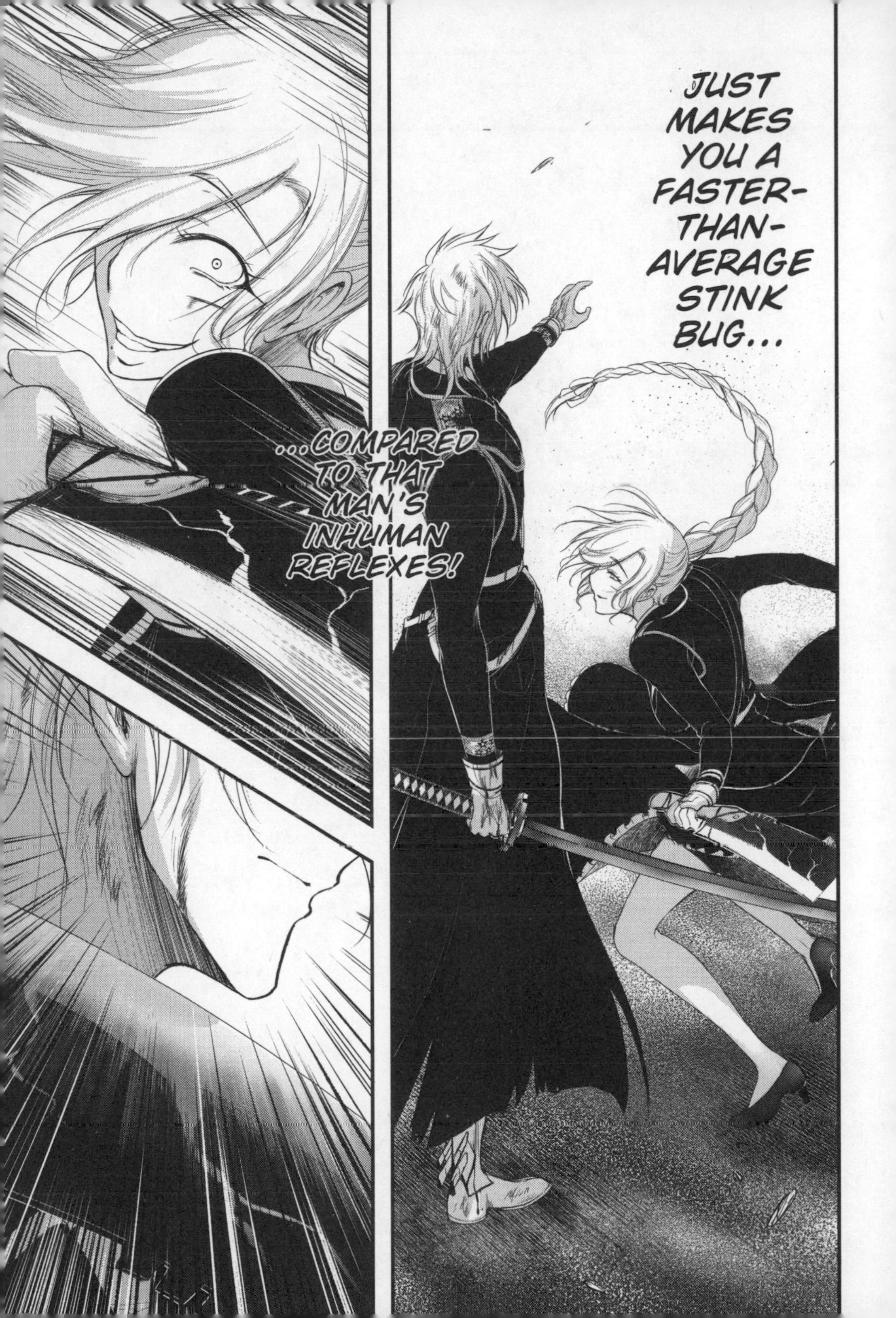
JUST MAKES YOU A FASTER-THAN-AVERAGE STINK BUG...
...COMPARED TO THAT MAN'S INHUMAN REFLEXES!

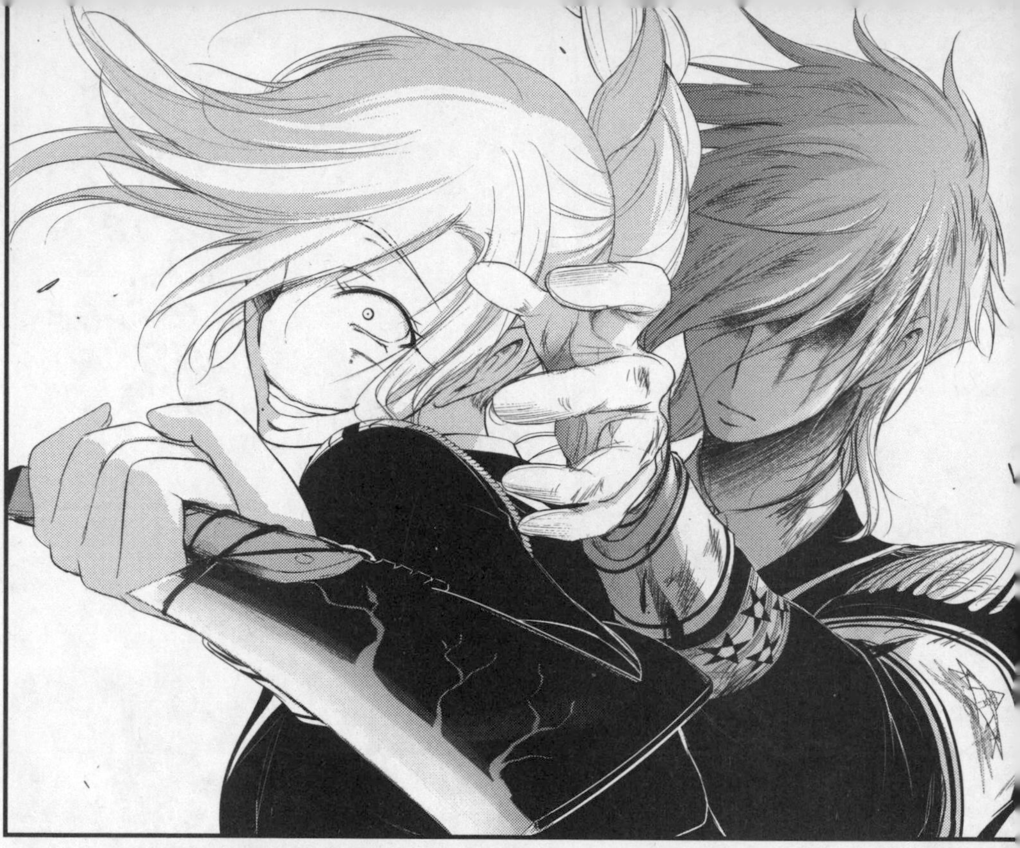
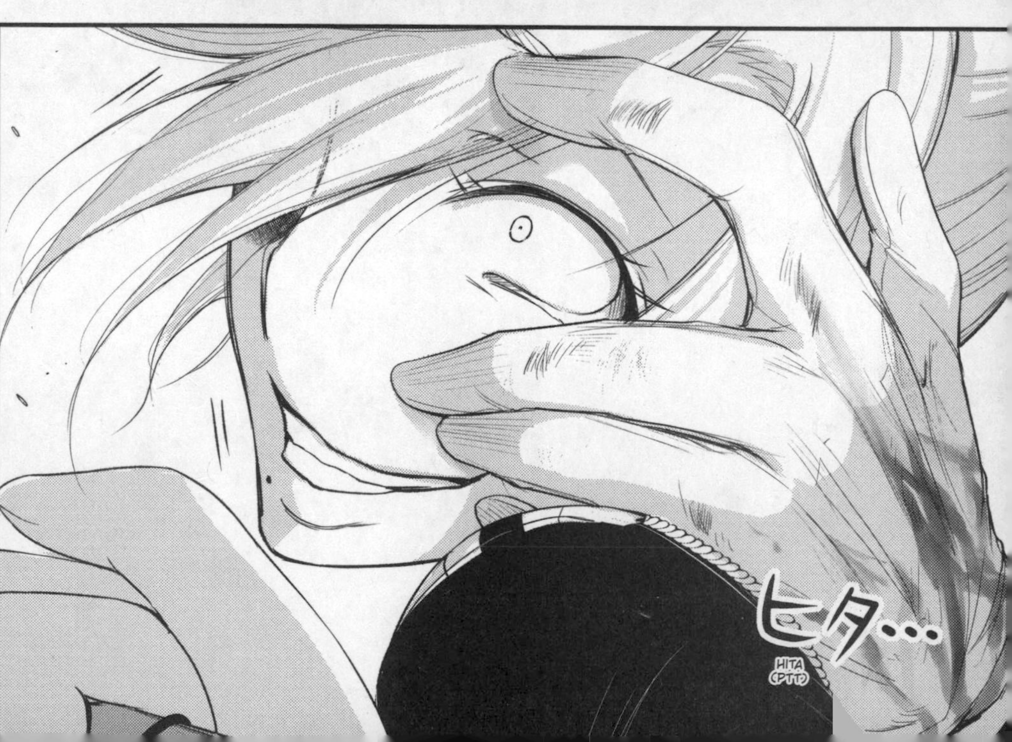
ヒタ…
HITA
(PTTT)

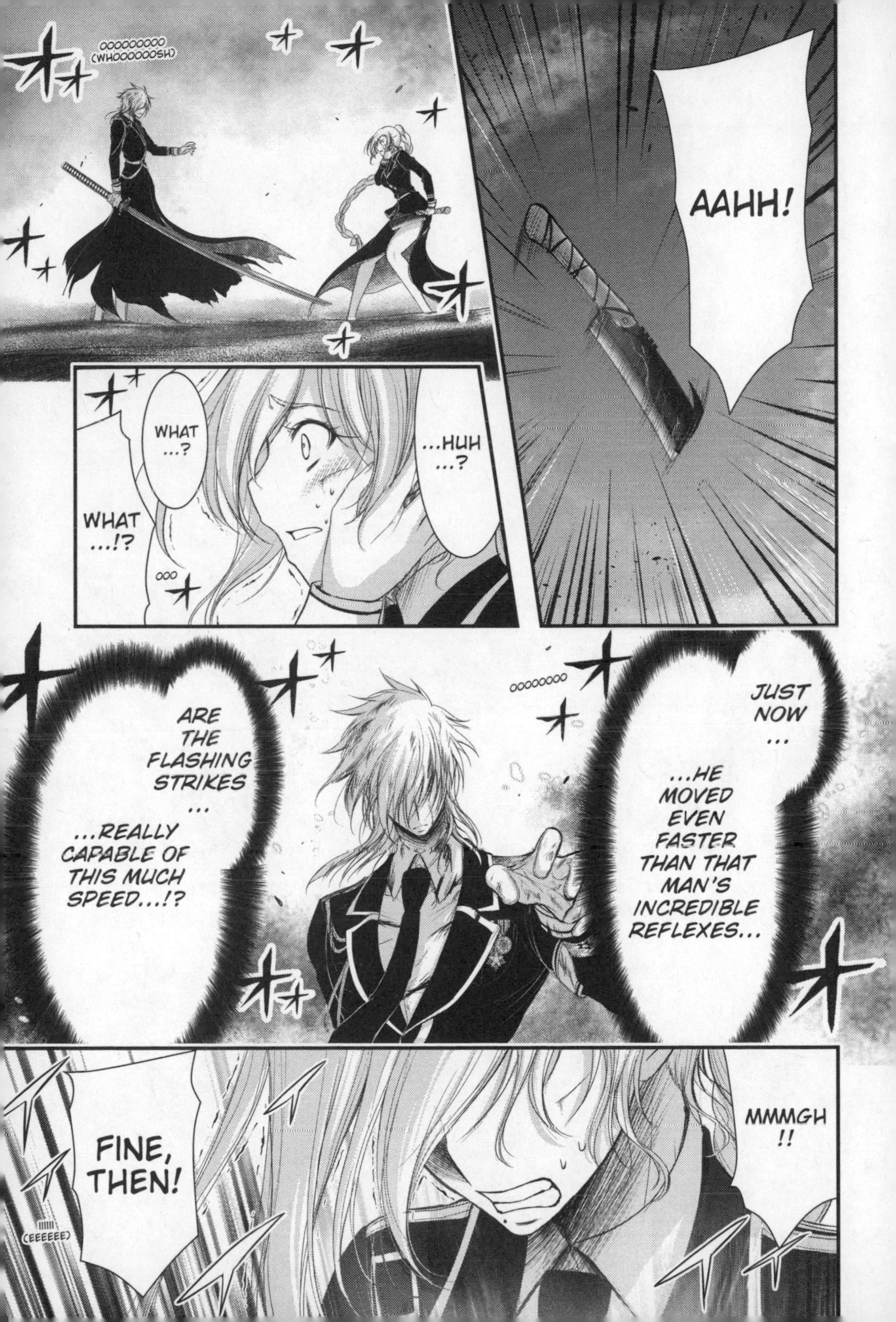
AAHH!
OOOOOOOOO (WHOOOOOOSH)
...HUH ...?
WHAT ...?
WHAT ...!?
OOO
OOOOOOOOO
JUST NOW ...
...HE MOVED EVEN FASTER THAN THAT MAN'S INCREDIBLE REFLEXES...
ARE THE FLASHING STRIKES ...
...REALLY CAPABLE OF THIS MUCH SPEED...!?
MMMGH !!
FINE, THEN!
(EEEEEEE)

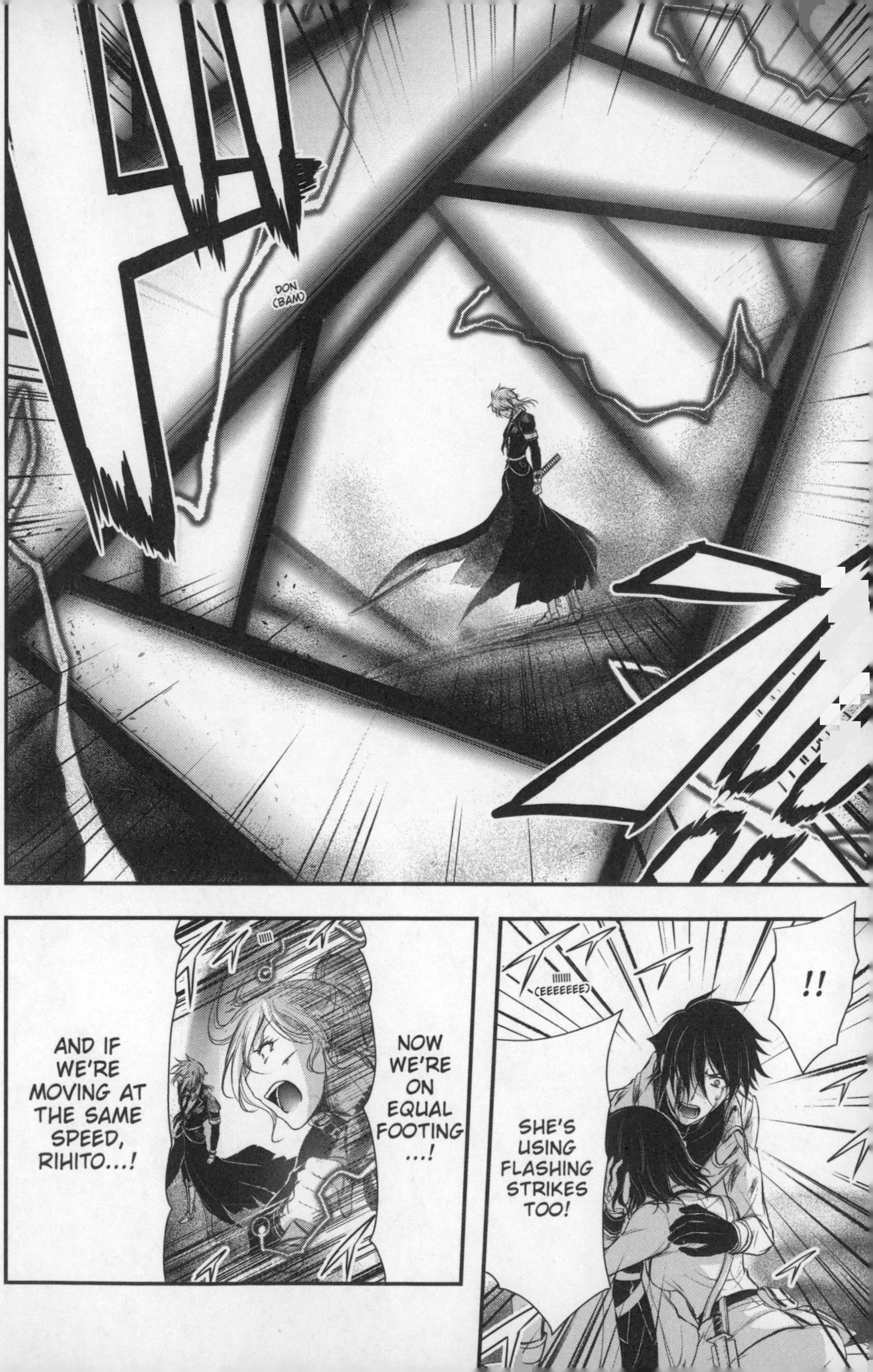
DON (BAM)
!!
(EEEEEEE)
SHE'S USING FLASHING STRIKES TOO!
NOW WE'RE ON EQUAL FOOTING...!
AND IF WE'RE MOVING AT THE SAME SPEED, RIHITO...!

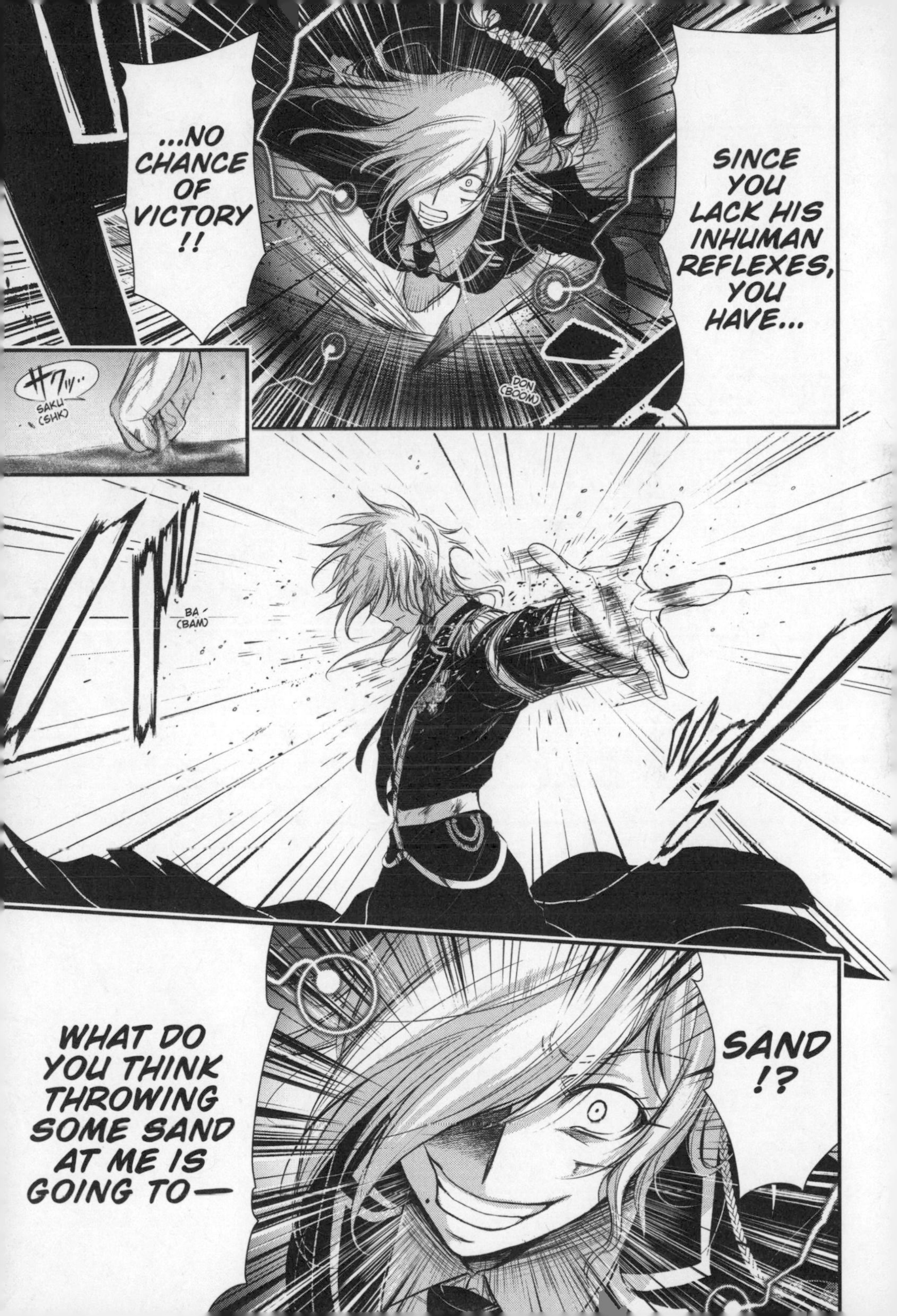
SINCE YOU LACK HIS INHUMAN REFLEXES, YOU HAVE...
...NO CHANCE OF VICTORY!!
DON (BOOM)
SAKU (SHK)
BA (BAM)
SAND!?
WHAT DO YOU THINK THROWING SOME SAND AT ME IS GOING TO—

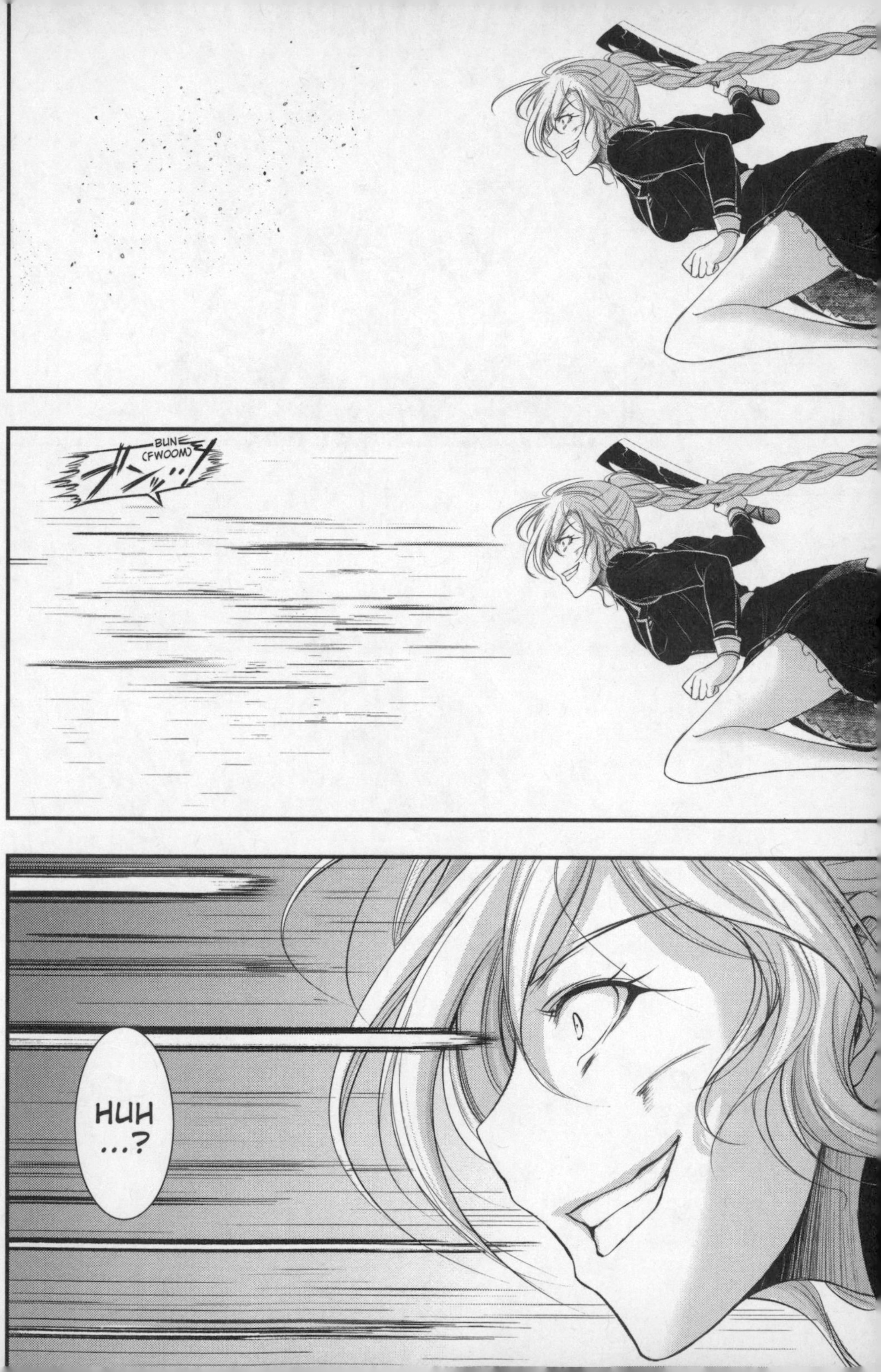
ブンッ!
BUN (FWOOM)
HUH ...?

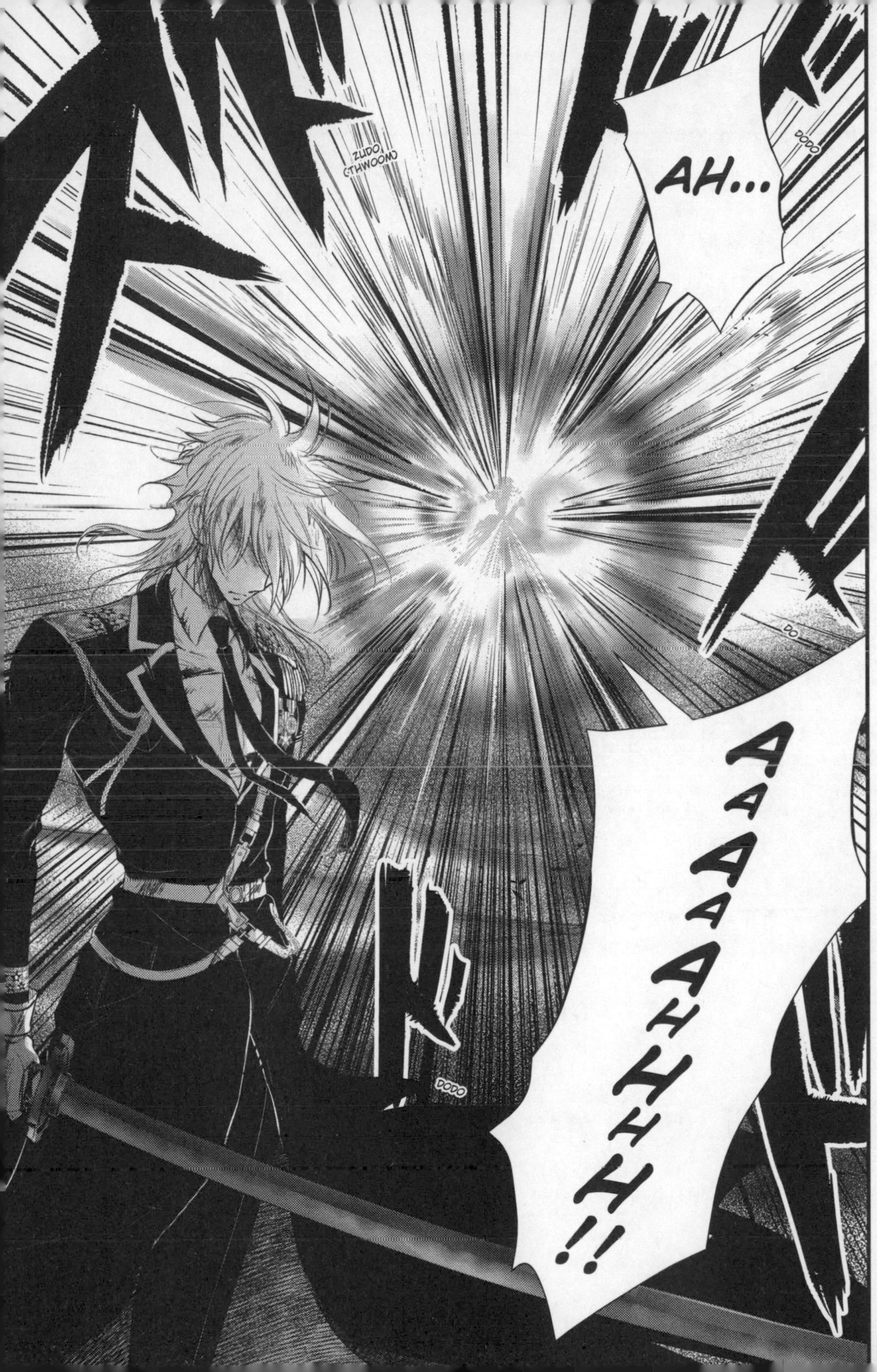
DODO
AH...
ZUDO (THWOOM)
DO
AAAAAAHHHHH!!
DODO

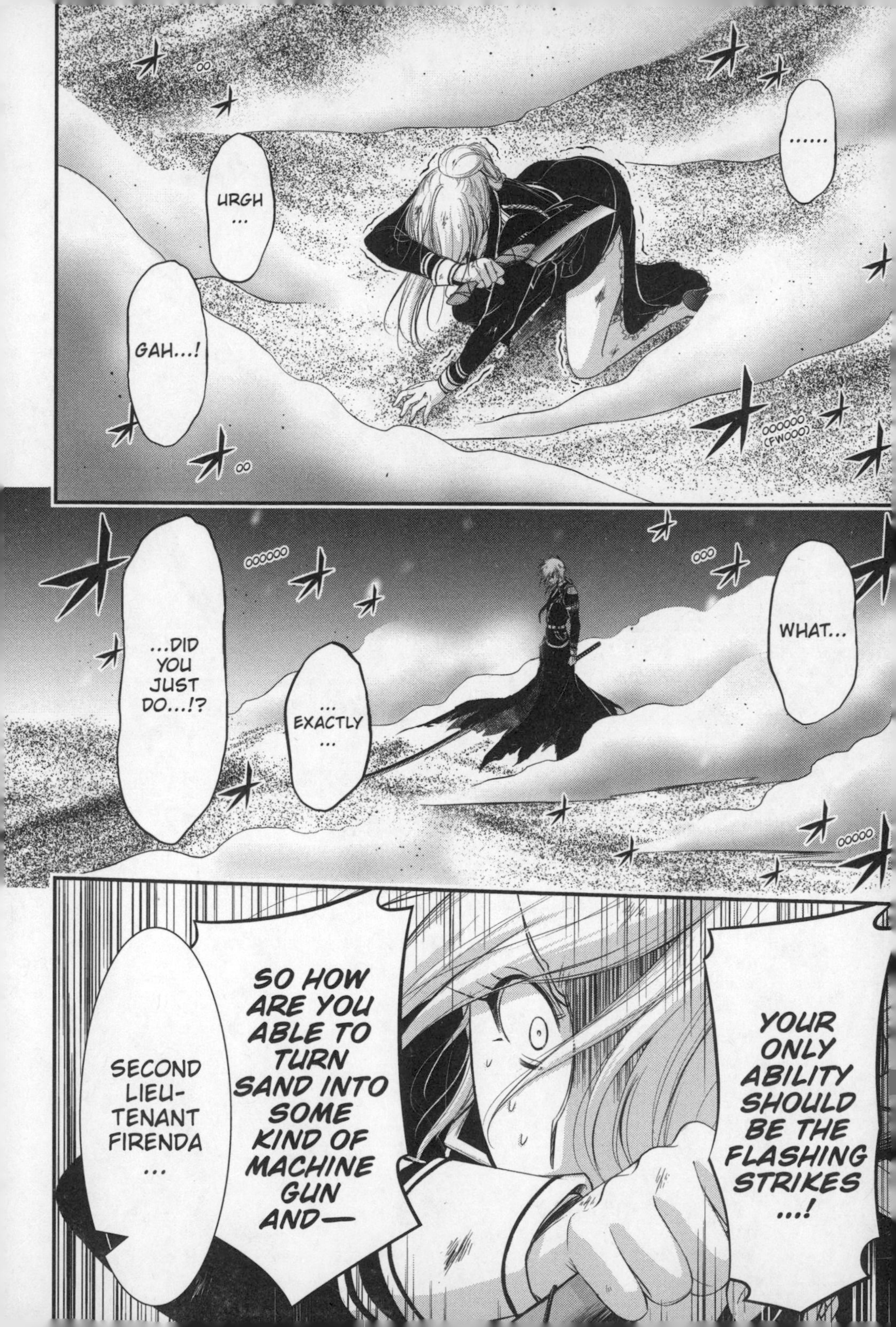

......
URGH ...
GAH...!
OOOOOO (FWOOO)
OO
WHAT...
... EXACTLY ...
...DID YOU JUST DO...!?
OOOOO
YOUR ONLY ABILITY SHOULD BE THE FLASHING STRIKES ...!
SO HOW ARE YOU ABLE TO TURN SAND INTO SOME KIND OF MACHINE GUN AND—
SECOND LIEU-TENANT FIRENDA ...

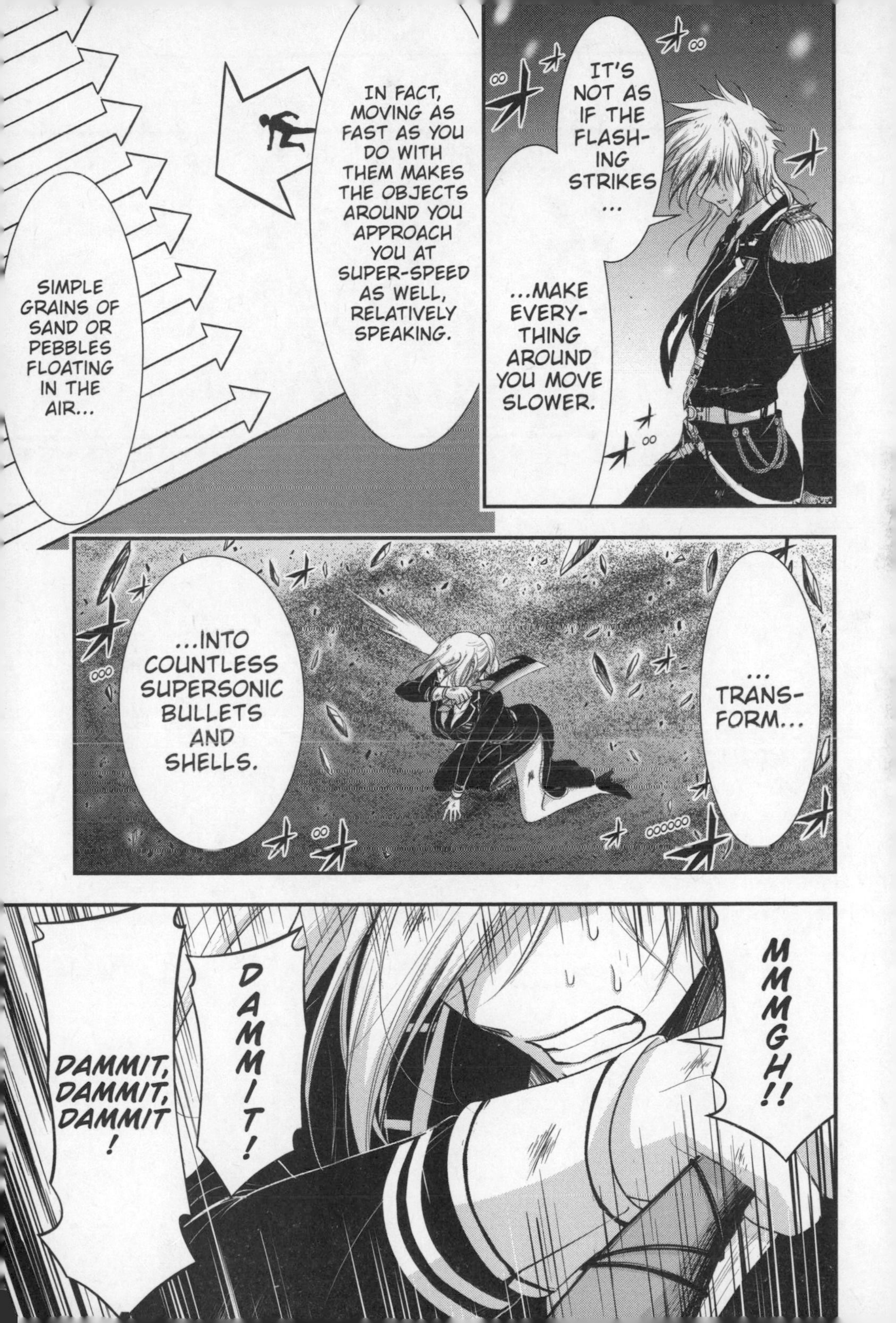
IT'S NOT AS IF THE FLASHING STRIKES...
...MAKE EVERYTHING AROUND YOU MOVE SLOWER.
IN FACT, MOVING AS FAST AS YOU DO WITH THEM MAKES THE OBJECTS AROUND YOU APPROACH YOU AT SUPER-SPEED AS WELL, RELATIVELY SPEAKING.
SIMPLE GRAINS OF SAND OR PEBBLES FLOATING IN THE AIR...
...TRANSFORM...
...INTO COUNTLESS SUPERSONIC BULLETS AND SHELLS.
MMMGH!!
DAMMIT!
DAMMIT, DAMMIT, DAMMIT!

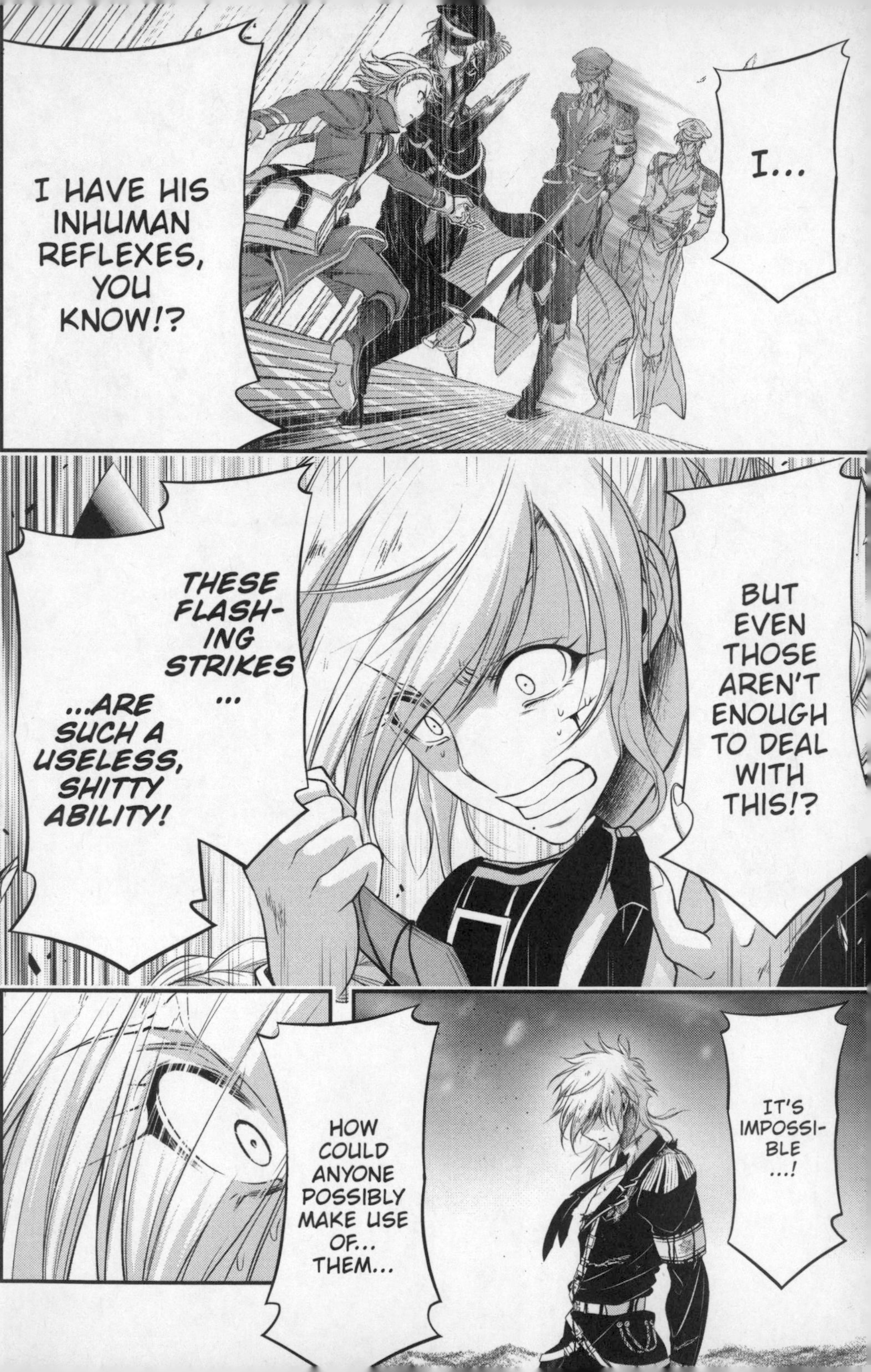
I...
I HAVE HIS INHUMAN REFLEXES, YOU KNOW!?
BUT EVEN THOSE AREN'T ENOUGH TO DEAL WITH THIS!?
THESE FLASH-ING STRIKES...
...ARE SUCH A USELESS, SHITTY ABILITY!
IT'S IMPOSSI-BLE...!
HOW COULD ANYONE POSSIBLY MAKE USE OF... THEM...

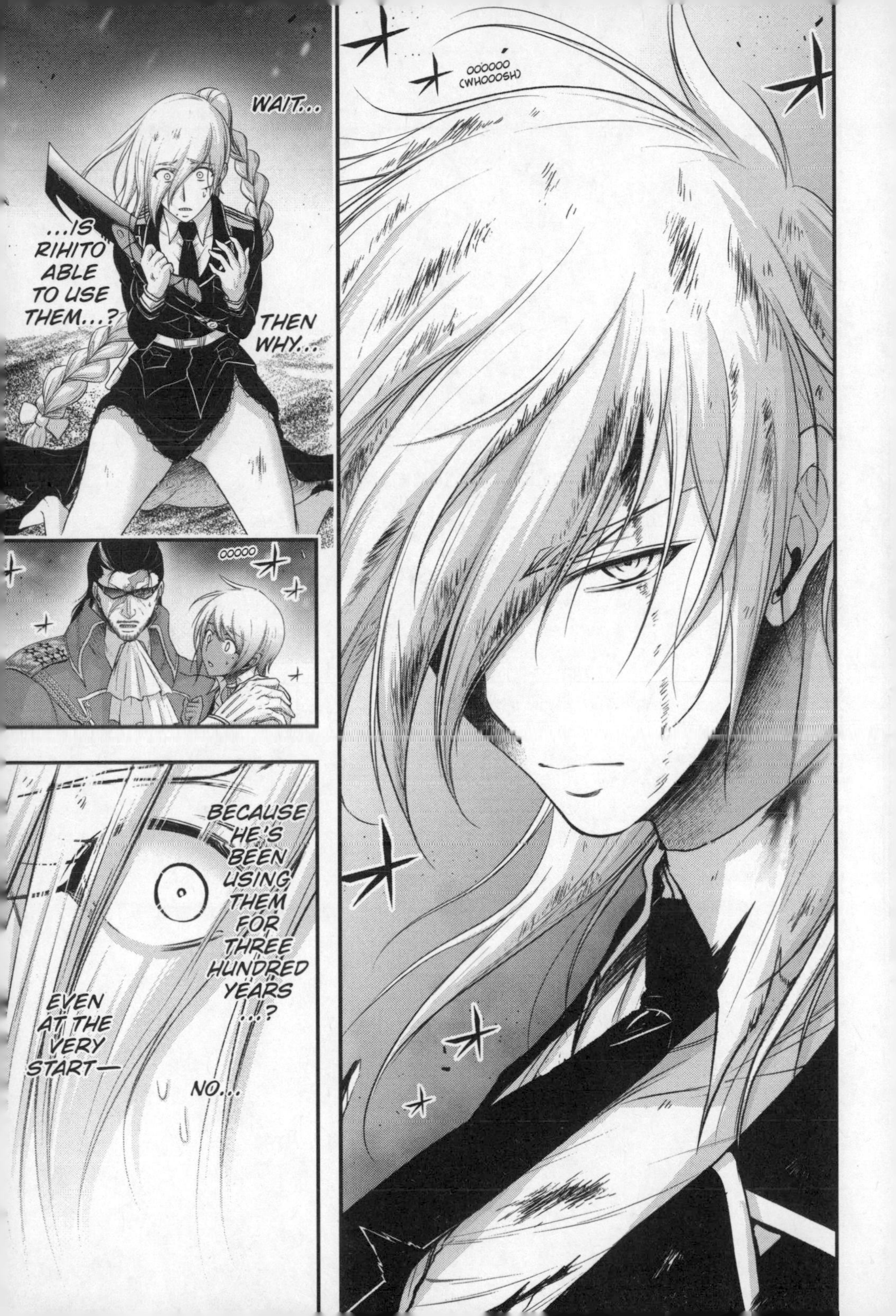
OOOOOO
(WHOOOSH)
WAIT...
...IS RIHITO ABLE TO USE THEM...?
THEN WHY...
OOOOO
BECAUSE HE'S BEEN USING THEM FOR THREE HUNDRED YEARS...?
EVEN AT THE VERY START—
NO...

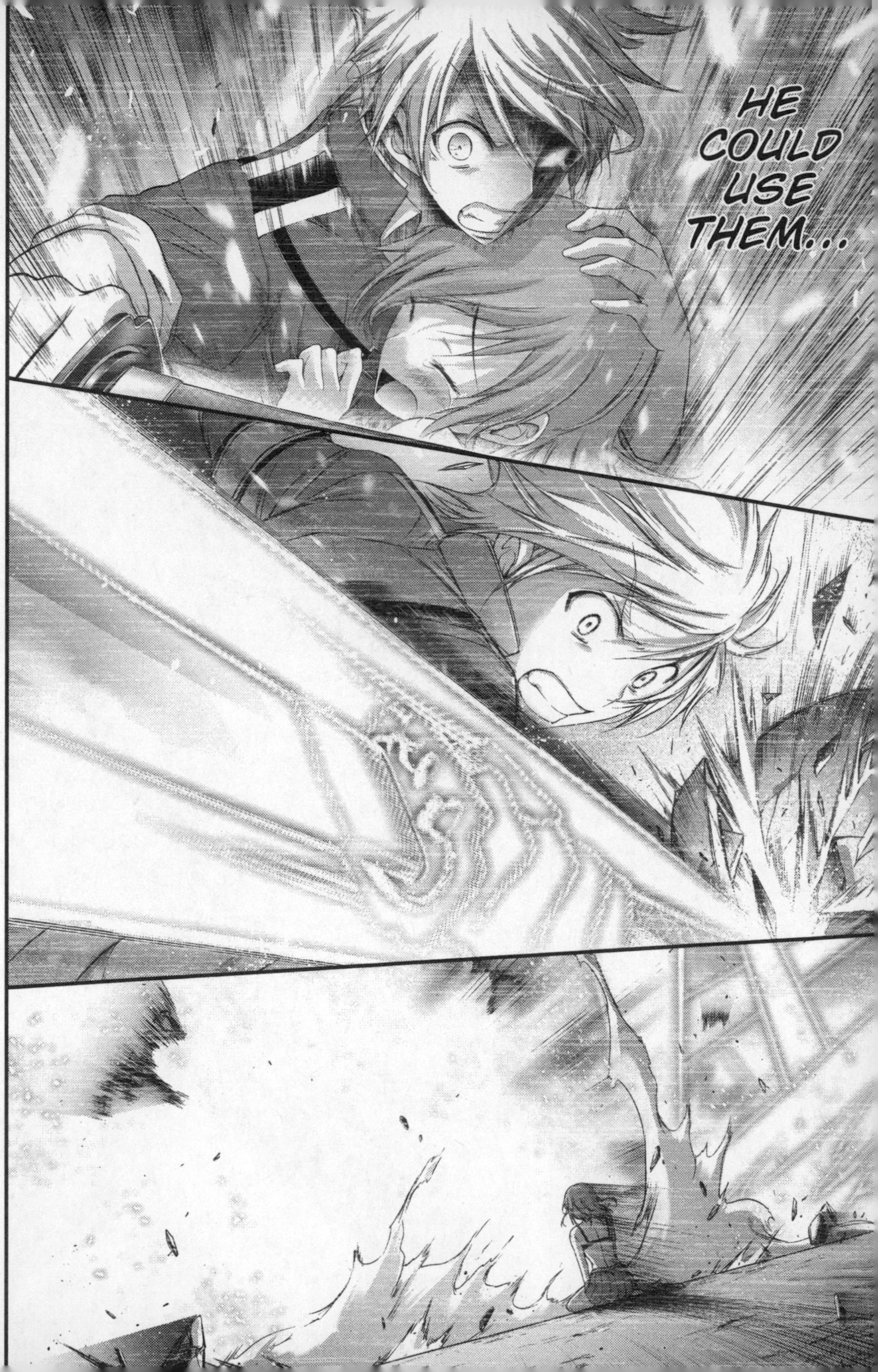
HE COULD USE THEM...

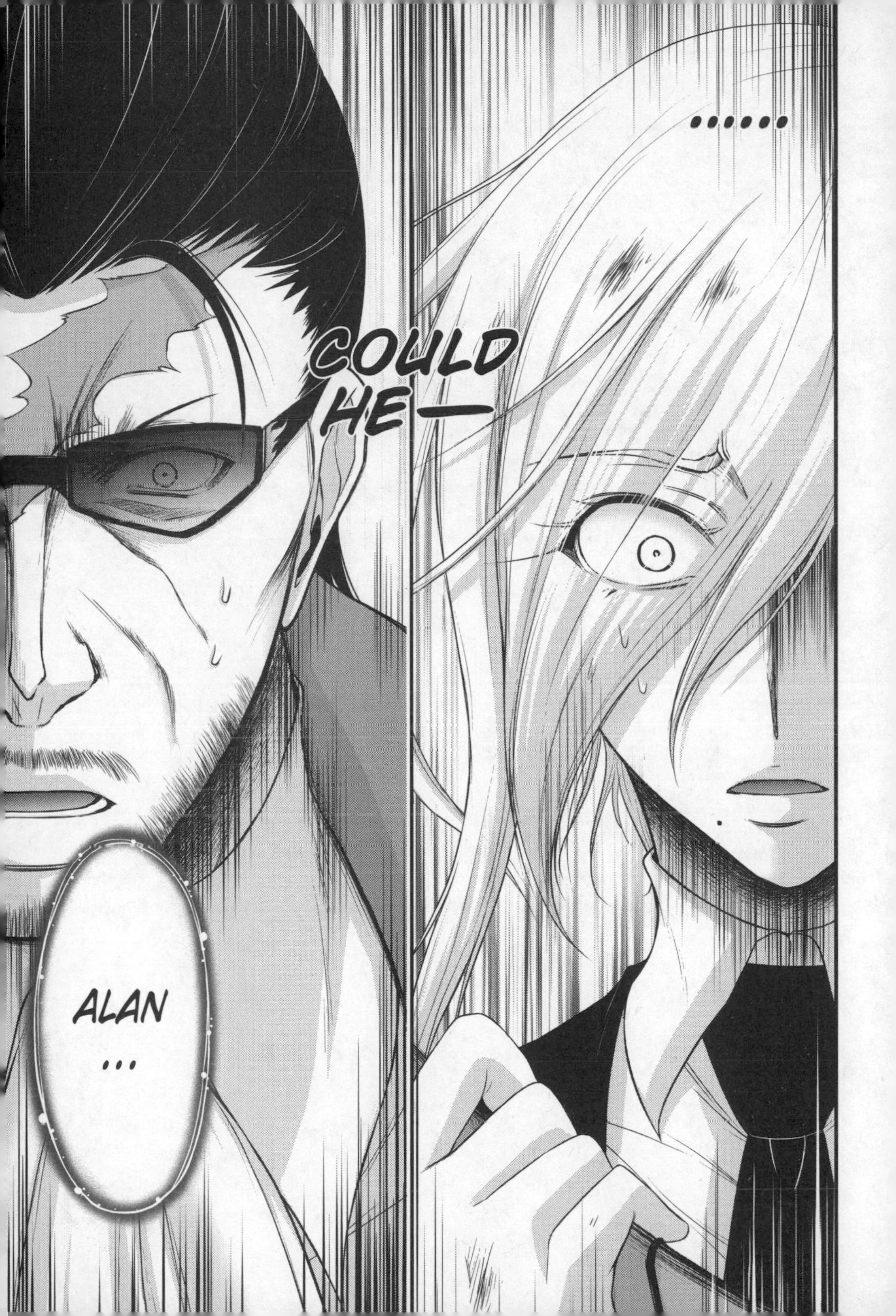
......
COULD HE—
ALAN ...

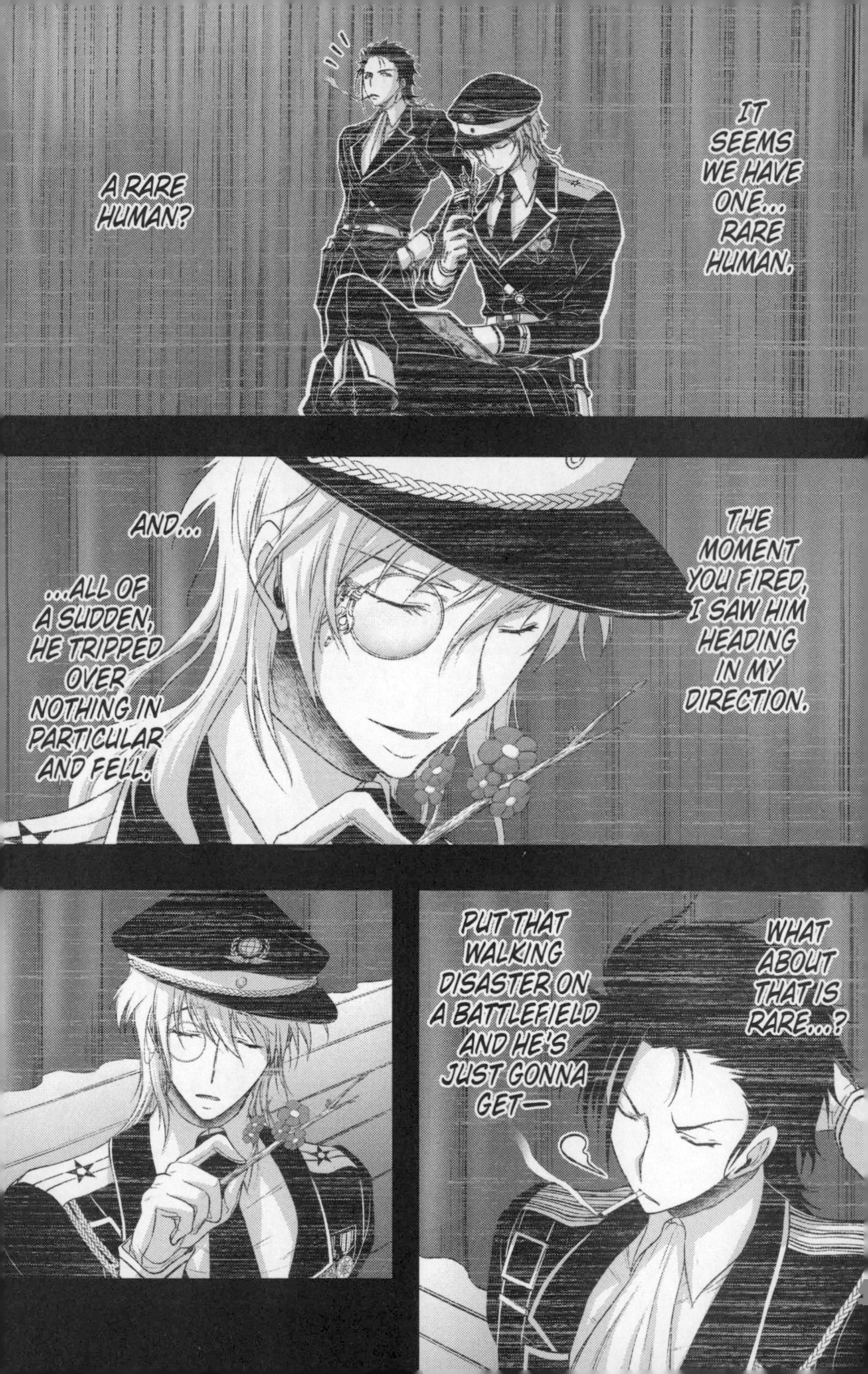
IT SEEMS WE HAVE ONE... RARE HUMAN.
A RARE HUMAN?
THE MOMENT YOU FIRED, I SAW HIM HEADING IN MY DIRECTION.
AND...
...ALL OF A SUDDEN, HE TRIPPED OVER NOTHING IN PARTICULAR AND FELL.
WHAT ABOUT THAT IS RARE...?
PUT THAT WALKING DISASTER ON A BATTLEFIELD AND HE'S JUST GONNA GET—

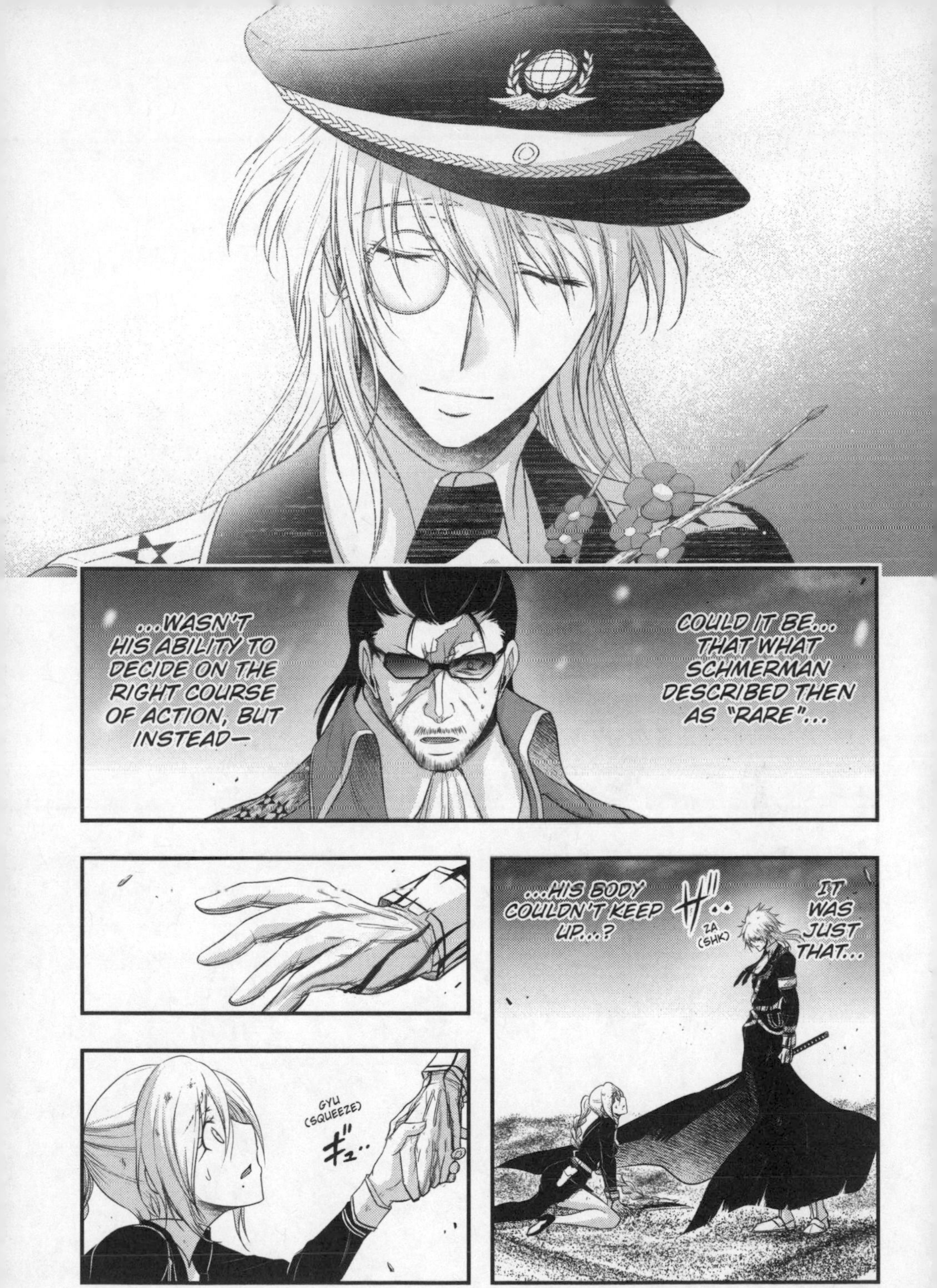
COULD IT BE... THAT WHAT SCHMERMAN DESCRIBED THEN AS "RARE"...
...WASN'T HIS ABILITY TO DECIDE ON THE RIGHT COURSE OF ACTION, BUT INSTEAD—
IT WAS JUST THAT...
ZA (SHK)
...HIS BODY COULDN'T KEEP UP...?
GYU (SQUEEZE)

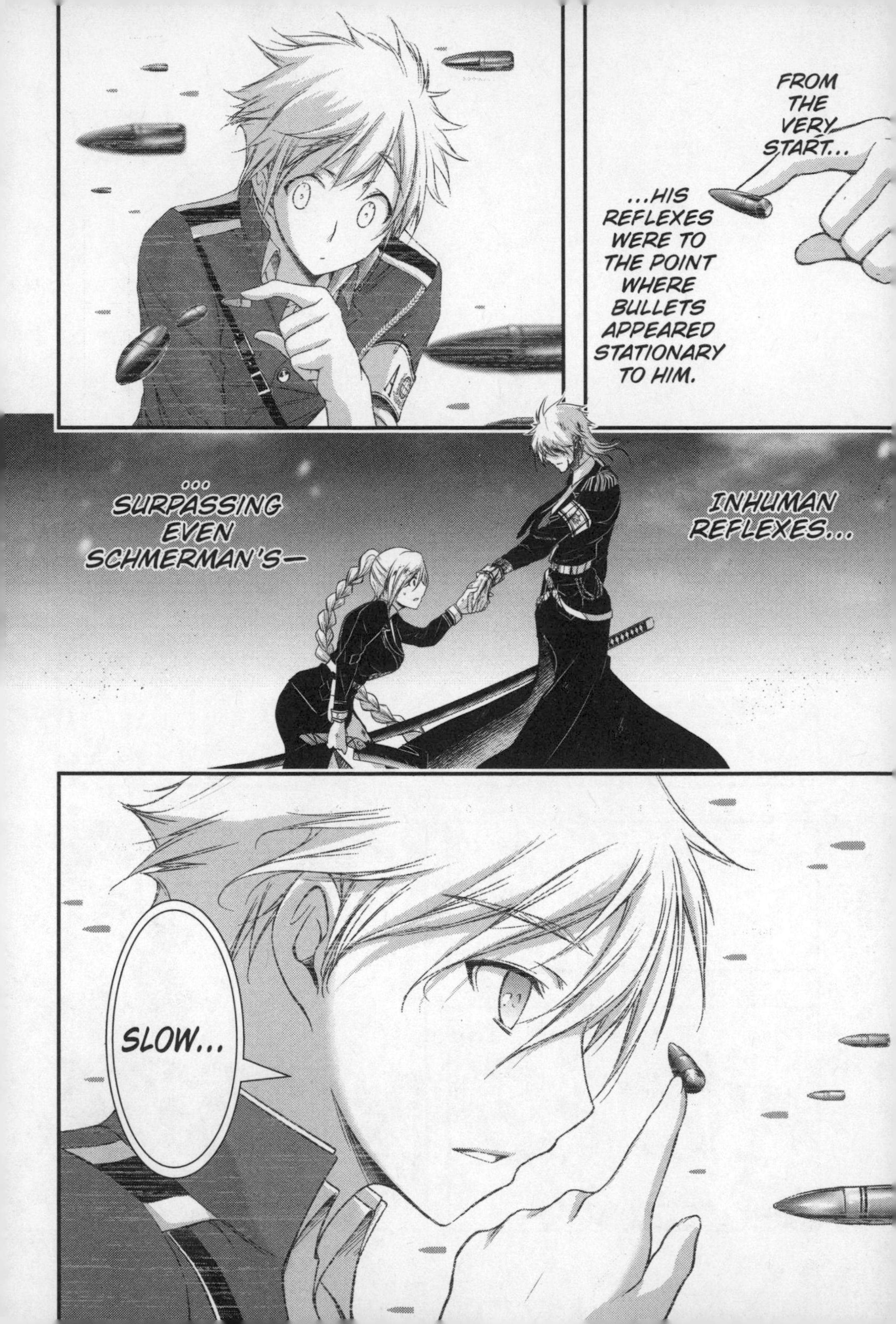
FROM THE VERY START...
...HIS REFLEXES WERE TO THE POINT WHERE BULLETS APPEARED STATIONARY TO HIM.
INHUMAN REFLEXES...
...SURPASSING EVEN SCHMERMAN'S—
SLOW...

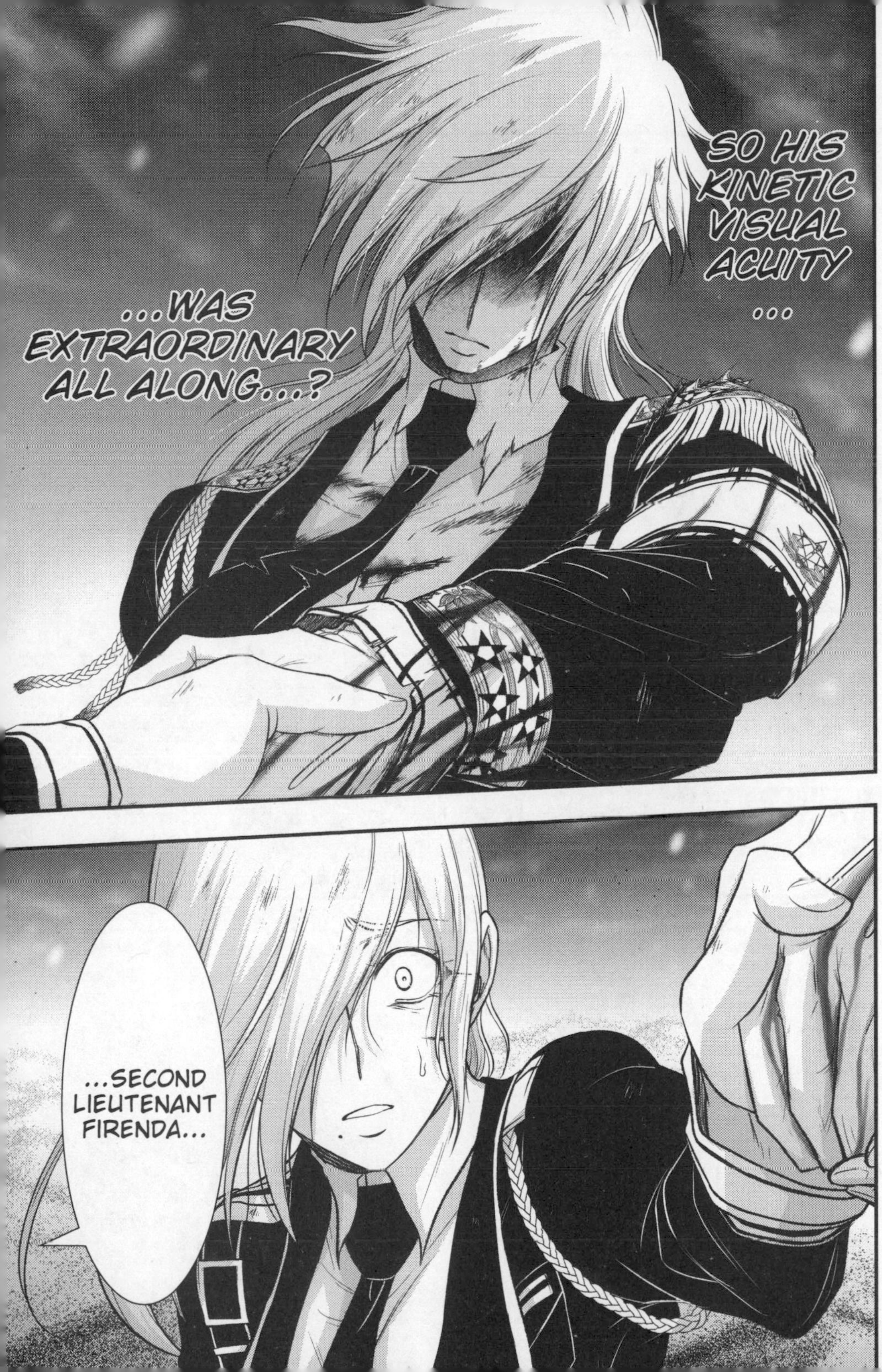
SO HIS KINETIC VISUAL ACUITY ...
...WAS EXTRAORDINARY ALL ALONG...?
...SECOND LIEUTENANT FIRENDA...

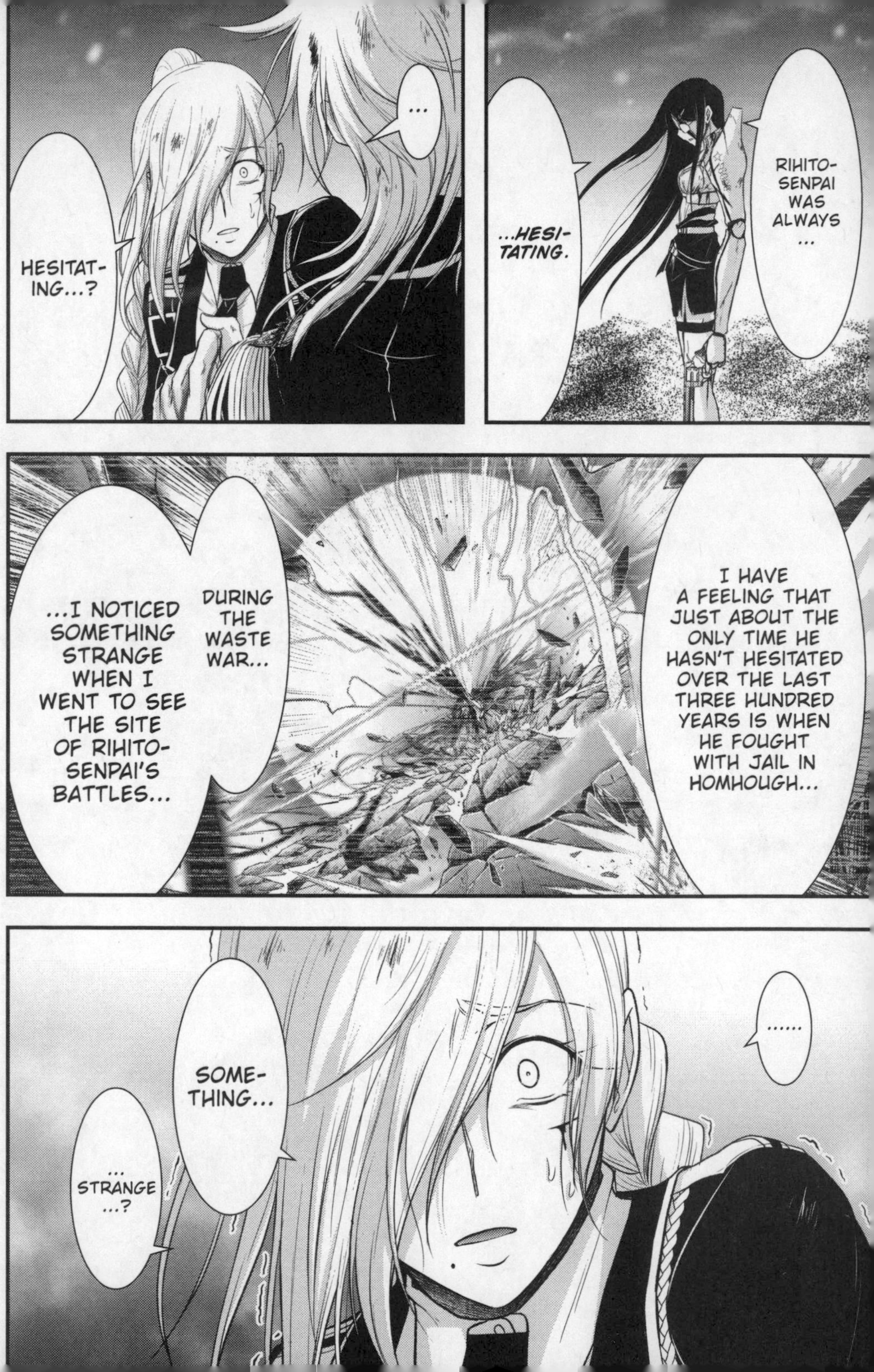
RIHITO-SENPAI WAS ALWAYS ...
...HESI-TATING.
...
HESITAT-ING...?
I HAVE A FEELING THAT JUST ABOUT THE ONLY TIME HE HASN'T HESITATED OVER THE LAST THREE HUNDRED YEARS IS WHEN HE FOUGHT WITH JAIL IN HOMHOUGH...
DURING THE WASTE WAR...
...I NOTICED SOMETHING STRANGE WHEN I WENT TO SEE THE SITE OF RIHITO-SENPAI'S BATTLES...
......
SOME-THING...
...STRANGE...?

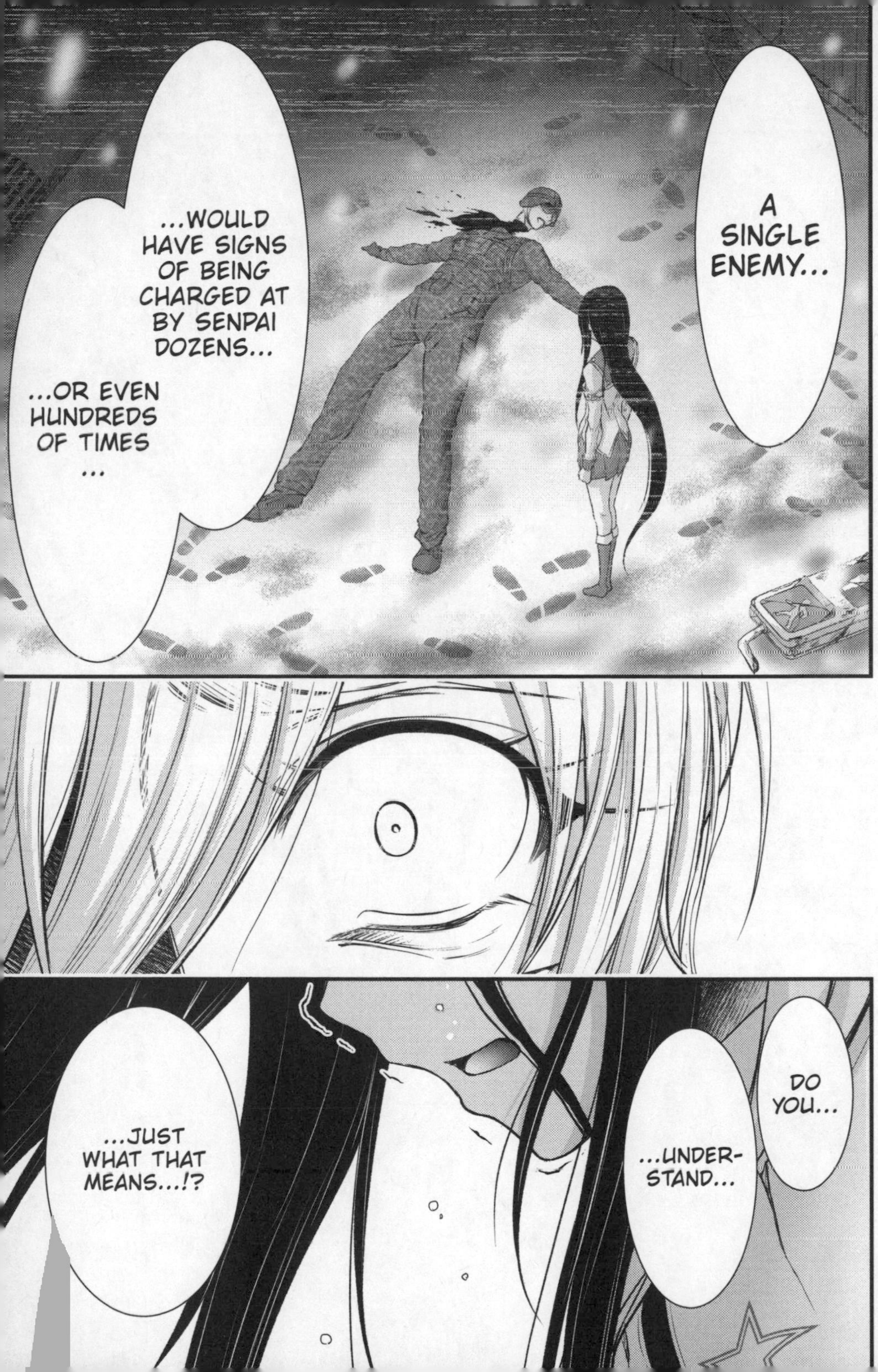
A SINGLE ENEMY...
...WOULD HAVE SIGNS OF BEING CHARGED AT BY SENPAI DOZENS...
...OR EVEN HUNDREDS OF TIMES ...
DO YOU...
...UNDER-STAND...
...JUST WHAT THAT MEANS...!?

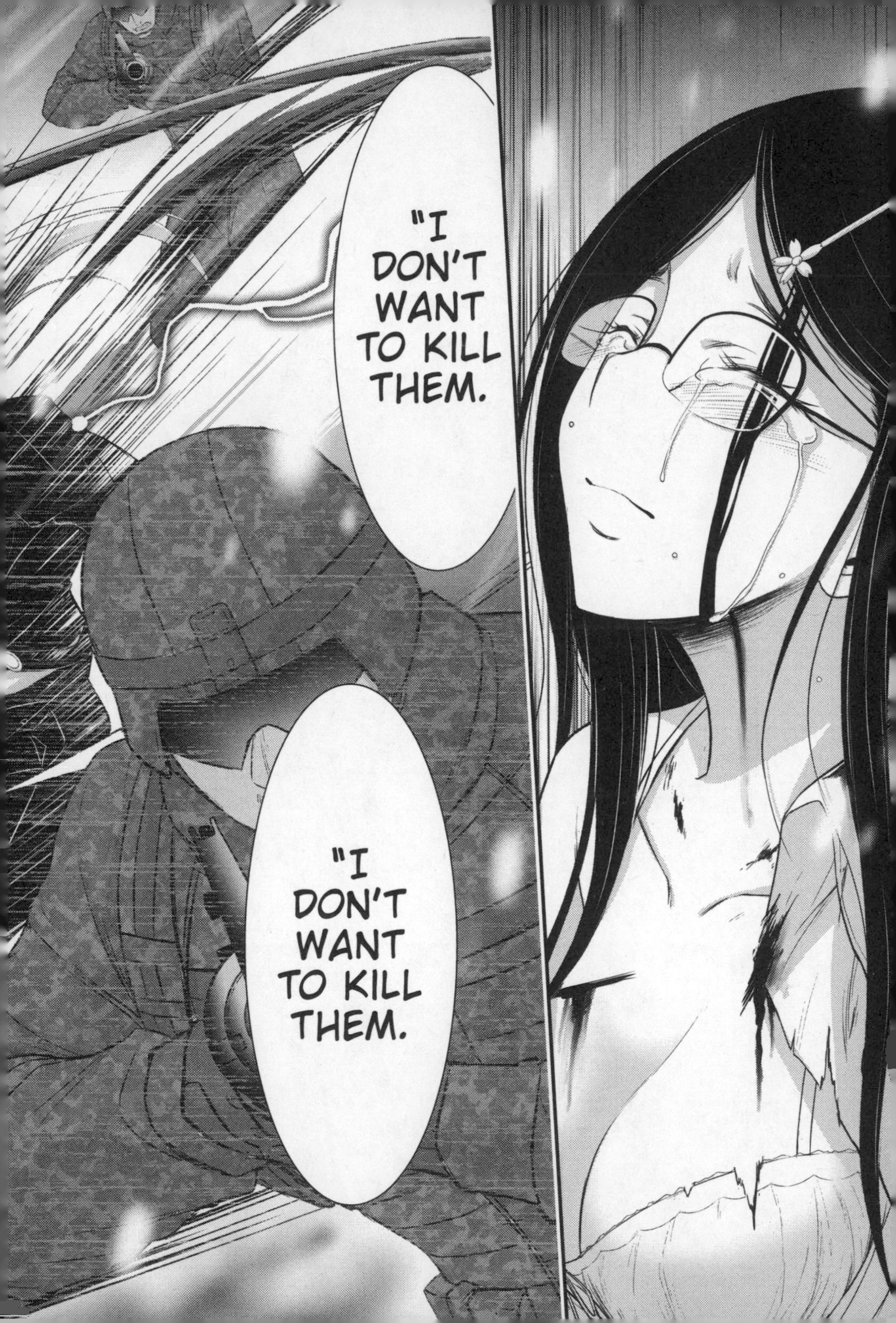
"I DON'T WANT TO KILL THEM.
"I DON'T WANT TO KILL THEM.

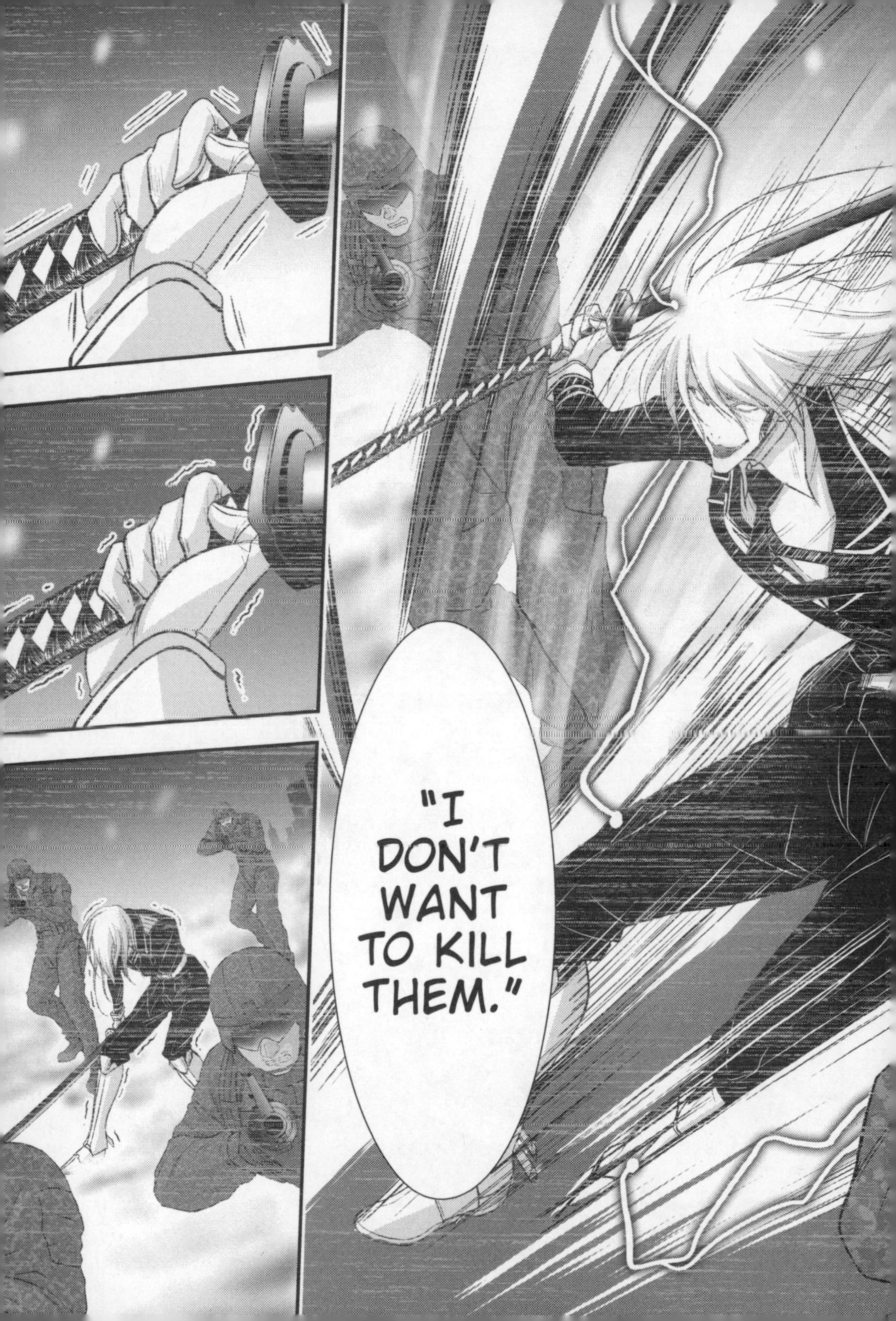
"I DON'T WANT TO KILL THEM."

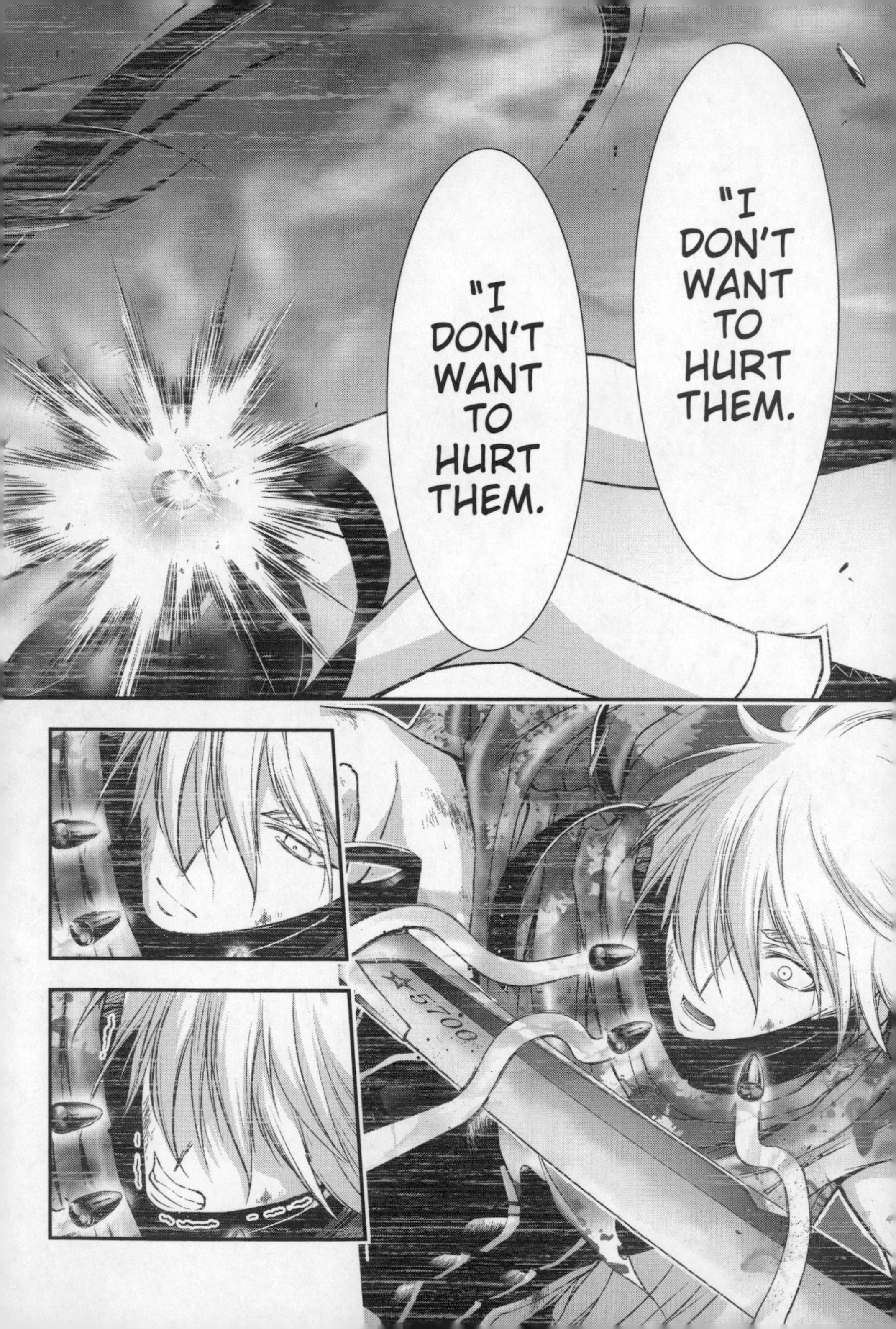
"I DON'T WANT TO HURT THEM.
"I DON'T WANT TO HURT THEM.

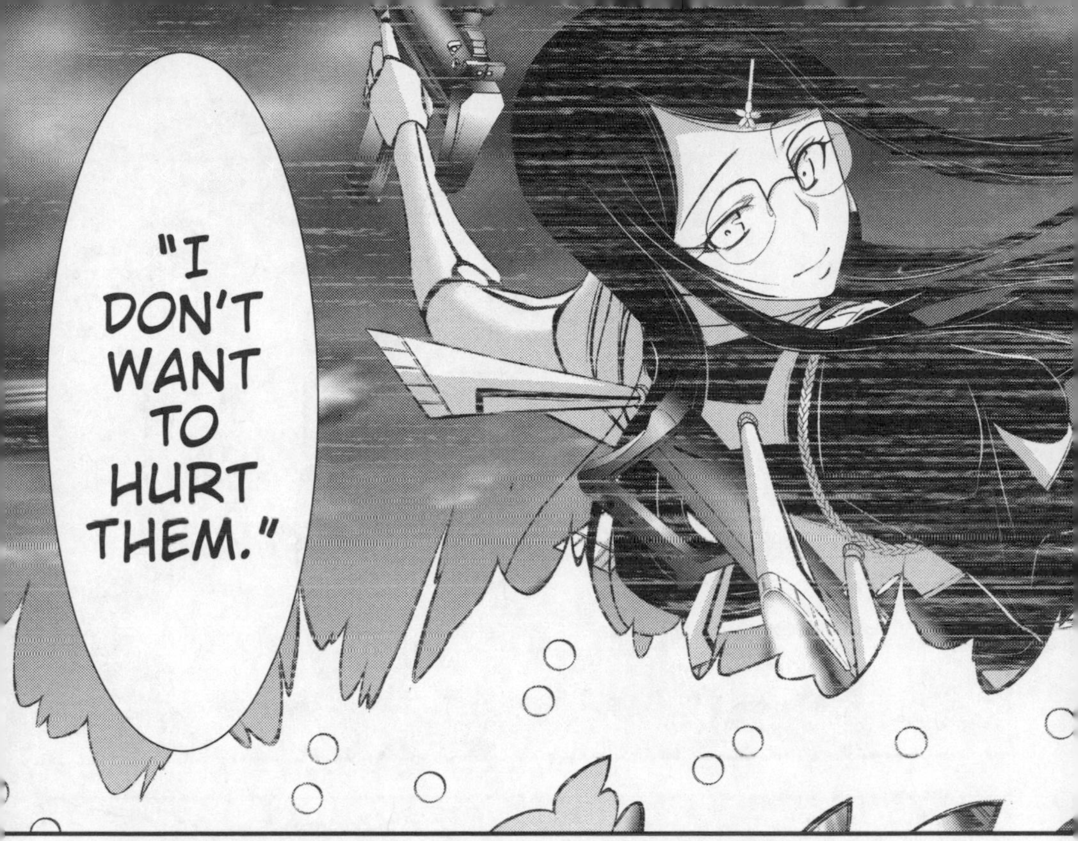
"I DON'T WANT TO HURT THEM."
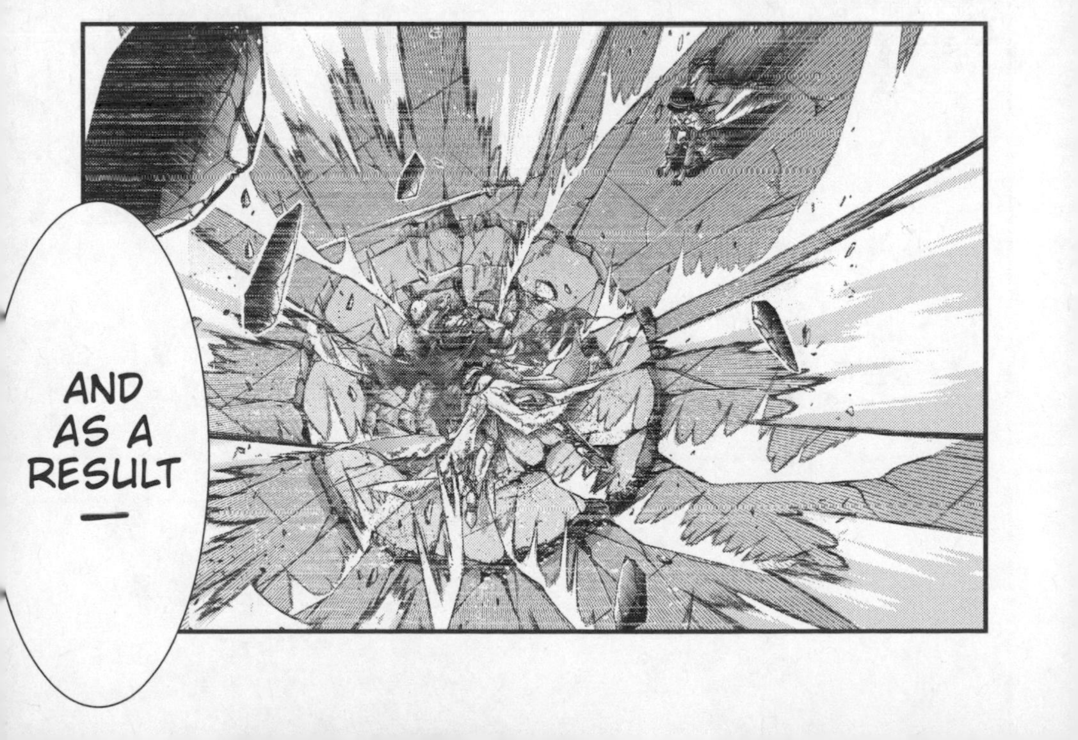
AND AS A RESULT —

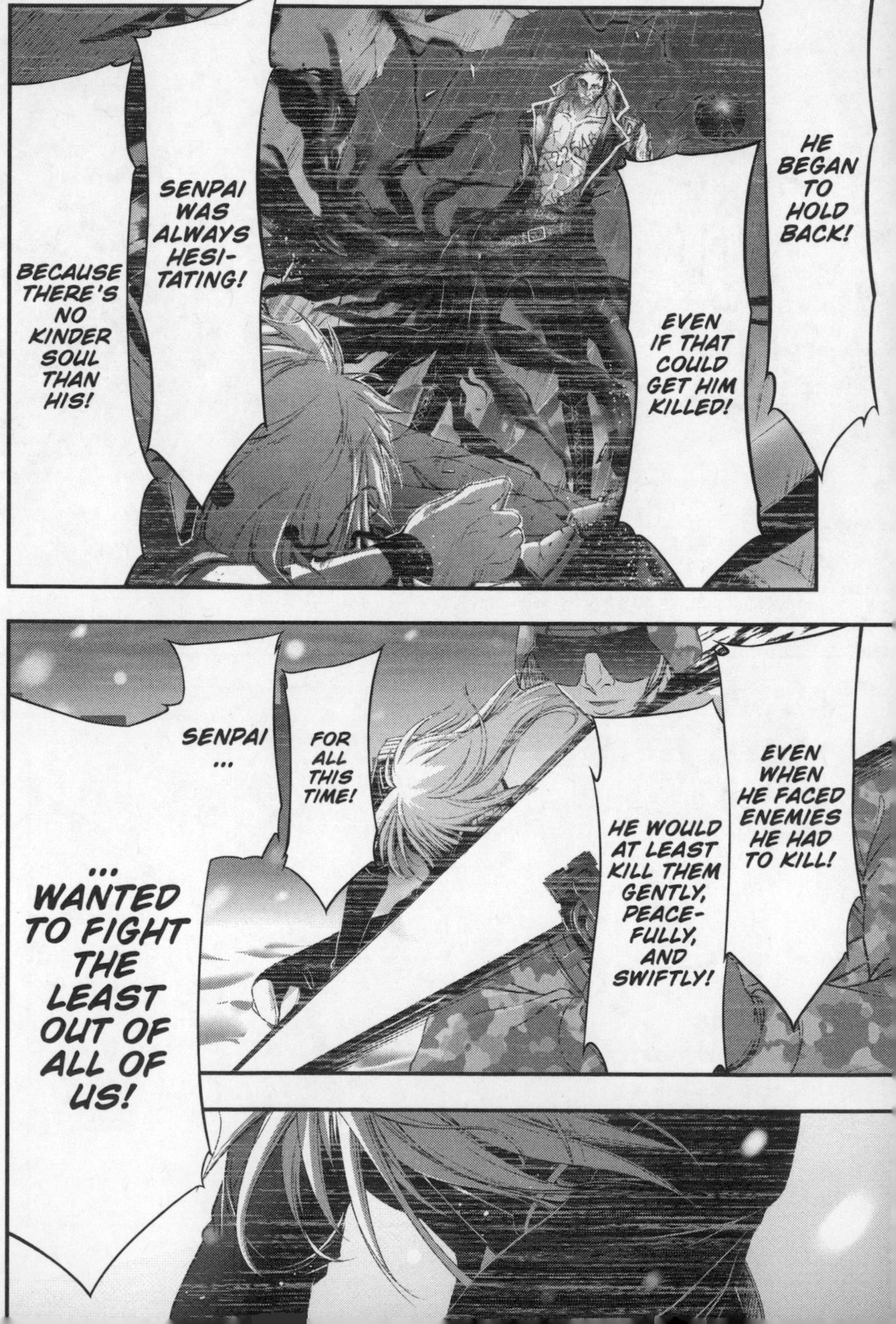
HE BEGAN TO HOLD BACK!
EVEN IF THAT COULD GET HIM KILLED!
SENPAI WAS ALWAYS HESITATING!
BECAUSE THERE'S NO KINDER SOUL THAN HIS!
EVEN WHEN HE FACED ENEMIES HE HAD TO KILL!
HE WOULD AT LEAST KILL THEM GENTLY, PEACEFULLY, AND SWIFTLY!
FOR ALL THIS TIME!
SENPAI ...
... WANTED TO FIGHT THE LEAST OUT OF ALL OF US!

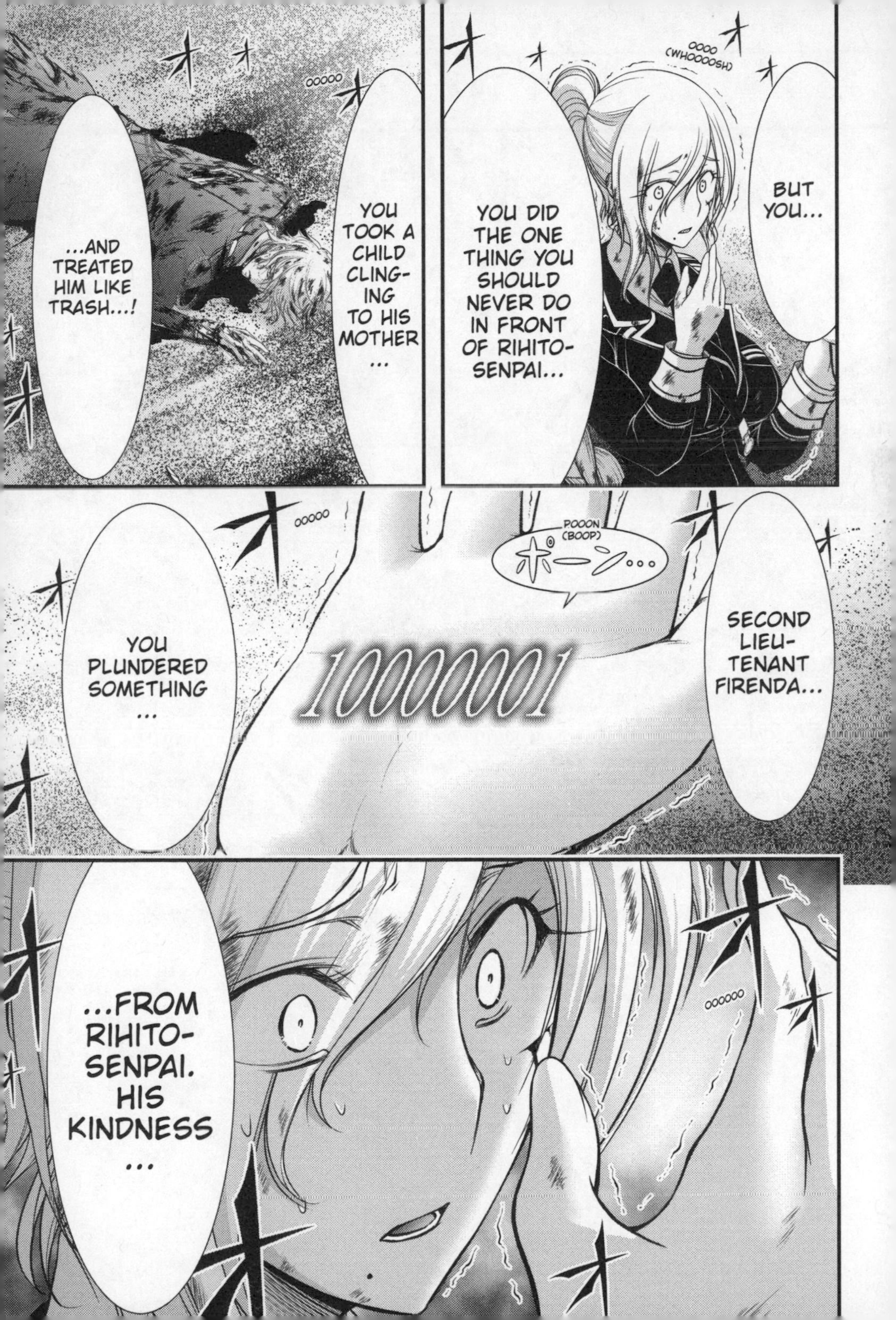

OOOO (WHOOOOSH)
BUT YOU...
YOU DID THE ONE THING YOU SHOULD NEVER DO IN FRONT OF RIHITO-SENPAI...
OOOOO
YOU TOOK A CHILD CLINGING TO HIS MOTHER...
...AND TREATED HIM LIKE TRASH...!
SECOND LIEUTENANT FIRENDA...
POOON (BOOP)
ポーン...
10000001
OOOOO
YOU PLUNDERED SOMETHING...
OOOOOO
...FROM RIHITO-SENPAI. HIS KINDNESS...

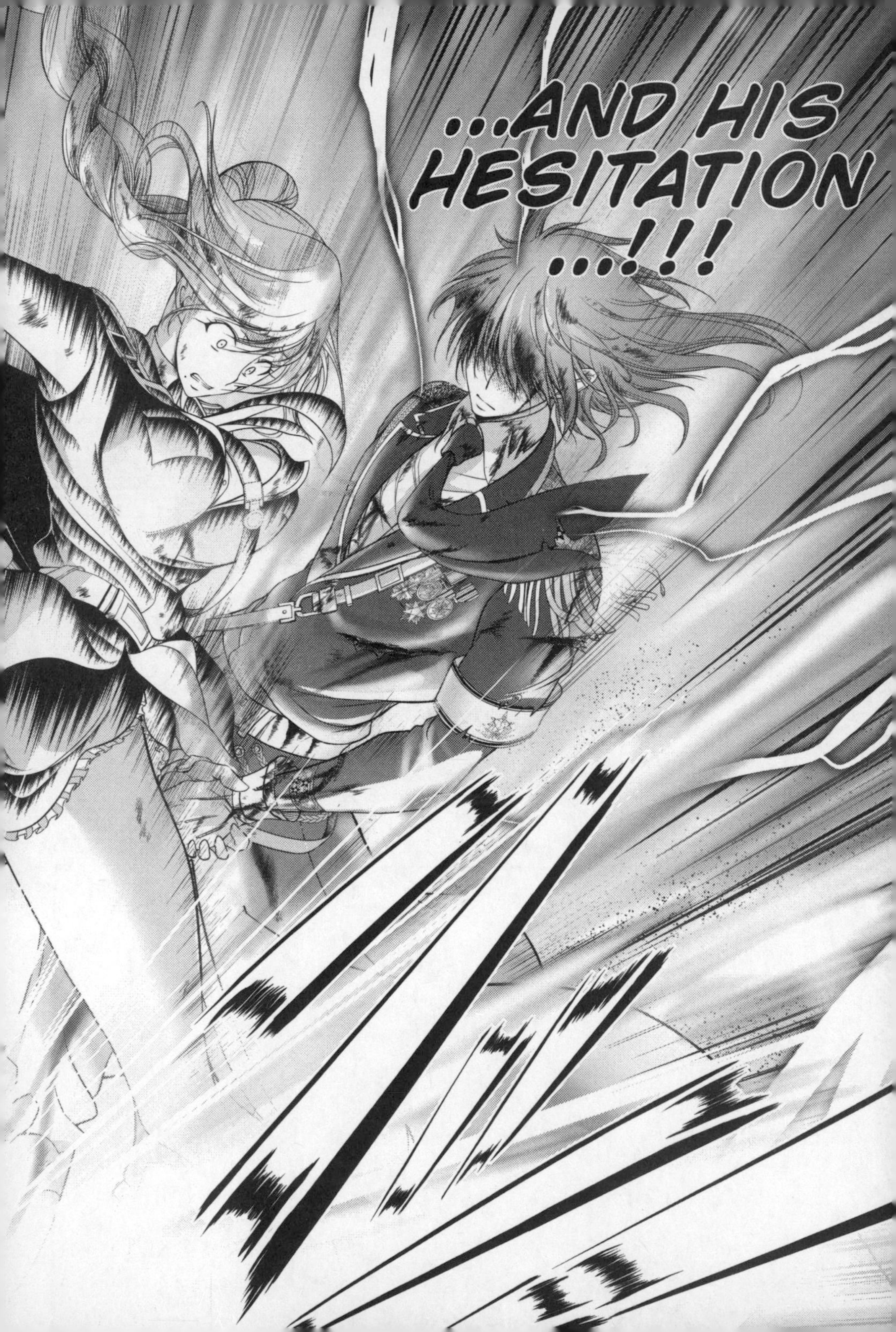
...AND HIS HESITATION ...!!!

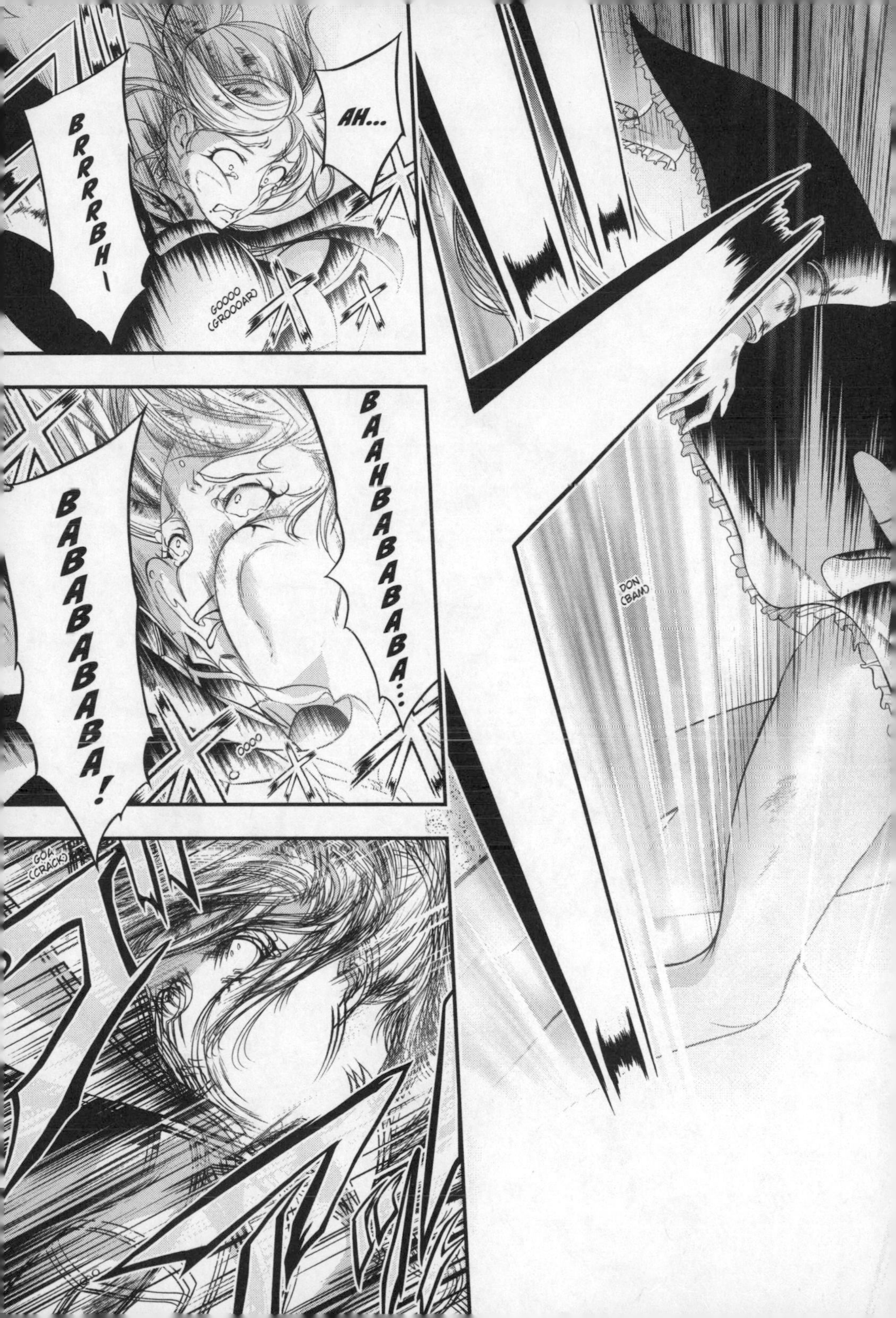
DON
(BAM)
AH...
BRRRRBH!
GOOOO
(GROOOAR)
BAAHBABABABABA...
BABABABABA!
GOA
(CRACK)

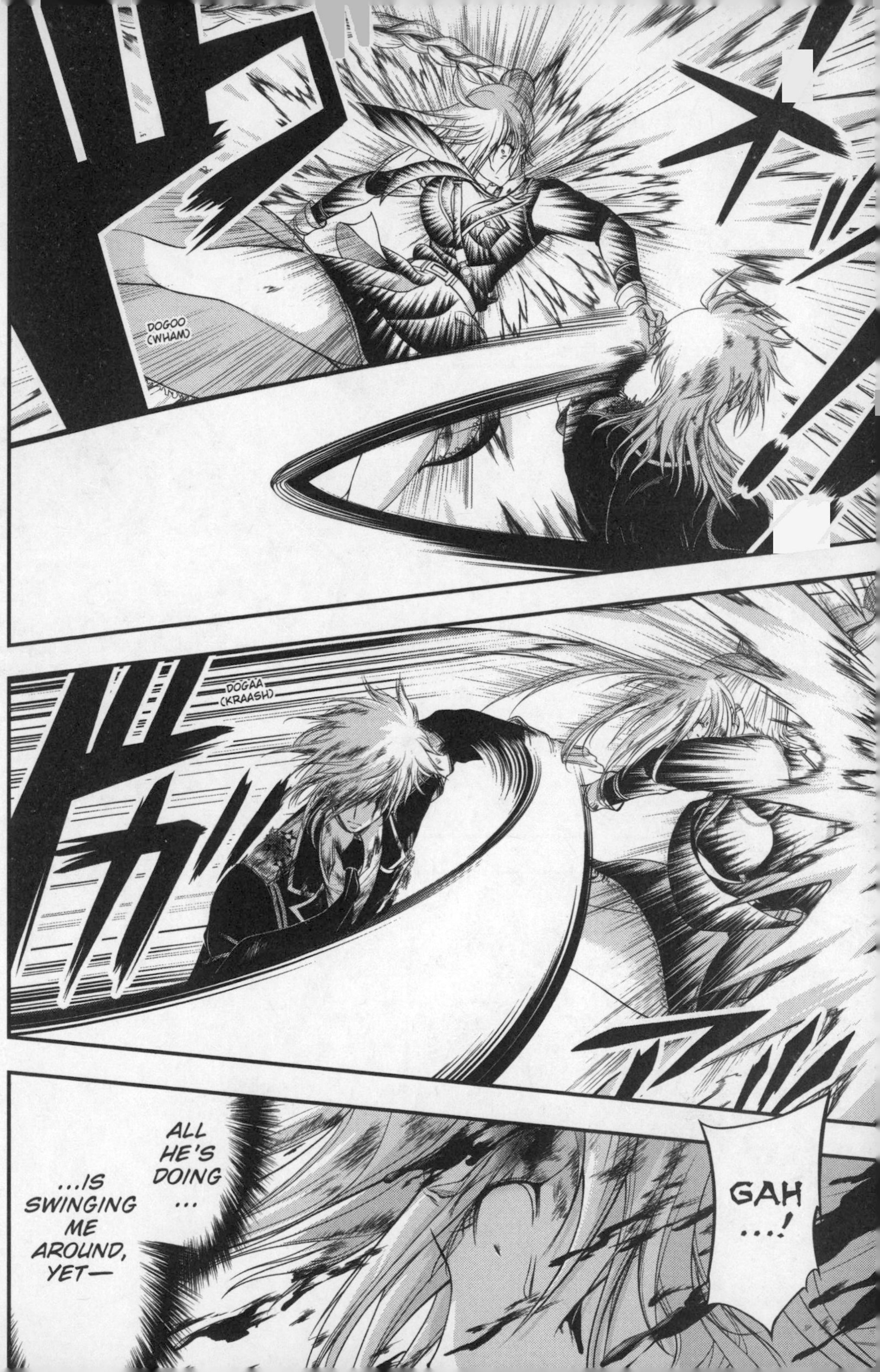
DOGOO
(WHAM)
DOGAA
(KRAASH)
GAH ...!
ALL HE'S DOING...
...IS SWINGING ME AROUND, YET—

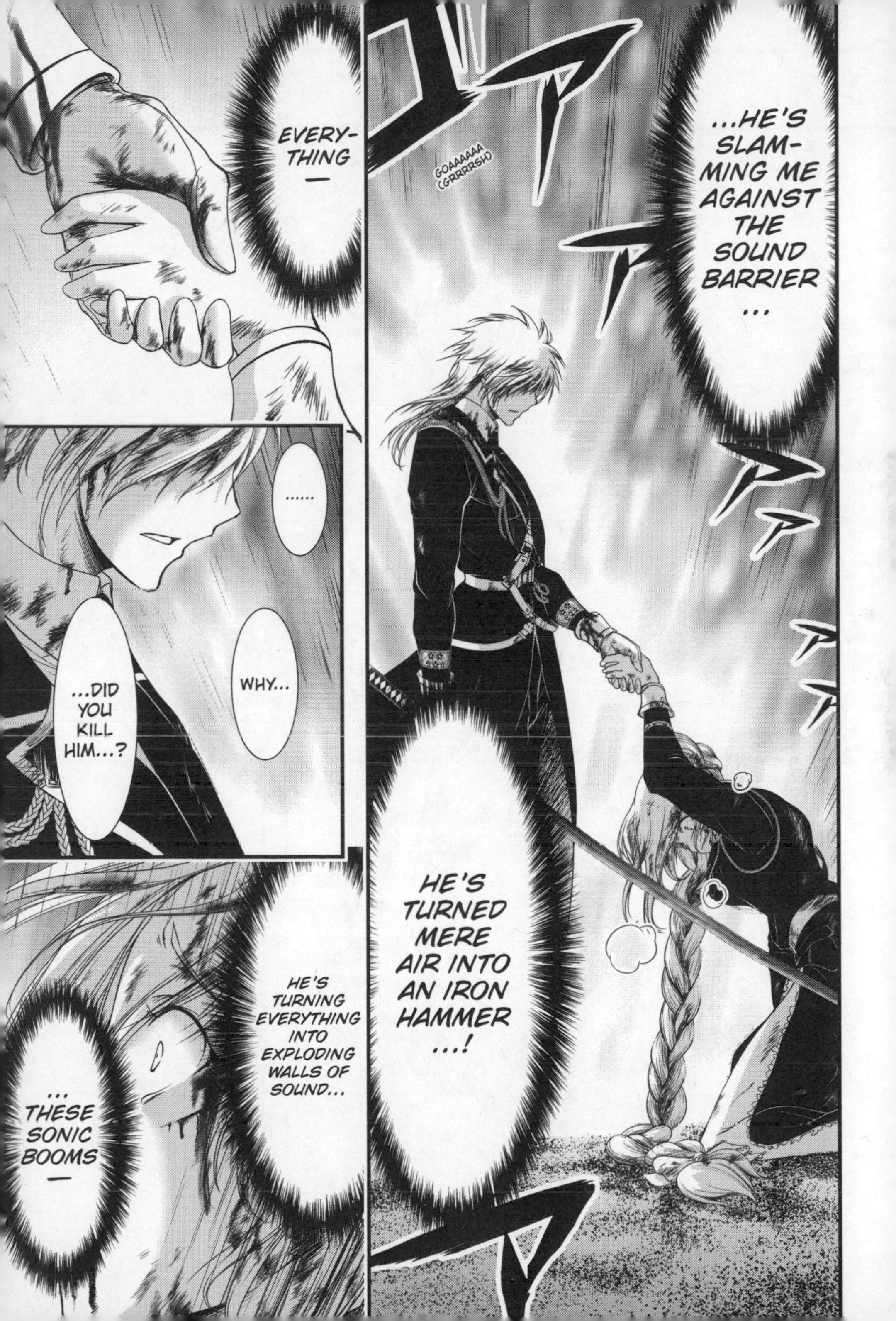
...HE'S SLAMMING ME AGAINST THE SOUND BARRIER...
GOAAAAAA (GRRRRSH)
HE'S TURNED MERE AIR INTO AN IRON HAMMER...!
EVERYTHING —
......
WHY...
...DID YOU KILL HIM...?
HE'S TURNING EVERYTHING INTO EXPLODING WALLS OF SOUND...
... THESE SONIC BOOMS —

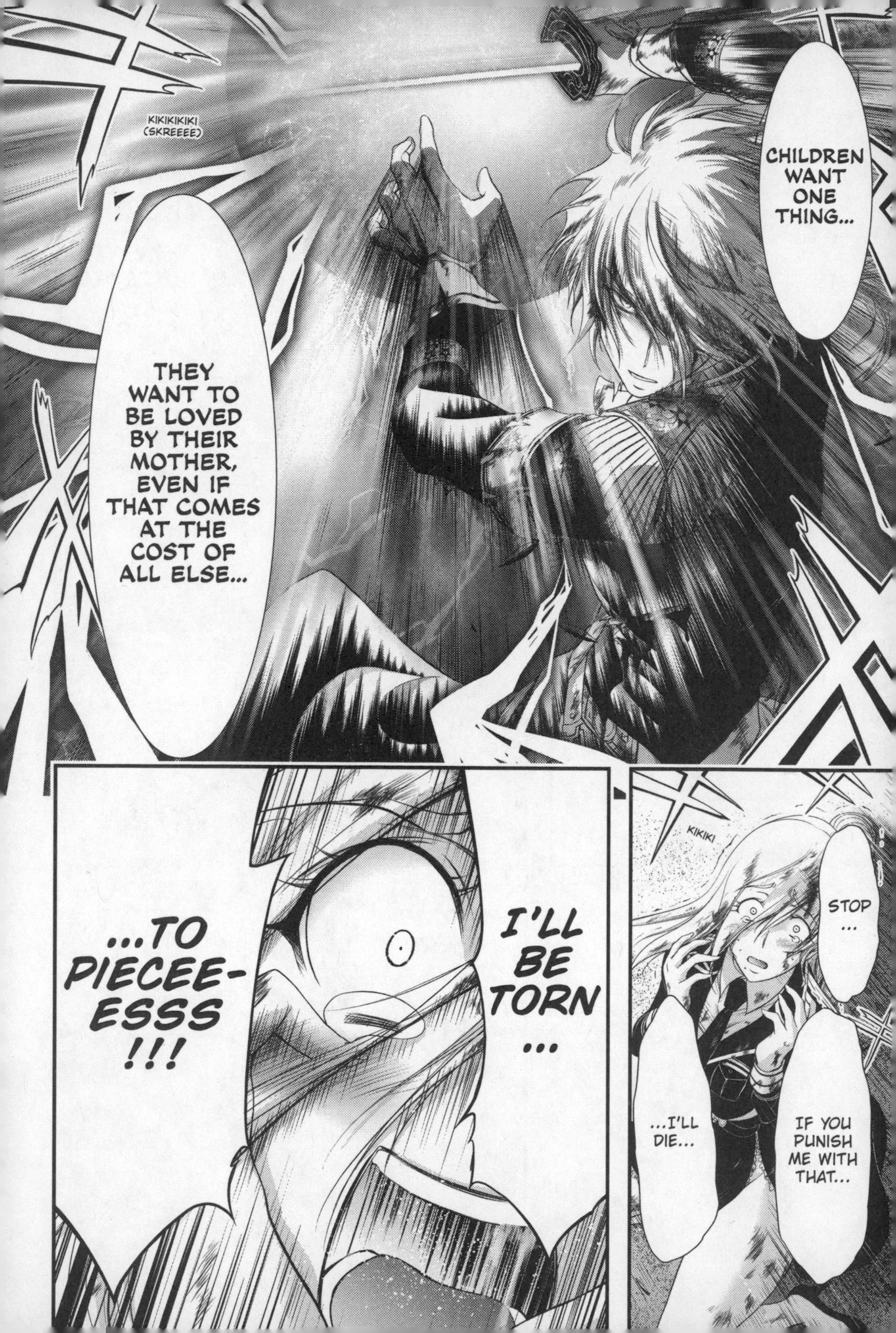
CHILDREN WANT ONE THING...
KIKIKIKIKI (SKREEEE)
THEY WANT TO BE LOVED BY THEIR MOTHER, EVEN IF THAT COMES AT THE COST OF ALL ELSE...
KIKIKI
STOP...
IF YOU PUNISH ME WITH THAT...
...I'LL DIE...
I'LL BE TORN...
...TO PIECEE-ESSS!!!

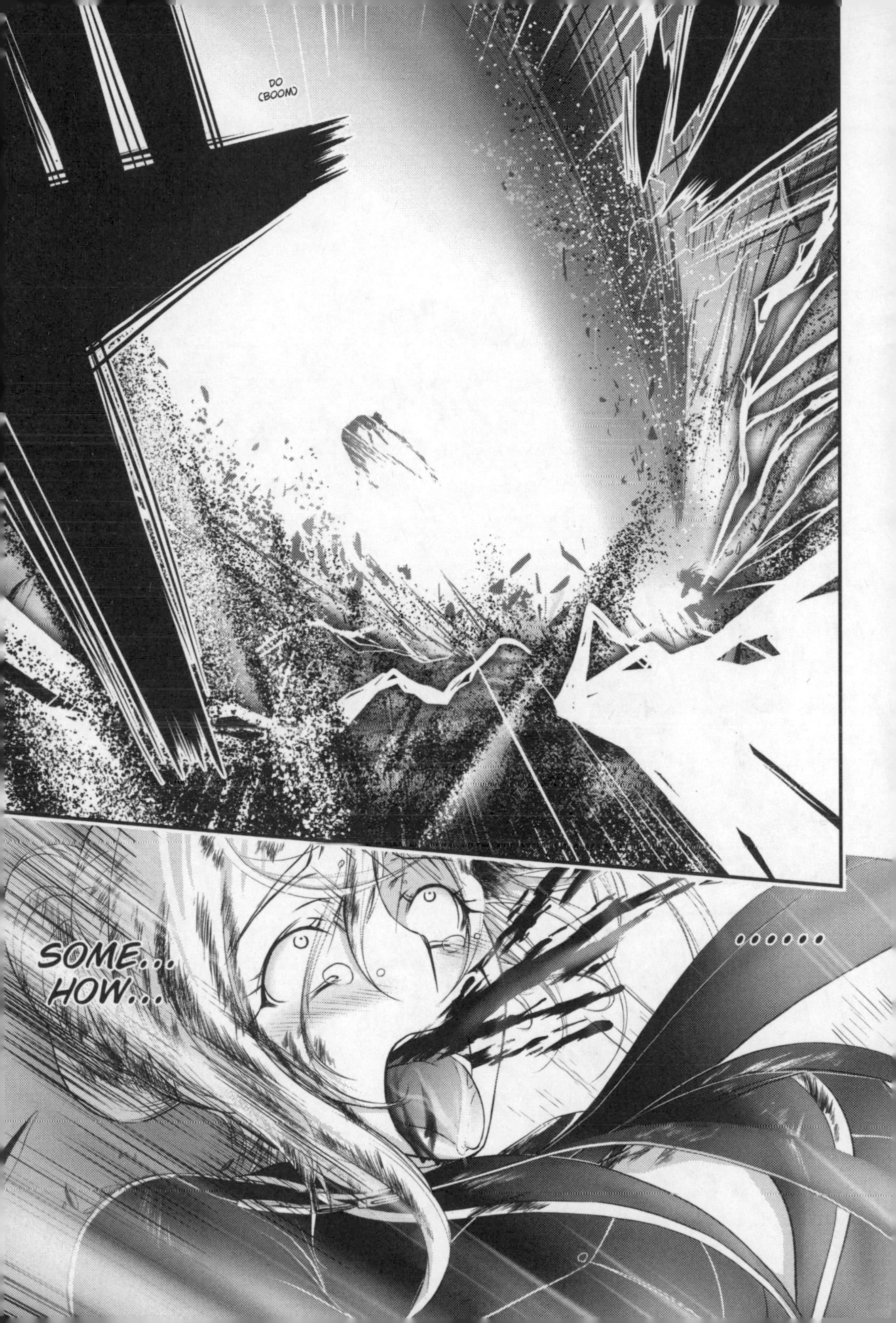
DO
(BOOM)
......
SOME... HOW...

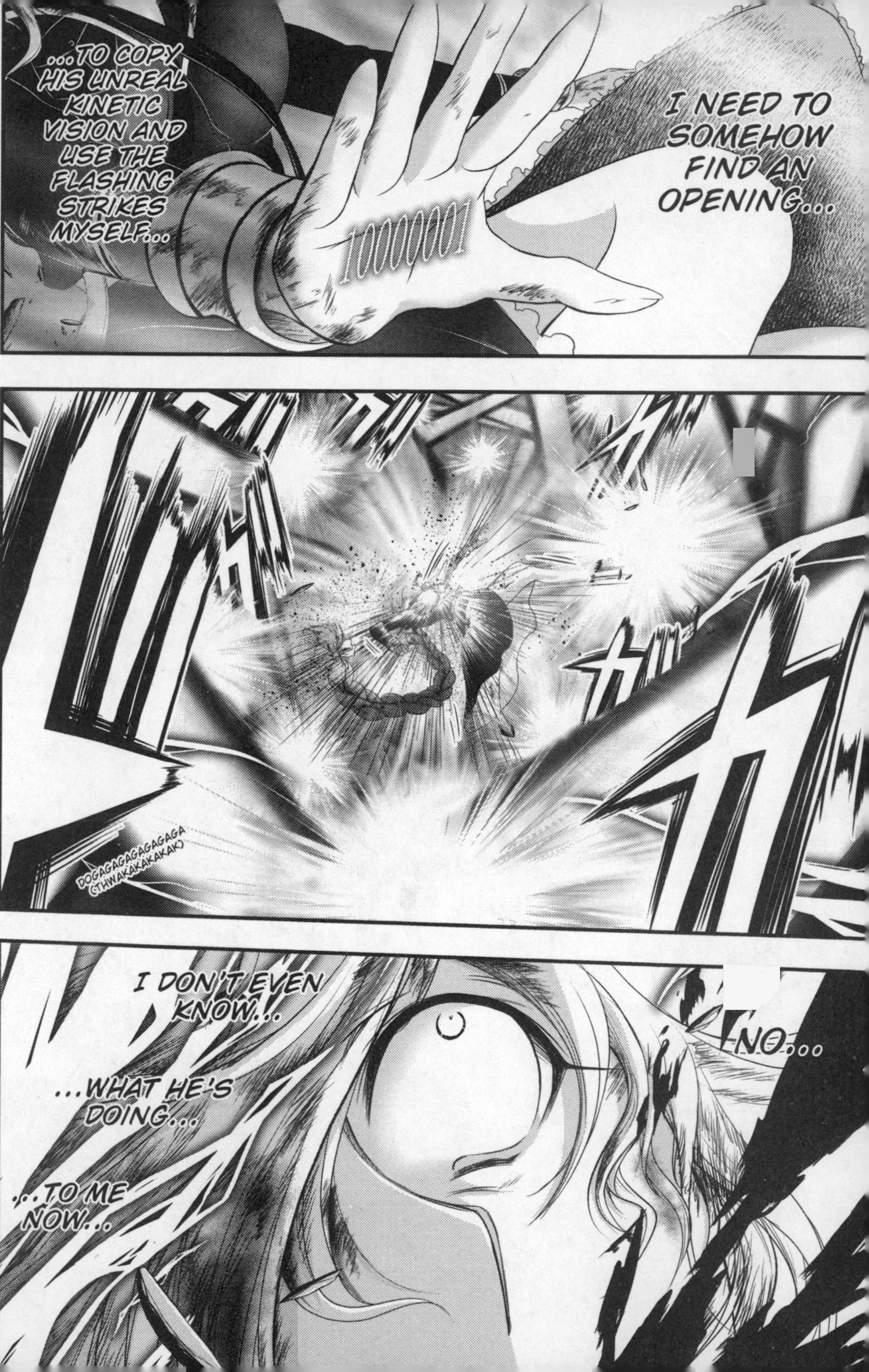
I NEED TO SOMEHOW FIND AN OPENING...
...TO COPY HIS UNREAL KINETIC VISION AND USE THE FLASHING STRIKES MYSELF...
10000001
DOGAGAGAGAGAGAGA (THWAKAKAKAKAK)
NO...
I DON'T EVEN KNOW...
...WHAT HE'S DOING...
...TO ME NOW...

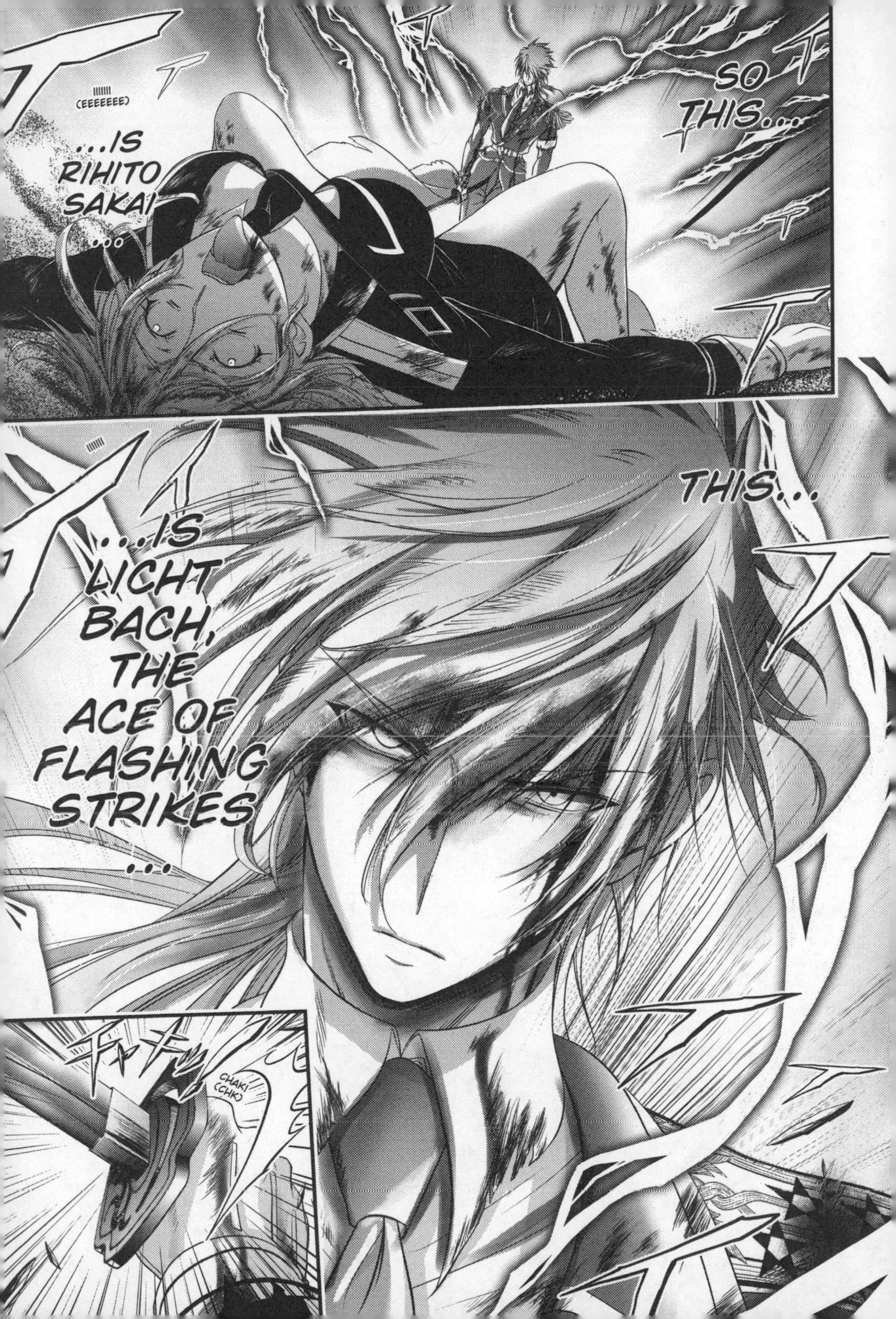
SO THIS...
IIIIII (EEEEEEE)
...IS RIHITO SAKAI...
THIS...
...IS LICHT BACH, THE ACE OF FLASHING STRIKES...
CHAKI (CHK)

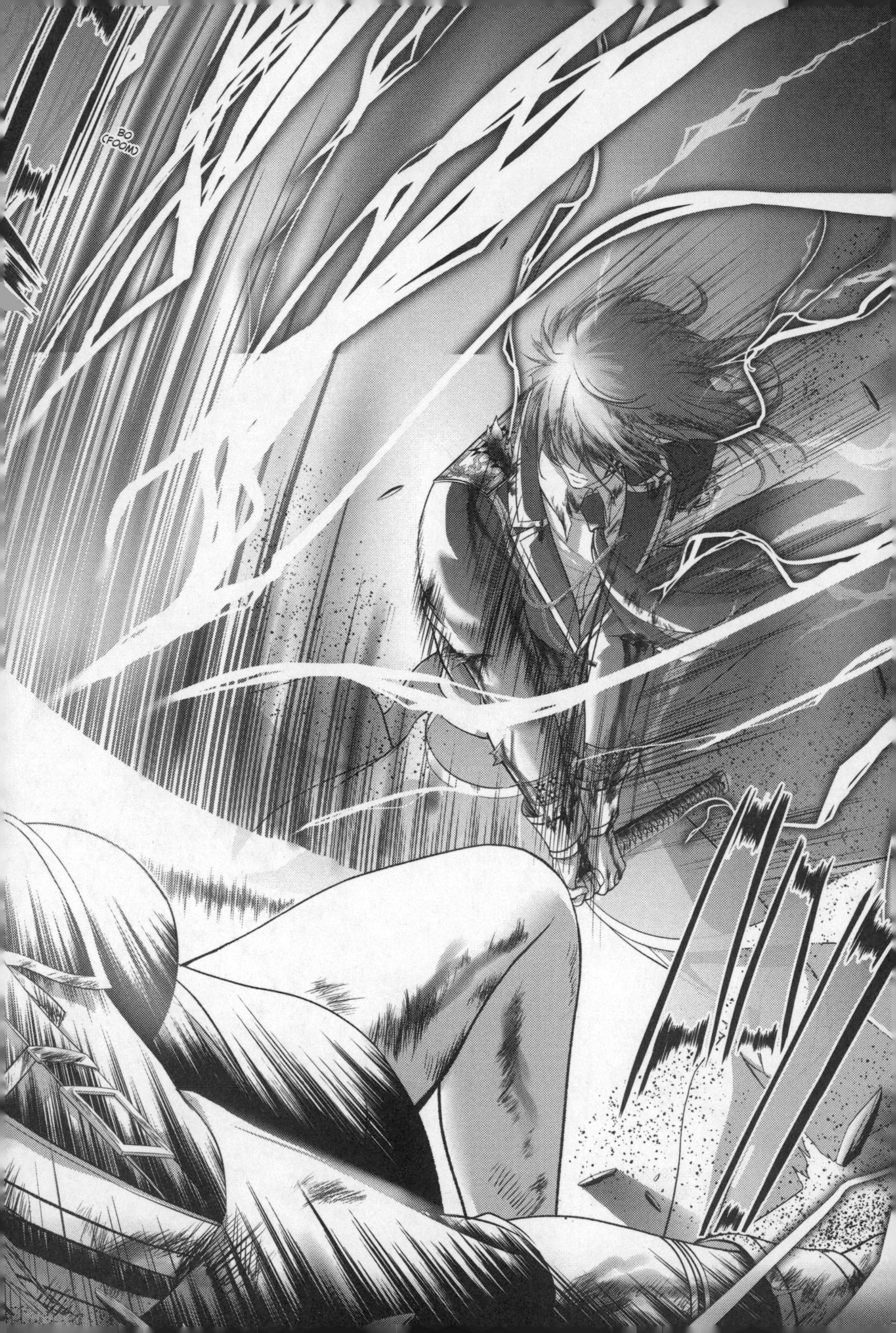
BO
(FOOM)

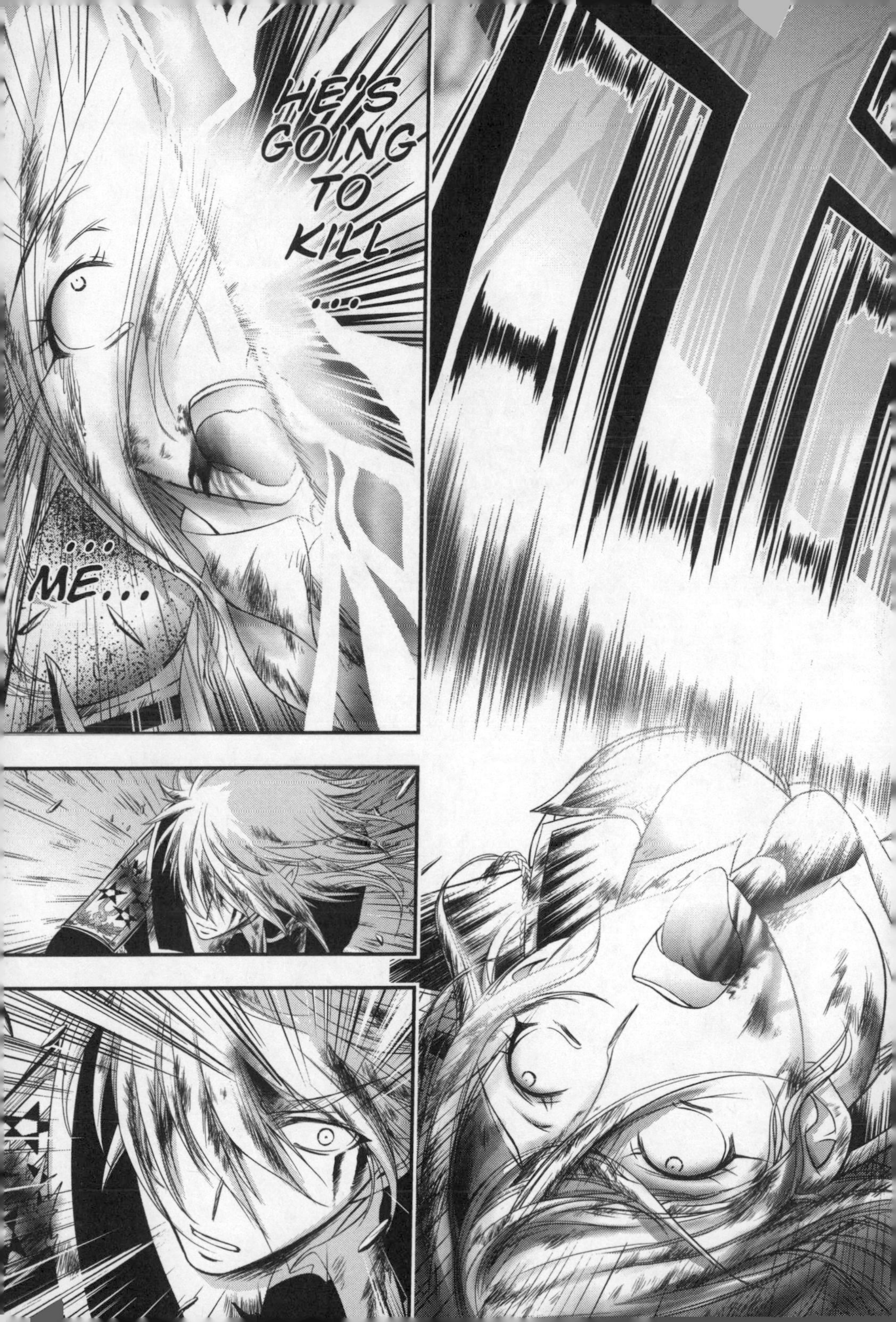
HE'S GOING TO KILL ...
... ME...

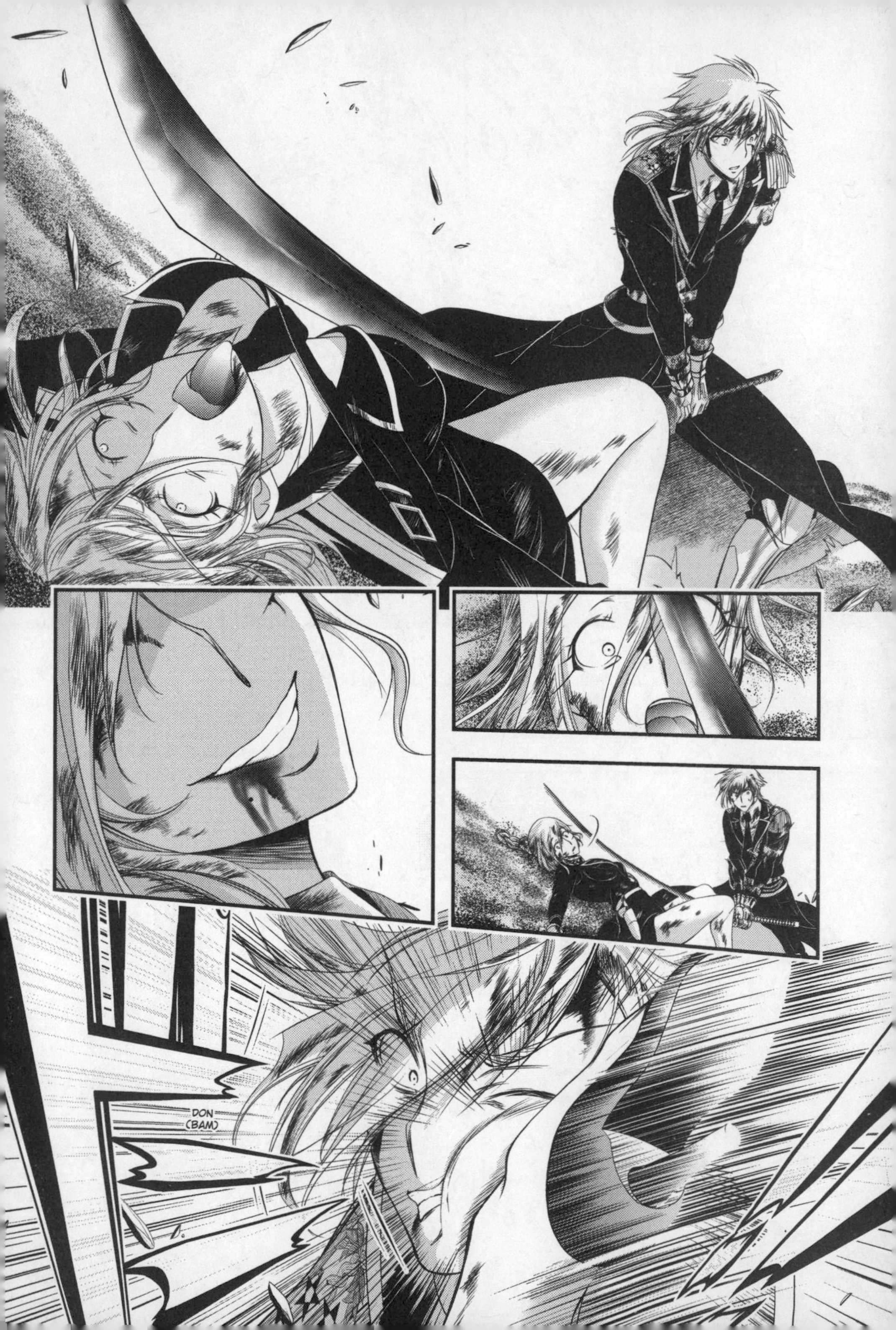
DON
(BAM)

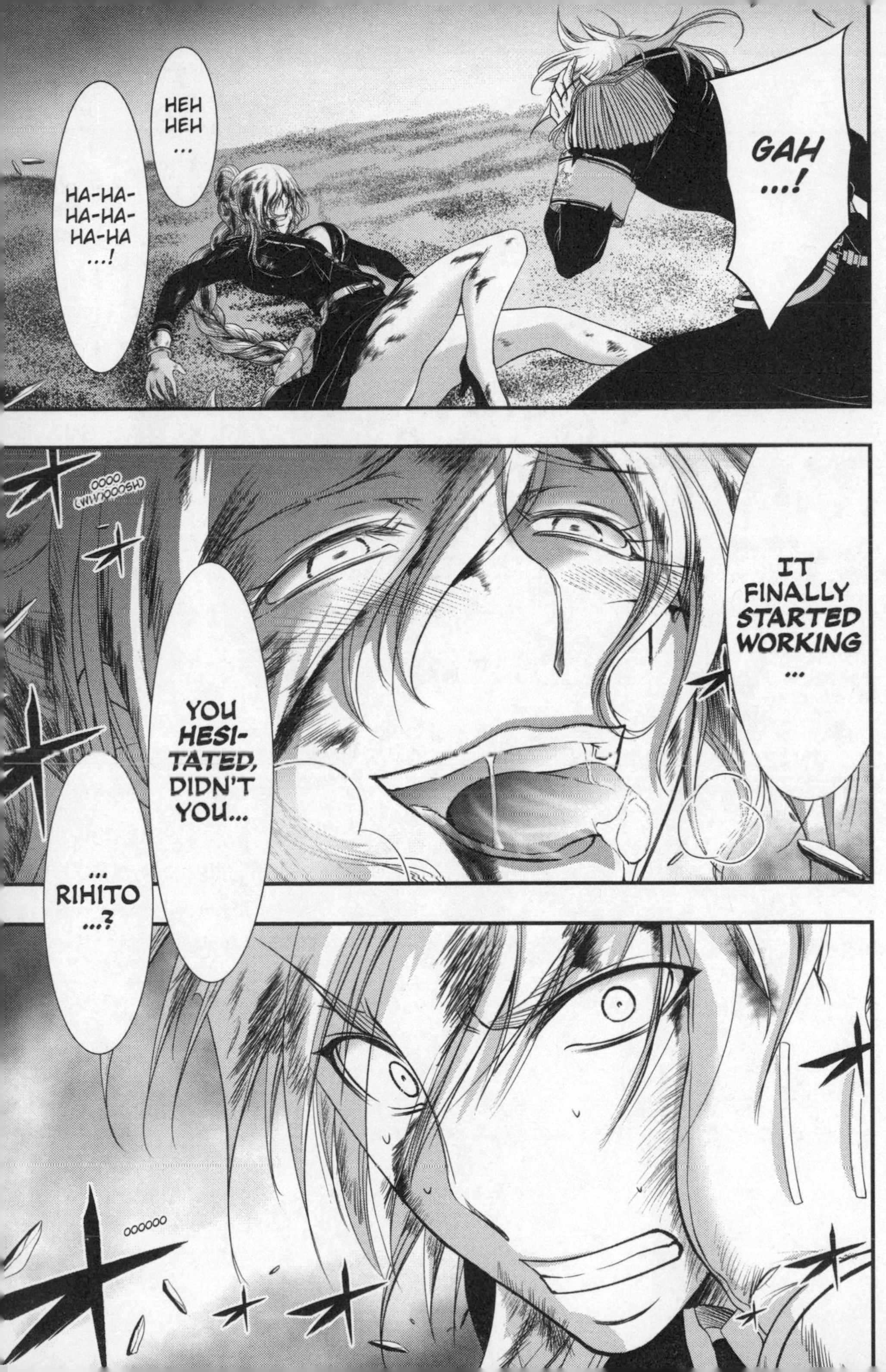
GAH ...!
HEH HEH ...
HA-HA-HA-HA-HA-HA ...!
IT FINALLY STARTED WORKING ...
OOOO (WHOOOSH)
YOU HESI-TATED, DIDN'T YOU...
... RIHITO ...?
OOOOOO

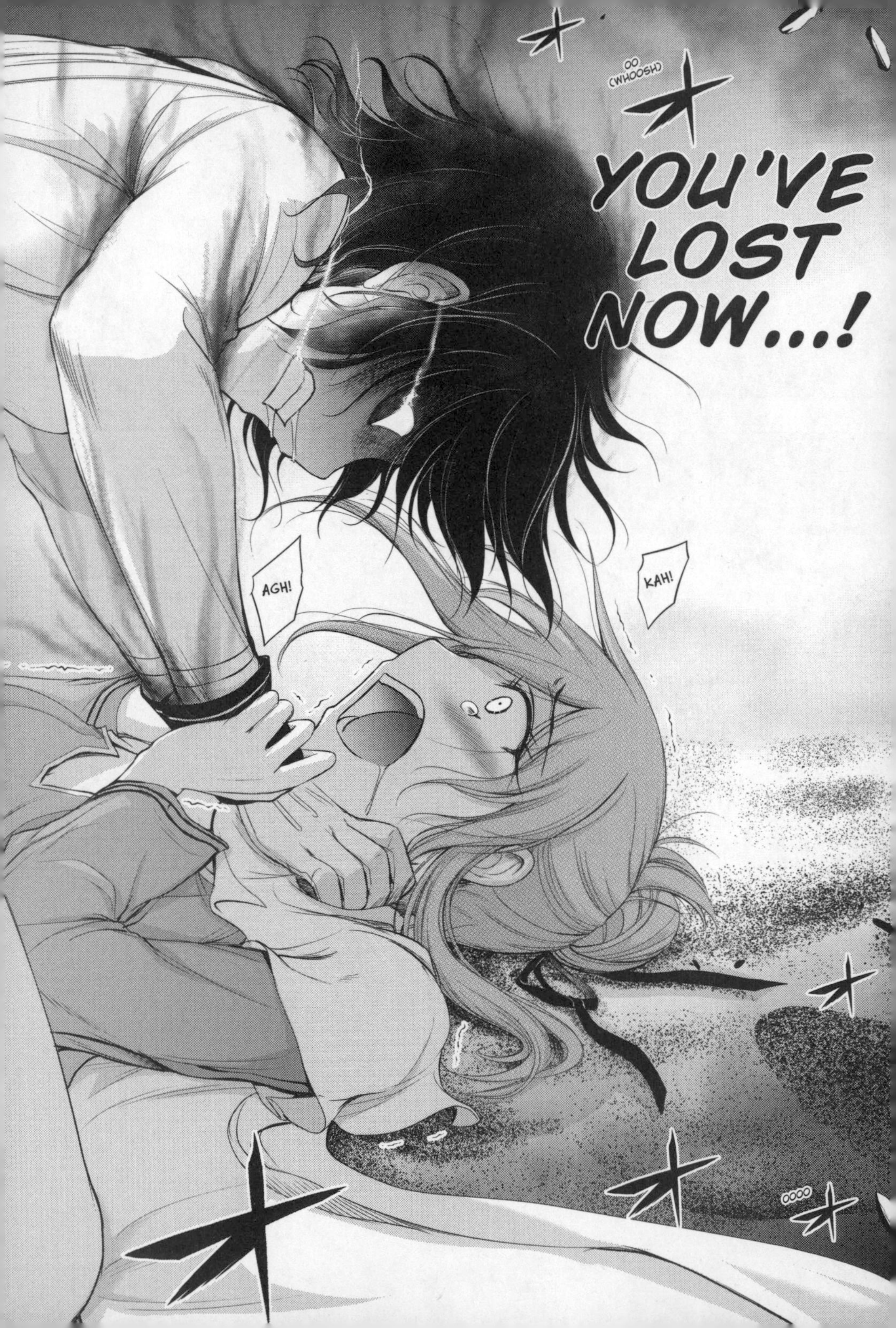
OO
(WHOOSH)
YOU'VE LOST NOW...!
KAH!
AGH!
OOOO

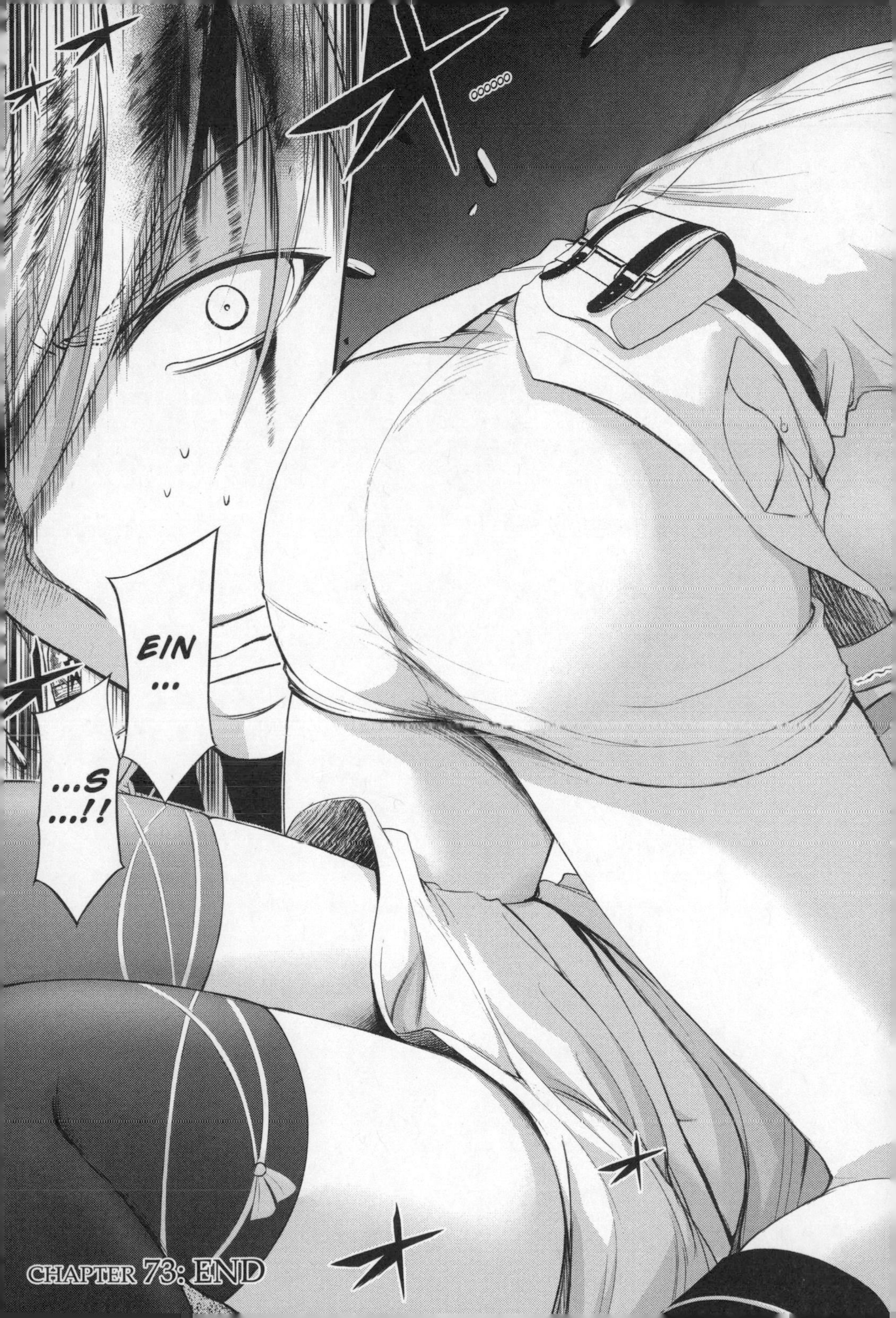
......
EIN ...
...S ...!!
CHAPTER 73: END

PLUNDERER

CHAPTER 74

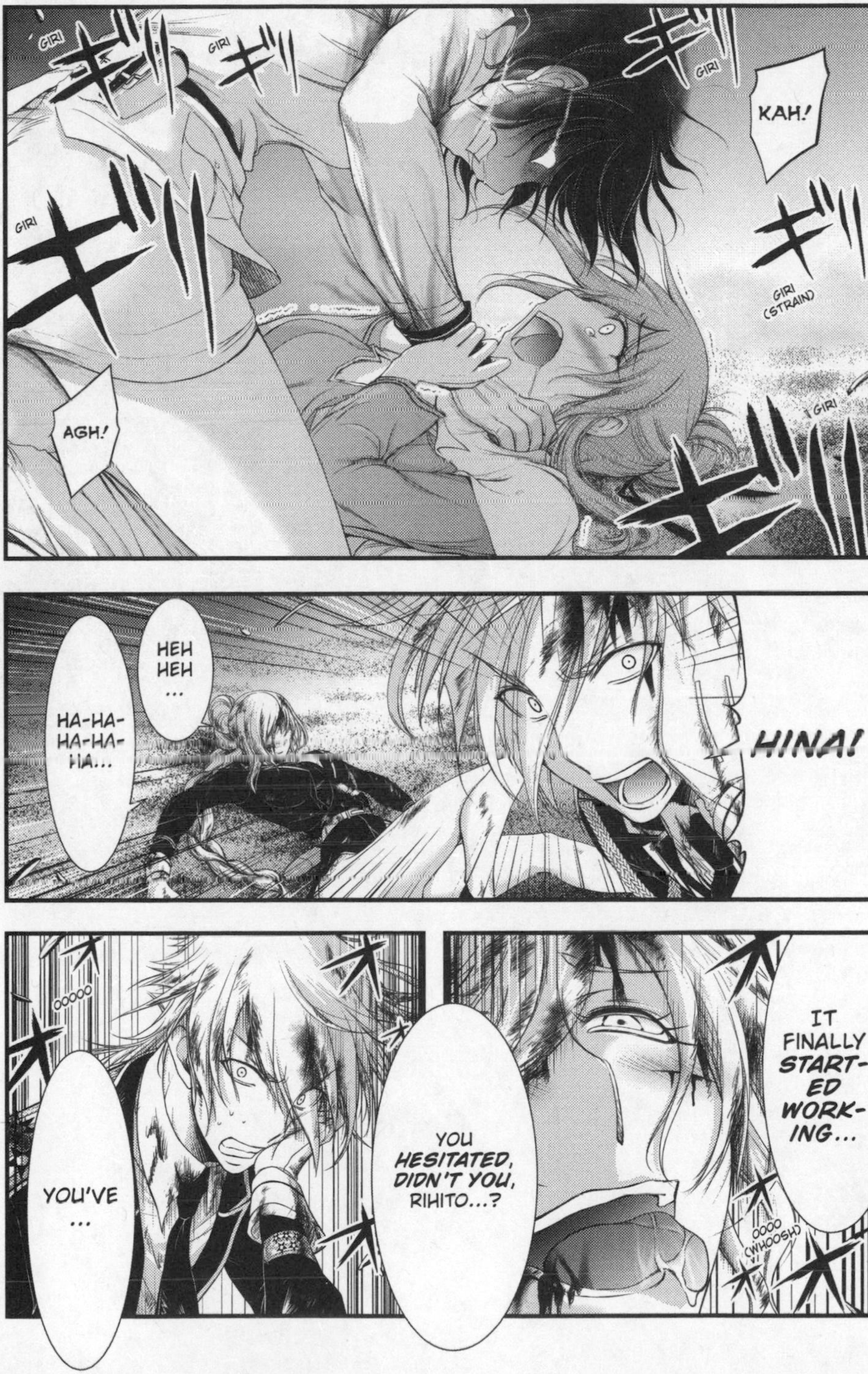
GIRI
KAH!
GIRI (STRAIN)
GIRI
GIRI
GIRI
AGH!
GIRI
HINA!
HEH HEH ...
HA-HA-HA-HA...
IT FINALLY STARTED-ED WORKING-ING...
OOOO (WHOOSH)
YOU HESITATED, DIDN'T YOU, RIHITO...?
YOU'VE ...
OOOOO

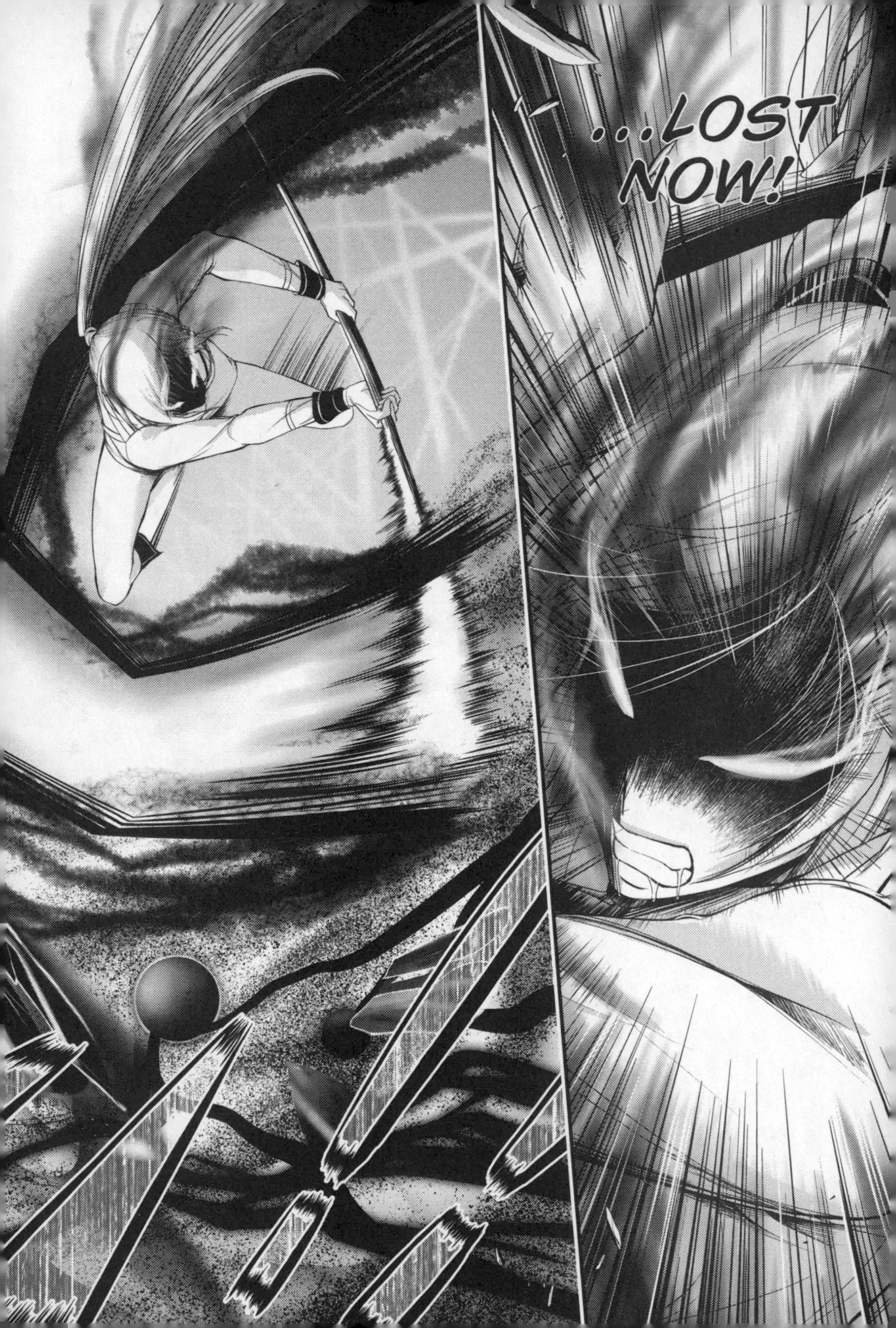
...LOST NOW!

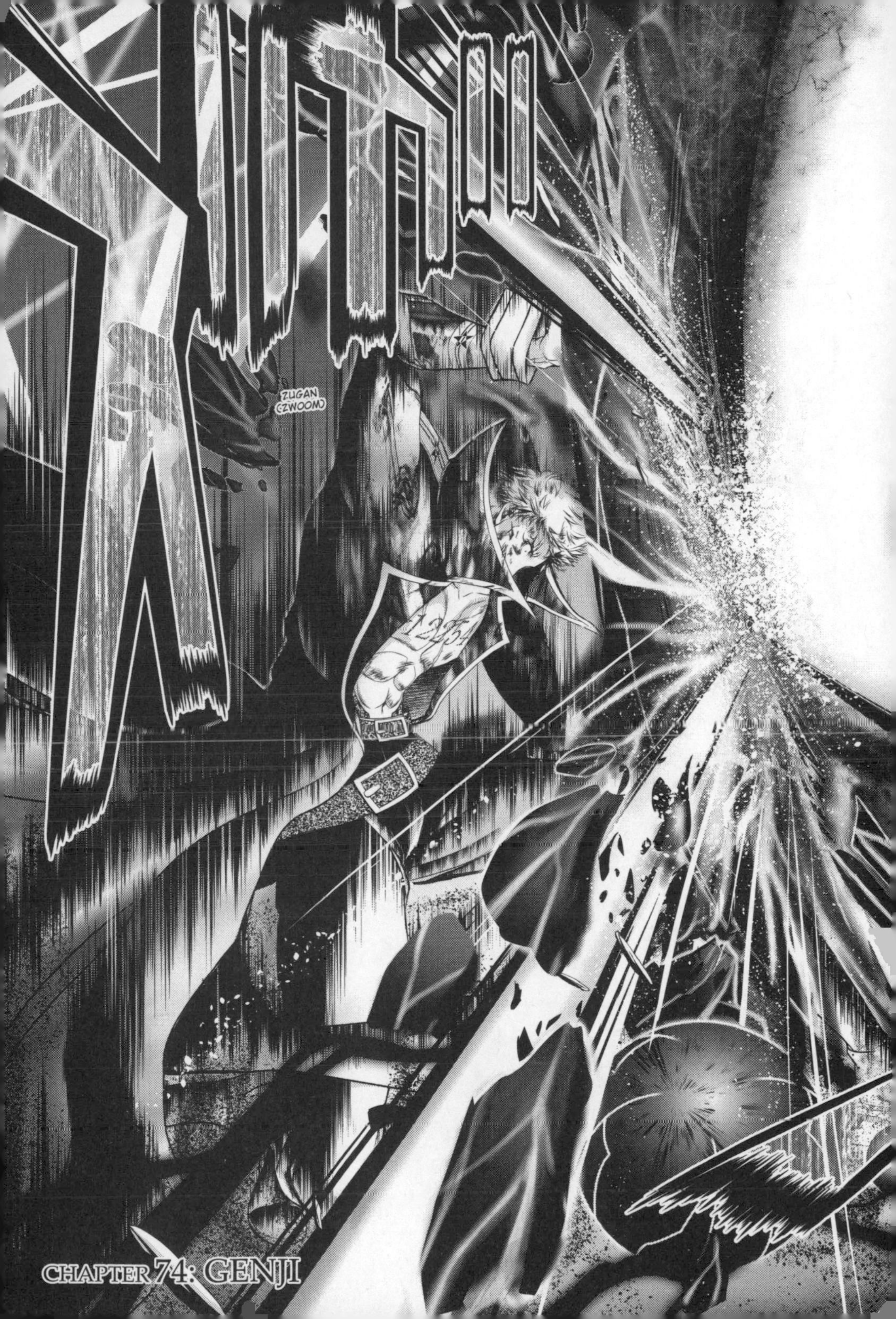
ZUGAN
(ZWOOM)

CHAPTER 74: GENJI

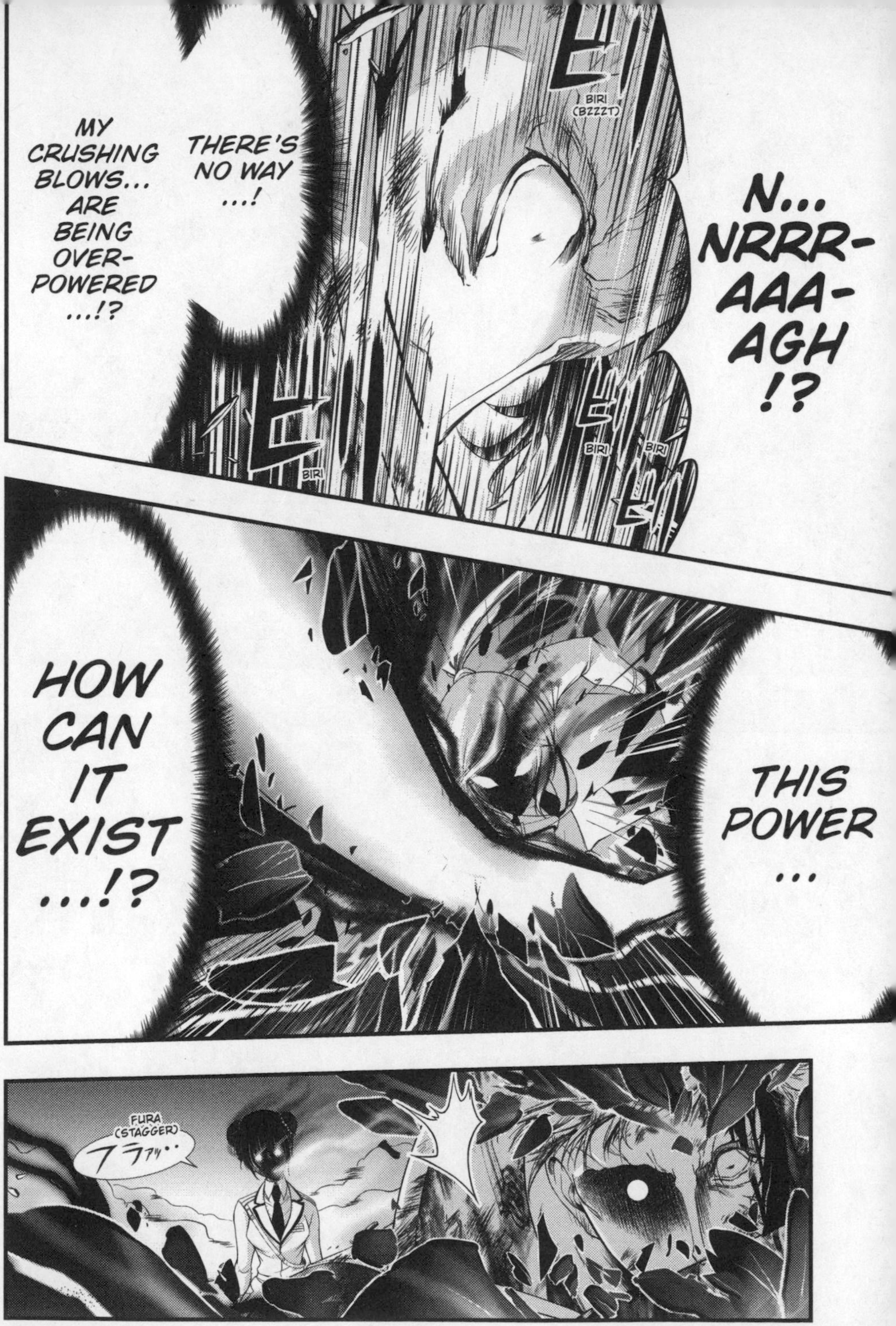
BIRI (BZZZT)
N... NRRRR-AAAA-AGH!?
THERE'S NO WAY...!
MY CRUSHING BLOWS... ARE BEING OVER-POWERED...!?
BIRI
BIRI
BIRI
THIS POWER...
HOW CAN IT EXIST...!?
FURA (STAGGER)
フラッ・・

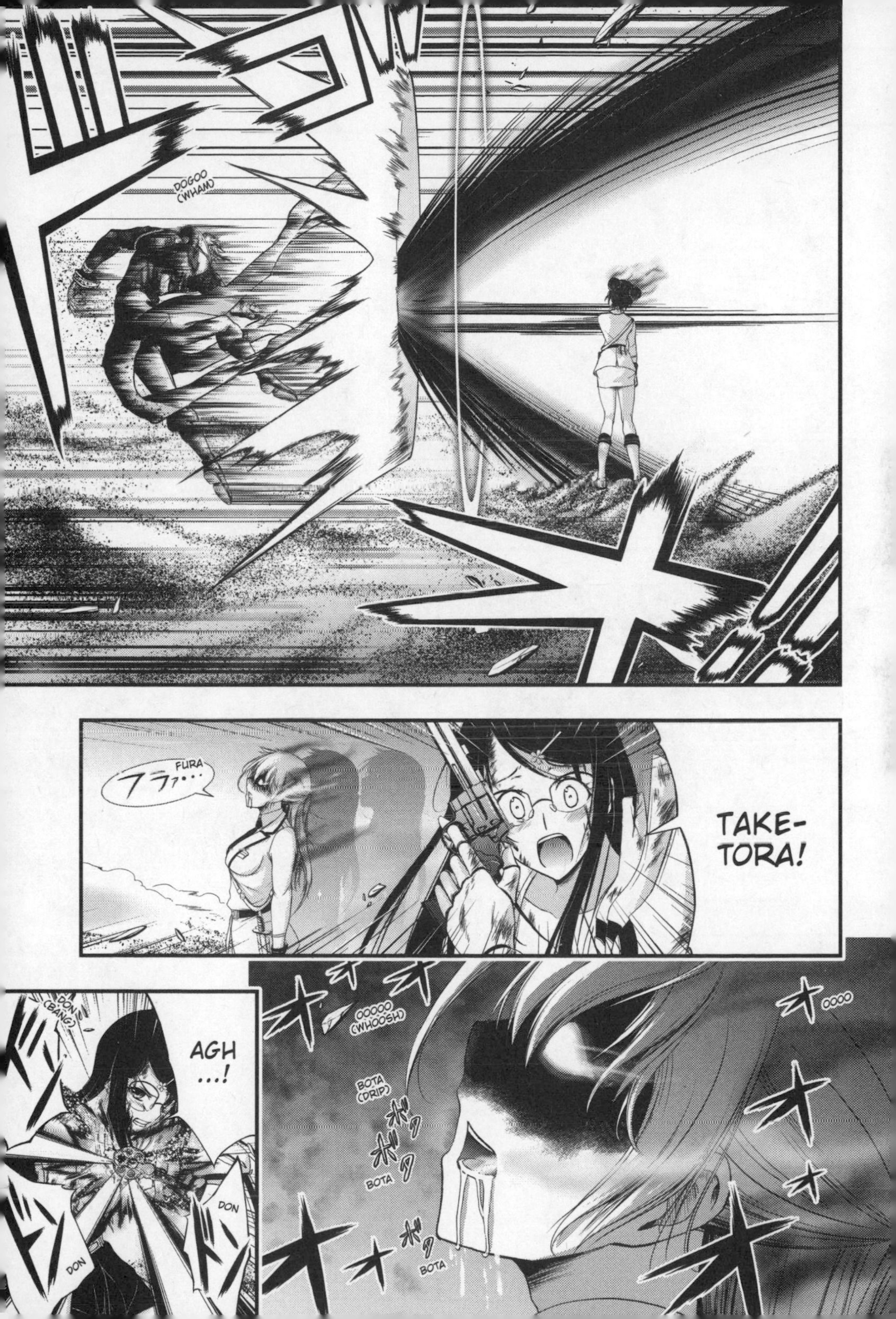
DOGOO (WHAM)
TAKE-TORA!
FURA
フラァ…
OOOO
OOOOO (WHOOSH)
BOTA (DRIP)
BOTA
BOTA
DON (BANG)
AGH ...!
DON
DON

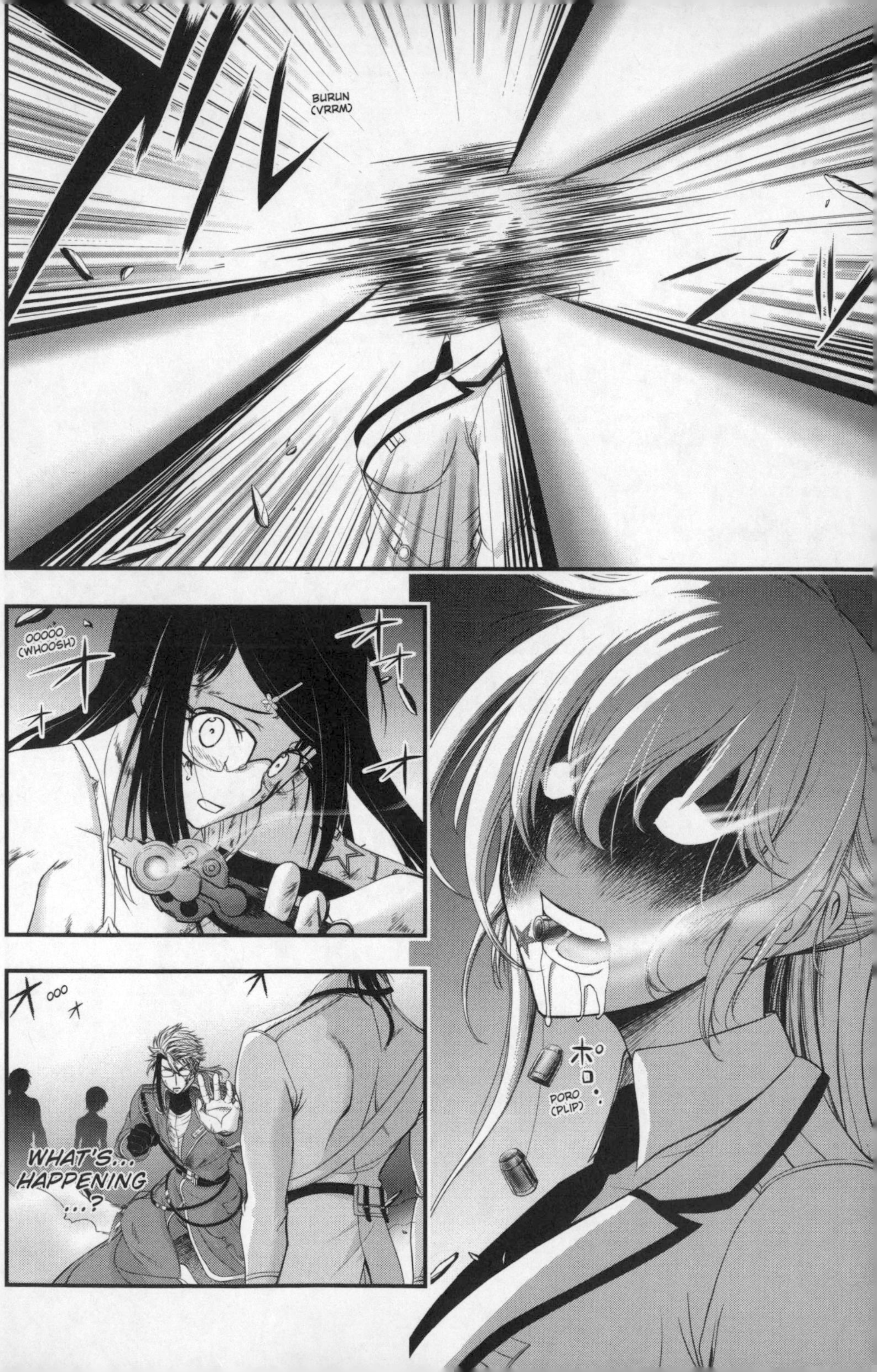
BURUN (VRRM)
PORO (PLIP)
OOOOO (WHOOSH)
OOO
WHAT'S... HAPPENING ...?

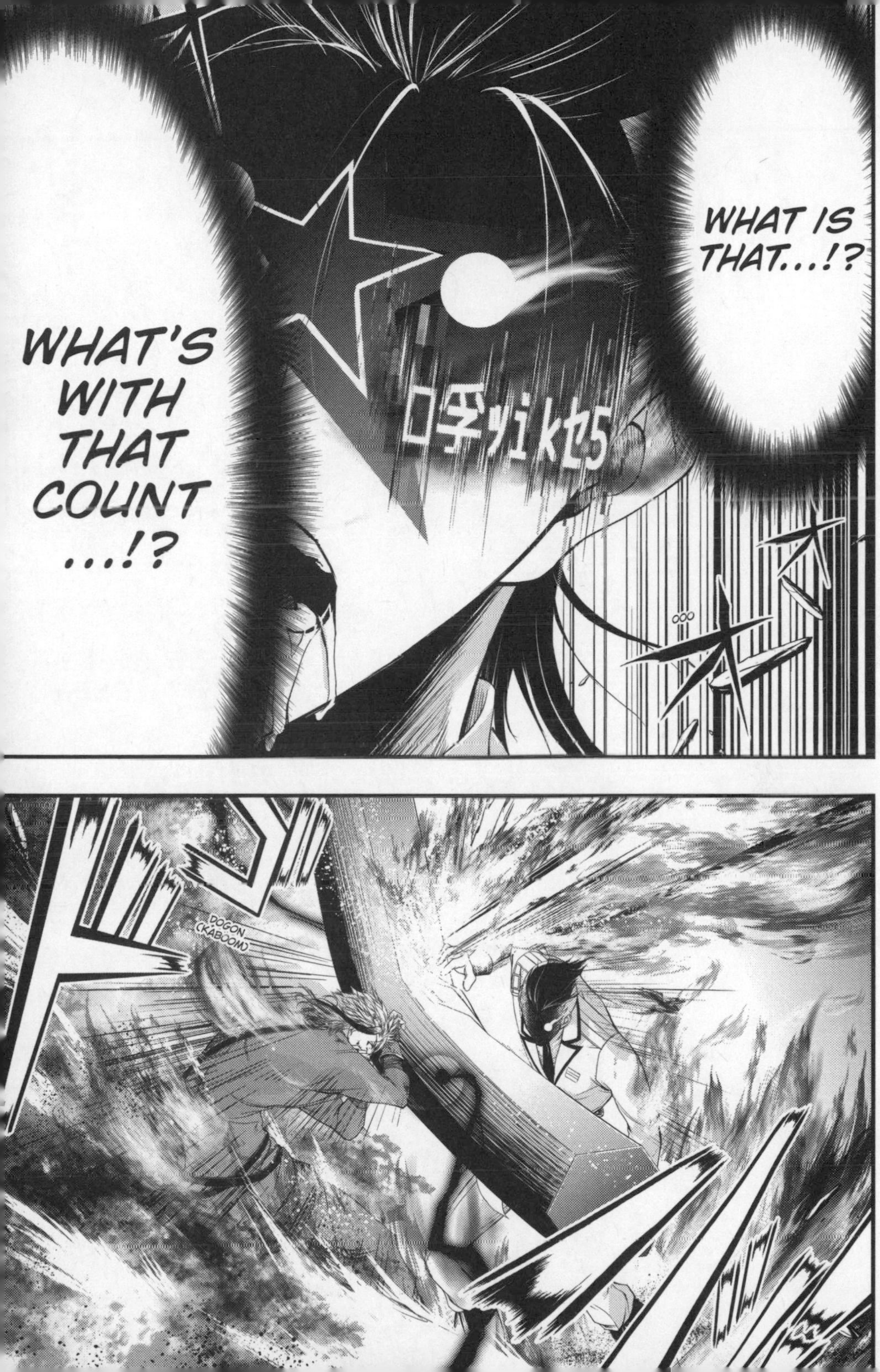
WHAT IS THAT...!?
WHAT'S WITH THAT COUNT...!?
DOGON (KABOOM)

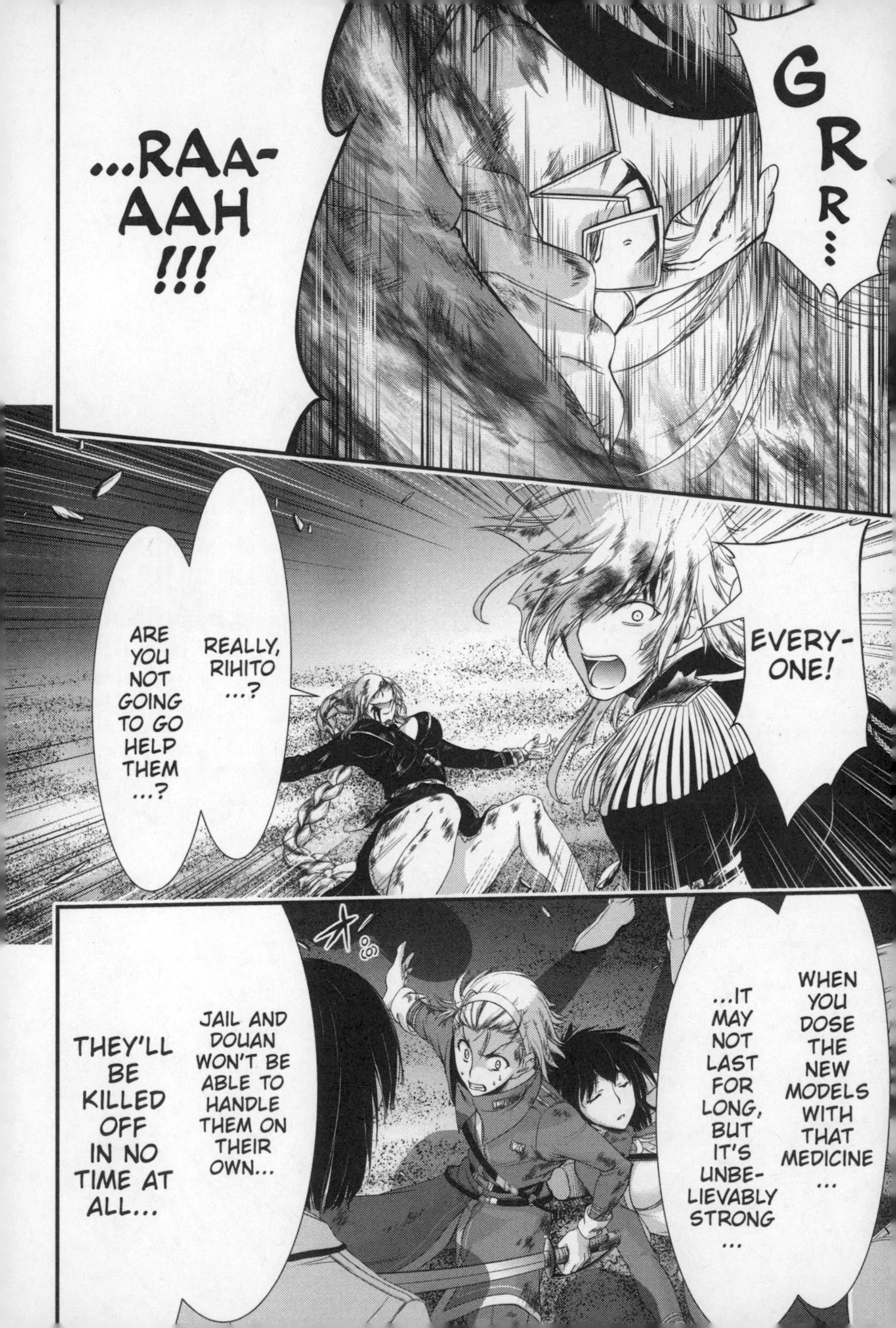
GRR...
...RAA-AAH!!!
EVERY-ONE!
REALLY, RIHITO...?
ARE YOU NOT GOING TO GO HELP THEM...?
WHEN YOU DOSE THE NEW MODELS WITH THAT MEDICINE...
...IT MAY NOT LAST FOR LONG, BUT IT'S UNBELIEVABLY STRONG...
JAIL AND DOUAN WON'T BE ABLE TO HANDLE THEM ON THEIR OWN...
THEY'LL BE KILLED OFF IN NO TIME AT ALL...

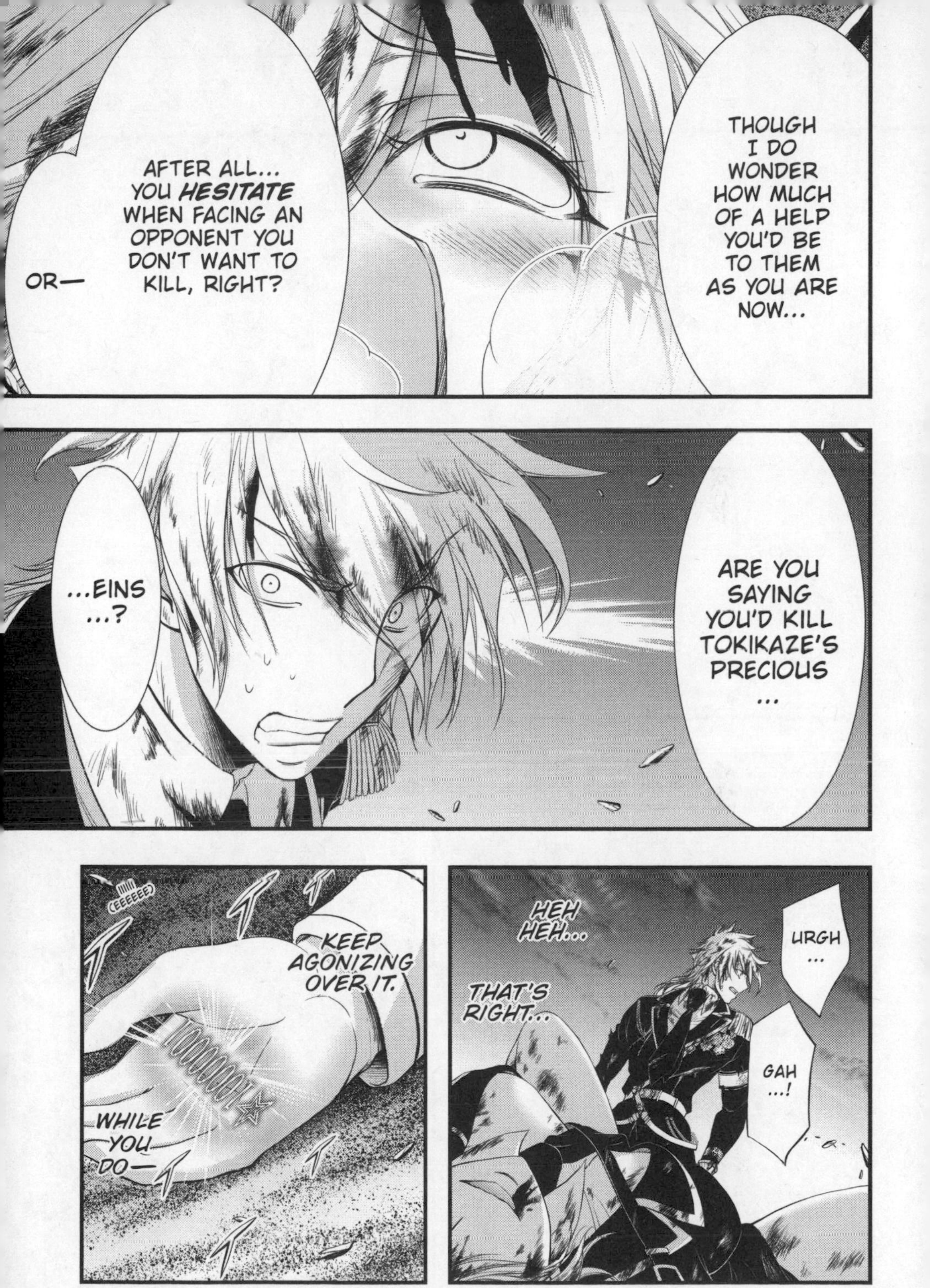
THOUGH I DO WONDER HOW MUCH OF A HELP YOU'D BE TO THEM AS YOU ARE NOW...
AFTER ALL... YOU *HESITATE* WHEN FACING AN OPPONENT YOU DON'T WANT TO KILL, RIGHT?
OR—
ARE YOU SAYING YOU'D KILL TOKIKAZE'S PRECIOUS ...
...EINS ...?
URGH ...
HEH HEH...
GAH ...!
THAT'S RIGHT...
(EEEEEE)
KEEP AGONIZING OVER IT.
WHILE YOU DO—

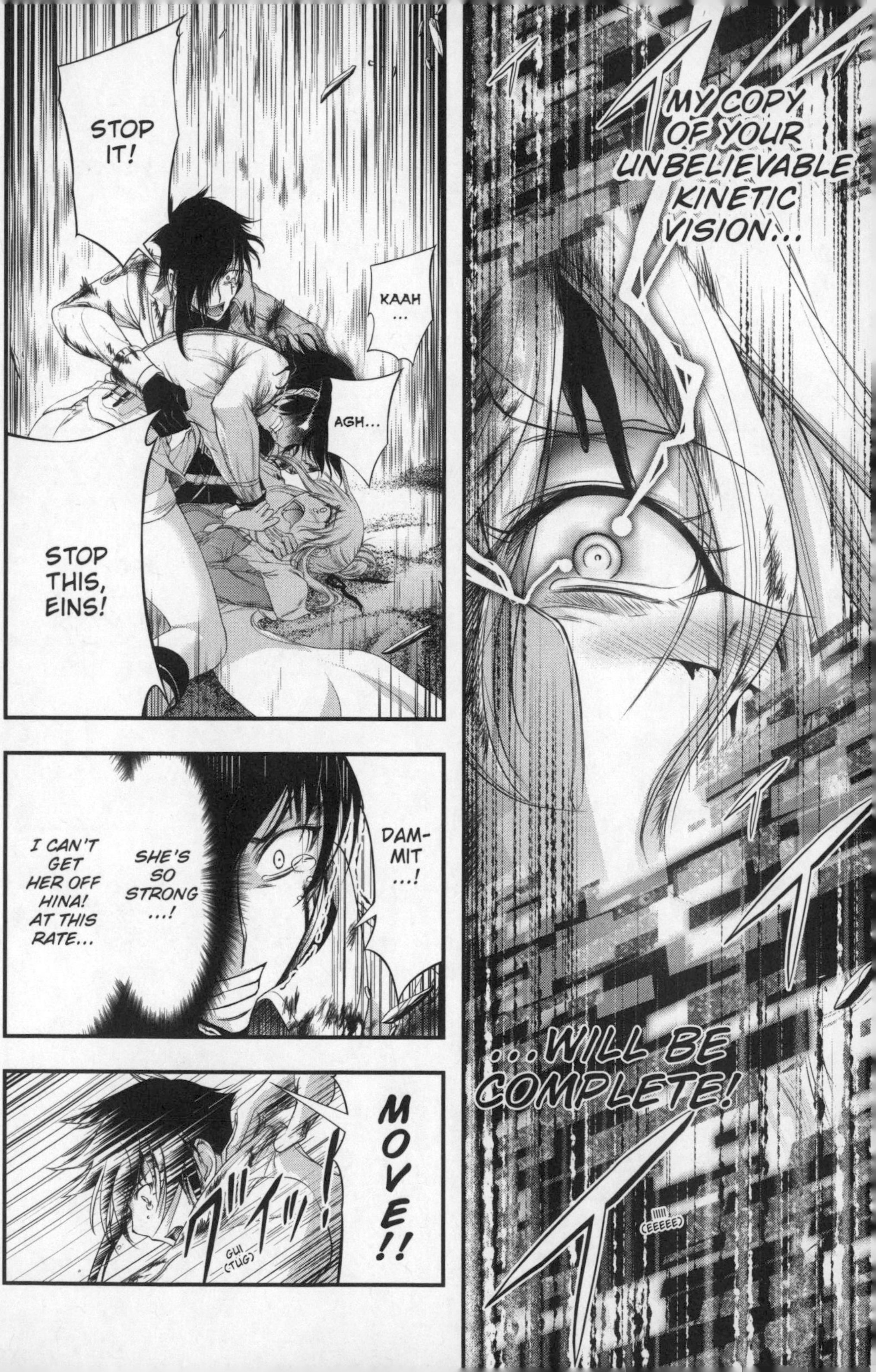

MY COPY OF YOUR UNBELIEVABLE KINETIC VISION...
...WILL BE COMPLETE!
(EEEEE)
STOP IT!
KAAH ...
AGH...
STOP THIS, EINS!
DAM-MIT ...!
SHE'S SO STRONG ...!
I CAN'T GET HER OFF HINA! AT THIS RATE...
MOVE!!
GUI (TUG)

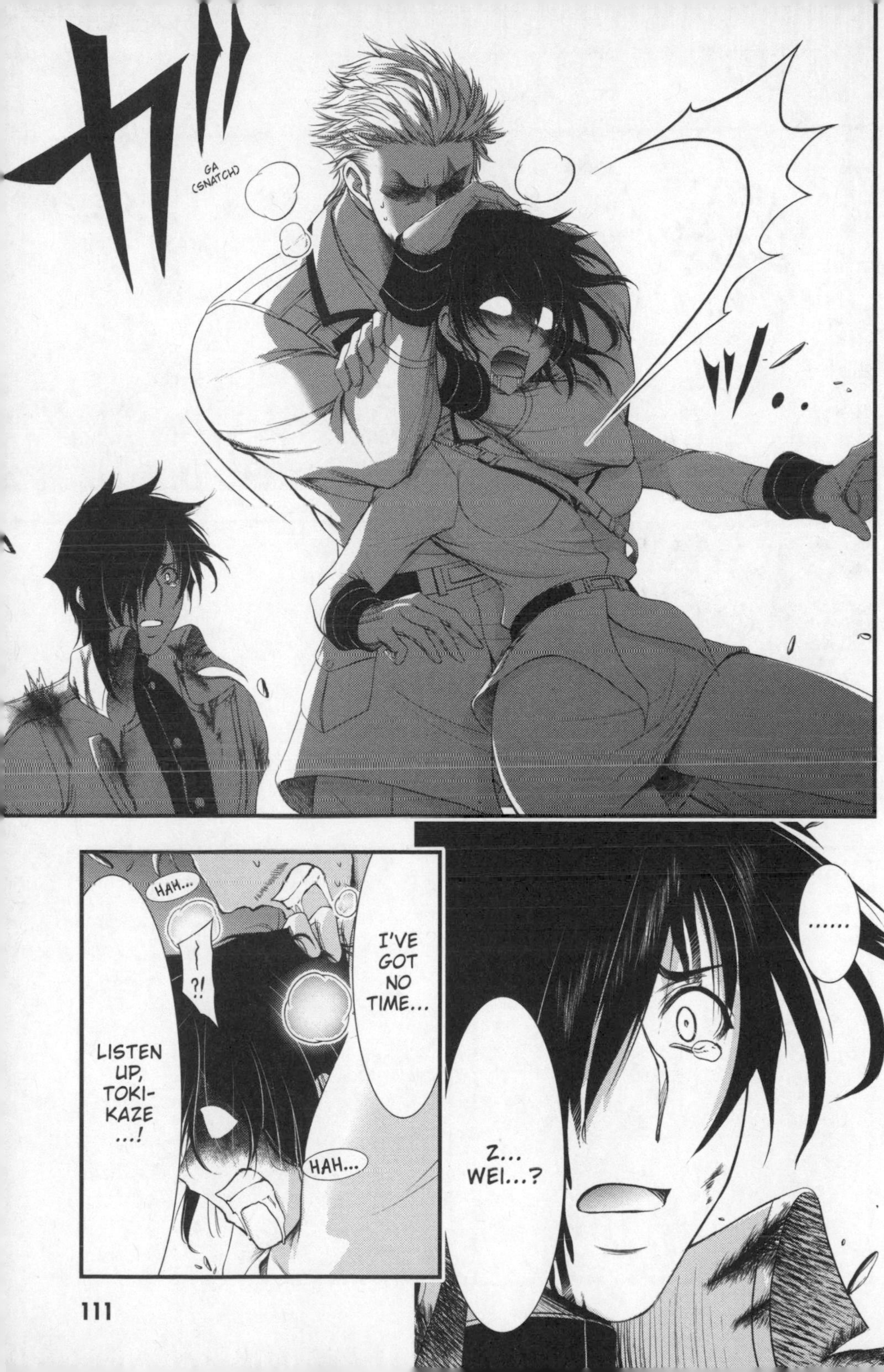
GA
(SNATCH)
......
Z... WEI...?
I'VE GOT NO TIME...
HAH...
?!
LISTEN UP, TOKI-KAZE ...!
HAH...

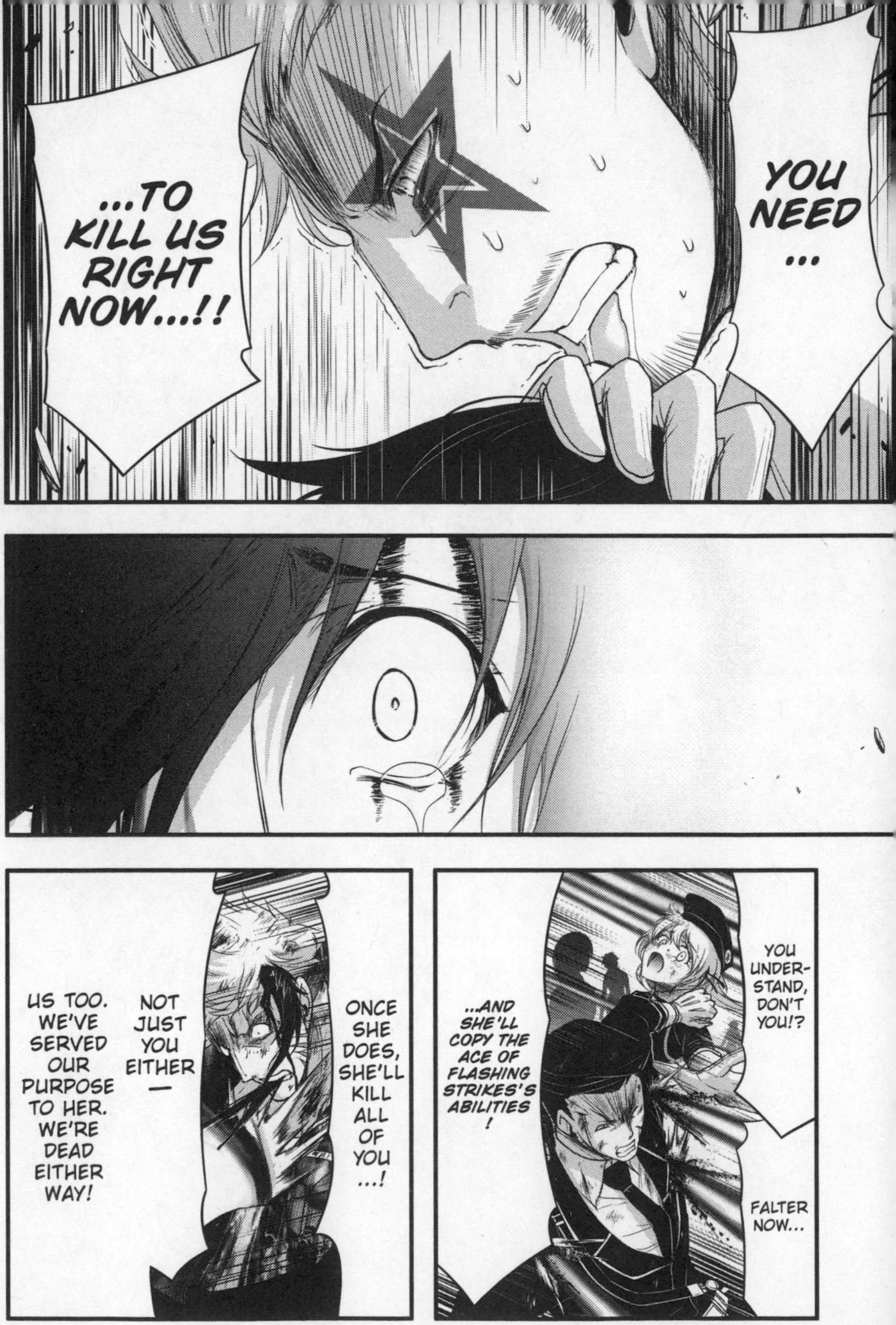
YOU NEED ...
...TO KILL US RIGHT NOW...!!
YOU UNDER-STAND, DON'T YOU!?
FALTER NOW...
...AND SHE'LL COPY THE ACE OF FLASHING STRIKES'S ABILITIES!
ONCE SHE DOES, SHE'LL KILL ALL OF YOU...!
NOT JUST YOU EITHER—
US TOO. WE'VE SERVED OUR PURPOSE TO HER. WE'RE DEAD EITHER WAY!

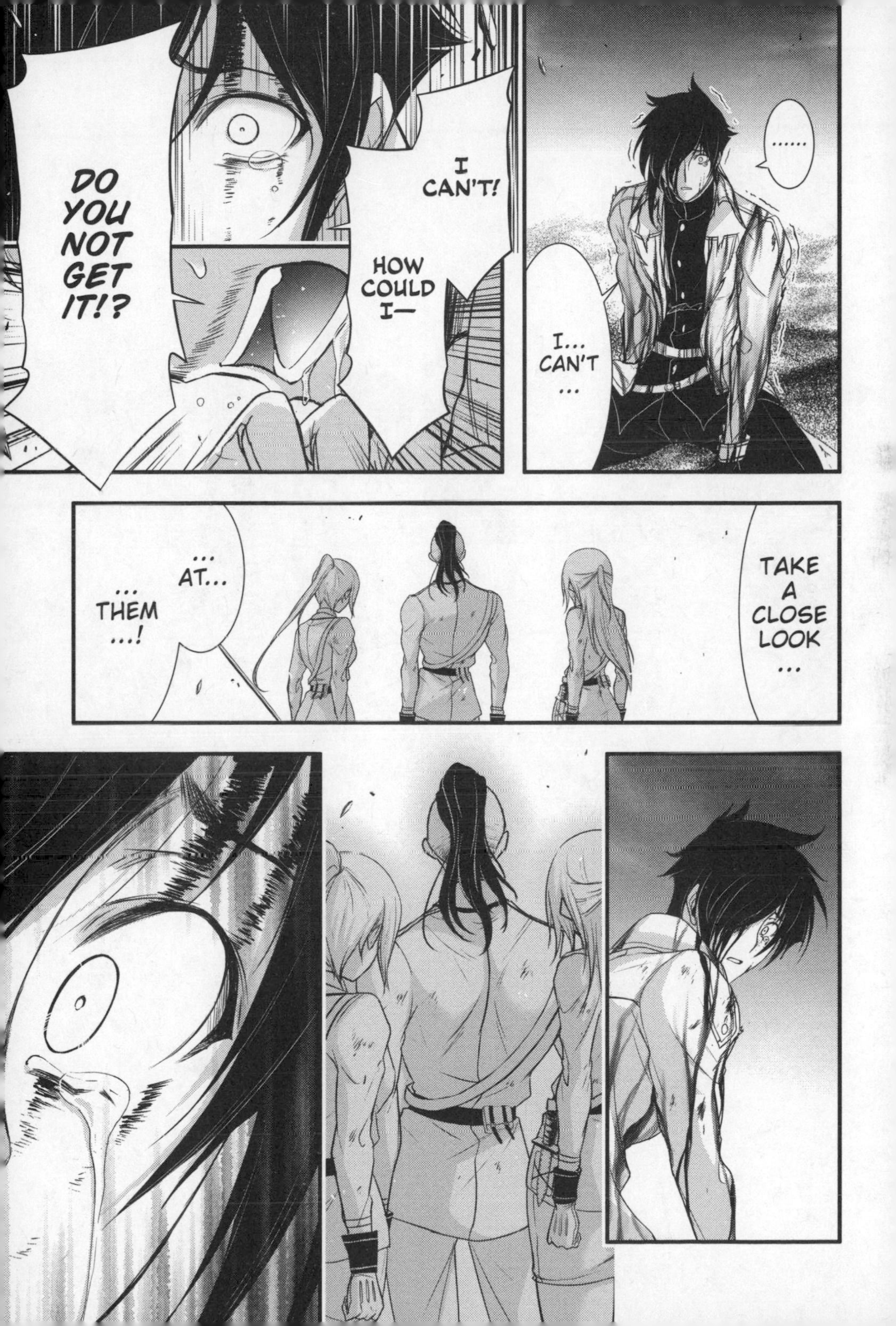
......
I... CAN'T ...
I CAN'T!
HOW COULD I—
DO YOU NOT GET IT!?
TAKE A CLOSE LOOK ...
... AT...
... THEM ...!

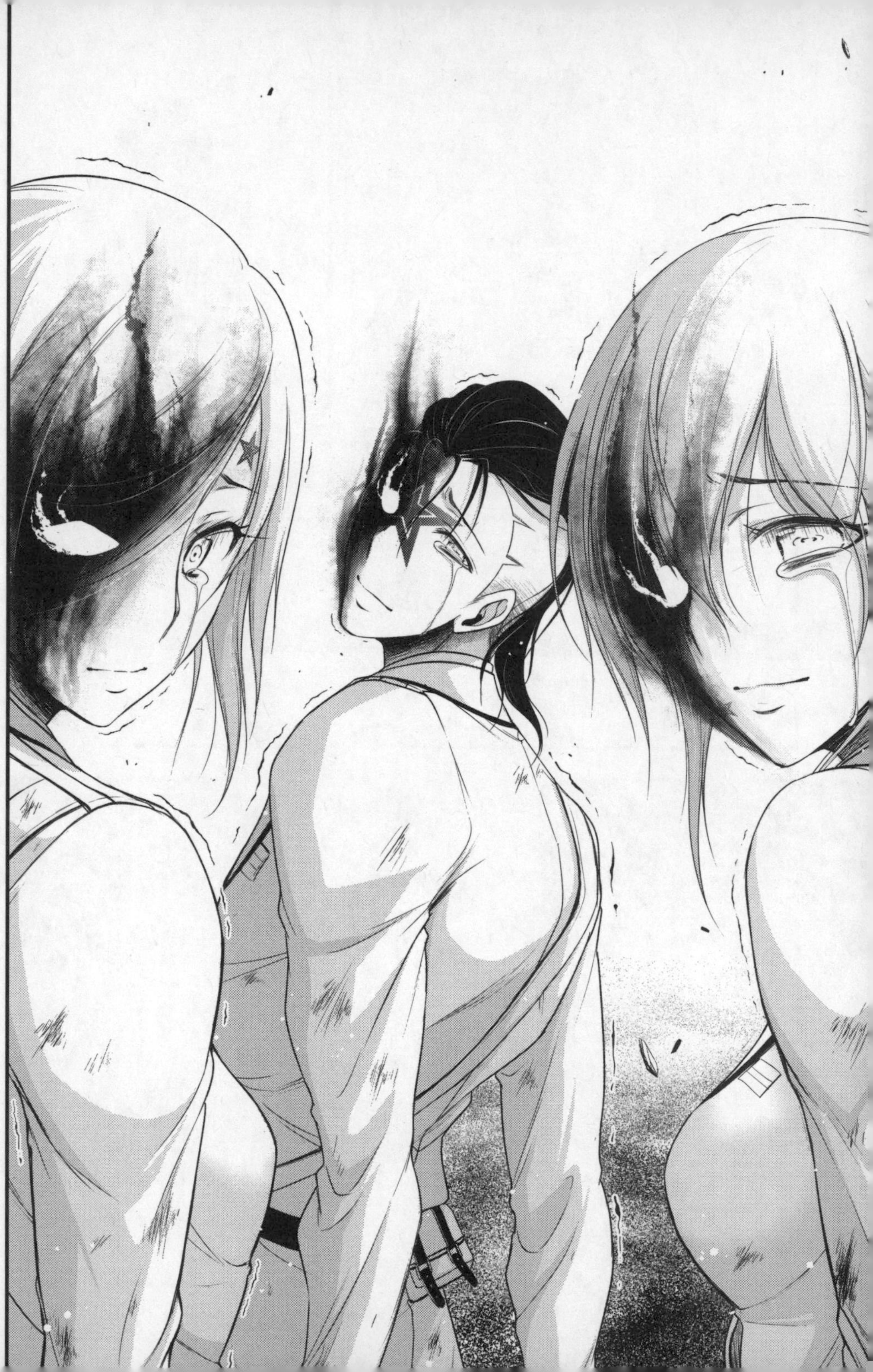

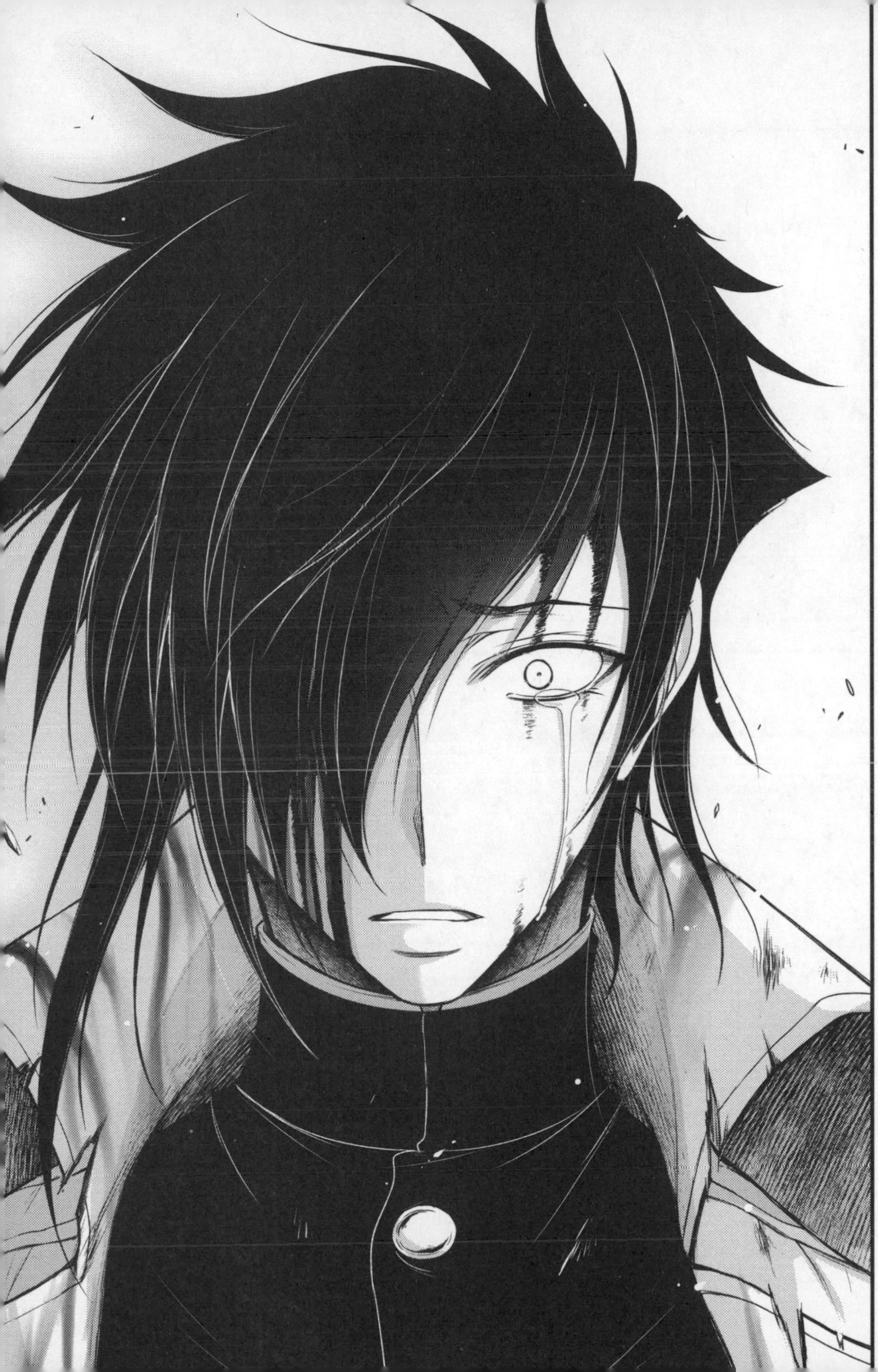

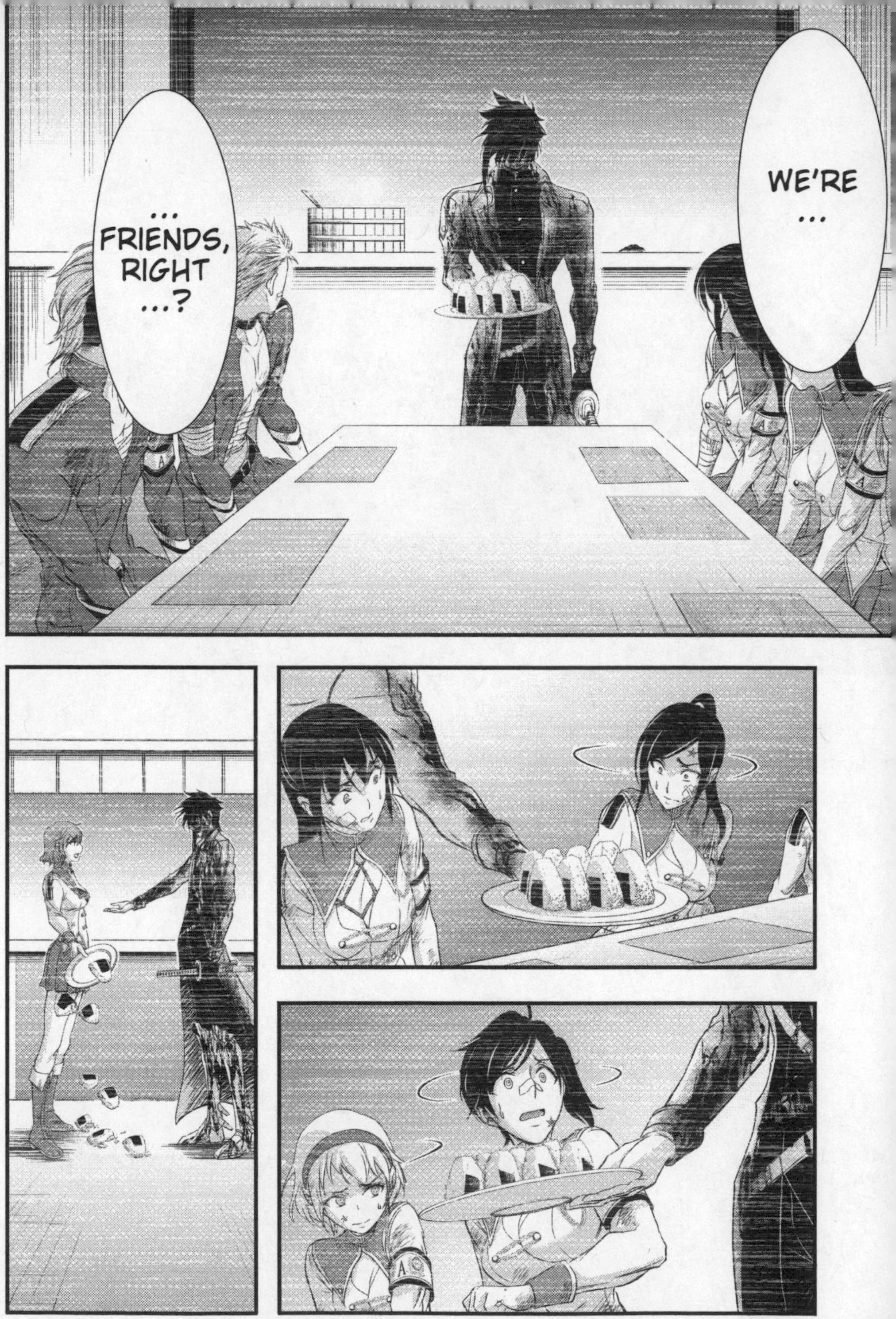
WE'RE
...
...
FRIENDS,
RIGHT
...?

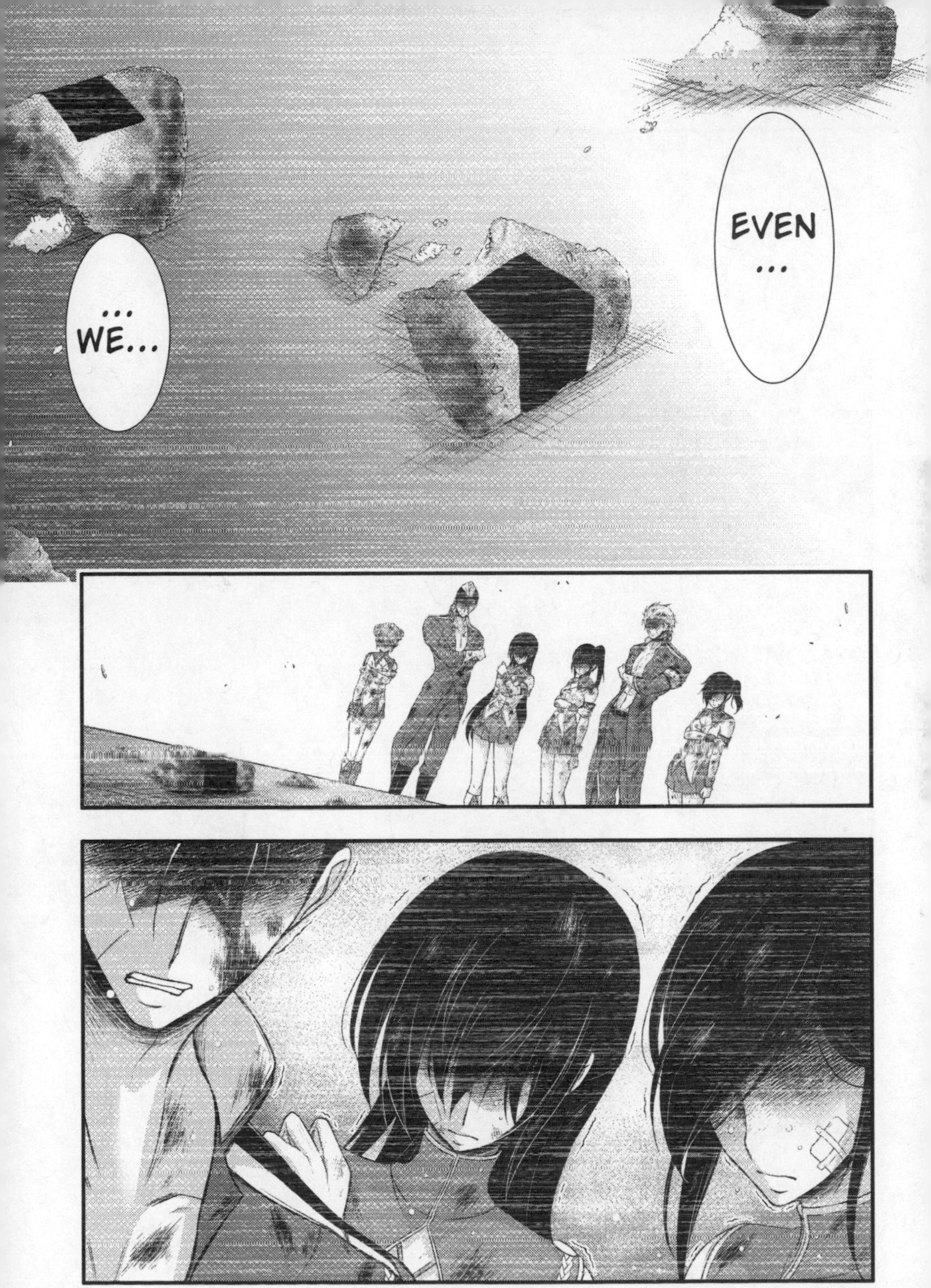
EVEN ...
... WE...

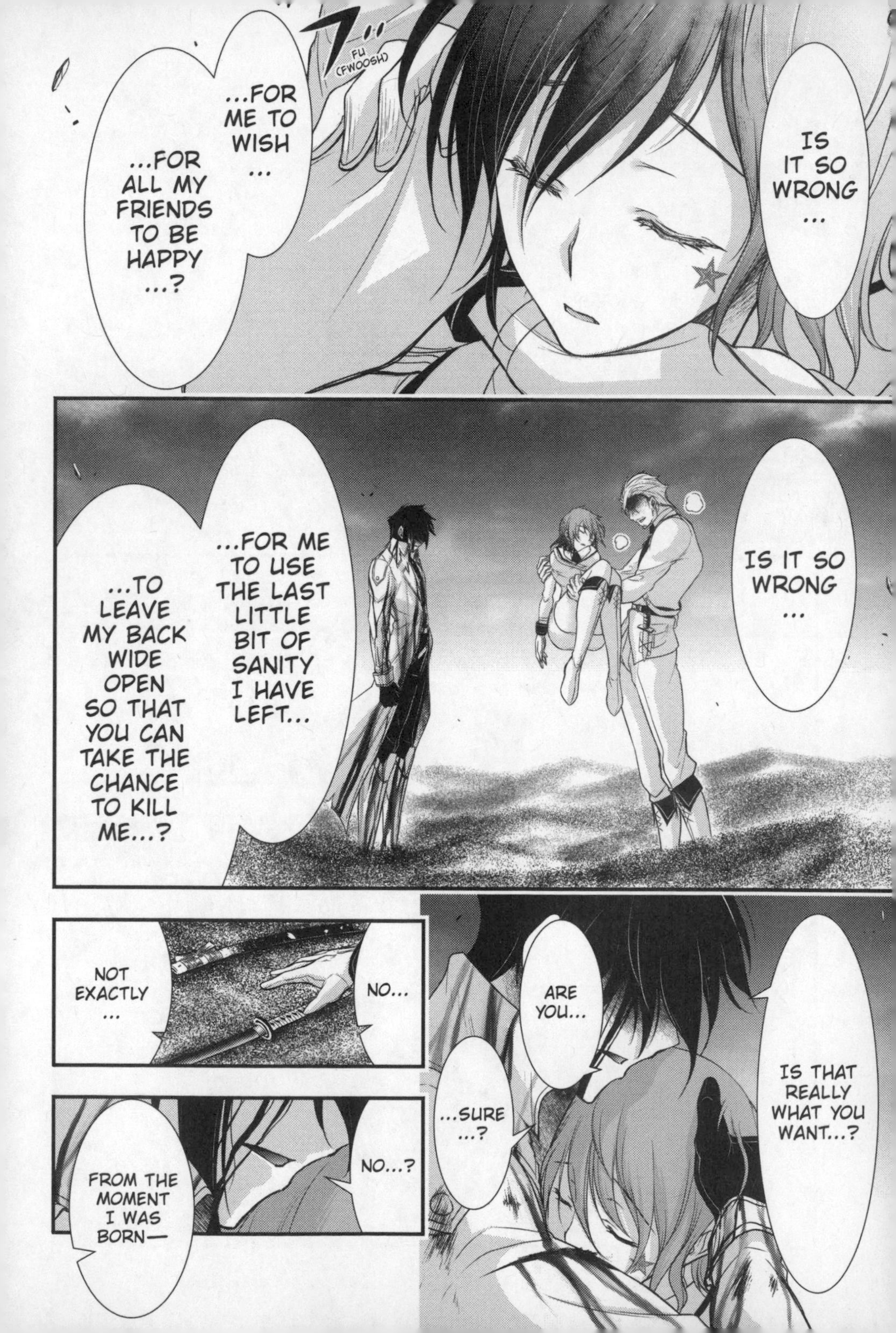
IS IT SO WRONG ...
FU (FWOOSH)
...FOR ME TO WISH ...
...FOR ALL MY FRIENDS TO BE HAPPY ...?
IS IT SO WRONG ...
...FOR ME TO USE THE LAST LITTLE BIT OF SANITY I HAVE LEFT...
...TO LEAVE MY BACK WIDE OPEN SO THAT YOU CAN TAKE THE CHANCE TO KILL ME...?
IS THAT REALLY WHAT YOU WANT...?
ARE YOU...
...SURE ...?
NO...
NOT EXACTLY ...
NO...?
FROM THE MOMENT I WAS BORN—

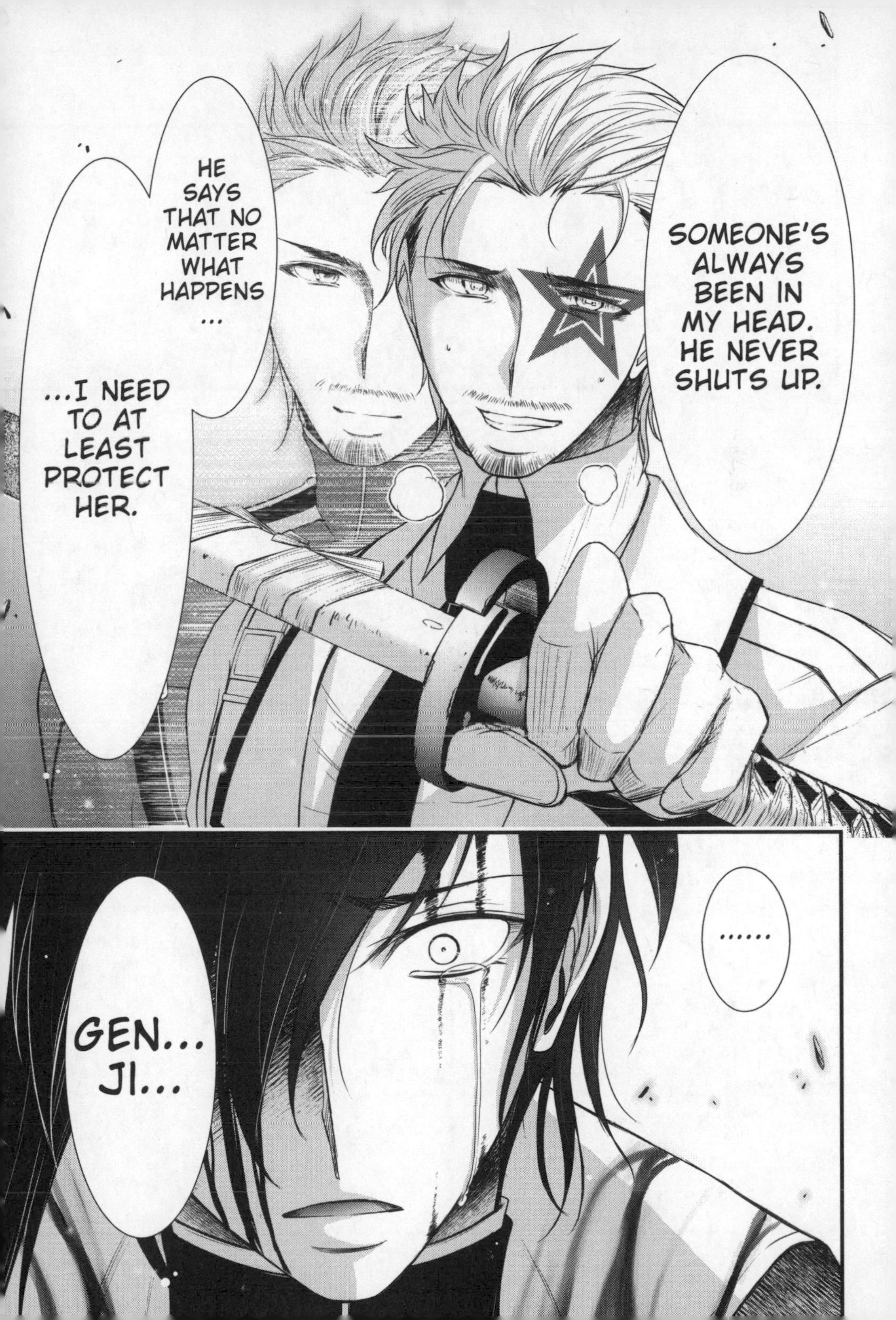
SOMEONE'S ALWAYS BEEN IN MY HEAD. HE NEVER SHUTS UP.
HE SAYS THAT NO MATTER WHAT HAPPENS...
...I NEED TO AT LEAST PROTECT HER.
......
GEN... JI...

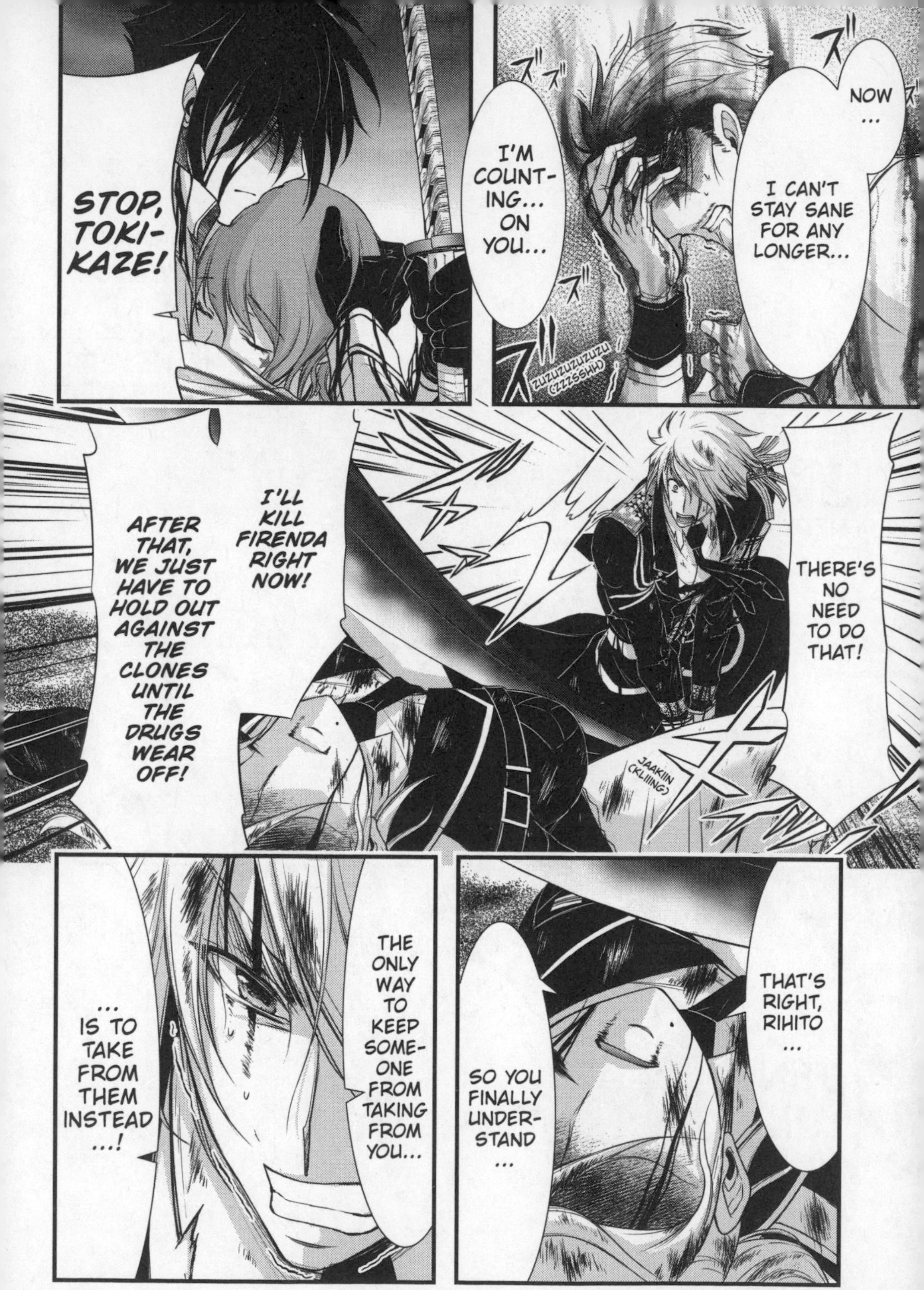
NOW ...
I CAN'T STAY SANE FOR ANY LONGER...
I'M COUNTING... ON YOU...
ZUZUZUZUZUZU (ZZZZSSHH)
STOP, TOKI-KAZE!
THERE'S NO NEED TO DO THAT!
JAAKIIN (KLIIING)
I'LL KILL FIRENDA RIGHT NOW!
AFTER THAT, WE JUST HAVE TO HOLD OUT AGAINST THE CLONES UNTIL THE DRUGS WEAR OFF!
THAT'S RIGHT, RIHITO ...
SO YOU FINALLY UNDERSTAND ...
THE ONLY WAY TO KEEP SOMEONE FROM TAKING FROM YOU...
... IS TO TAKE FROM THEM INSTEAD ...!

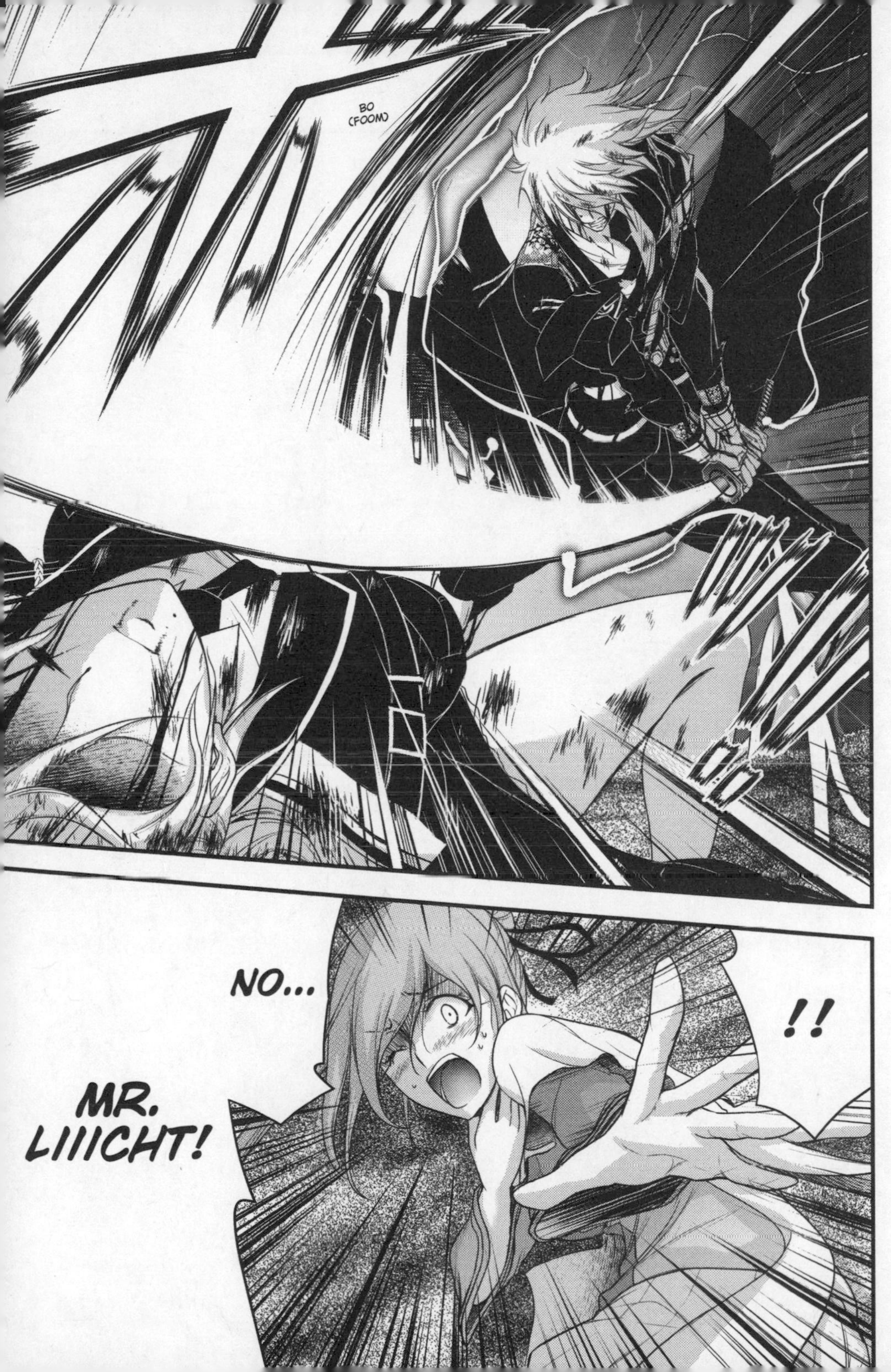
BO
(FOOM)
!!
NO...
MR. LIIICHT!

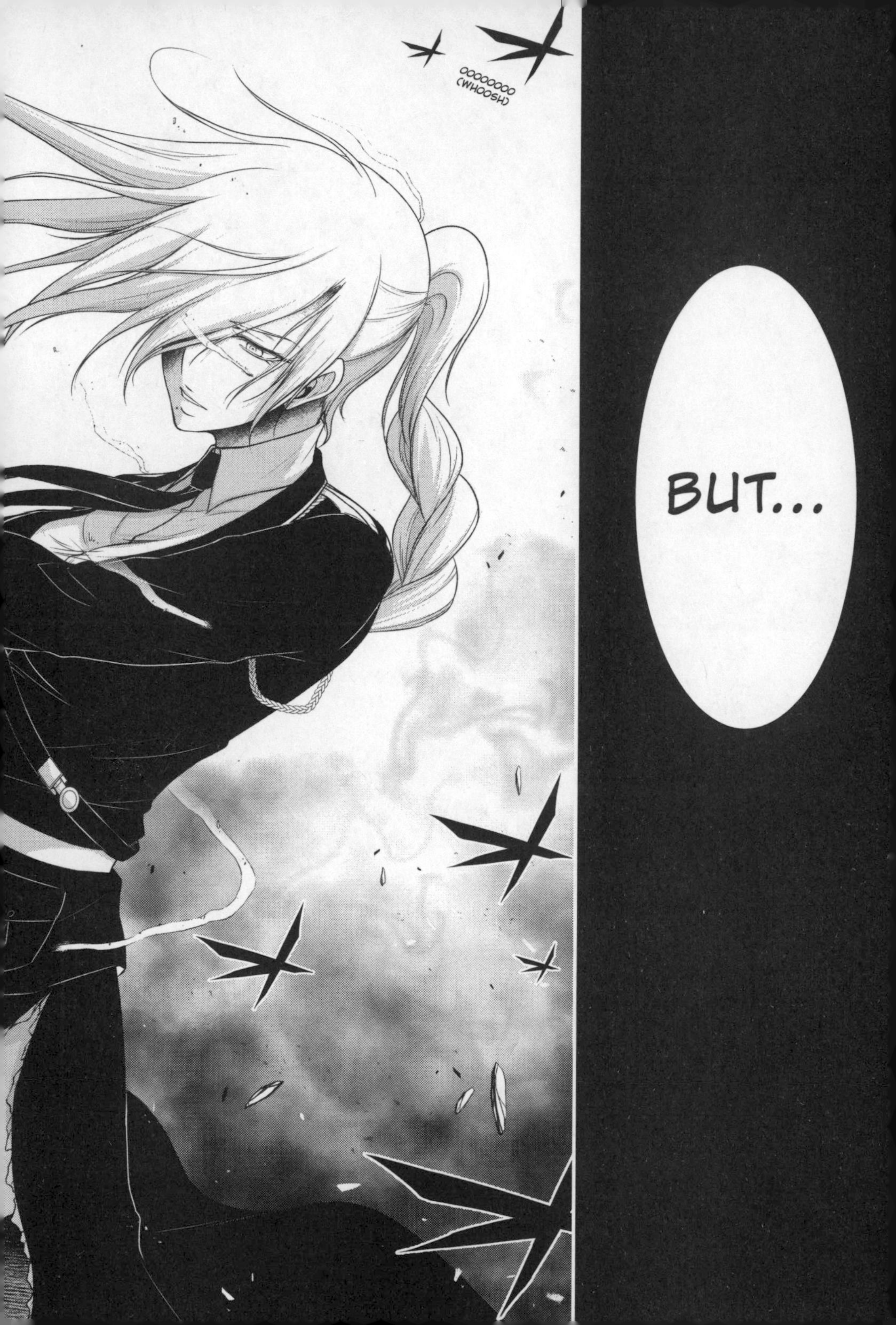
BUT...
OOOOOOOO
(WHOOSH)

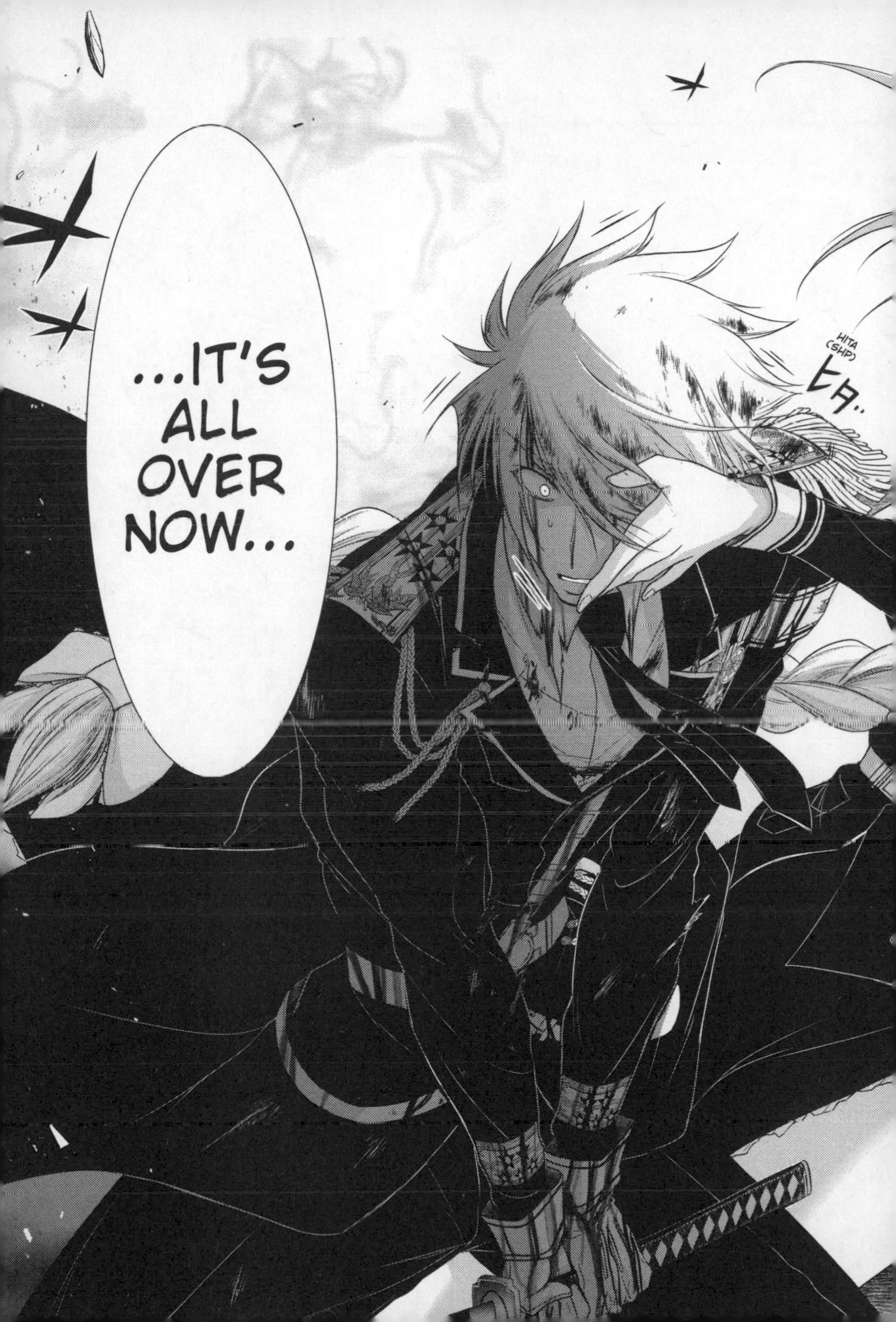
...IT'S ALL OVER NOW...
HITA (SHP)
ヒタ..

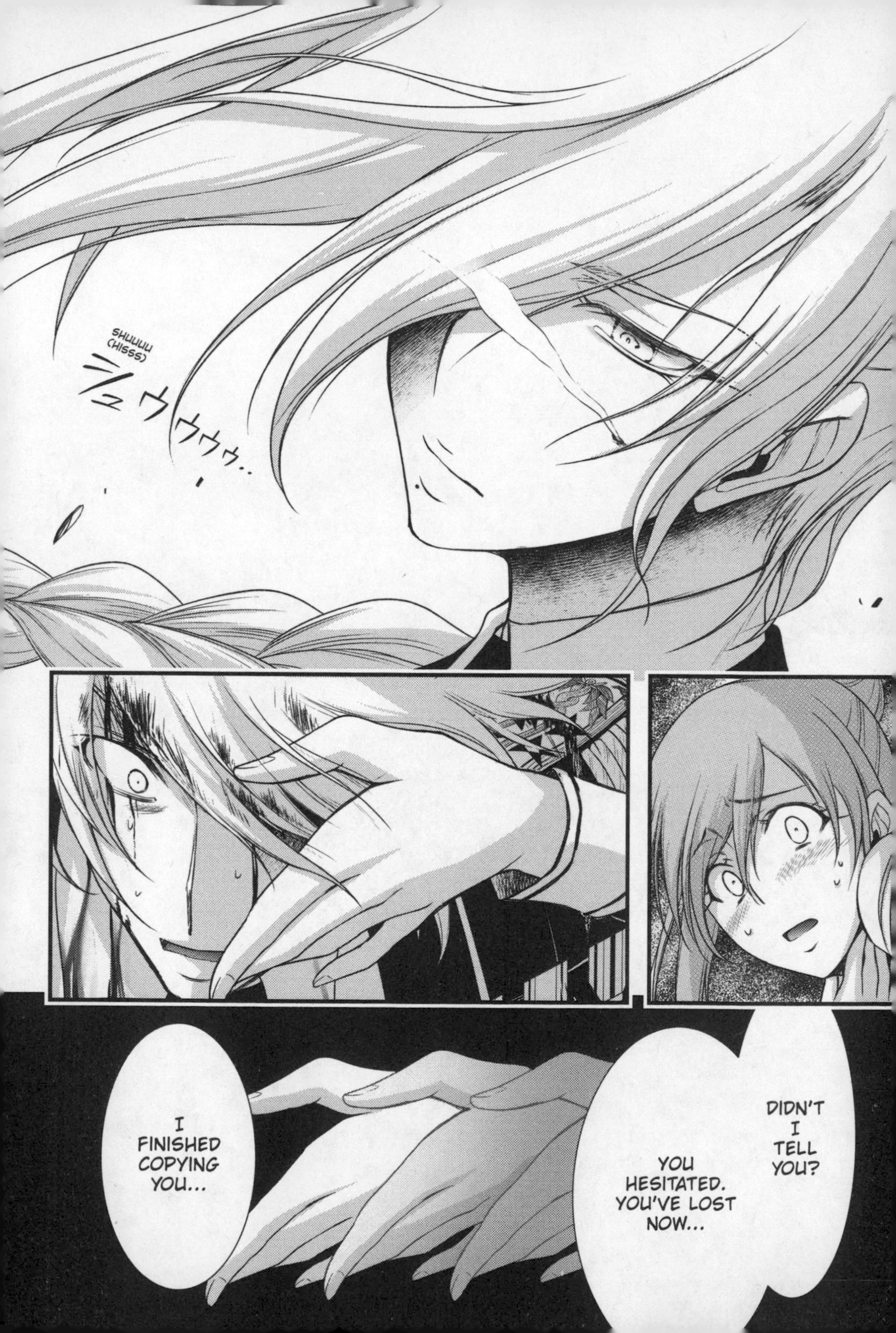
SHUUUU (HISSS)
シュウウウウ..
DIDN'T I TELL YOU?
YOU HESITATED. YOU'VE LOST NOW...
I FINISHED COPYING YOU...

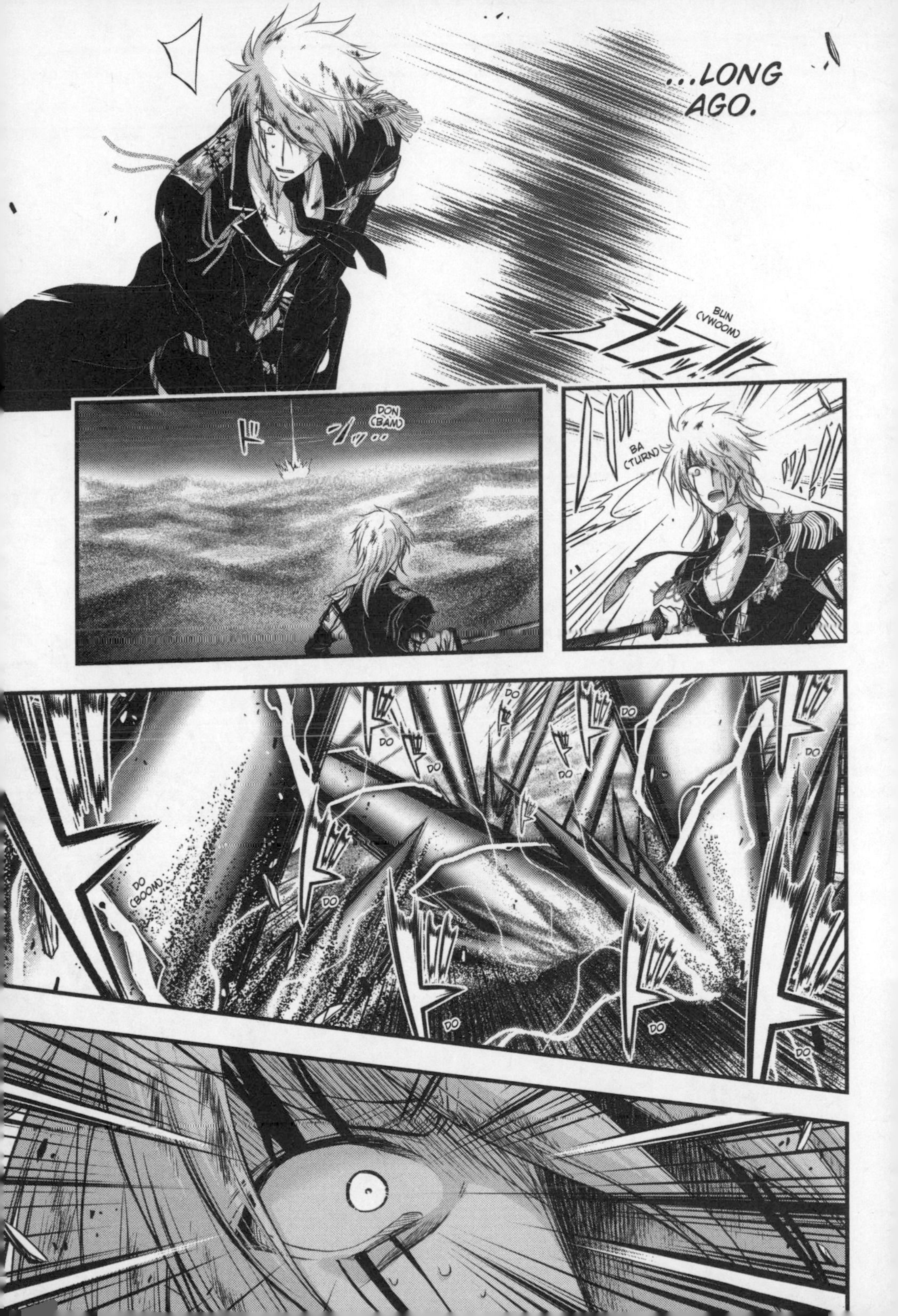
...LONG AGO.
BUN (VWOOM)
BA (TURN)
DON (BAM)
DO
DO
DO
DO
DO
DO (BOOM)
DO
DO
DO
DO

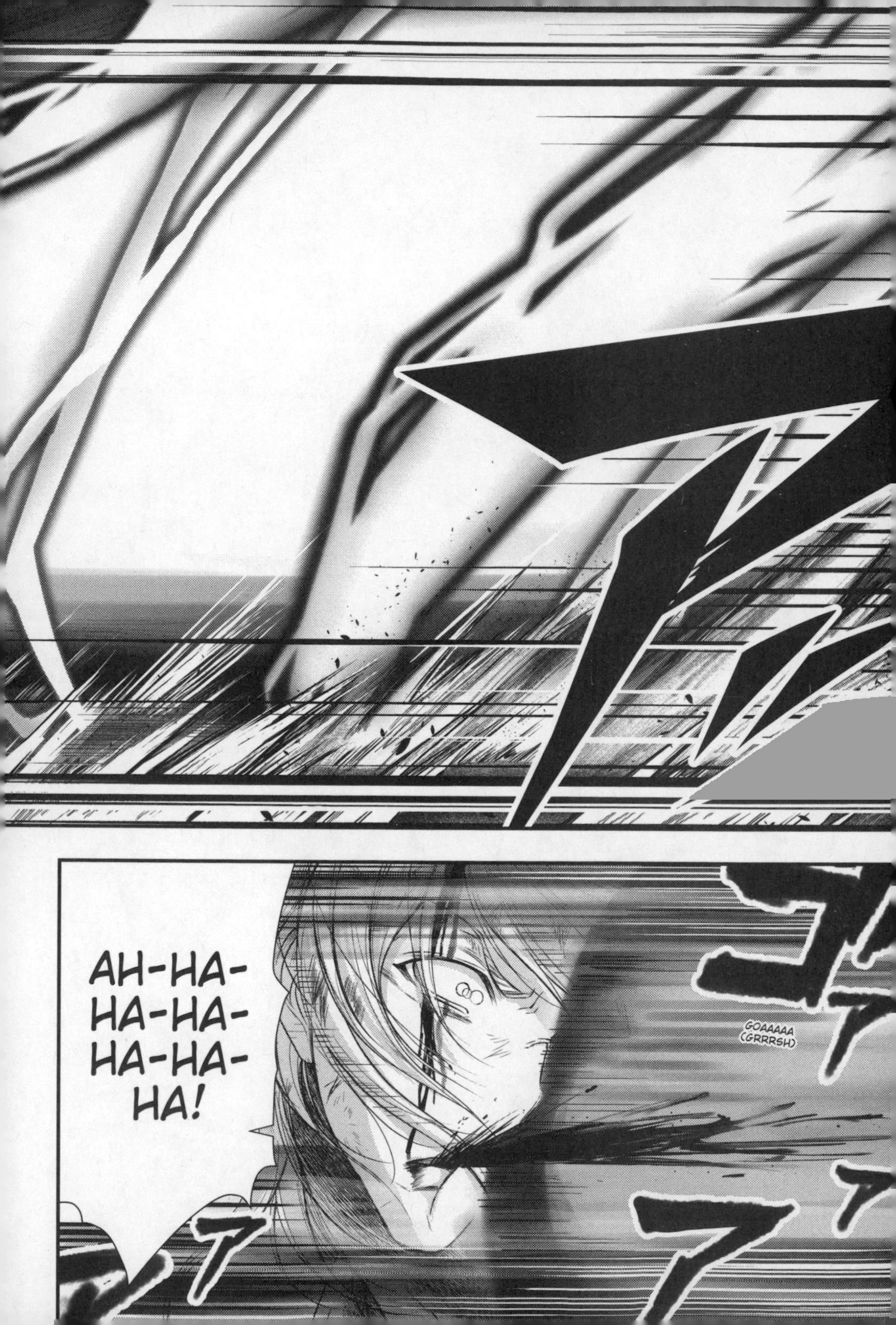
GOAAAAA (GRRRSH)
AH-HA-HA-HA-HA-HA-HA-HA-HA!

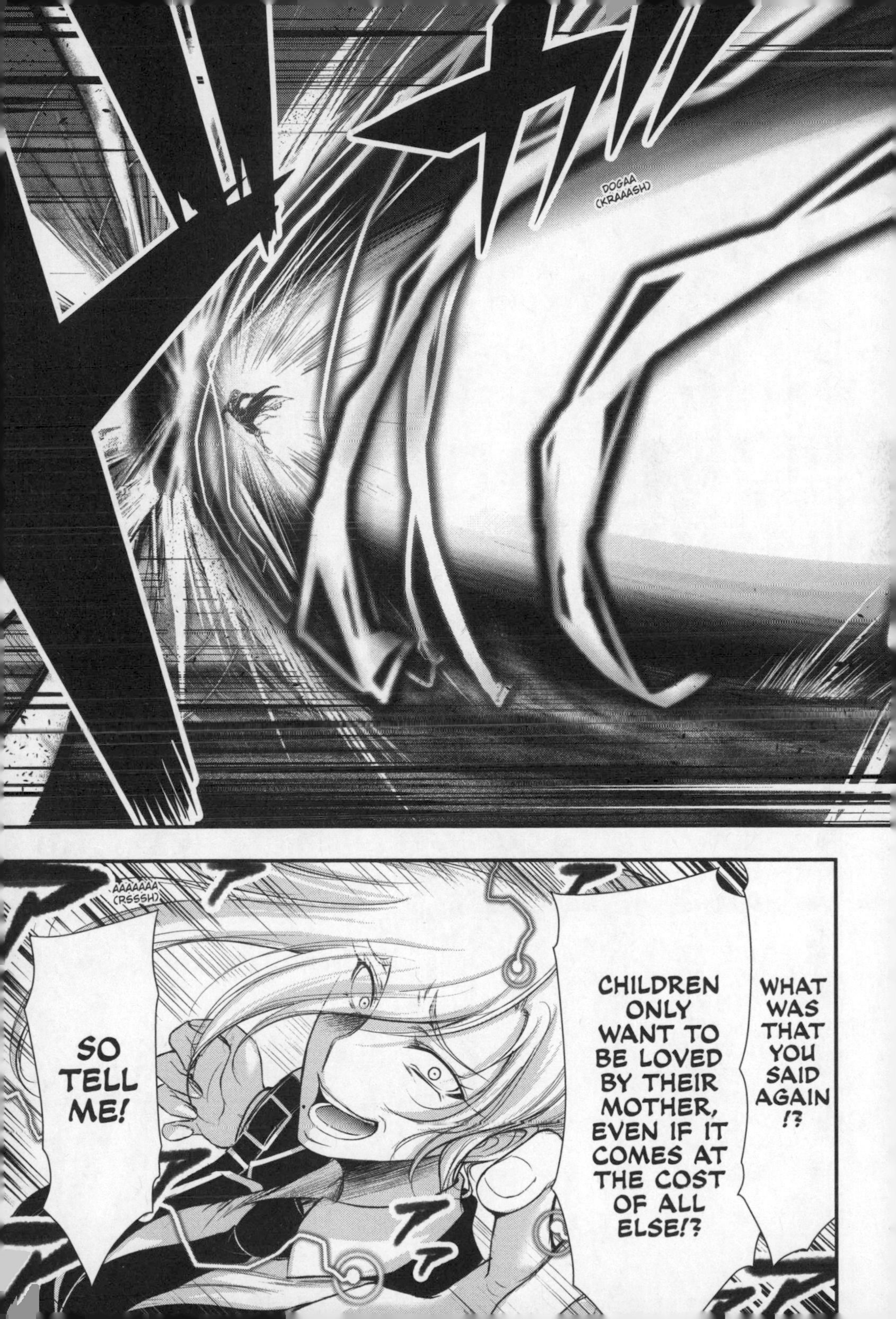
DOGAA (KRAAASH)
WHAT WAS THAT YOU SAID AGAIN!?
CHILDREN ONLY WANT TO BE LOVED BY THEIR MOTHER, EVEN IF IT COMES AT THE COST OF ALL ELSE!?
AAAAAAA (RSSSH)
SO TELL ME!

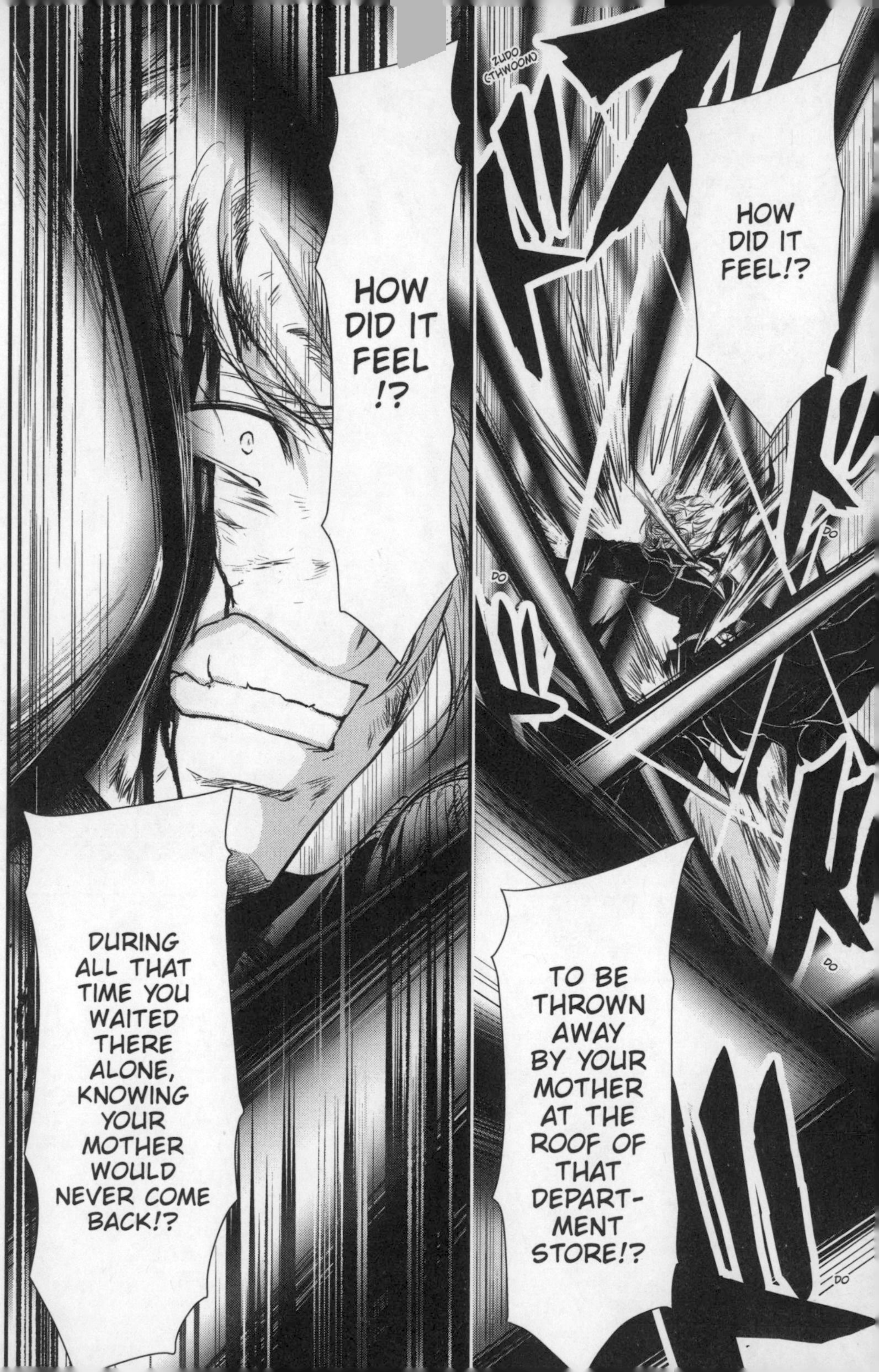
ZUDO (THWOOM)
HOW DID IT FEEL!?
DO
DO
DO
DO
TO BE THROWN AWAY BY YOUR MOTHER AT THE ROOF OF THAT DEPART-MENT STORE!?
HOW DID IT FEEL!?
DURING ALL THAT TIME YOU WAITED THERE ALONE, KNOWING YOUR MOTHER WOULD NEVER COME BACK!?

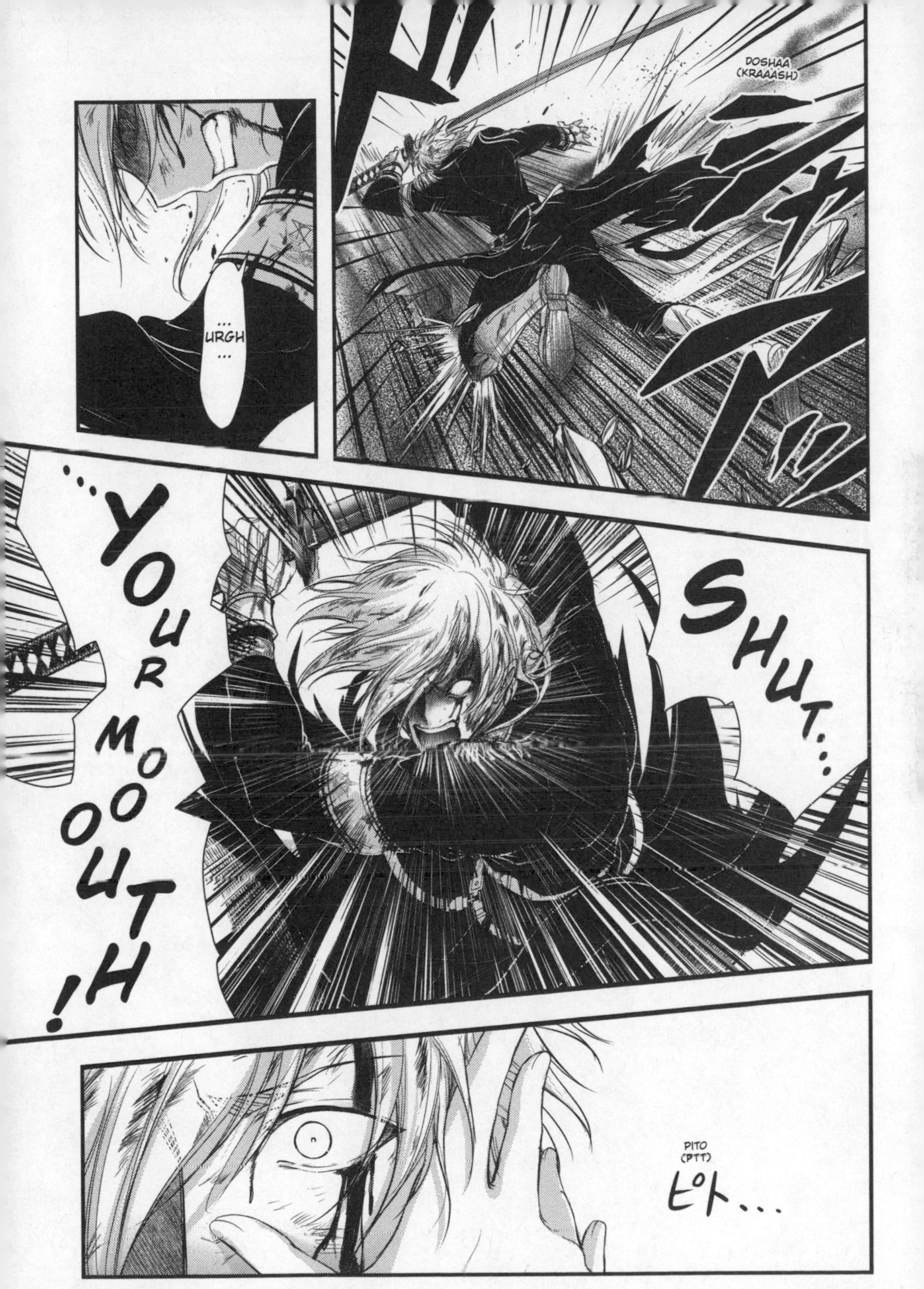
DOSHAA
(KRAAASH)
...URGH...
SHUT...
...YOUR MOOOOUTH!
PITO
(PTT)
ピト...

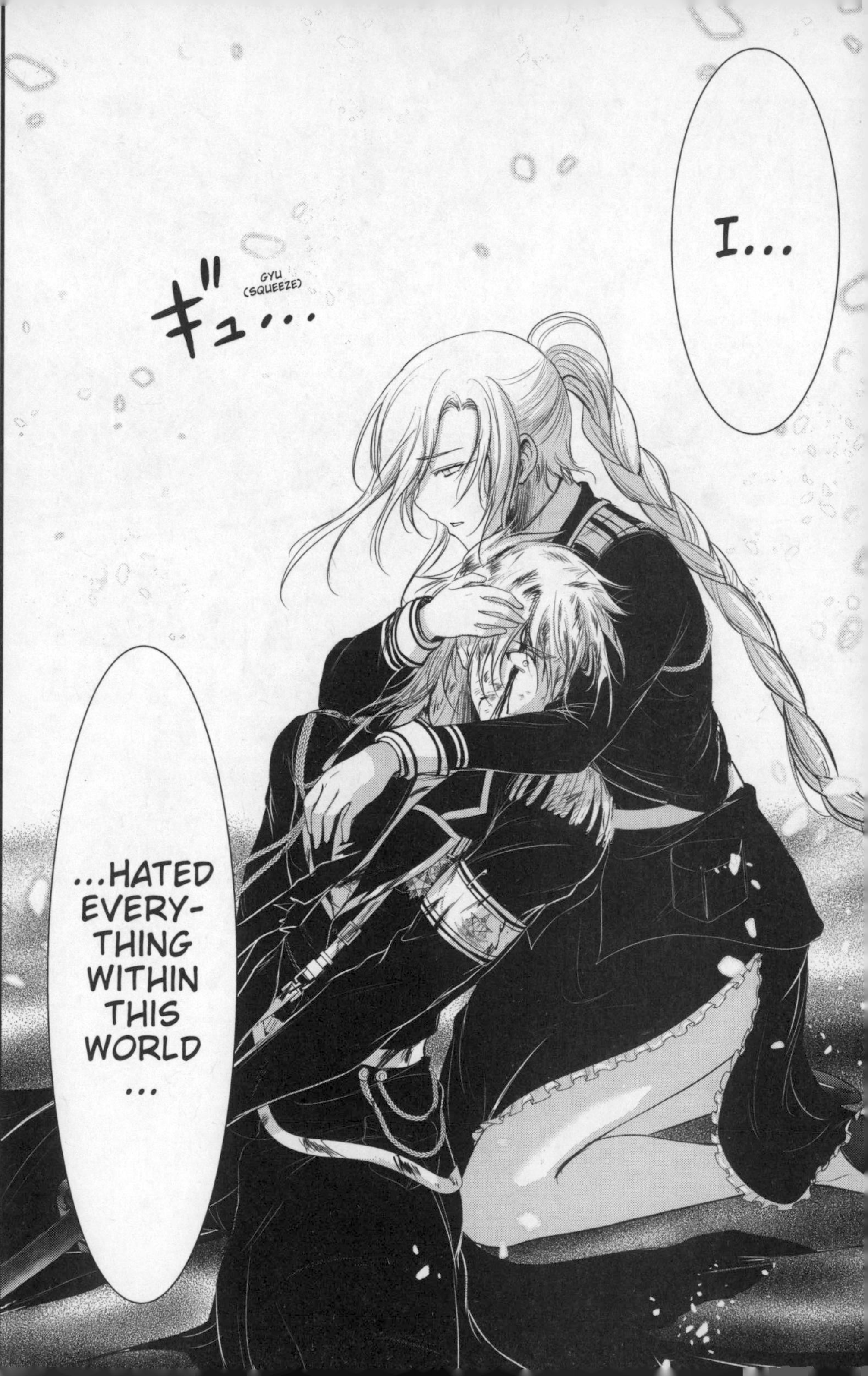
I...
ギュ...
GYU (SQUEEZE)
...HATED EVERY-THING WITHIN THIS WORLD ...

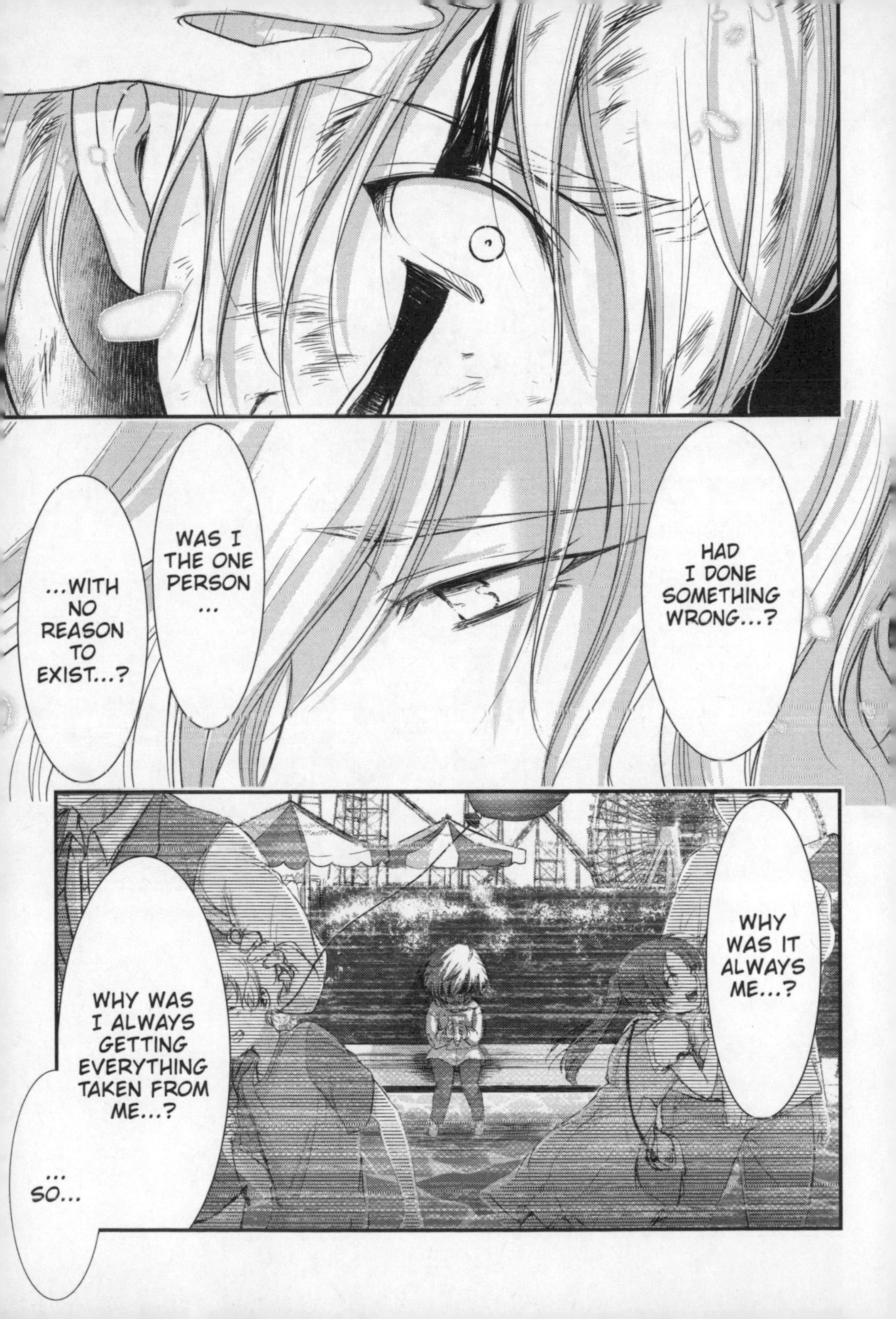
HAD I DONE SOMETHING WRONG...?
WAS I THE ONE PERSON ...
...WITH NO REASON TO EXIST...?
WHY WAS IT ALWAYS ME...?
WHY WAS I ALWAYS GETTING EVERYTHING TAKEN FROM ME...?
... SO...

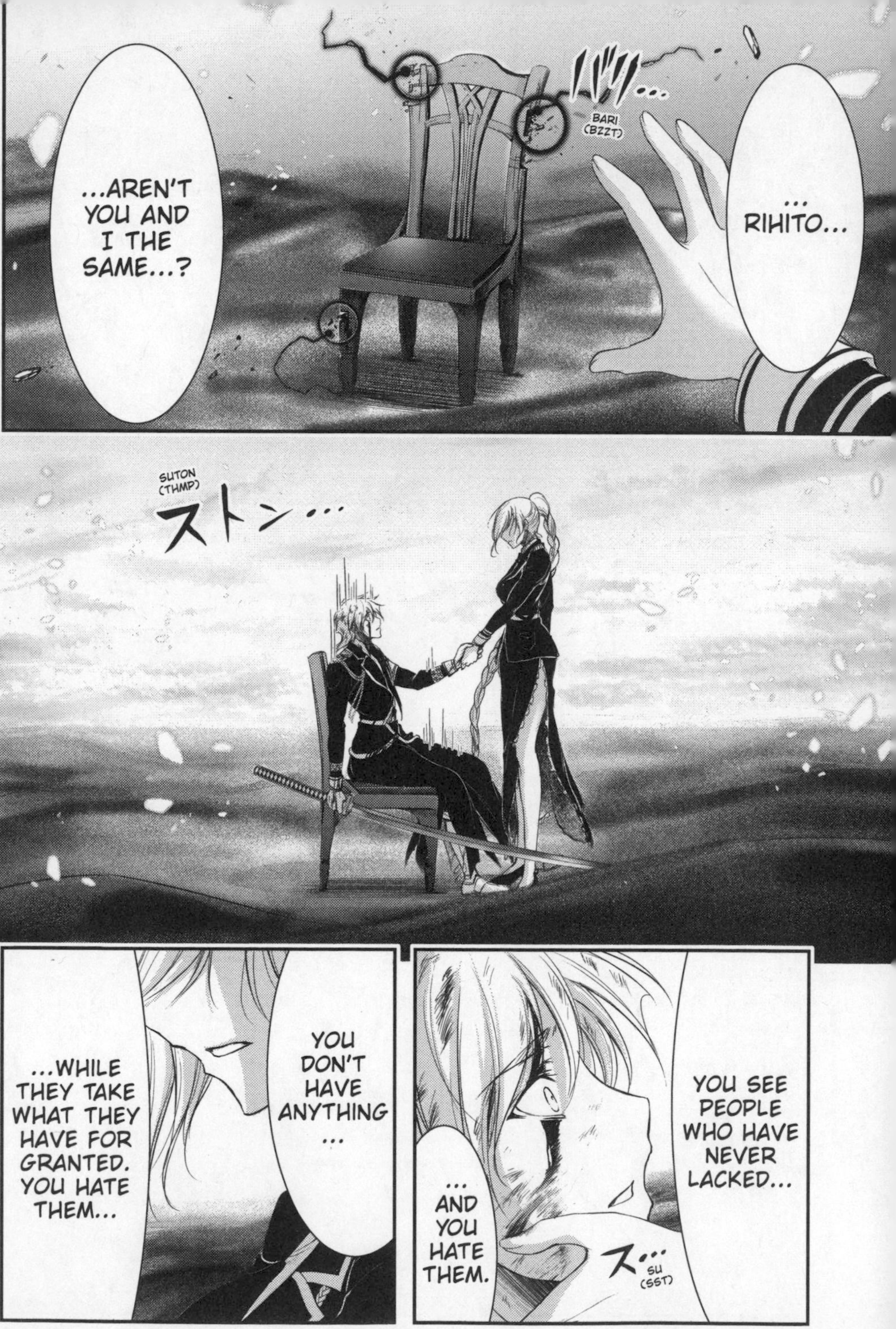
... RIHITO...
BARI (BZZT)
...AREN'T YOU AND I THE SAME...?
SUTON (THMP)
ストン...
YOU SEE PEOPLE WHO HAVE NEVER LACKED...
... AND YOU HATE THEM.
ス...
SU (SST)
YOU DON'T HAVE ANYTHING ...
...WHILE THEY TAKE WHAT THEY HAVE FOR GRANTED. YOU HATE THEM...

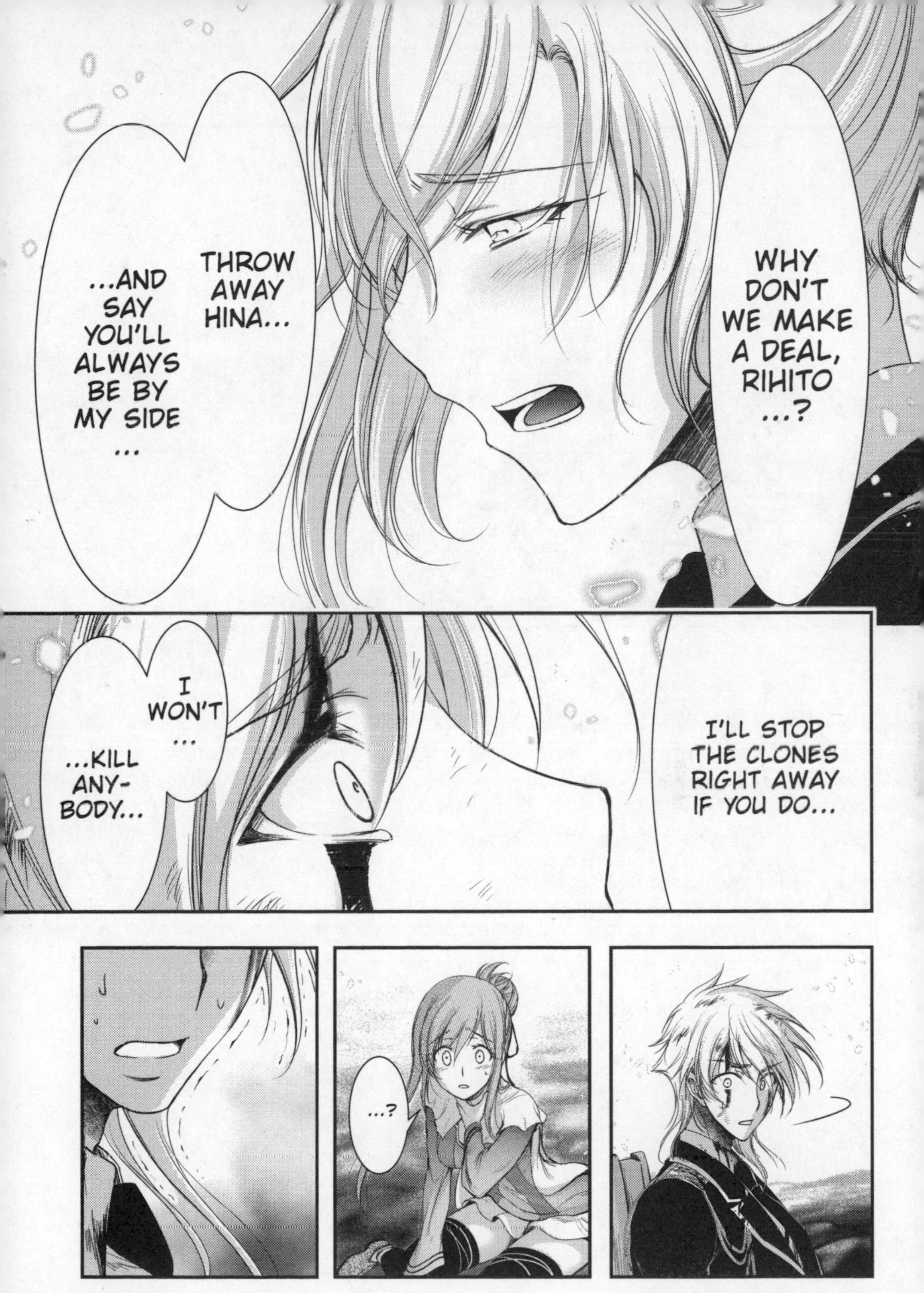
WHY DON'T WE MAKE A DEAL, RIHITO ...?
THROW AWAY HINA...
...AND SAY YOU'LL ALWAYS BE BY MY SIDE ...
I'LL STOP THE CLONES RIGHT AWAY IF YOU DO...
I WON'T ...
...KILL ANY-BODY...
...?

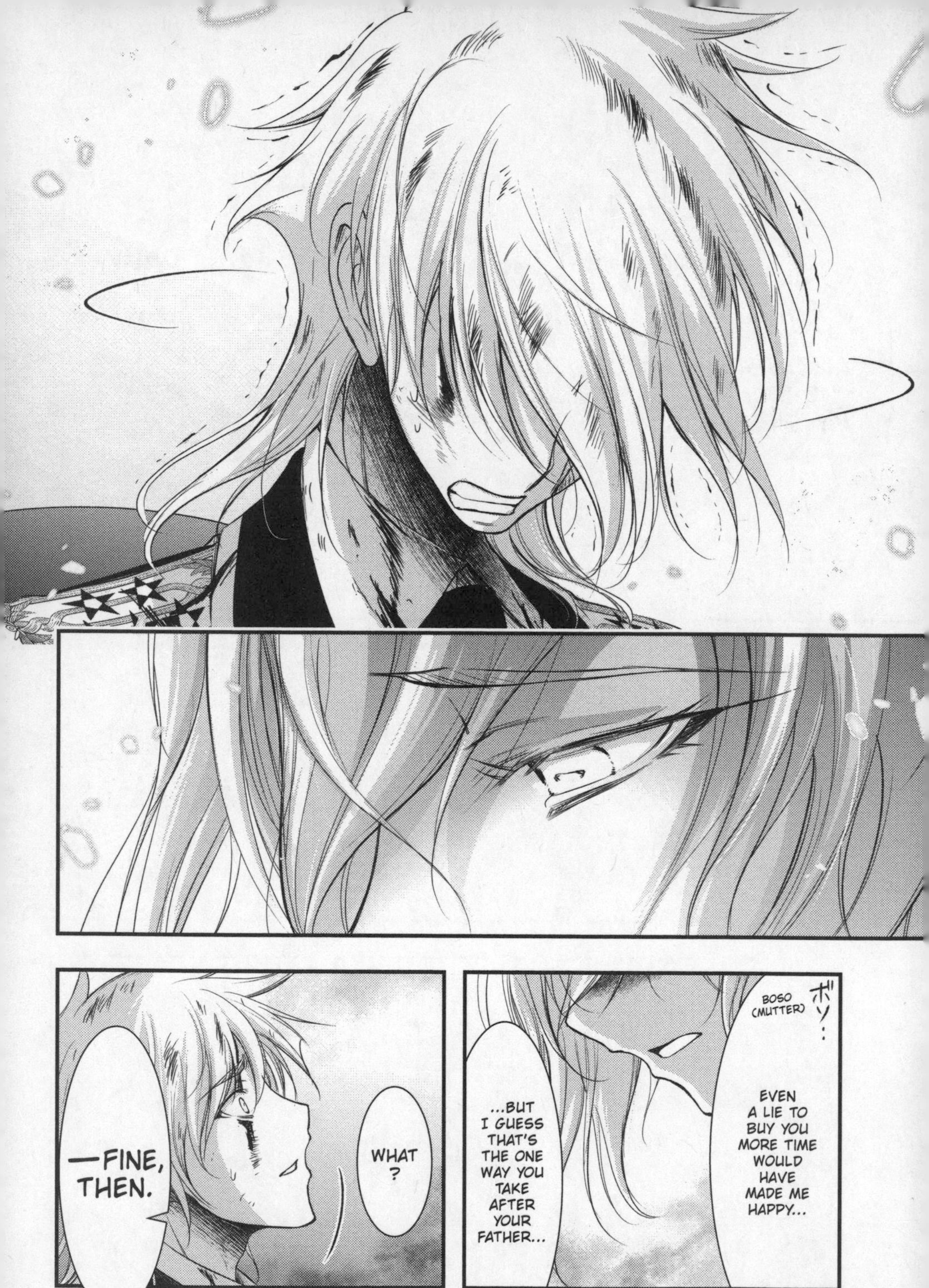
ボソ…
BOSO (MUTTER)
EVEN A LIE TO BUY YOU MORE TIME WOULD HAVE MADE ME HAPPY...
...BUT I GUESS THAT'S THE ONE WAY YOU TAKE AFTER YOUR FATHER...
WHAT?
—FINE, THEN.

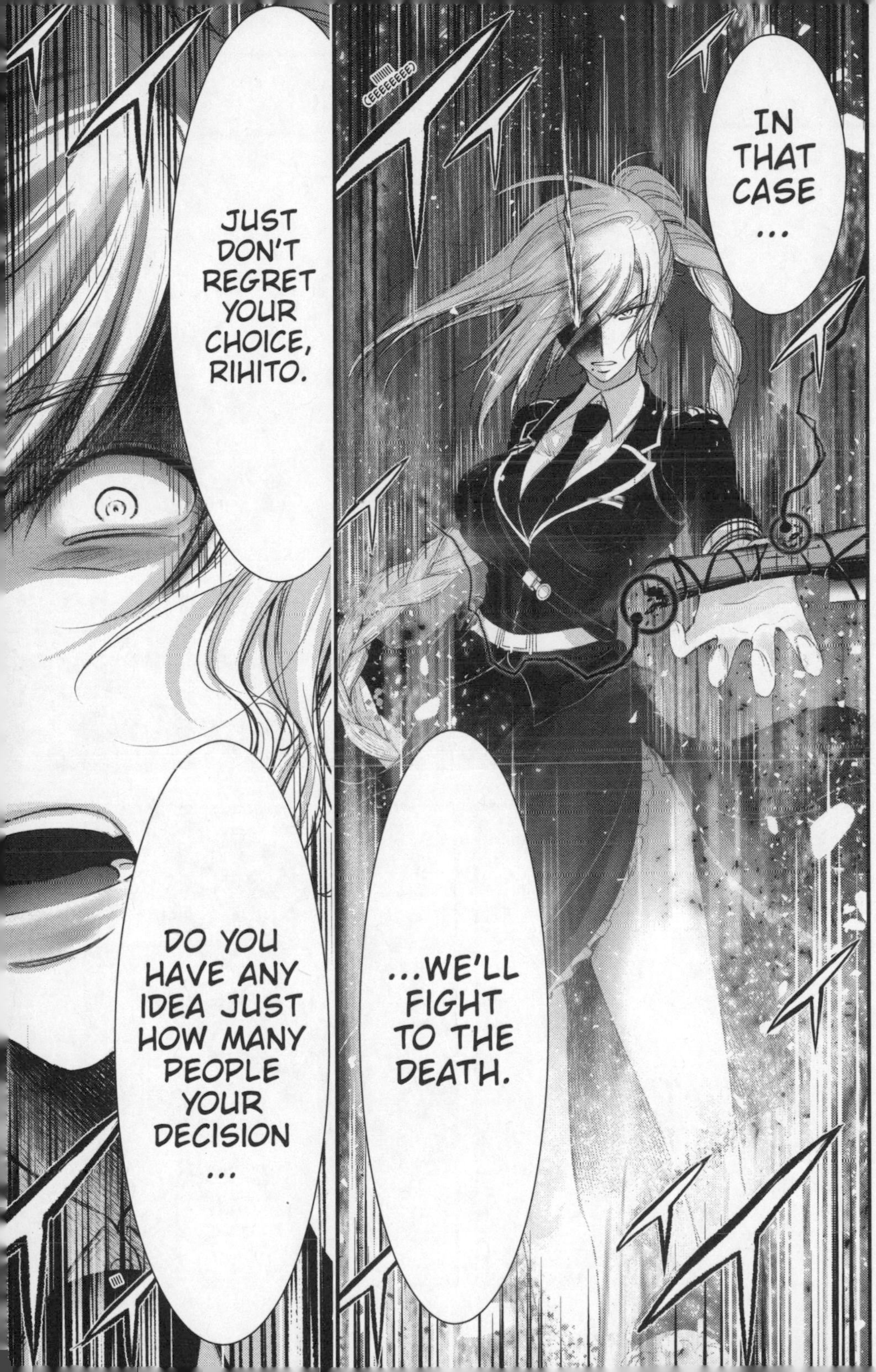
IN THAT CASE...
...WE'LL FIGHT TO THE DEATH.
JUST DON'T REGRET YOUR CHOICE, RIHITO.
DO YOU HAVE ANY IDEA JUST HOW MANY PEOPLE YOUR DECISION...

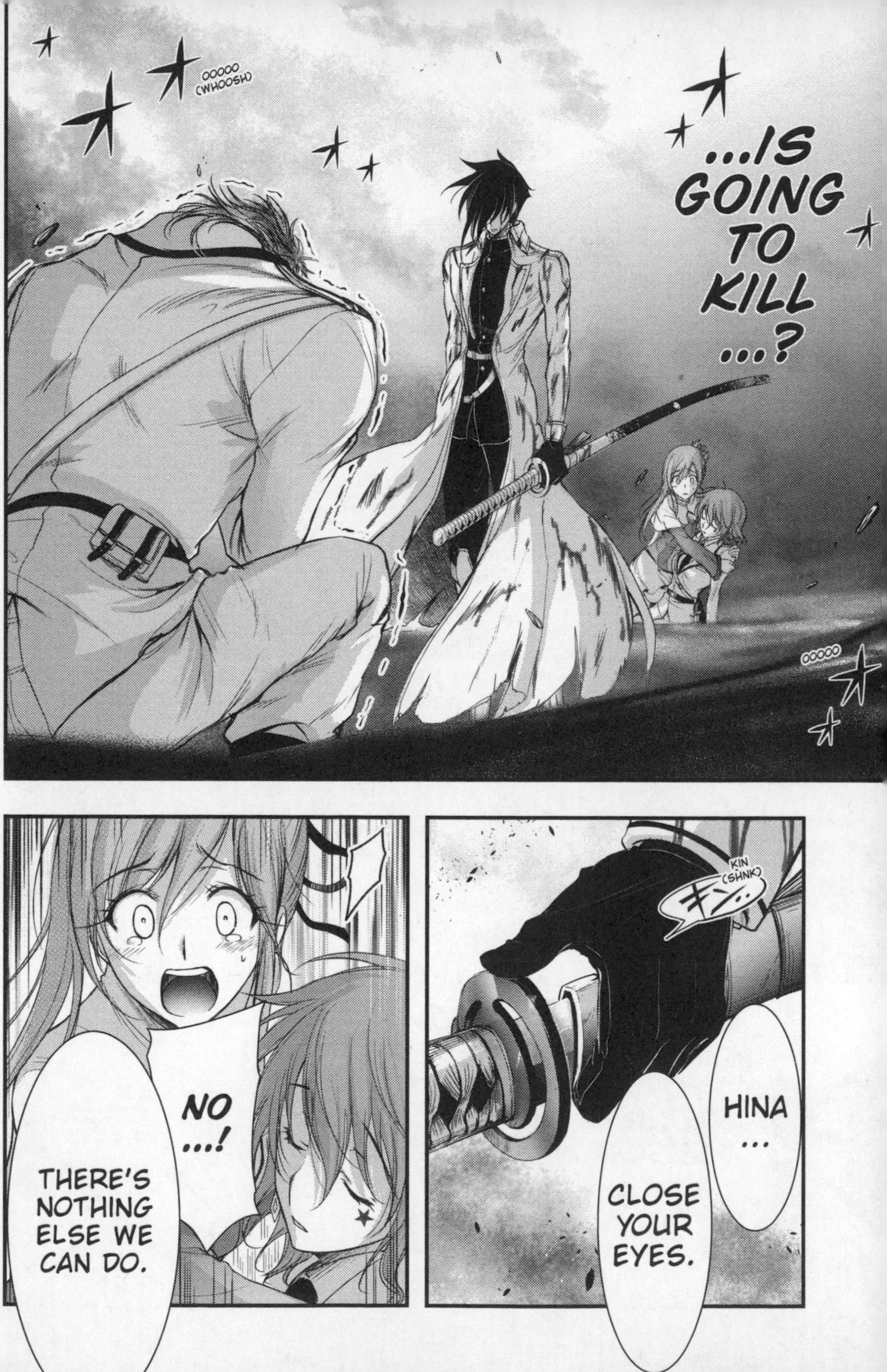
...IS GOING TO KILL ...?
OOOOO (WHOOSH)
OOOOO
KIN (SHNK)
HINA ...
CLOSE YOUR EYES.
NO ...!
THERE'S NOTHING ELSE WE CAN DO.

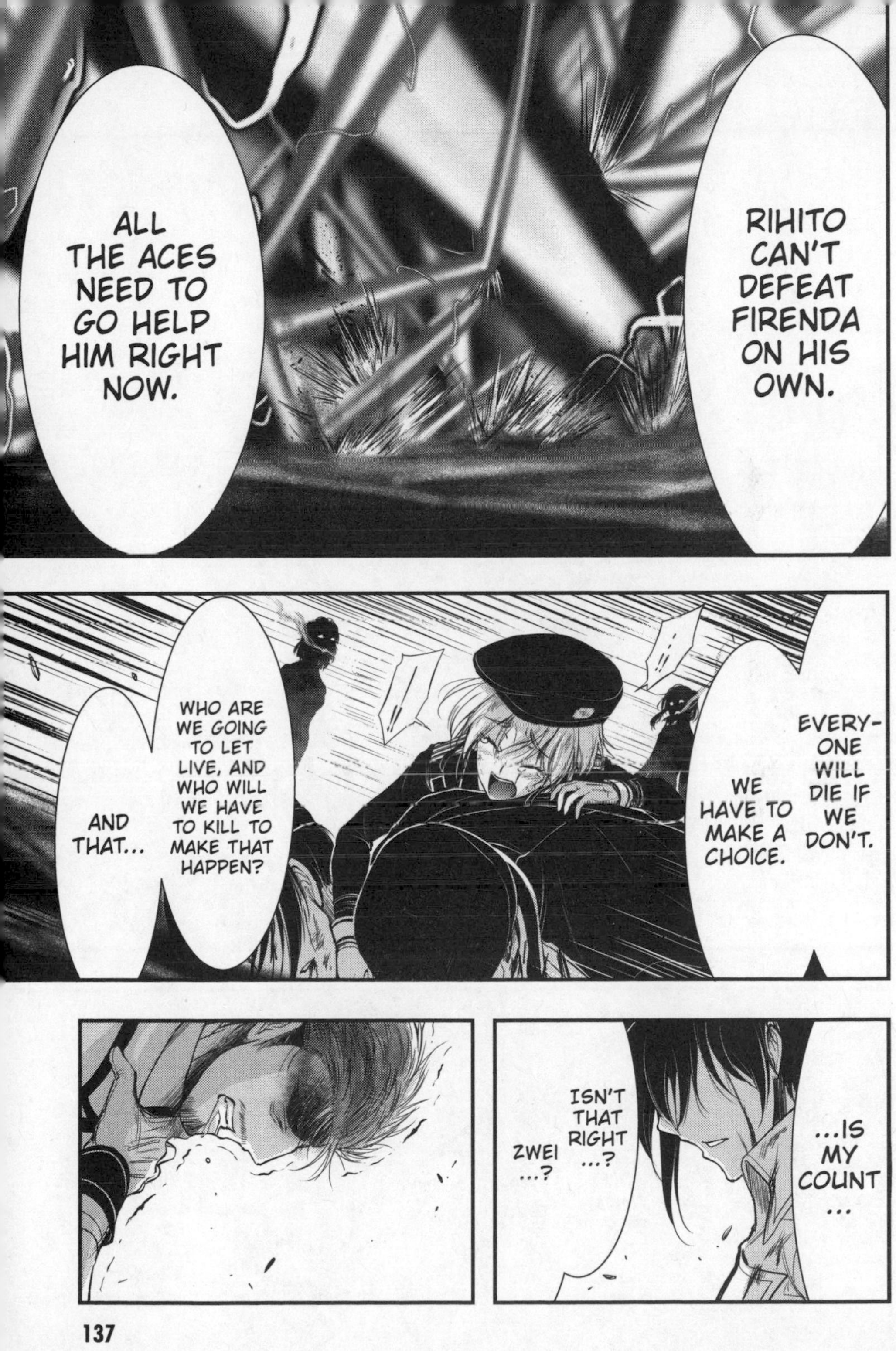
RIHITO CAN'T DEFEAT FIRENDA ON HIS OWN.
ALL THE ACES NEED TO GO HELP HIM RIGHT NOW.
EVERY-ONE WILL DIE IF WE DON'T.
WE HAVE TO MAKE A CHOICE.
!!
!!
WHO ARE WE GOING TO LET LIVE, AND WHO WILL WE HAVE TO KILL TO MAKE THAT HAPPEN?
AND THAT...
...IS MY COUNT...
ISN'T THAT RIGHT...?
ZWEI...?

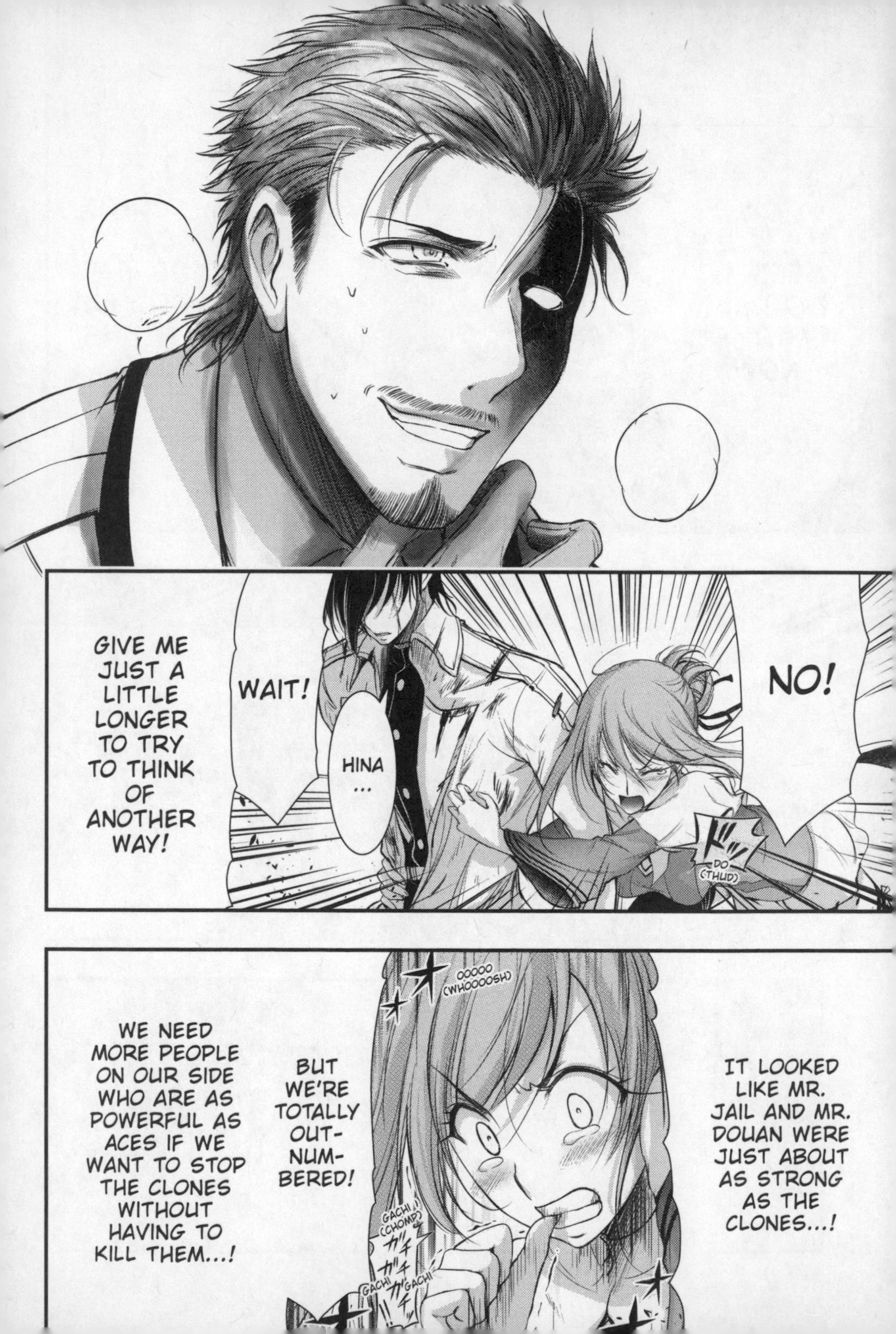
NO!
DO (THUD)
HINA...
WAIT!
GIVE ME JUST A LITTLE LONGER TO TRY TO THINK OF ANOTHER WAY!
IT LOOKED LIKE MR. JAIL AND MR. DOUAN WERE JUST ABOUT AS STRONG AS THE CLONES...!
OOOOO (WHOOOOSH)
BUT WE'RE TOTALLY OUT-NUM-BERED!
WE NEED MORE PEOPLE ON OUR SIDE WHO ARE AS POWERFUL AS ACES IF WE WANT TO STOP THE CLONES WITHOUT HAVING TO KILL THEM...!
GACHI (CHOMP)
GACHI GACHI

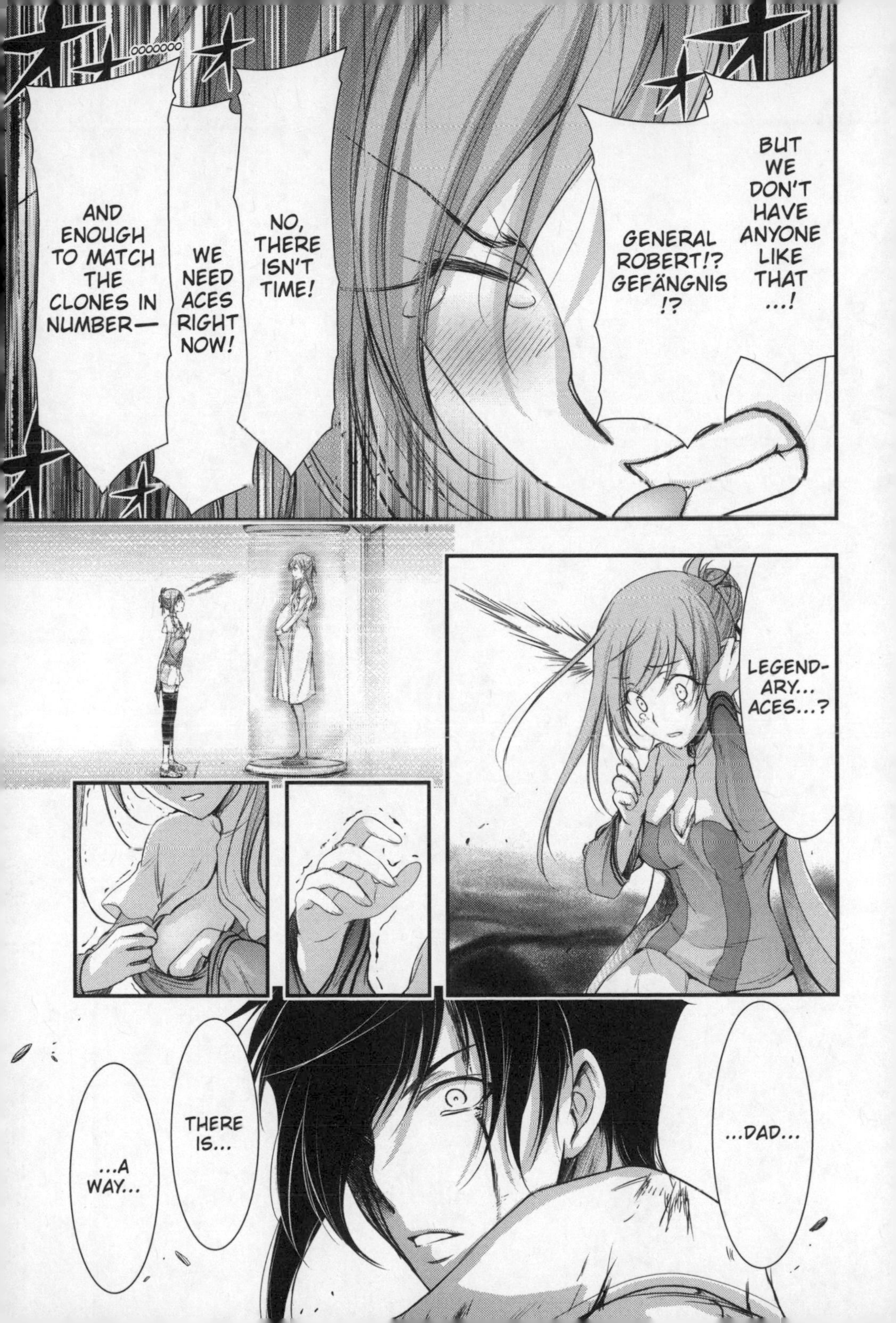
BUT WE DON'T HAVE ANYONE LIKE THAT ...!
GENERAL ROBERT!? GEFÄNGNIS !?
NO, THERE ISN'T TIME!
WE NEED ACES RIGHT NOW!
AND ENOUGH TO MATCH THE CLONES IN NUMBER—
LEGENDARY... ACES...?
...DAD...
THERE IS...
...A WAY...

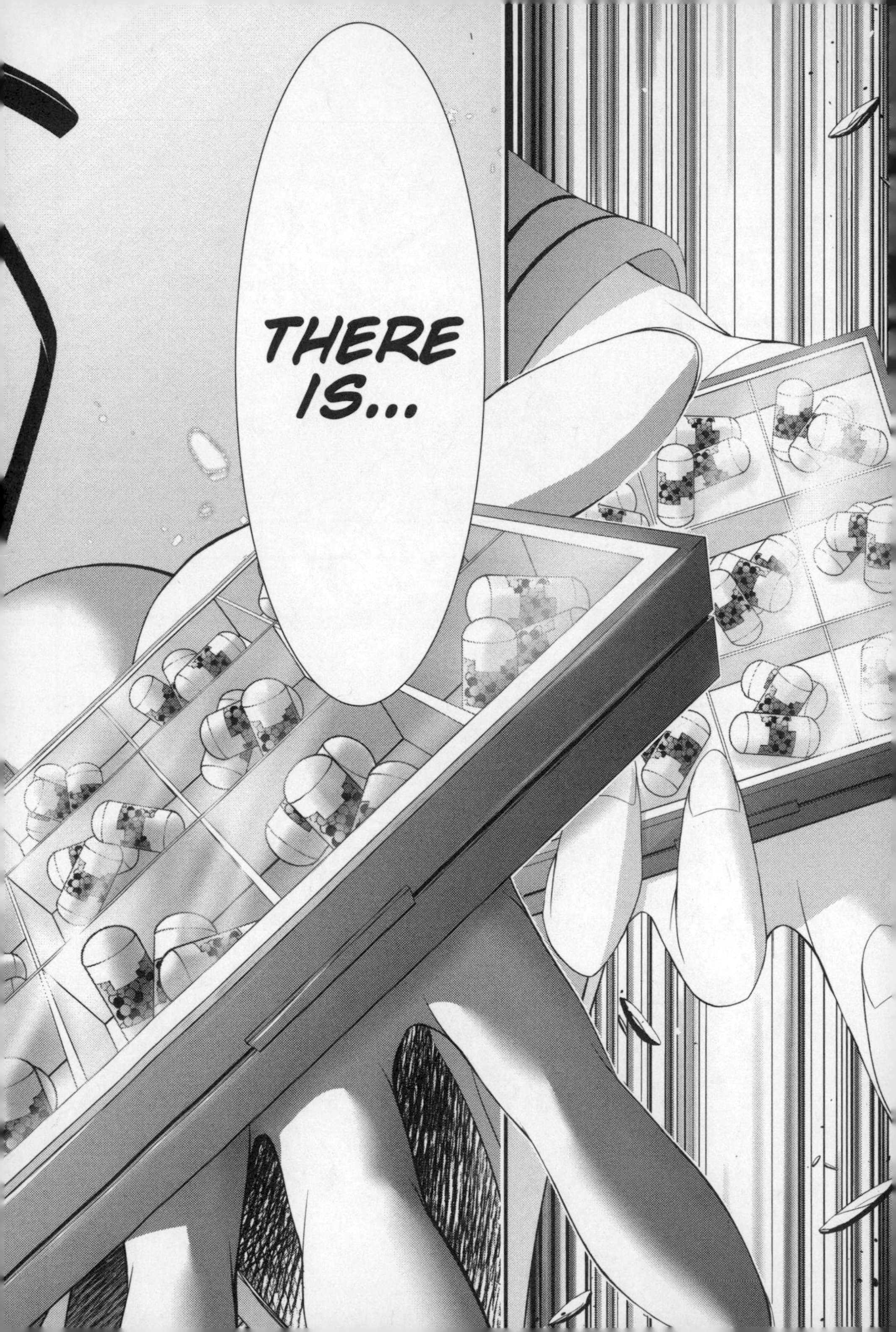
THERE IS...

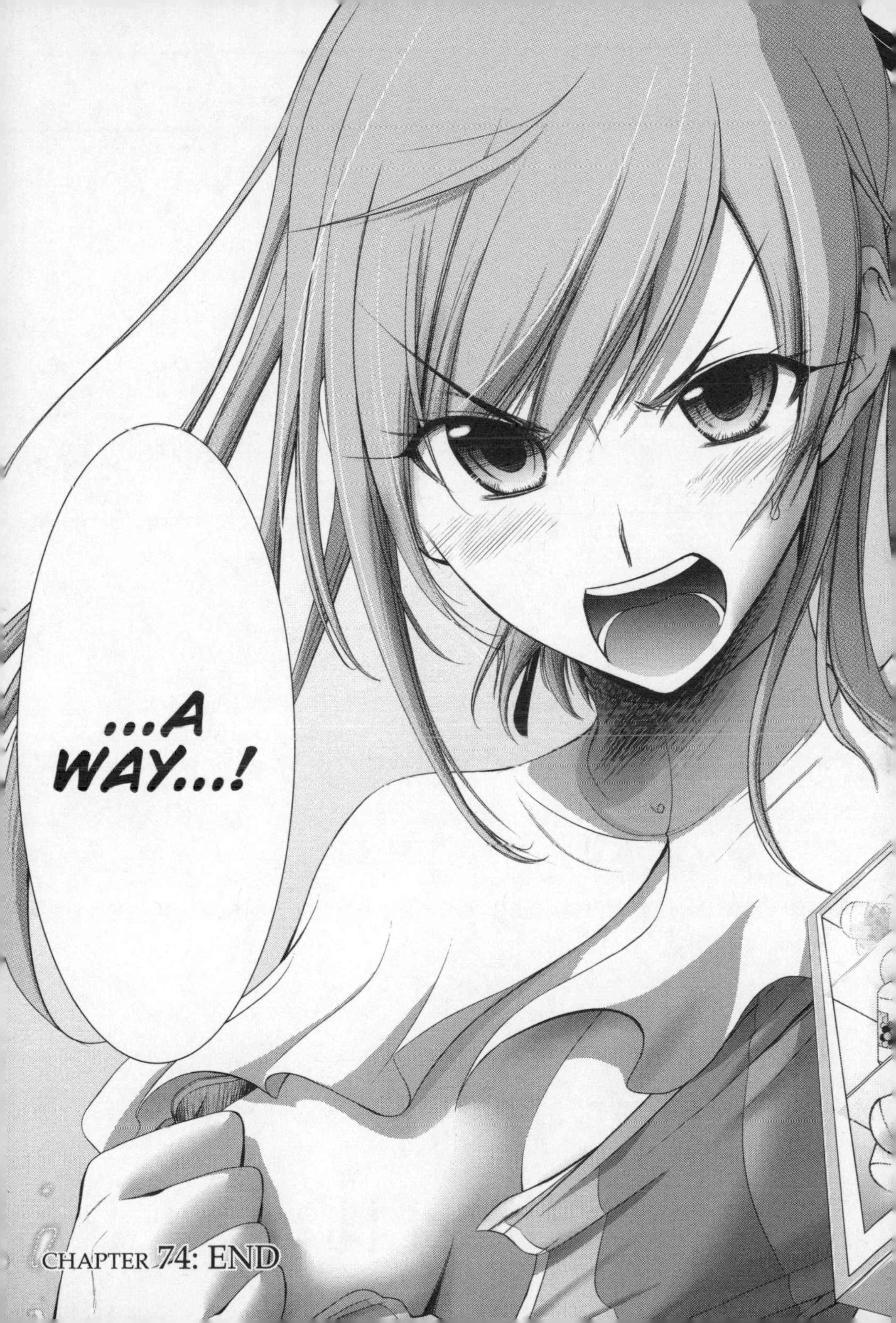
...A WAY...!
CHAPTER 74: END

PLUNDERER

CHAPTER 75

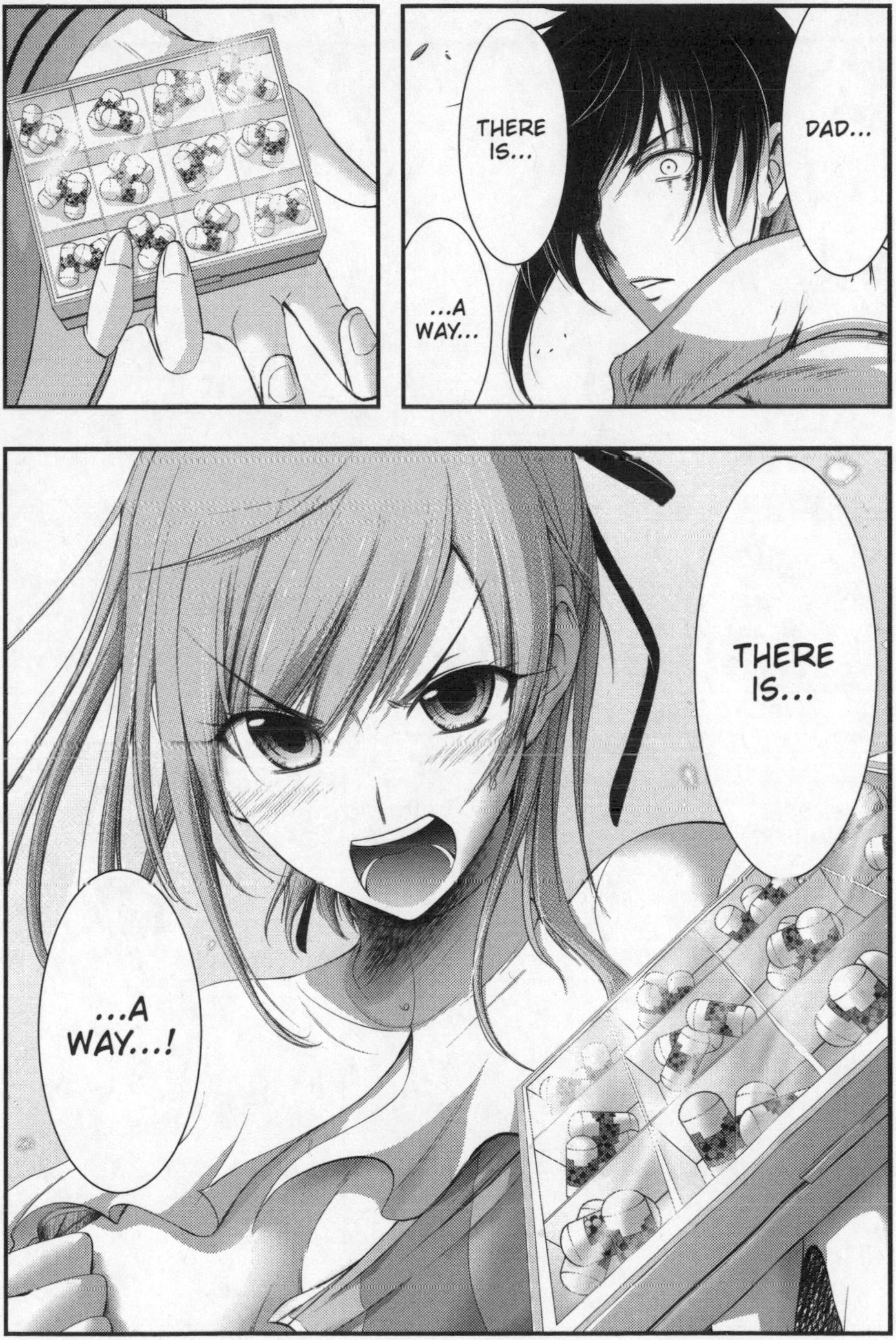
DAD...
THERE IS...
...A WAY...
THERE IS...
...A WAY...!

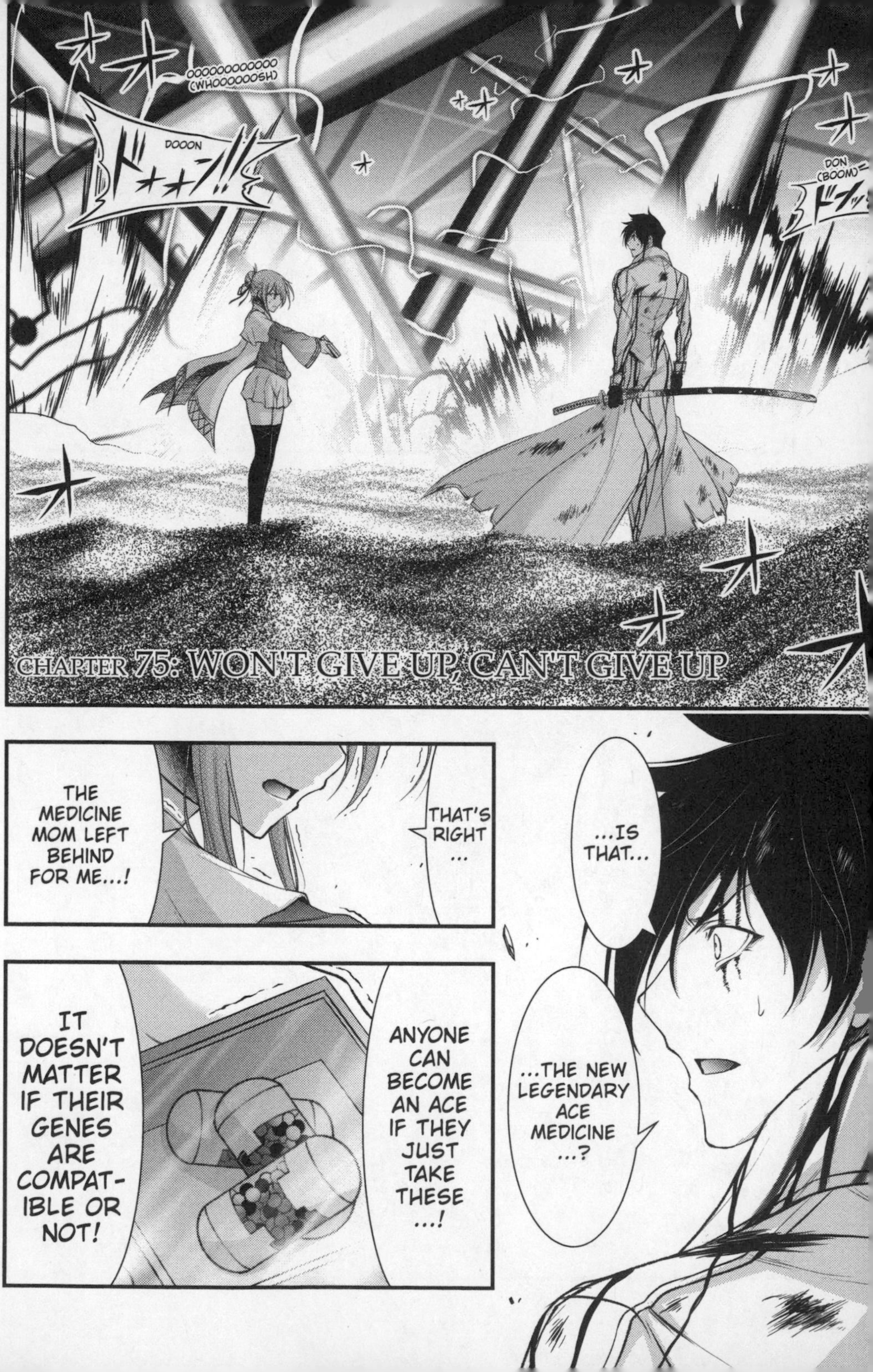

DON (BOOM)
ドッ
OOOOOOOOOOOO (WHOOOOOOSH)
DOOON
ドォォン!!
CHAPTER 75: WON'T GIVE UP, CAN'T GIVE UP
...IS THAT...
...THE NEW LEGENDARY ACE MEDICINE ...?
THAT'S RIGHT ...
THE MEDICINE MOM LEFT BEHIND FOR ME...!
ANYONE CAN BECOME AN ACE IF THEY JUST TAKE THESE ...!
IT DOESN'T MATTER IF THEIR GENES ARE COMPATIBLE OR NOT!

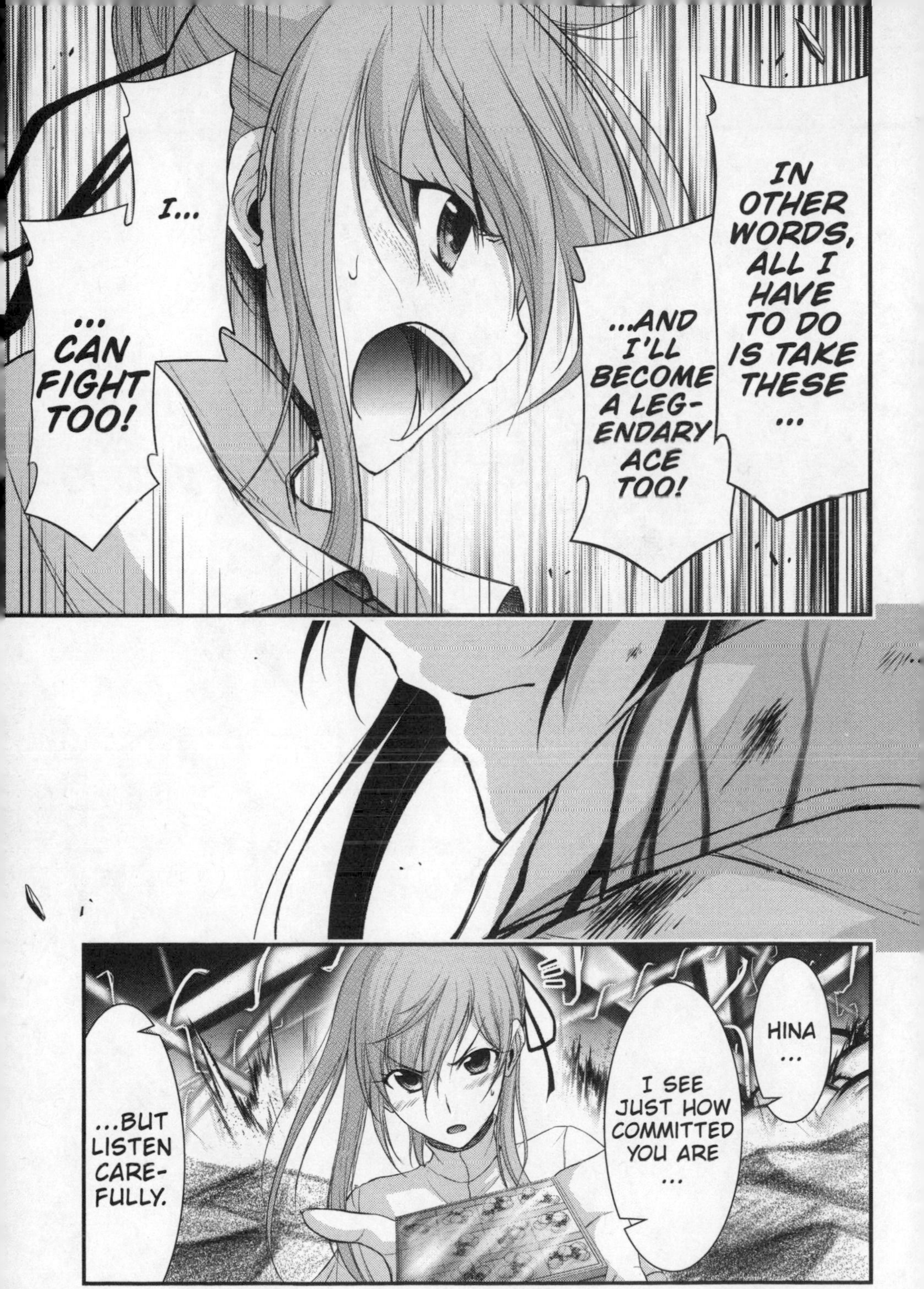
IN OTHER WORDS, ALL I HAVE TO DO IS TAKE THESE ...
...AND I'LL BECOME A LEG-ENDARY ACE TOO!
I...
...CAN FIGHT TOO!
HINA ...
I SEE JUST HOW COMMITTED YOU ARE ...
...BUT LISTEN CARE-FULLY.

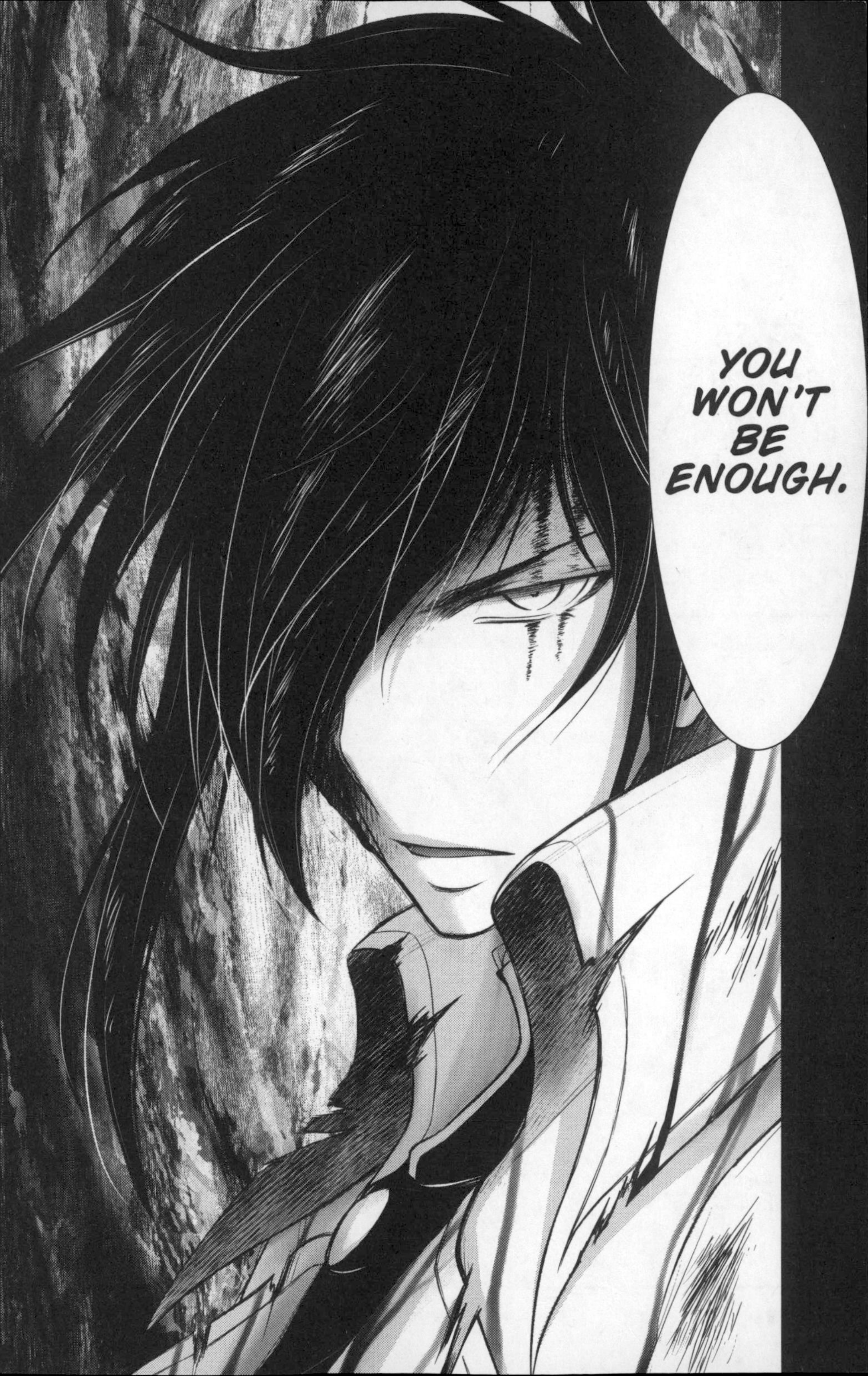
YOU WON'T BE ENOUGH.

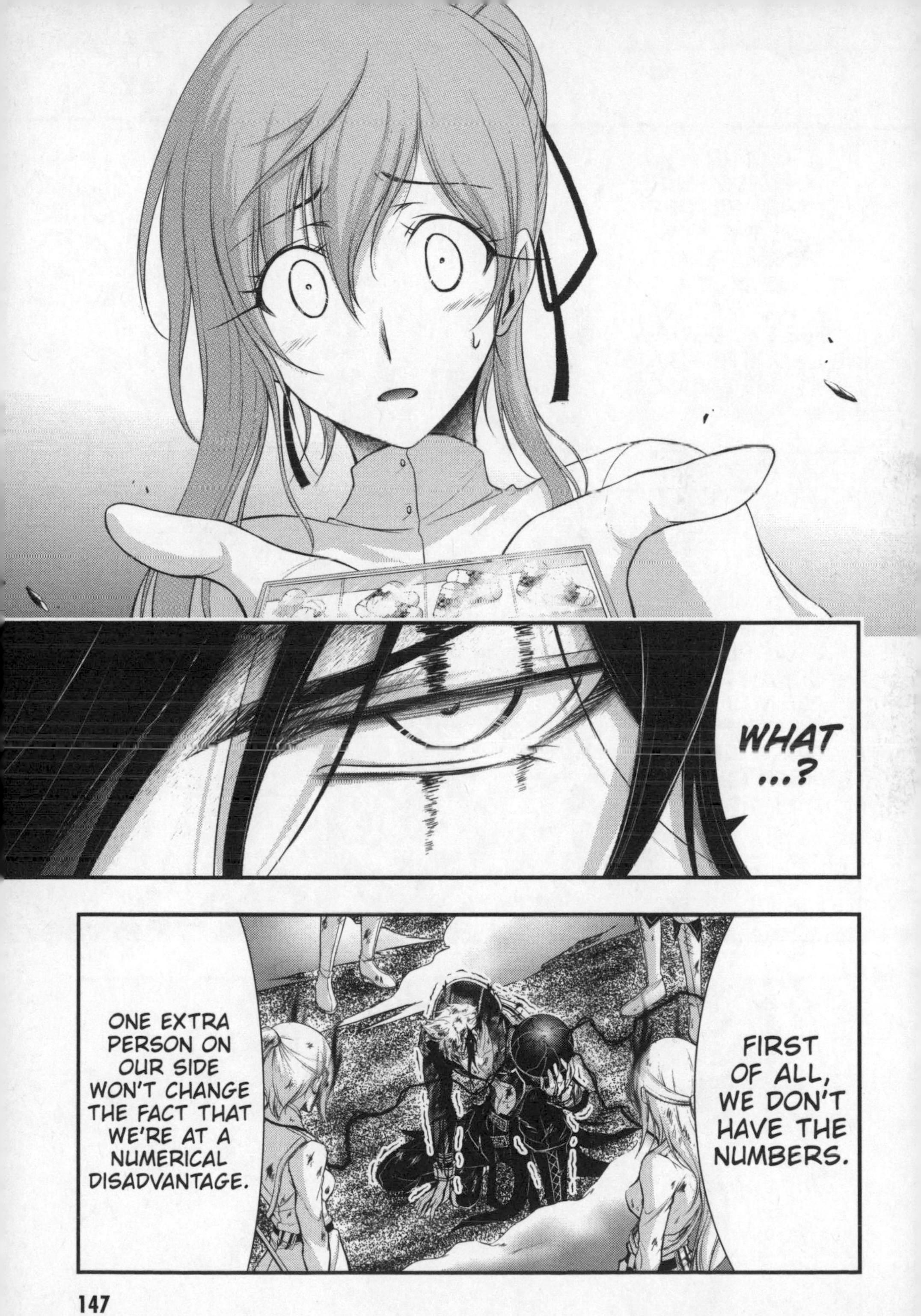
WHAT ...?
FIRST OF ALL, WE DON'T HAVE THE NUMBERS.
ONE EXTRA PERSON ON OUR SIDE WON'T CHANGE THE FACT THAT WE'RE AT A NUMERICAL DISADVANTAGE.

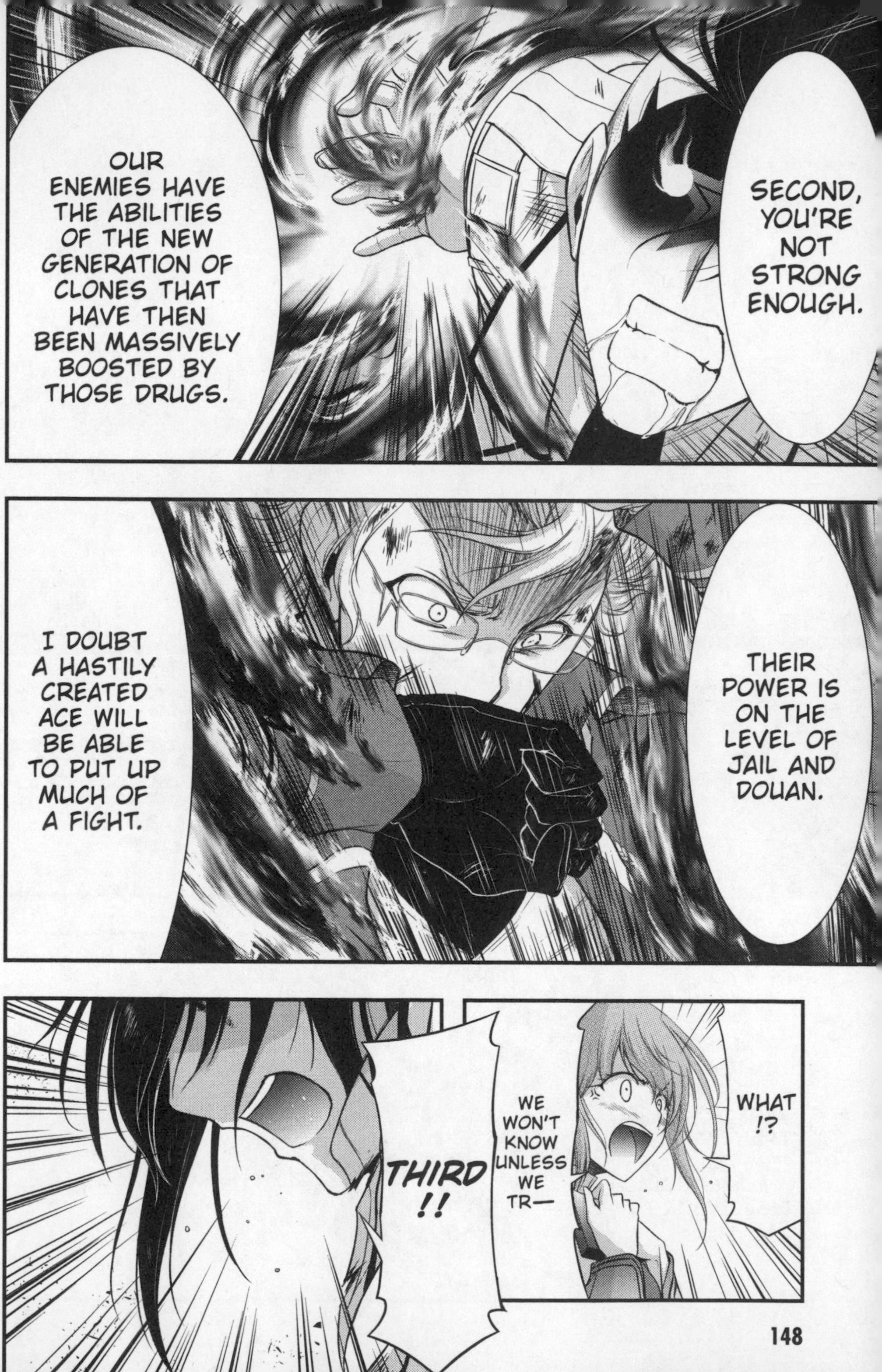
SECOND, YOU'RE NOT STRONG ENOUGH.
OUR ENEMIES HAVE THE ABILITIES OF THE NEW GENERATION OF CLONES THAT HAVE THEN BEEN MASSIVELY BOOSTED BY THOSE DRUGS.
THEIR POWER IS ON THE LEVEL OF JAIL AND DOUAN.
I DOUBT A HASTILY CREATED ACE WILL BE ABLE TO PUT UP MUCH OF A FIGHT.
WHAT!?
WE WON'T KNOW UNLESS WE TR—
THIRD!!

CAN'T YOU TELL JUST FROM HAVING WATCHED FIRENDA JUST NOW!?

THE WAY HER FAILED ATTEMPT AT USING THE FLASHING STRIKES BACK-FIRED!?

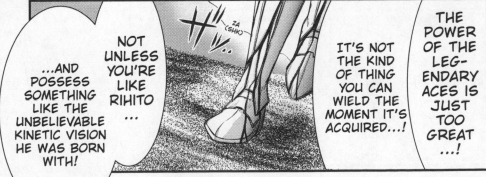

ZA (SHK)

THE POWER OF THE LEGENDARY ACES IS JUST TOO GREAT ...!

IT'S NOT THE KIND OF THING YOU CAN WIELD THE MOMENT IT'S ACQUIRED...!

NOT UNLESS YOU'RE LIKE RIHITO...

...AND POSSESS SOMETHING LIKE THE UNBELIEVABLE KINETIC VISION HE WAS BORN WITH!

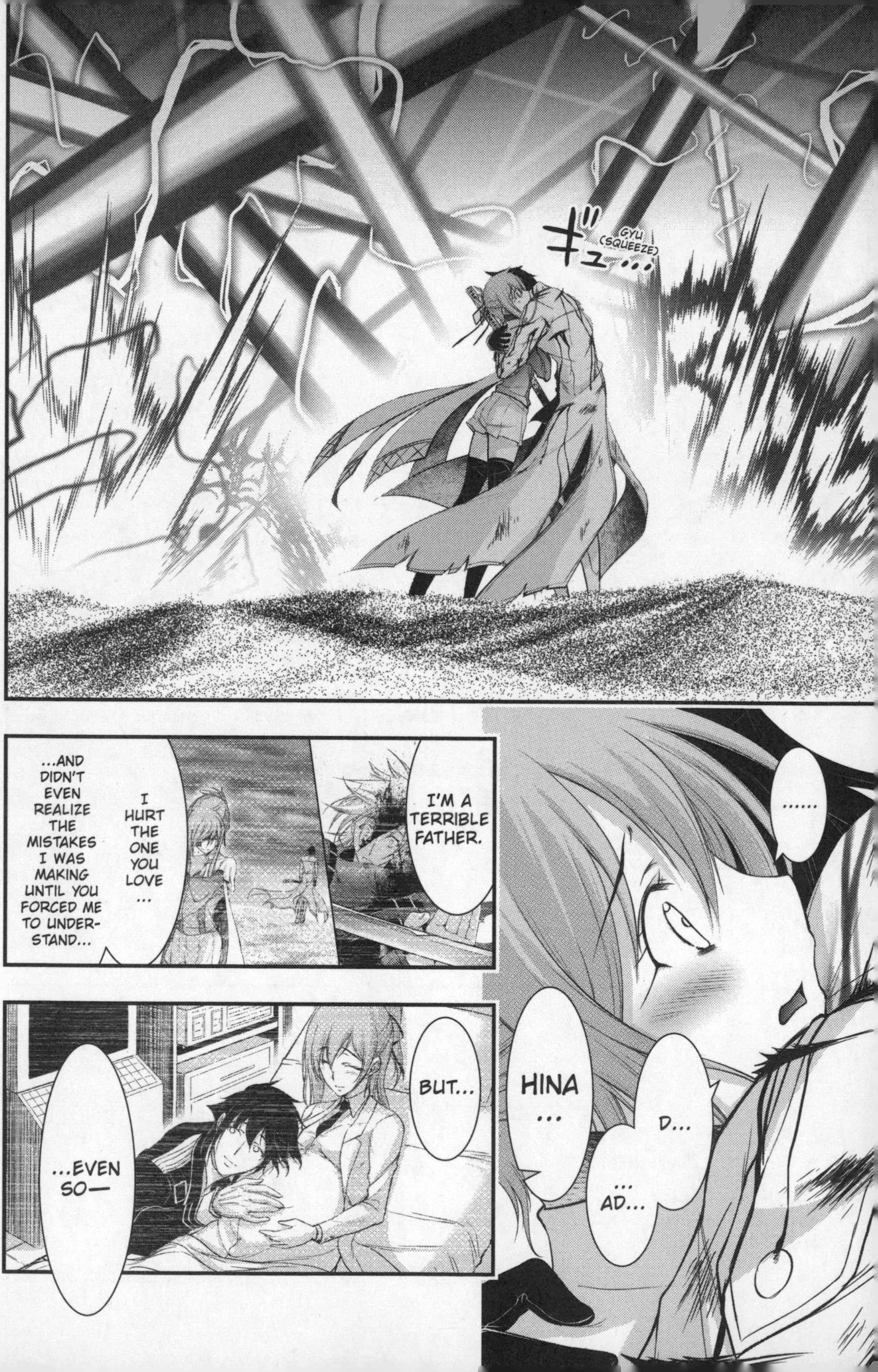
ギュ…
GYU (SQUEEZE)
......
D... ...AD...
HINA...
I'M A TERRIBLE FATHER.
I HURT THE ONE YOU LOVE...
...AND DIDN'T EVEN REALIZE THE MISTAKES I WAS MAKING UNTIL YOU FORCED ME TO UNDERSTAND...
BUT...
...EVEN SO—

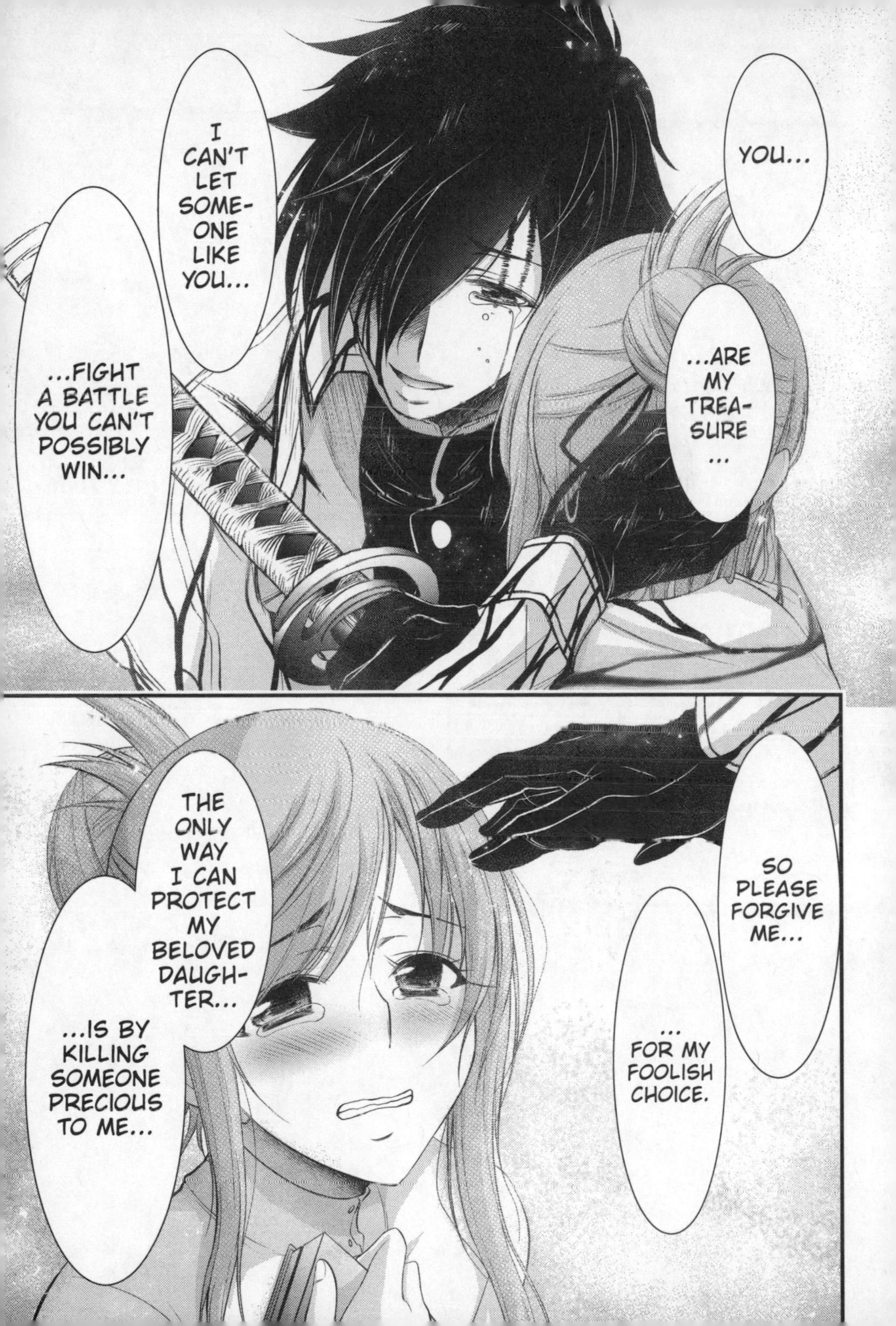
YOU...
...ARE MY TREASURE...
I CAN'T LET SOMEONE LIKE YOU...
...FIGHT A BATTLE YOU CAN'T POSSIBLY WIN...
SO PLEASE FORGIVE ME...
...FOR MY FOOLISH CHOICE.
THE ONLY WAY I CAN PROTECT MY BELOVED DAUGHTER...
...IS BY KILLING SOMEONE PRECIOUS TO ME...

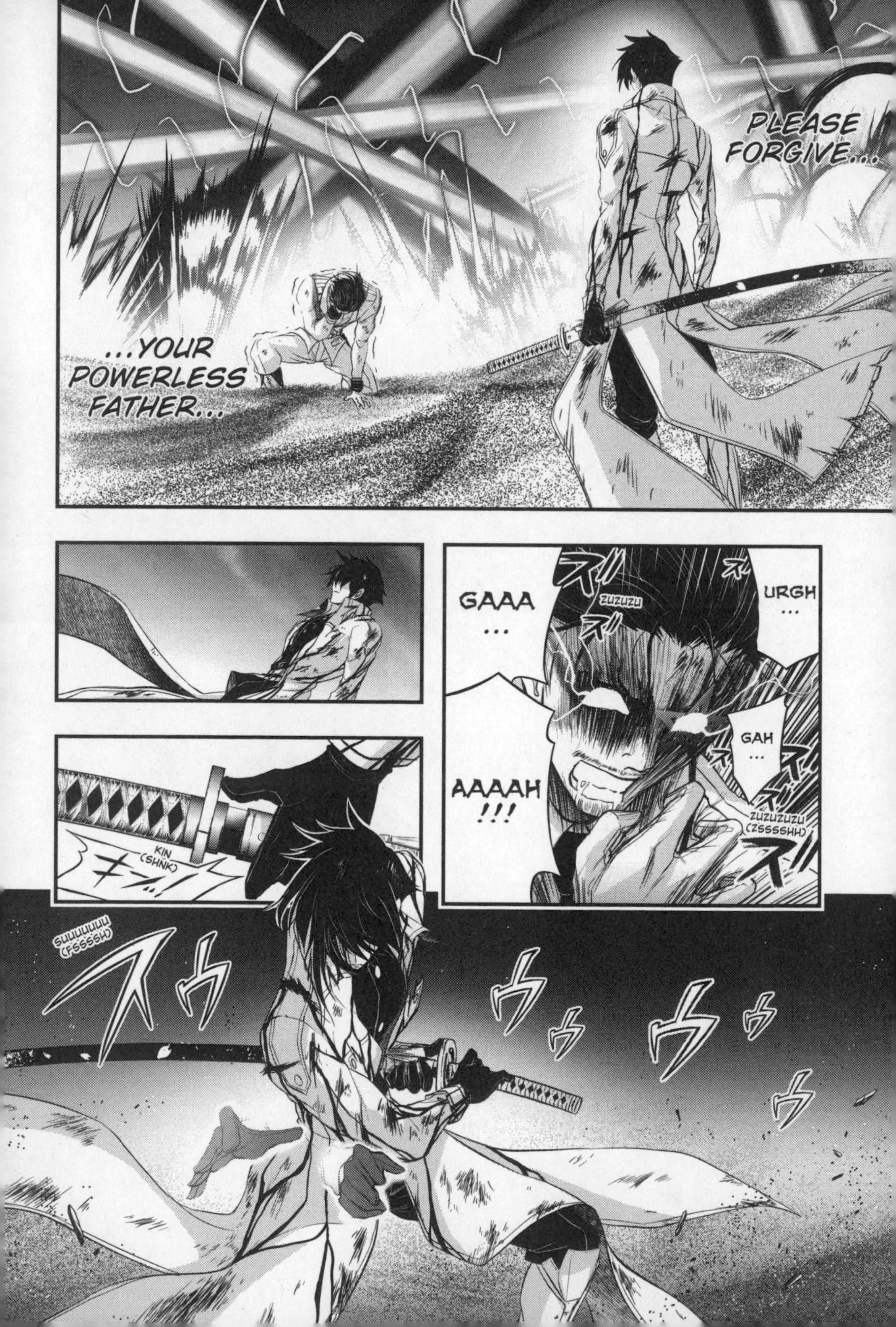
PLEASE FORGIVE...
...YOUR POWERLESS FATHER...
URGH ...
zuzuzu
GAAA ...
GAH ...
zuzuzuzu (ZSSSSHH)
AAAAH !!!
KIN (SHNK)
suuuuuuu (FSSSSH)

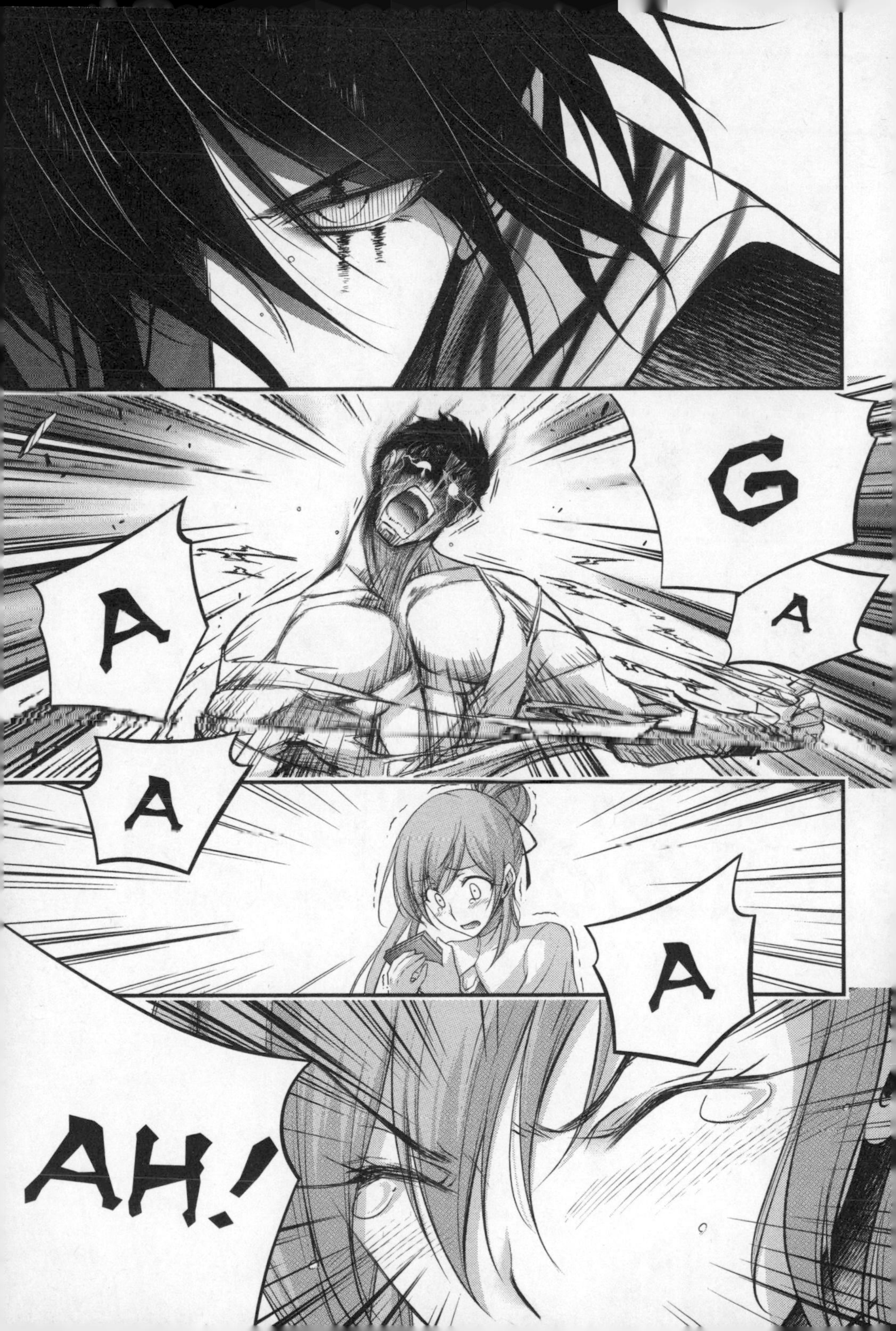
G
A
A
A
A
AH!

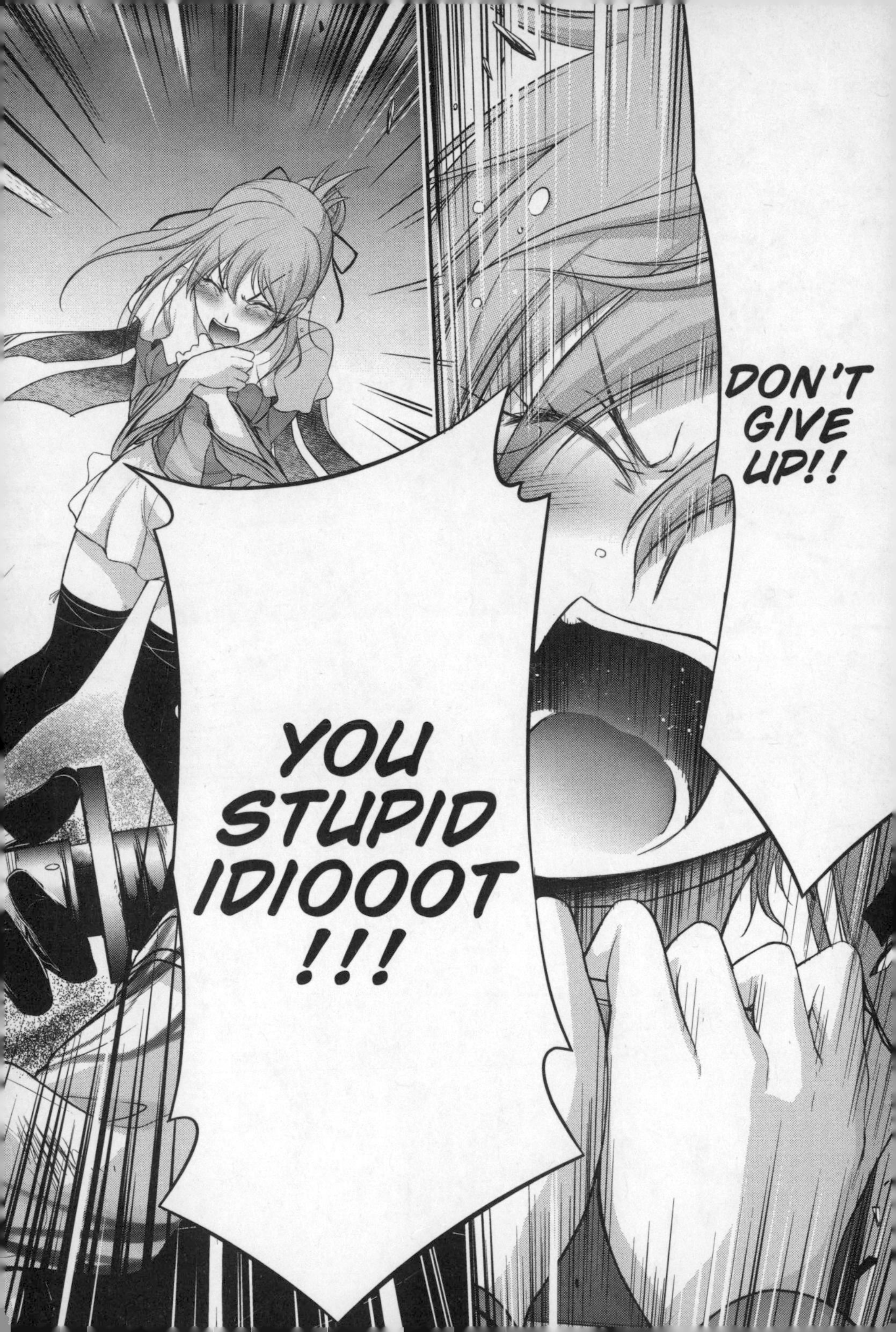
DON'T GIVE UP!!
YOU STUPID IDIOOOT!!!

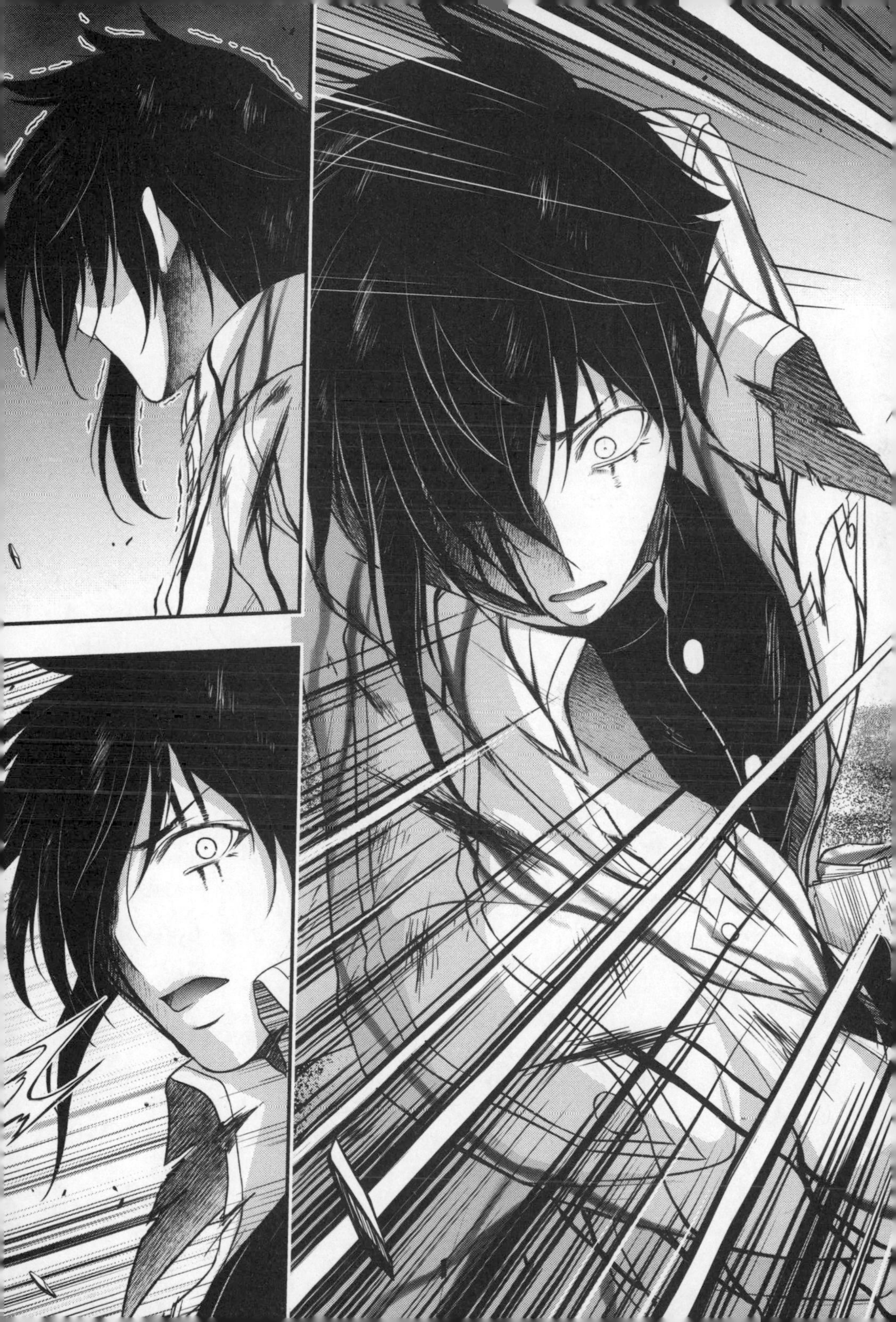

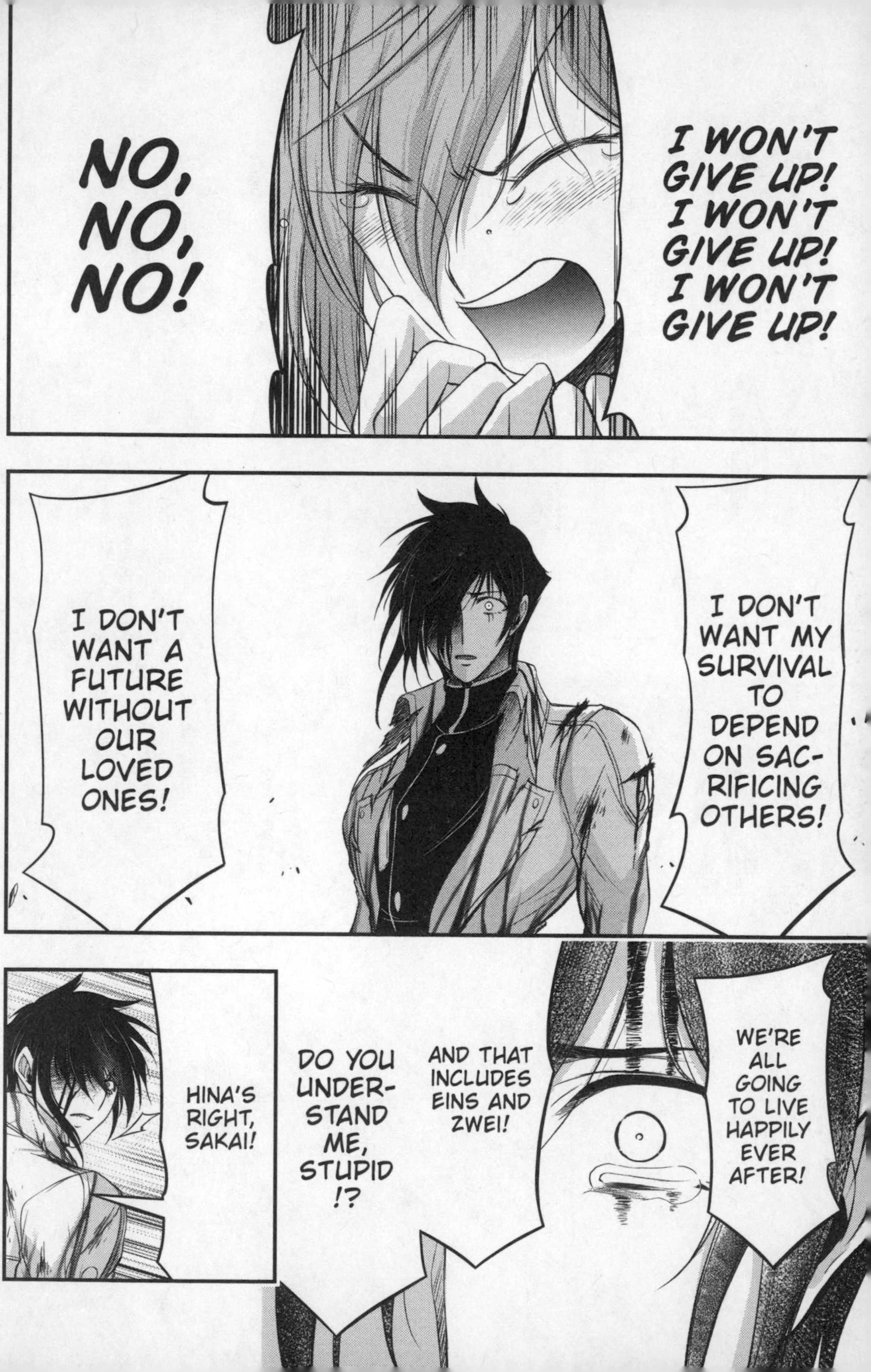
I WON'T GIVE UP! I WON'T GIVE UP! I WON'T GIVE UP!
NO, NO, NO!
I DON'T WANT MY SURVIVAL TO DEPEND ON SACRIFICING OTHERS!
I DON'T WANT A FUTURE WITHOUT OUR LOVED ONES!
WE'RE ALL GOING TO LIVE HAPPILY EVER AFTER!
AND THAT INCLUDES EINS AND ZWEI!
DO YOU UNDERSTAND ME, STUPID!?
HINA'S RIGHT, SAKAI!

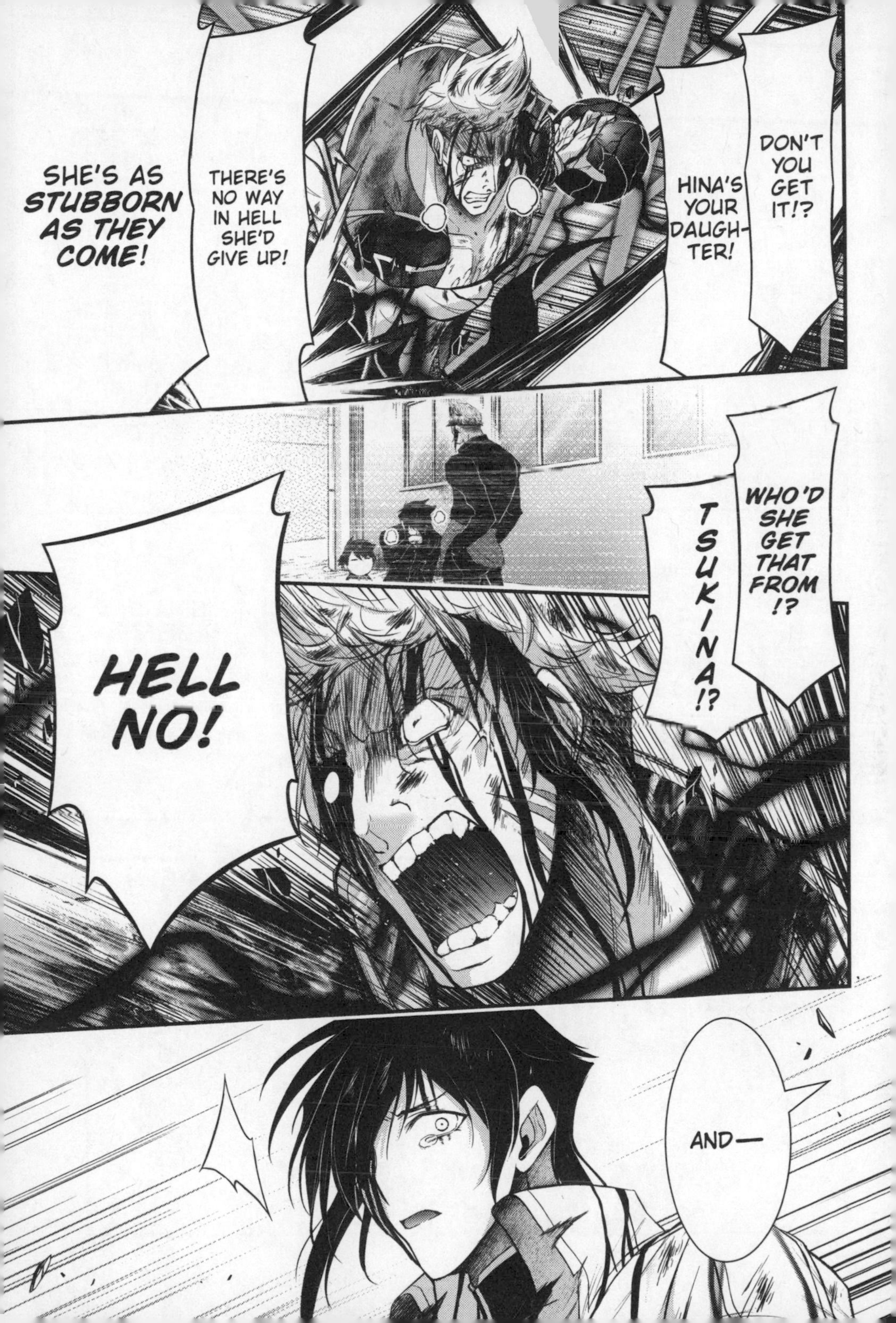
DON'T YOU GET IT!?
HINA'S YOUR DAUGHTER!
THERE'S NO WAY IN HELL SHE'D GIVE UP!
SHE'S AS STUBBORN AS THEY COME!
WHO'D SHE GET THAT FROM!?
TSUKINA!?
HELL NO!
AND—

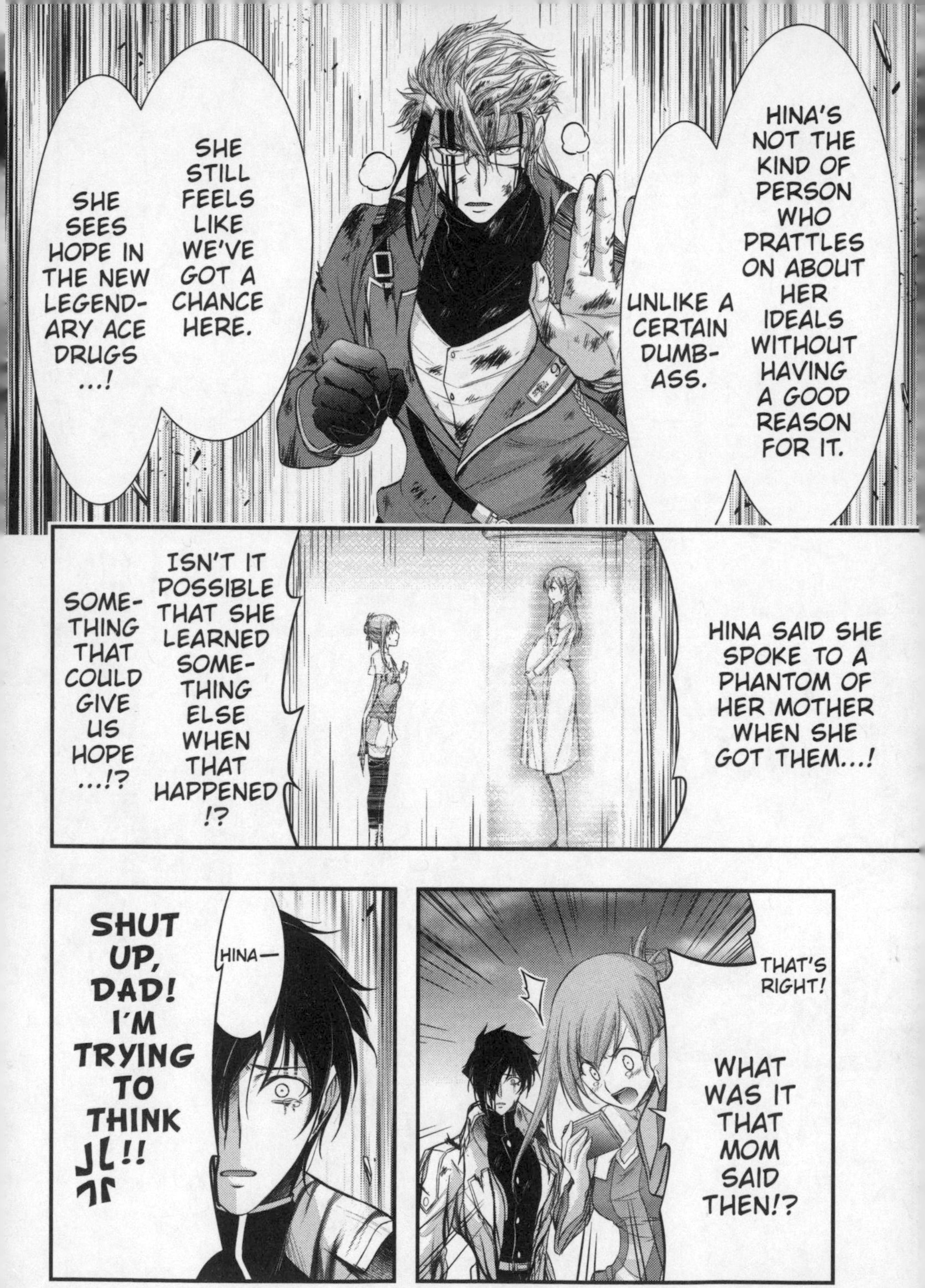
HINA'S NOT THE KIND OF PERSON WHO PRATTLES ON ABOUT HER IDEALS WITHOUT HAVING A GOOD REASON FOR IT.
UNLIKE A CERTAIN DUMB-ASS.
SHE STILL FEELS LIKE WE'VE GOT A CHANCE HERE.
SHE SEES HOPE IN THE NEW LEGEND-ARY ACE DRUGS ...!
HINA SAID SHE SPOKE TO A PHANTOM OF HER MOTHER WHEN SHE GOT THEM...!
ISN'T IT POSSIBLE THAT SHE LEARNED SOME-THING ELSE WHEN THAT HAPPENED!?
SOME-THING THAT COULD GIVE US HOPE ...!?
THAT'S RIGHT!
WHAT WAS IT THAT MOM SAID THEN!?
HINA—
SHUT UP, DAD! I'M TRYING TO THINK!!

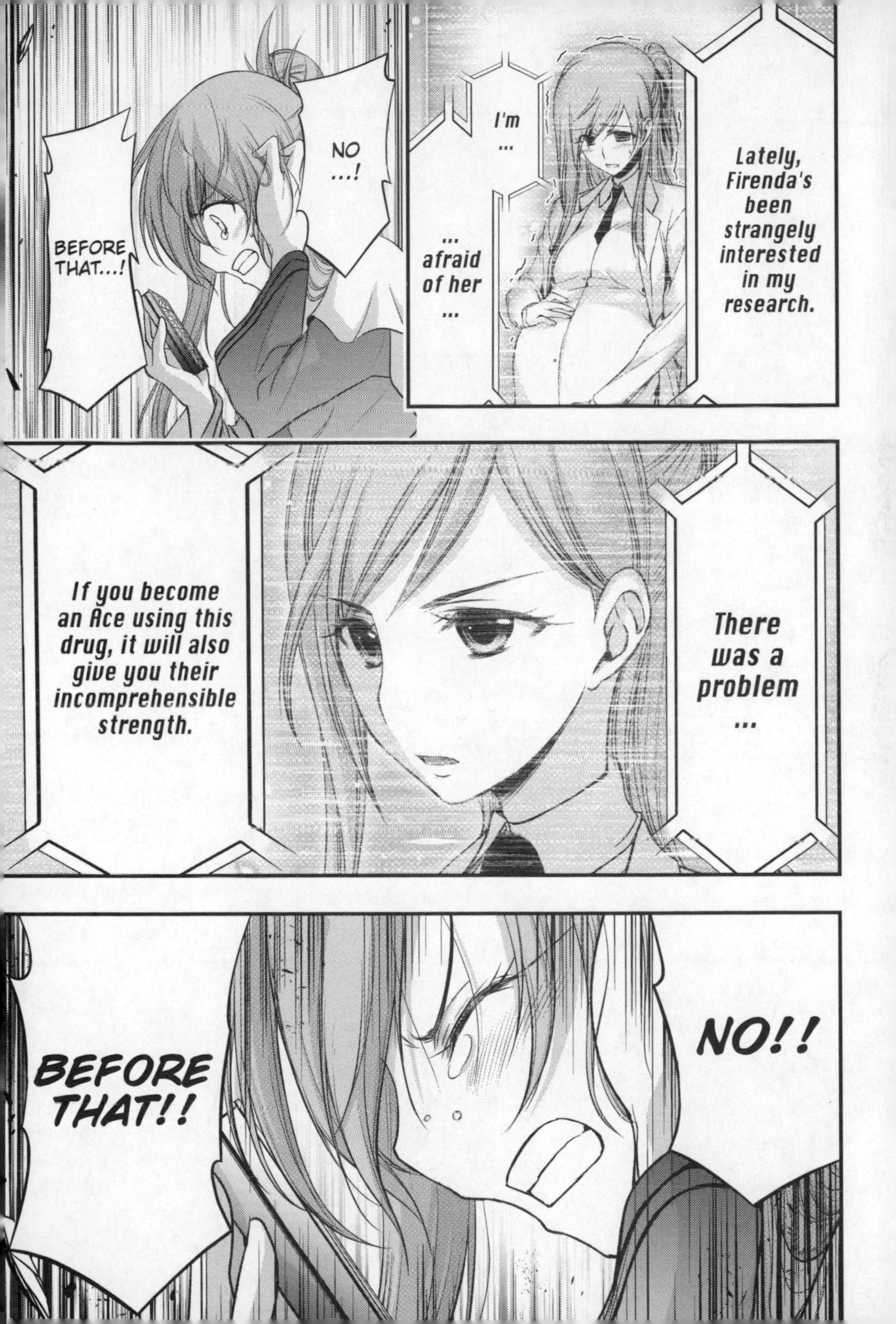
Lately, Firenda's been strangely interested in my research.
I'm ... ... afraid of her ...
NO ...!
BEFORE THAT...!
There was a problem ...
If you become an Ace using this drug, it will also give you their incomprehensible strength.
NO!!
BEFORE THAT!!

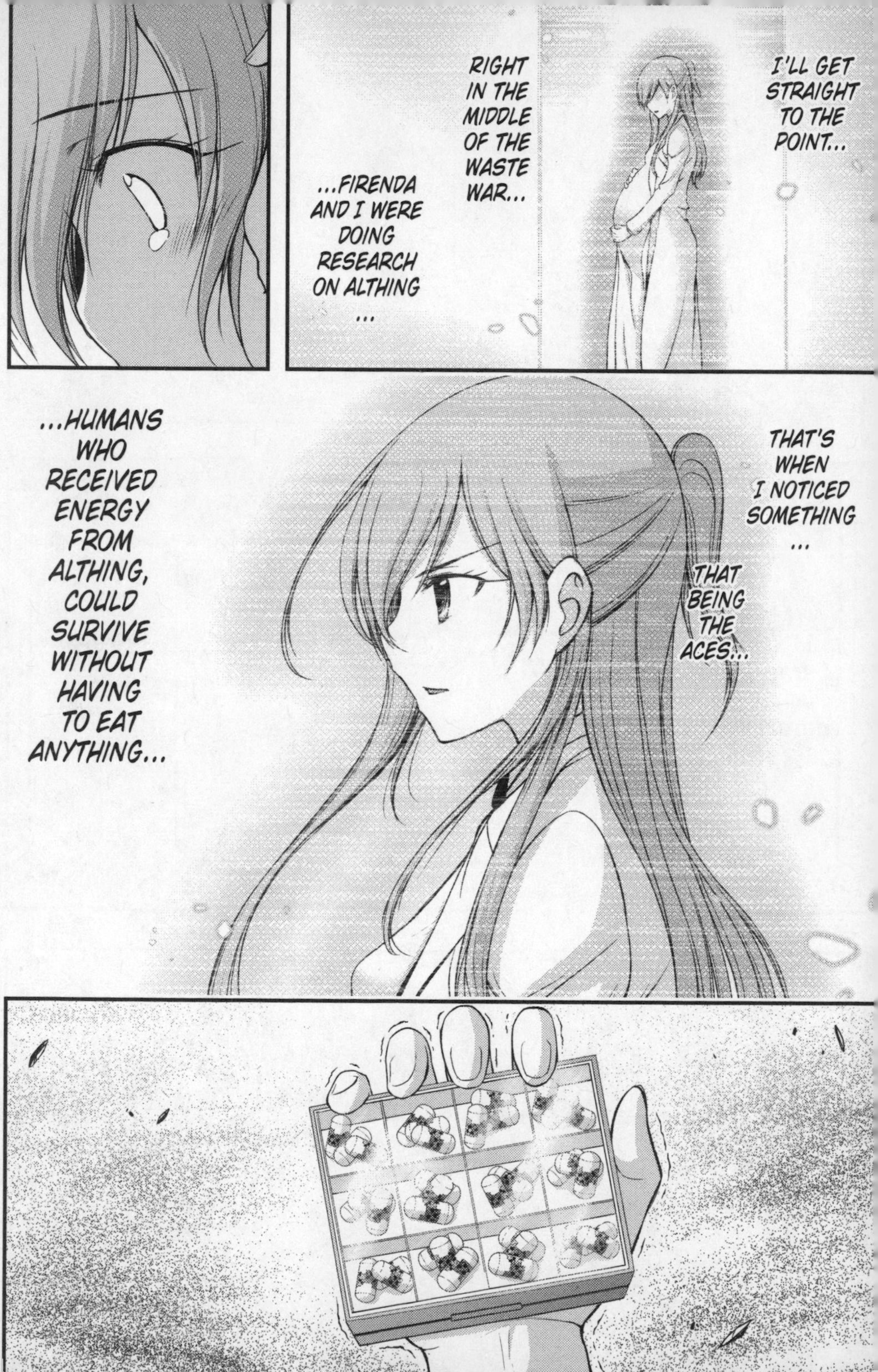
I'LL GET STRAIGHT TO THE POINT...
RIGHT IN THE MIDDLE OF THE WASTE WAR...
...FIRENDA AND I WERE DOING RESEARCH ON ALTHING...
THAT'S WHEN I NOTICED SOMETHING...
THAT BEING THE ACES...
...HUMANS WHO RECEIVED ENERGY FROM ALTHING, COULD SURVIVE WITHOUT HAVING TO EAT ANYTHING...

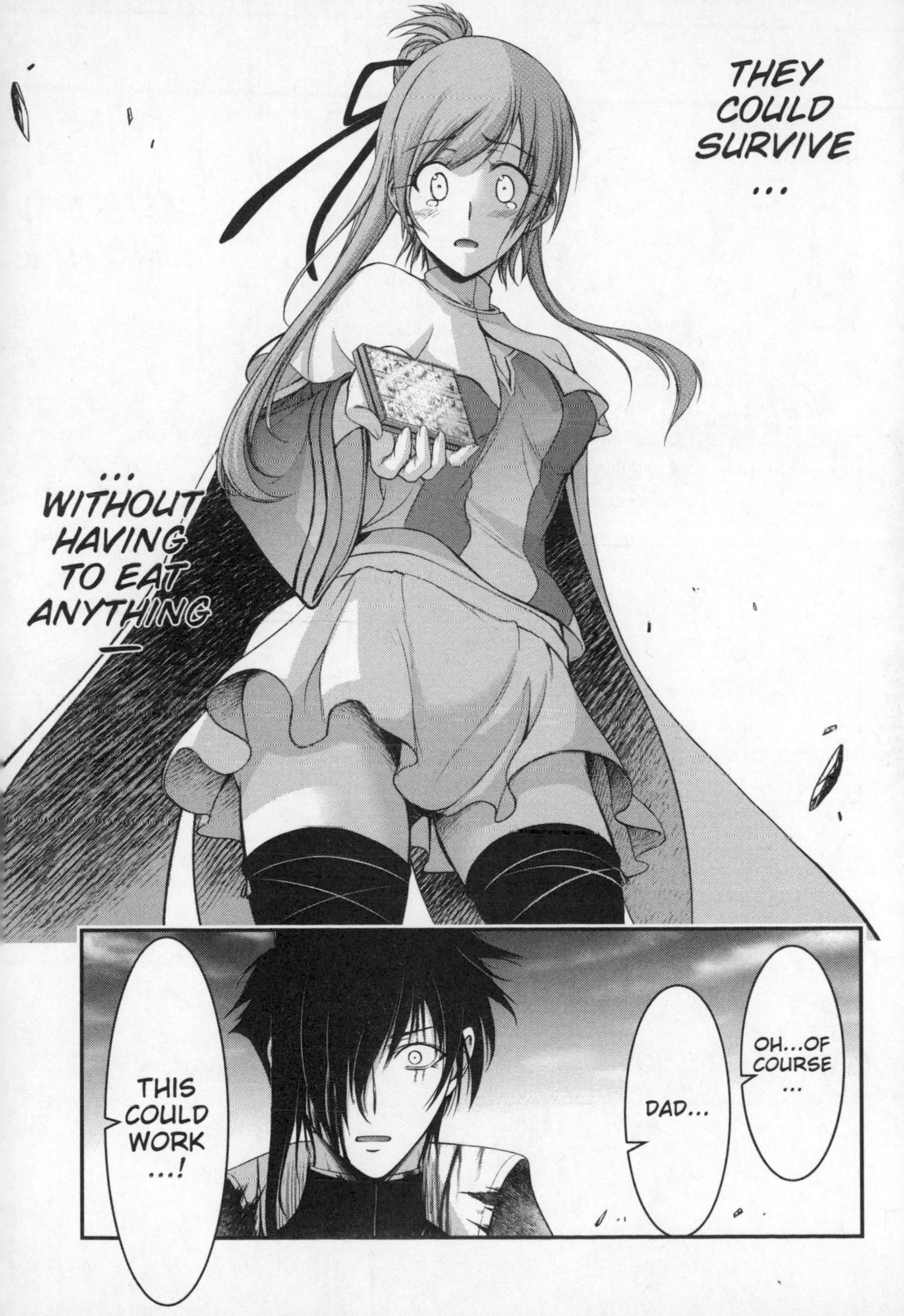
THEY COULD SURVIVE ...
... WITHOUT HAVING TO EAT ANYTHING
OH...OF COURSE ...
DAD...
THIS COULD WORK ...!

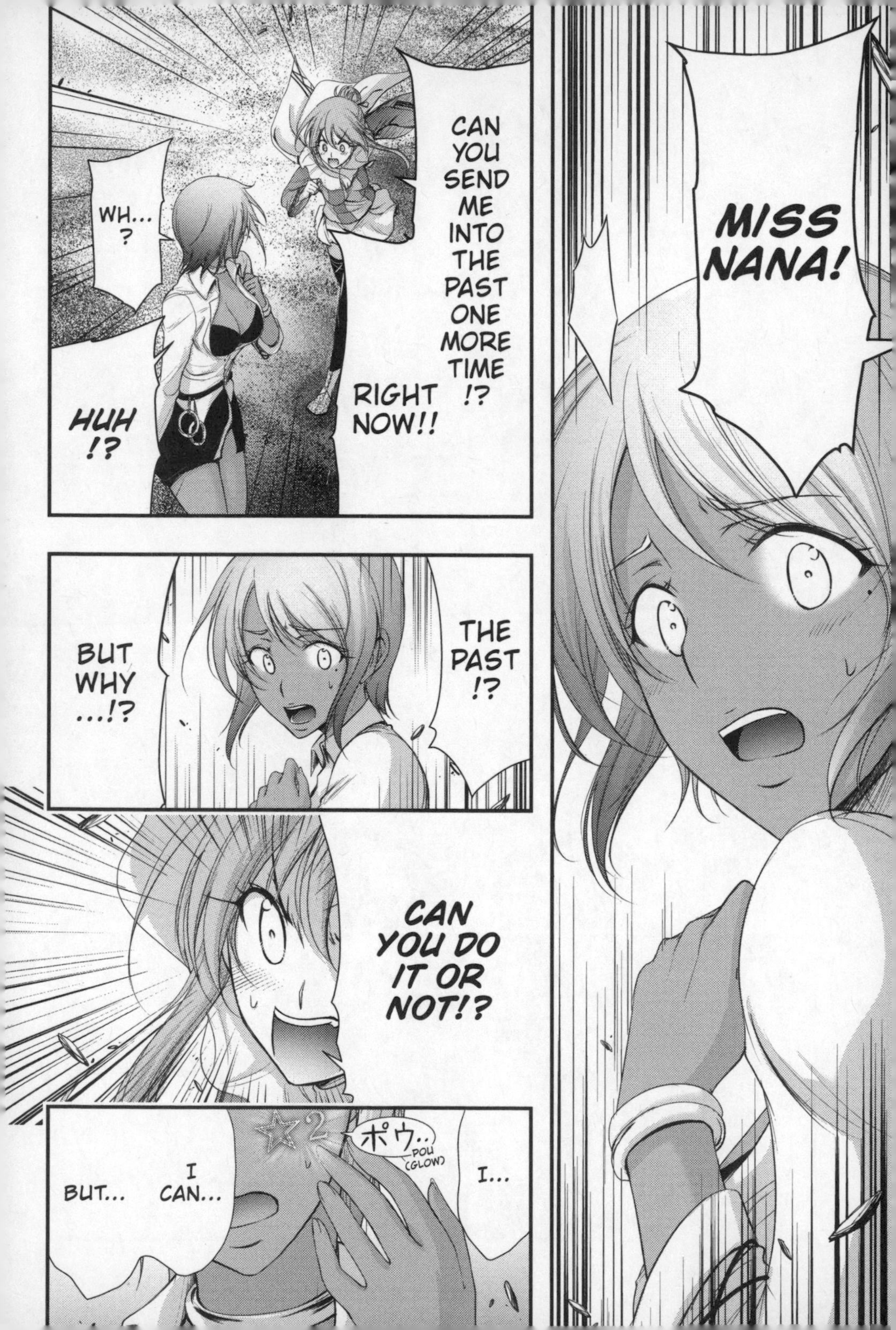

MISS NANA!
CAN YOU SEND ME INTO THE PAST ONE MORE TIME!?
RIGHT NOW!!
WH...?
HUH!?
THE PAST!?
BUT WHY...!?
CAN YOU DO IT OR NOT!?
I...
ポウ..
POU (GLOW)
I CAN...
BUT...

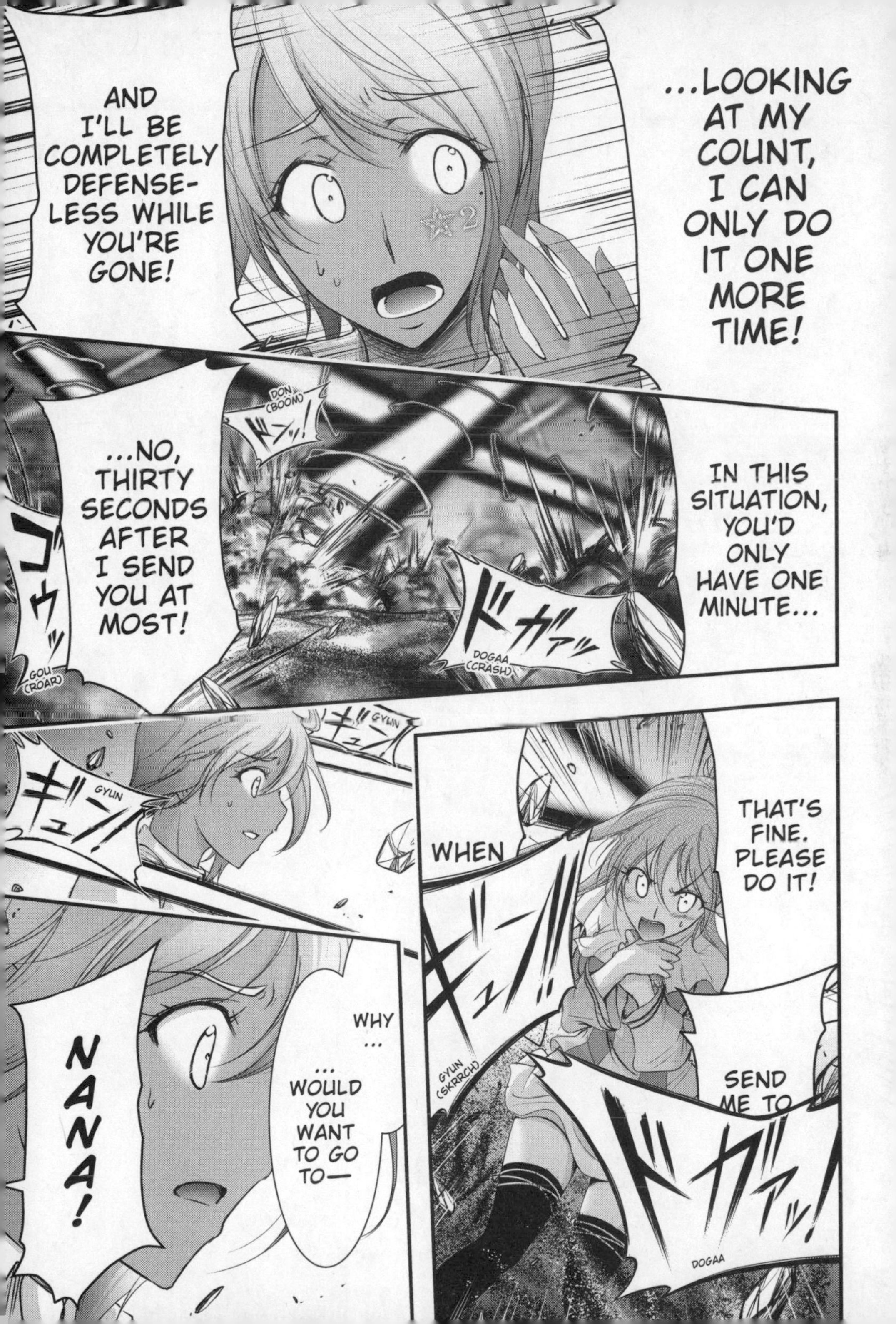
...LOOKING AT MY COUNT, I CAN ONLY DO IT ONE MORE TIME!
AND I'LL BE COMPLETELY DEFENSELESS WHILE YOU'RE GONE!
IN THIS SITUATION, YOU'D ONLY HAVE ONE MINUTE...
ドガァッ
DOGAA (CRASH)
ドンッ!
DON (BOOM)
...NO, THIRTY SECONDS AFTER I SEND YOU AT MOST!
ゴウッ
GOU (ROAR)
THAT'S FINE. PLEASE DO IT!
WHEN
ギュッ!!
GYUN (SKRRCH)
SEND ME TO
ドガァッ!
DOGAA
ギュン!
GYUN
ギューン!
GYUN
WHY...
...WOULD YOU WANT TO GO TO—
NANA!

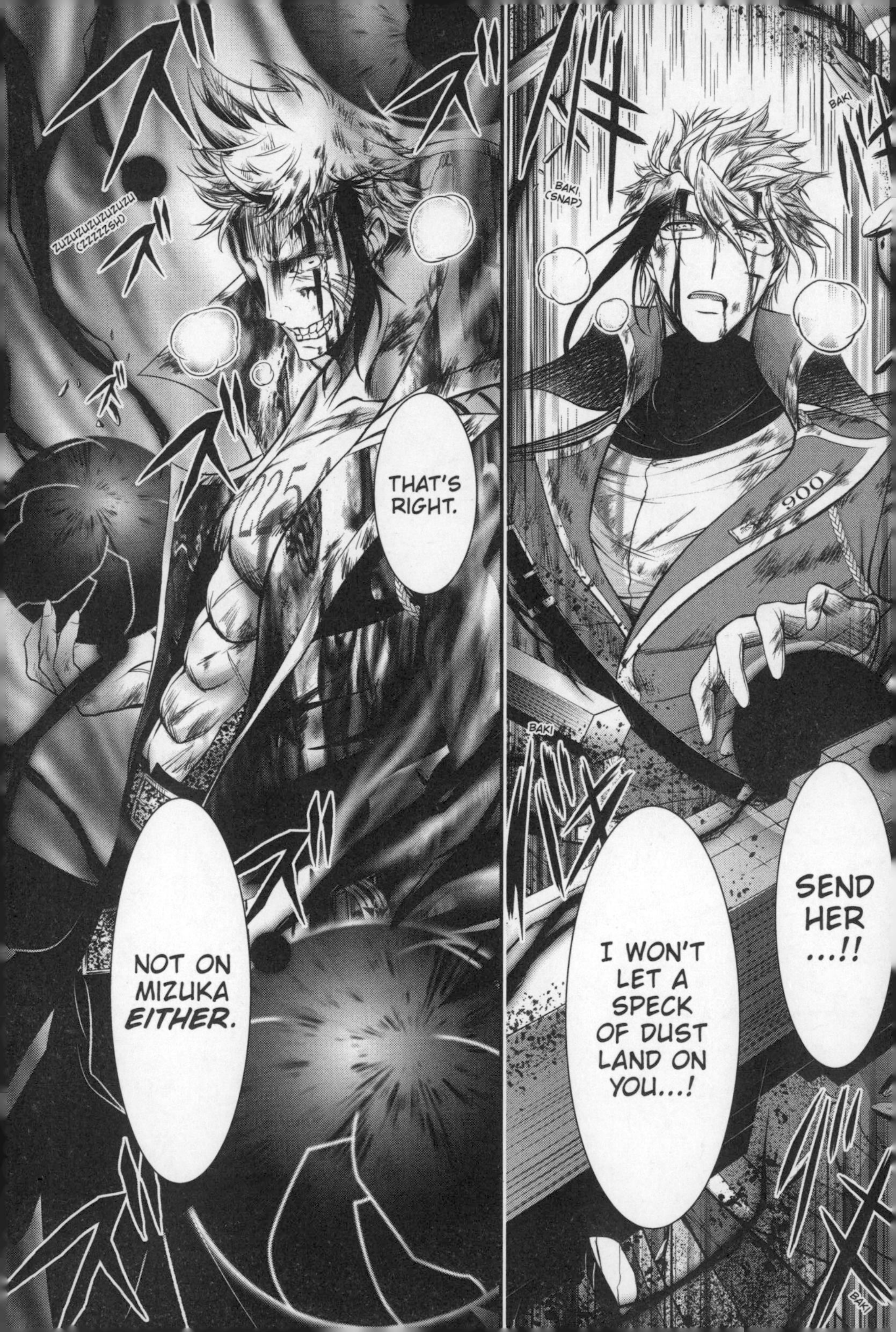
BAKI
BAKI (SNAP)
SEND HER ...!!
I WON'T LET A SPECK OF DUST LAND ON YOU...!
BAKI
BAKI
ZUZUZUZUZUZUZU (ZZZZZSH)
THAT'S RIGHT.
NOT ON MIZUKA *EITHER.*

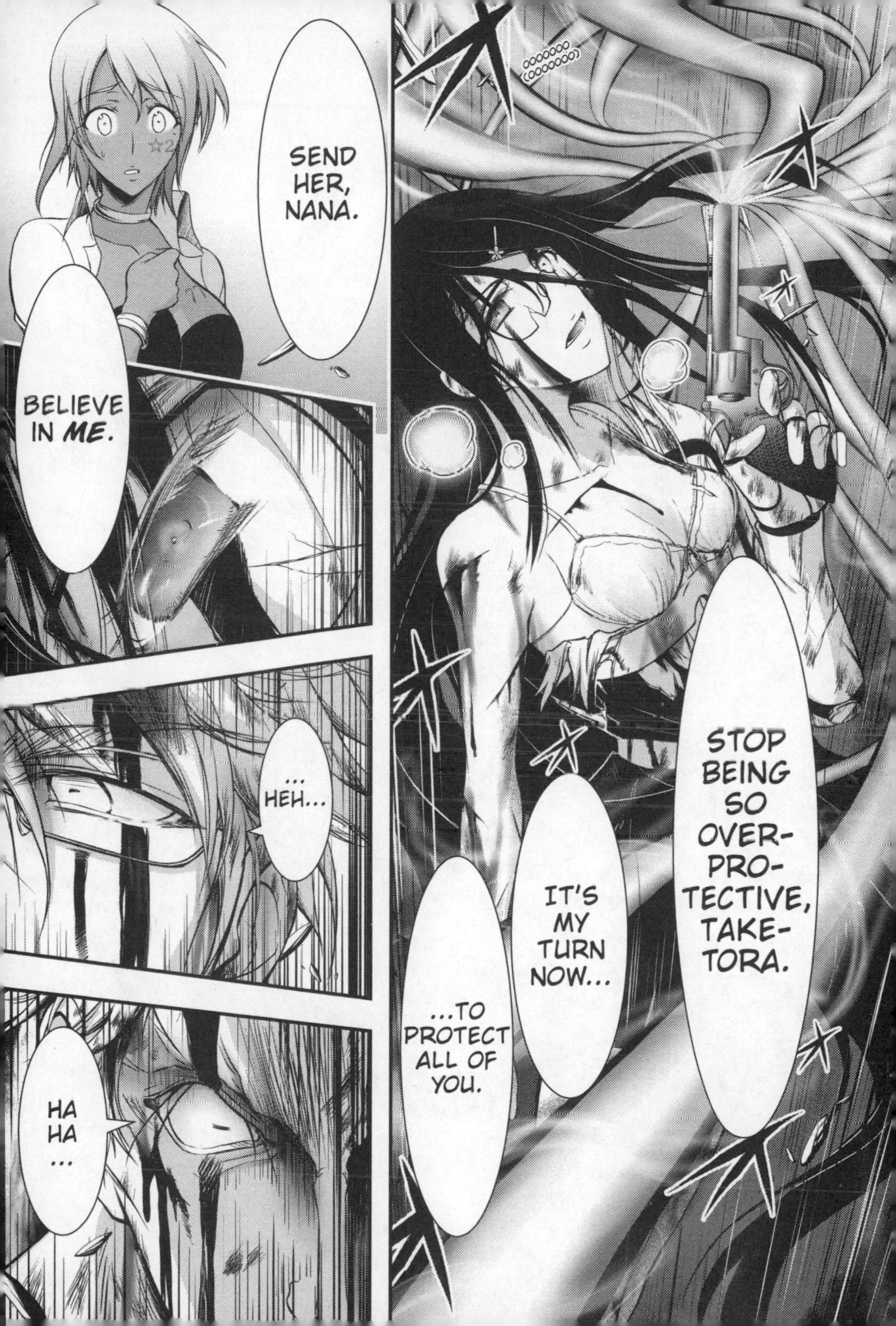
OOOOOOOO
(OOOOOOOO)
STOP BEING SO OVER-PROTECTIVE, TAKE-TORA.
IT'S MY TURN NOW...
...TO PROTECT ALL OF YOU.
SEND HER, NANA.
BELIEVE IN *ME*.
... HEH...
HA HA ...

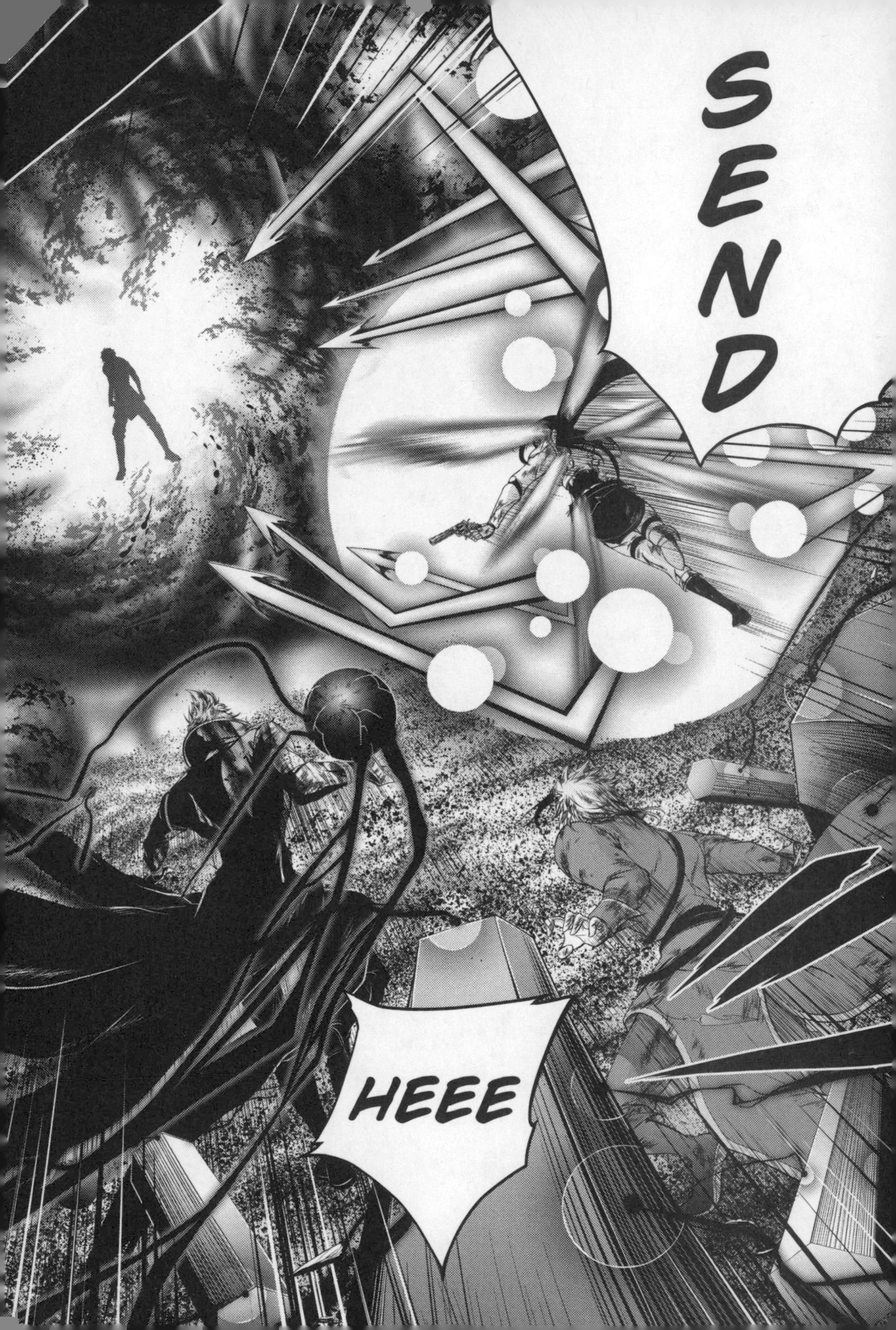
SEND
HEEE

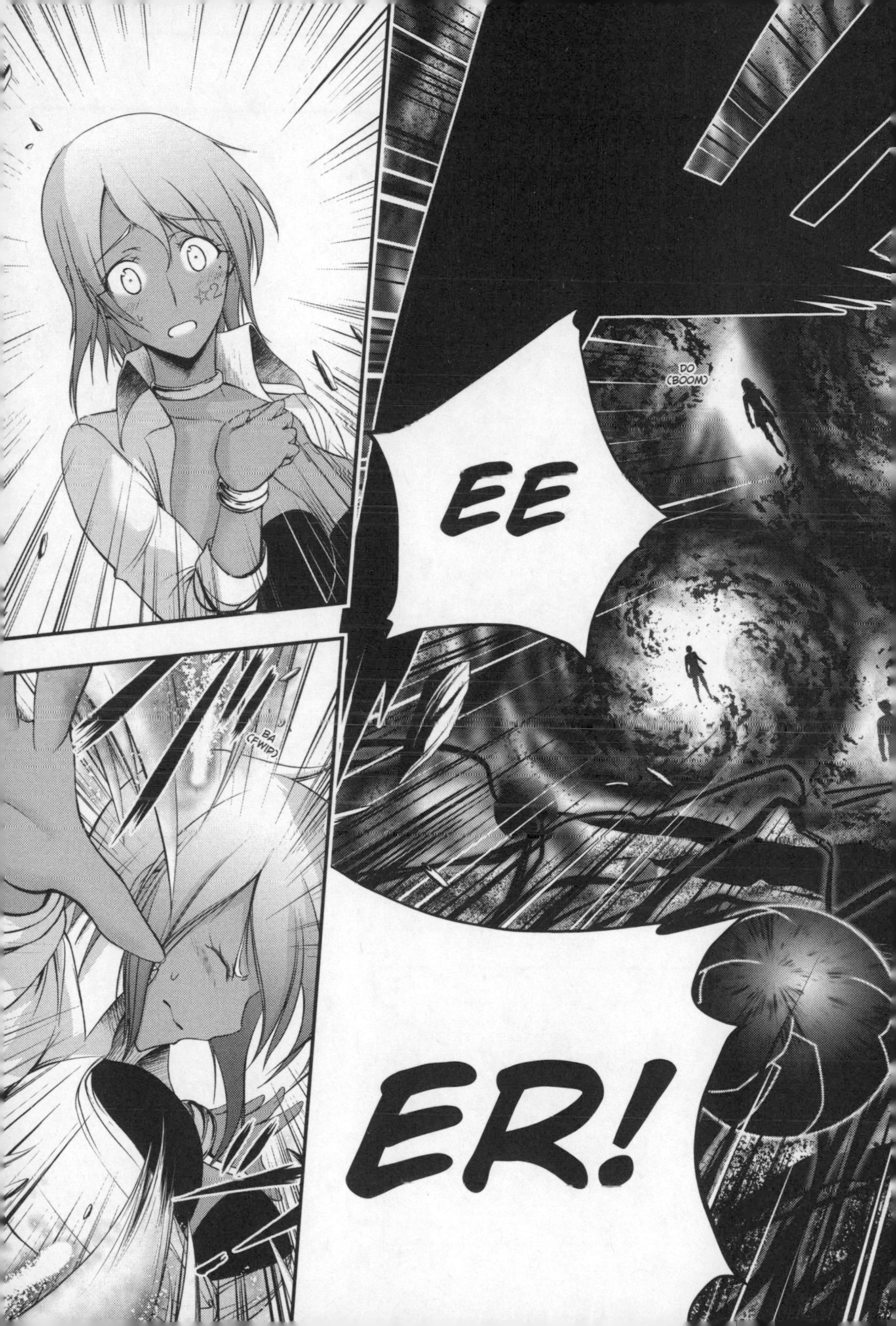
DO (BOOM)
EE
ER!
BA (FWIP)

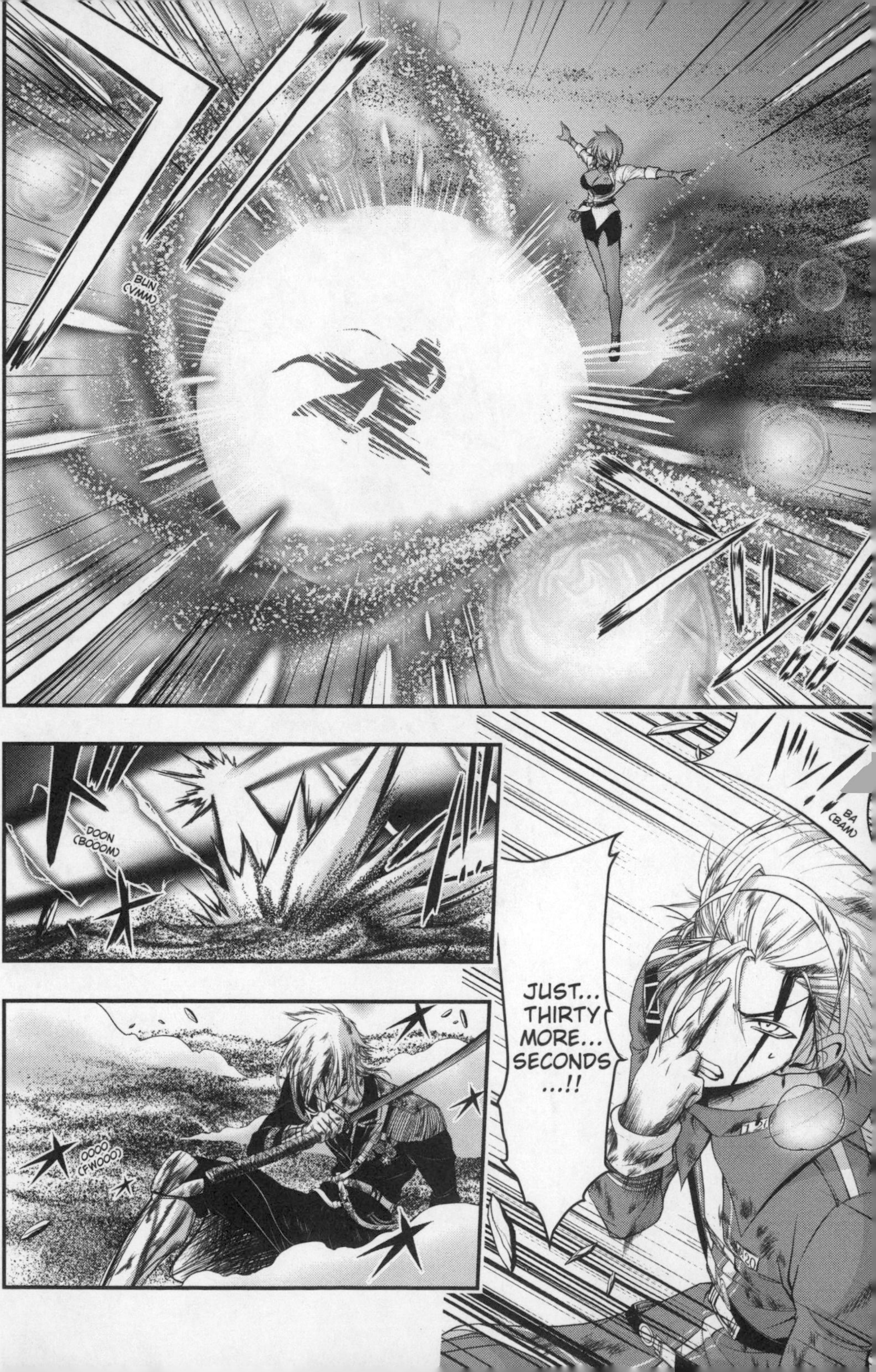
BUN (VMM)
BA (BAM)
JUST... THIRTY MORE... SECONDS ...!!
DOON (BOOOM)
OOOO (FWOOO)

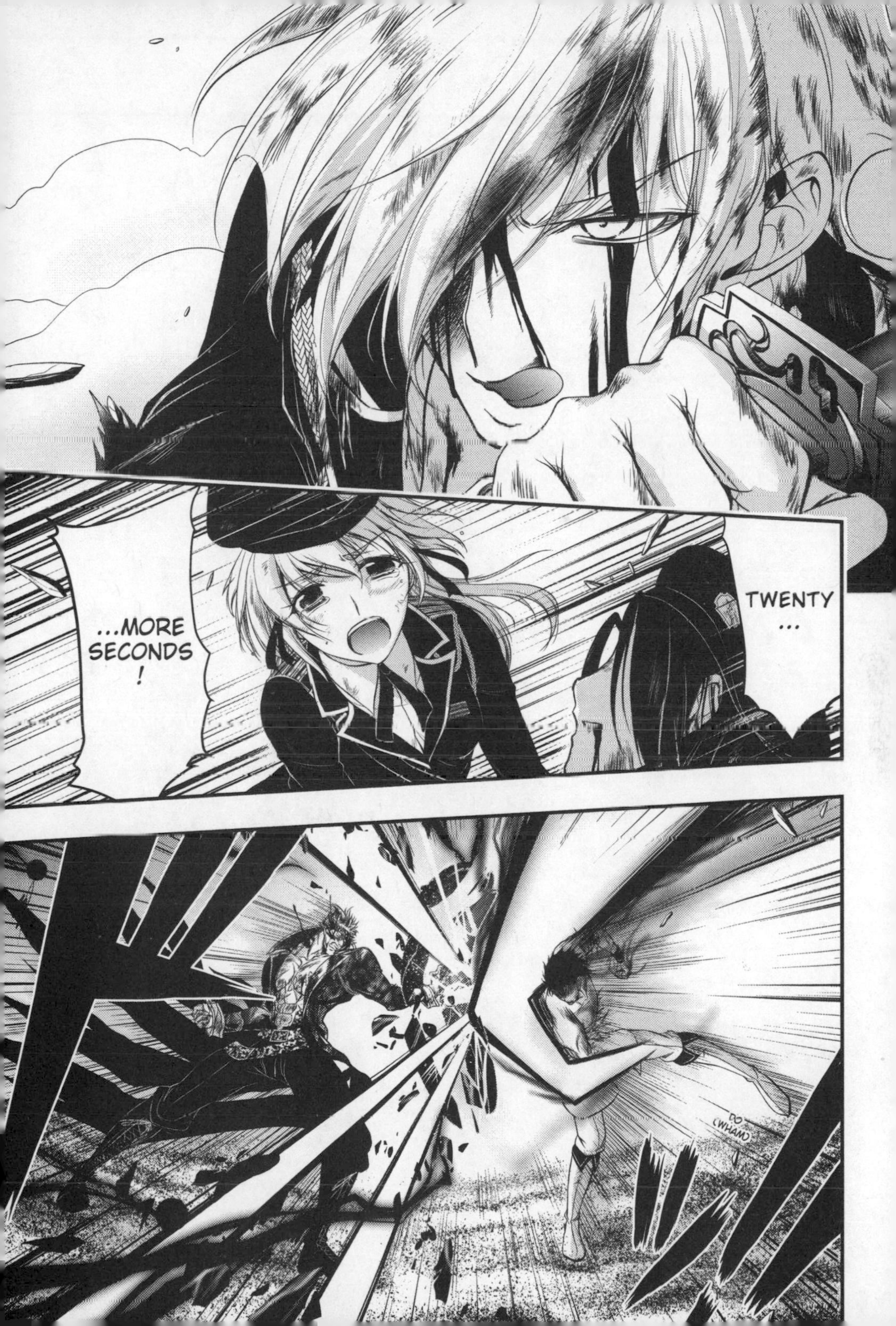
TWENTY ...
...MORE SECONDS !
DO
(WHAM)

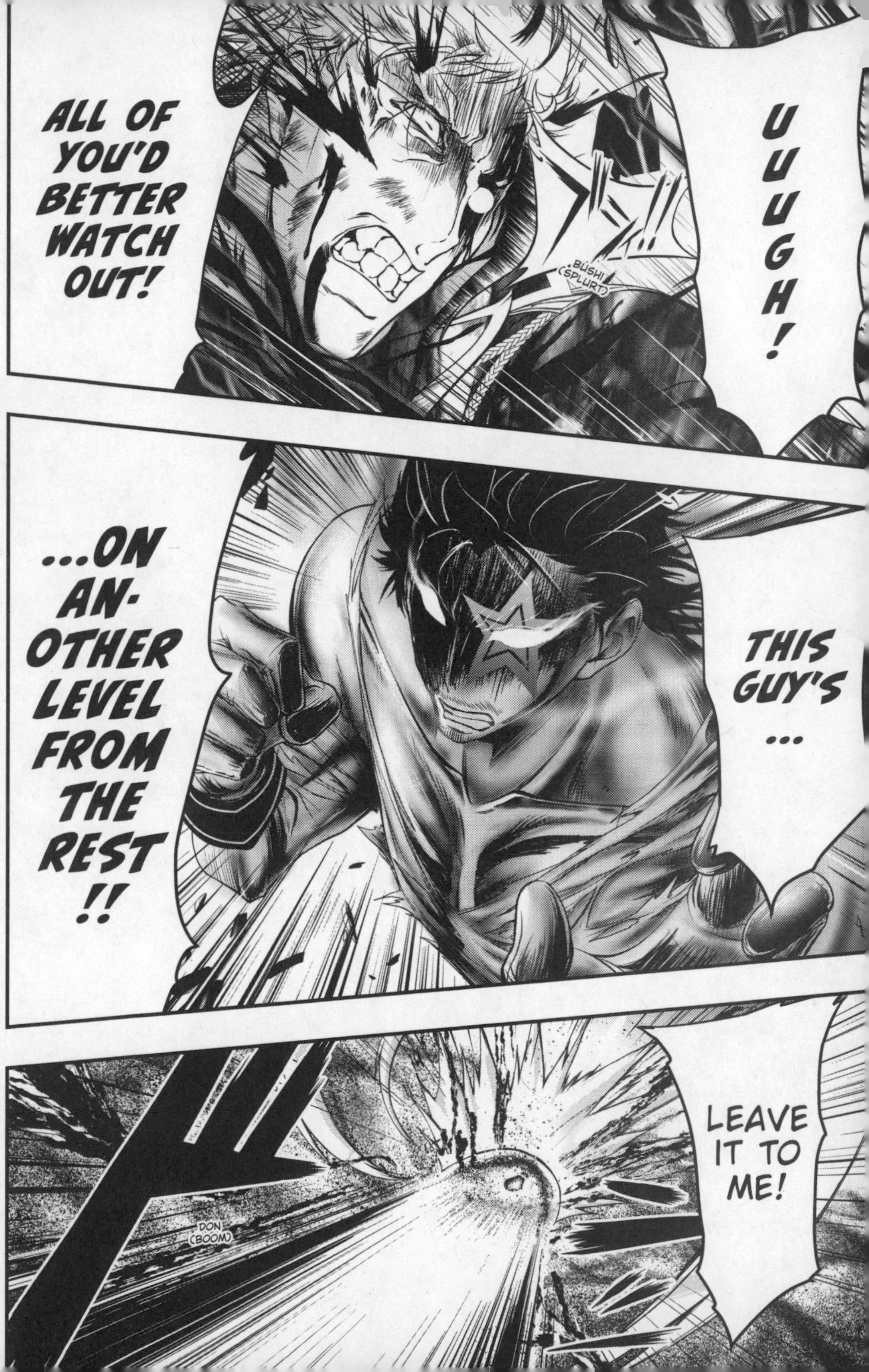
UUUGH!
BÜSHI (SPLURT)
ALL OF YOU'D BETTER WATCH OUT!
THIS GUY'S ...
...ON AN-OTHER LEVEL FROM THE REST!!
LEAVE IT TO ME!
DON (BOOM)

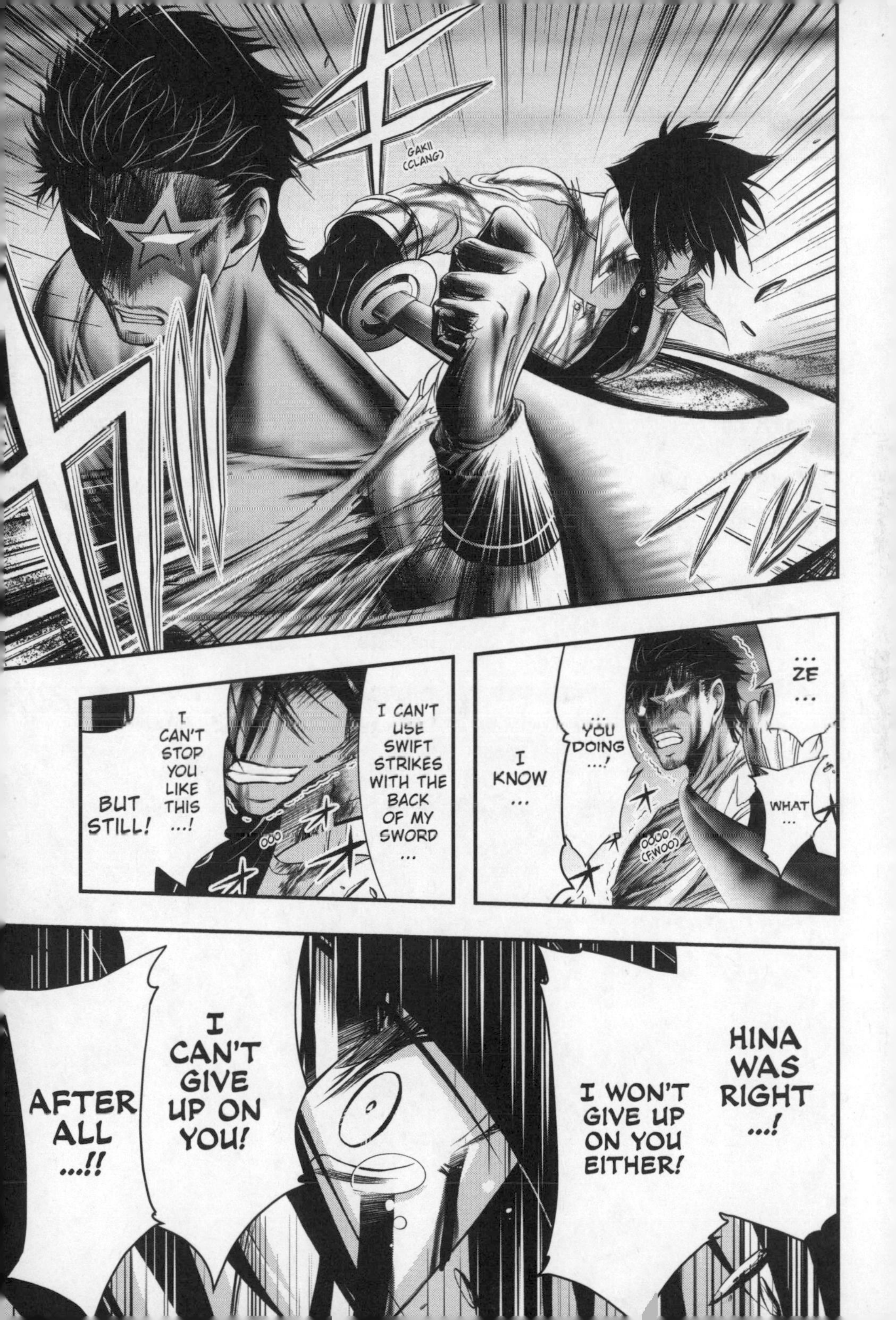
GAKII (CLANG)
... ZE ...
WHAT ...
... YOU DOING ...!
OOOO (FWOO)
I KNOW ...
I CAN'T USE SWIFT STRIKES WITH THE BACK OF MY SWORD ...
I CAN'T STOP YOU LIKE THIS ...!
BUT STILL!
OOO
HINA WAS RIGHT ...!
I WON'T GIVE UP ON YOU EITHER!
I CAN'T GIVE UP ON YOU!
AFTER ALL ...!!

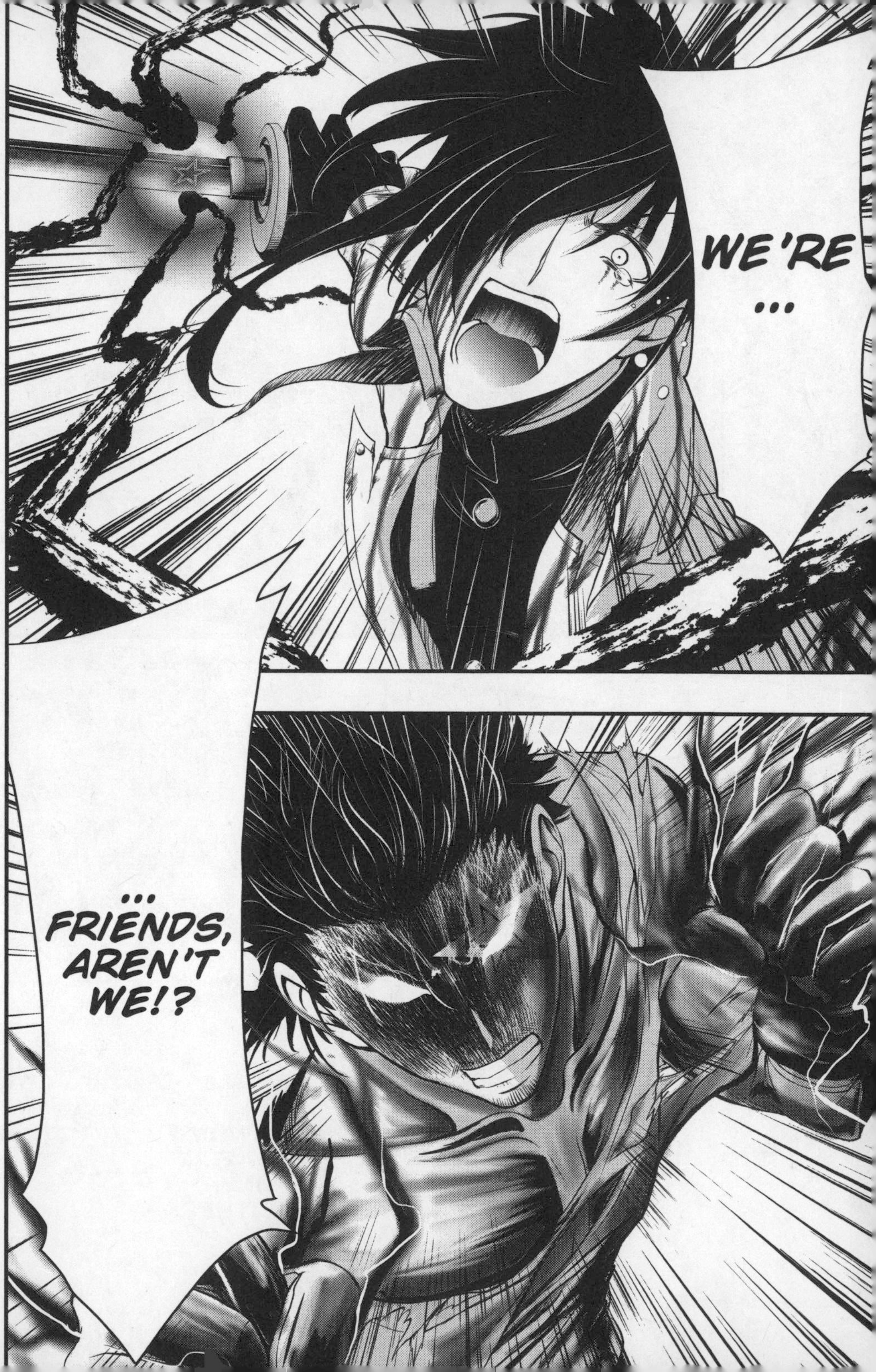
WE'RE ...
... FRIENDS, AREN'T WE!?

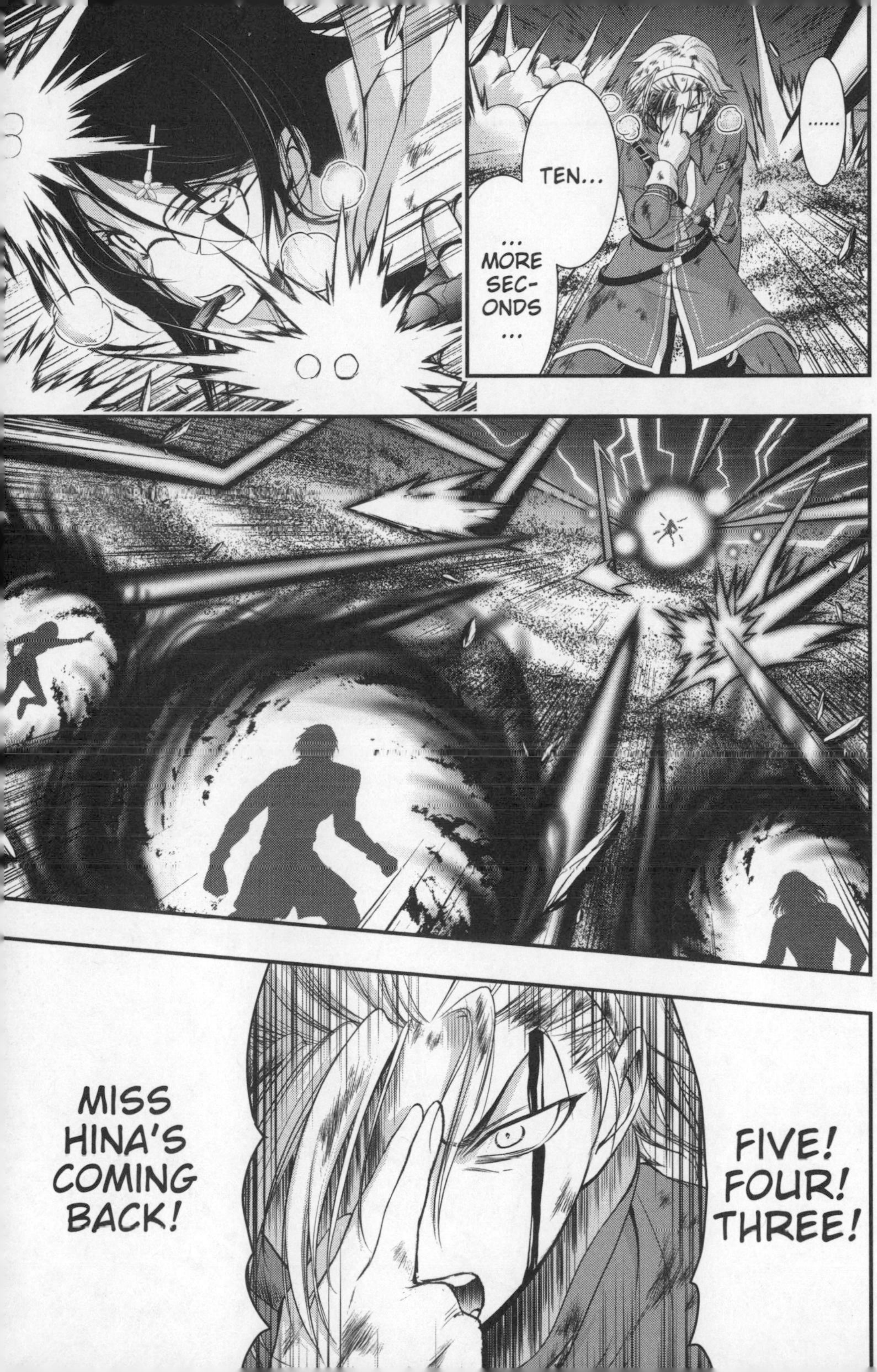
......
TEN...
...MORE SECONDS...
FIVE! FOUR! THREE!
MISS HINA'S COMING BACK!

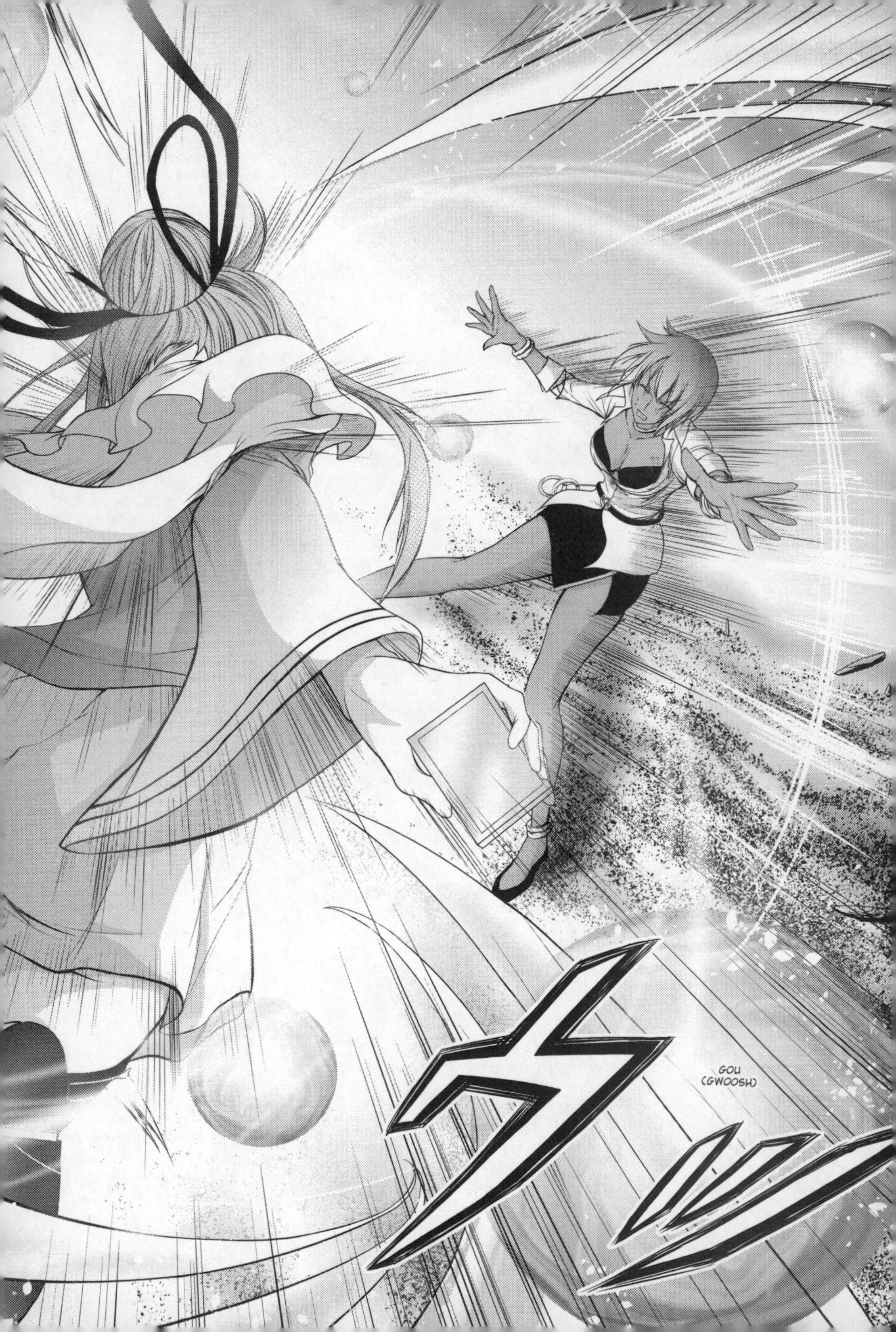
GOU
(GWOOSH)

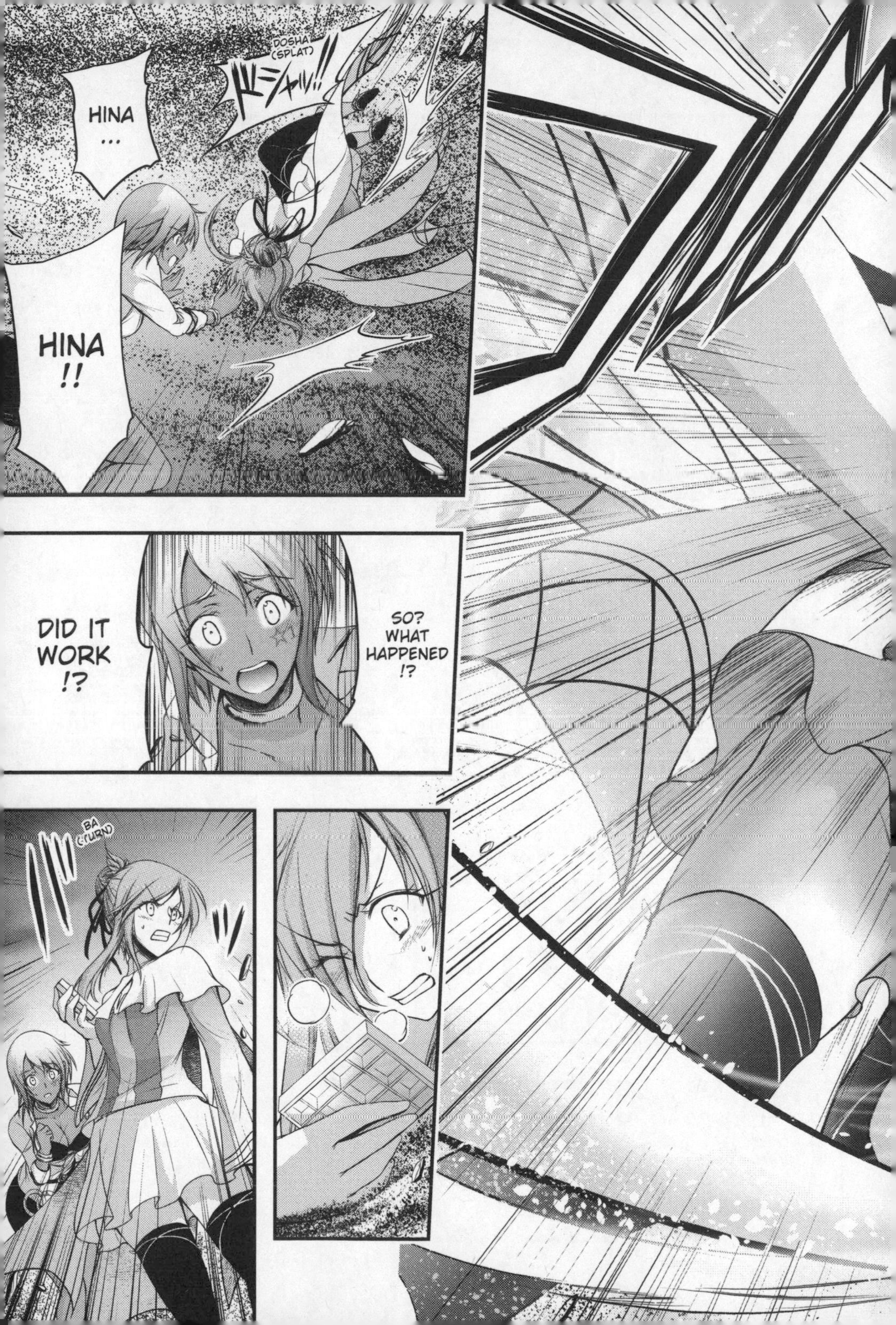
DOSHA (SPLAT)
HINA ...
HINA !!
SO? WHAT HAPPENED !?
DID IT WORK !?
BA (TURN)

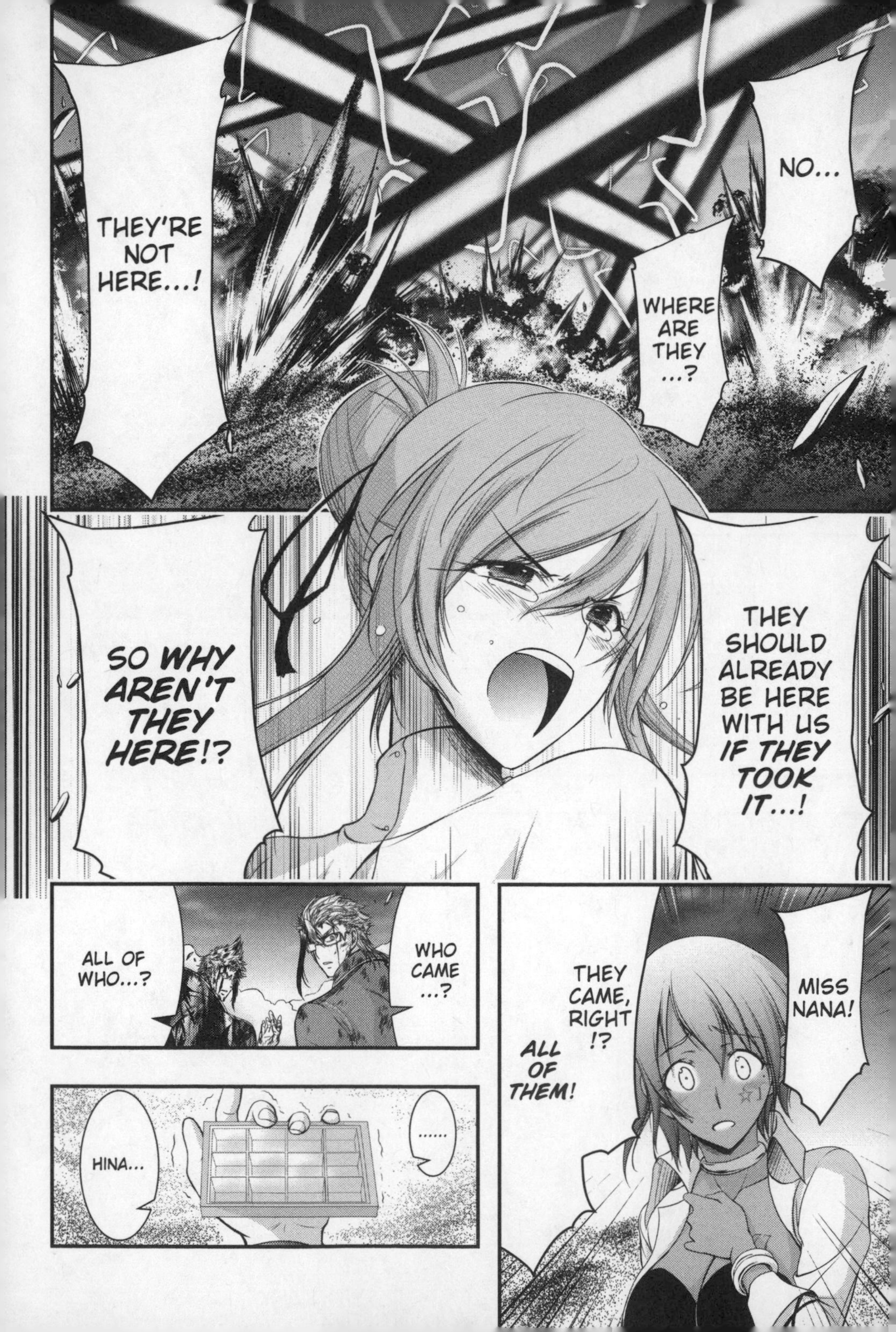
NO...
WHERE ARE THEY ...?
THEY'RE NOT HERE...!
THEY SHOULD ALREADY BE HERE WITH US IF THEY TOOK IT...!
SO WHY AREN'T THEY HERE!?
MISS NANA!
THEY CAME, RIGHT !?
ALL OF THEM!
WHO CAME ...?
ALL OF WHO...?
......
HINA...

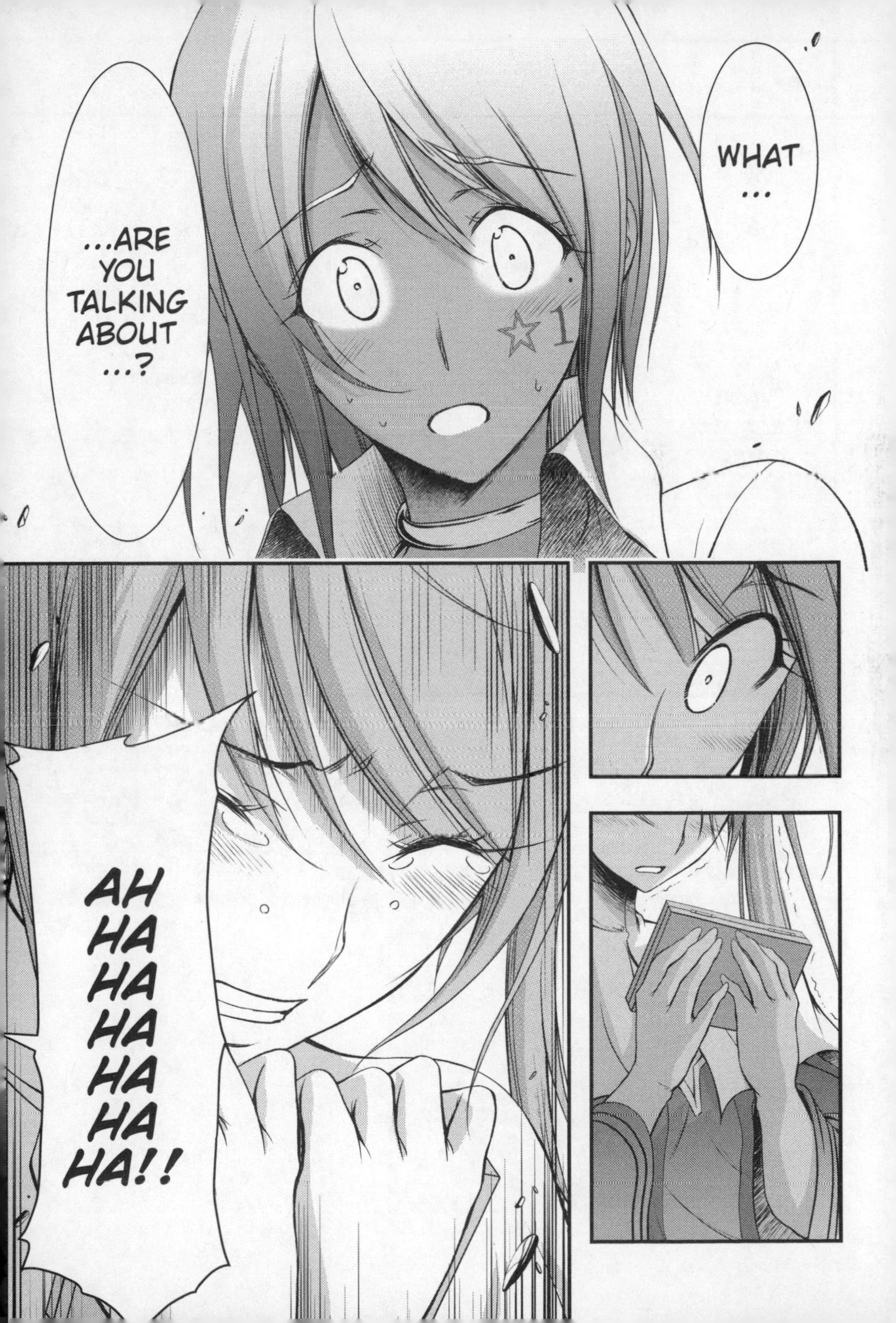
WHAT ...
...ARE YOU TALKING ABOUT ...?
AH HA HA HA HA HA HA HA!!

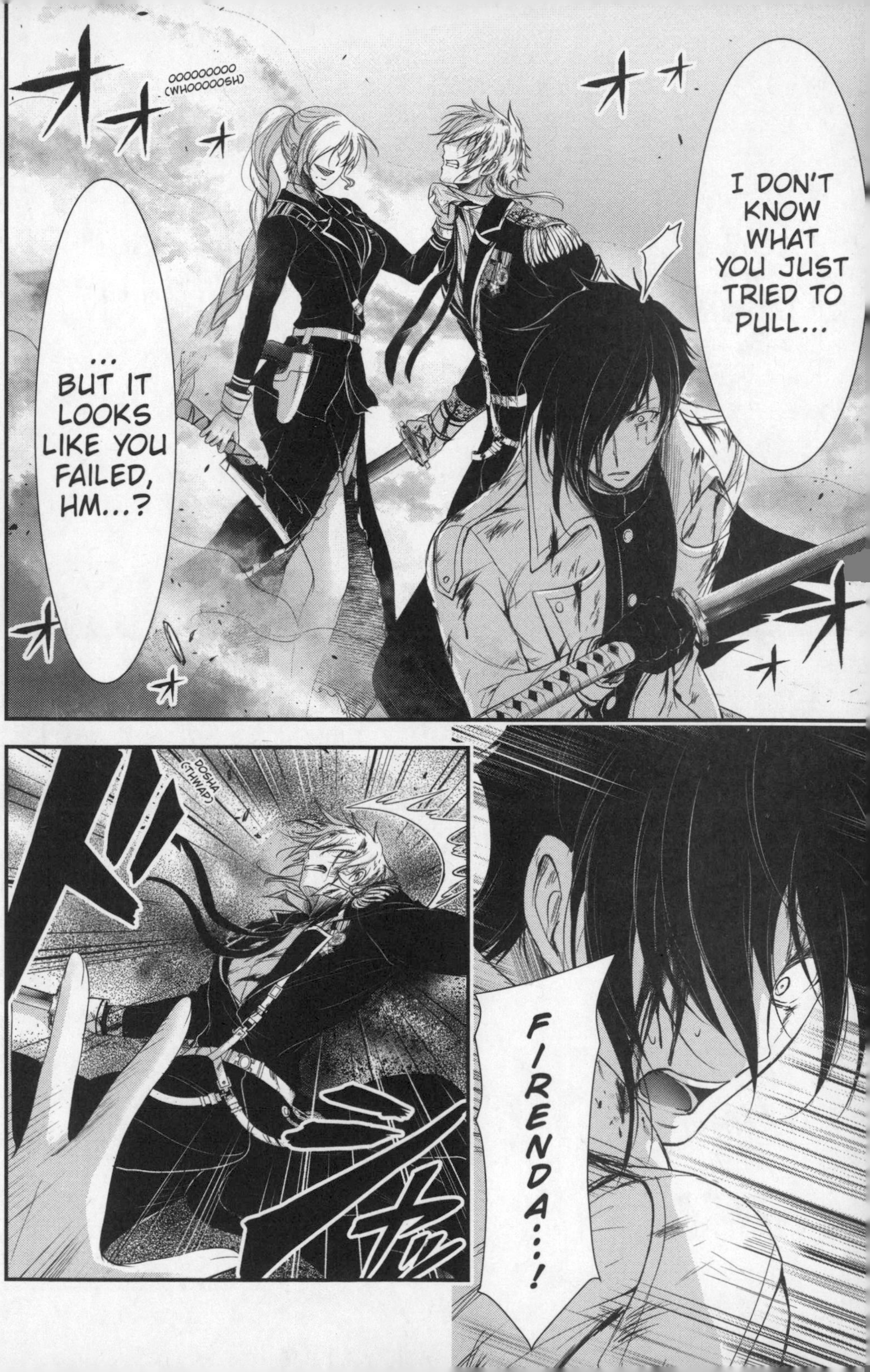
I DON'T KNOW WHAT YOU JUST TRIED TO PULL...
OOOOOOOOO (WHOOOOOSH)
... BUT IT LOOKS LIKE YOU FAILED, HM...?
FIRENDA...!
DOSHA (THWAP)

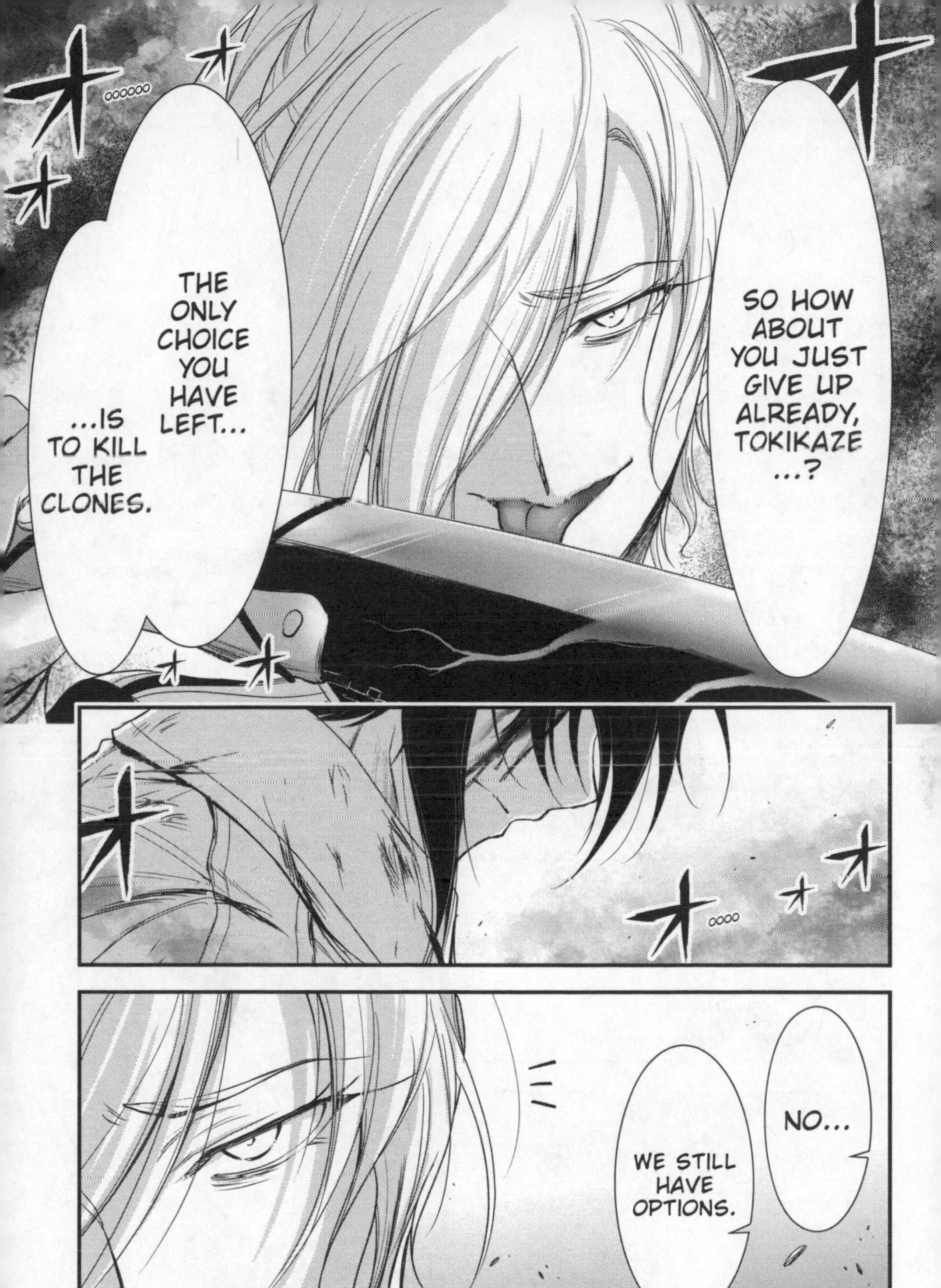
SO HOW ABOUT YOU JUST GIVE UP ALREADY, TOKIKAZE ...?
oooooo
THE ONLY CHOICE YOU HAVE LEFT...
...IS TO KILL THE CLONES.
oooo
NO...
WE STILL HAVE OPTIONS.

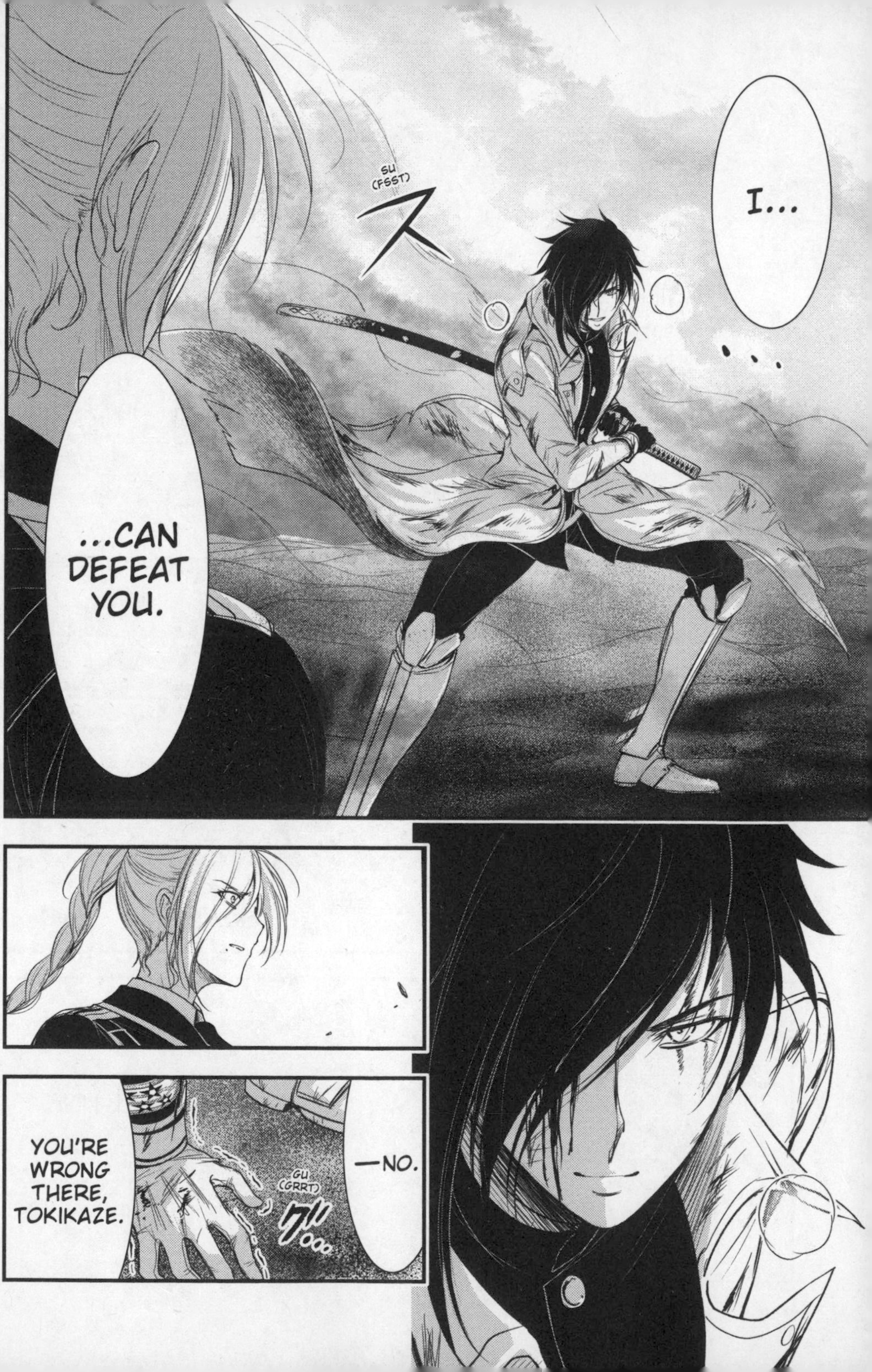
I...
...
SU (FSST)
...CAN DEFEAT YOU.
—NO.
GU (GRRT)
YOU'RE WRONG THERE, TOKIKAZE.

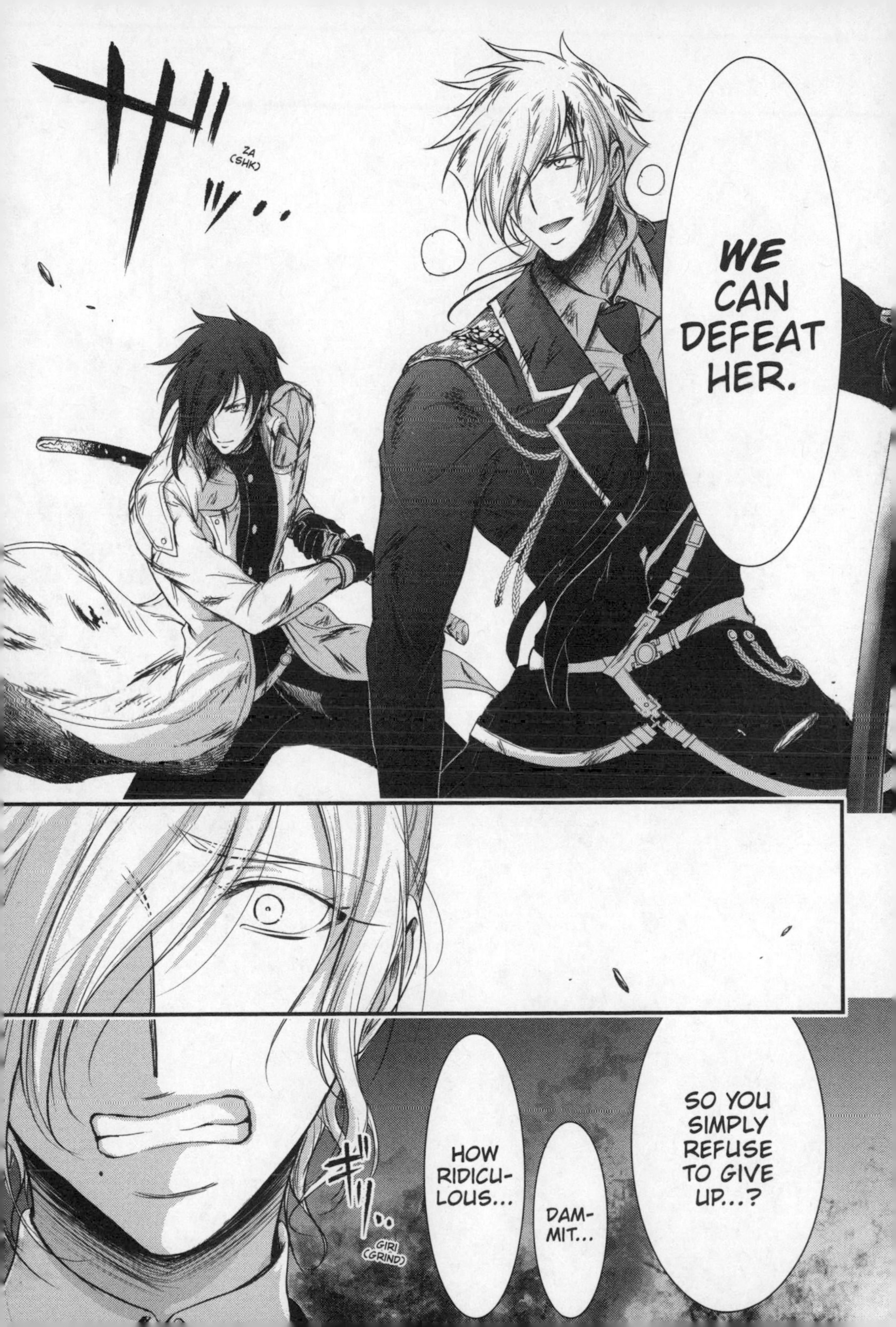
WE CAN DEFEAT HER.
ZA (SHK)
SO YOU SIMPLY REFUSE TO GIVE UP...?
DAM-MIT...
HOW RIDICU-LOUS...
GIRI (GRIND)

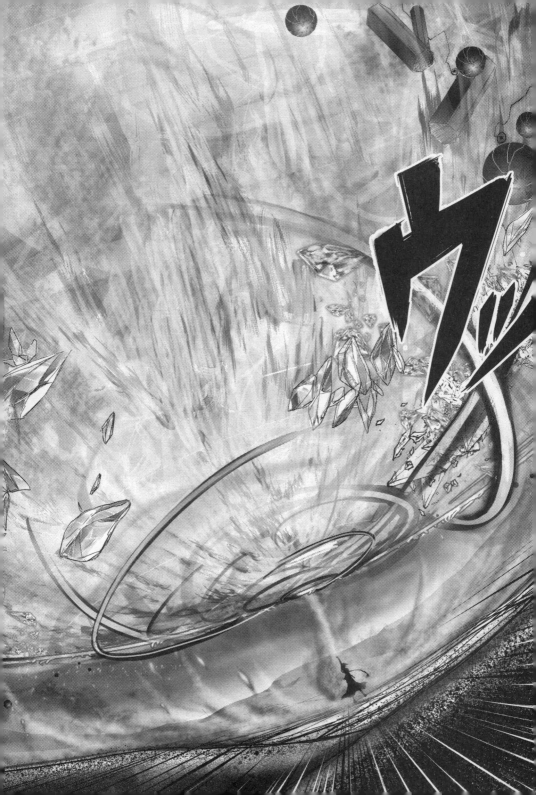

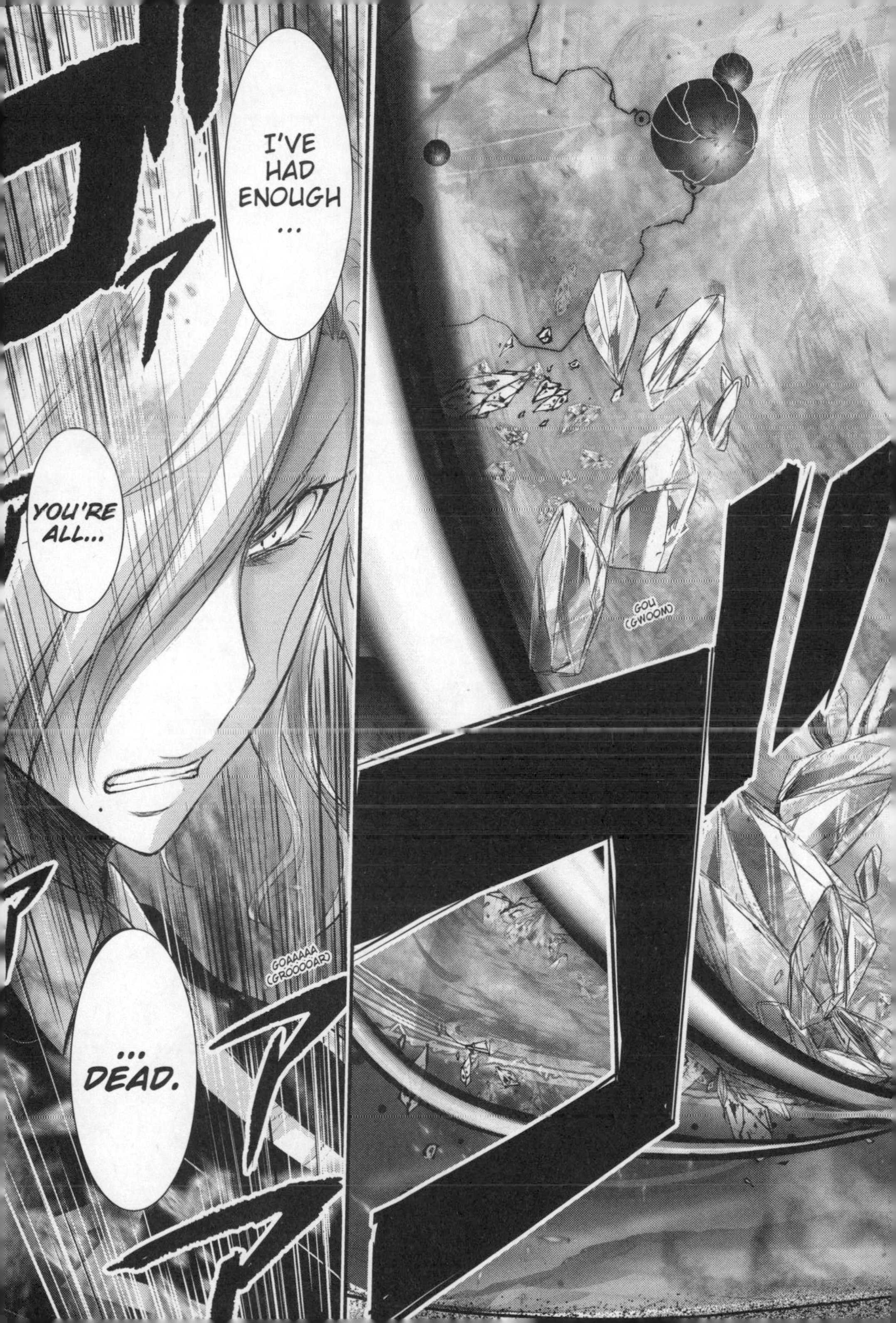
GOU (GWOOM)
I'VE HAD ENOUGH...
YOU'RE ALL...
GOAAAAA (GROOOOAR)
...DEAD.

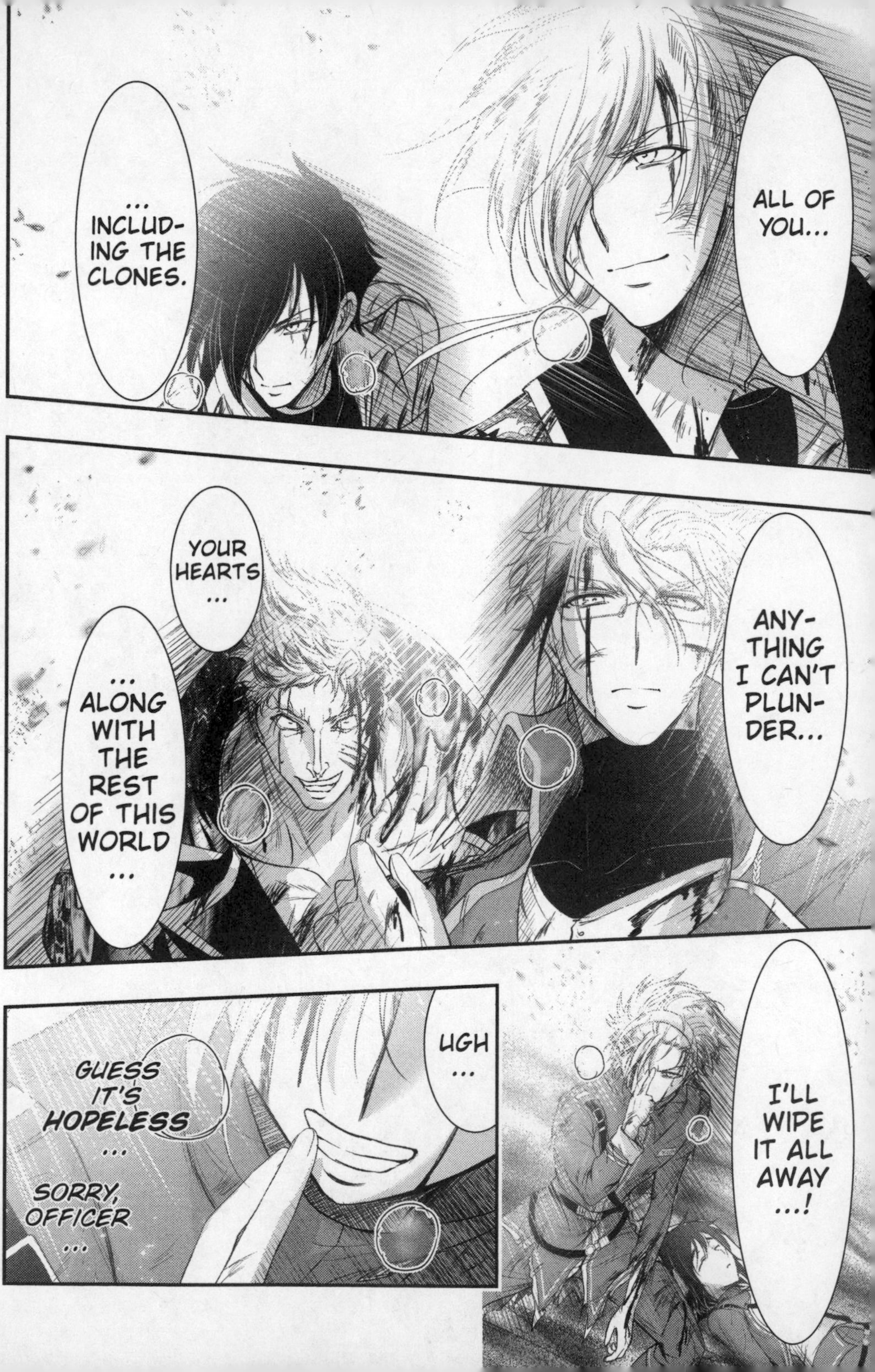
ALL OF YOU...
... INCLUDING THE CLONES.
ANYTHING I CAN'T PLUNDER...
YOUR HEARTS ...
... ALONG WITH THE REST OF THIS WORLD ...
I'LL WIPE IT ALL AWAY ...!
UGH ...
GUESS IT'S HOPELESS ...
SORRY, OFFICER ...

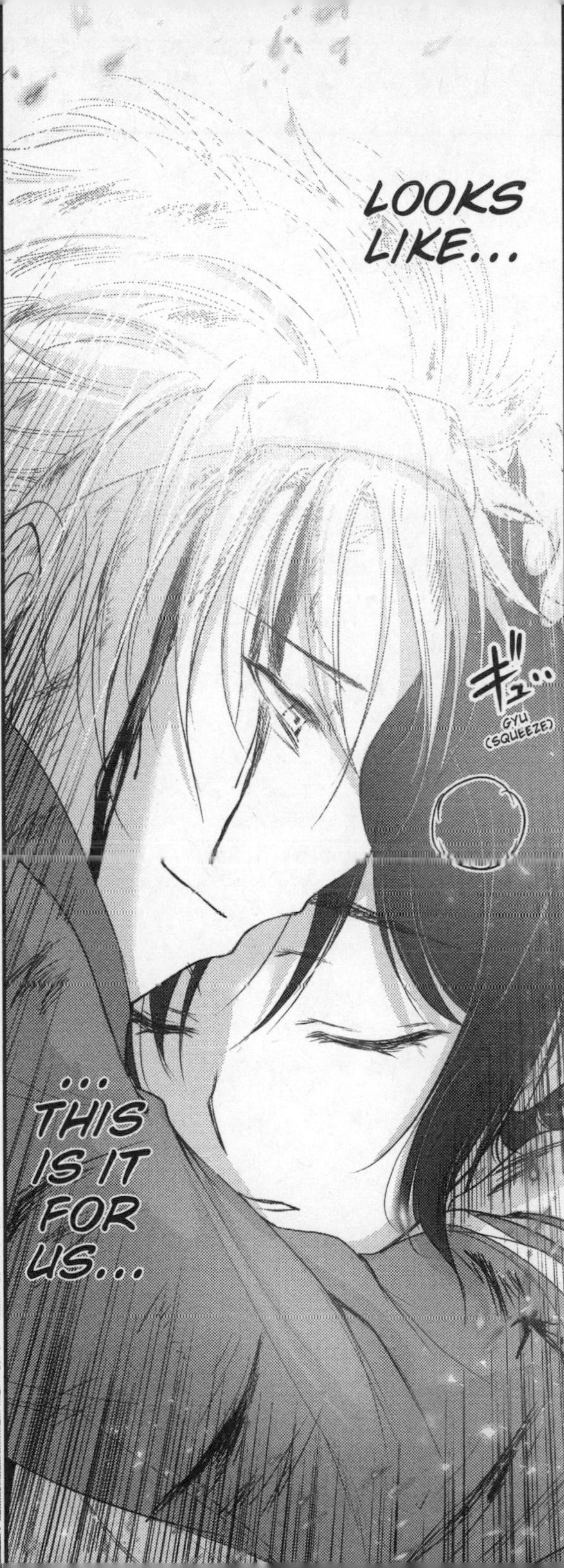
LOOKS LIKE...
ギュ..
GYU (SQUEEZE)
...THIS IS IT FOR US...
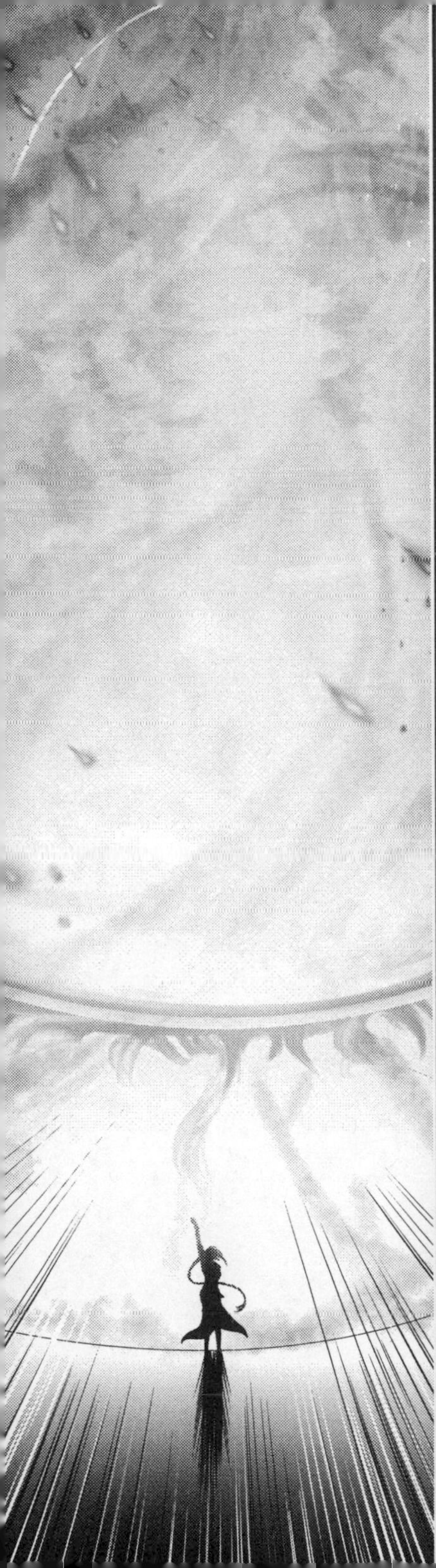

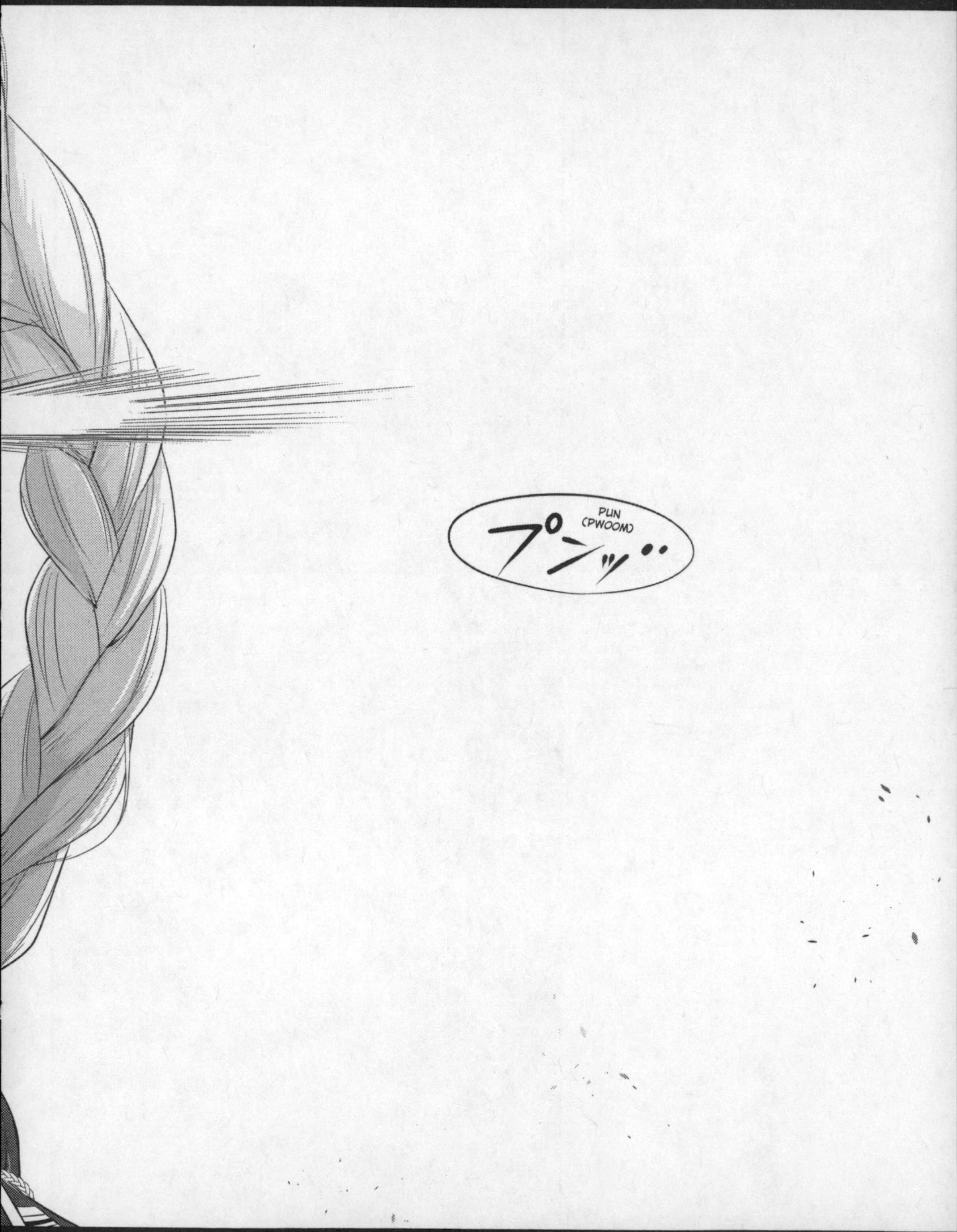
PUN
(PWOOM)
プンッ

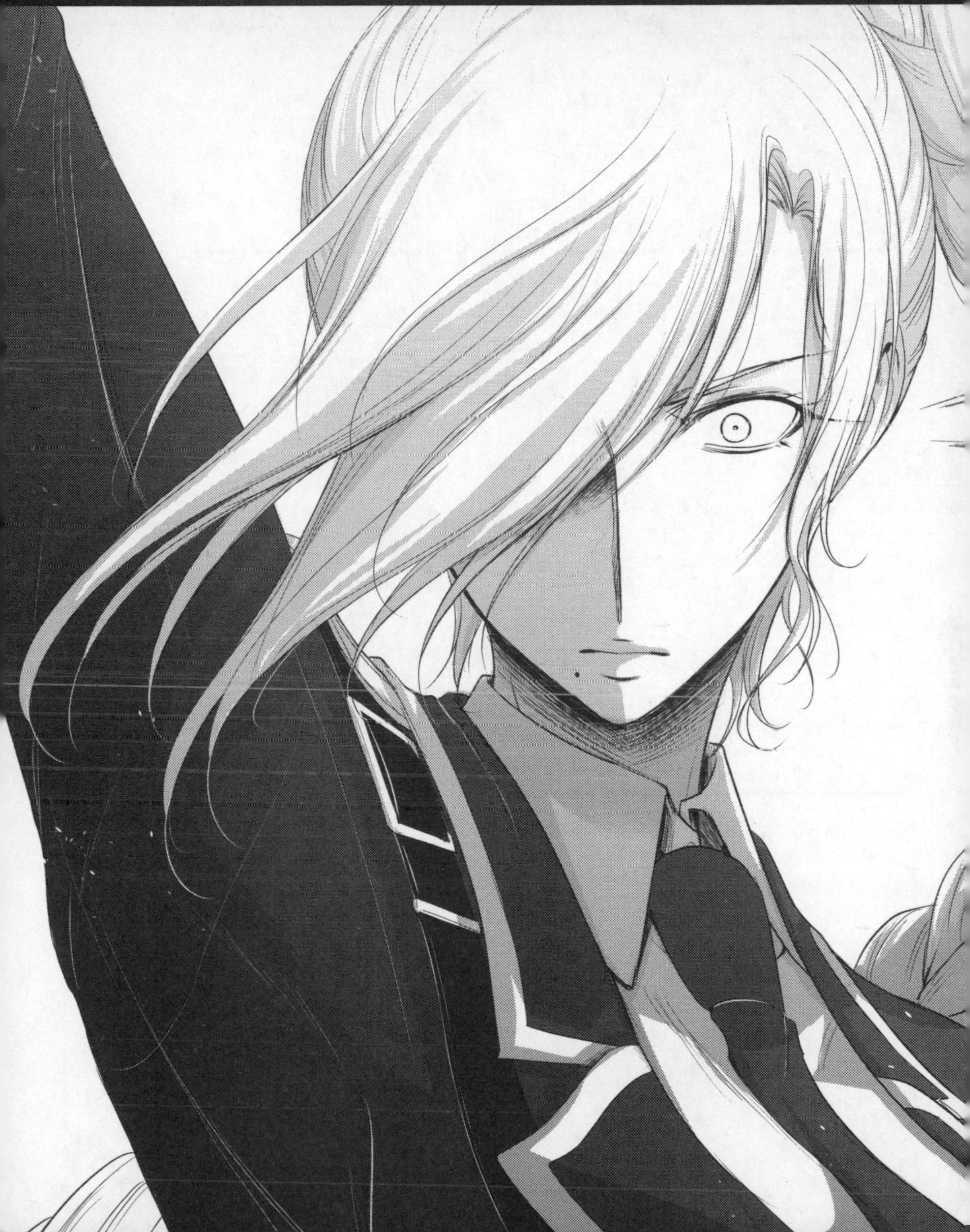

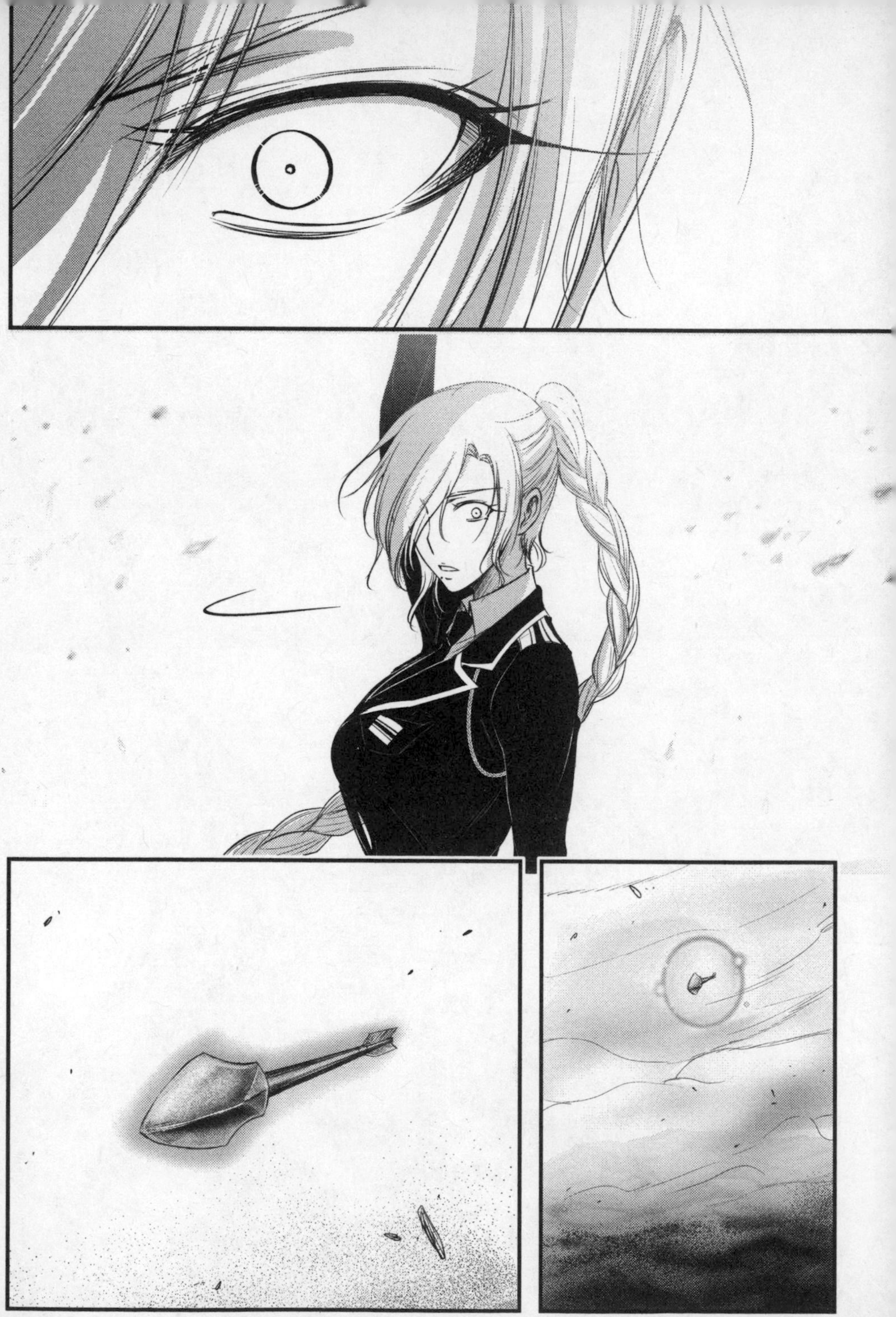

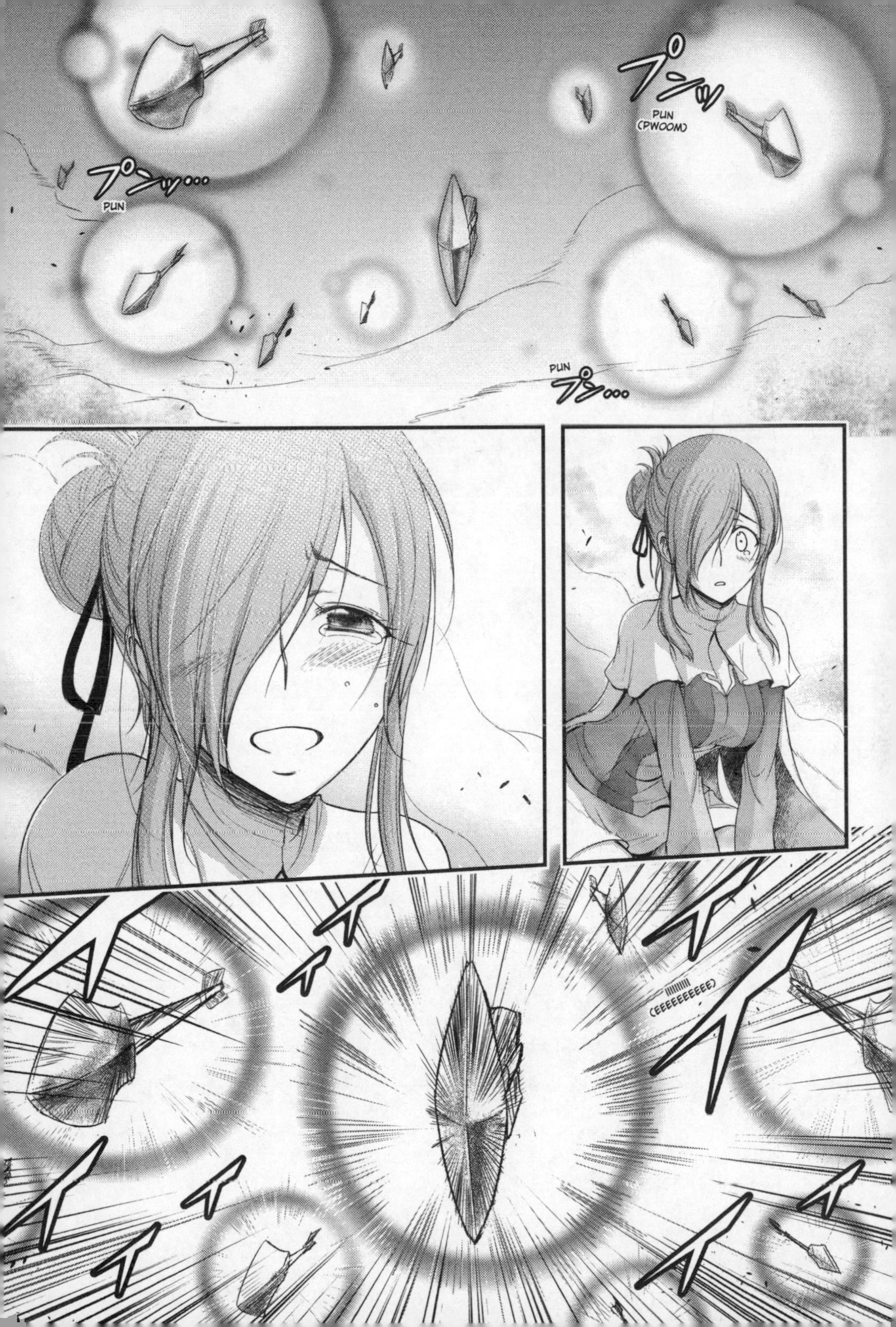
プンッ
PUN
(PWOOM)
プンッ…
PUN
PUN
プン…
IIIIIIIIIII
(EEEEEEEEEEE)

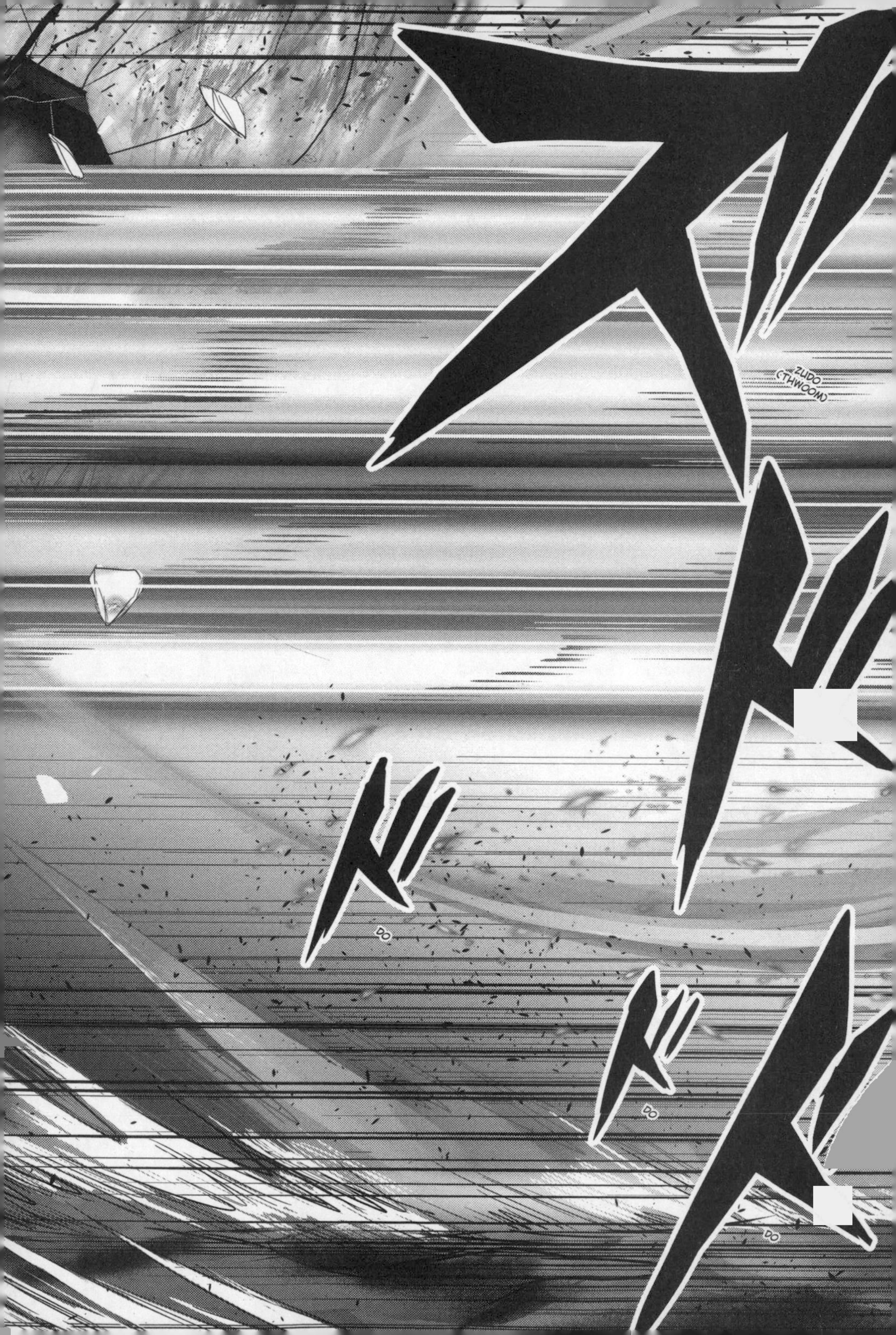
ZUDO
(THWOOM)
DO
DO
DO

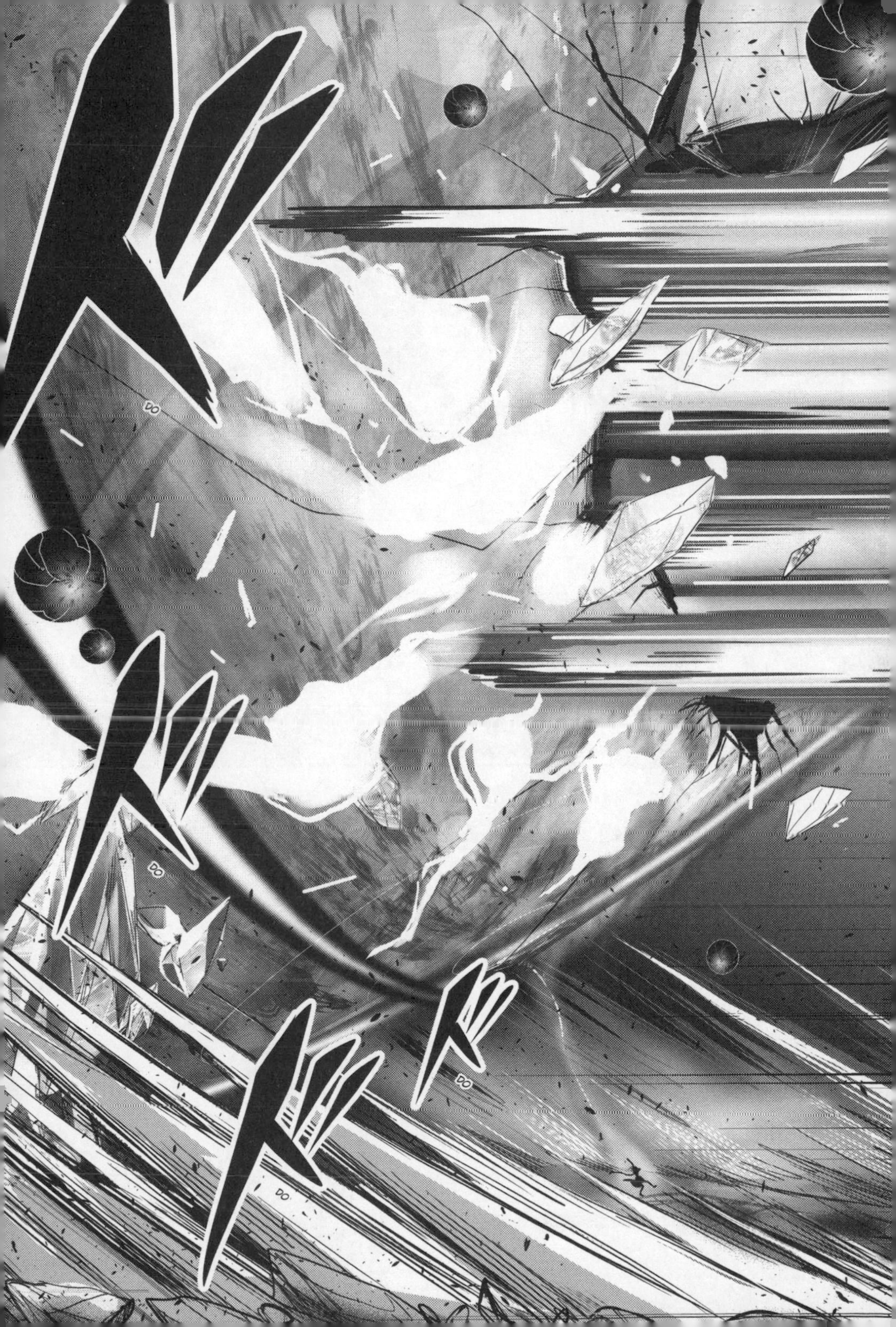
DO
DO
DO
DO

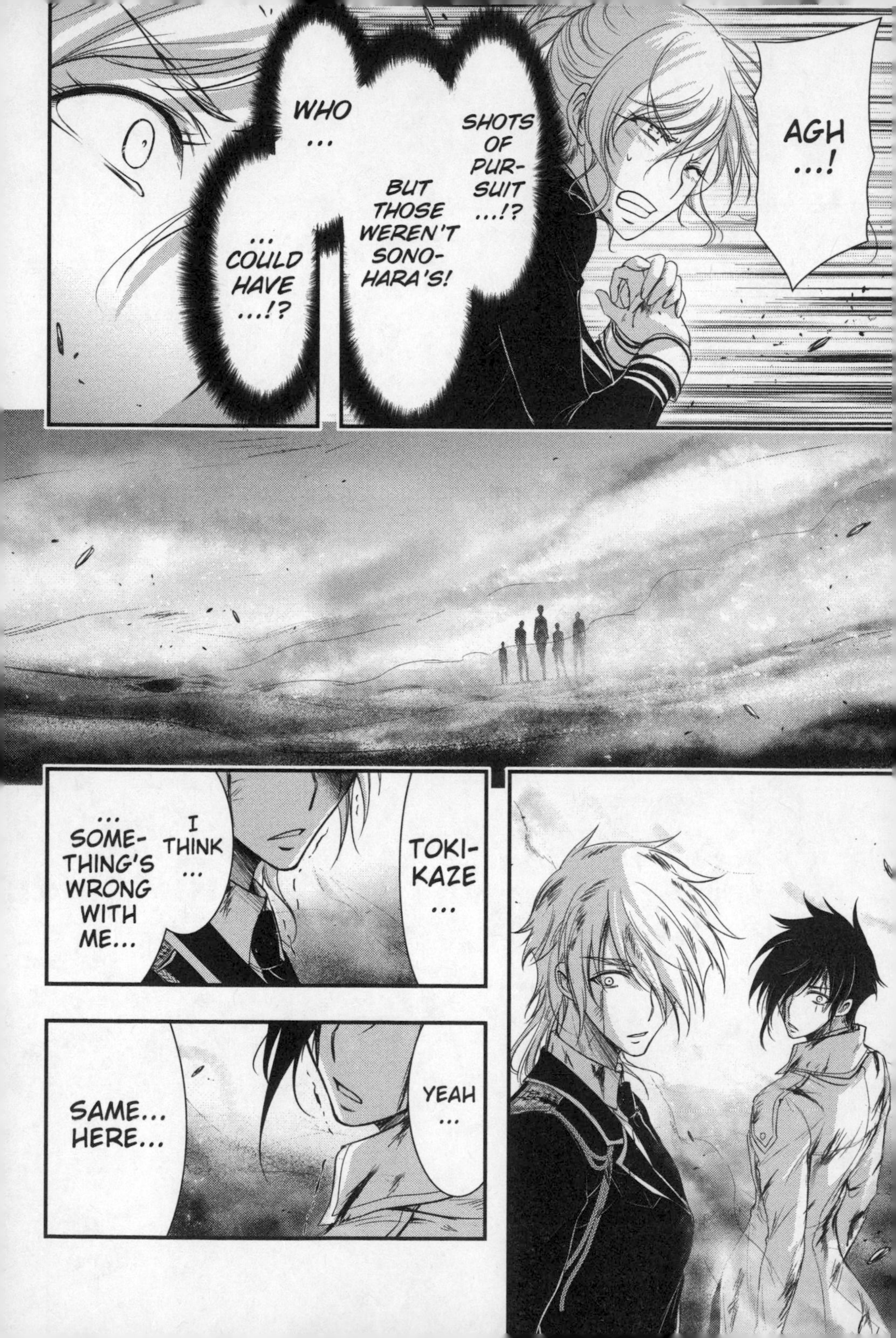
AGH ...!
SHOTS OF PUR-SUIT ...!?
BUT THOSE WEREN'T SONO-HARA'S!
WHO ...
... COULD HAVE ...!?
TOKI-KAZE ...
I THINK ...
... SOME-THING'S WRONG WITH ME...
YEAH ...
SAME... HERE...

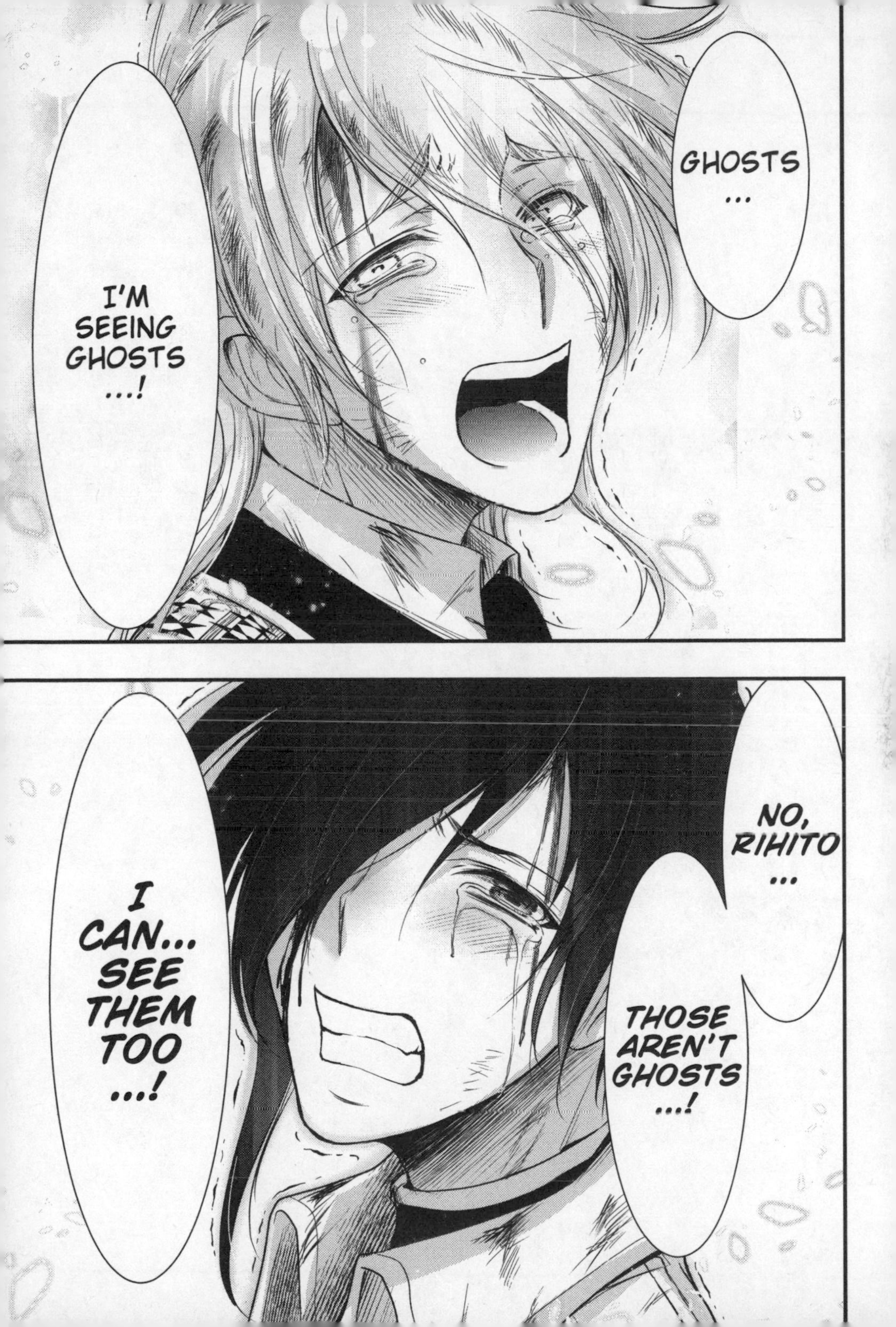
GHOSTS ...
I'M SEEING GHOSTS ...!
NO, RIHITO ...
THOSE AREN'T GHOSTS ...!
I CAN... SEE THEM TOO ...!

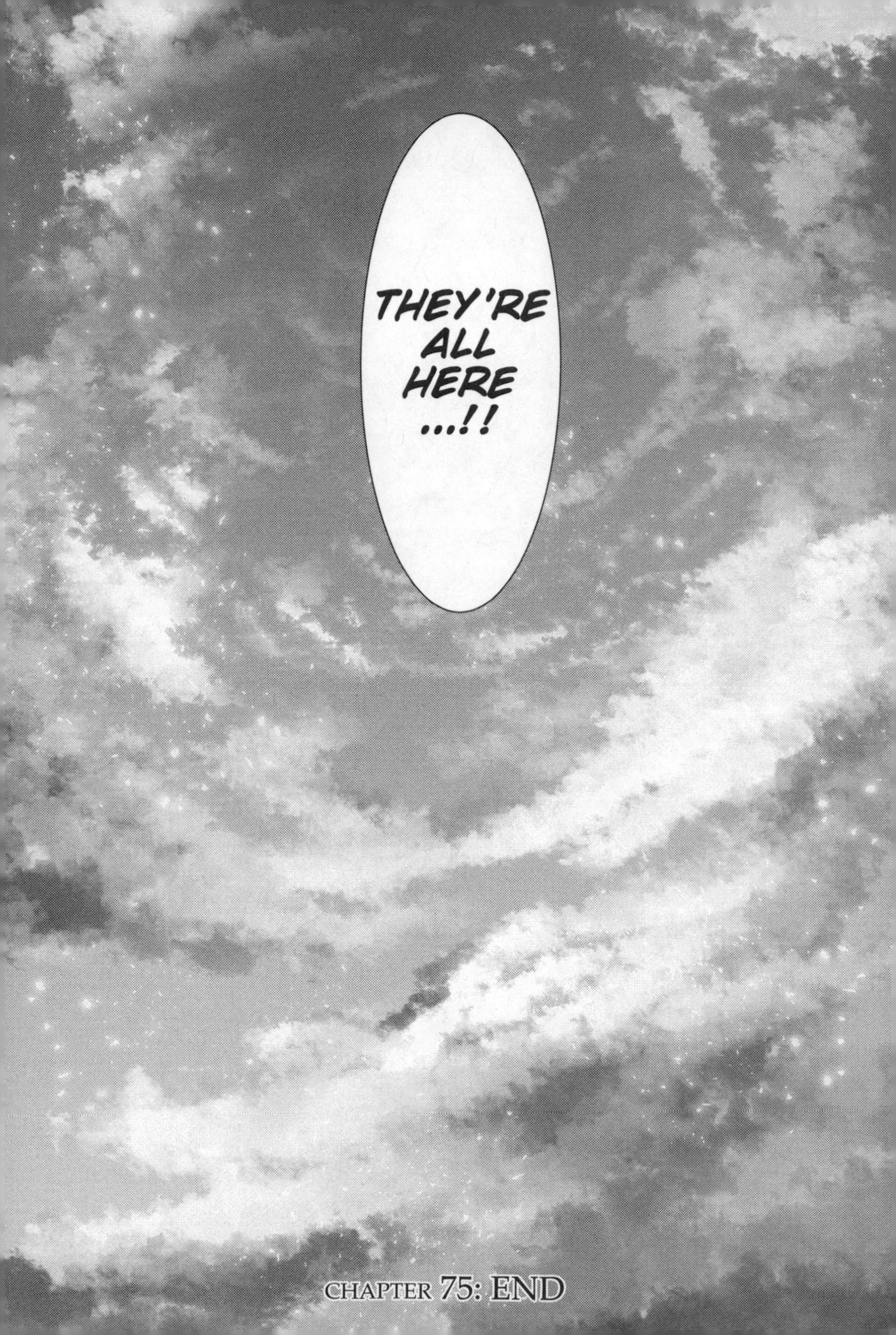
THEY'RE ALL HERE ...!!

CHAPTER 75: END

PLUNDERER

PLUNDERER

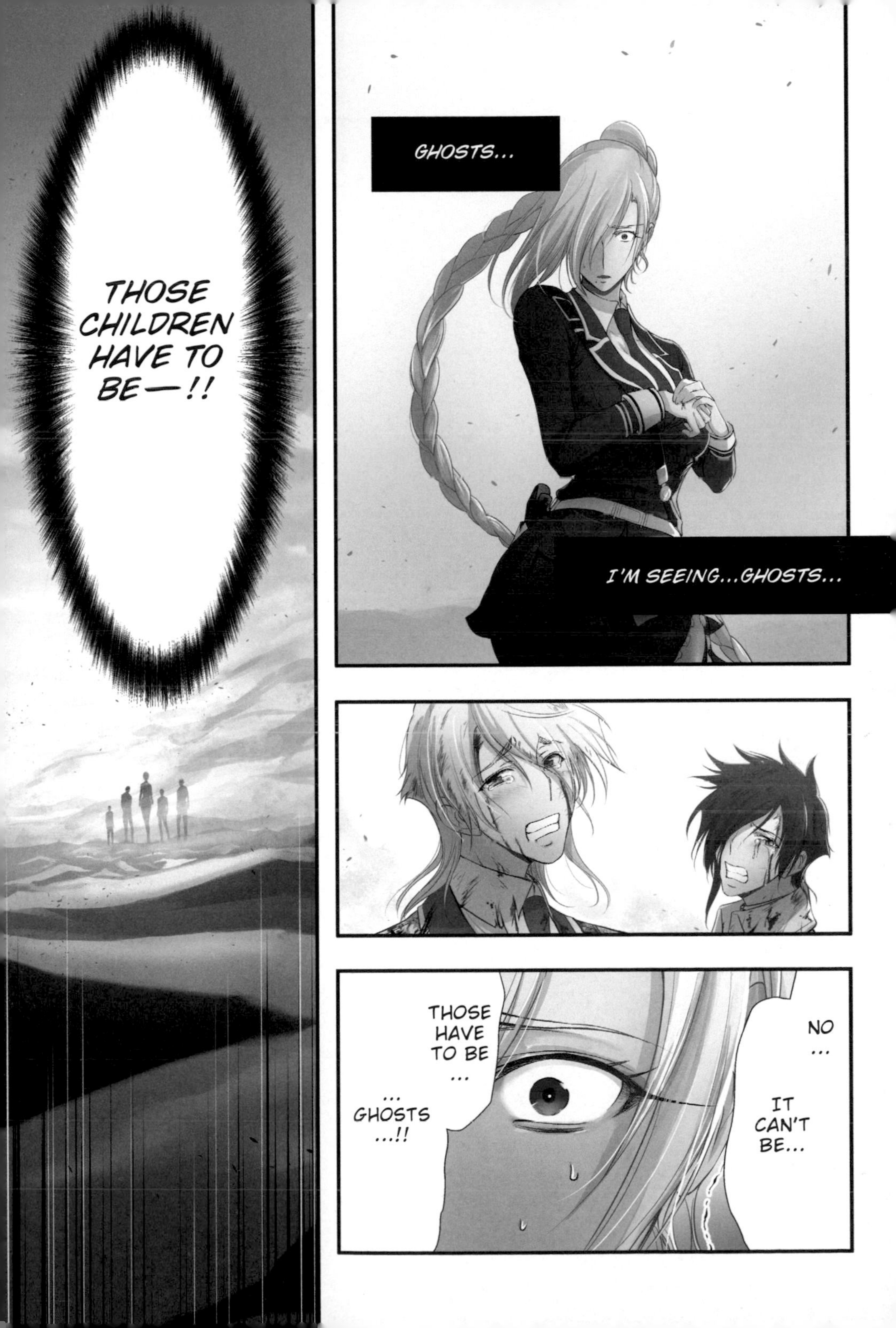
GHOSTS...
I'M SEEING...GHOSTS...
NO ... IT CAN'T BE...
THOSE HAVE TO BE ... ...GHOSTS ...!!
THOSE CHILDREN HAVE TO BE—!!

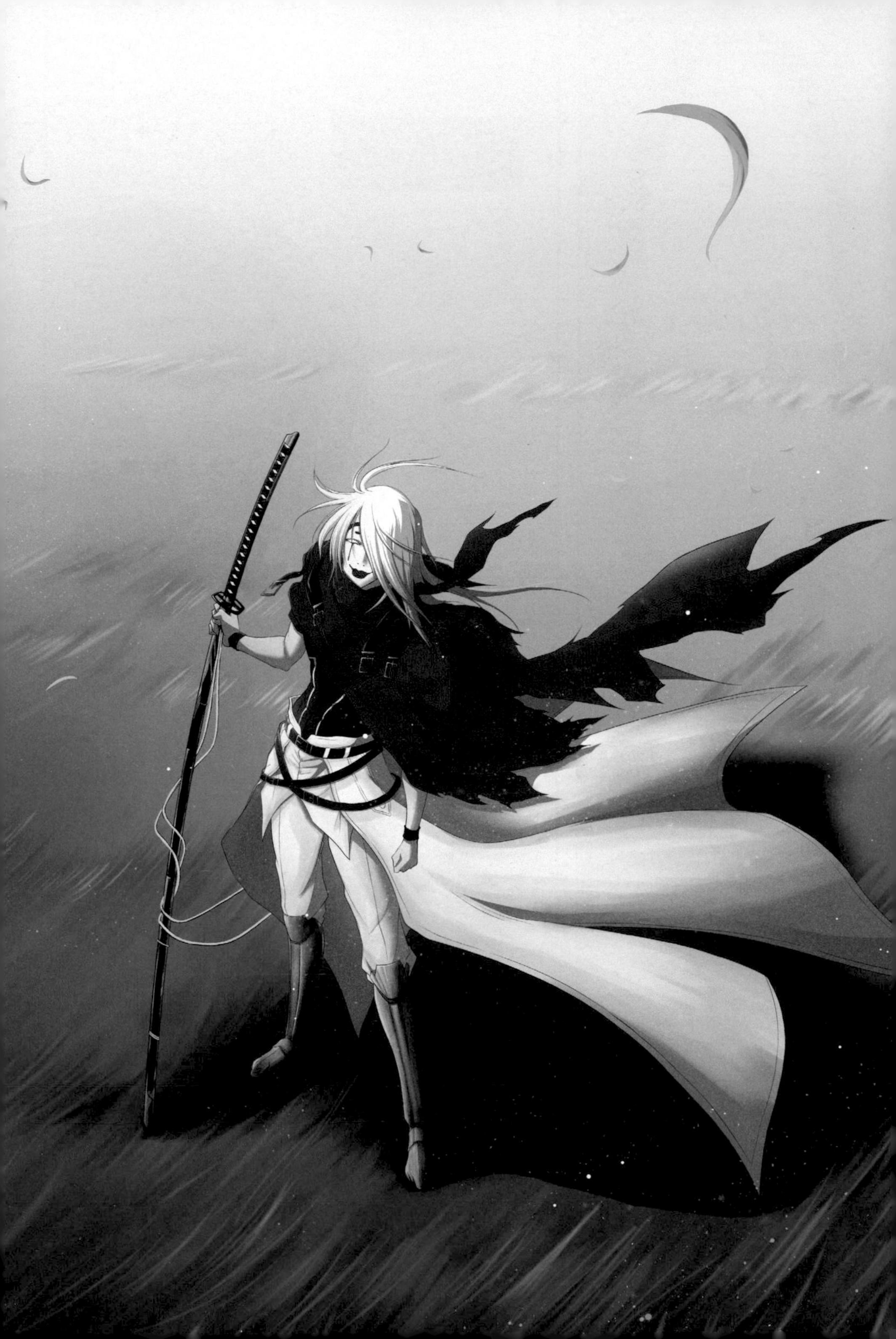

CHAPTER 76: FAIR

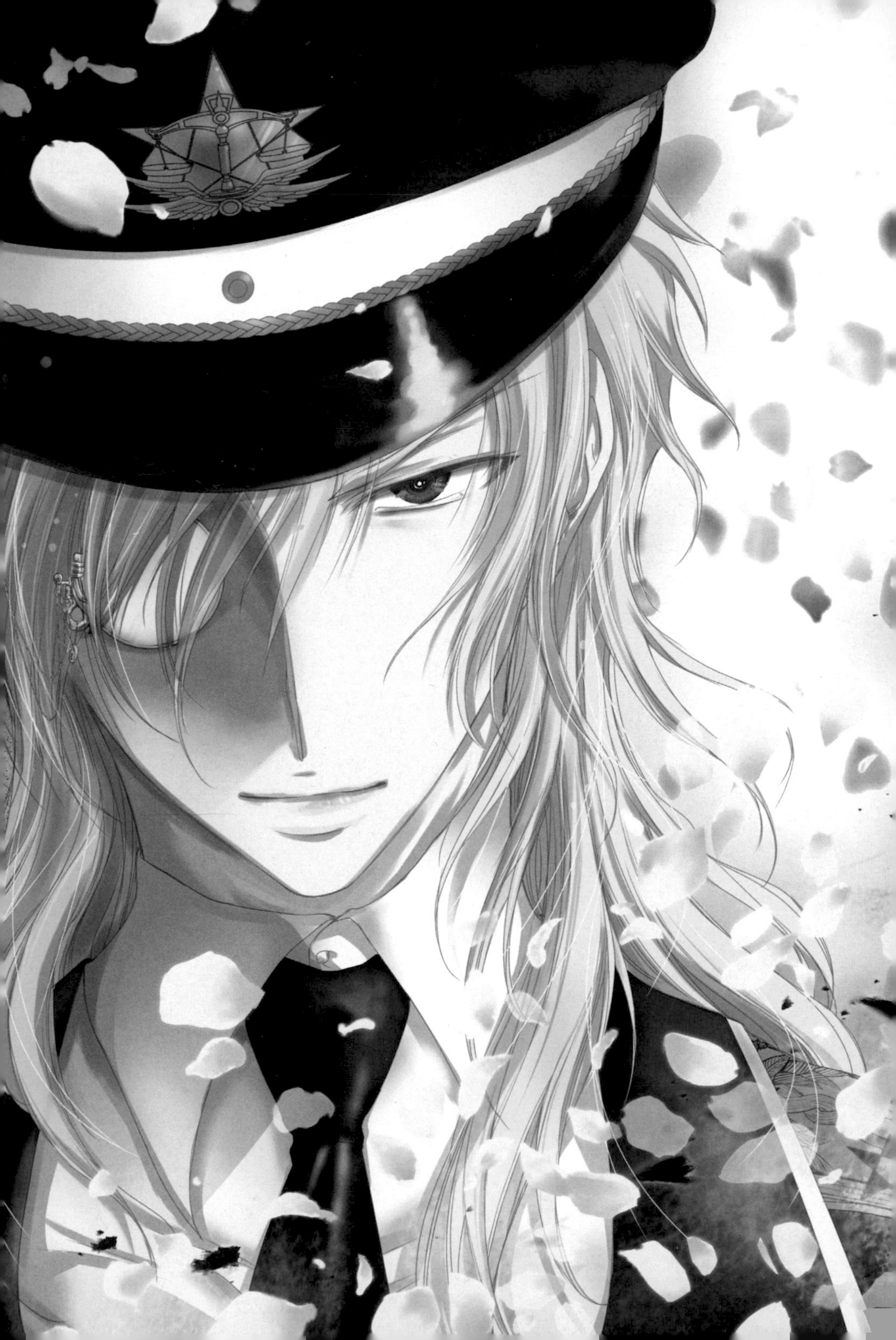

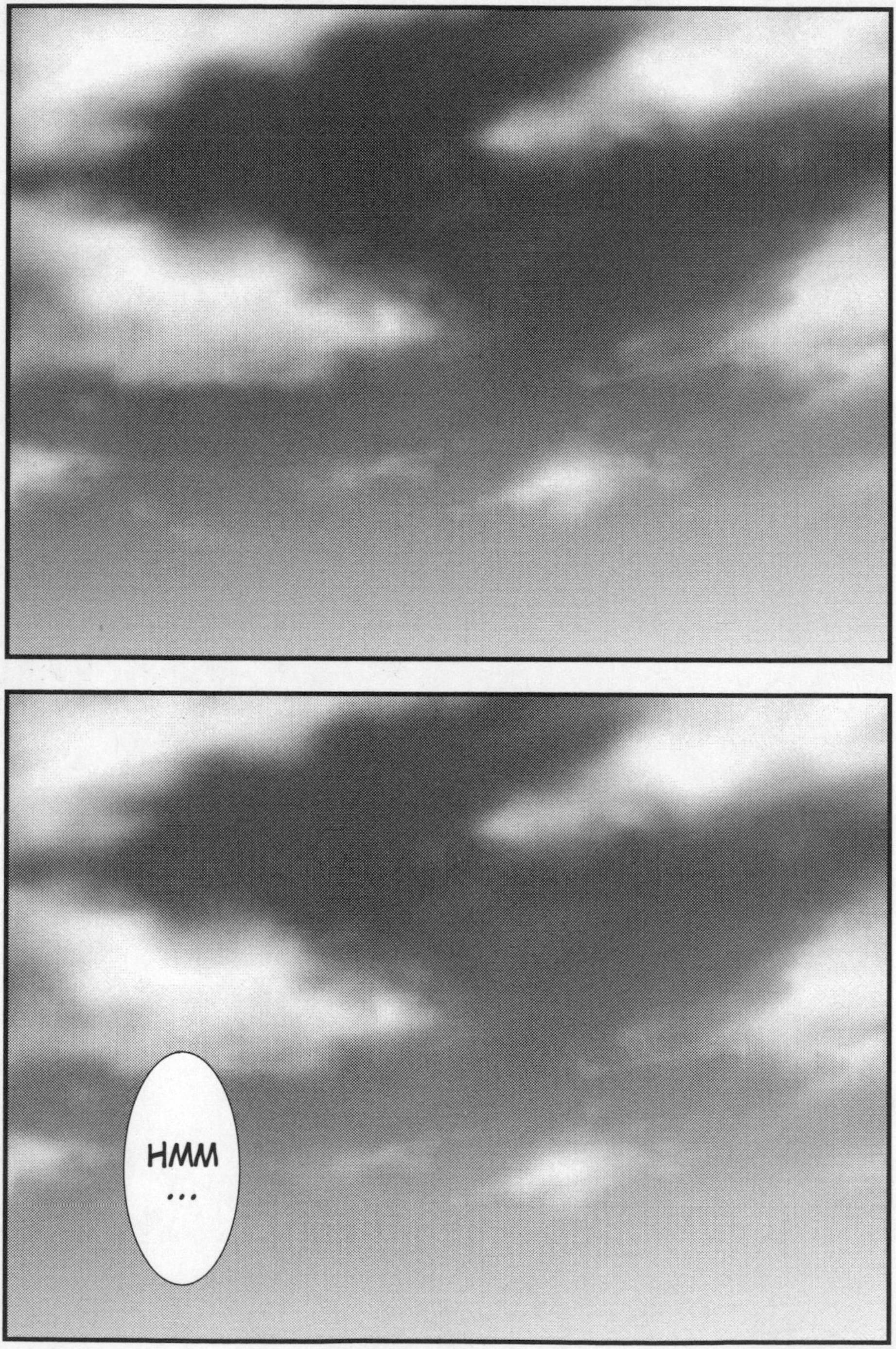
HMM
...

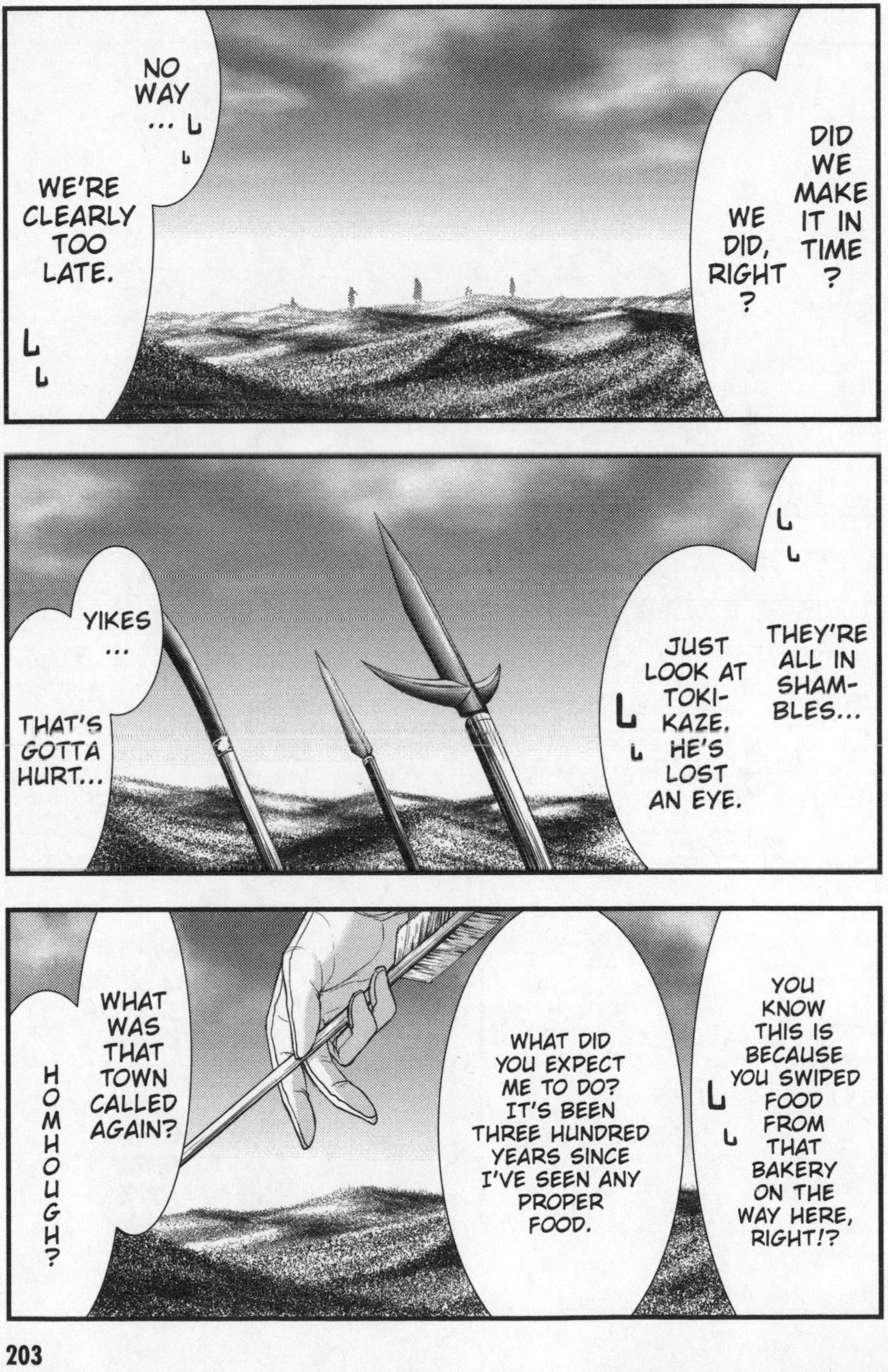
DID WE MAKE IT IN TIME?
WE DID, RIGHT?
NO WAY...
WE'RE CLEARLY TOO LATE.
THEY'RE ALL IN SHAMBLES...
JUST LOOK AT TOKI-KAZE. HE'S LOST AN EYE.
YIKES...
THAT'S GOTTA HURT...
YOU KNOW THIS IS BECAUSE YOU SWIPED FOOD FROM THAT BAKERY ON THE WAY HERE, RIGHT!?
WHAT DID YOU EXPECT ME TO DO? IT'S BEEN THREE HUNDRED YEARS SINCE I'VE SEEN ANY PROPER FOOD.
WHAT WAS THAT TOWN CALLED AGAIN?
HOMHOUGH?

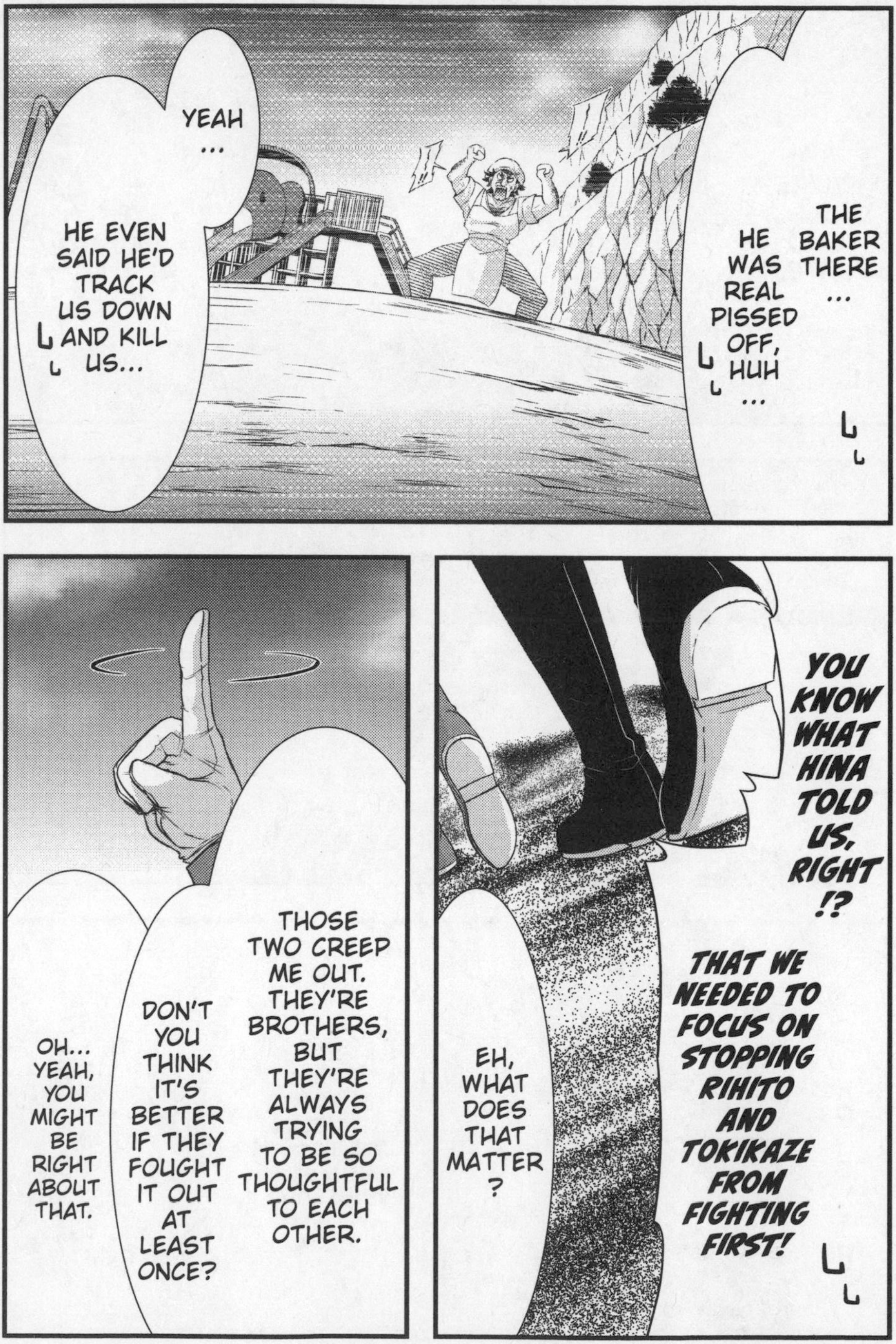
THE BAKER THERE ... HE WAS REAL PISSED OFF, HUH ...
YEAH ... HE EVEN SAID HE'D TRACK US DOWN AND KILL US...
YOU KNOW WHAT HINA TOLD US, RIGHT!?
THAT WE NEEDED TO FOCUS ON STOPPING RIHITO AND TOKIKAZE FROM FIGHTING FIRST!
EH, WHAT DOES THAT MATTER?
THOSE TWO CREEP ME OUT. THEY'RE BROTHERS, BUT THEY'RE ALWAYS TRYING TO BE SO THOUGHTFUL TO EACH OTHER.
DON'T YOU THINK IT'S BETTER IF THEY FOUGHT IT OUT AT LEAST ONCE?
OH... YEAH, YOU MIGHT BE RIGHT ABOUT THAT.

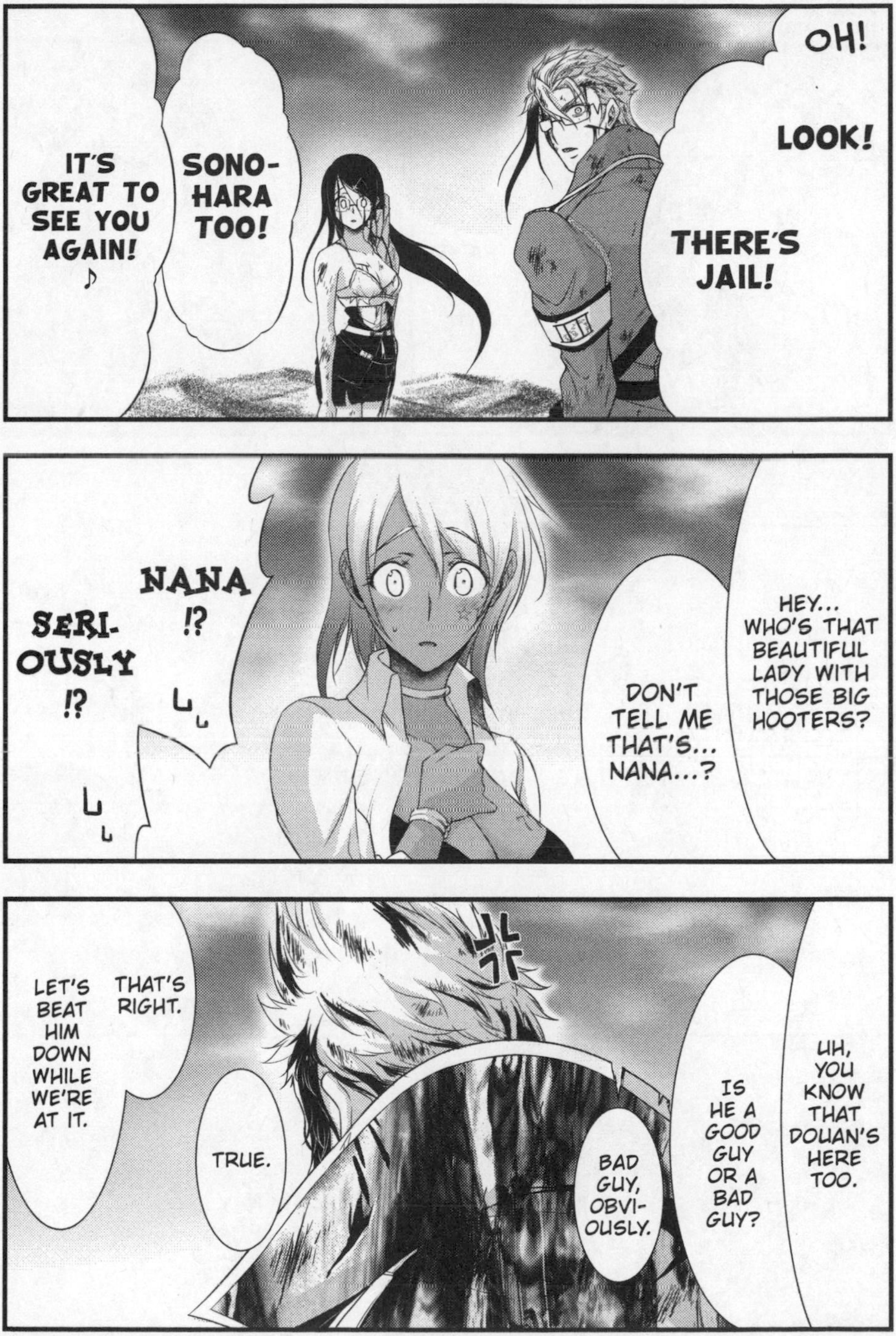
OH! LOOK! THERE'S JAIL!
SONO-HARA TOO!
IT'S GREAT TO SEE YOU AGAIN! ♪
HEY... WHO'S THAT BEAUTIFUL LADY WITH THOSE BIG HOOTERS?
DON'T TELL ME THAT'S... NANA...?
NANA !?
SERI-OUSLY !?
UH, YOU KNOW THAT DOUAN'S HERE TOO.
IS HE A GOOD GUY OR A BAD GUY?
BAD GUY, OBVI-OUSLY.
TRUE.
THAT'S RIGHT.
LET'S BEAT HIM DOWN WHILE WE'RE AT IT.

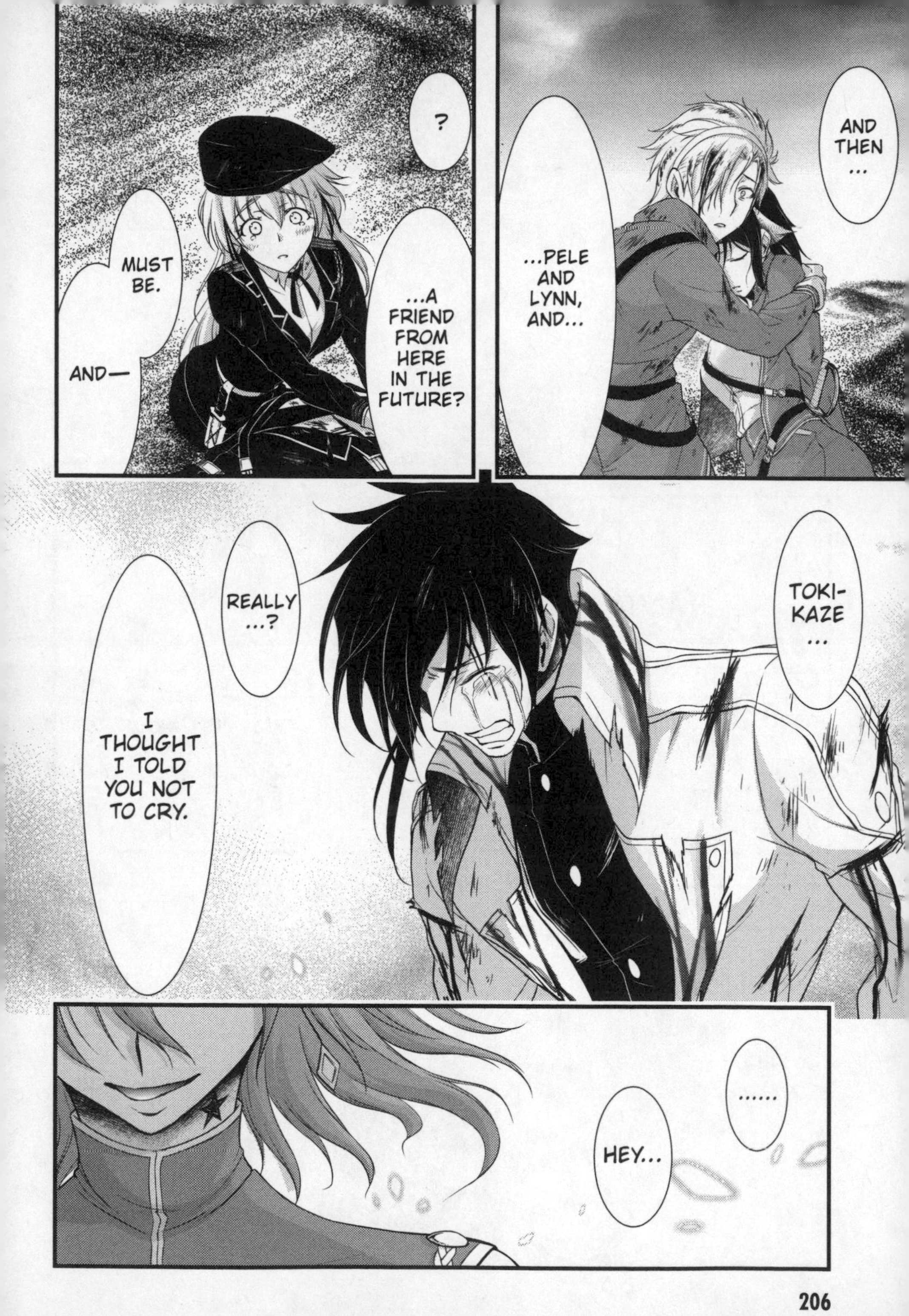
AND THEN ...
...PELE AND LYNN, AND...
?
...A FRIEND FROM HERE IN THE FUTURE?
MUST BE.
AND—
TOKI-KAZE ...
REALLY ...?
I THOUGHT I TOLD YOU NOT TO CRY.
......
HEY...

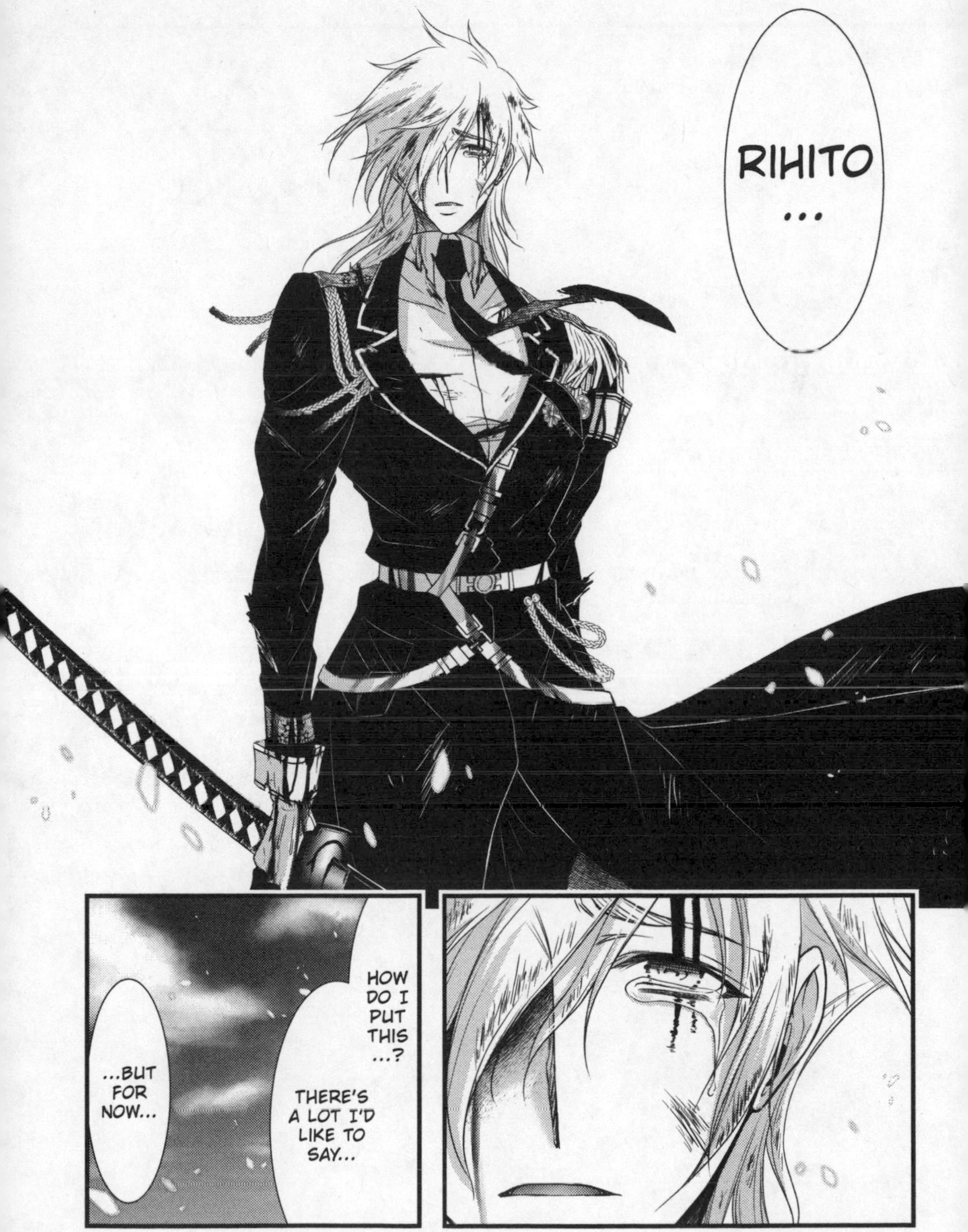
RIHITO
...
HOW DO I PUT THIS...?
THERE'S A LOT I'D LIKE TO SAY...
...BUT FOR NOW...

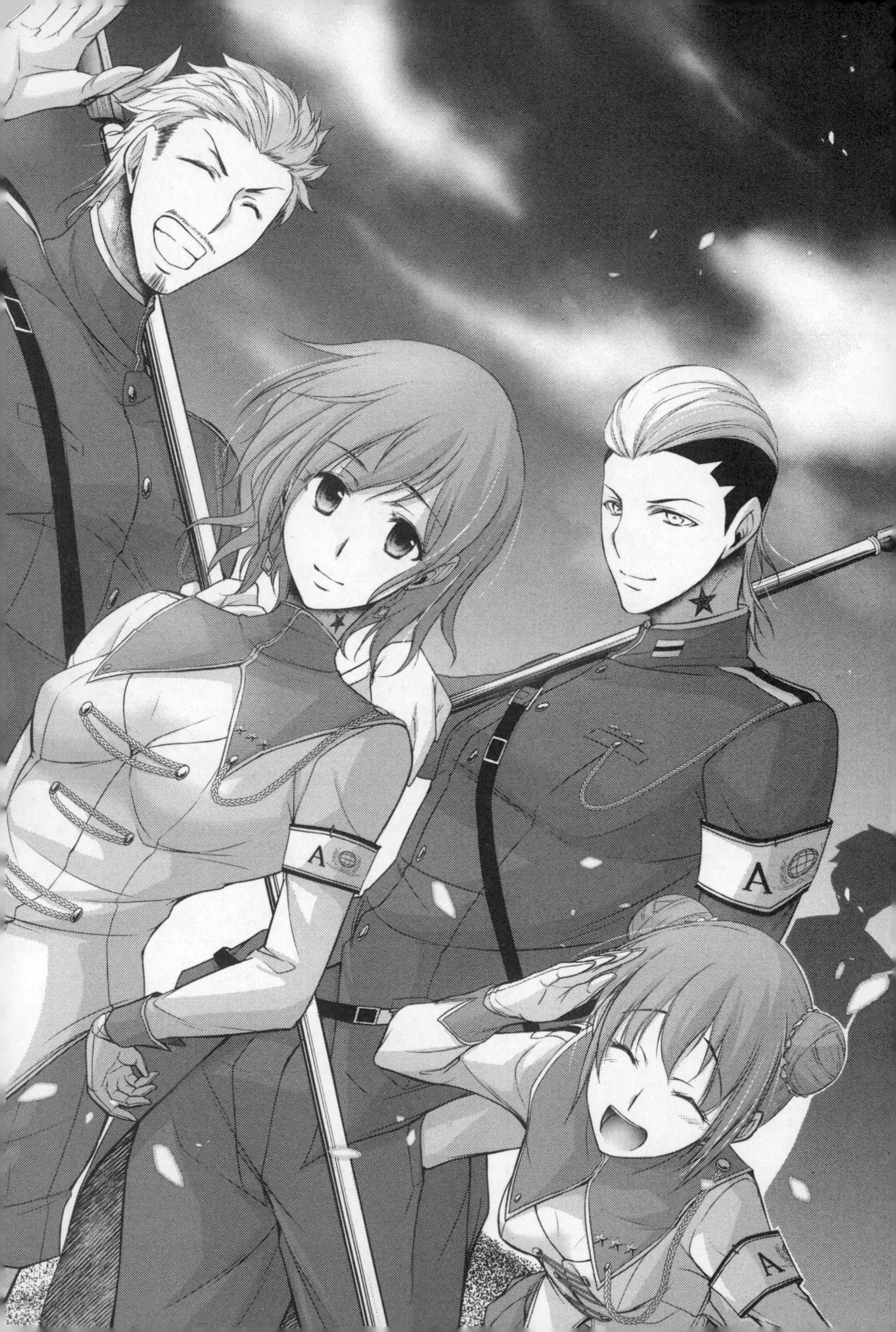

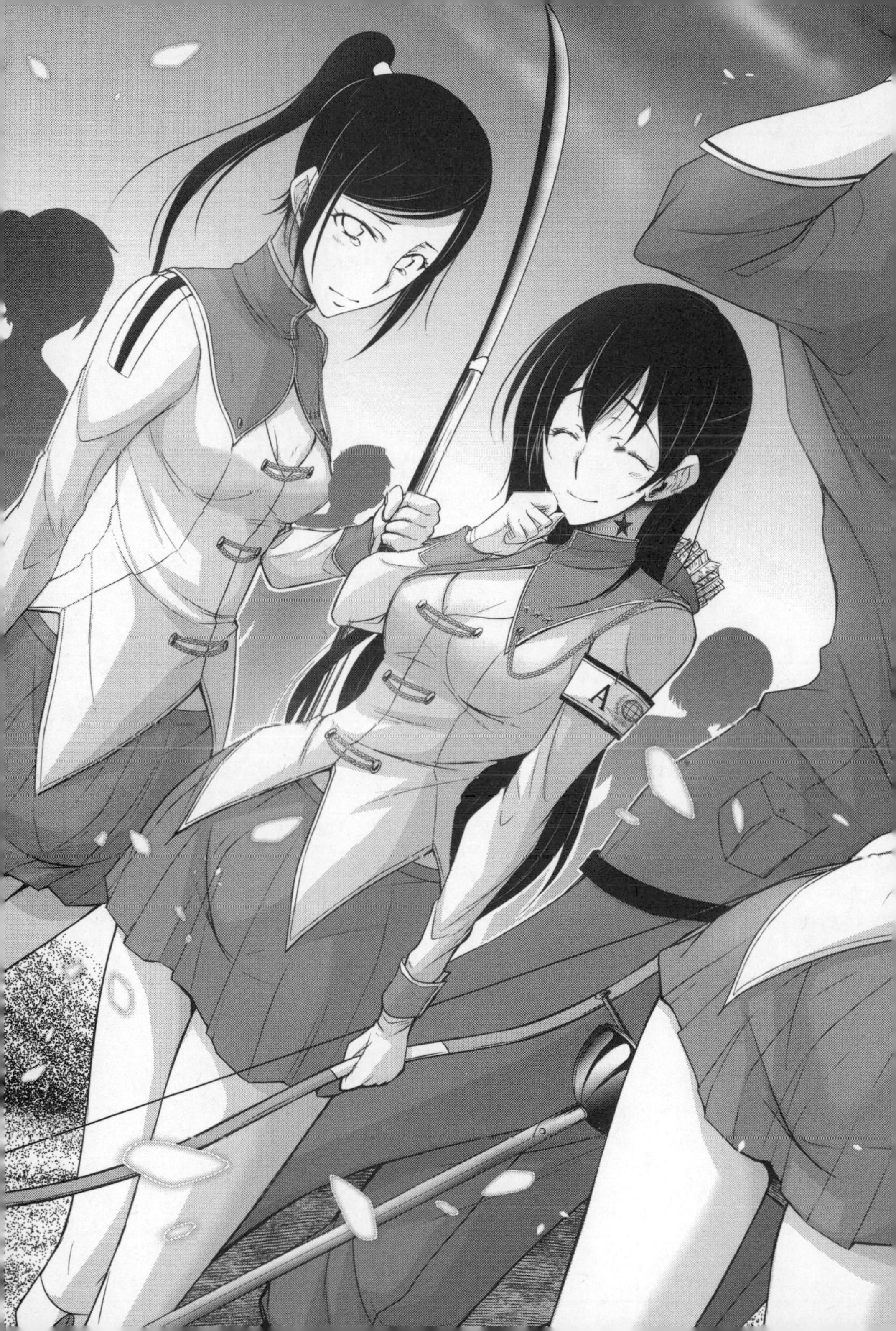

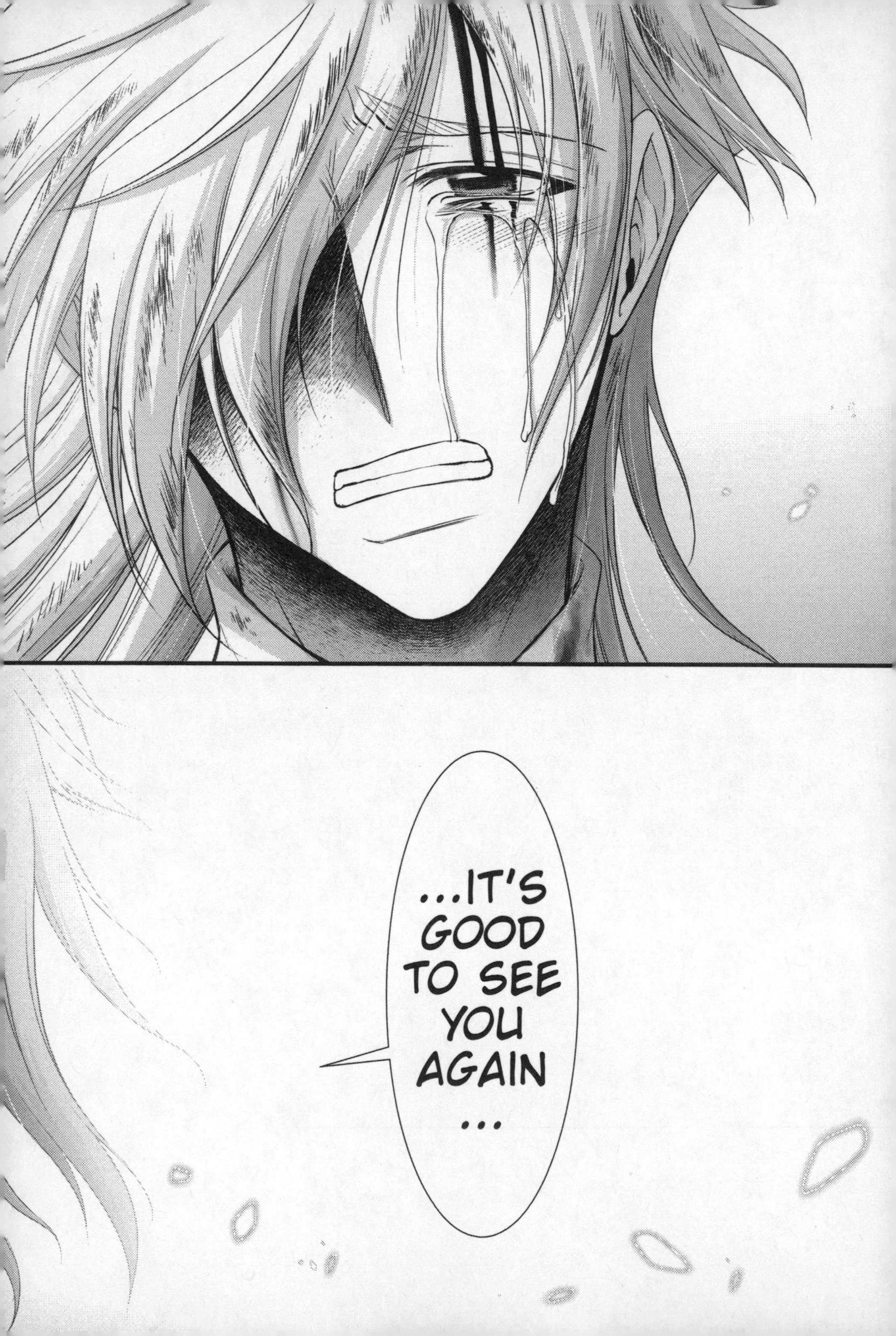
...IT'S GOOD TO SEE YOU AGAIN ...

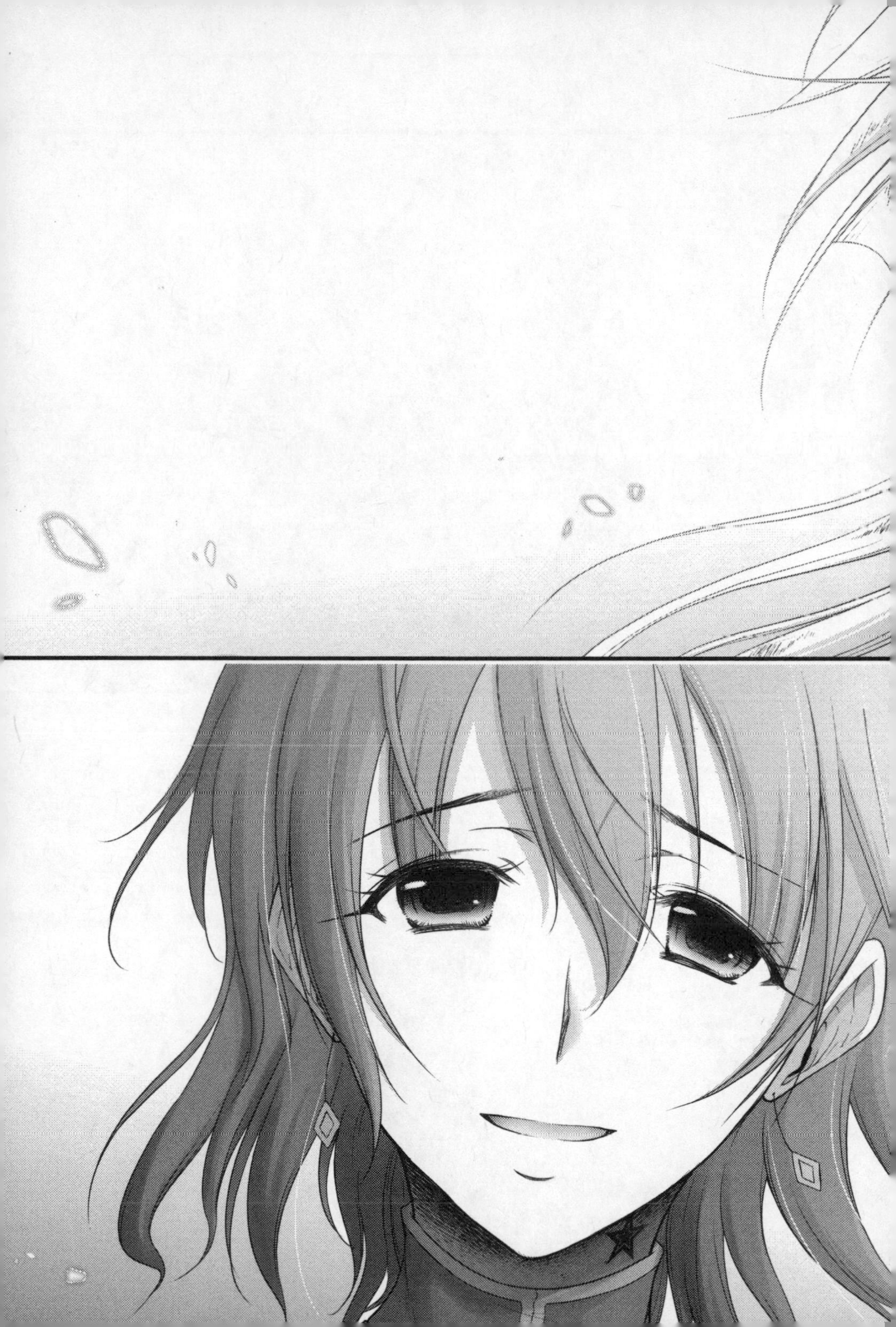

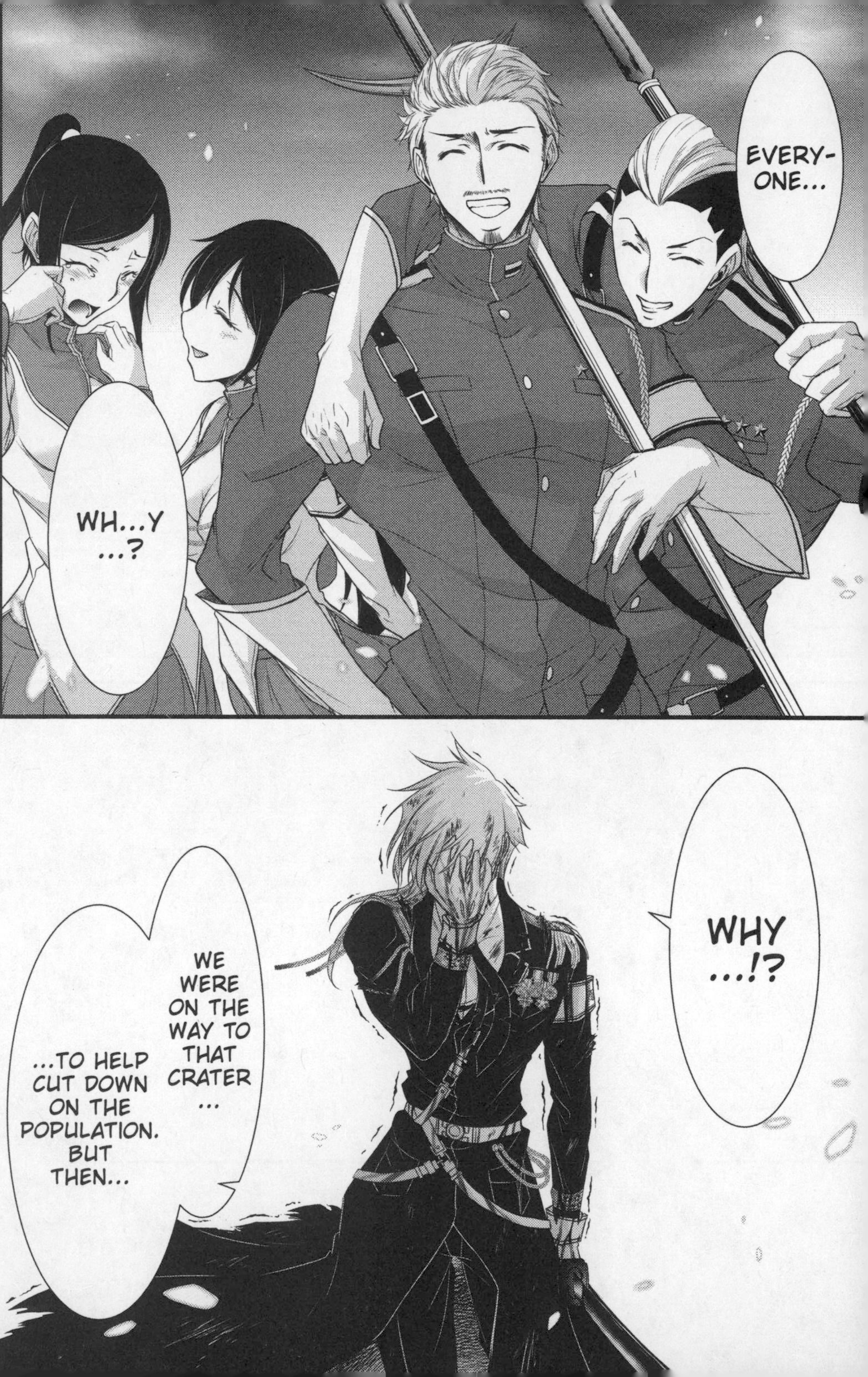
EVERY-ONE...
WH...Y ...?
WHY ...!?
WE WERE ON THE WAY TO THAT CRATER ...
...TO HELP CUT DOWN ON THE POPULATION. BUT THEN...

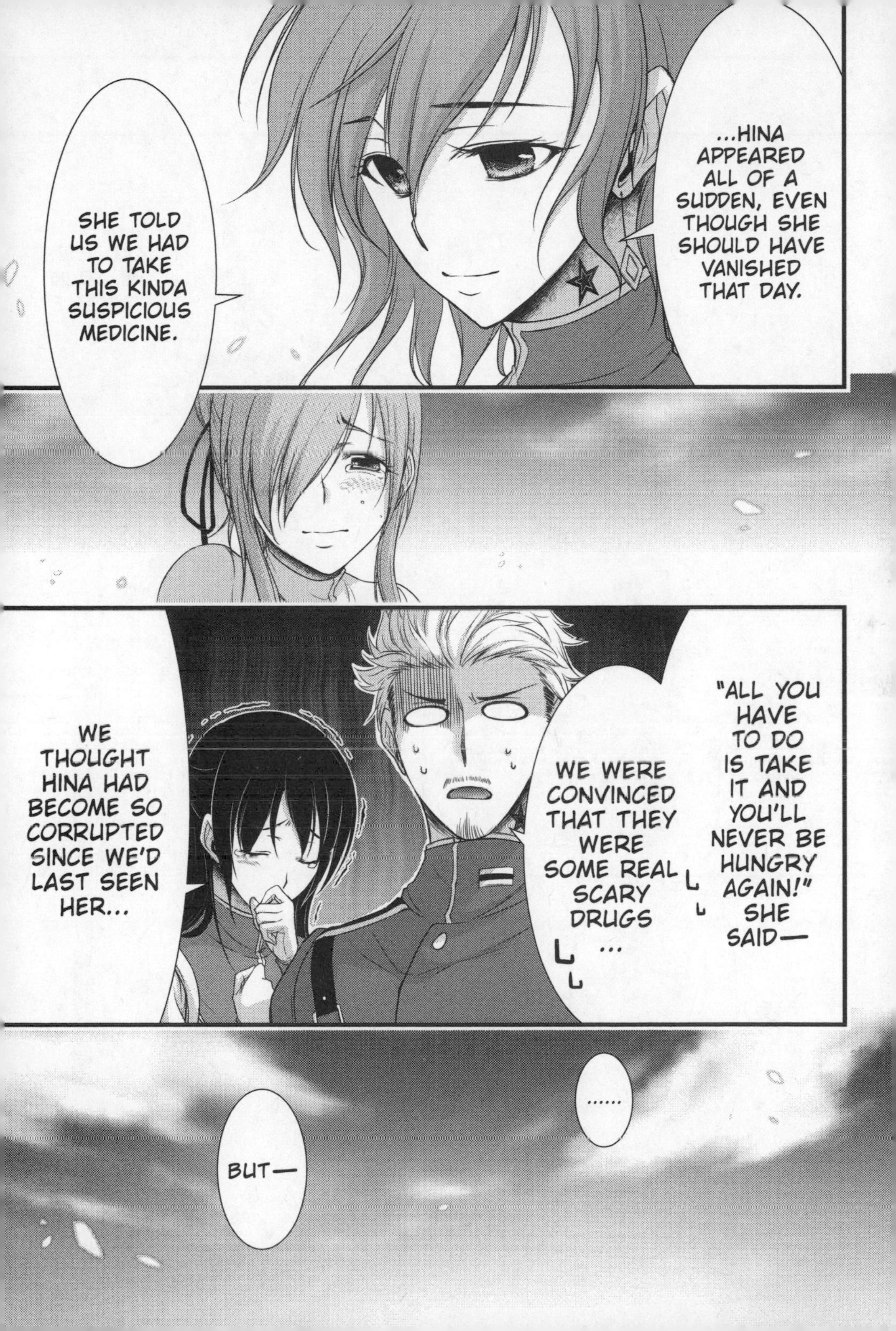
...HINA APPEARED ALL OF A SUDDEN, EVEN THOUGH SHE SHOULD HAVE VANISHED THAT DAY.
SHE TOLD US WE HAD TO TAKE THIS KINDA SUSPICIOUS MEDICINE.
"ALL YOU HAVE TO DO IS TAKE IT AND YOU'LL NEVER BE HUNGRY AGAIN!" SHE SAID—
WE WERE CONVINCED THAT THEY WERE SOME REAL SCARY DRUGS...
WE THOUGHT HINA HAD BECOME SO CORRUPTED SINCE WE'D LAST SEEN HER...
......
BUT—

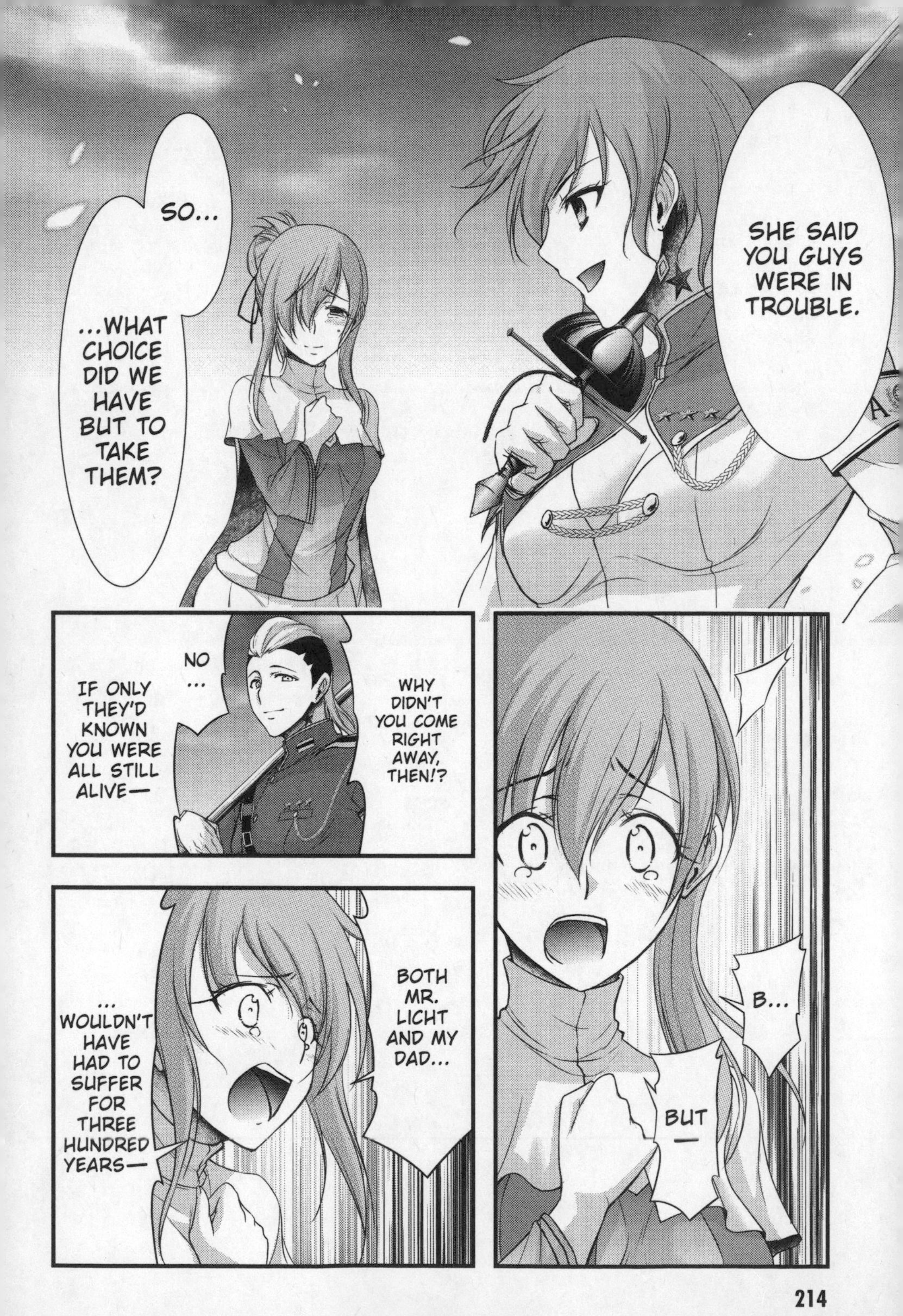
SHE SAID YOU GUYS WERE IN TROUBLE.
SO...
...WHAT CHOICE DID WE HAVE BUT TO TAKE THEM?
B...
BUT—
WHY DIDN'T YOU COME RIGHT AWAY, THEN!?
NO...
IF ONLY THEY'D KNOWN YOU WERE ALL STILL ALIVE—
BOTH MR. LICHT AND MY DAD...
...WOULDN'T HAVE HAD TO SUFFER FOR THREE HUNDRED YEARS—

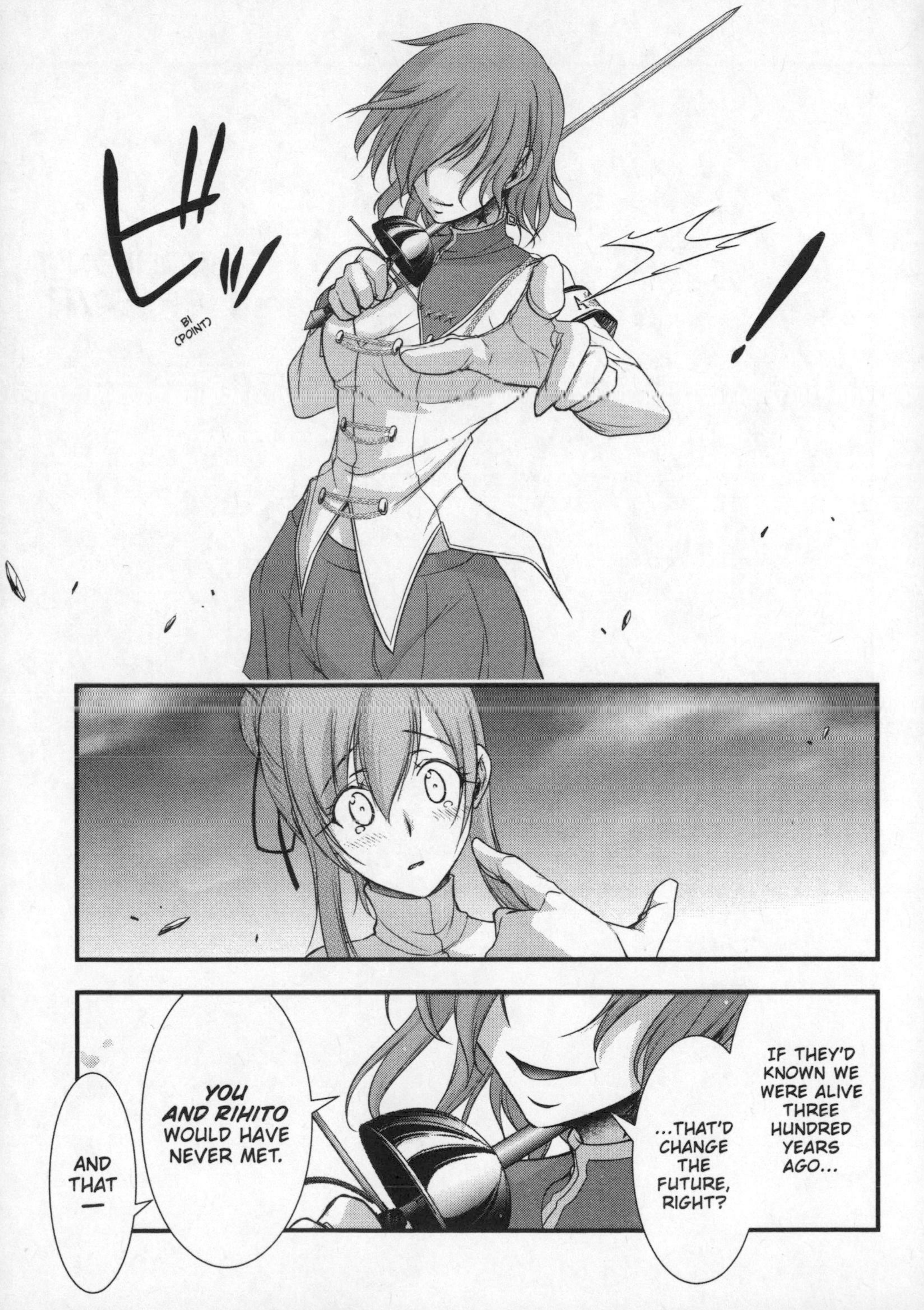
ビッ
BI (POINT)
IF THEY'D KNOWN WE WERE ALIVE THREE HUNDRED YEARS AGO...
...THAT'D CHANGE THE FUTURE, RIGHT?
YOU AND RIHITO WOULD HAVE NEVER MET.
AND THAT—

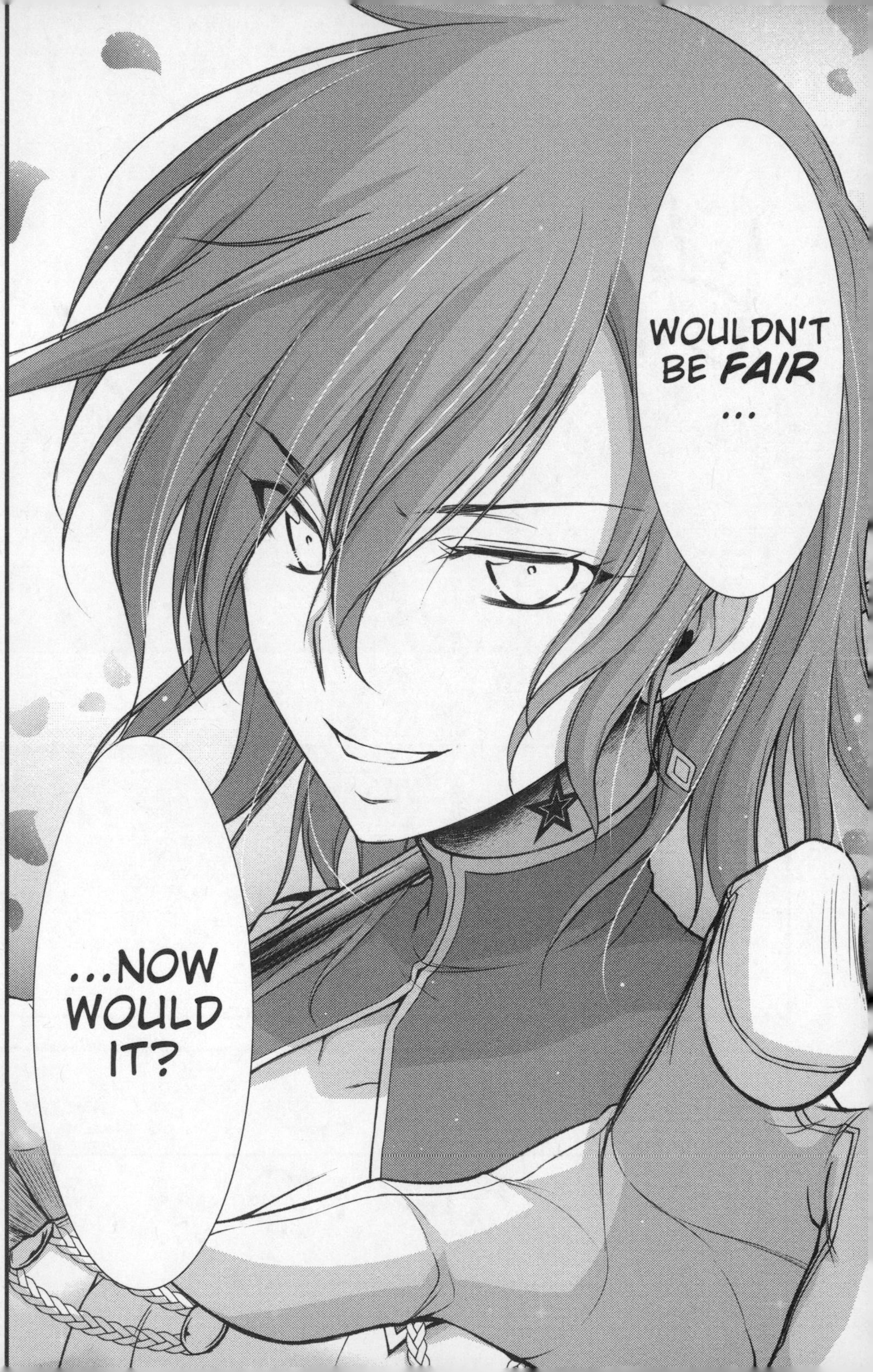
WOULDN'T BE **FAIR** ...
...NOW WOULD IT?

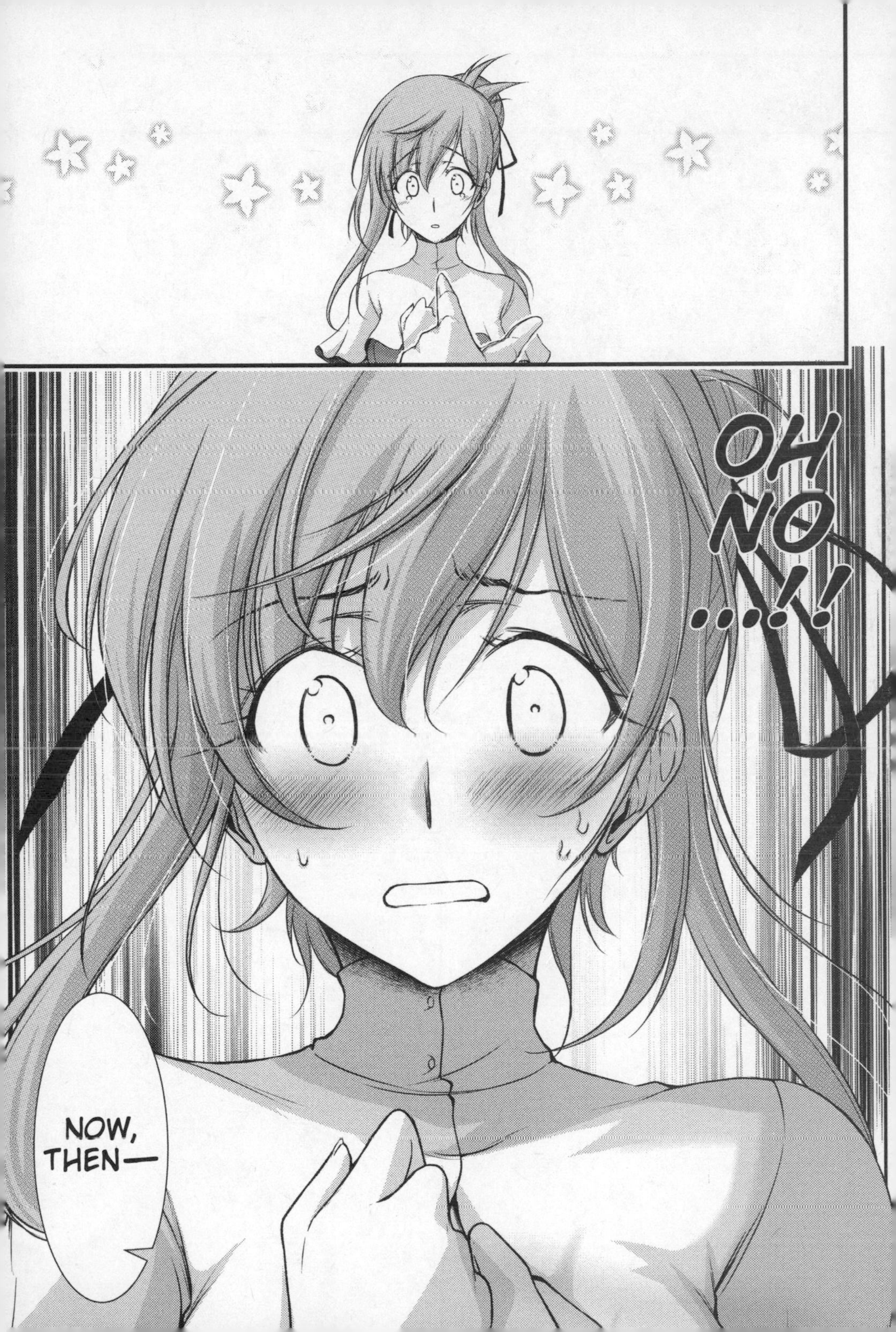
OH NO...!!
NOW, THEN—

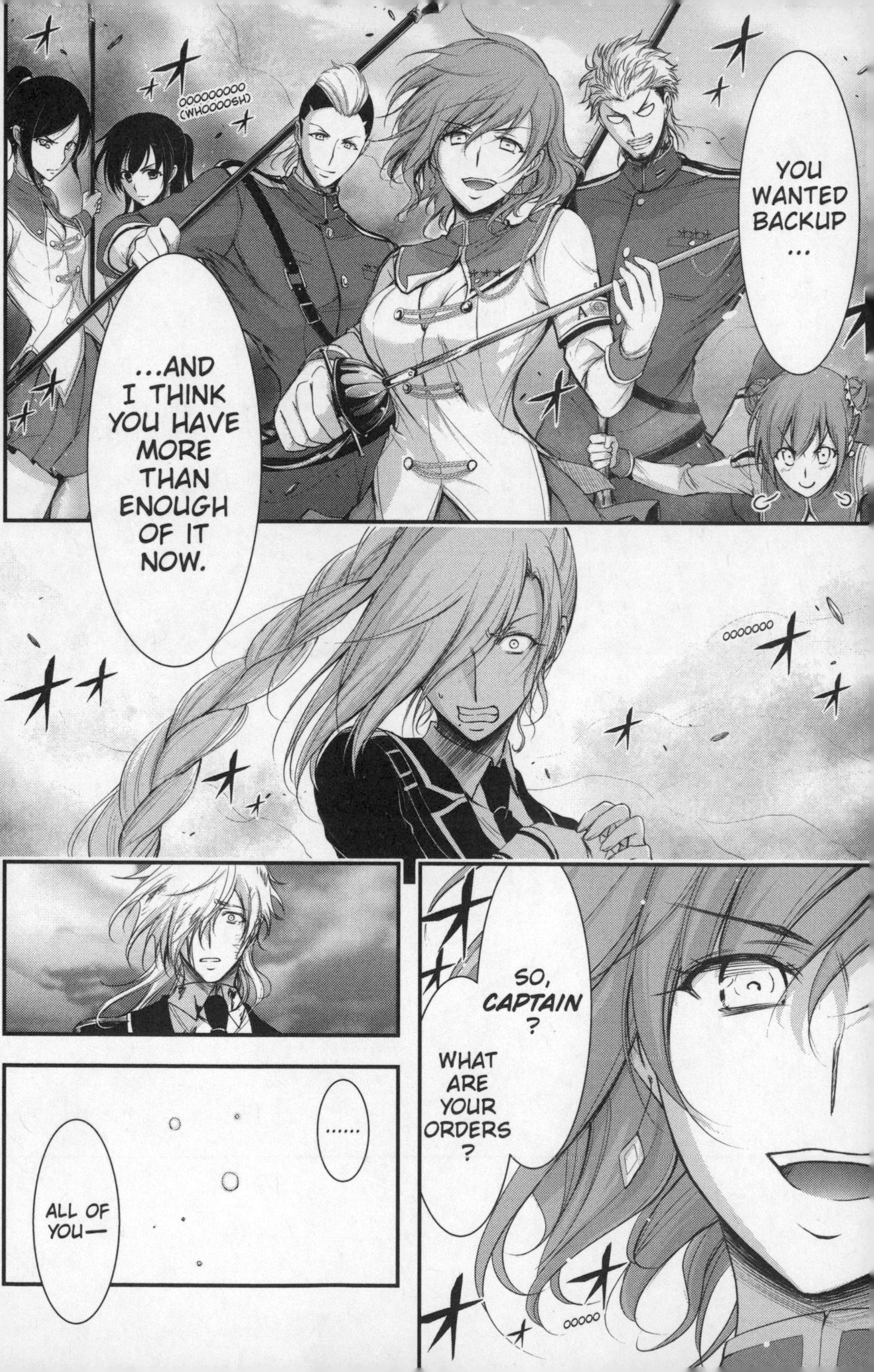
YOU WANTED BACKUP ...
OOOOOOOOO (WHOOOOSH)
...AND I THINK YOU HAVE MORE THAN ENOUGH OF IT NOW.
OOOOOOO
SO, CAPTAIN? WHAT ARE YOUR ORDERS?
OOOOO
......
ALL OF YOU—

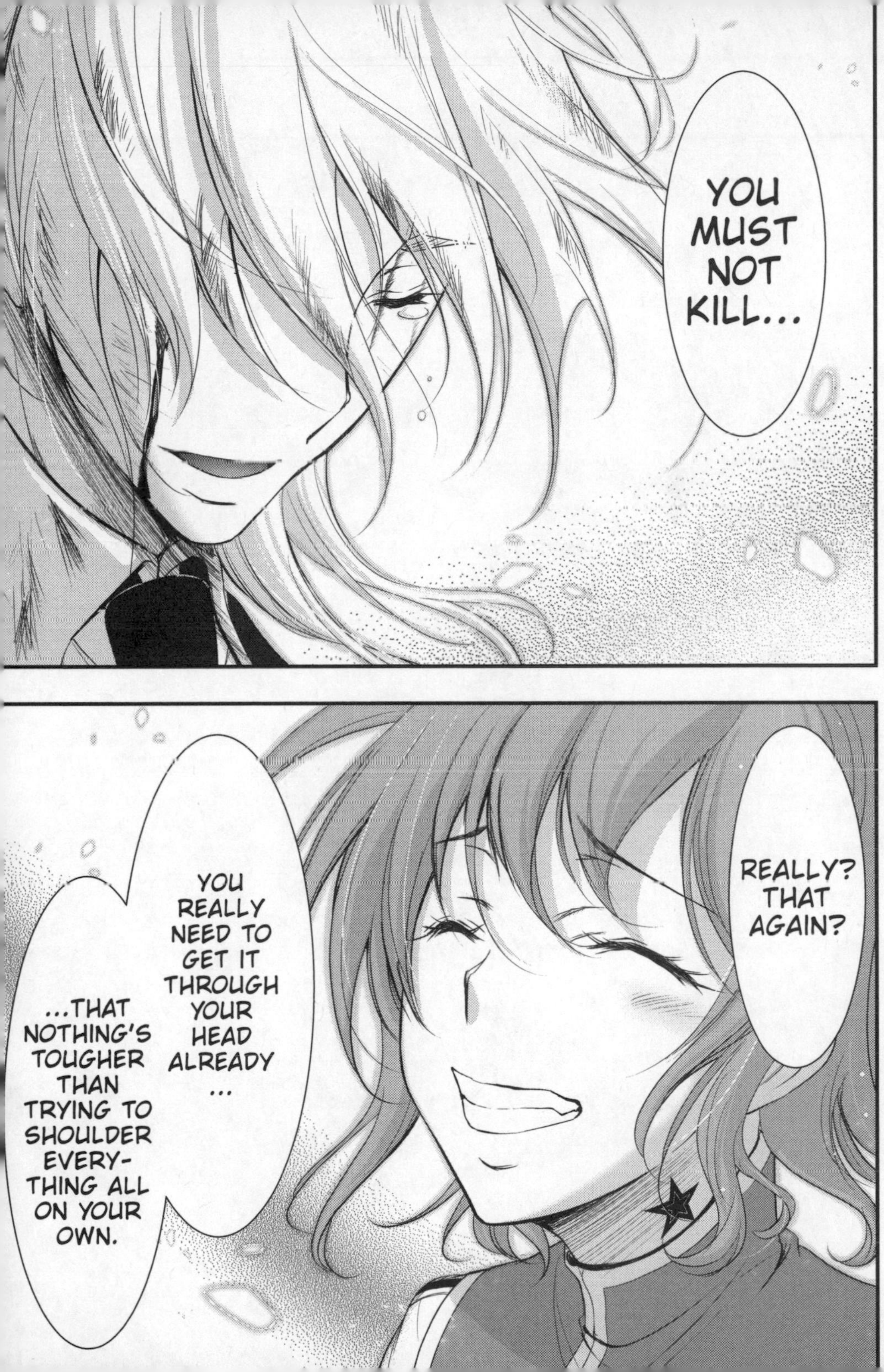
YOU MUST NOT KILL...
REALLY? THAT AGAIN?
YOU REALLY NEED TO GET IT THROUGH YOUR HEAD ALREADY ...
...THAT NOTHING'S TOUGHER THAN TRYING TO SHOULDER EVERY-THING ALL ON YOUR OWN.

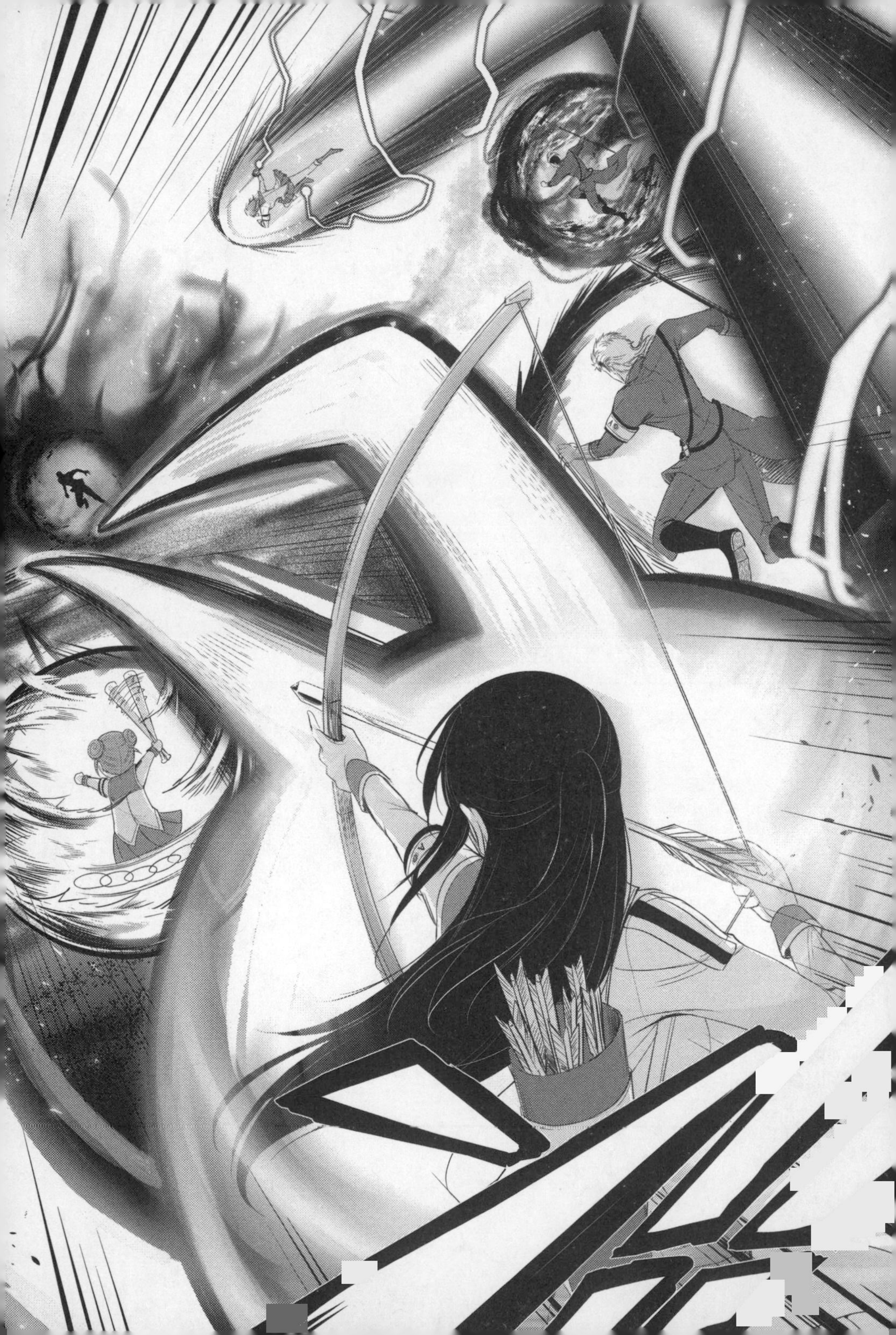

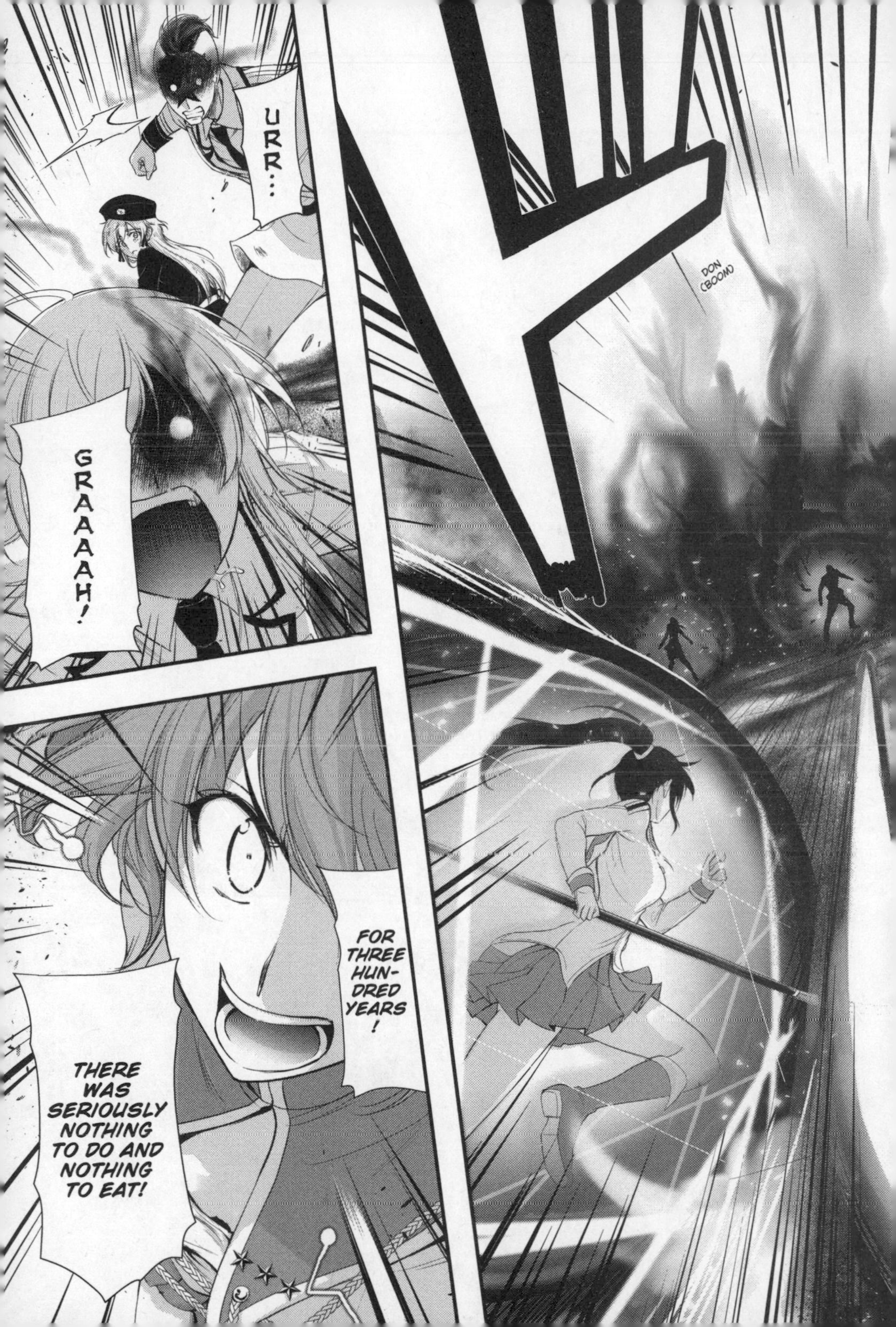
DON (BOOM)
URR...
GRAAAAH!
FOR THREE HUN-DRED YEARS!
THERE WAS SERIOUSLY NOTHING TO DO AND NOTHING TO EAT!

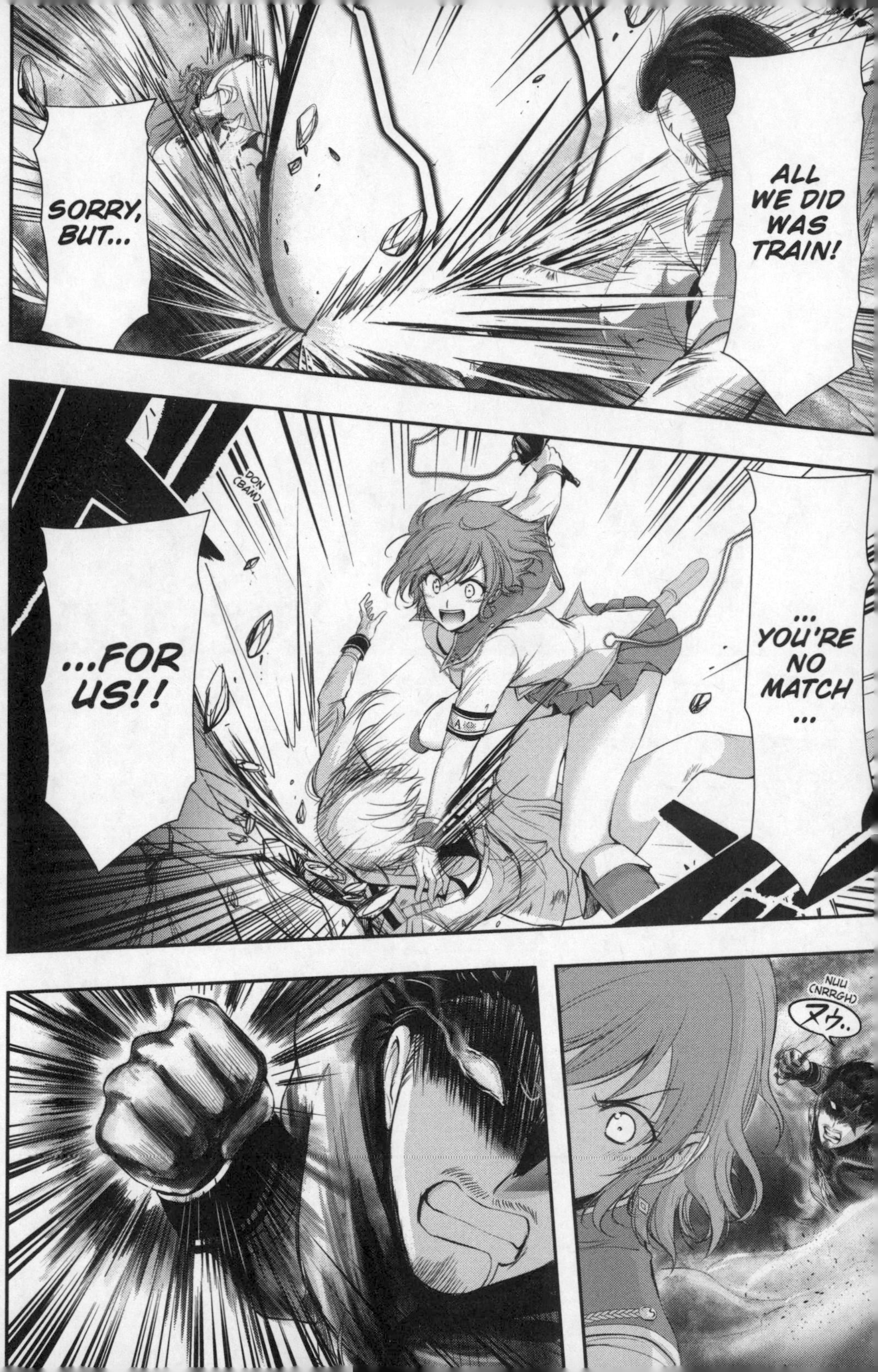
ALL WE DID WAS TRAIN!
SORRY, BUT...
... YOU'RE NO MATCH ...
DON (BAM)
...FOR US!!
NUU (NRRGH)
ヌウ..

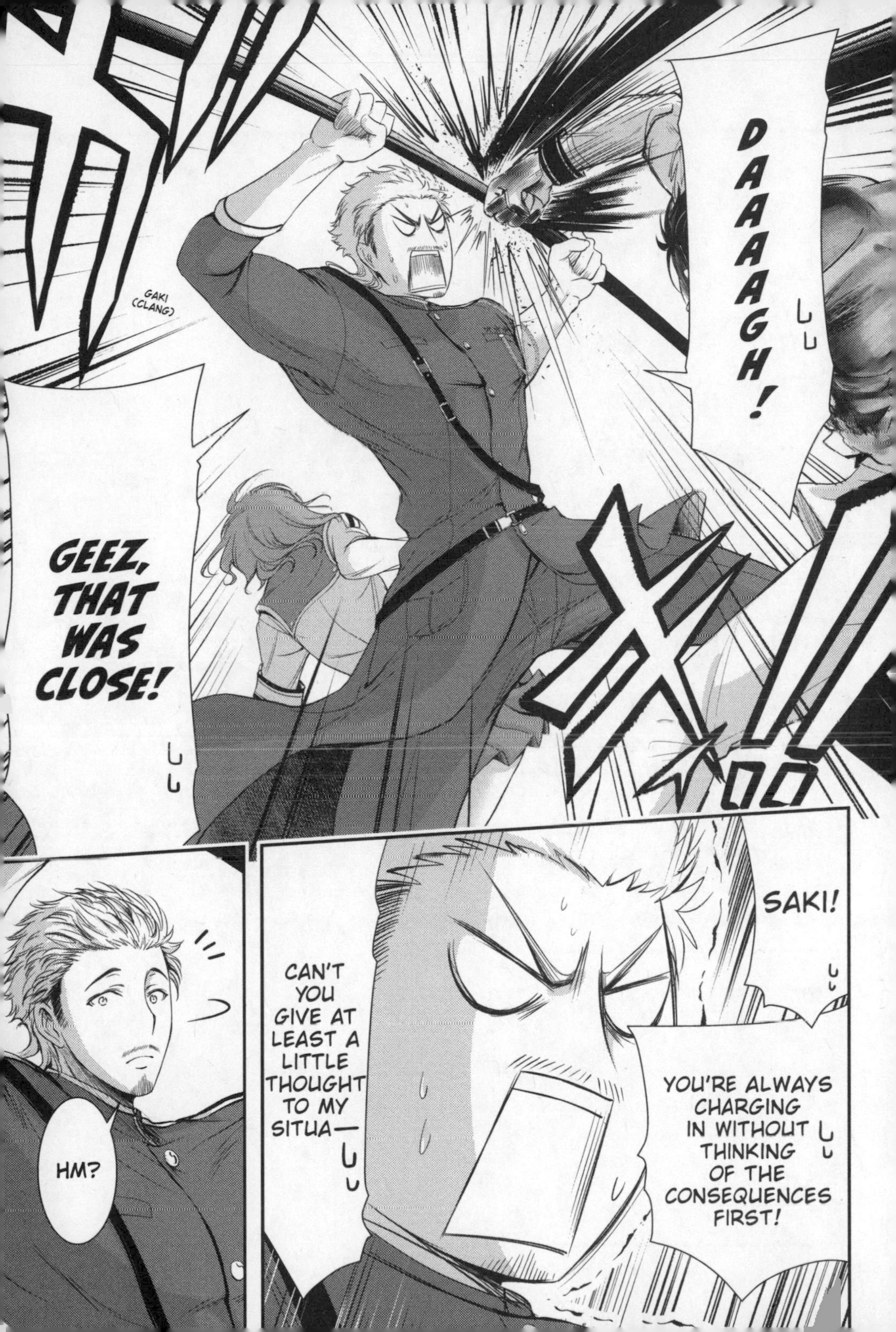
DAAAAAGH!
GAKI (CLANG)
GEEZ, THAT WAS CLOSE!
SAKI!
YOU'RE ALWAYS CHARGING IN WITHOUT THINKING OF THE CONSEQUENCES FIRST!
CAN'T YOU GIVE AT LEAST A LITTLE THOUGHT TO MY SITUA—
HM?

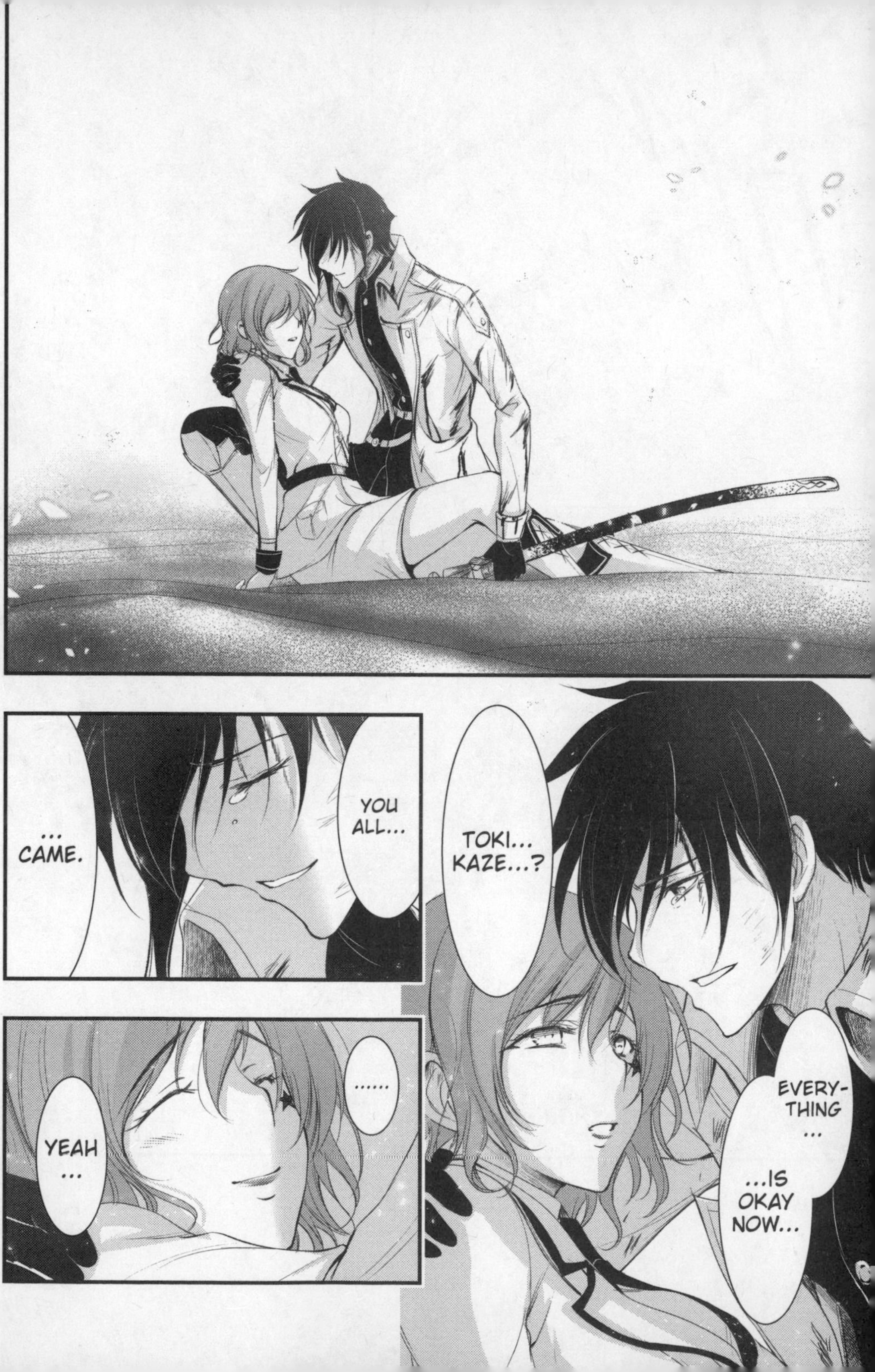
TOKI... KAZE...?
EVERY-THING... ...IS OKAY NOW...
YOU ALL...
...CAME.
......
YEAH...

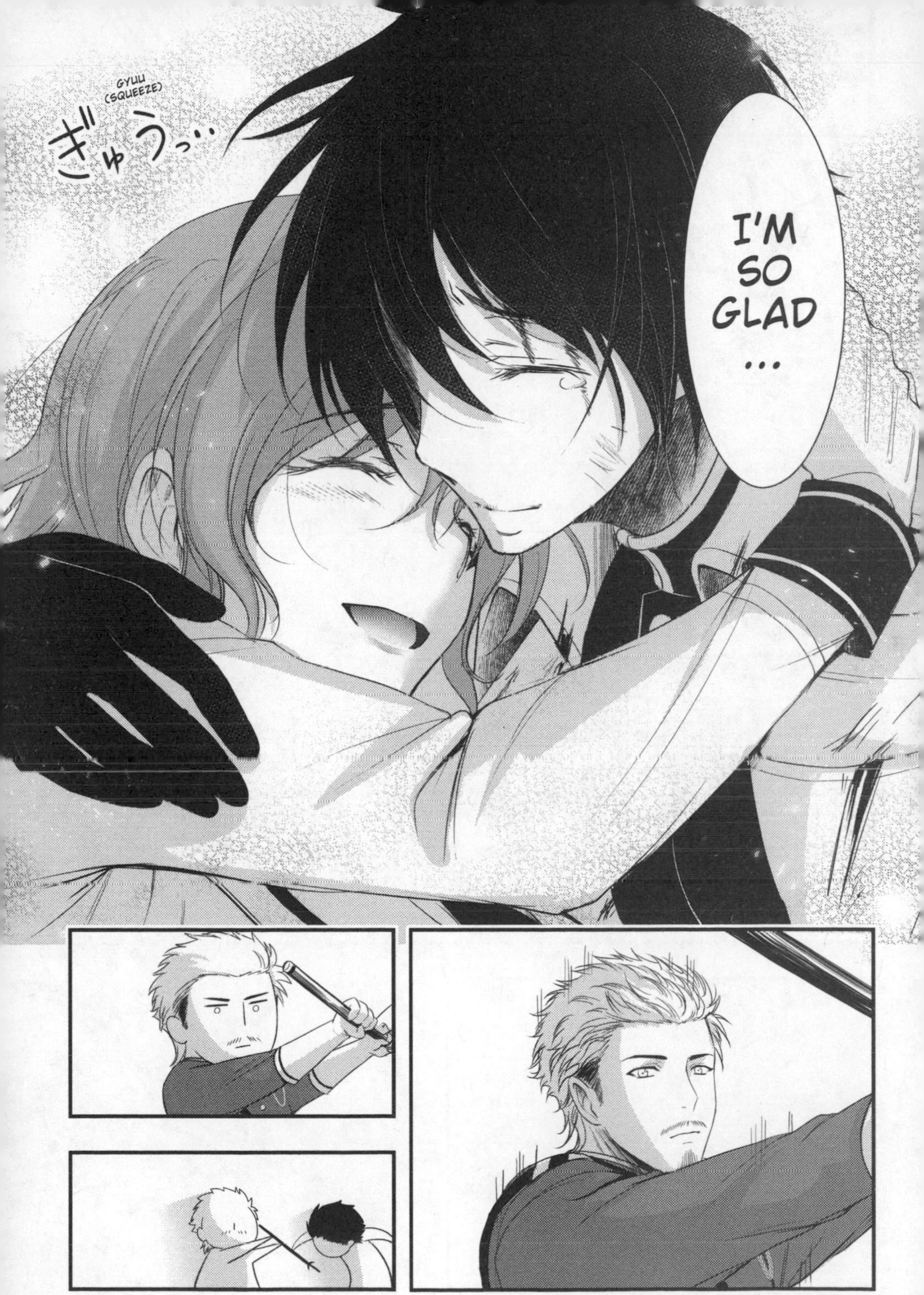
GYUU (SQUEEZE)
ぎゅうっ…
I'M SO GLAD ...

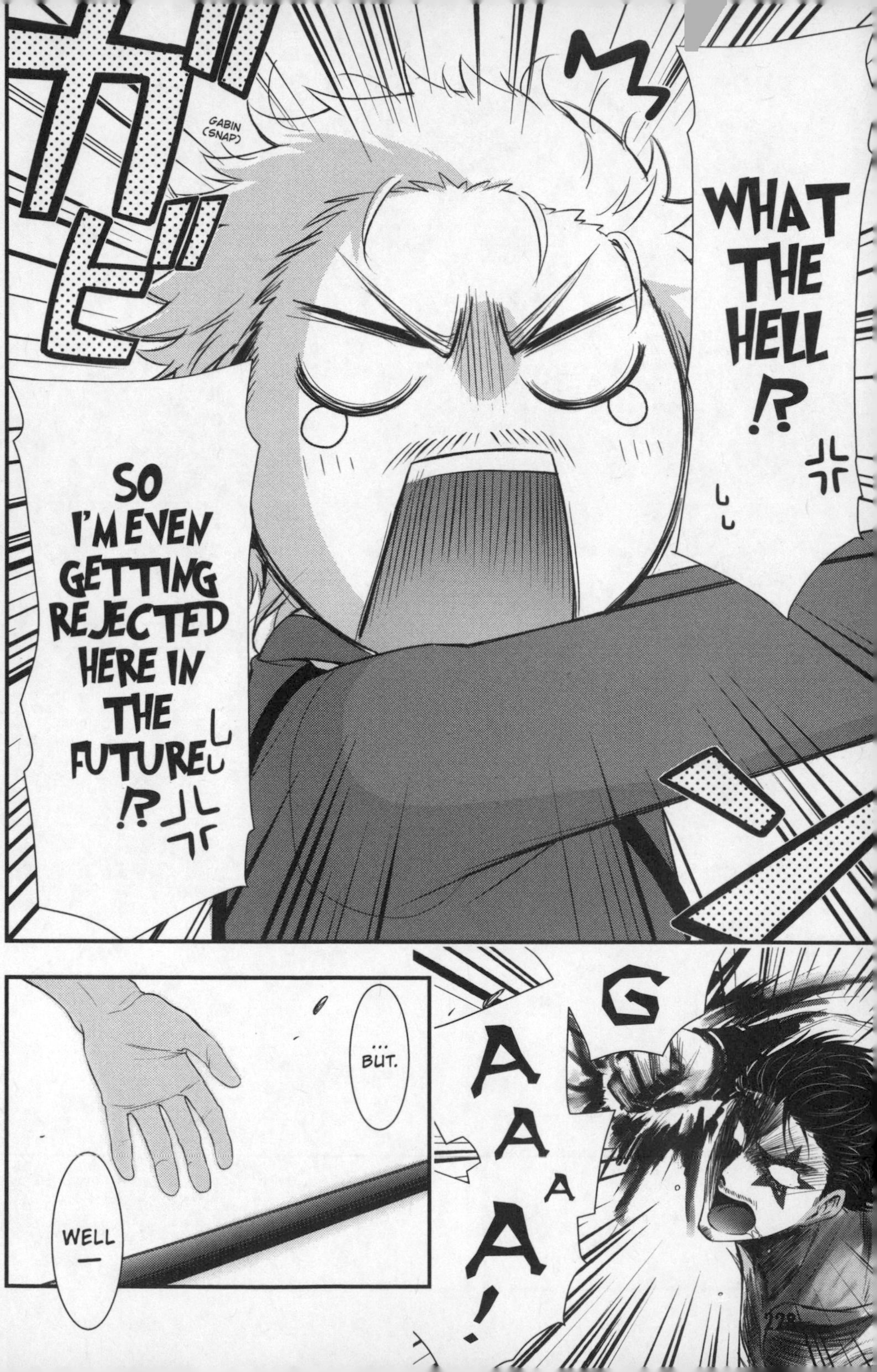
WHAT THE HELL!?
GABIN (SNAP)
SO I'M EVEN GETTING REJECTED HERE IN THE FUTURE!?
GAAAAA!
...BUT.
WELL—

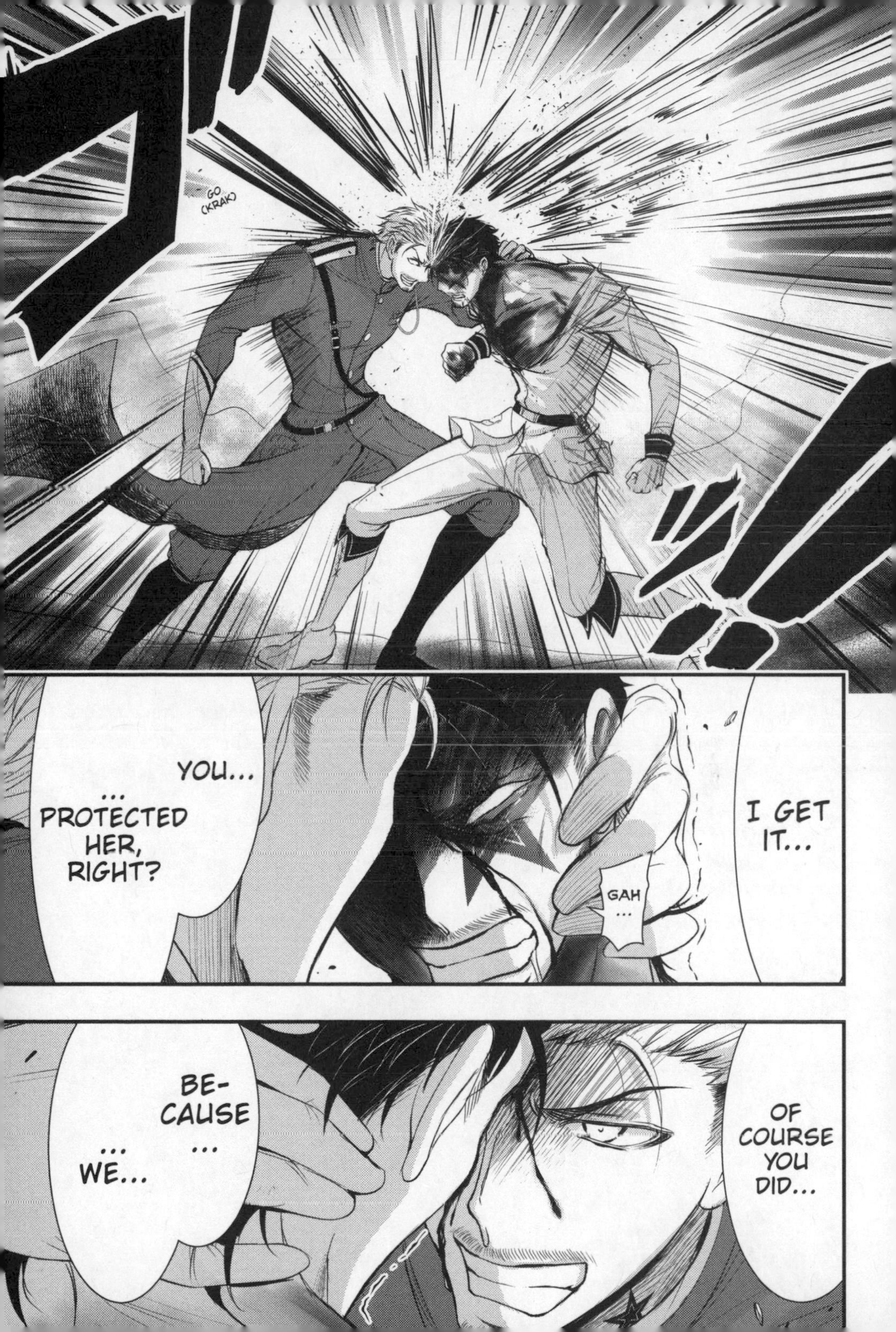
GO (KRAK)
I GET IT...
GAH...
YOU...
...PROTECTED HER, RIGHT?
OF COURSE YOU DID...
BE-CAUSE...
...WE...

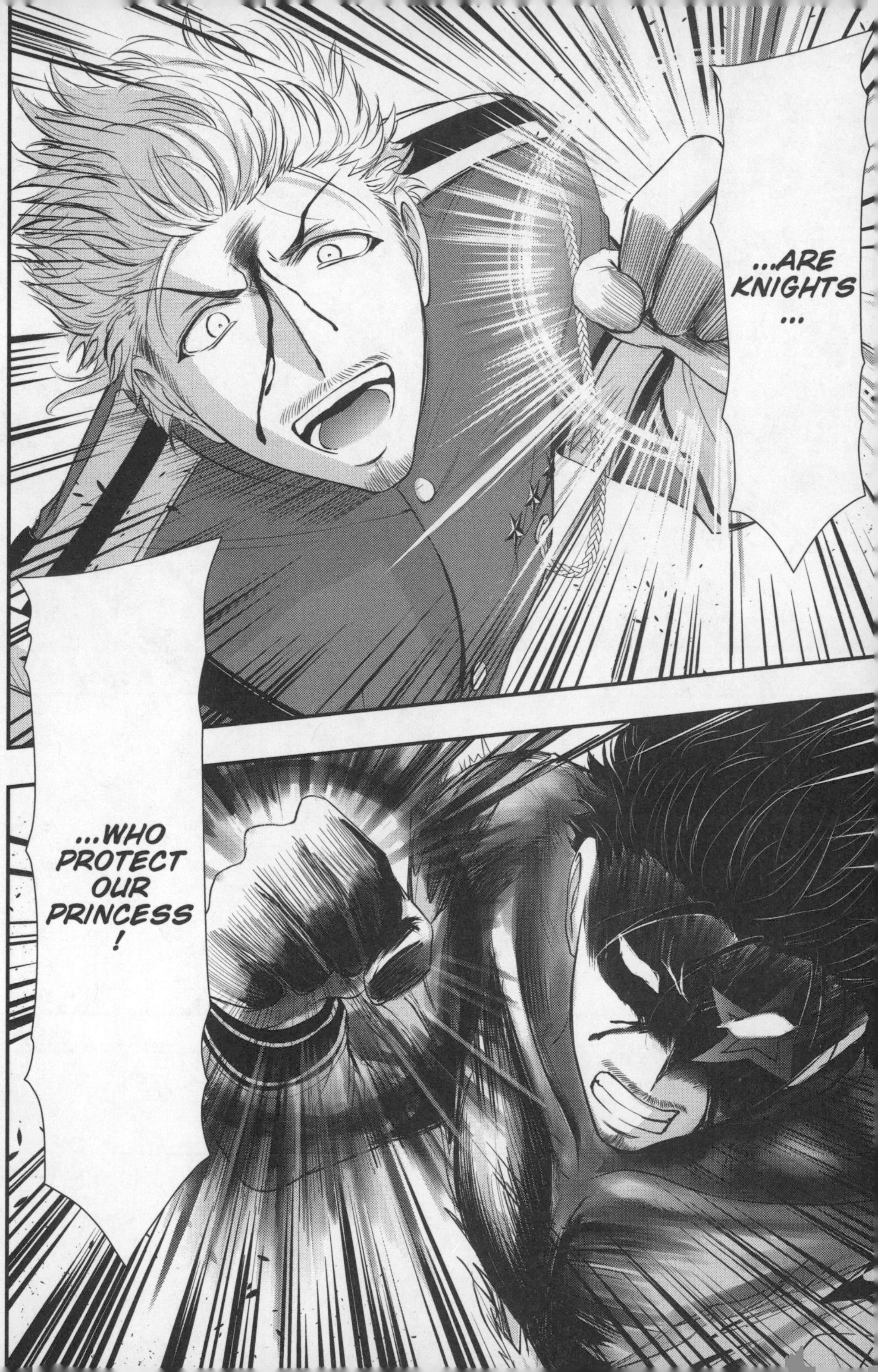
...ARE KNIGHTS ...
...WHO PROTECT OUR PRINCESS !

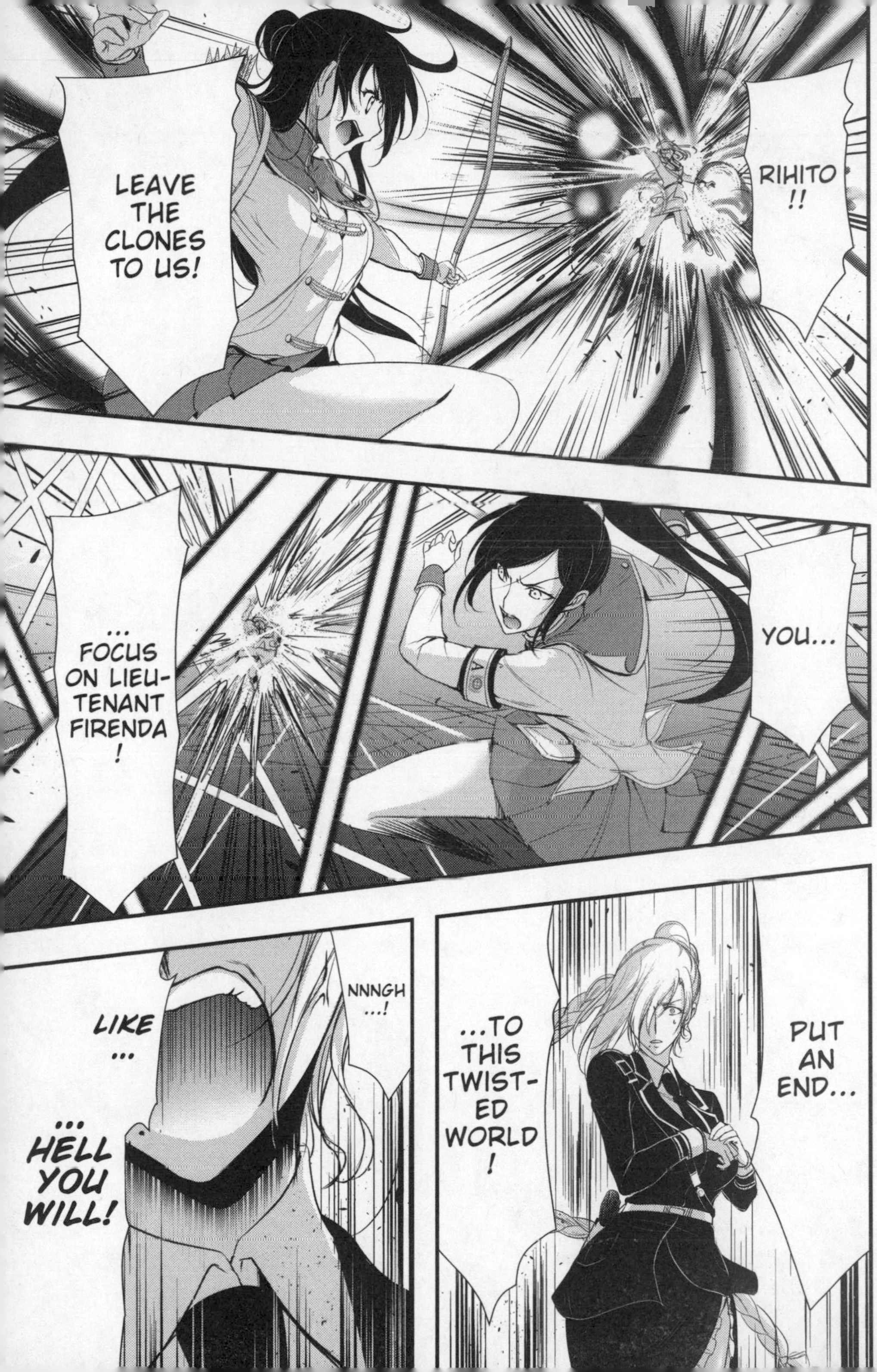
RIHITO !!
LEAVE THE CLONES TO US!
YOU...
...FOCUS ON LIEU-TENANT FIRENDA!
PUT AN END...
...TO THIS TWIST-ED WORLD!
NNNGH ...!
LIKE ...
... HELL YOU WILL!

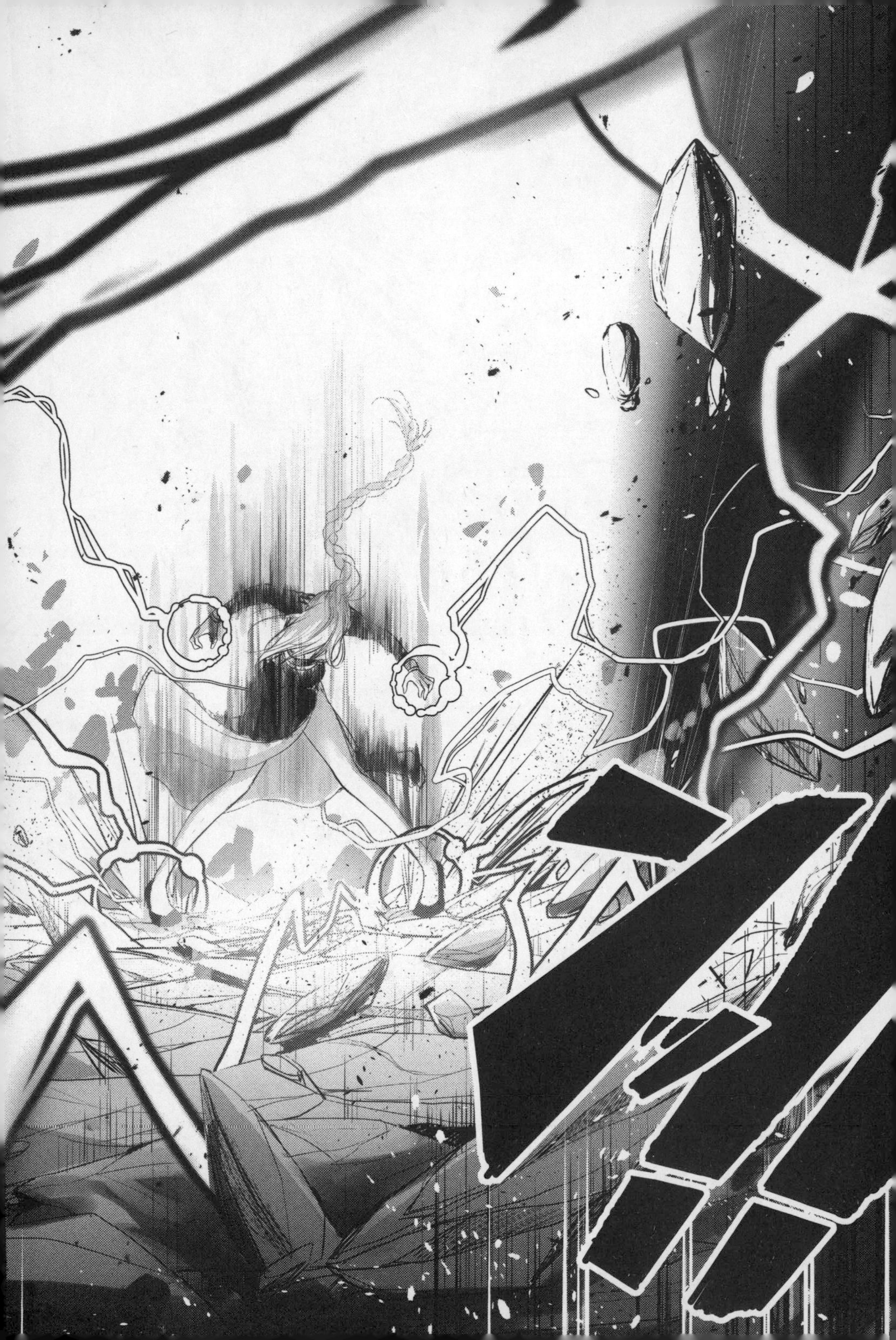

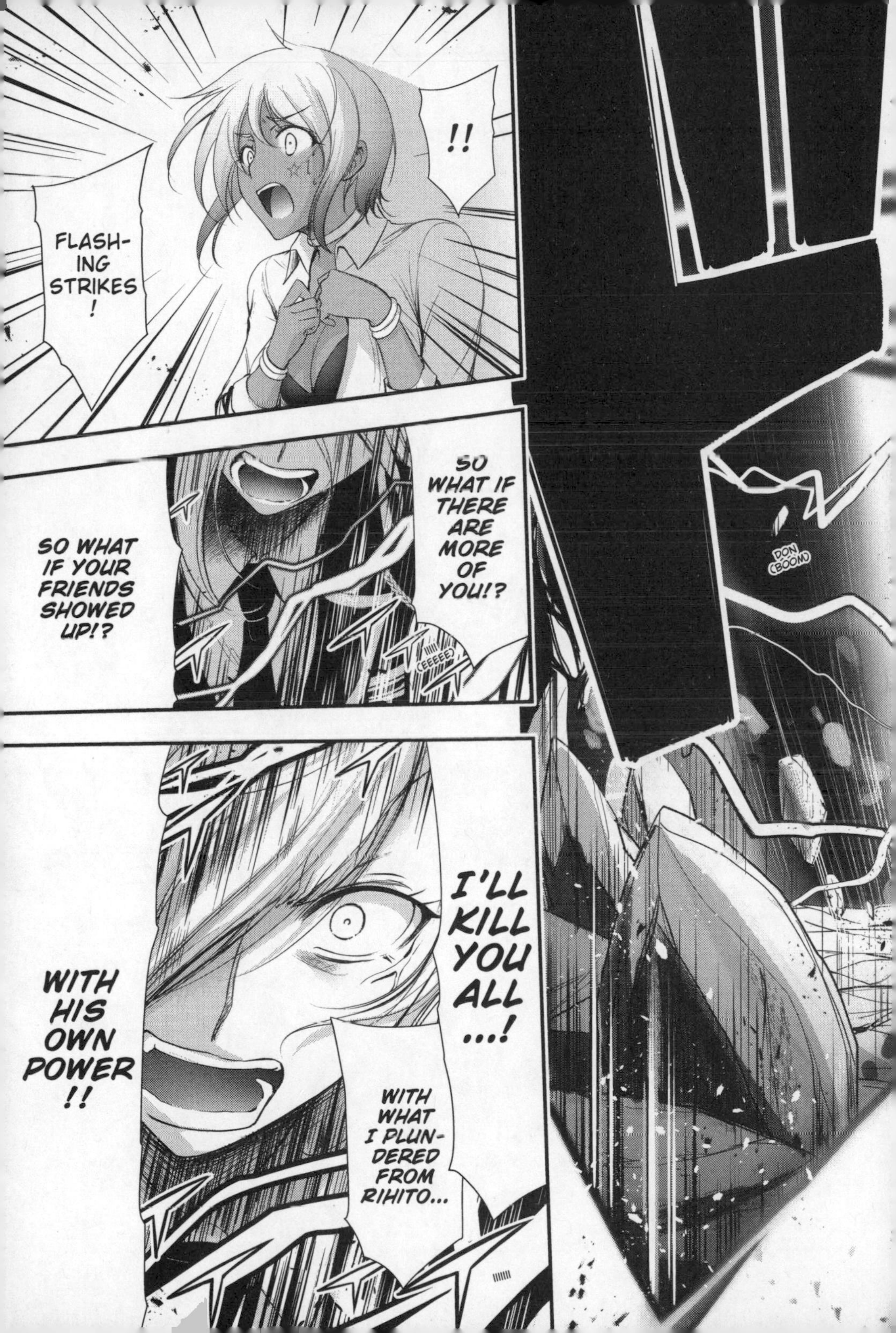
!!
FLASHING-STRIKES!
DON (BOOM)
SO WHAT IF THERE ARE MORE OF YOU!?
SO WHAT IF YOUR FRIENDS SHOWED UP!?
(EEEEE)
I'LL KILL YOU ALL...!
WITH WHAT I PLUNDERED FROM RIHITO...
WITH HIS OWN POWER!!

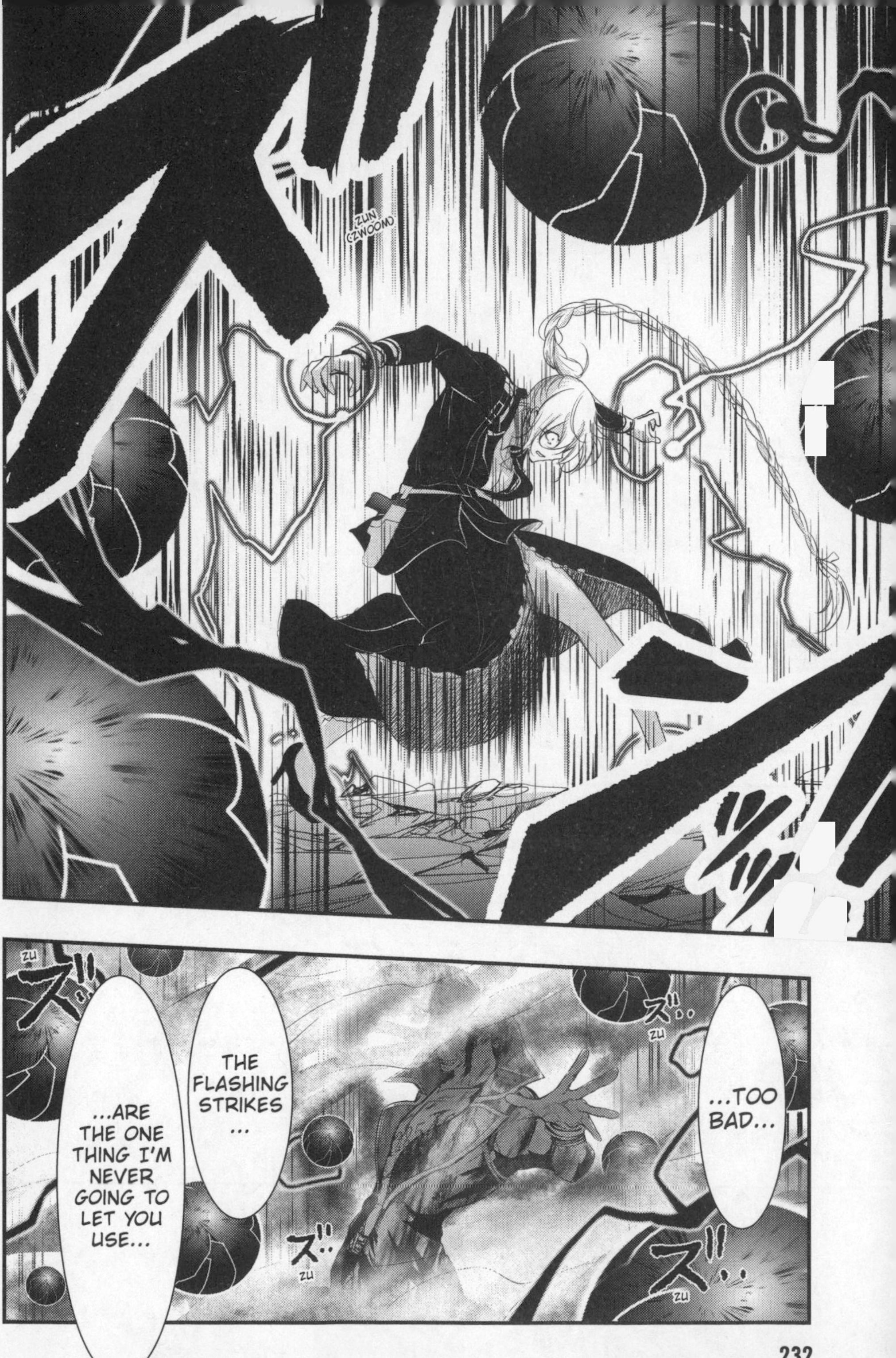
ZUN (ZWOOM)
...TOO BAD...
ZU
THE FLASHING STRIKES ...
...ARE THE ONE THING I'M NEVER GOING TO LET YOU USE...
ZU
ZU
ZU

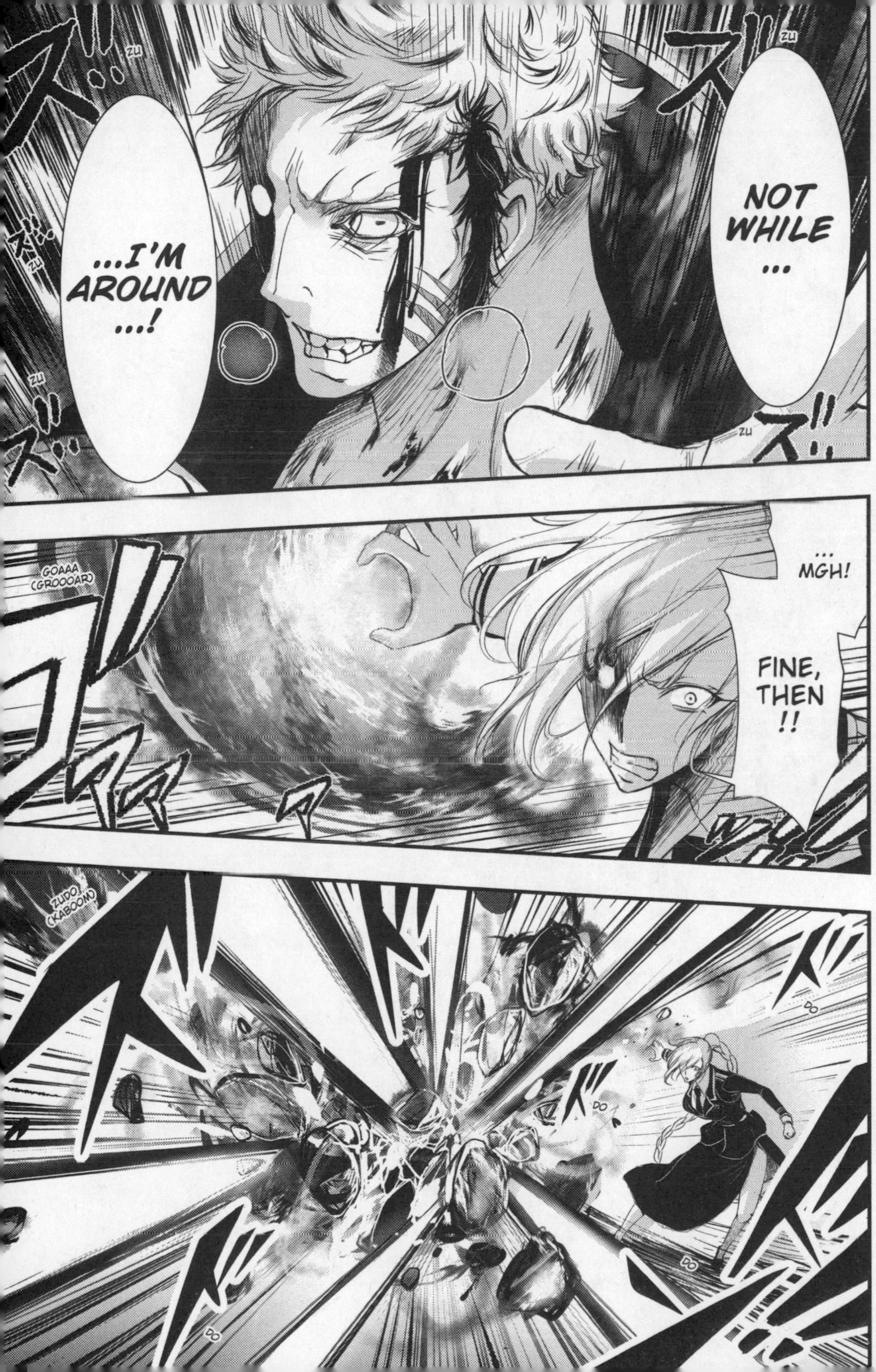
ZU
NOT WHILE ...
...I'M AROUND ...!
ZU
ZU
ZU
... MGH!
FINE, THEN !!
GOAAA (GROOOAR)
DO
DO
DO
ZUDO (KABOOM)
DO

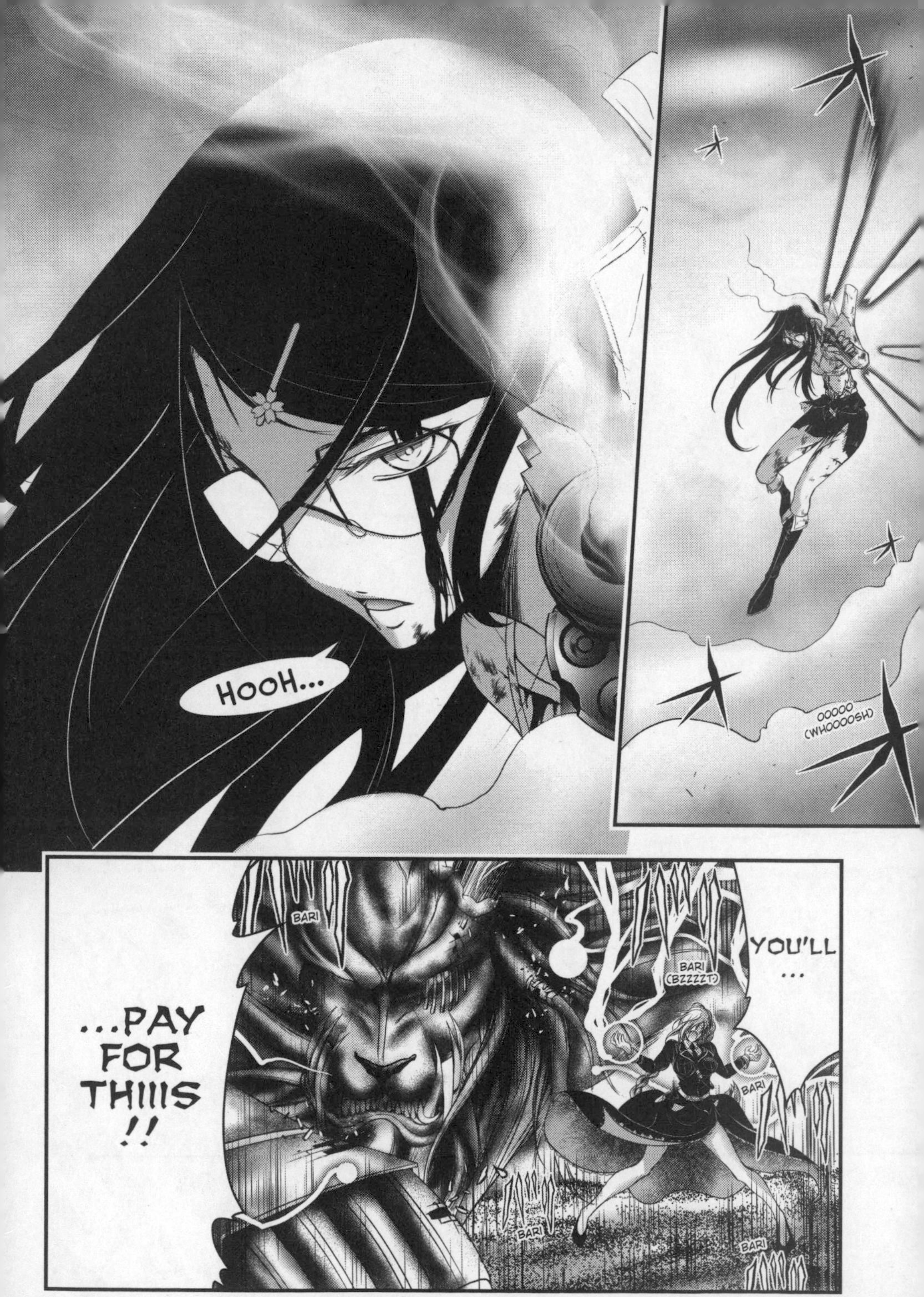
OOOOO (WHOOOOSH)
HOOH...
YOU'LL ...
BARI (BZZZZT)
BARI
BARI
...PAY FOR THIIIS!!
BARI
BARI

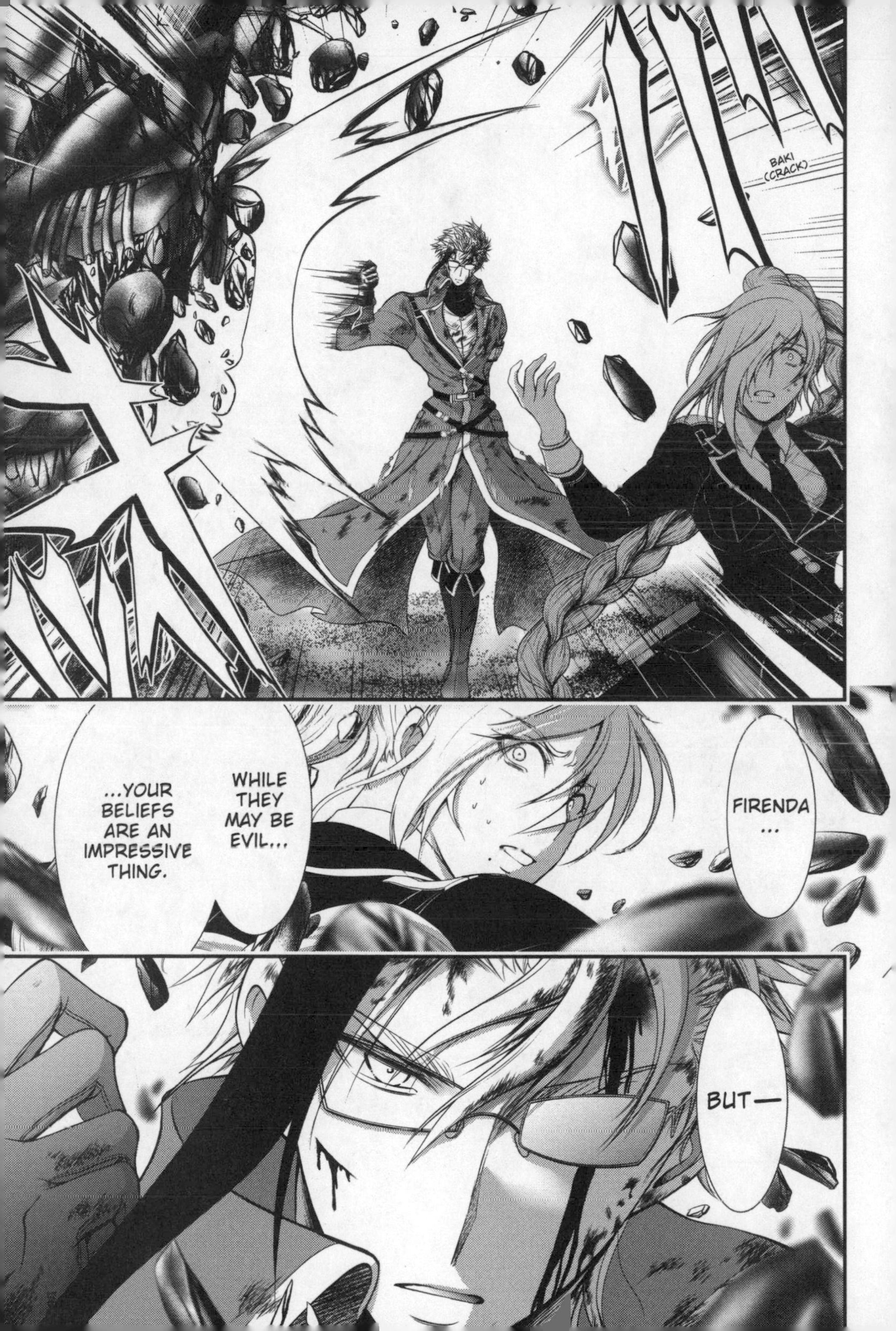
BAKI (CRACK)
FIRENDA...
WHILE THEY MAY BE EVIL...
...YOUR BELIEFS ARE AN IMPRESSIVE THING.
BUT—

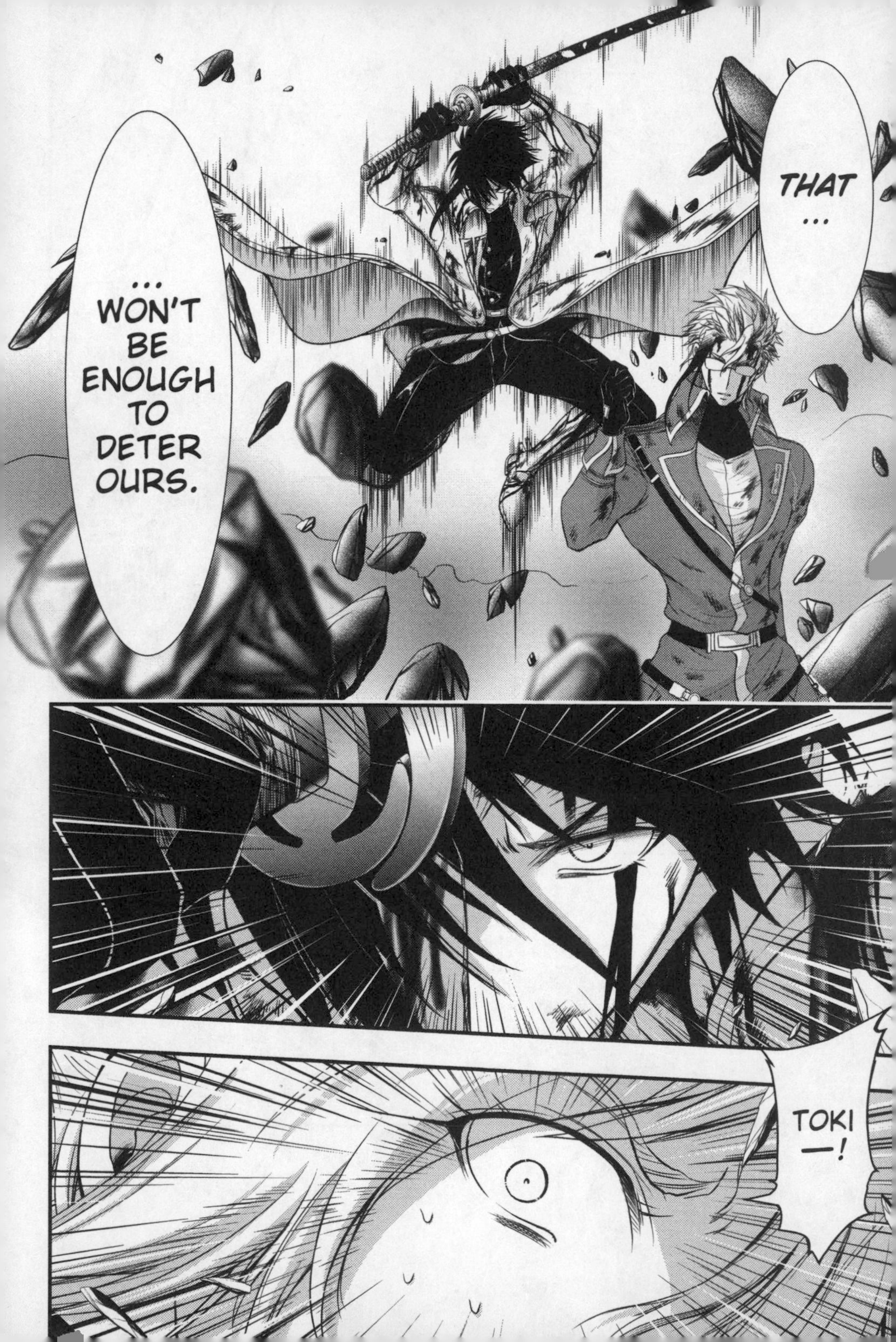
THAT ...
... WON'T BE ENOUGH TO DETER OURS.
TOKI —!

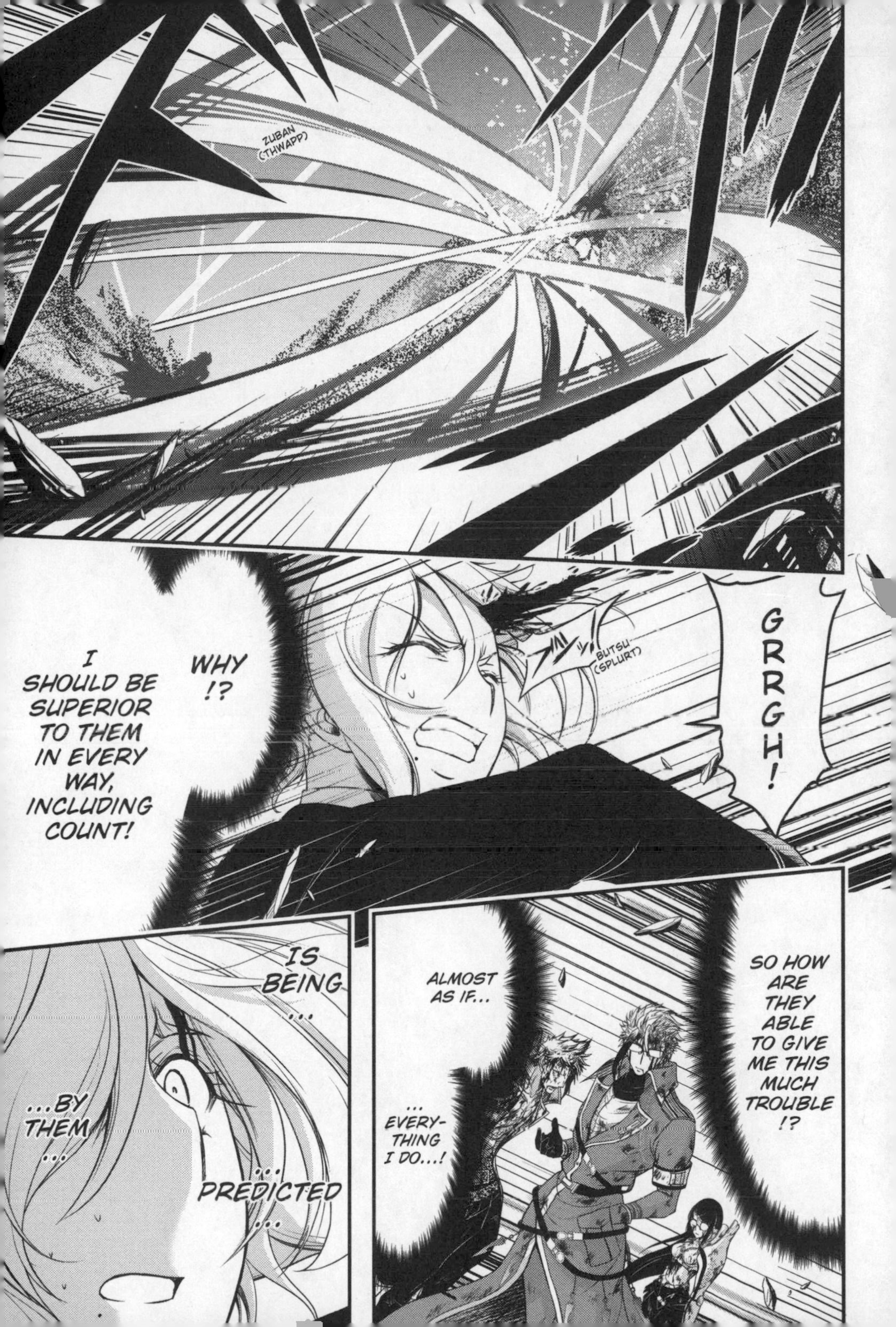
ZUBAN (THWAPP)
GRRGH!
BUTSU (SPLURT)
WHY!?
I SHOULD BE SUPERIOR TO THEM IN EVERY WAY, INCLUDING COUNT!
SO HOW ARE THEY ABLE TO GIVE ME THIS MUCH TROUBLE!?
ALMOST AS IF...
...EVERYTHING I DO...!
IS BEING...
...BY THEM...
...PREDICTED...

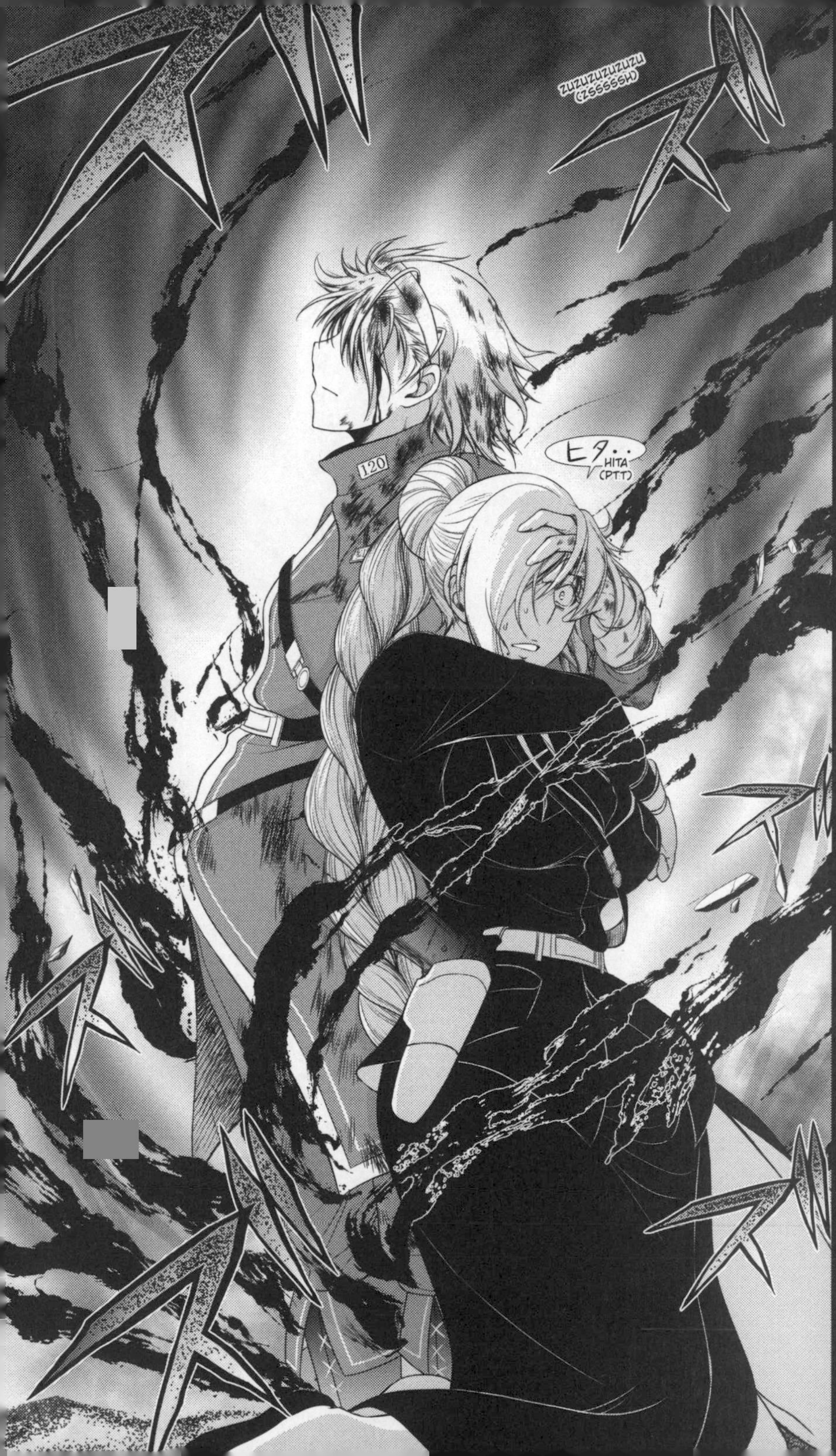
ZUZUZUZUZUZU
(ZSSSSSSH)
ヒタ‥
HITA
(PTT)

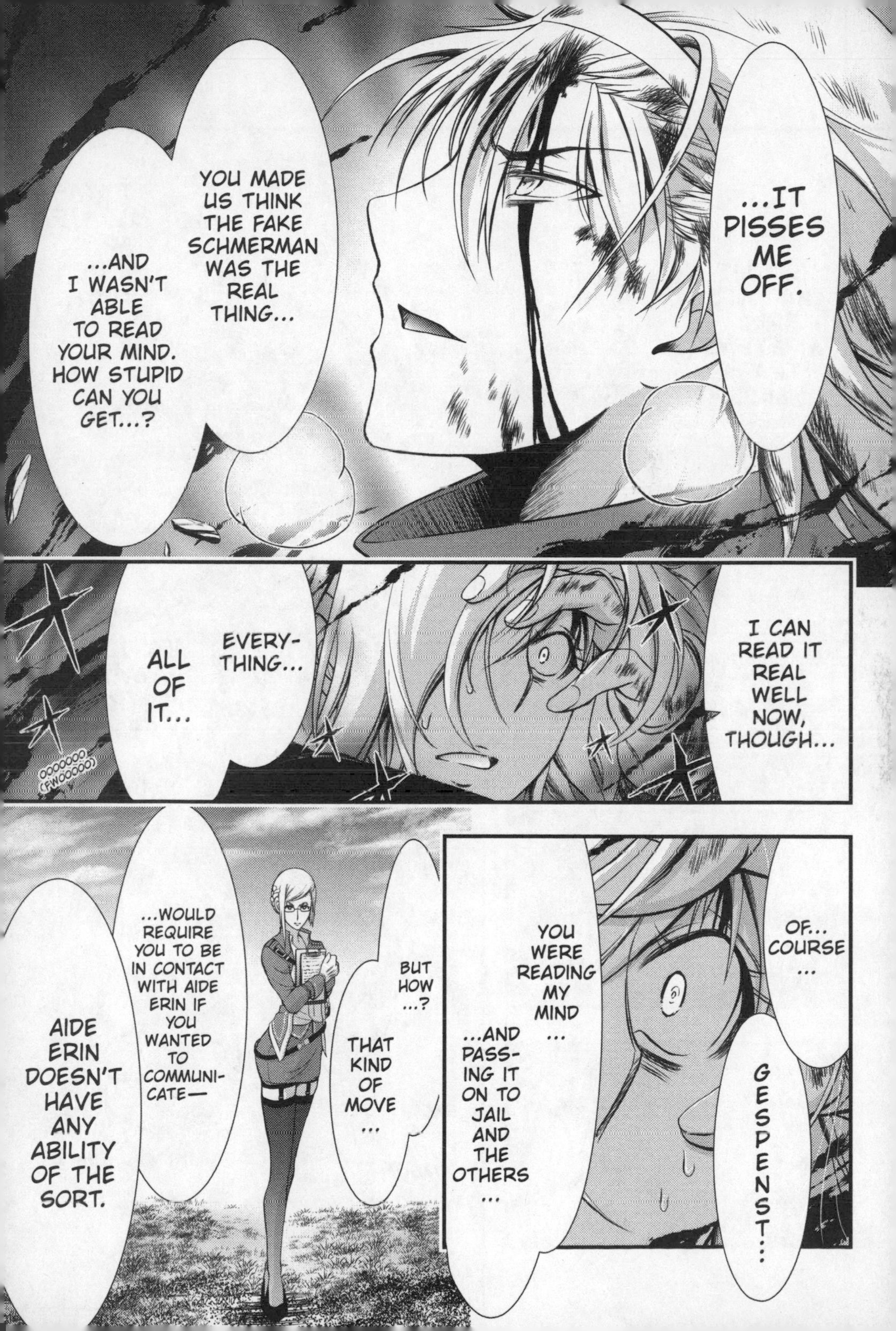
...IT PISSES ME OFF.
YOU MADE US THINK THE FAKE SCHMERMAN WAS THE REAL THING...
...AND I WASN'T ABLE TO READ YOUR MIND. HOW STUPID CAN YOU GET...?
I CAN READ IT REAL WELL NOW, THOUGH...
EVERY-THING...
ALL OF IT...
OF... COURSE...
GESPENST...
YOU WERE READING MY MIND...
...AND PASSING IT ON TO JAIL AND THE OTHERS...
BUT HOW...?
THAT KIND OF MOVE...
...WOULD REQUIRE YOU TO BE IN CONTACT WITH AIDE ERIN IF YOU WANTED TO COMMUNI-CATE—
AIDE ERIN DOESN'T HAVE ANY ABILITY OF THE SORT.

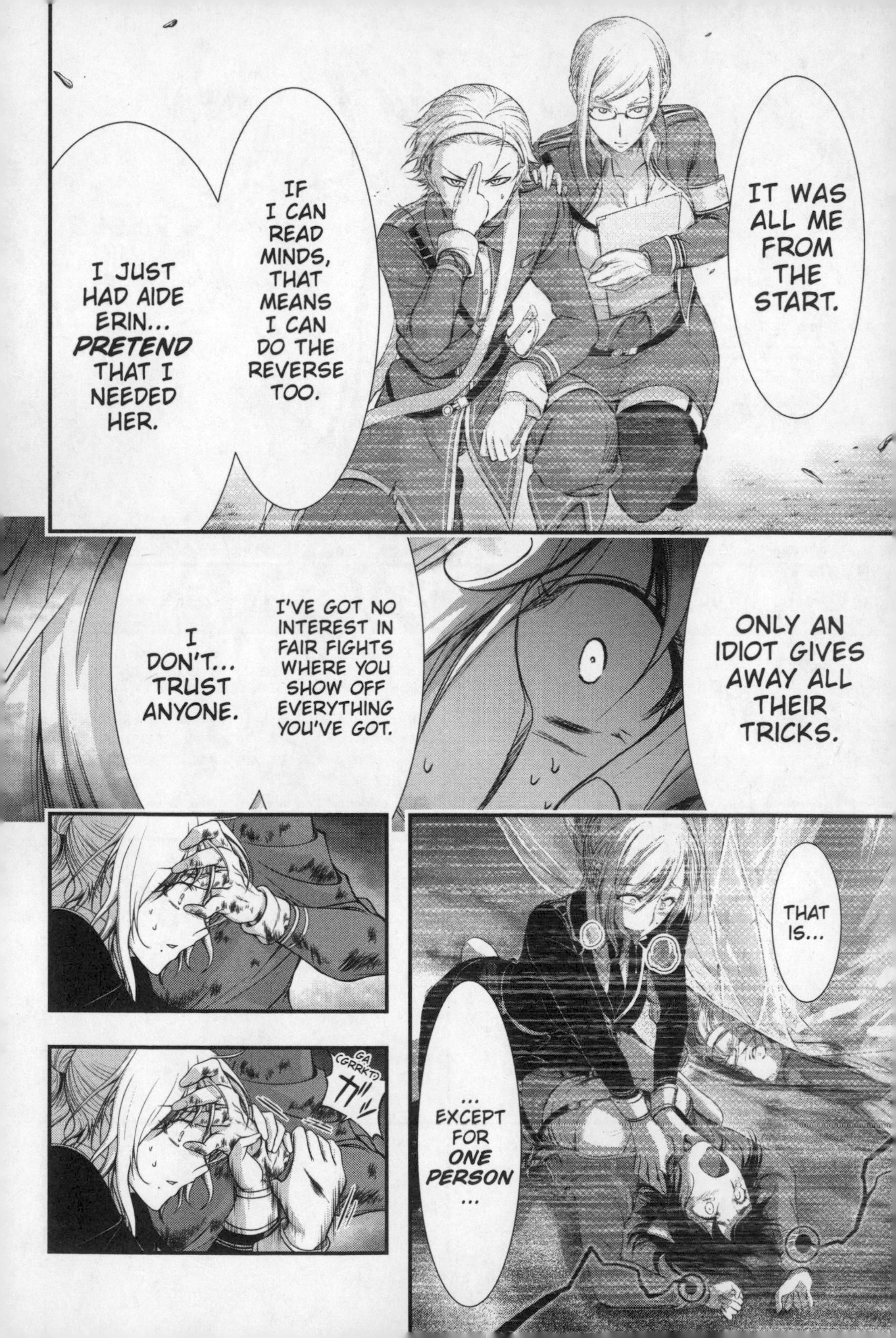
IT WAS ALL ME FROM THE START.
IF I CAN READ MINDS, THAT MEANS I CAN DO THE REVERSE TOO.
I JUST HAD AIDE ERIN... ***PRETEND*** THAT I NEEDED HER.
ONLY AN IDIOT GIVES AWAY ALL THEIR TRICKS.
I'VE GOT NO INTEREST IN FAIR FIGHTS WHERE YOU SHOW OFF EVERYTHING YOU'VE GOT.
I DON'T... TRUST ANYONE.
THAT IS...
...EXCEPT FOR ***ONE PERSON***...
GA (GRRKT)
ガッ

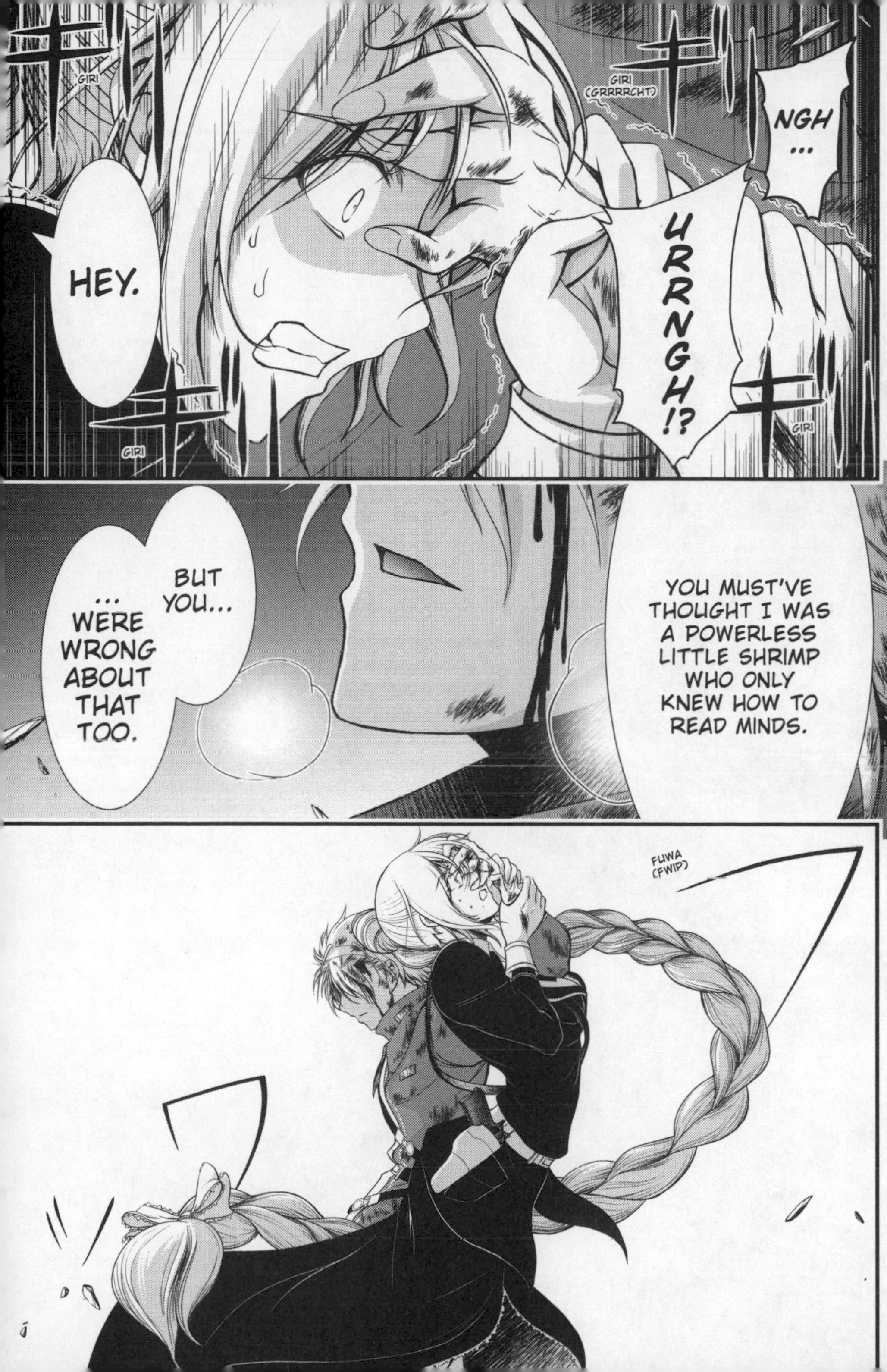
NGH...
URRNGH!?
GIRI (GRRRRCHT)
GIRI
GIRI
GIRI
HEY.
YOU MUST'VE THOUGHT I WAS A POWERLESS LITTLE SHRIMP WHO ONLY KNEW HOW TO READ MINDS.
BUT YOU...
...WERE WRONG ABOUT THAT TOO.
FUWA (FWIP)

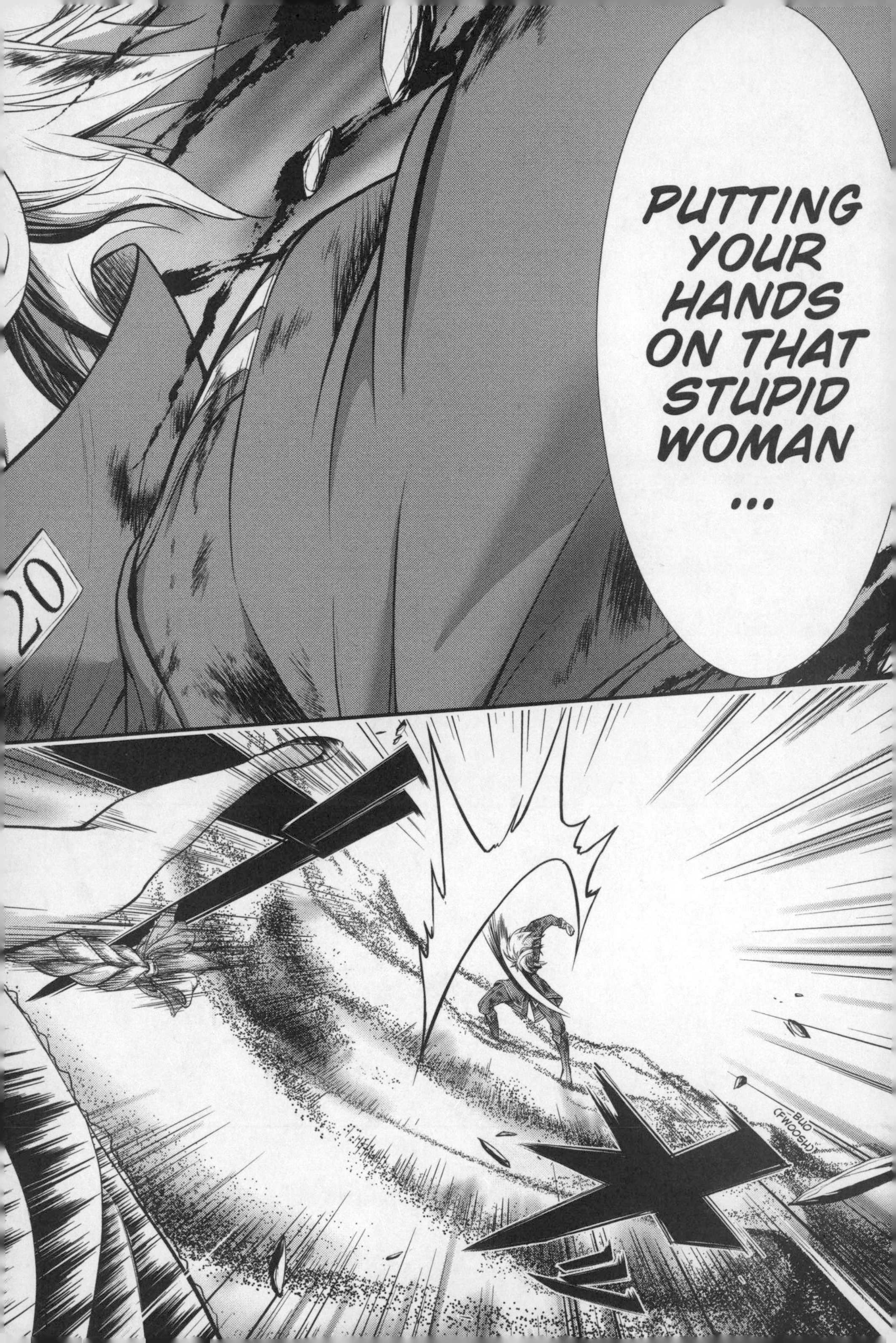
PUTTING YOUR HANDS ON THAT STUPID WOMAN ...
20
BUO (FWOOSH)

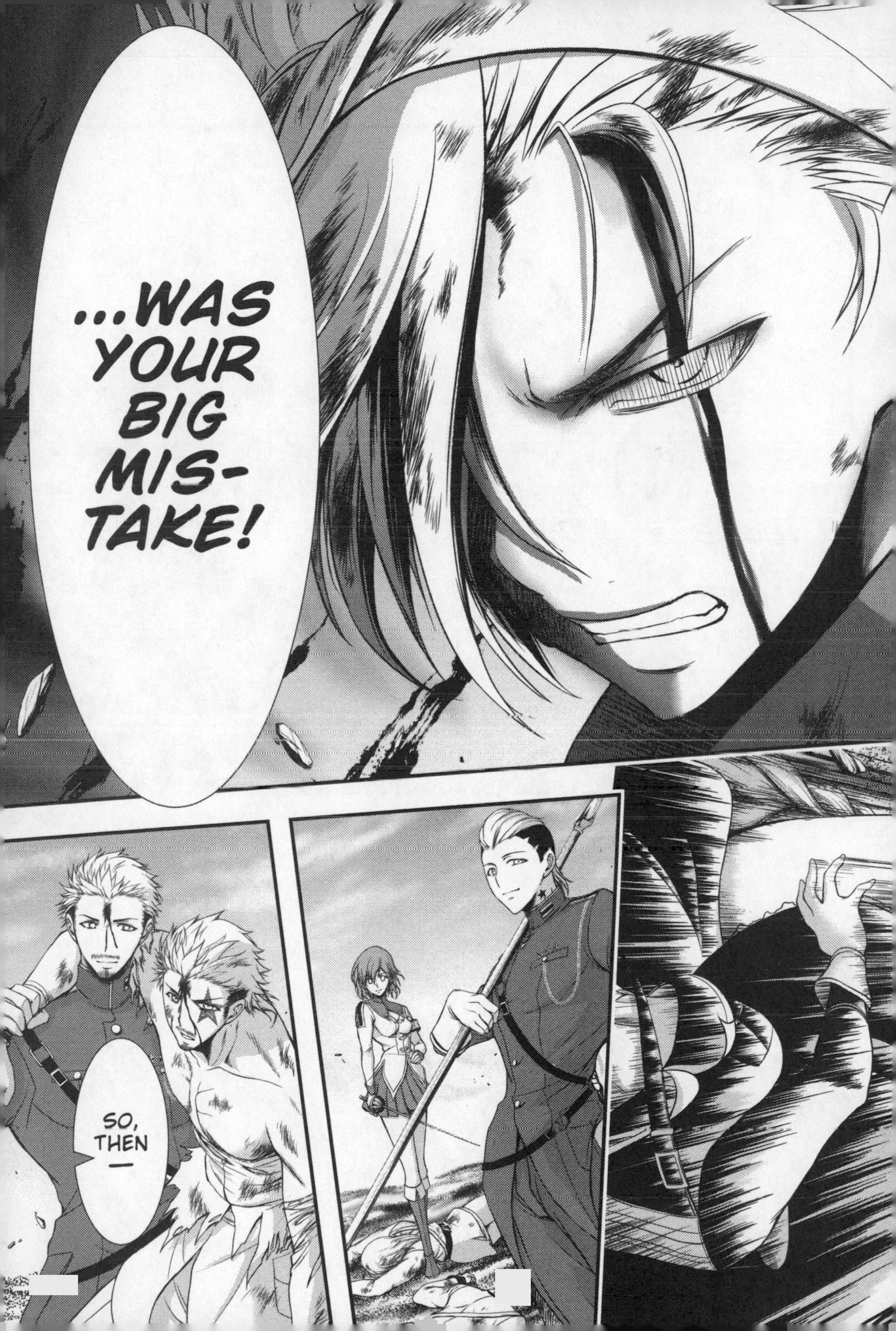
...WAS YOUR BIG MIS- TAKE!
SO, THEN —

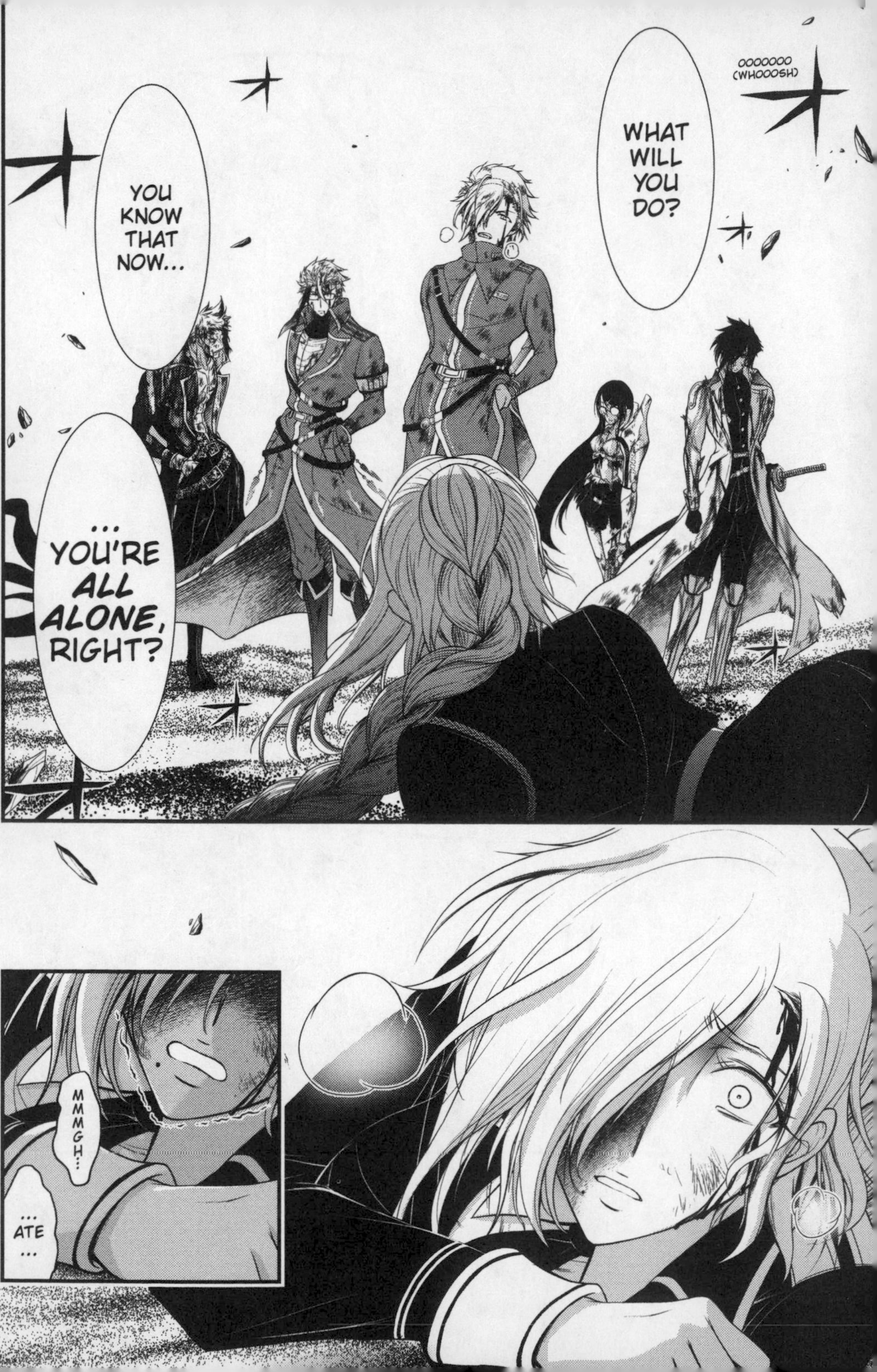
OOOOOOO (WHOOOSH)
WHAT WILL YOU DO?
YOU KNOW THAT NOW...
... YOU'RE *ALL ALONE*, RIGHT?
MMMGH...
... ATE ...

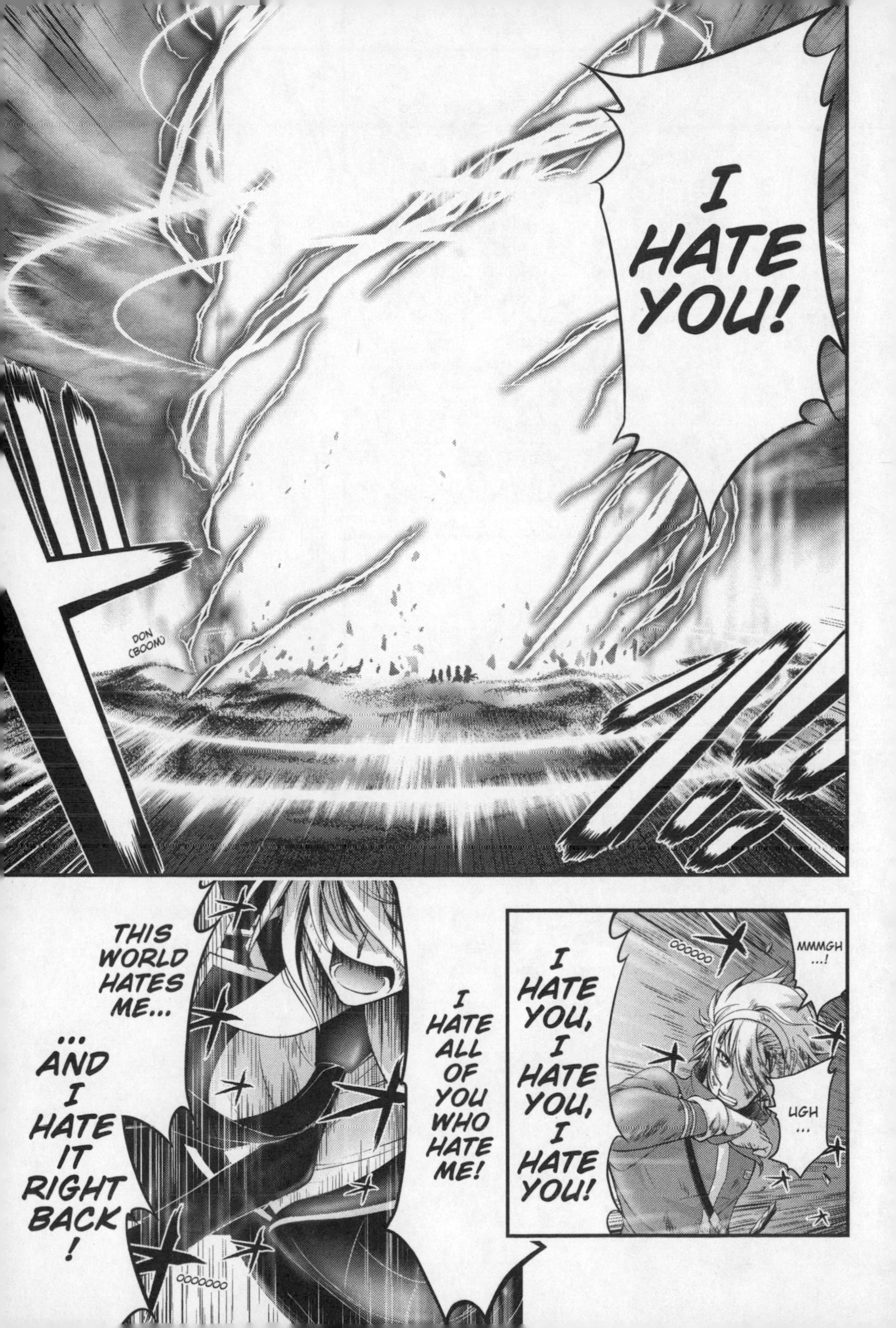
I HATE YOU!
DON (BOOM)
MMMGH ...!
OOOOOO
I HATE YOU, I HATE YOU, I HATE YOU!
UGH ...
I HATE ALL OF YOU WHO HATE ME!
THIS WORLD HATES ME...
... AND I HATE IT RIGHT BACK!
OOOOOOO

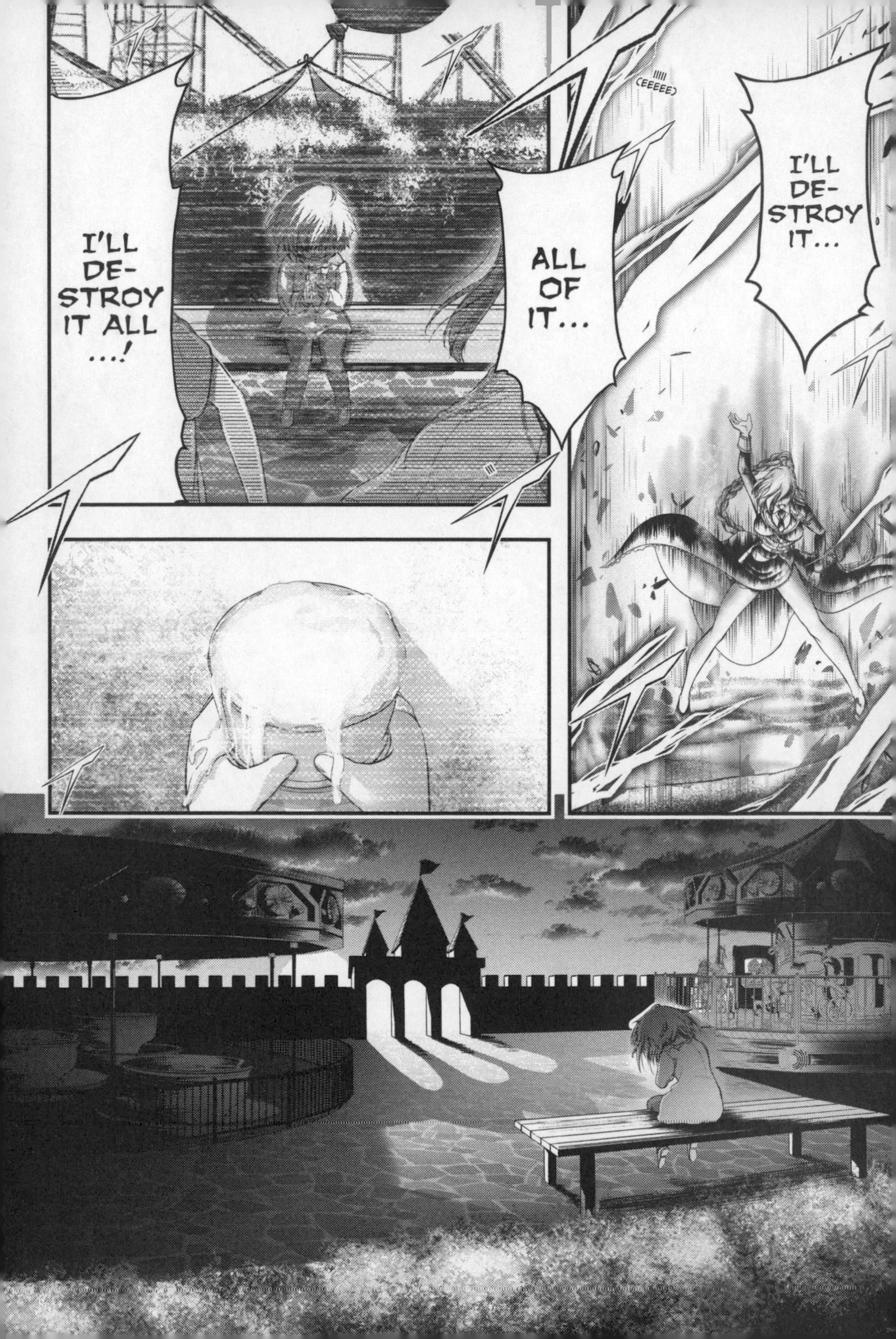

(EEEEE)
I'LL DE-STROY IT...
ALL OF IT...
I'LL DE-STROY IT ALL ...!

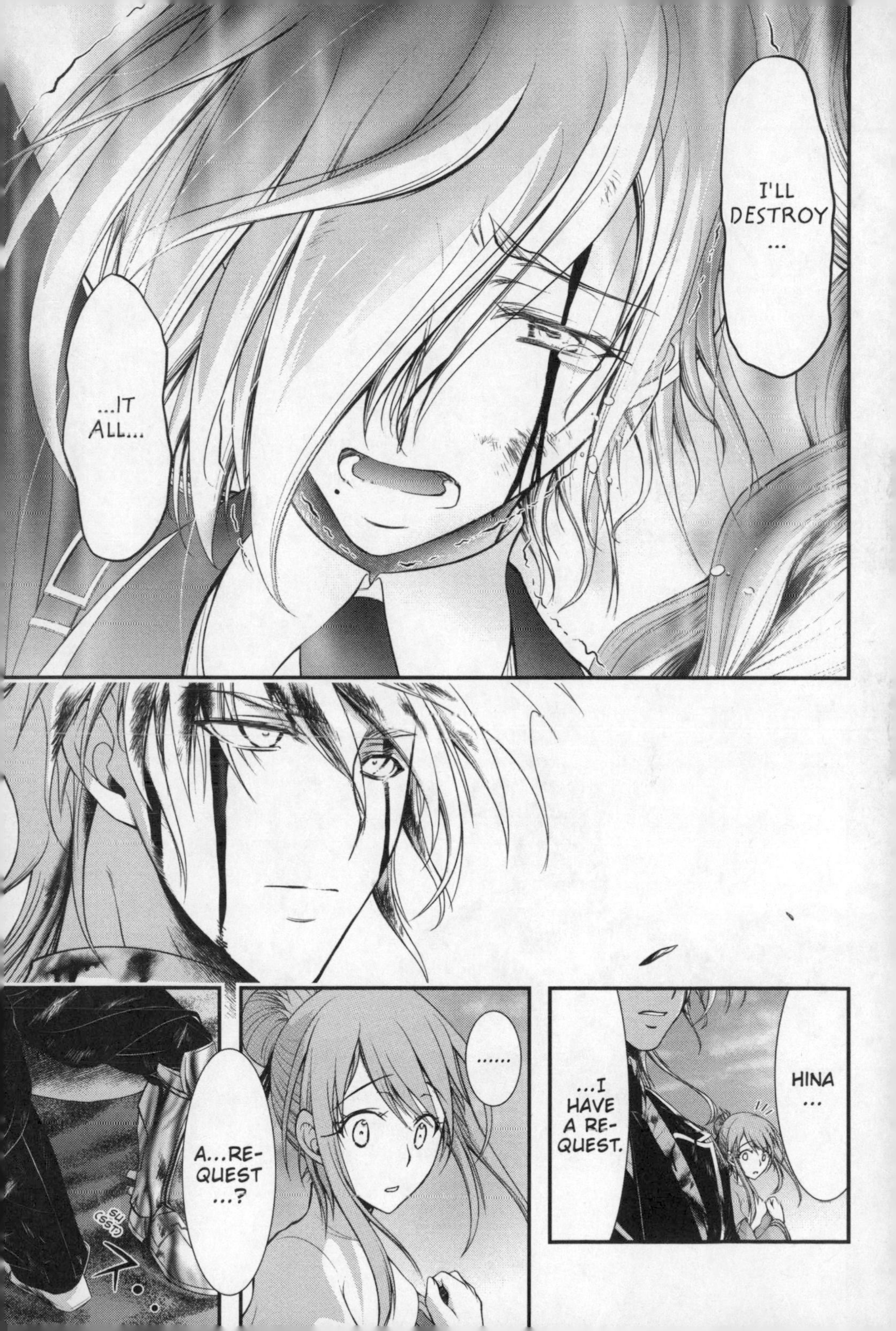
I'LL DESTROY ...
...IT ALL...
HINA ...
...I HAVE A RE-QUEST.
......
A...RE-QUEST ...?
SU (SST)

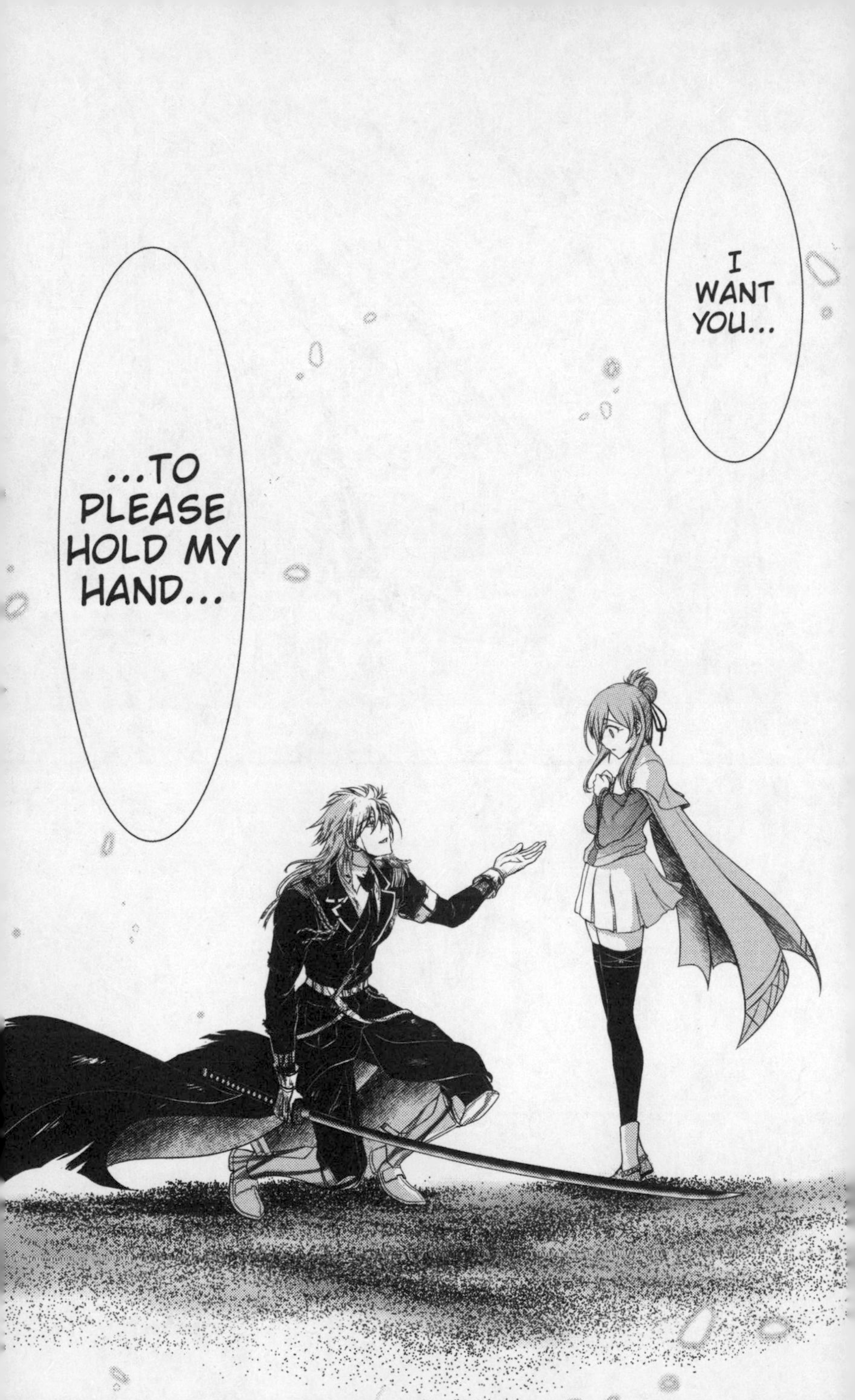
I WANT YOU...
...TO PLEASE HOLD MY HAND...

CHAPTER 76: END

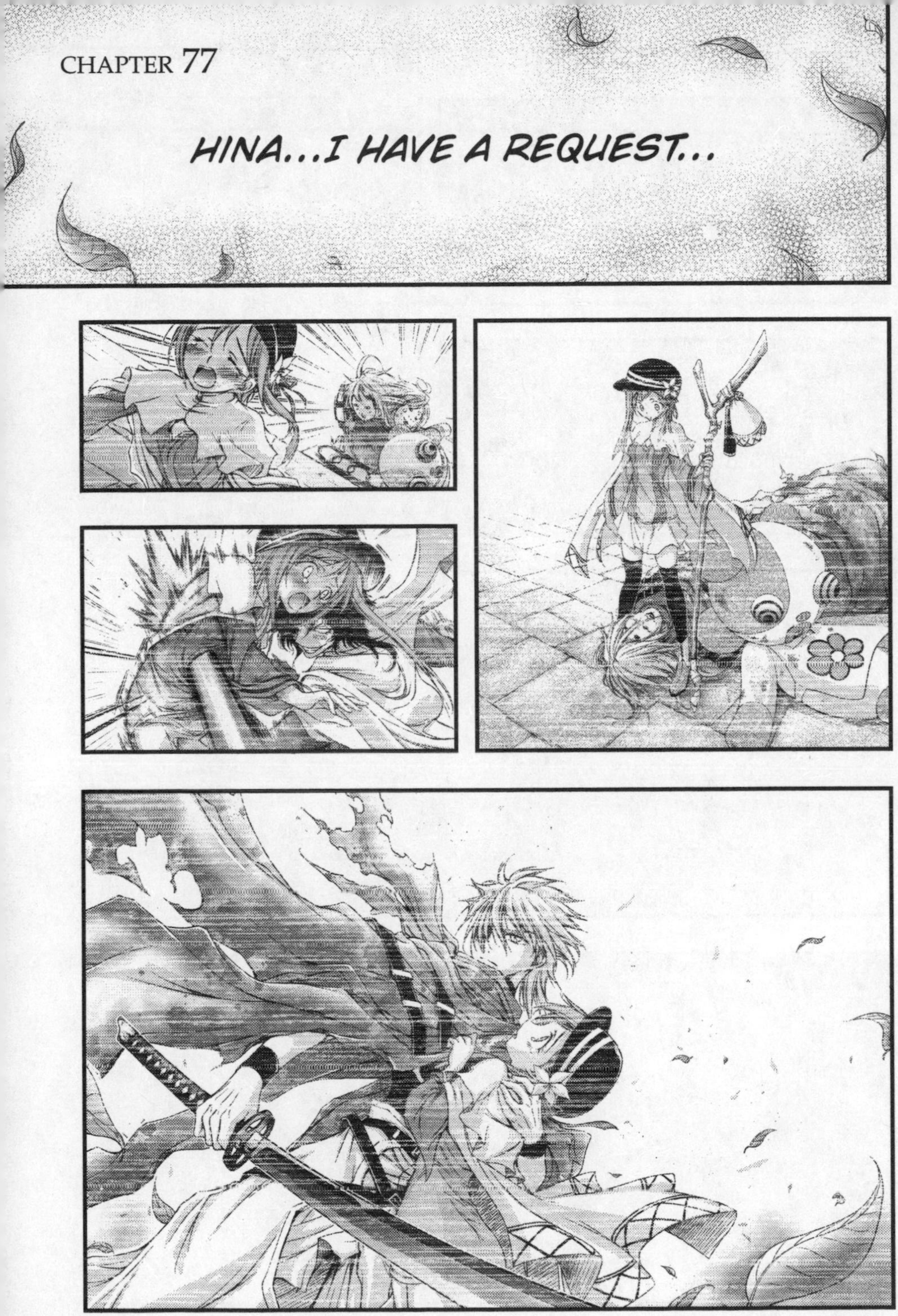
CHAPTER 77
HINA...I HAVE A REQUEST...

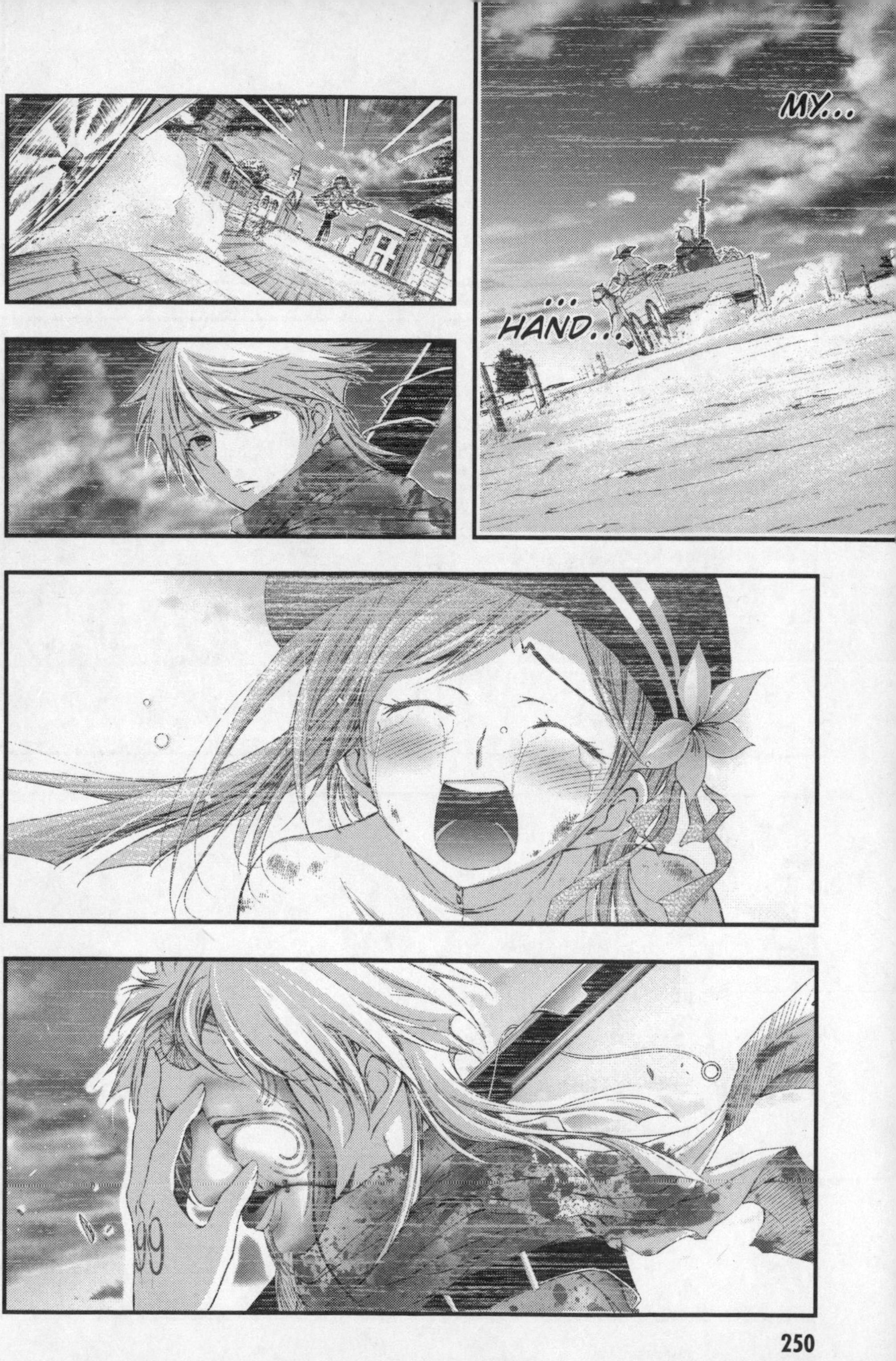
MY...
...HAND...

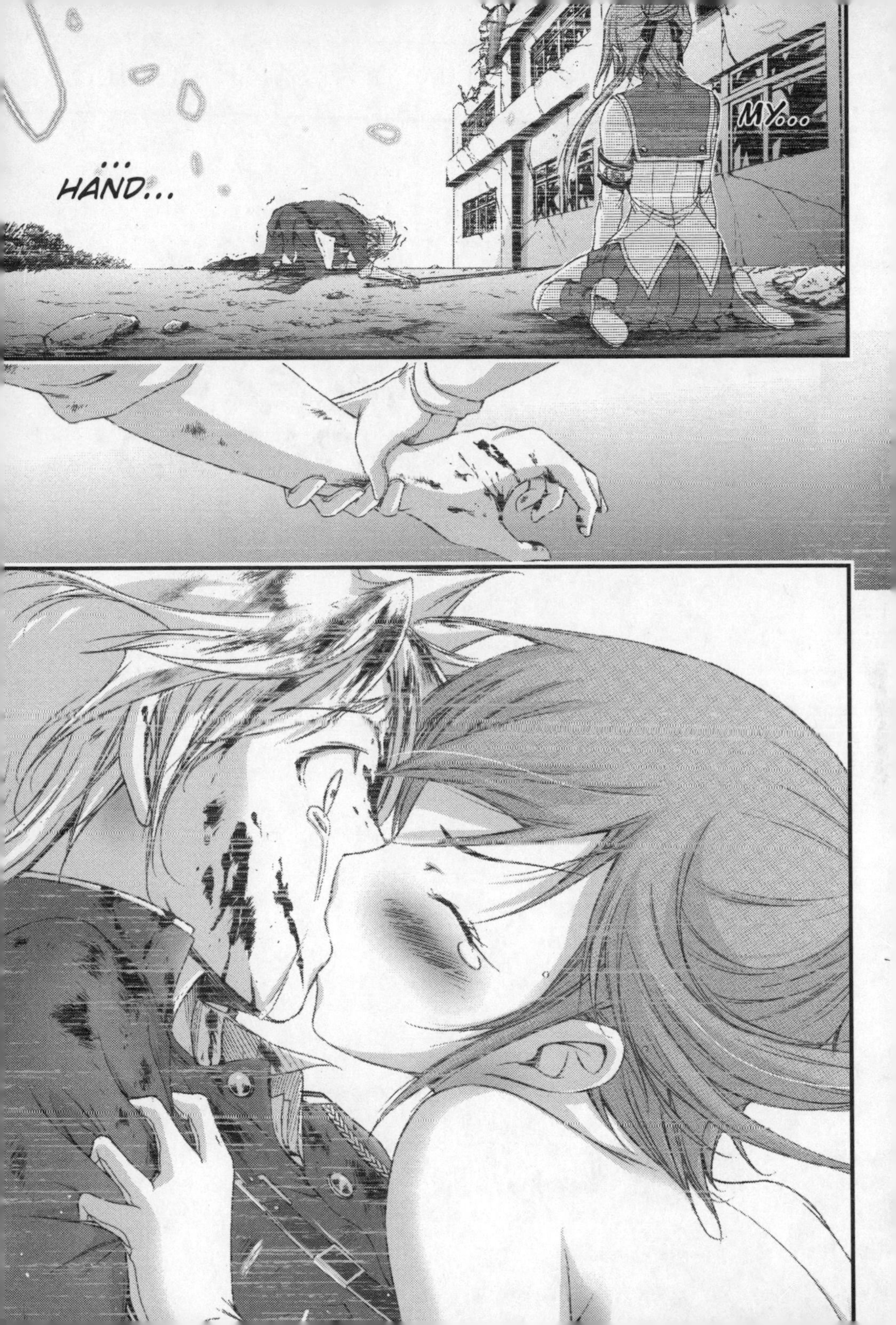
MY...
...HAND...

CHAPTER 77: STILL A CHILD

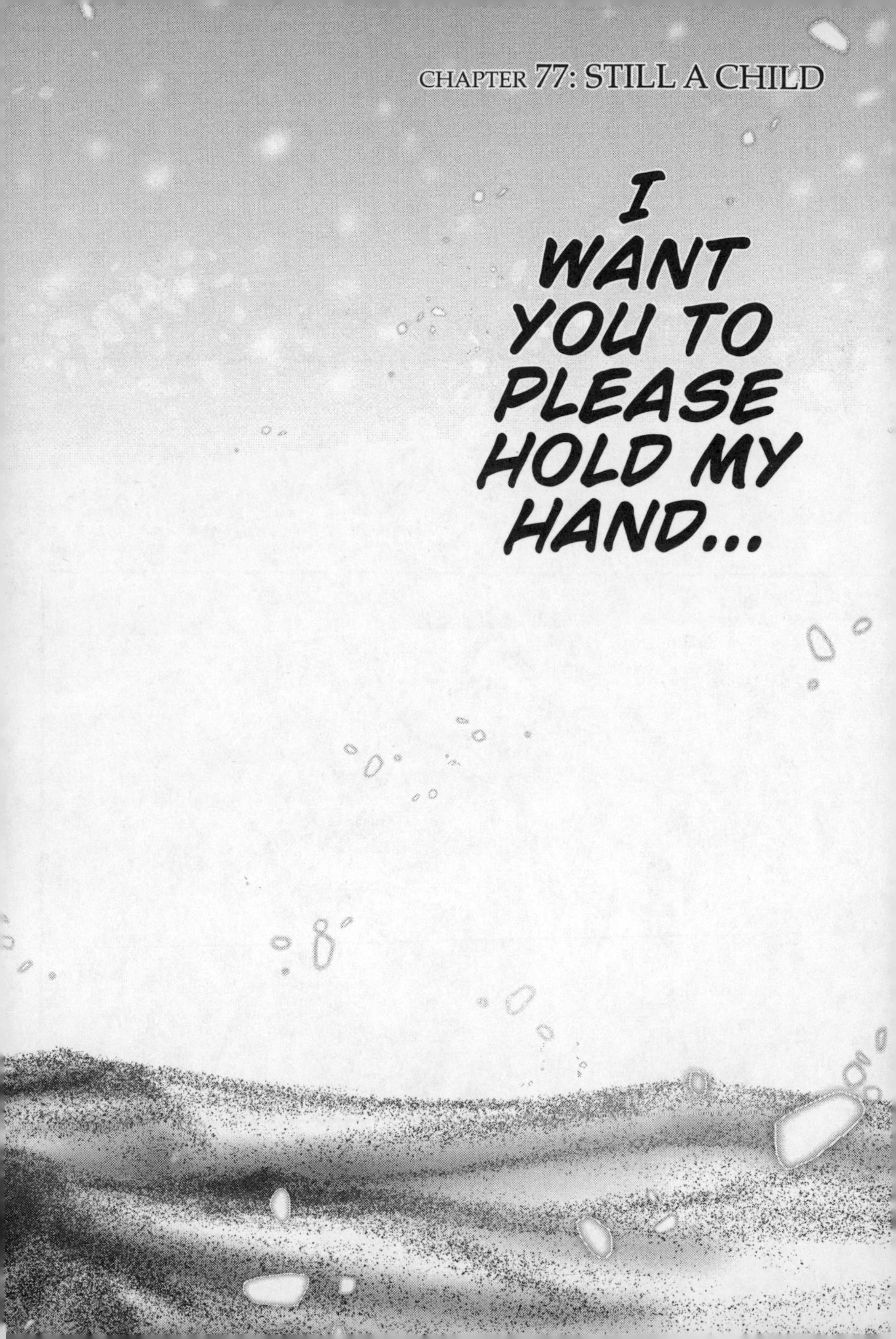
I WANT YOU TO PLEASE HOLD MY HAND...

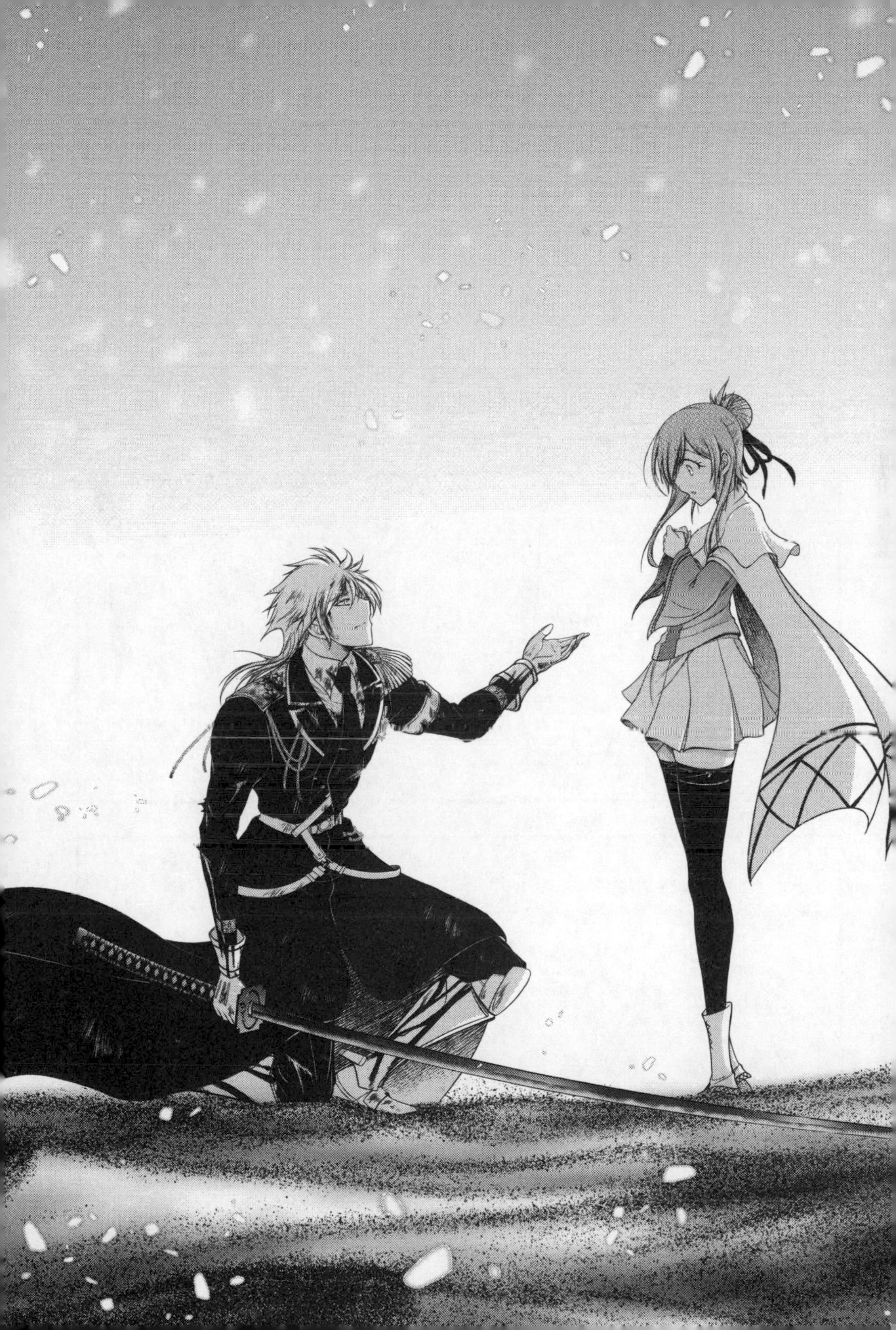

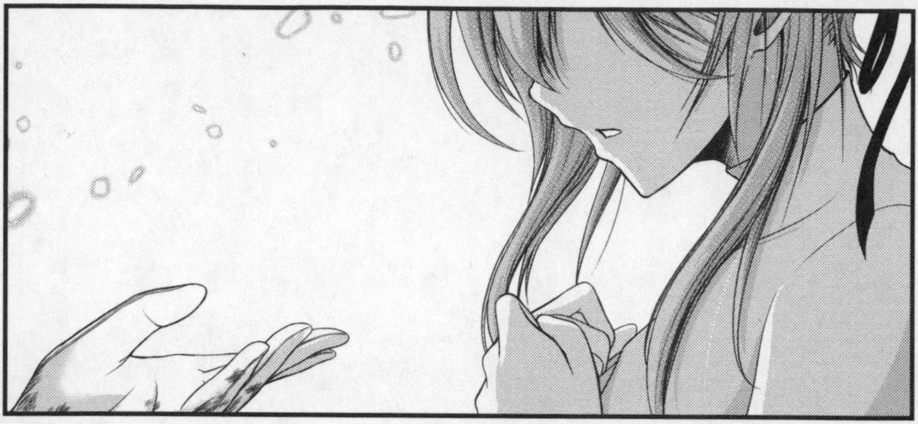

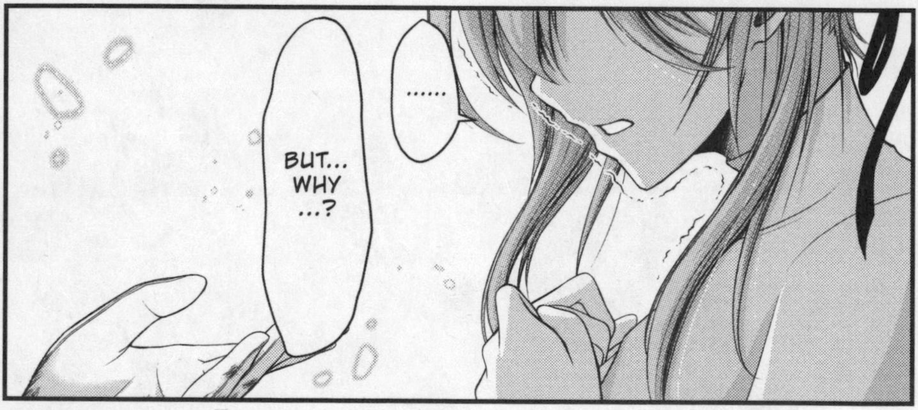
......
BUT... WHY ...?

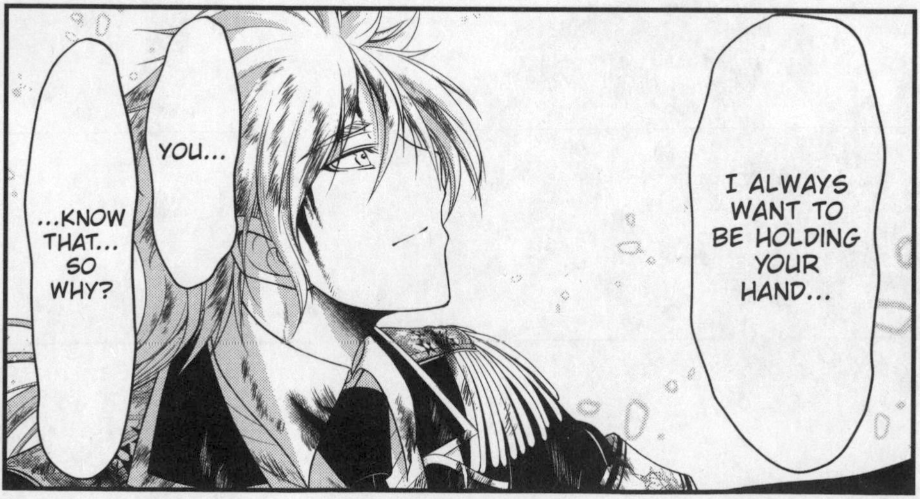
I ALWAYS WANT TO BE HOLDING YOUR HAND...
YOU...
...KNOW THAT... SO WHY?

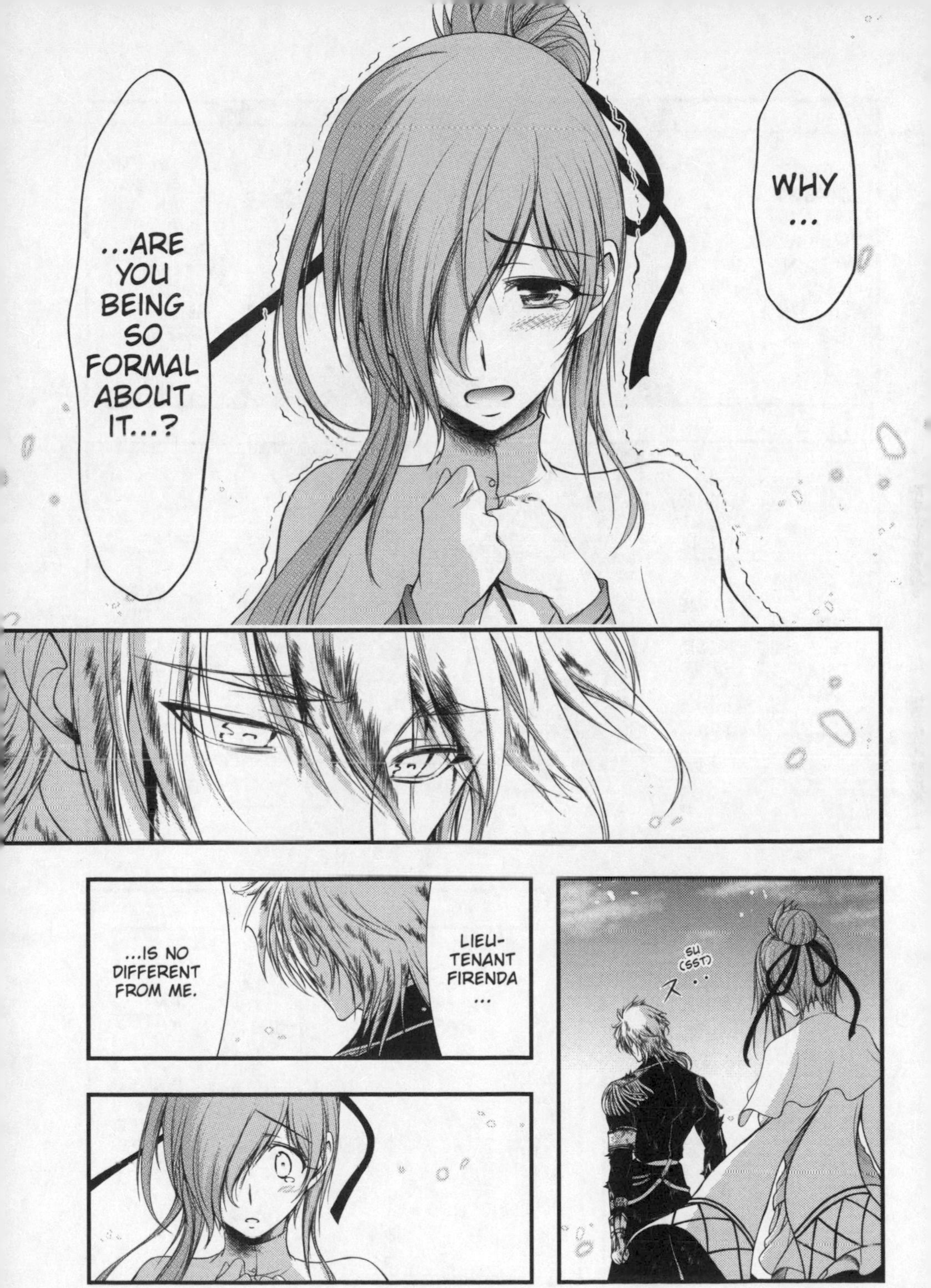
WHY...
...ARE YOU BEING SO FORMAL ABOUT IT...?
ス
SU (SST)
LIEU-TENANT FIRENDA...
...IS NO DIFFERENT FROM ME.

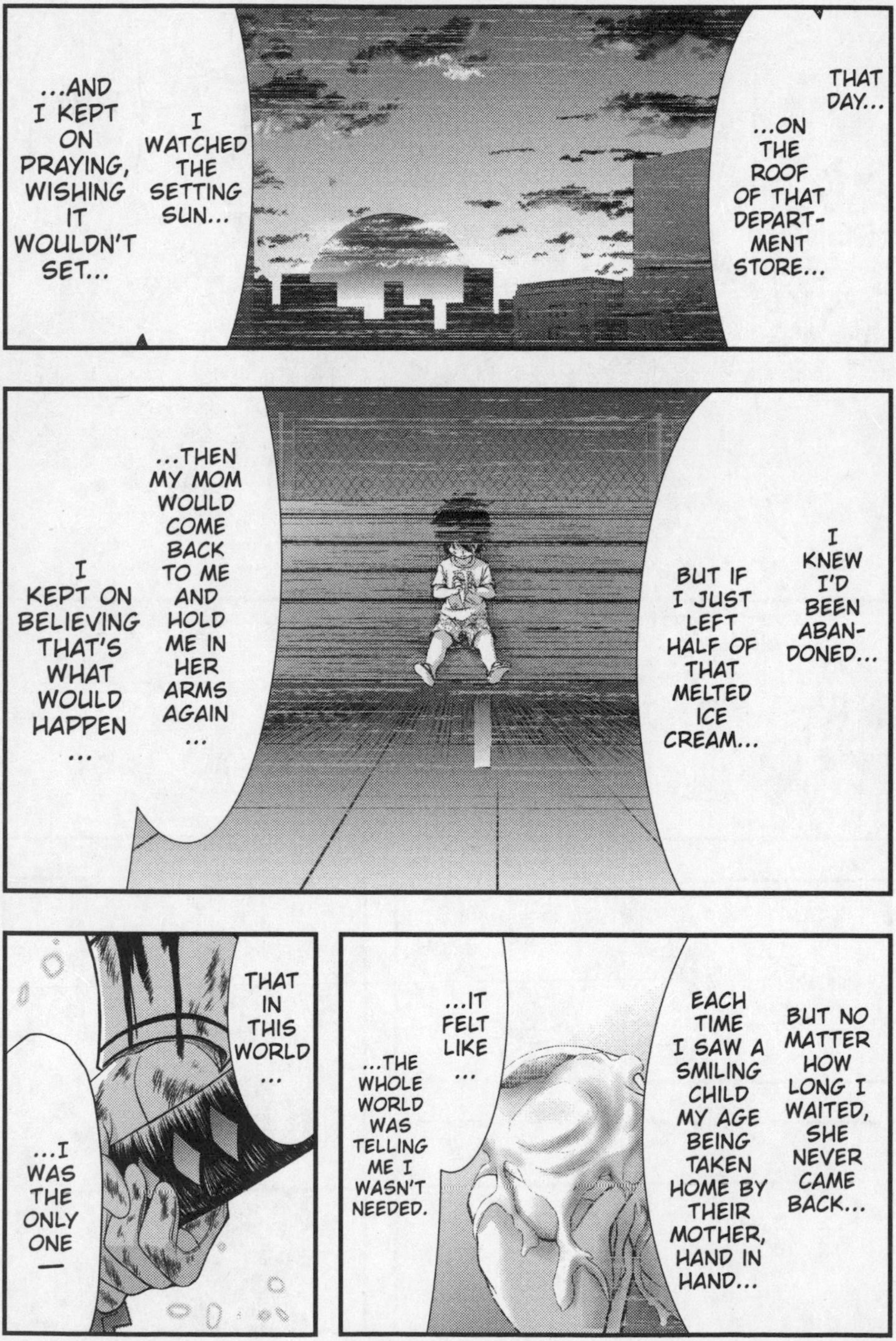
THAT DAY...
...ON THE ROOF OF THAT DEPARTMENT STORE...
I WATCHED THE SETTING SUN...
...AND I KEPT ON PRAYING, WISHING IT WOULDN'T SET...
I KNEW I'D BEEN ABANDONED...
BUT IF I JUST LEFT HALF OF THAT MELTED ICE CREAM...
...THEN MY MOM WOULD COME BACK TO ME AND HOLD ME IN HER ARMS AGAIN...
I KEPT ON BELIEVING THAT'S WHAT WOULD HAPPEN...
BUT NO MATTER HOW LONG I WAITED, SHE NEVER CAME BACK...
EACH TIME I SAW A SMILING CHILD MY AGE BEING TAKEN HOME BY THEIR MOTHER, HAND IN HAND...
...IT FELT LIKE...
...THE WHOLE WORLD WAS TELLING ME I WASN'T NEEDED.
THAT IN THIS WORLD...
...I WAS THE ONLY ONE —

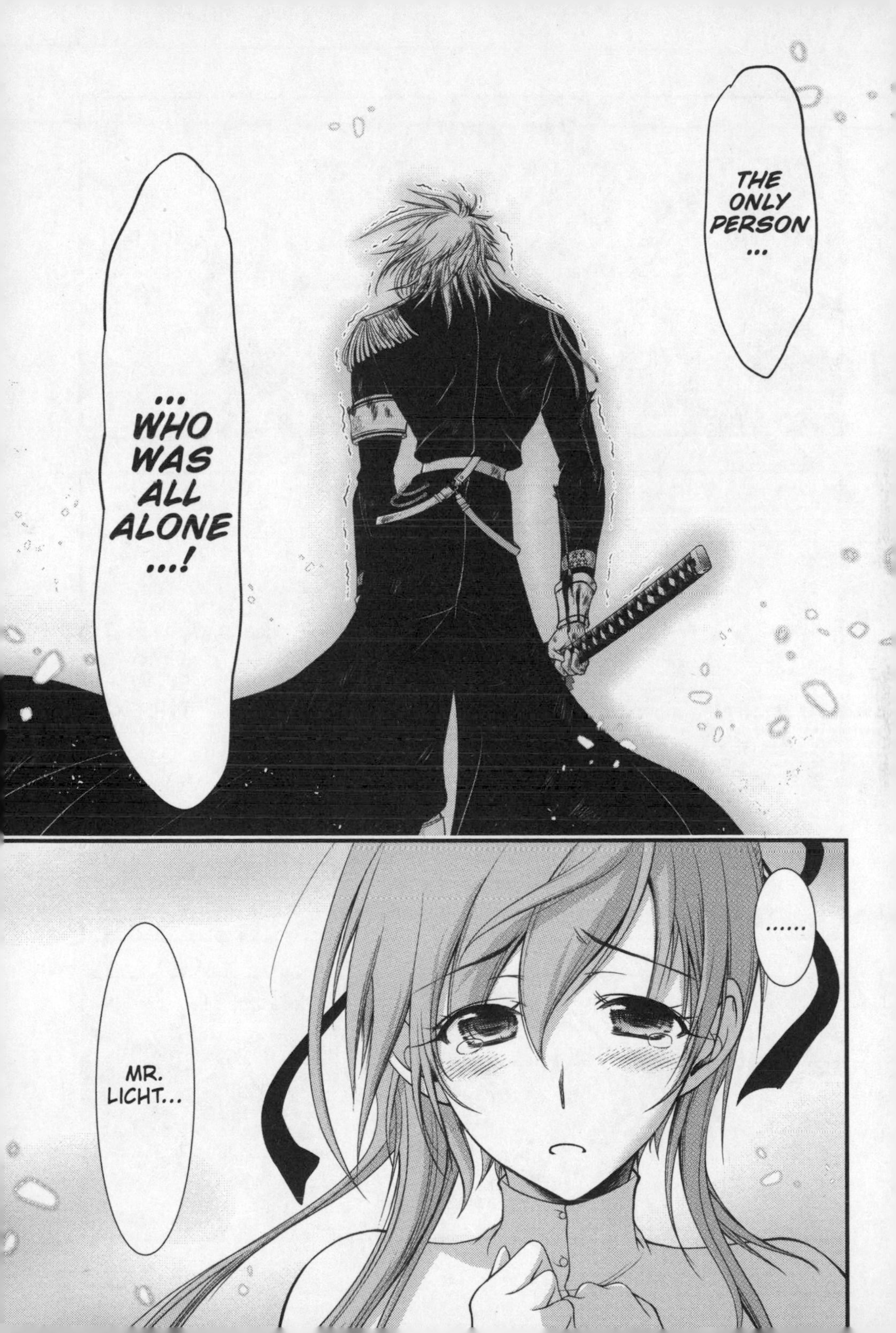
THE ONLY PERSON ...
... WHO WAS ALL ALONE ...!
......
MR. LICHT...

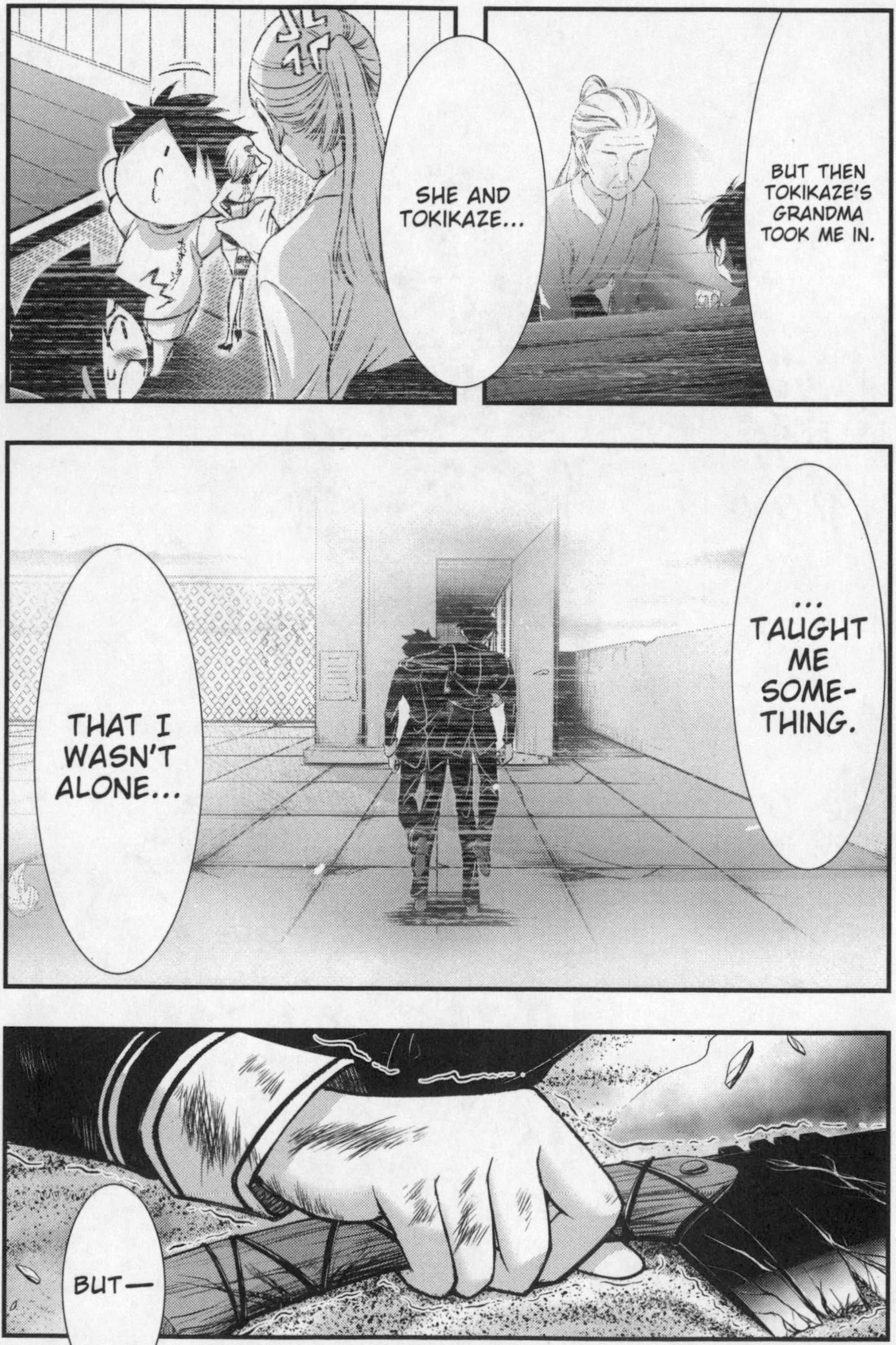
BUT THEN TOKIKAZE'S GRANDMA TOOK ME IN.
SHE AND TOKIKAZE...
...TAUGHT ME SOME-THING.
THAT I WASN'T ALONE...
BUT—

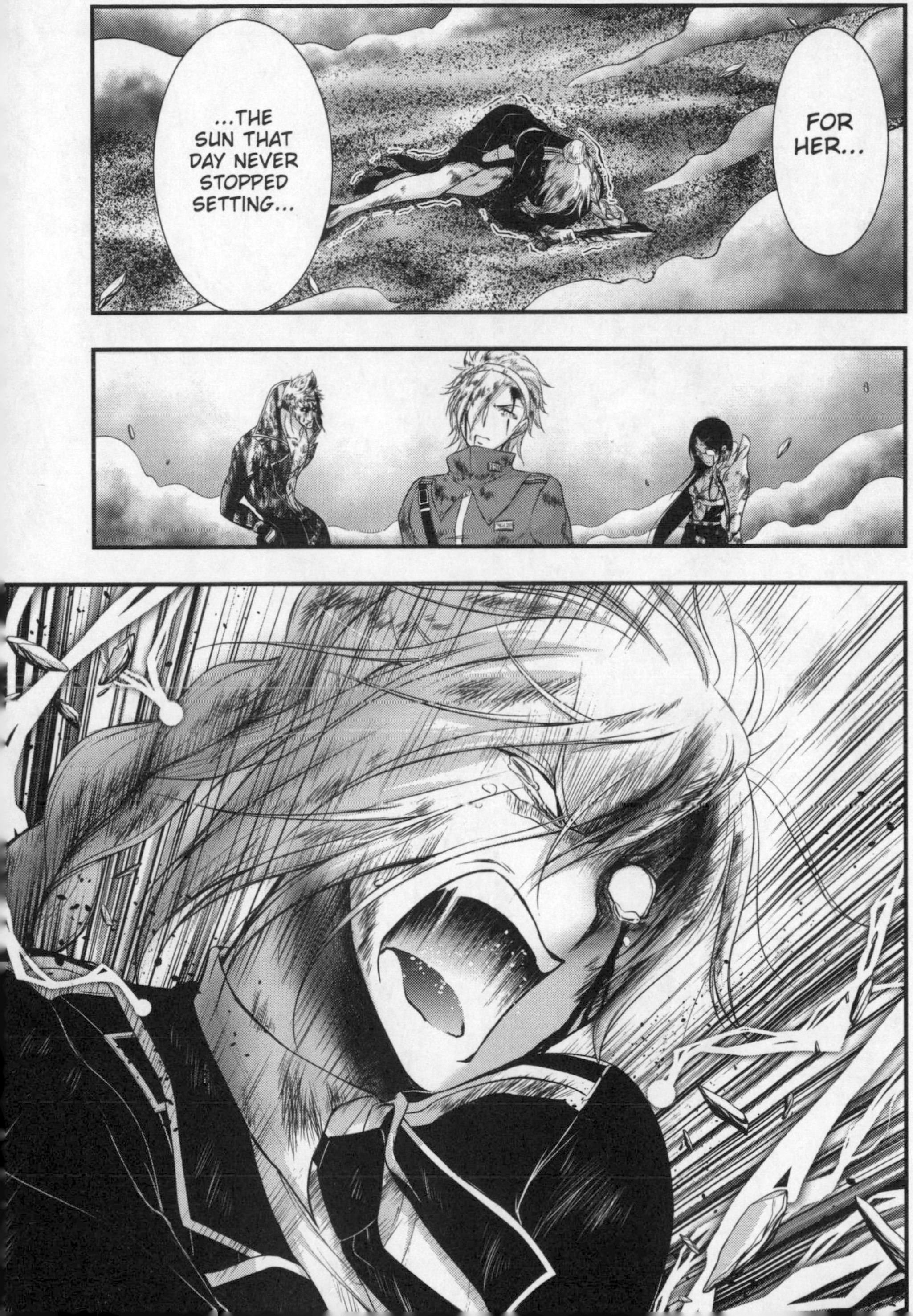
FOR HER...
...THE SUN THAT DAY NEVER STOPPED SETTING...

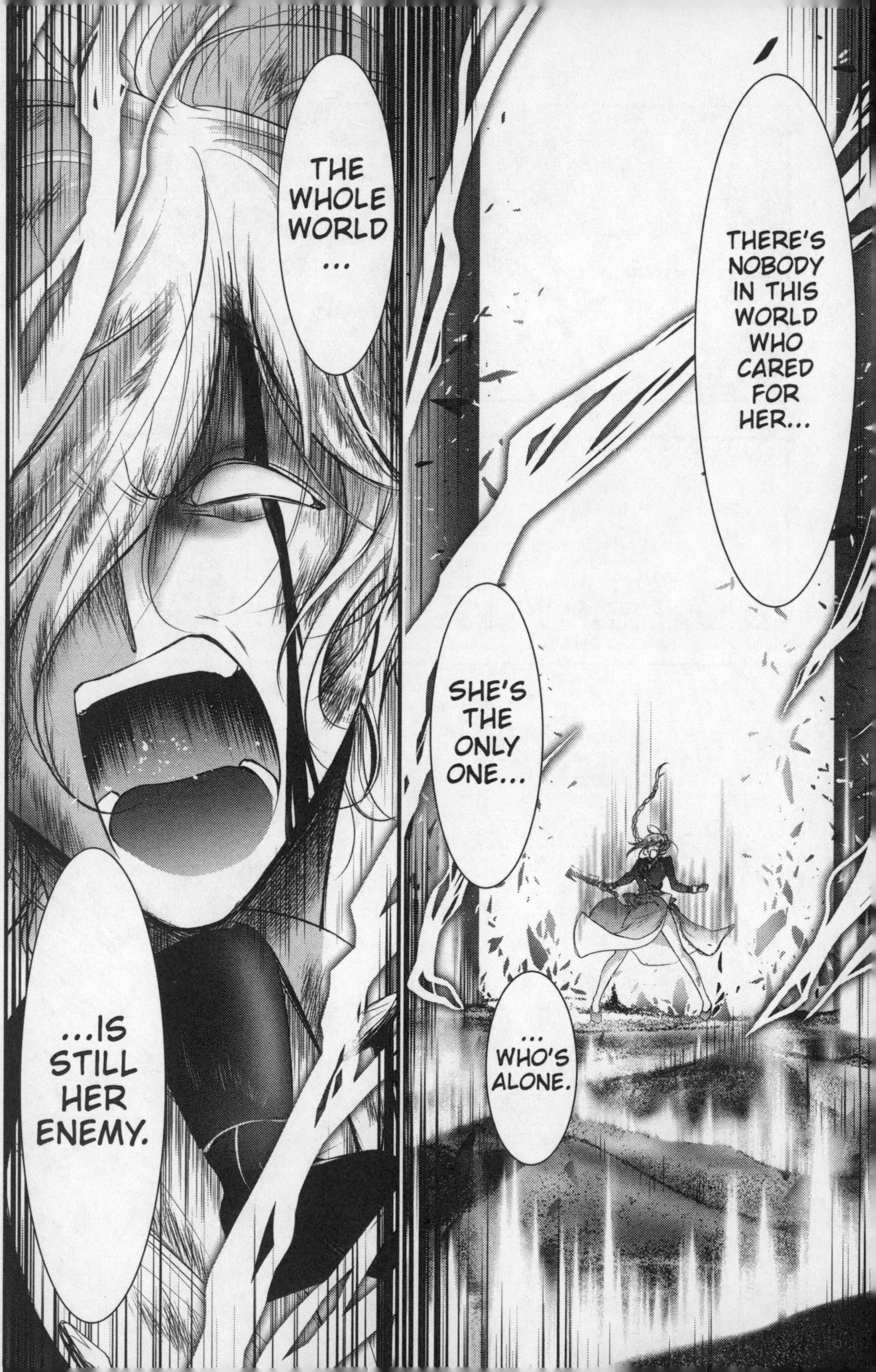
THERE'S NOBODY IN THIS WORLD WHO CARED FOR HER...
SHE'S THE ONLY ONE...
... WHO'S ALONE.
THE WHOLE WORLD ...
...IS STILL HER ENEMY.

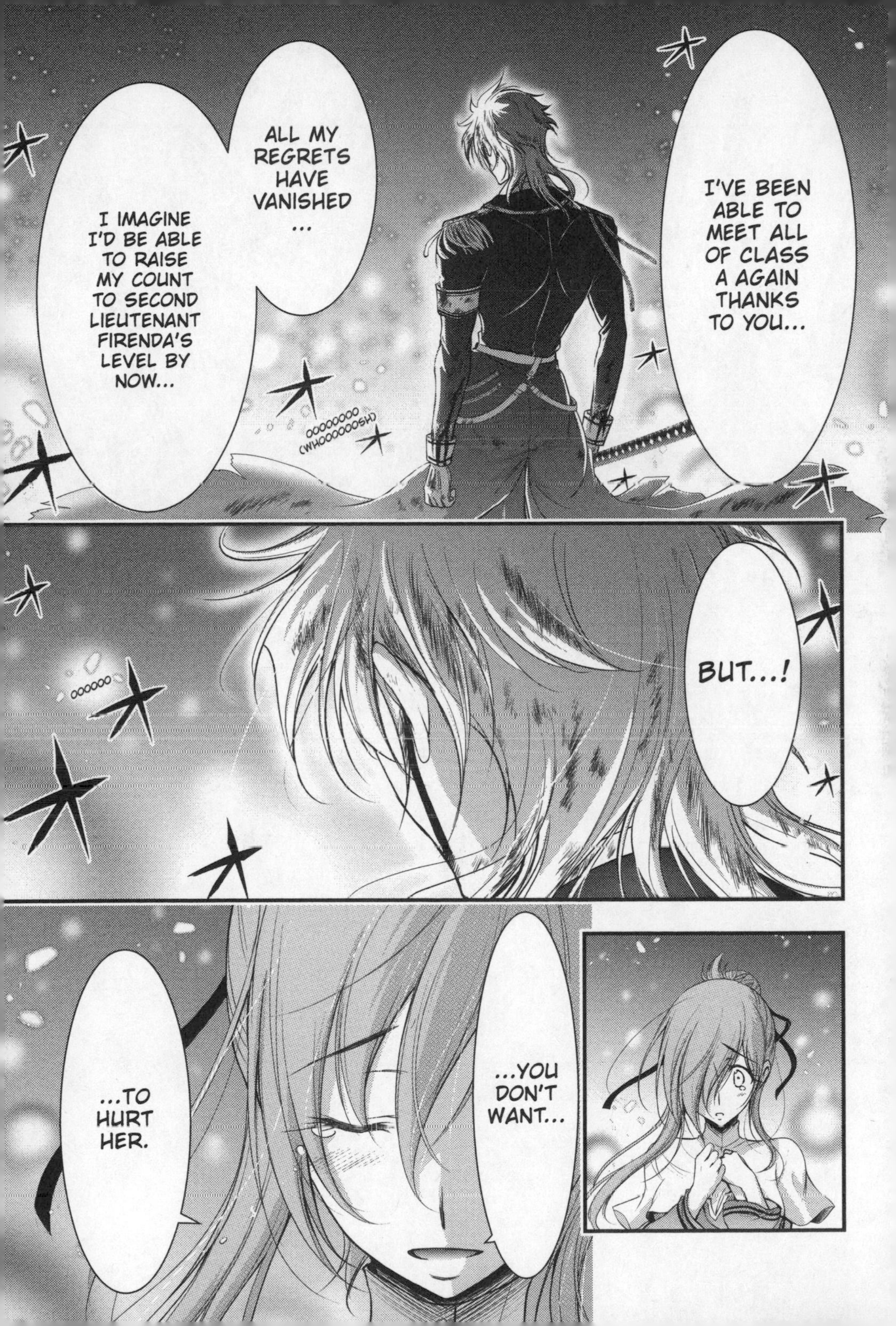
I'VE BEEN ABLE TO MEET ALL OF CLASS A AGAIN THANKS TO YOU...
ALL MY REGRETS HAVE VANISHED...
I IMAGINE I'D BE ABLE TO RAISE MY COUNT TO SECOND LIEUTENANT FIRENDA'S LEVEL BY NOW...
OOOOOOOO (WHOOOOOOSH)
BUT...!
OOOOOO
...YOU DON'T WANT...
...TO HURT HER.

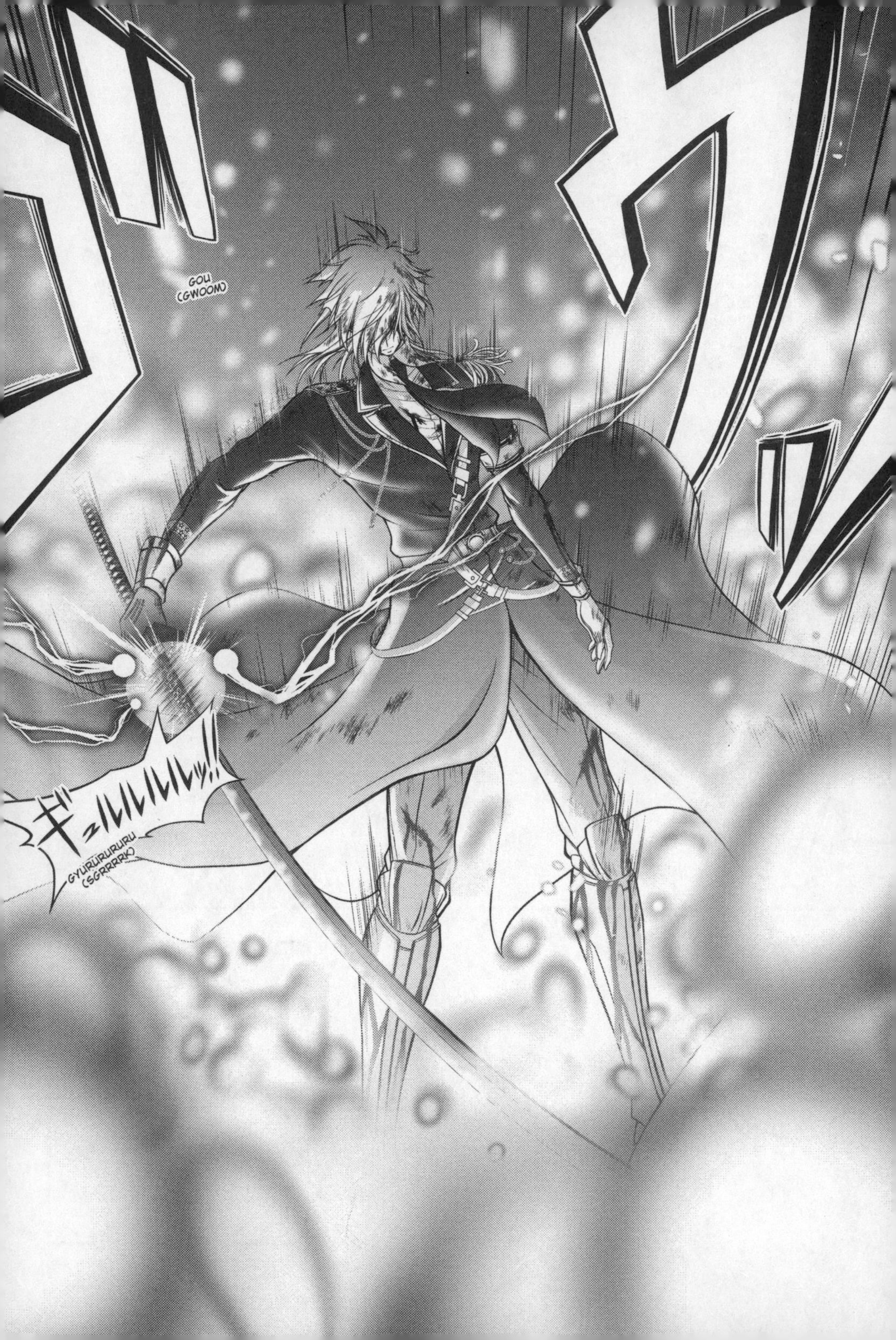
GOU
(GWOOM)
ギュルルルルルッ!!
GYURURURURU
(SGRRRRK)

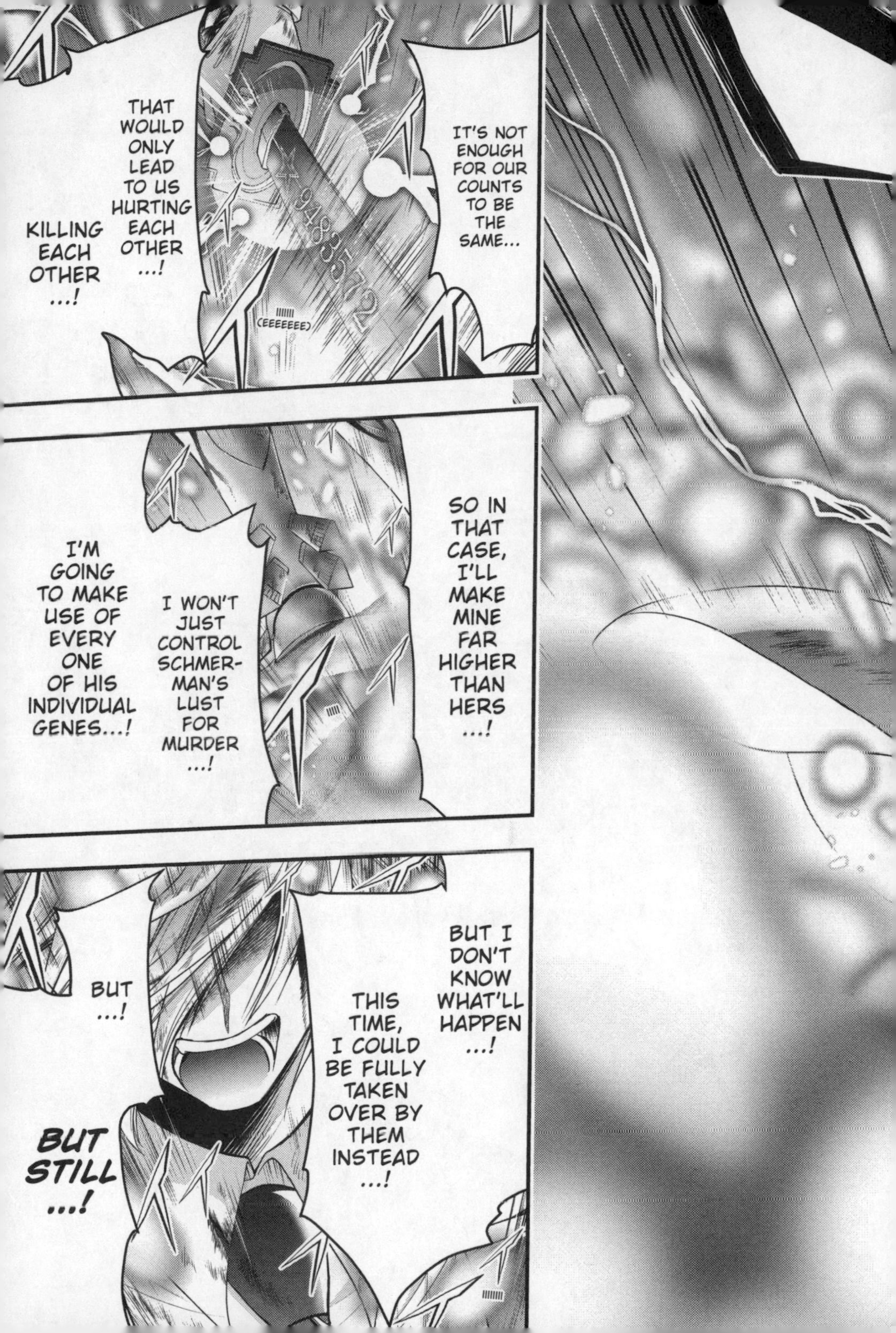
IT'S NOT ENOUGH FOR OUR COUNTS TO BE THE SAME...
THAT WOULD ONLY LEAD TO US HURTING EACH OTHER ...!
(EEEEEEE)
KILLING EACH OTHER ...!
SO IN THAT CASE, I'LL MAKE MINE FAR HIGHER THAN HERS ...!
I WON'T JUST CONTROL SCHMER-MAN'S LUST FOR MURDER ...!
I'M GOING TO MAKE USE OF EVERY ONE OF HIS INDIVIDUAL GENES...!
BUT I DON'T KNOW WHAT'LL HAPPEN ...!
THIS TIME, I COULD BE FULLY TAKEN OVER BY THEM INSTEAD ...!
BUT ...!
BUT STILL ...!

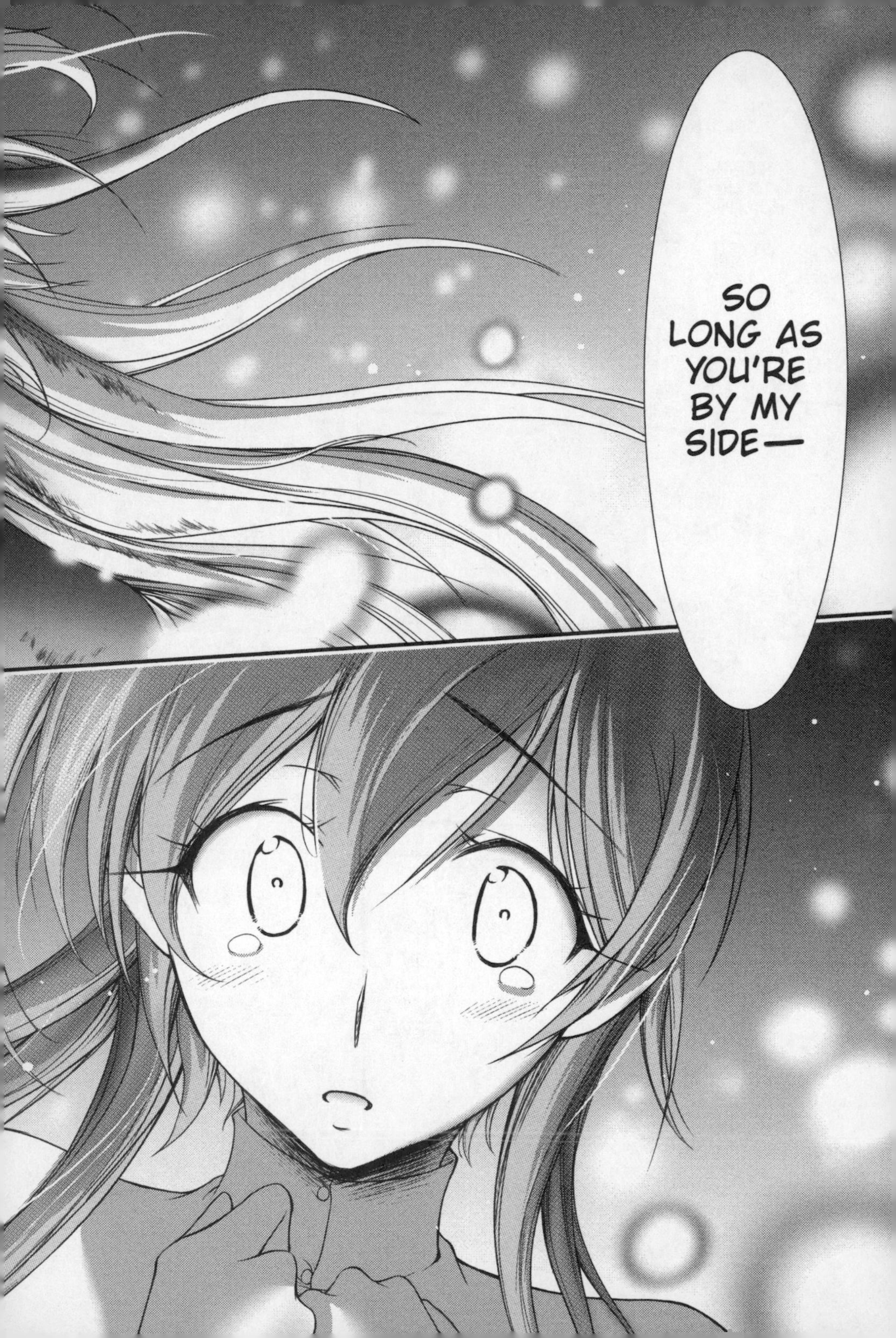
SO LONG AS YOU'RE BY MY SIDE—

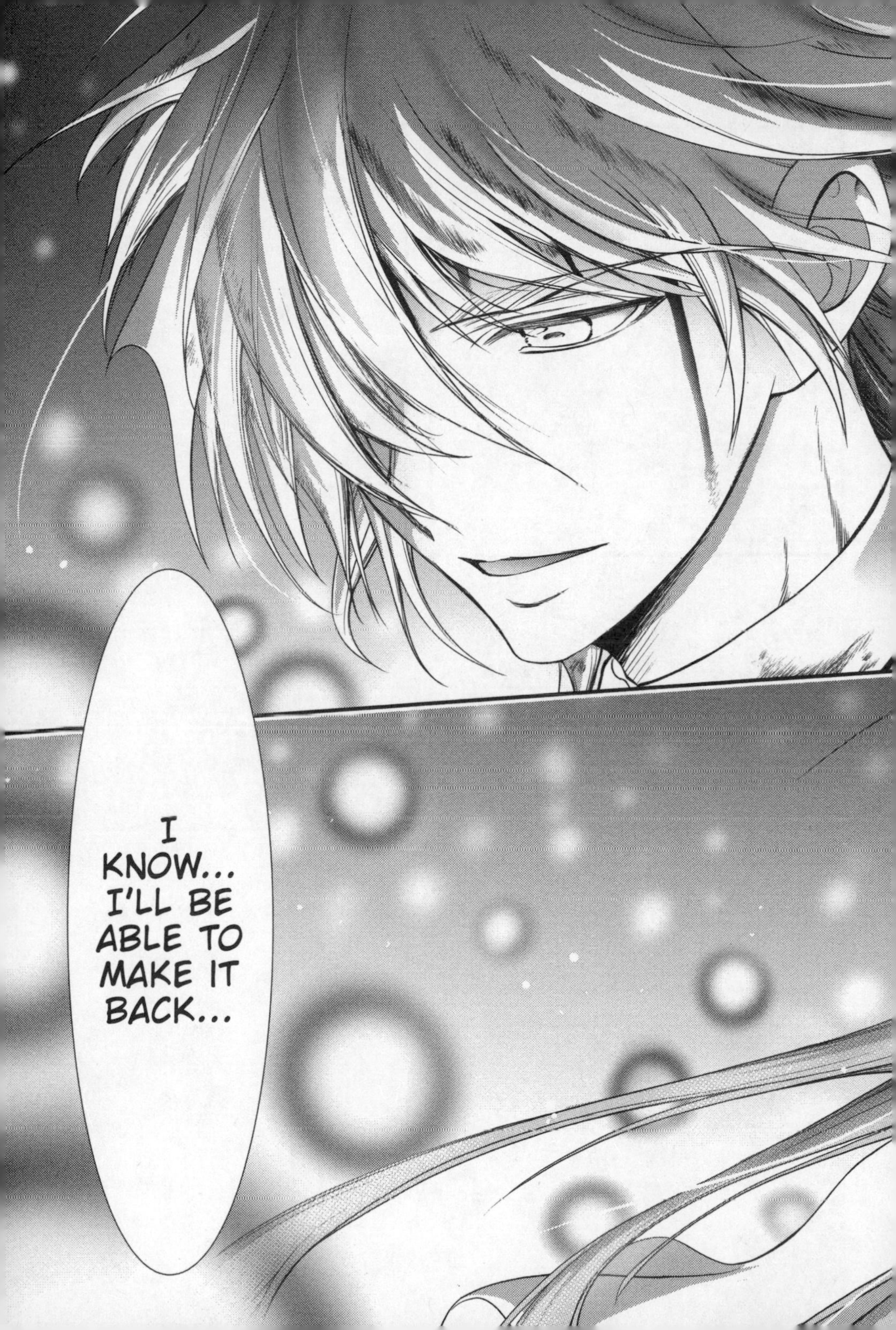
I KNOW... I'LL BE ABLE TO MAKE IT BACK...

RIGHT? JUST THINK ABOUT IT...

YOU'VE ALWAYS BEEN THERE FOR ME—

...HOW DARK A PLACE I WAS IN...

NO MATTER...

...HOW DEEP MY DESPAIR—

NO MATTER...

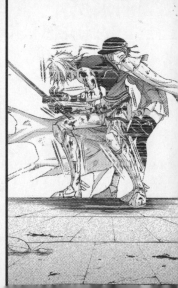

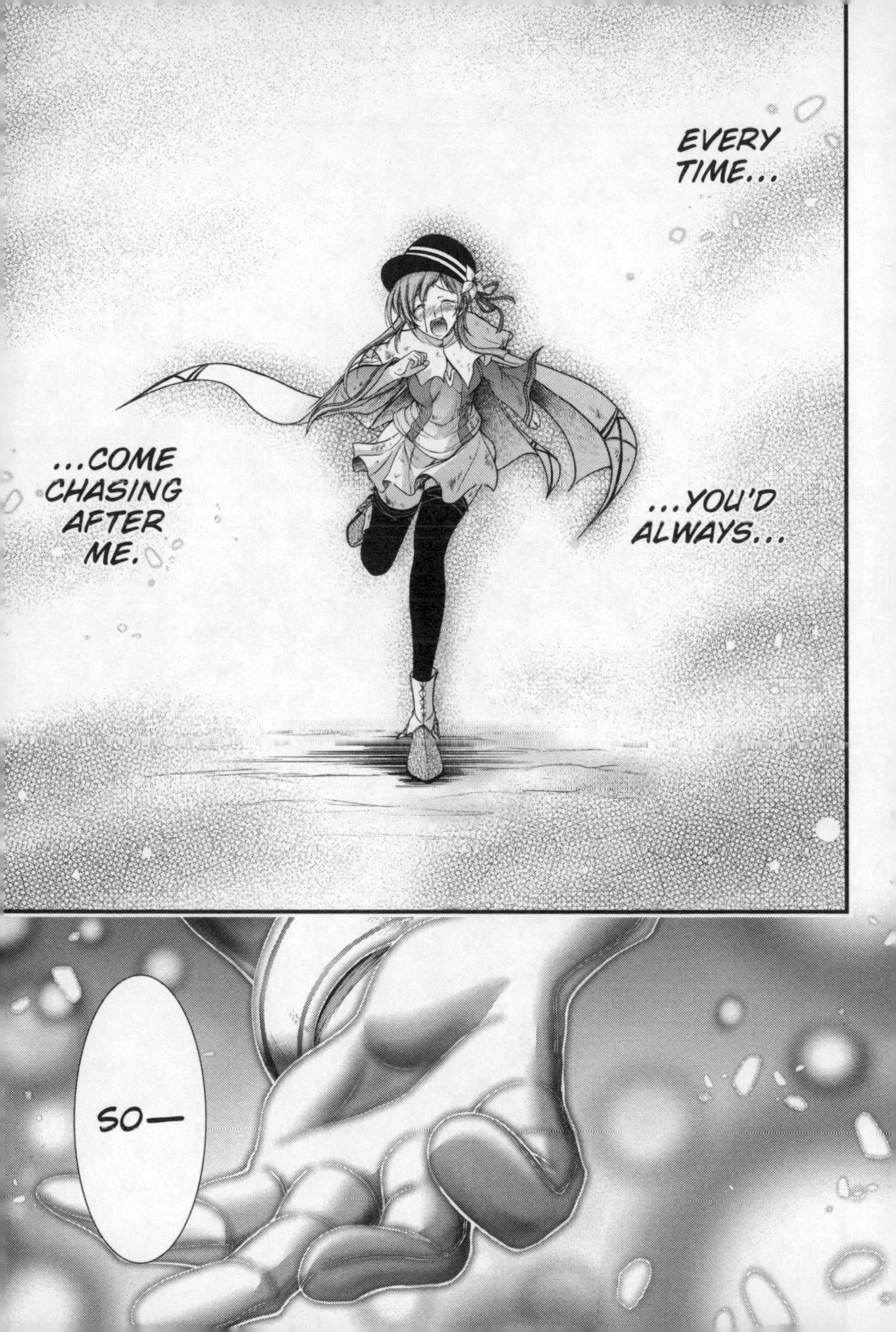
EVERY TIME...
...YOU'D ALWAYS...
...COME CHASING AFTER ME.
SO—

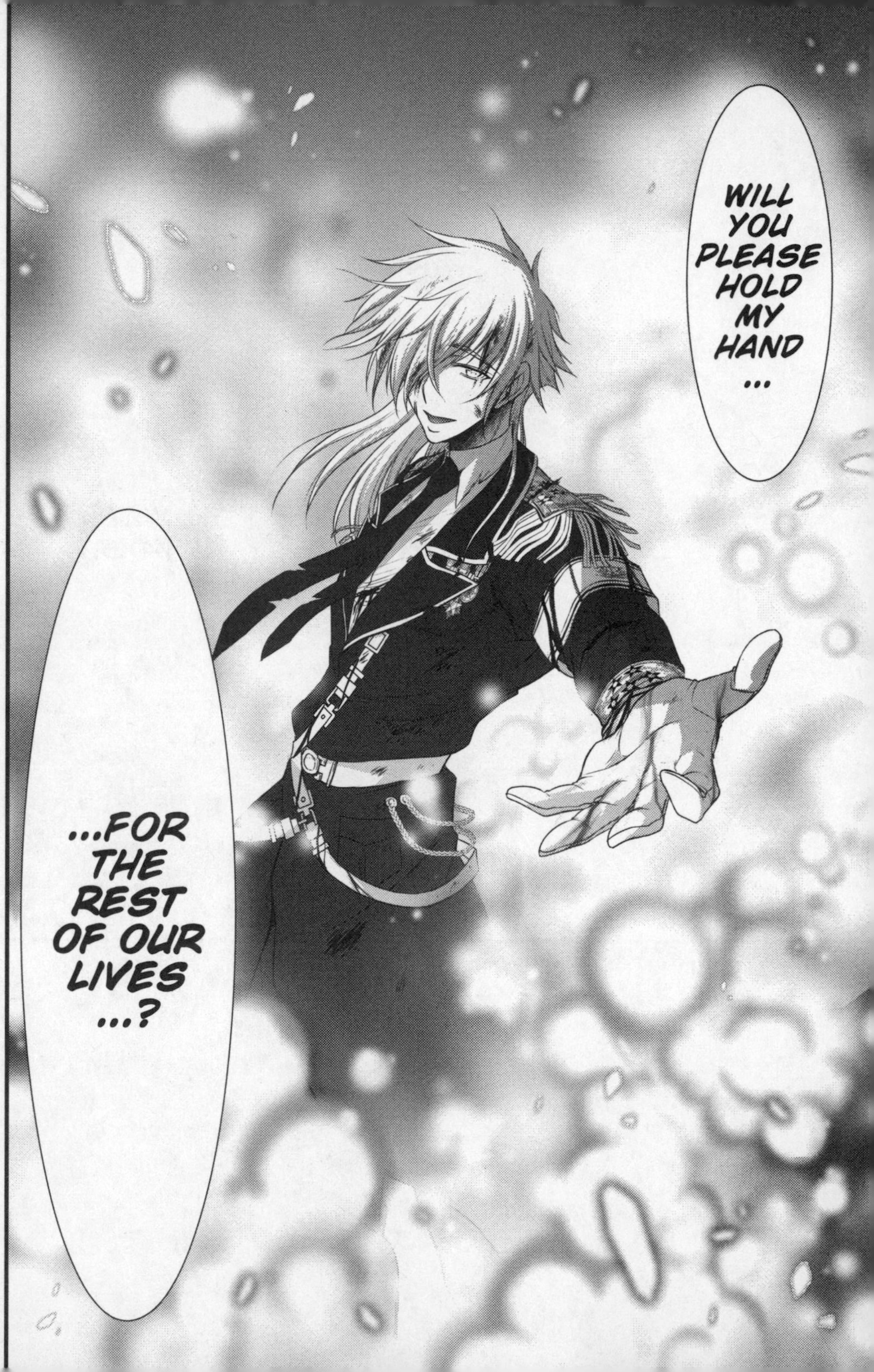
WILL YOU PLEASE HOLD MY HAND...
...FOR THE REST OF OUR LIVES...?

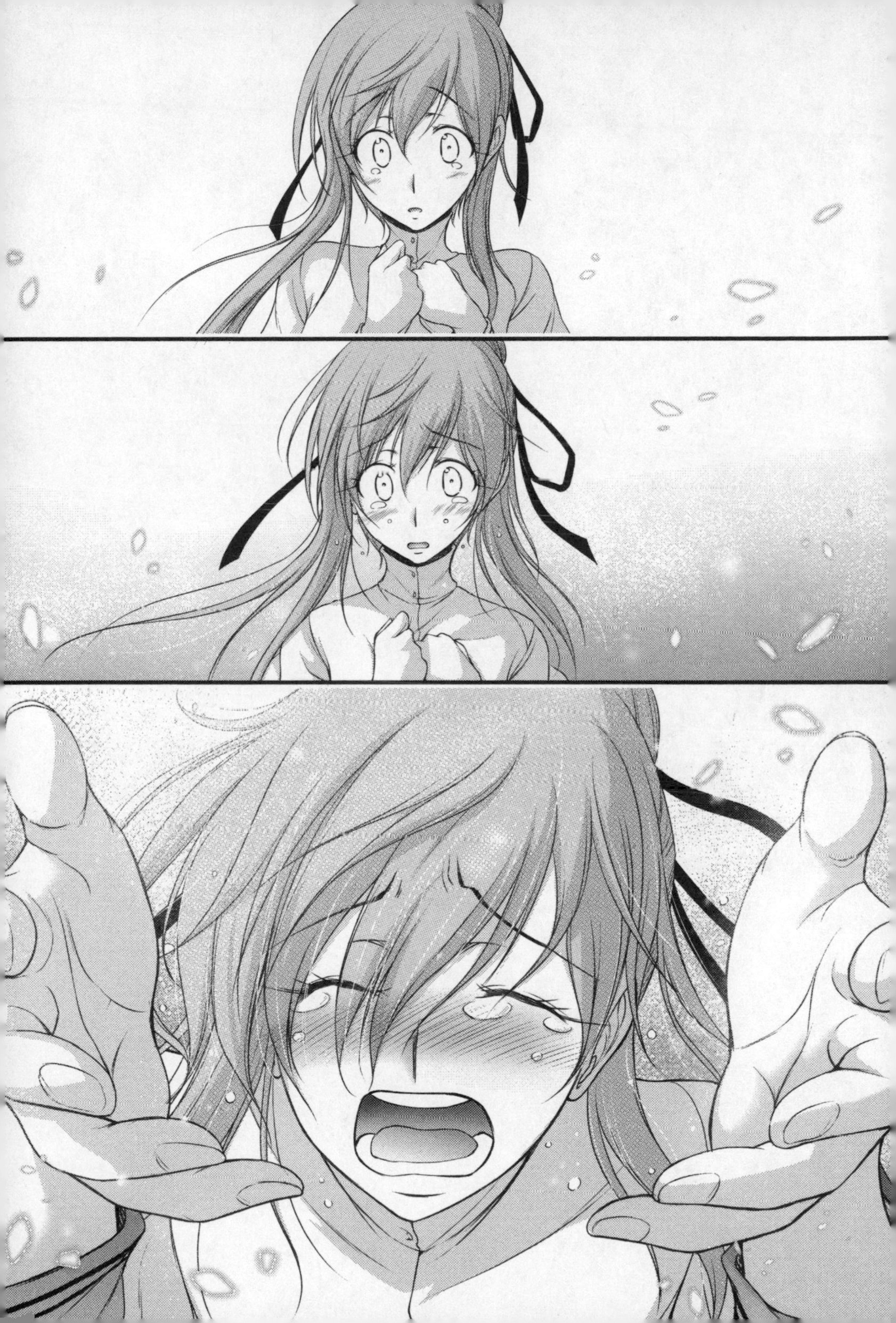

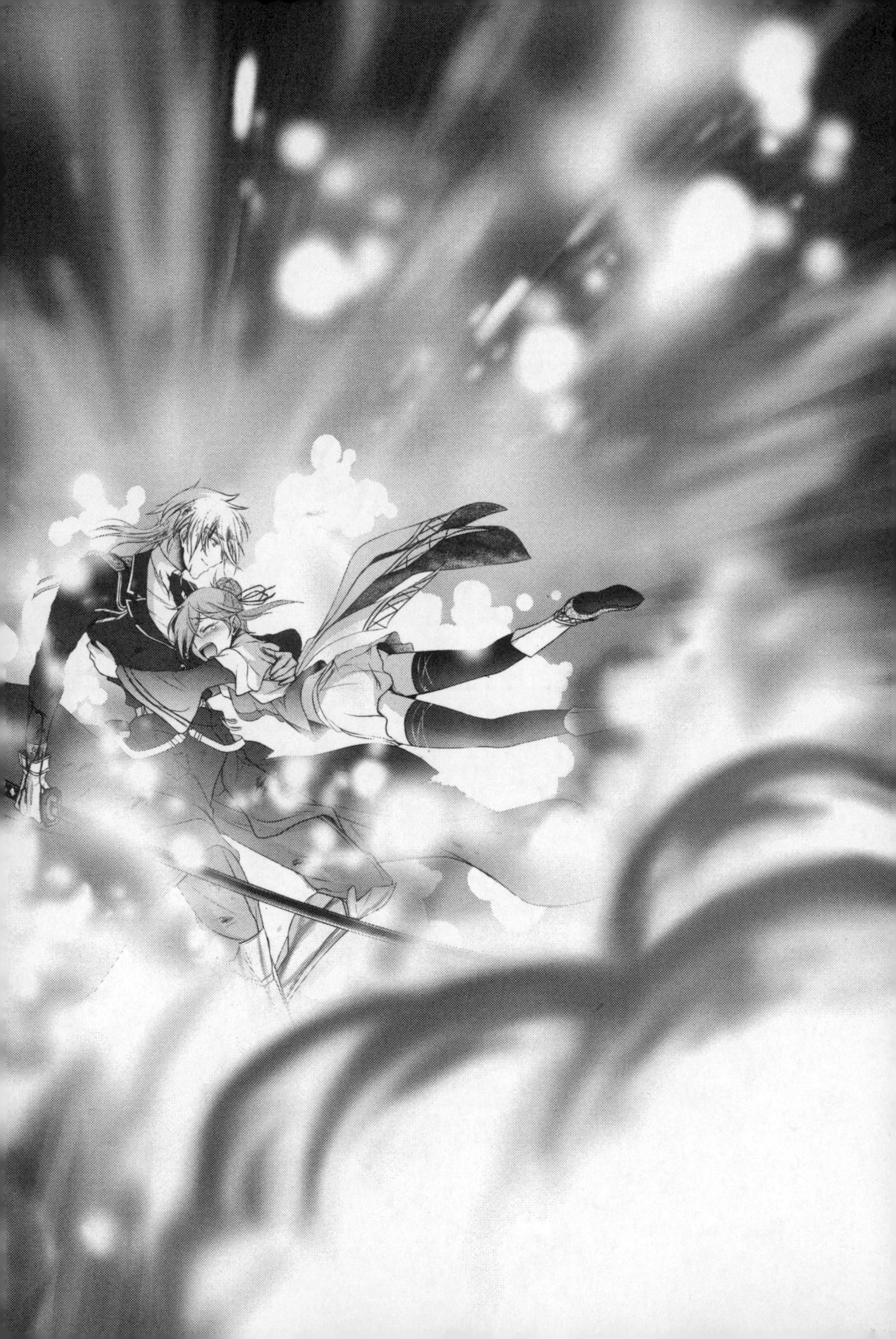

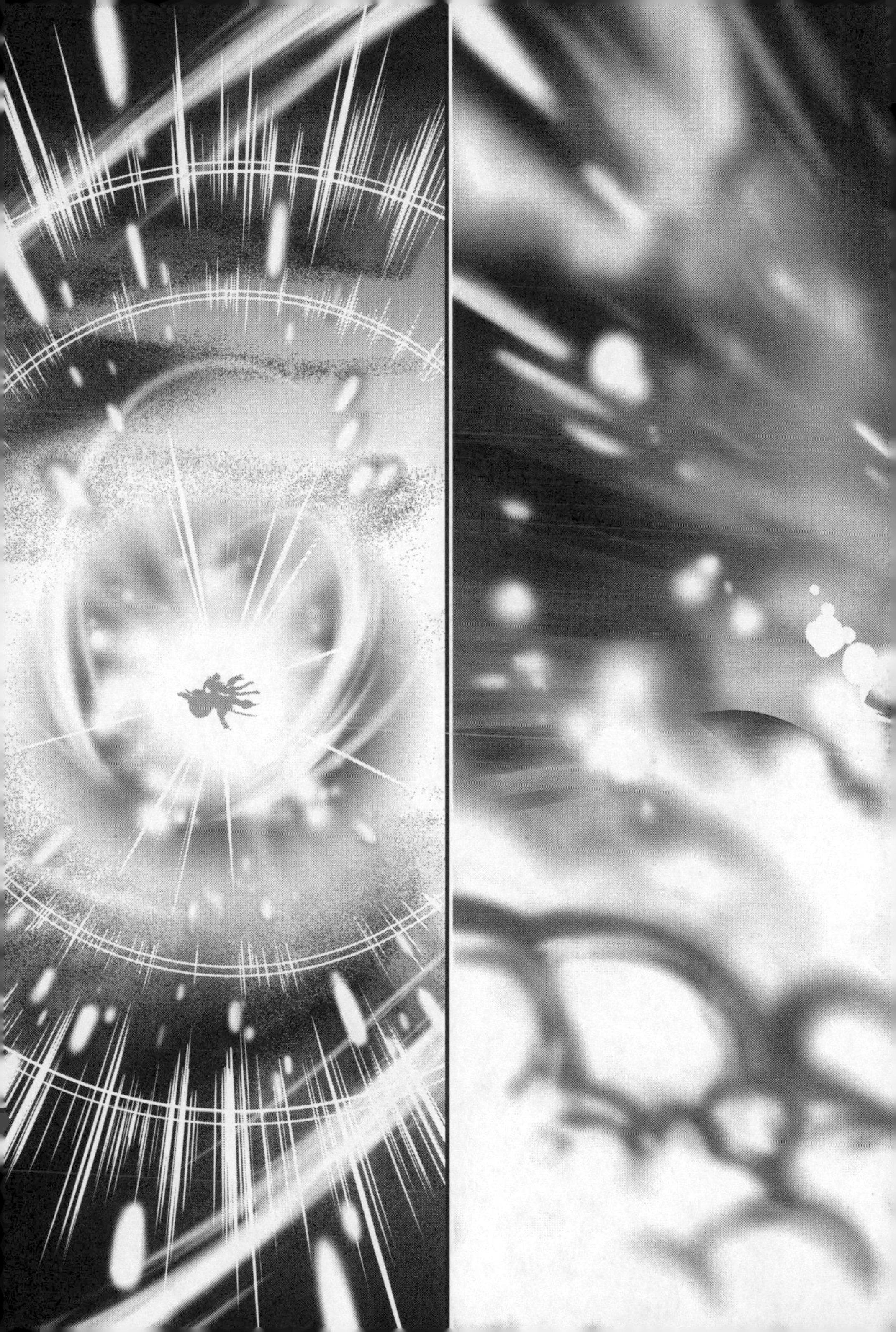

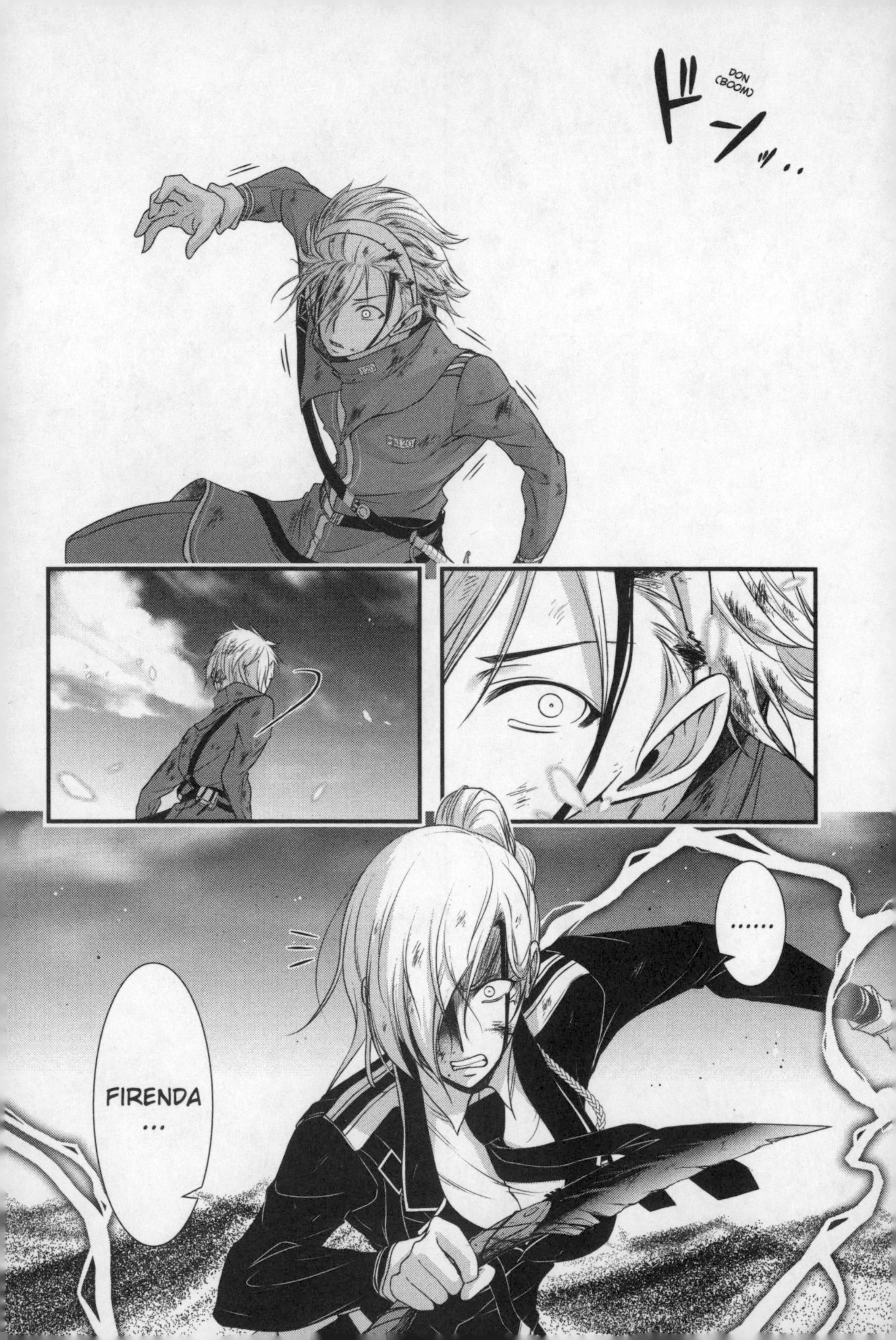
ドッッ..
DON (BOOM)
......
FIRENDA ...

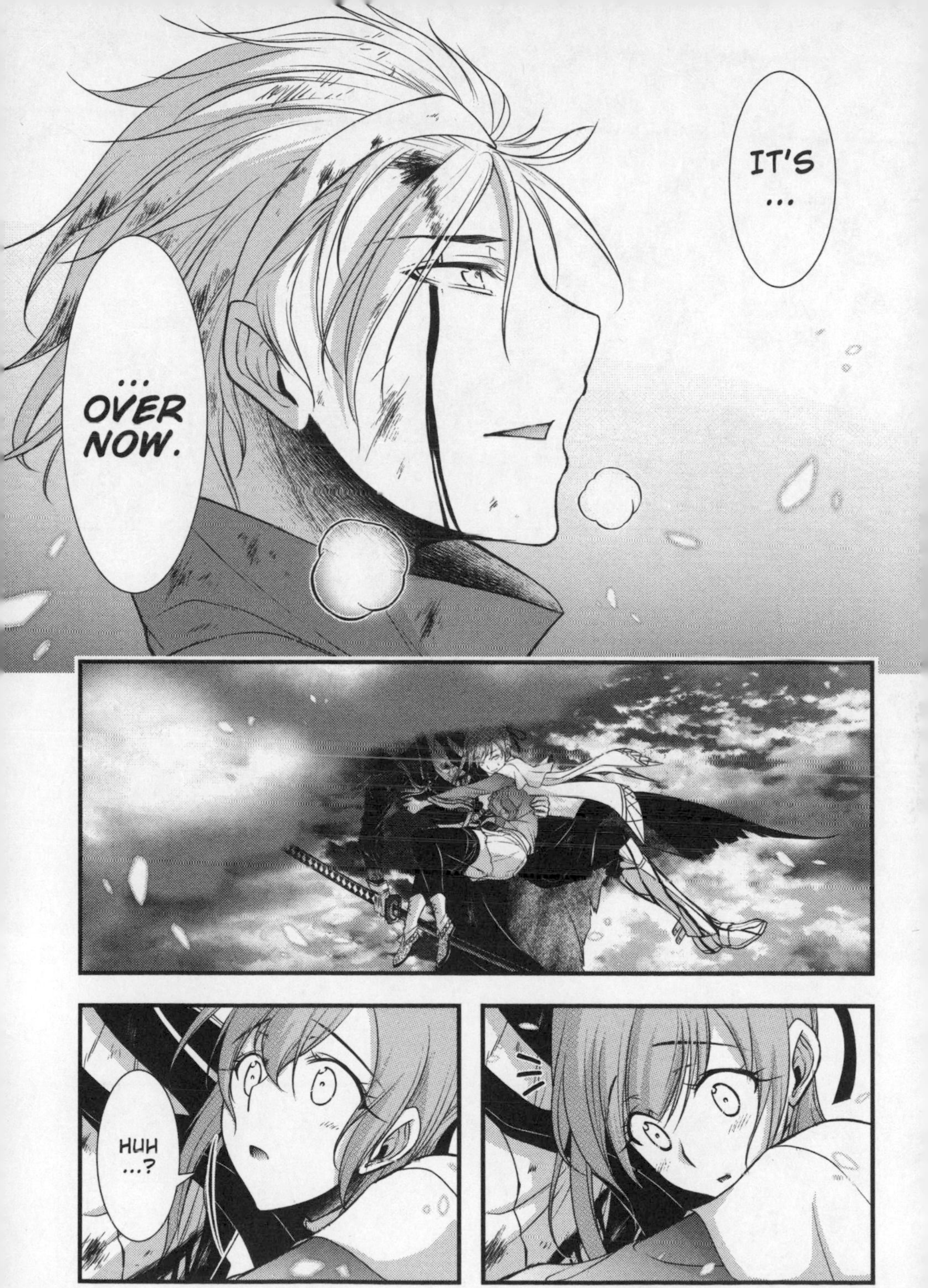
IT'S ...
... OVER NOW.
HUH ...?

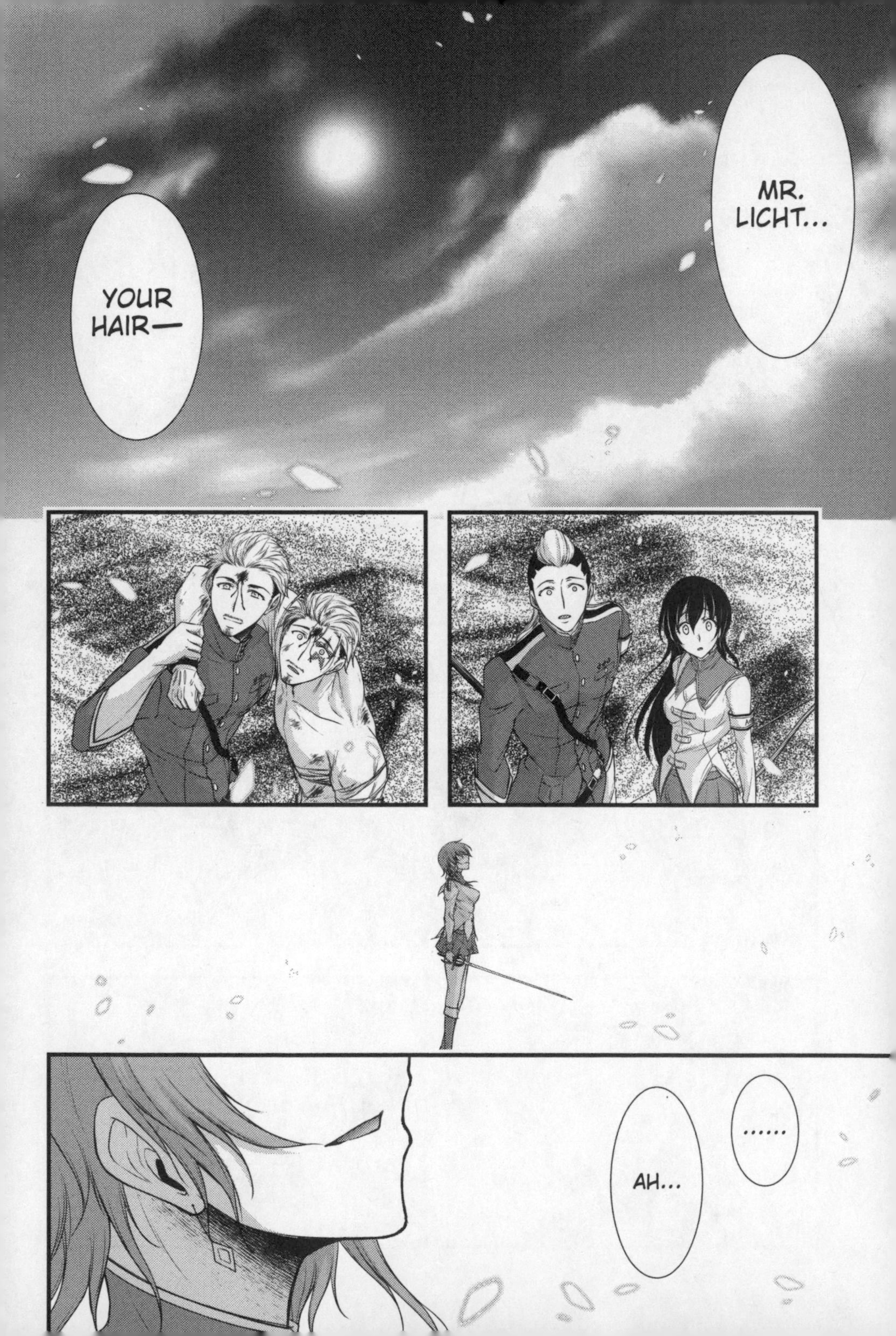
MR. LICHT...
YOUR HAIR—
......
AH...

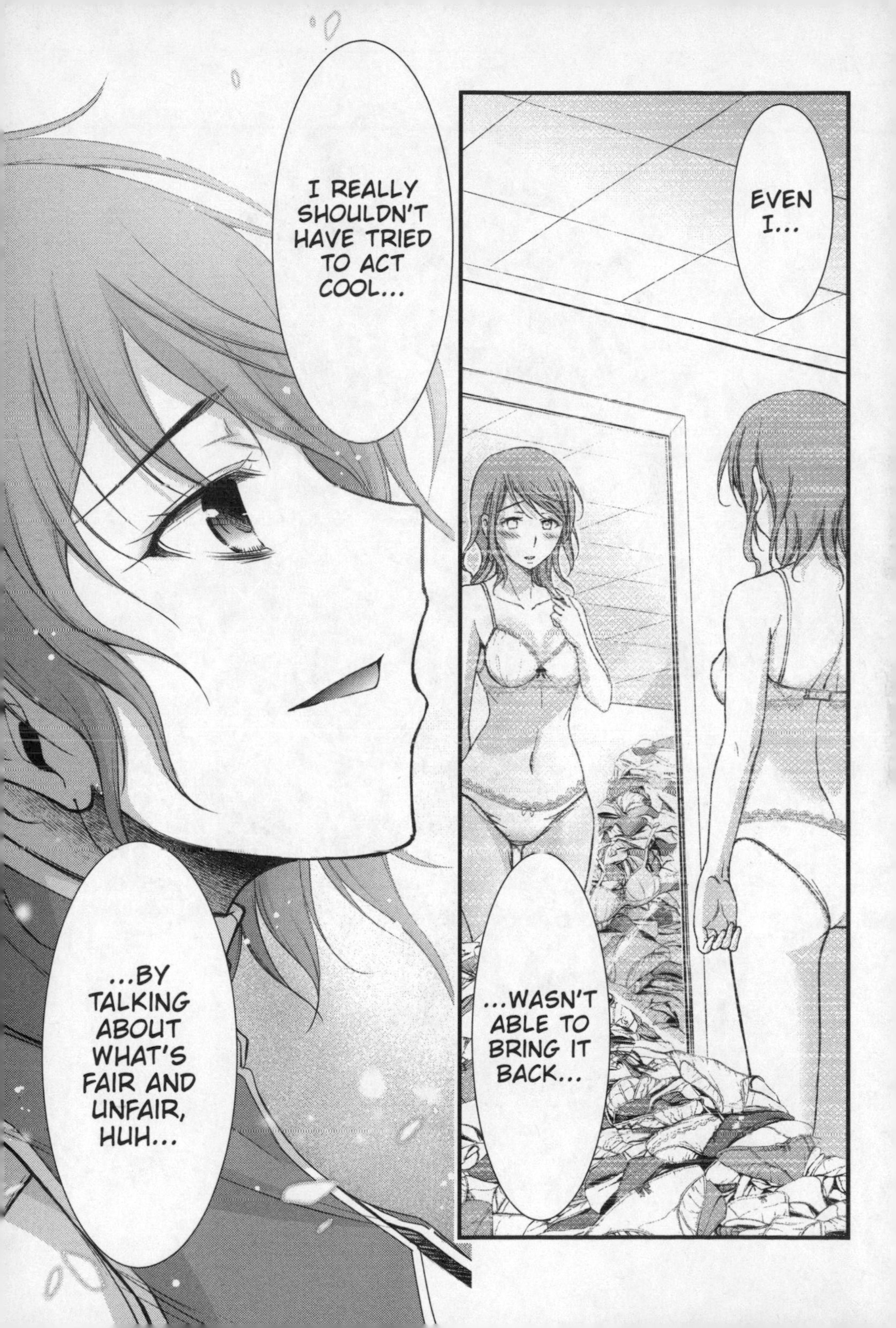
EVEN I...
...WASN'T ABLE TO BRING IT BACK...
I REALLY SHOULDN'T HAVE TRIED TO ACT COOL...
...BY TALKING ABOUT WHAT'S FAIR AND UNFAIR, HUH...

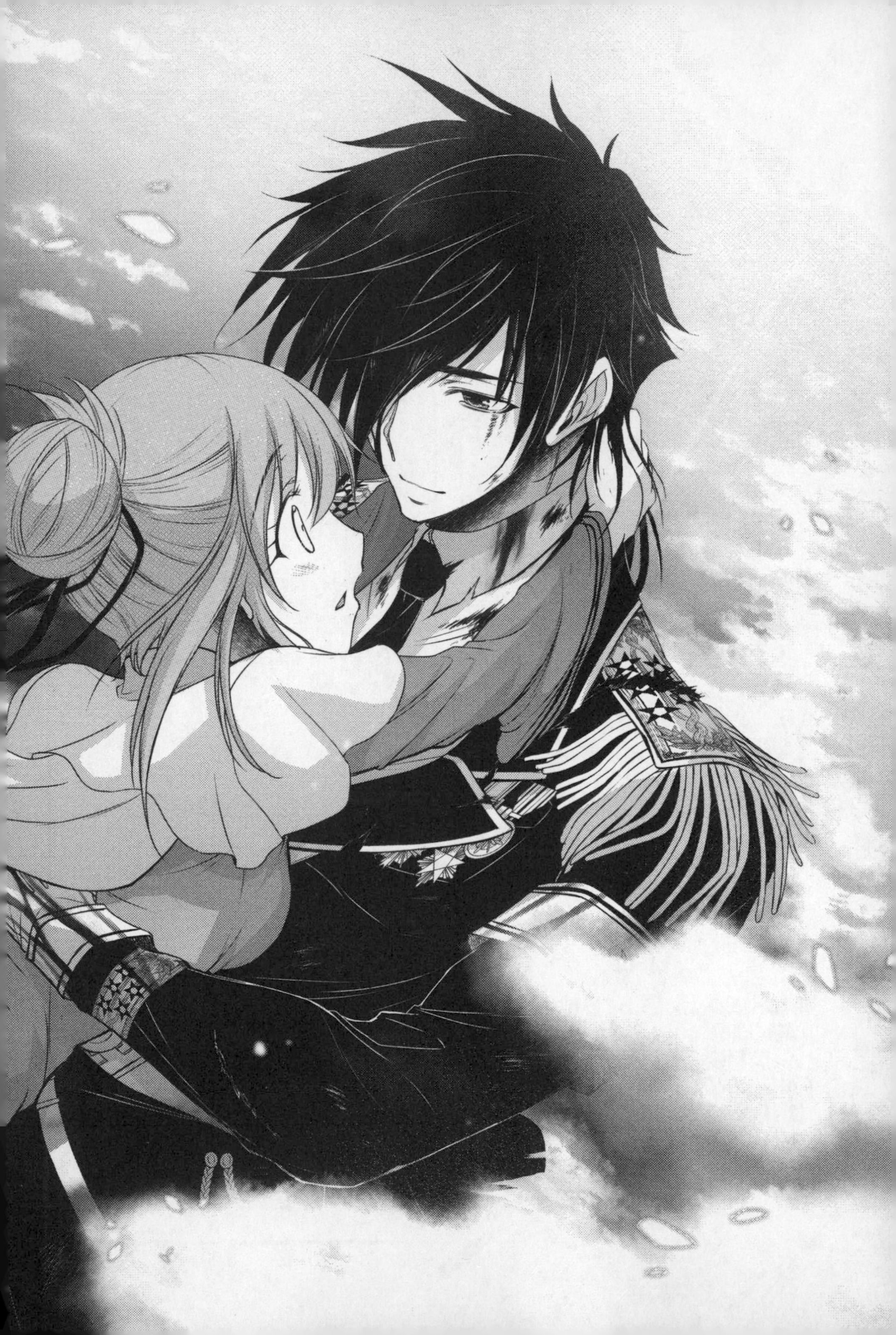

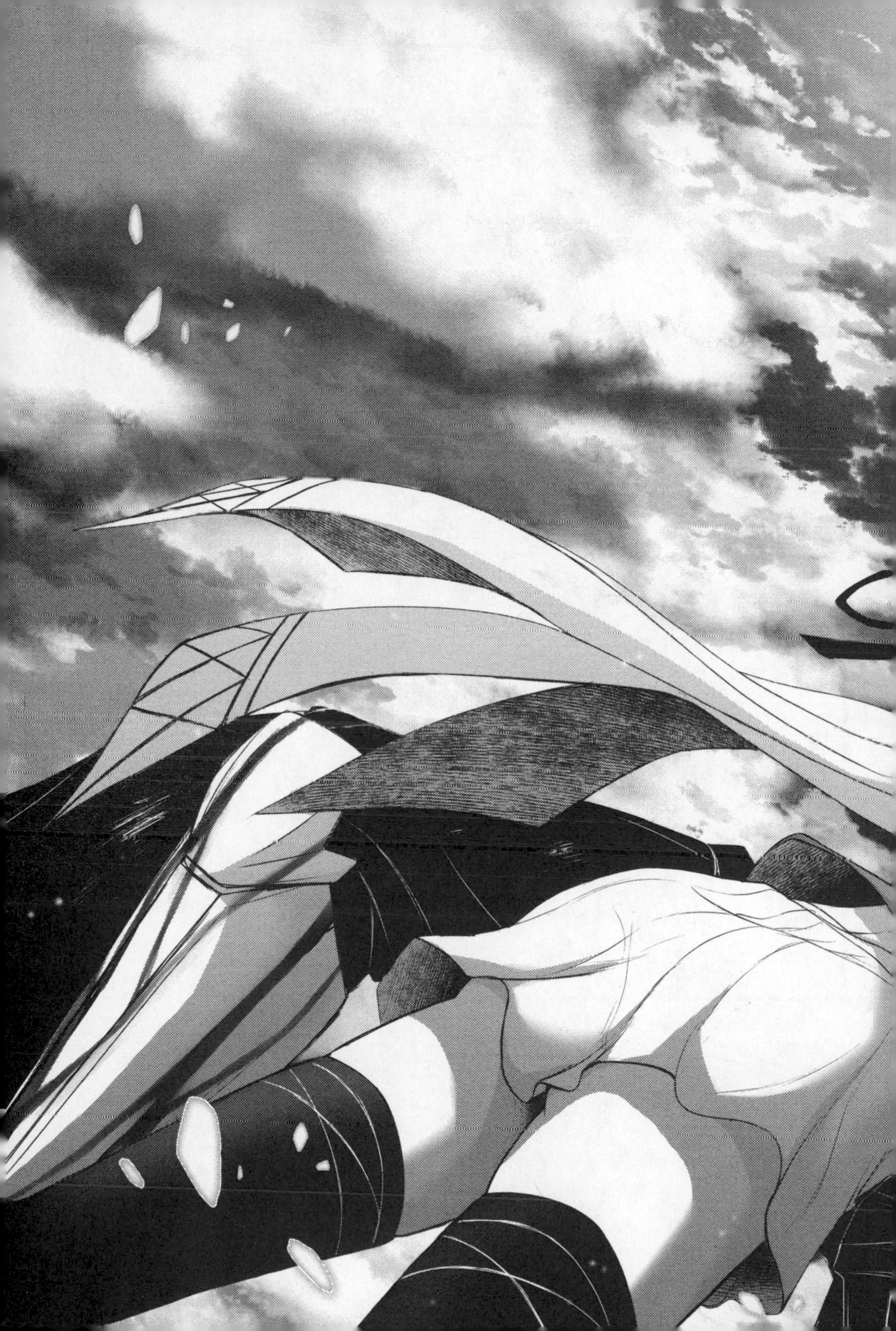

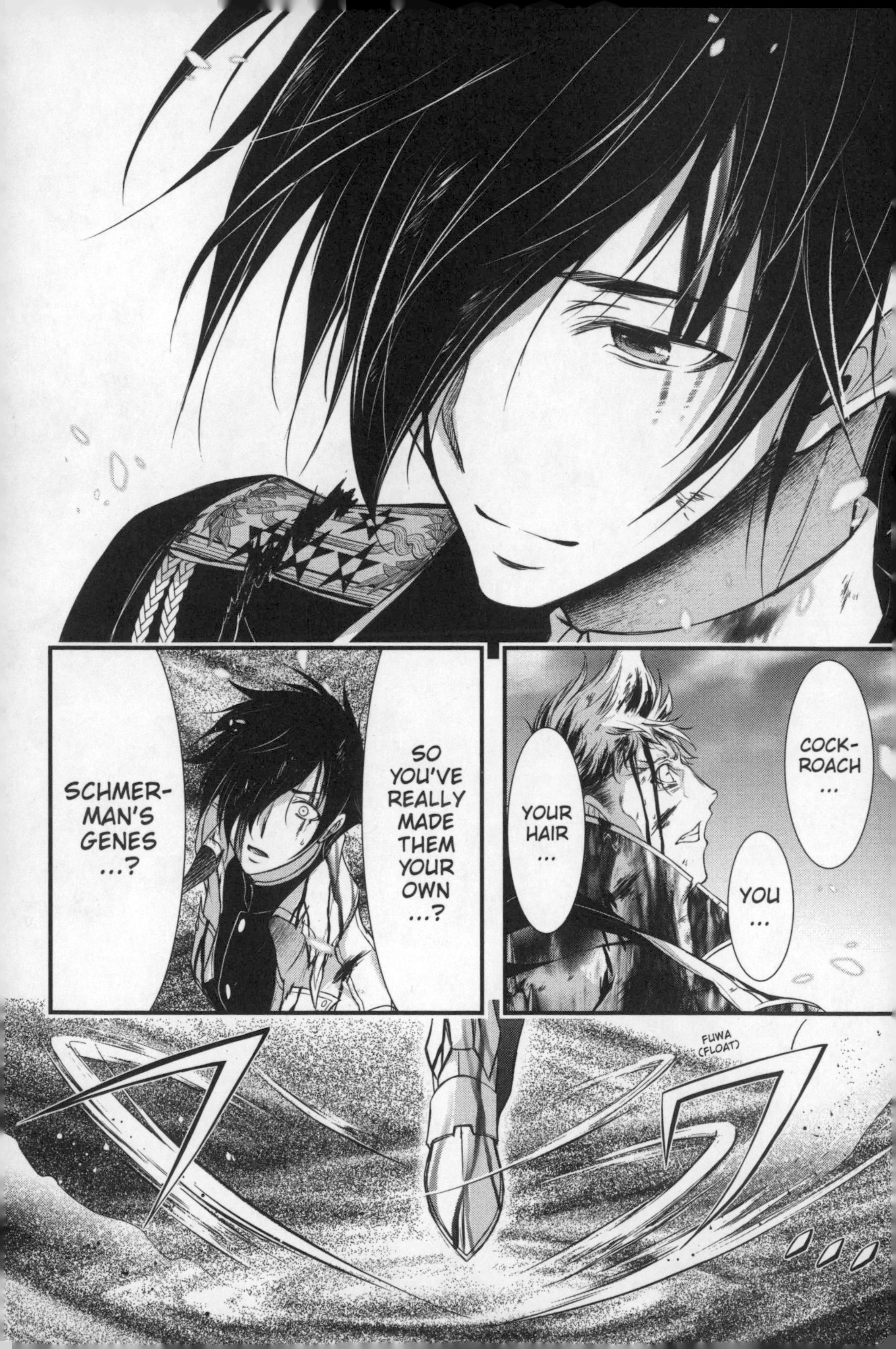
COCK-ROACH ...
YOU ...
YOUR HAIR ...
SO YOU'VE REALLY MADE THEM YOUR OWN ...?
SCHMER-MAN'S GENES ...?
FUWA (FLOAT)

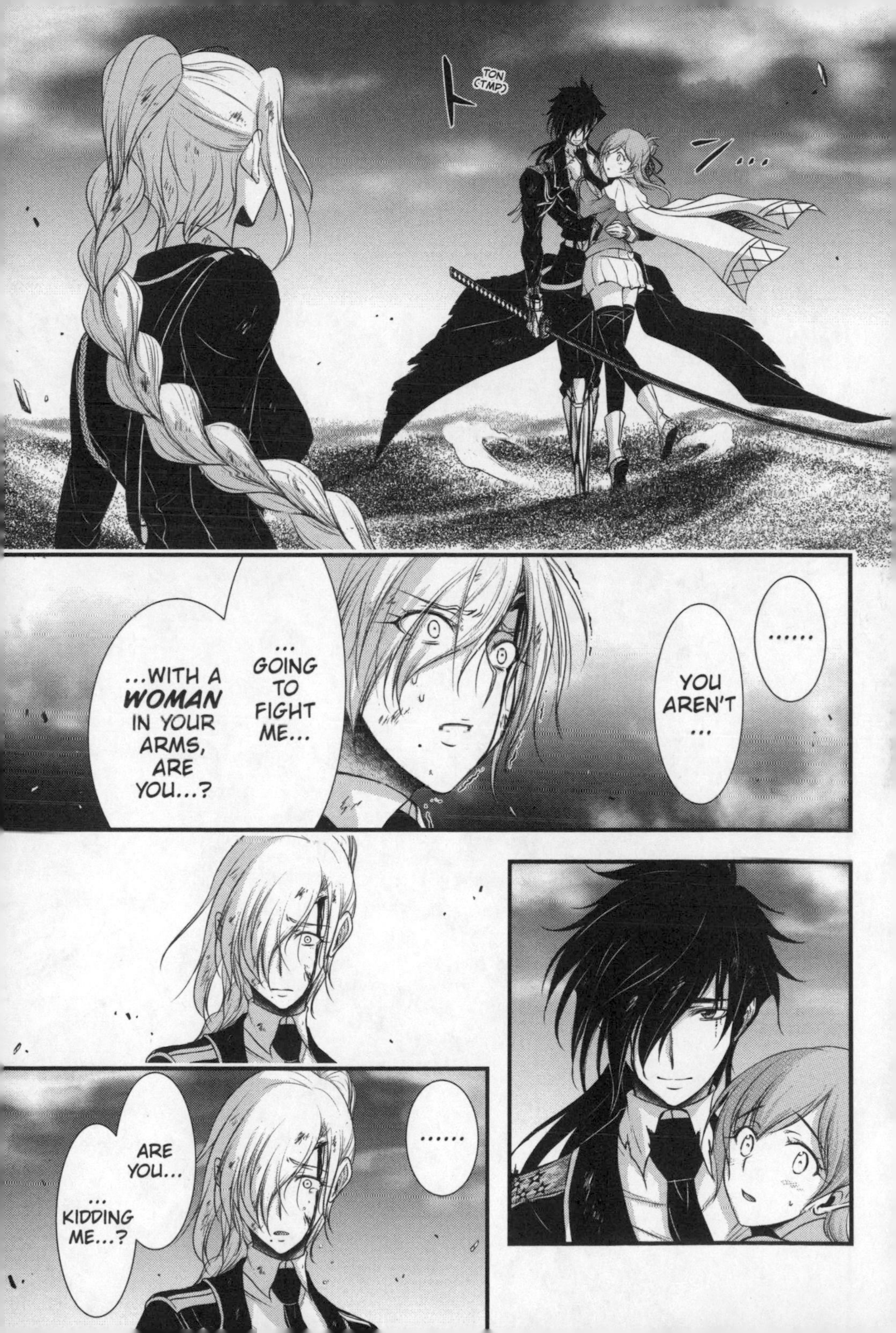

ト
TON (TMP)
ン...
......
YOU AREN'T ...
... GOING TO FIGHT ME...
...WITH A **WOMAN** IN YOUR ARMS, ARE YOU...?
......
ARE YOU...
... KIDDING ME...?

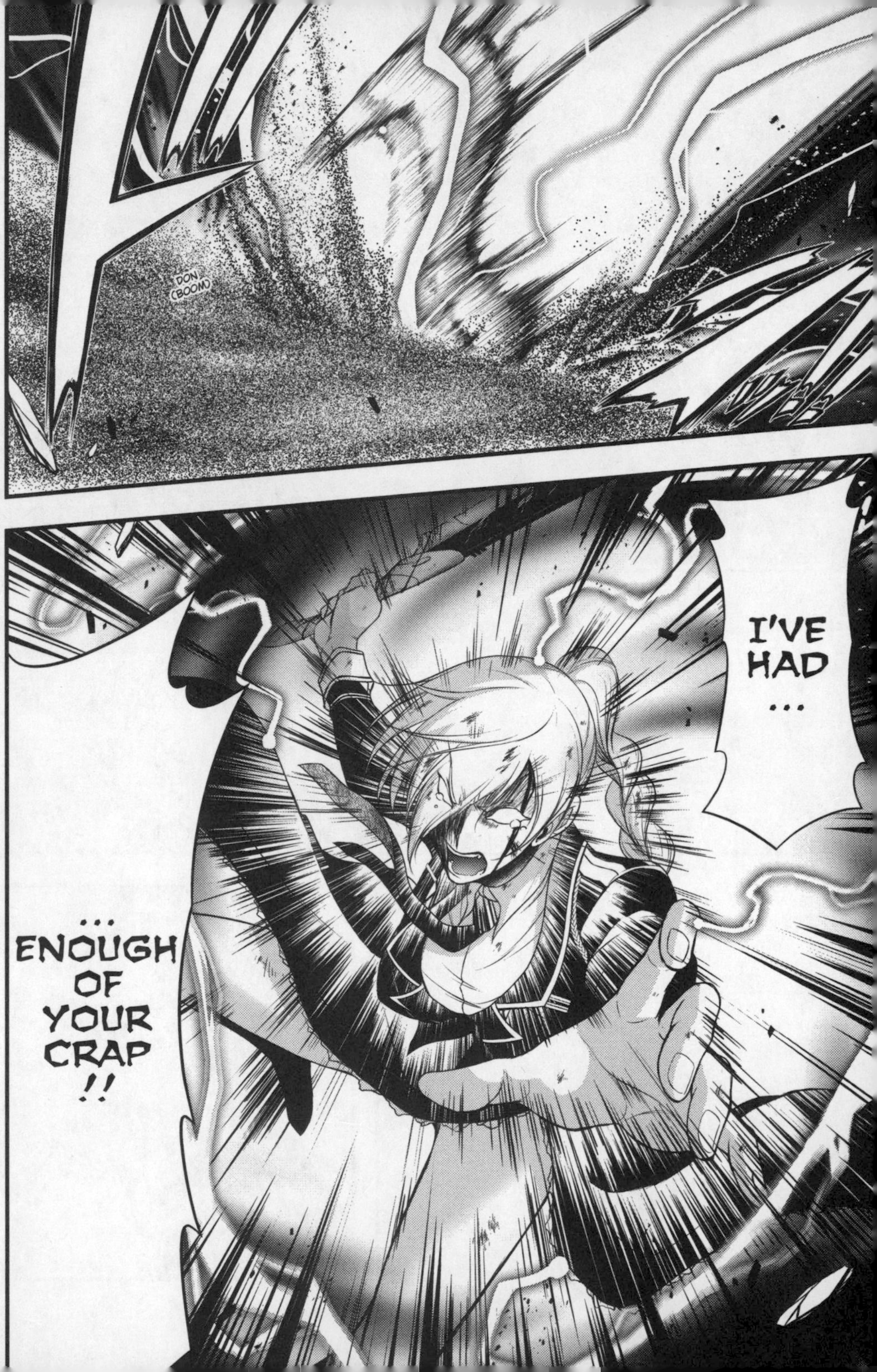
DON (BOOM)
I'VE HAD ...
... ENOUGH OF YOUR CRAP!!

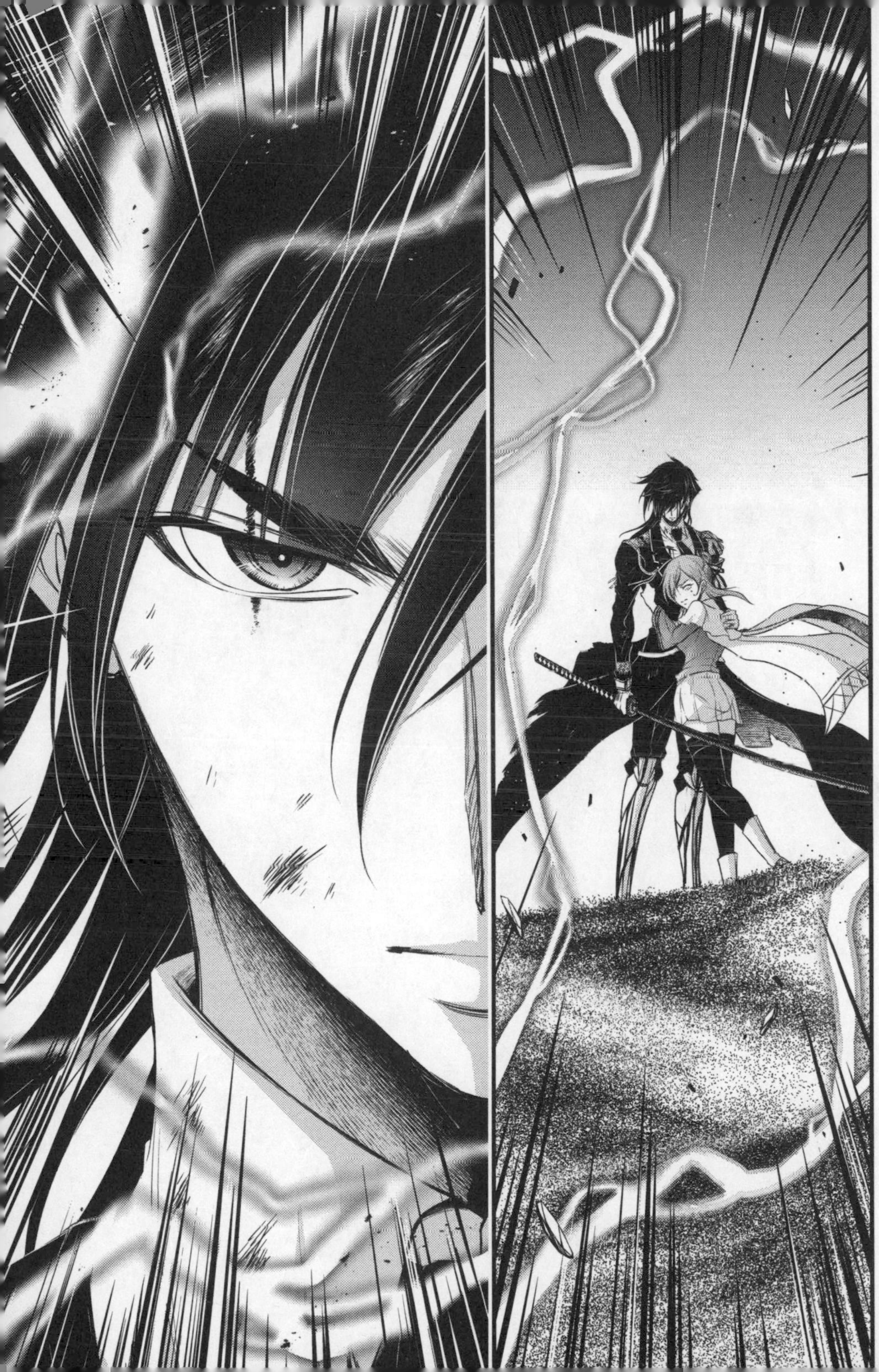

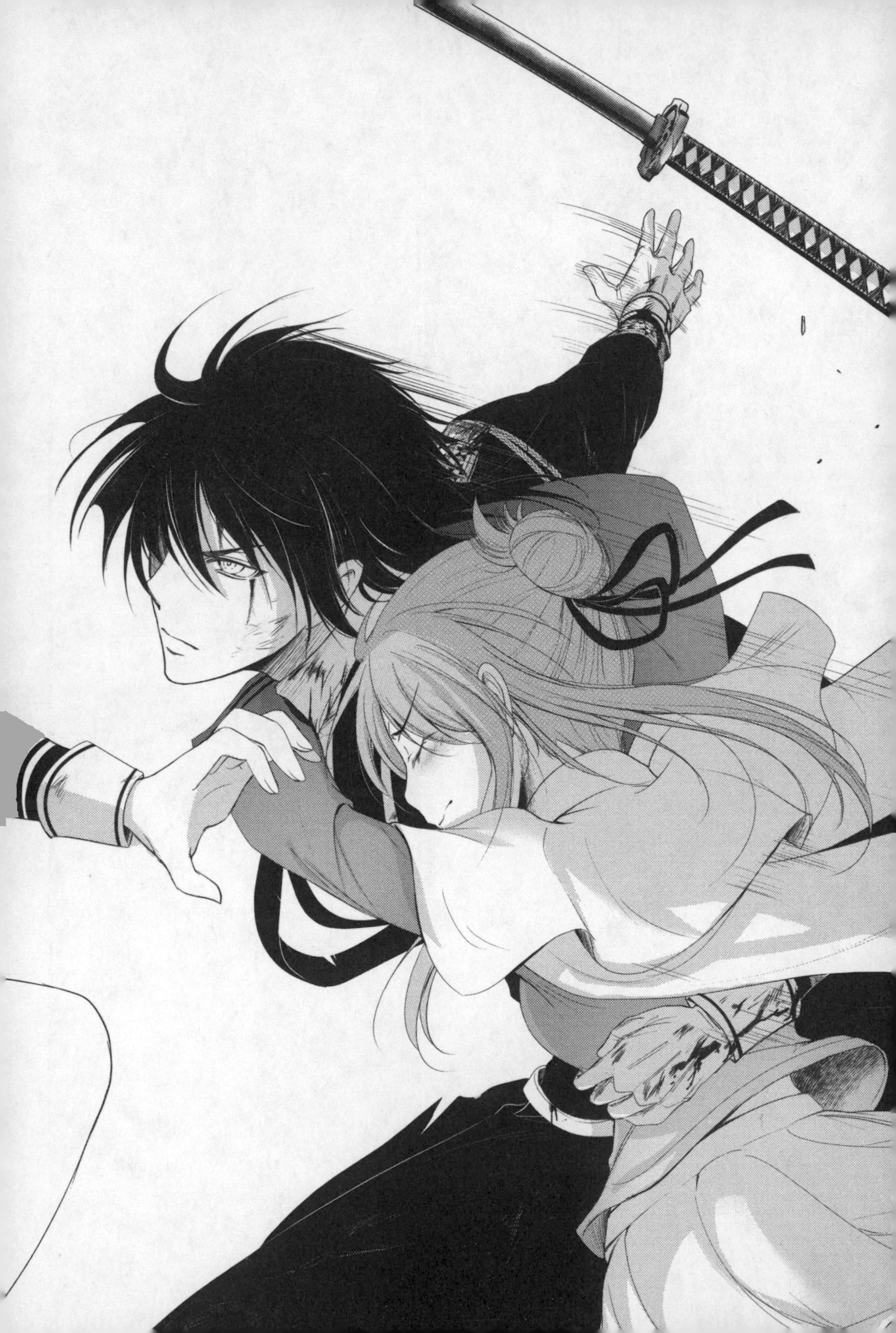

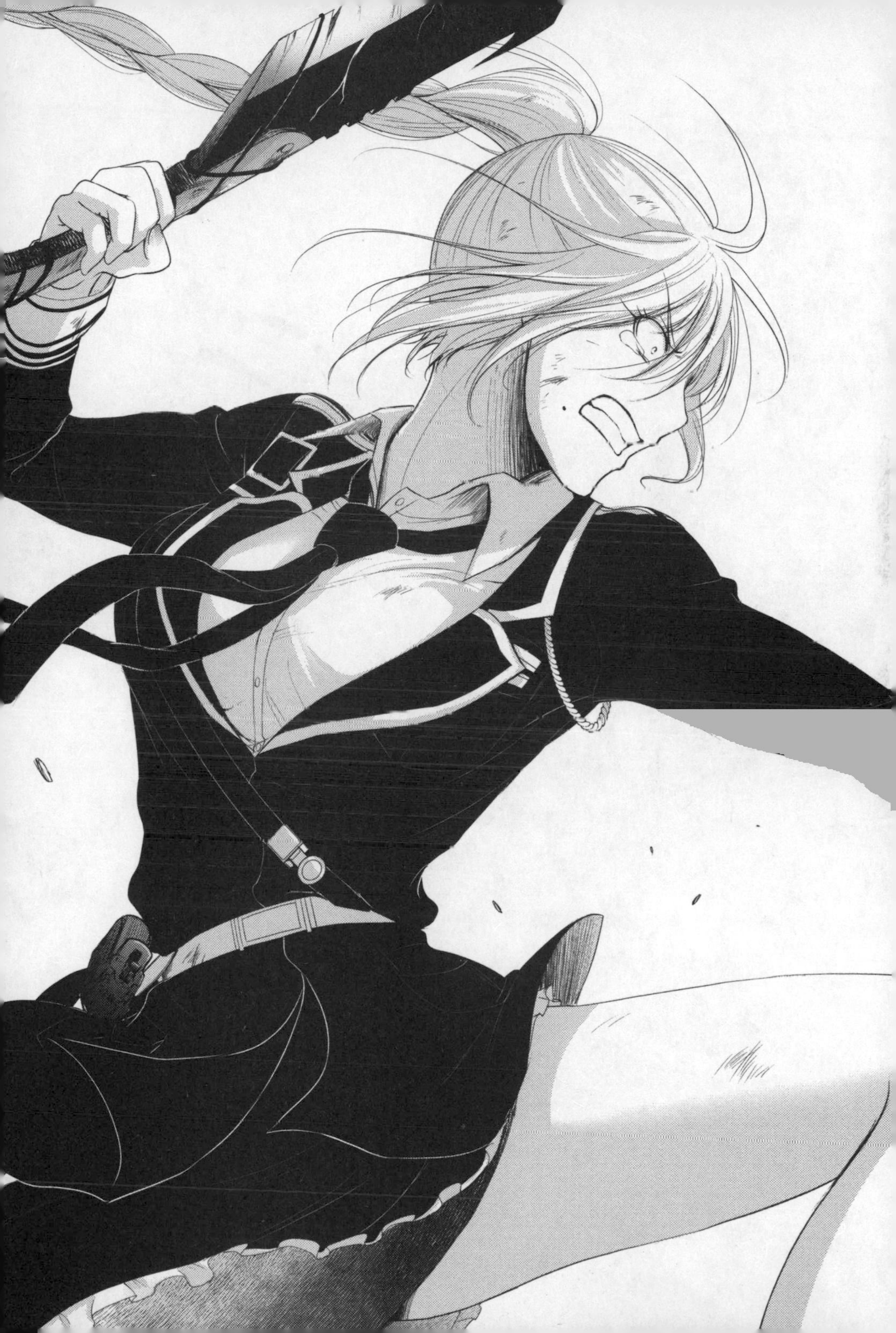

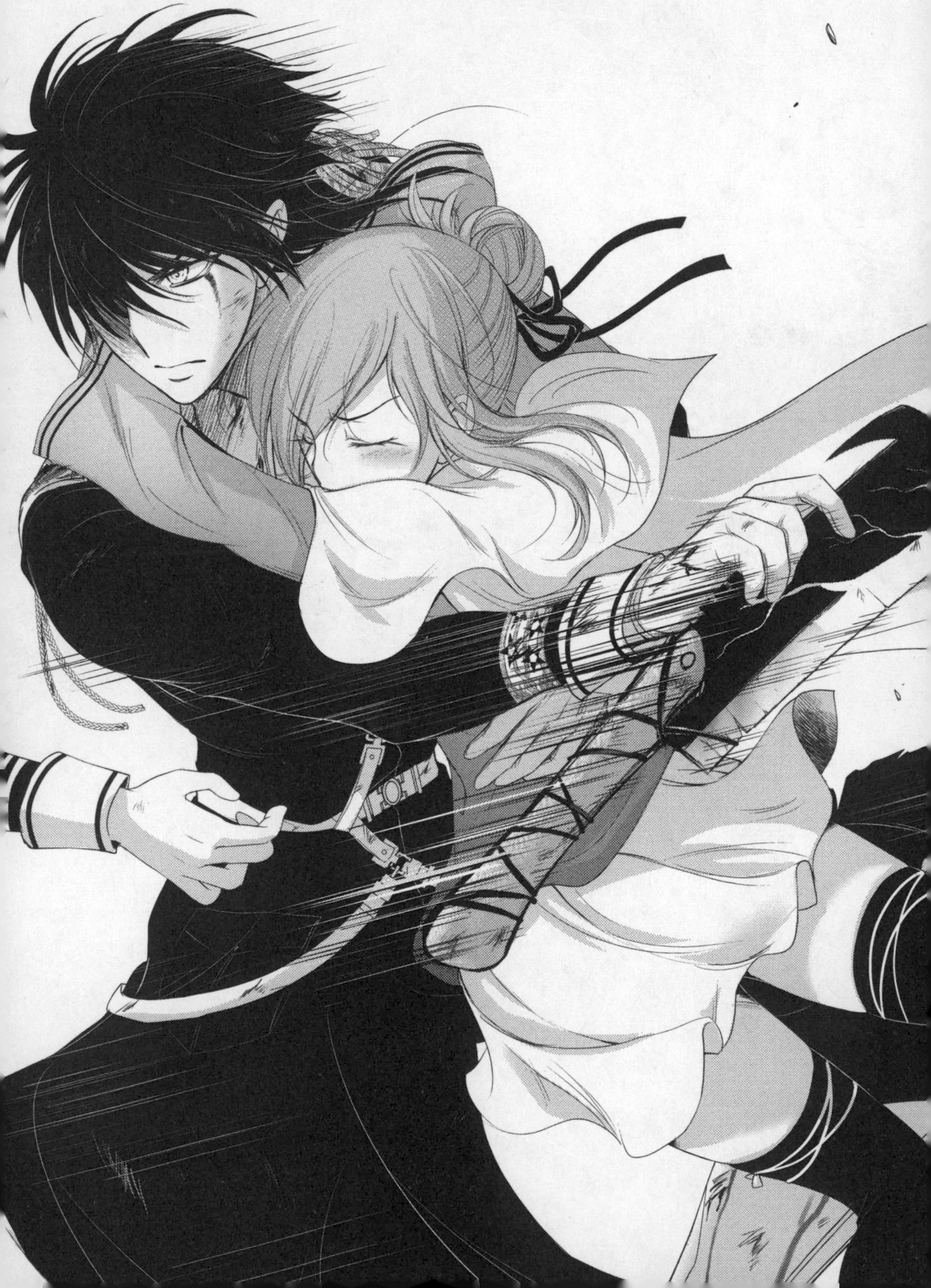

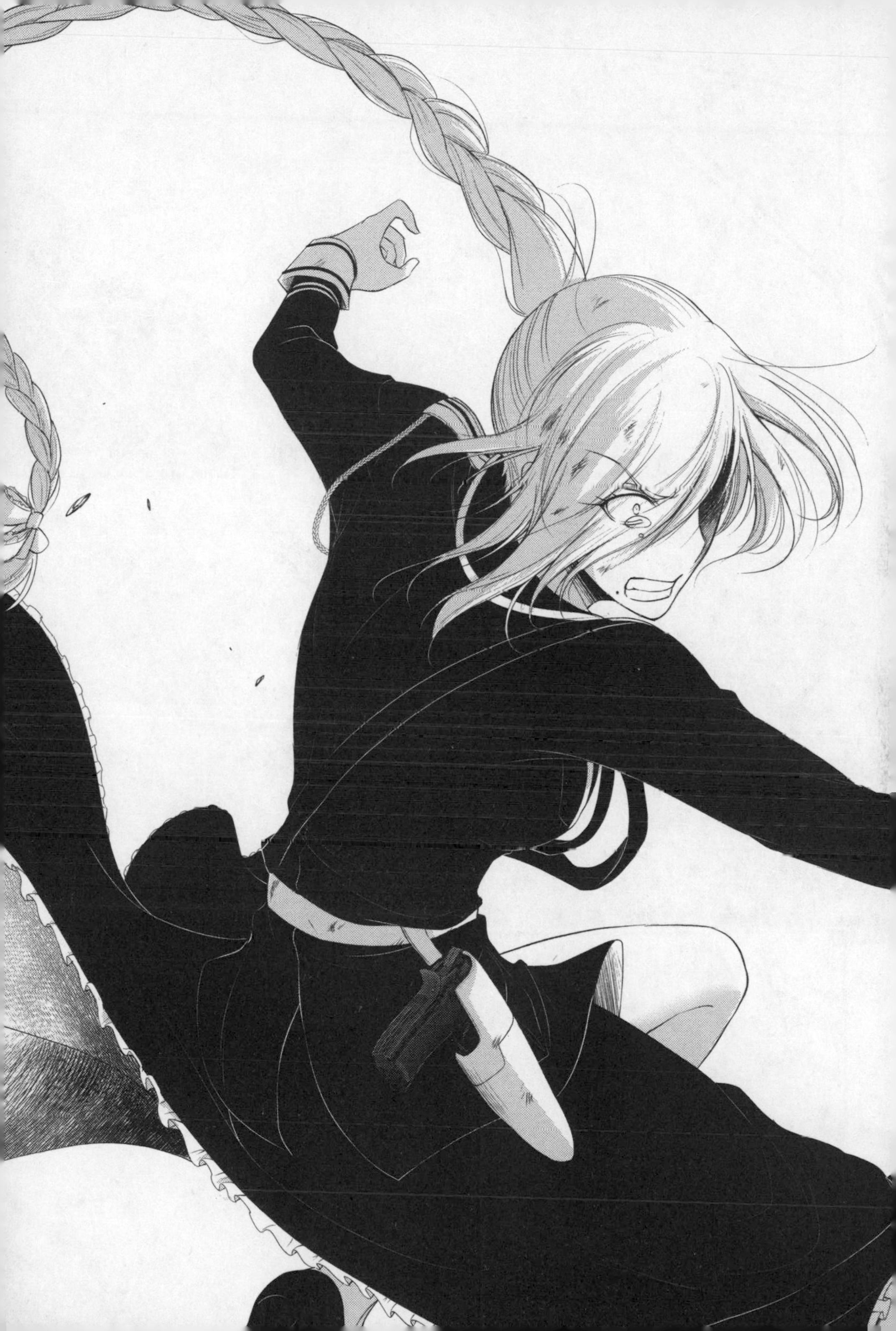

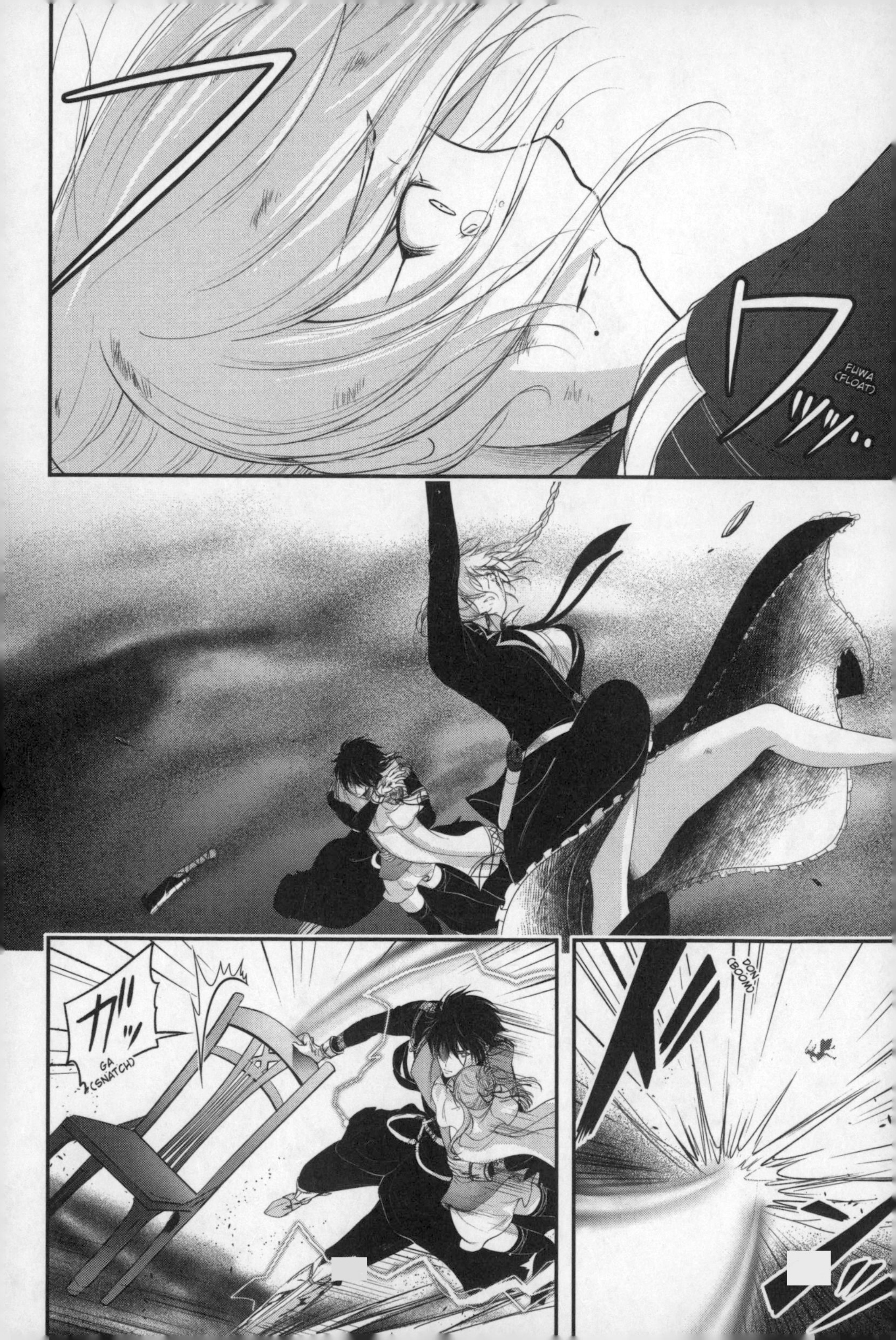
FUWA (FLOAT)
DON (BOOM)
GA (SNATCH)

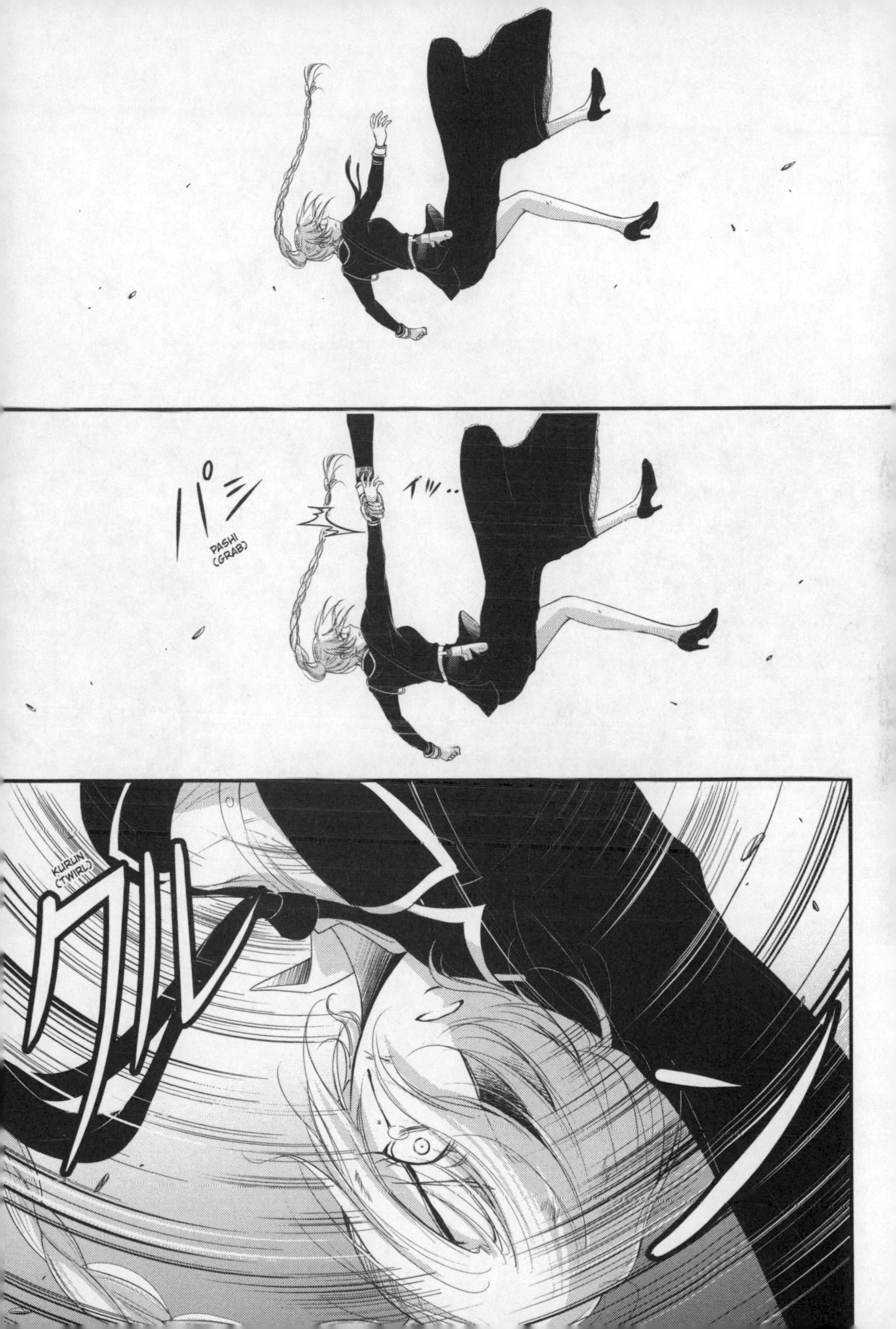
PASHI (GRAB)
KURUN (TWIRL)

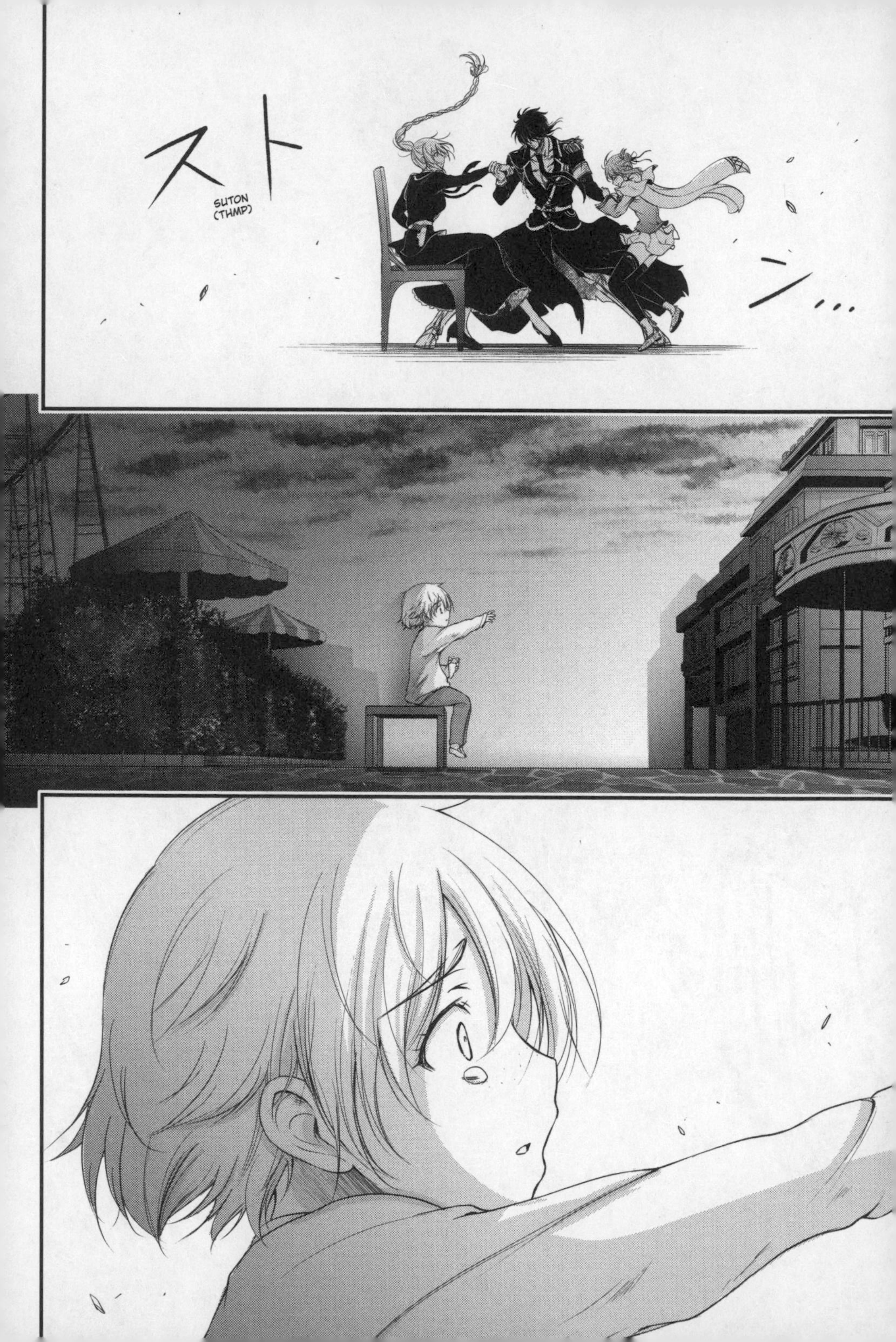

スト
SUTON (THMP)

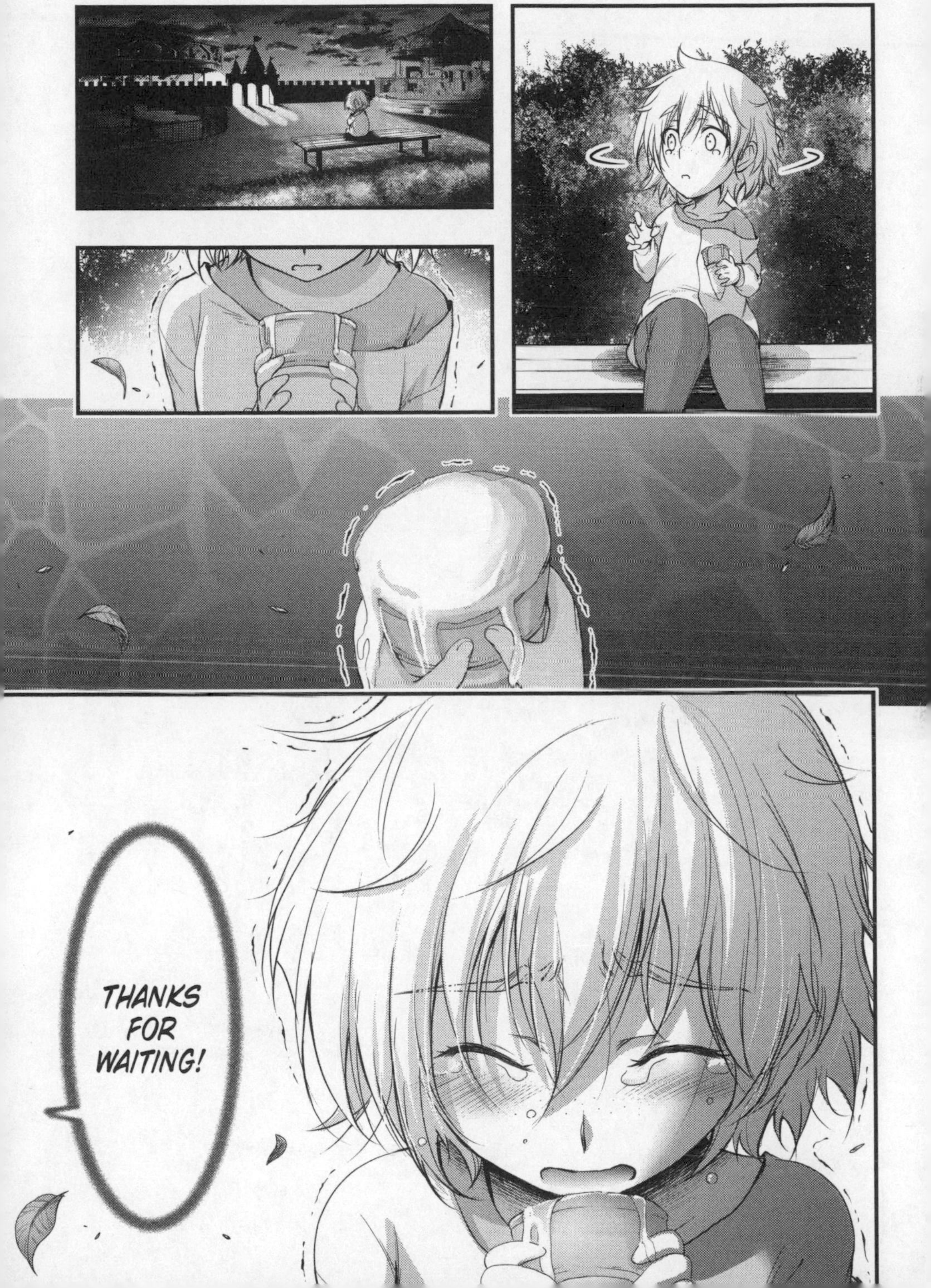
THANKS FOR WAITING!

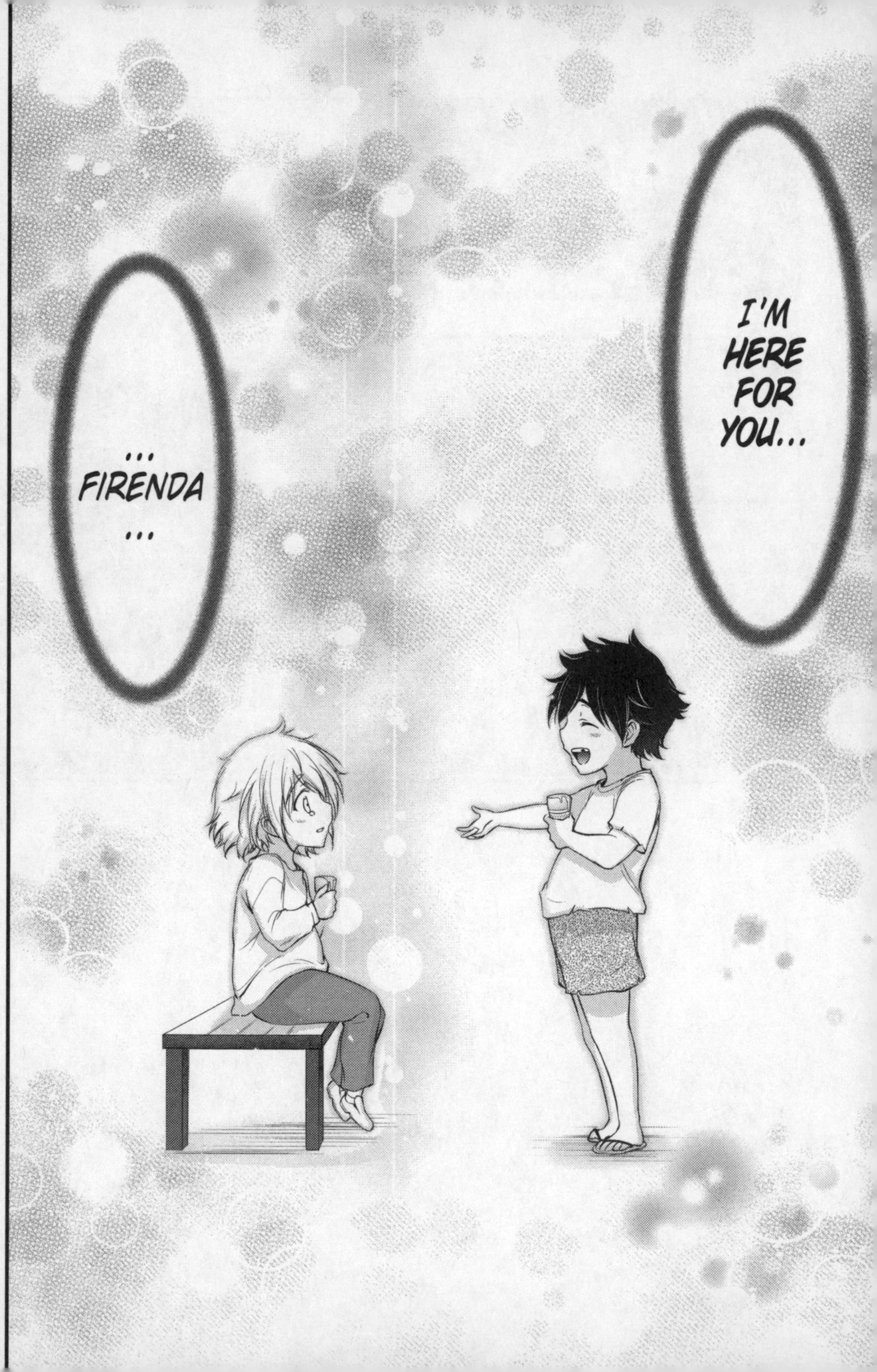
I'M HERE FOR YOU...
...FIRENDA...

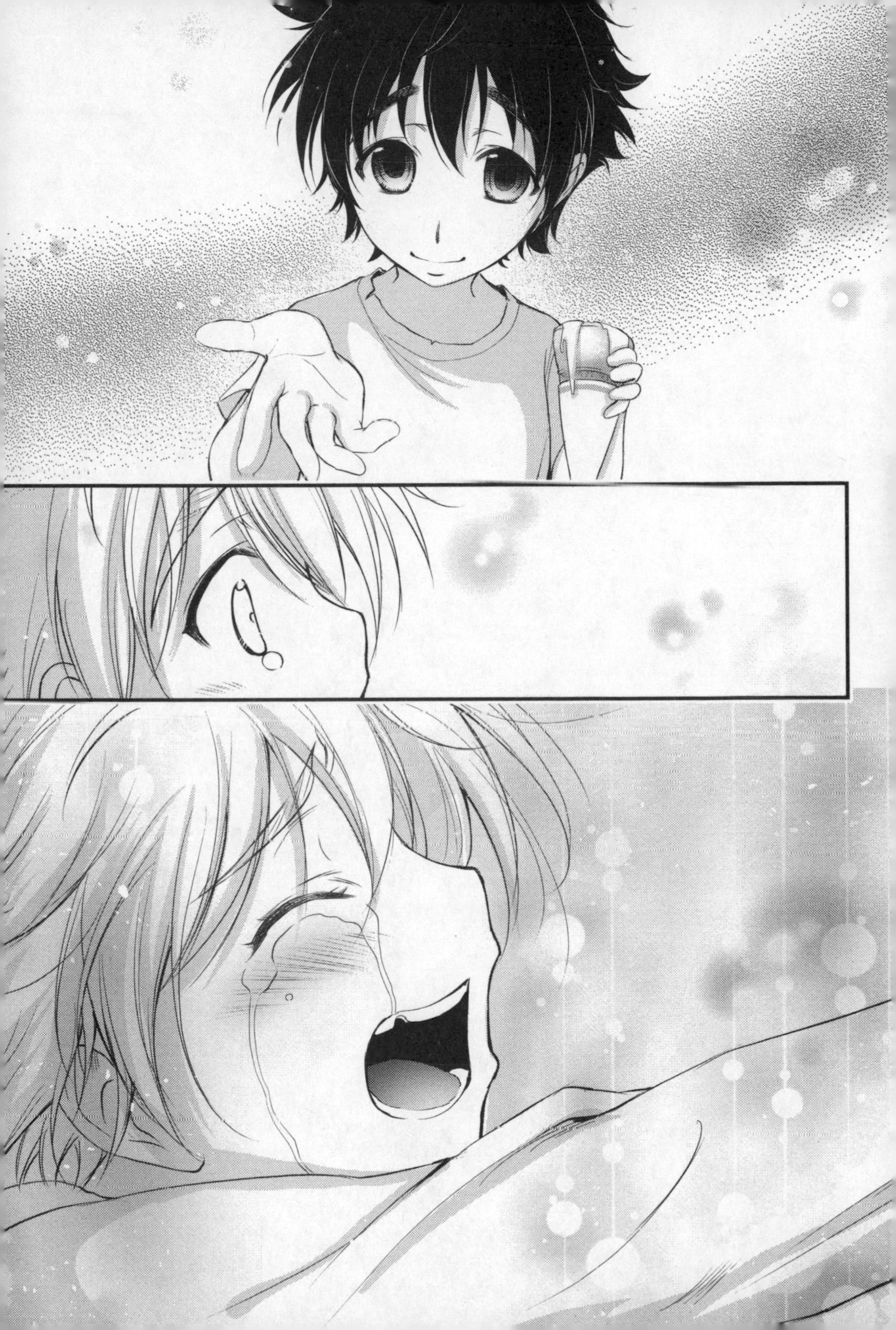

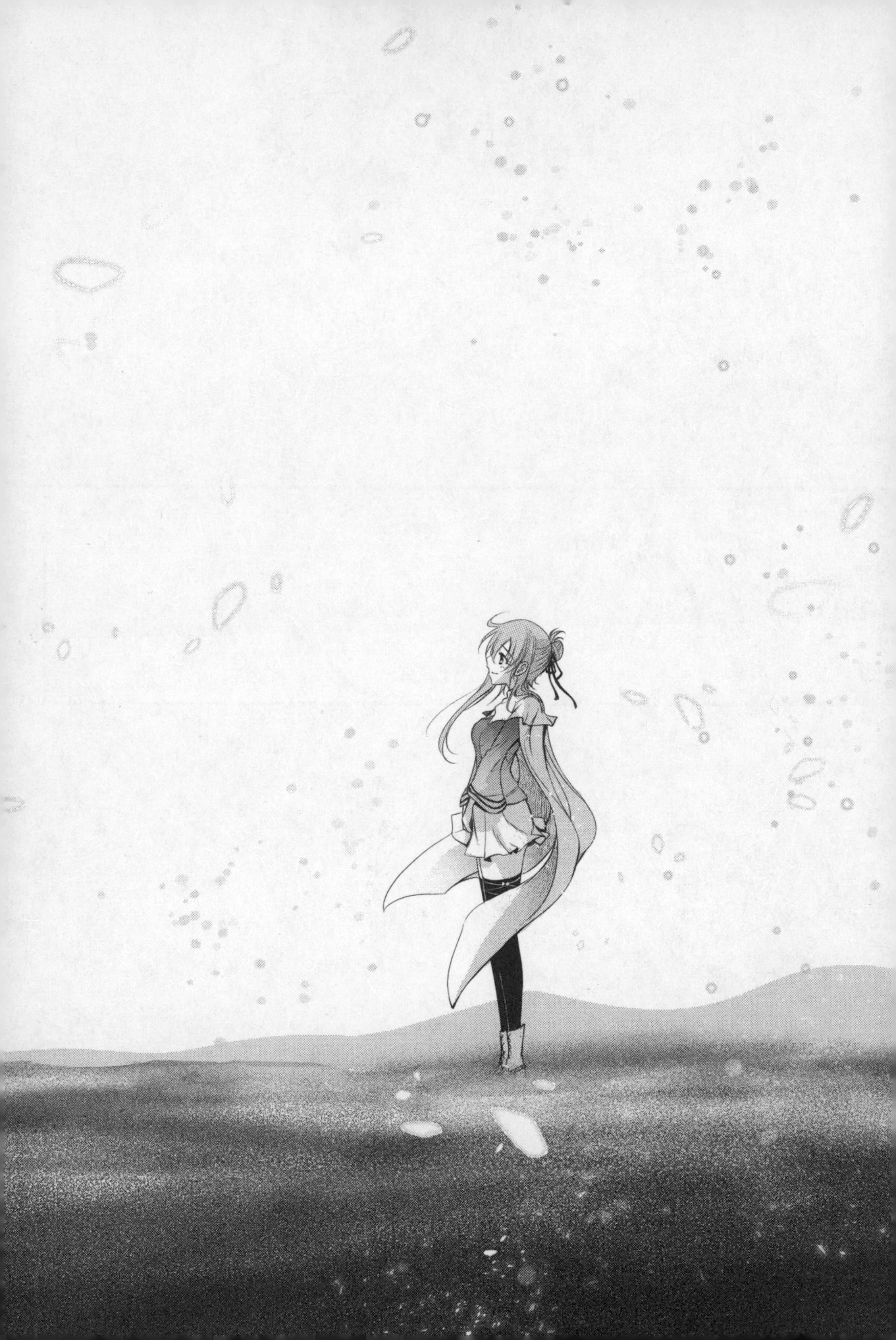

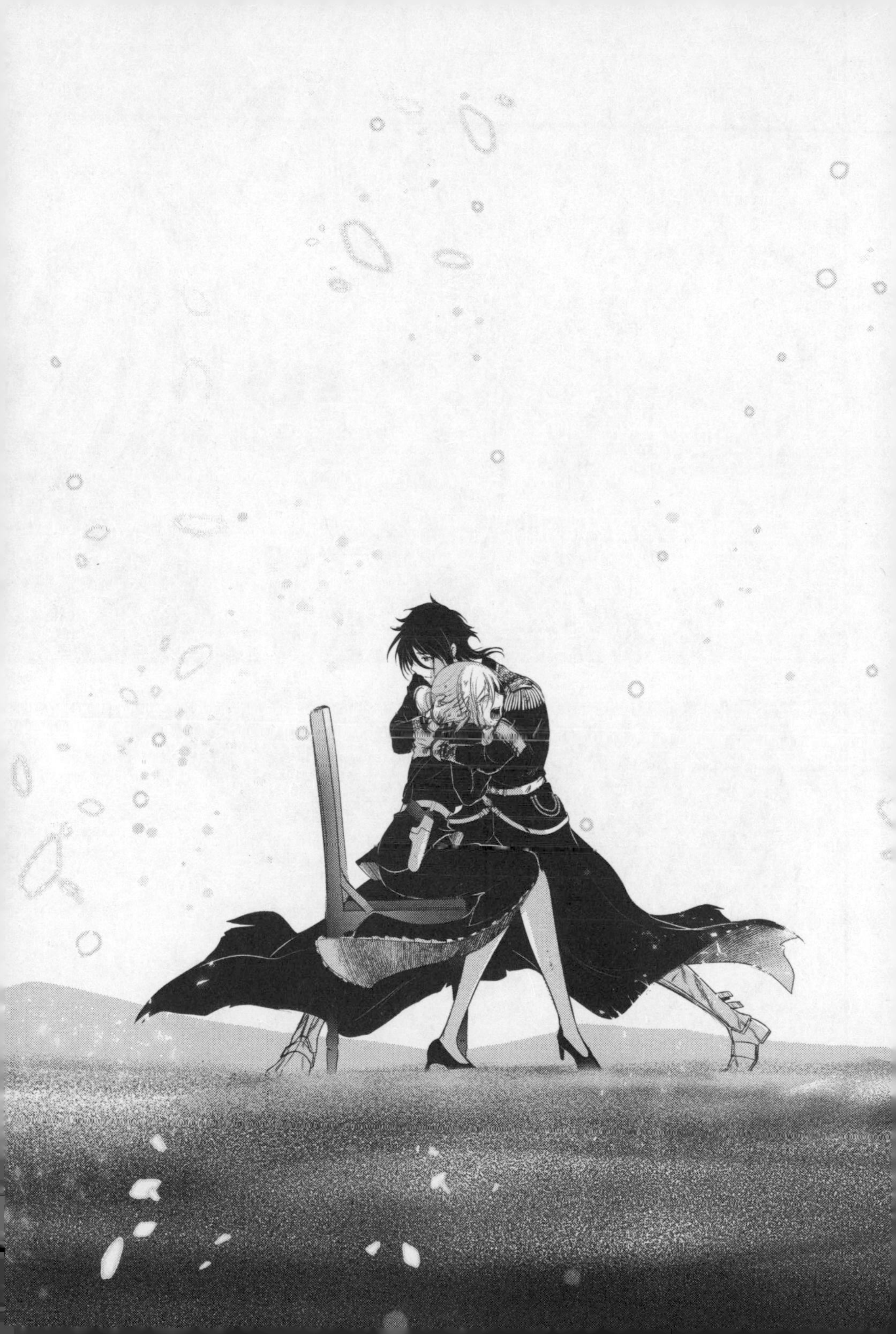

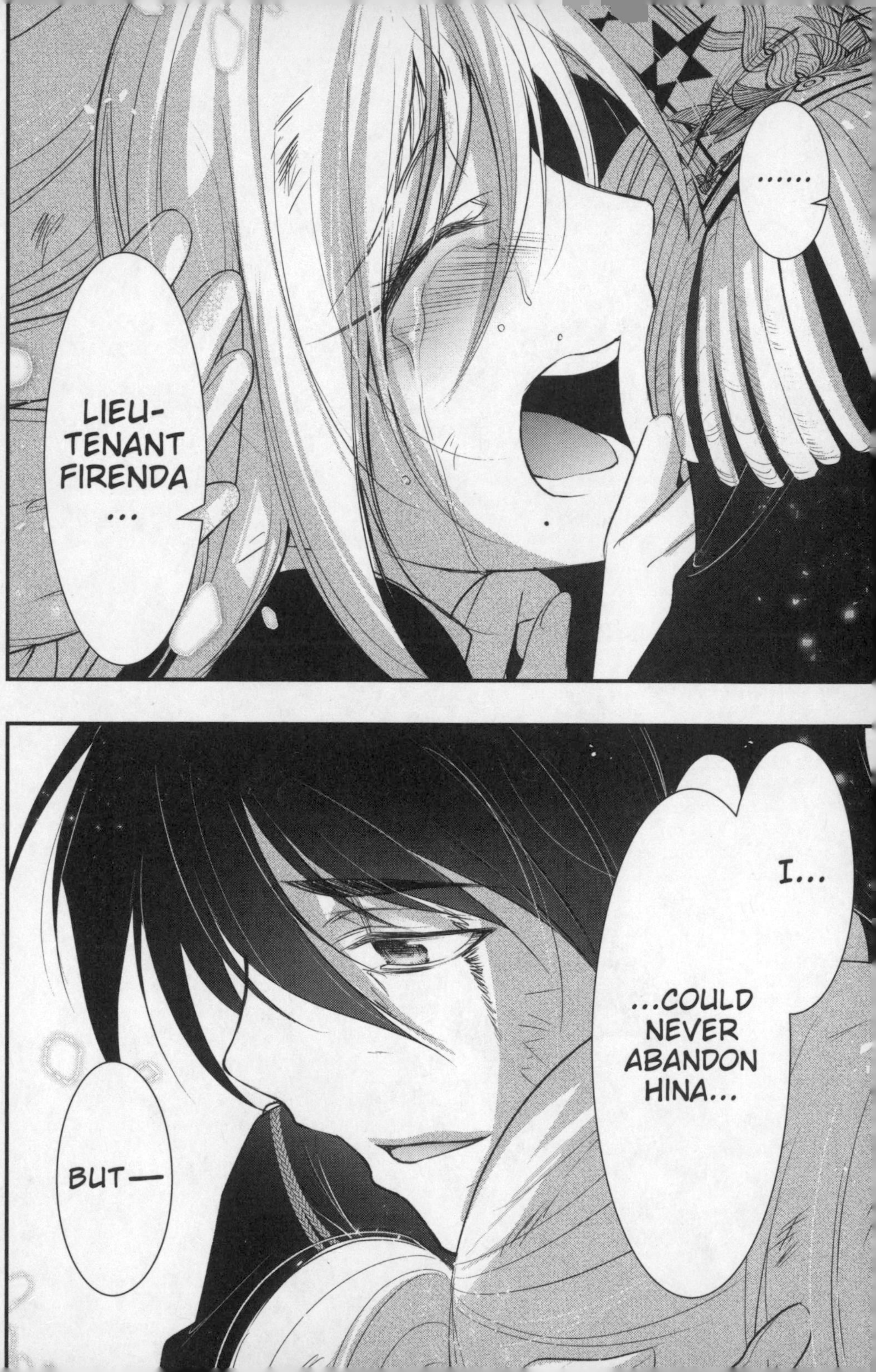
......
LIEU-TENANT FIRENDA ...
I...
...COULD NEVER ABANDON HINA...
BUT—

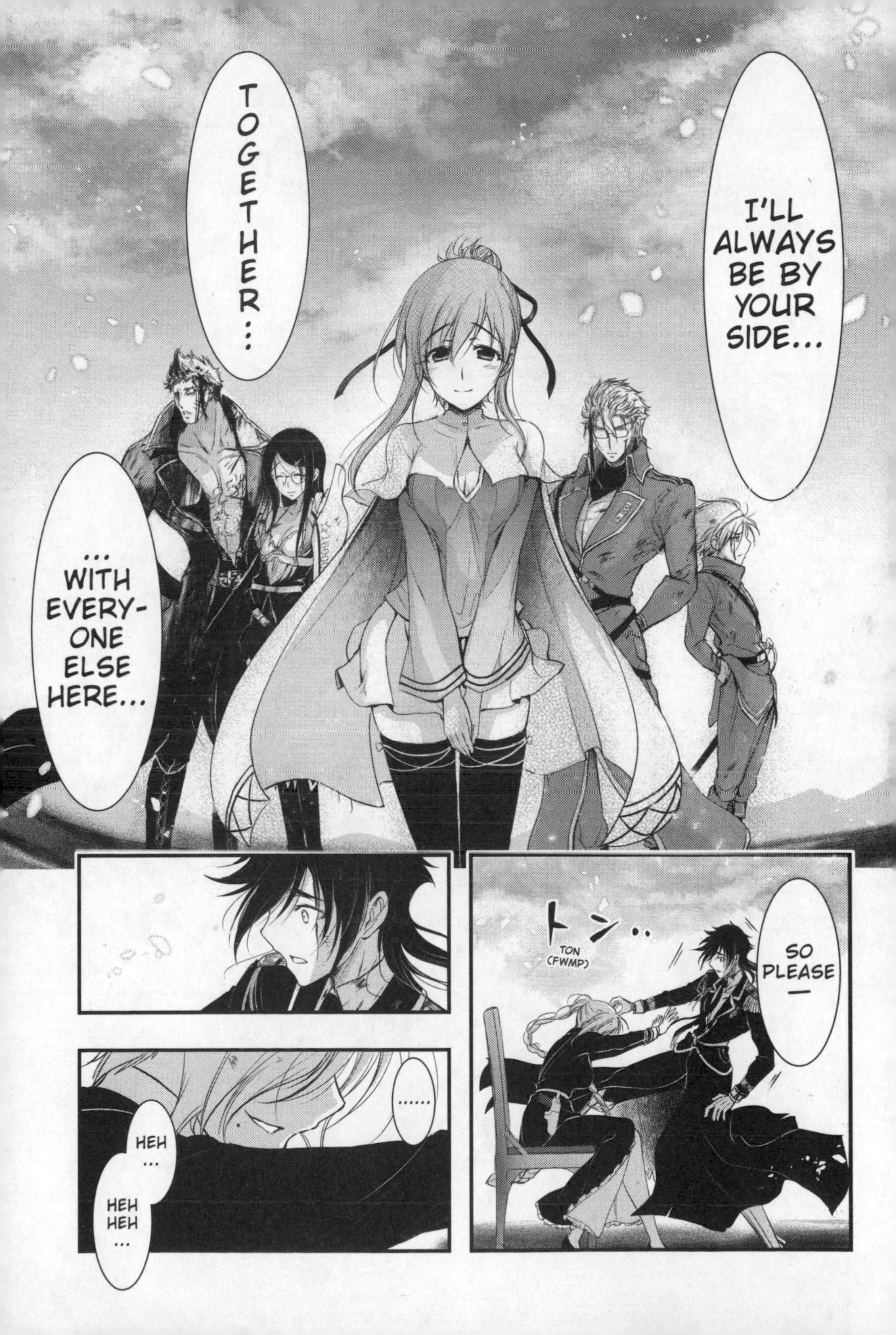
I'LL ALWAYS BE BY YOUR SIDE...
TOGETHER...
...WITH EVERY-ONE ELSE HERE...
トン..
TON (FWMP)
SO PLEASE—
......
HEH...
HEH HEH...

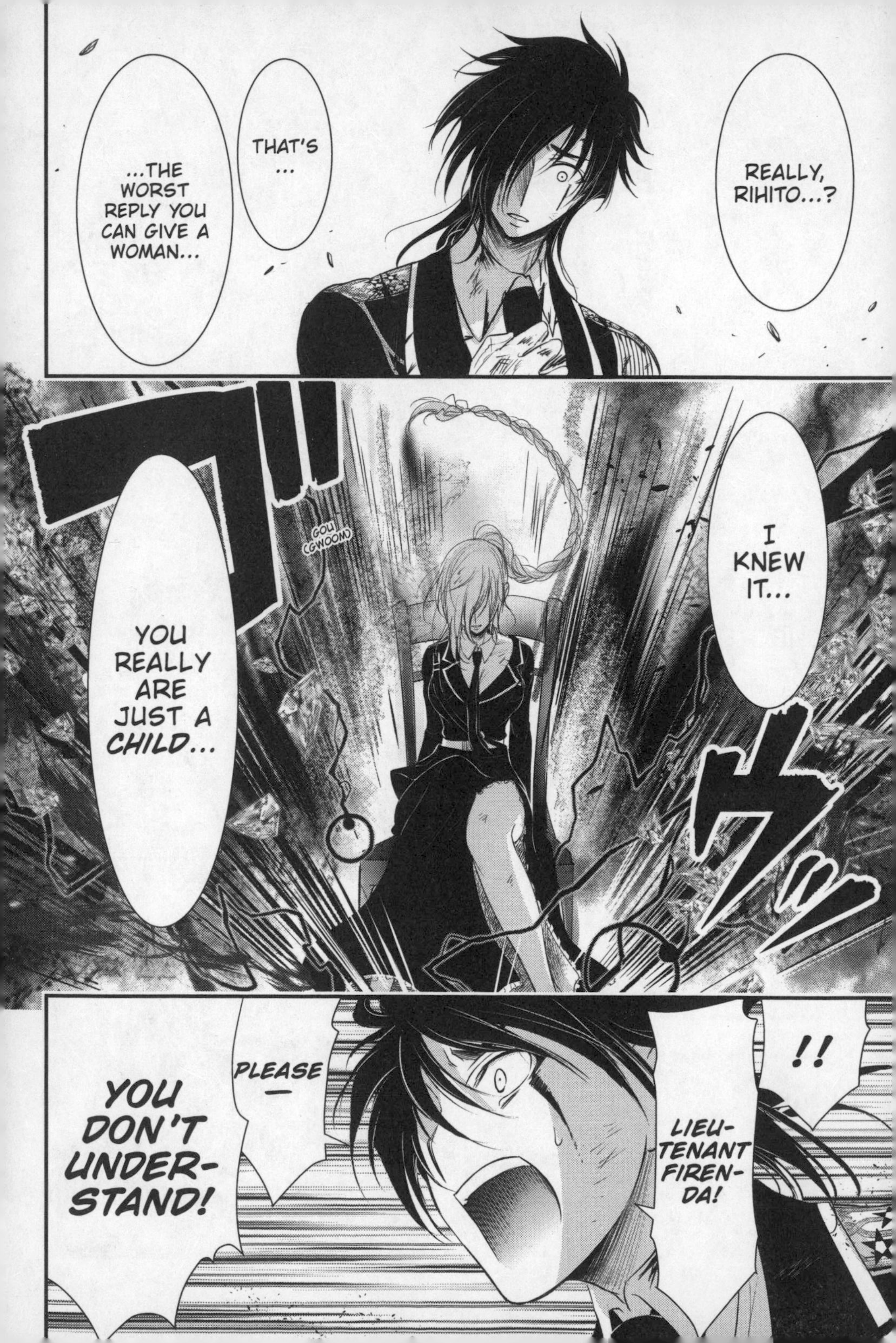
REALLY, RIHITO...?
THAT'S ...
...THE WORST REPLY YOU CAN GIVE A WOMAN...
I KNEW IT...
GOU (GWOOM)
YOU REALLY ARE JUST A CHILD...
!!
LIEU-TENANT FIREN-DA!
PLEASE —
YOU DON'T UNDER-STAND!

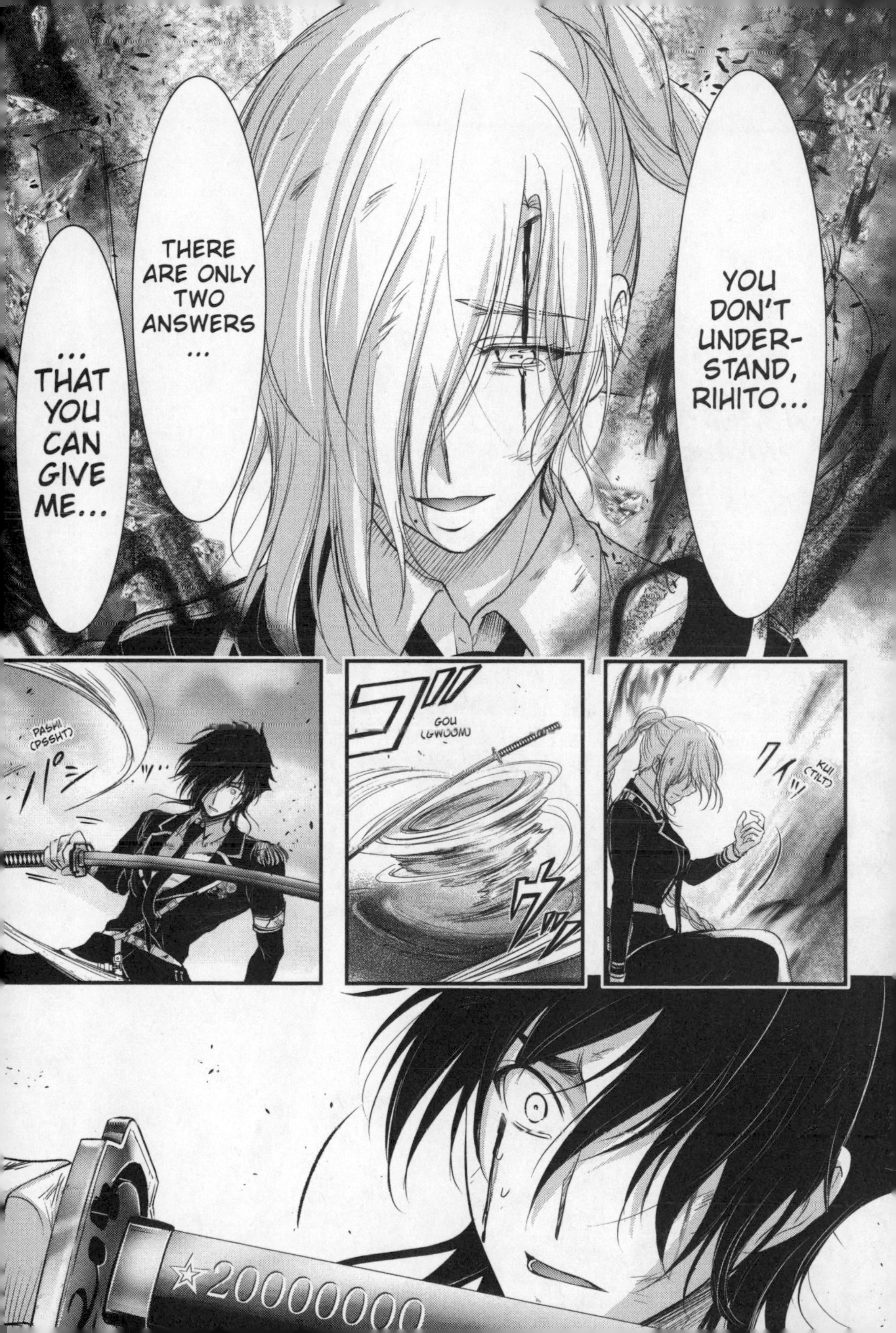
YOU DON'T UNDER-STAND, RIHITO...
THERE ARE ONLY TWO ANSWERS...
...THAT YOU CAN GIVE ME...
KUI (TILT)
GOU (GWOOM)
PASHI (PSSHT)
☆20000000

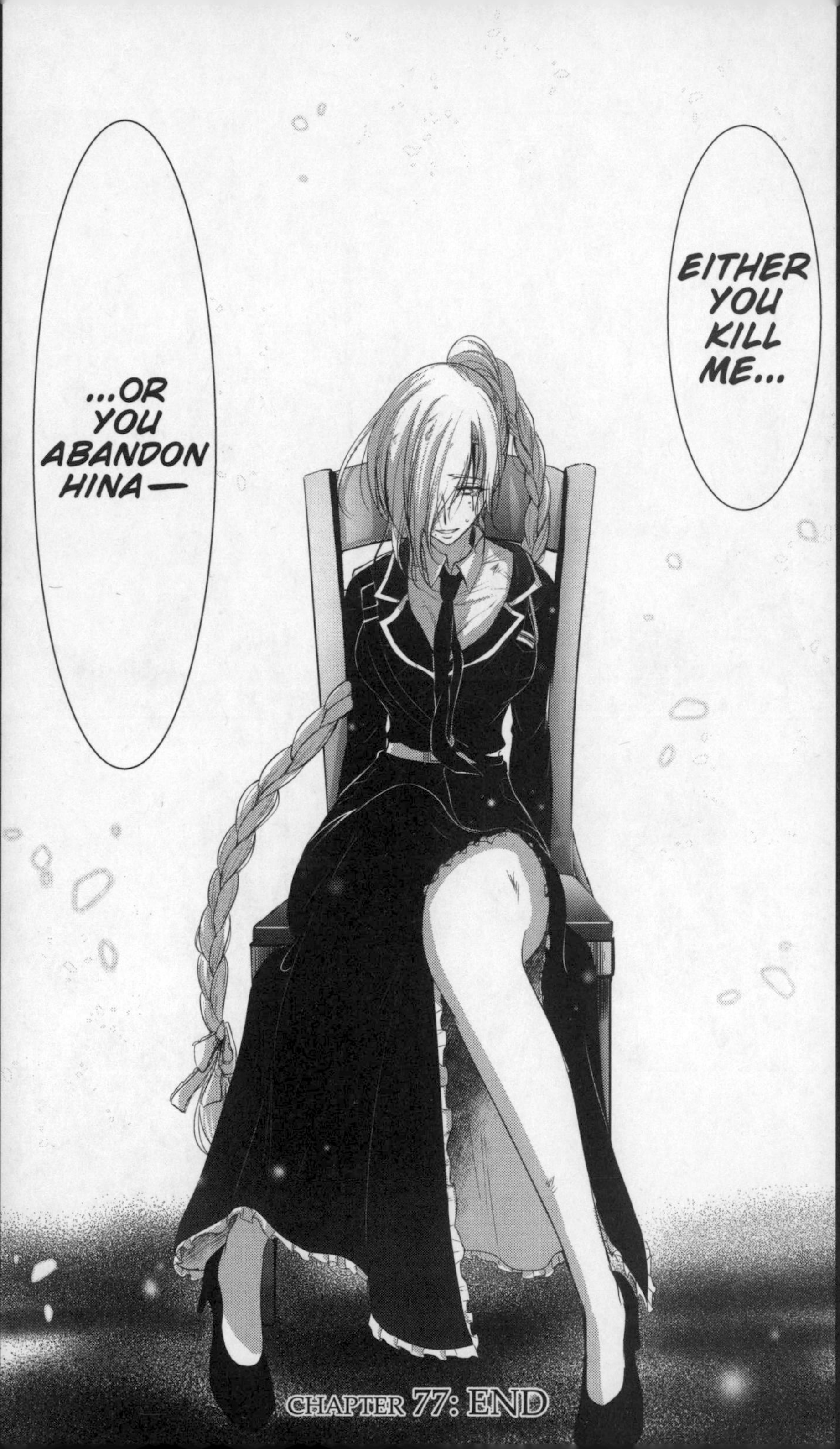
EITHER YOU KILL ME...
...OR YOU ABANDON HINA—
CHAPTER 77: END

CHAPTER 78

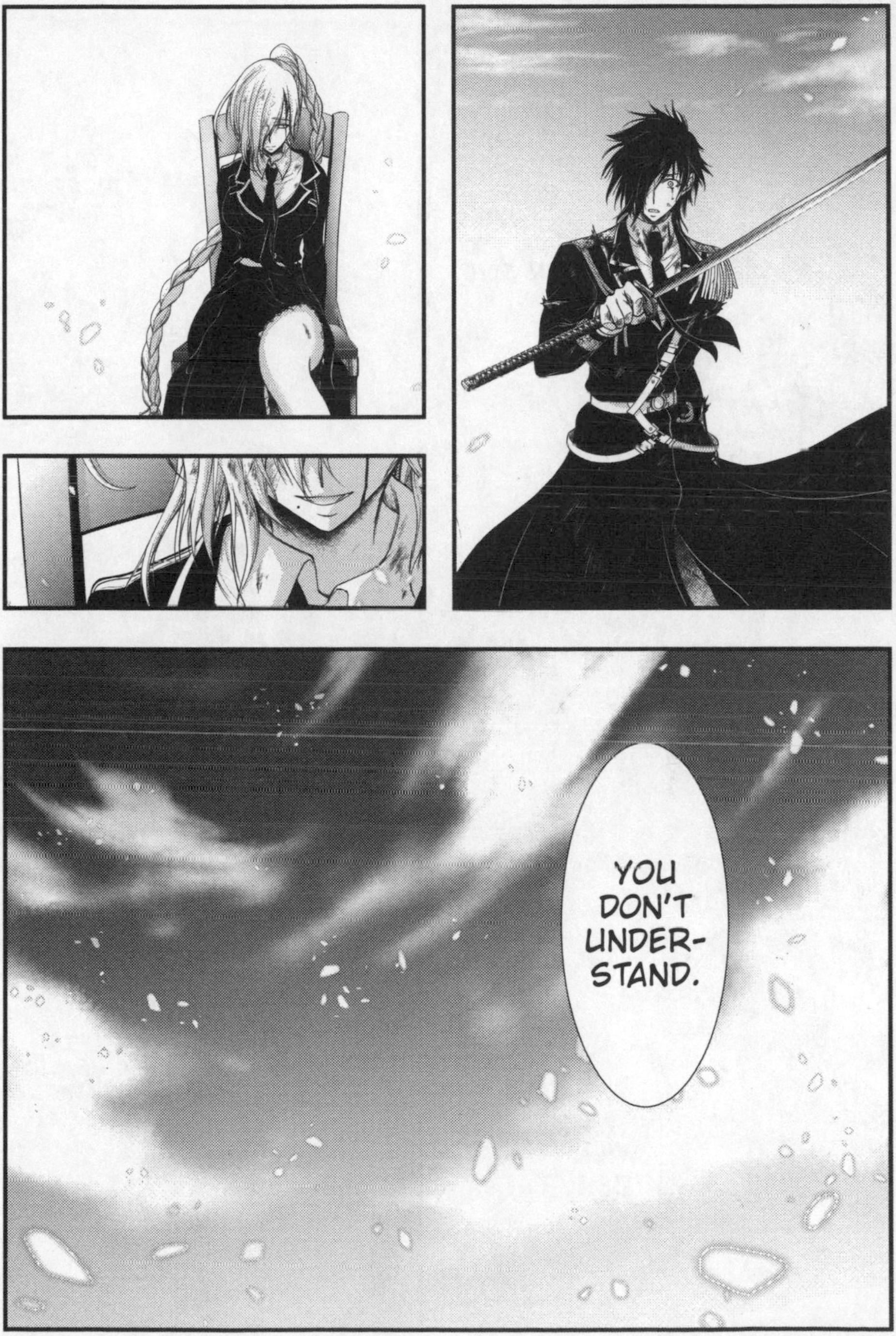
YOU DON'T UNDER-STAND.

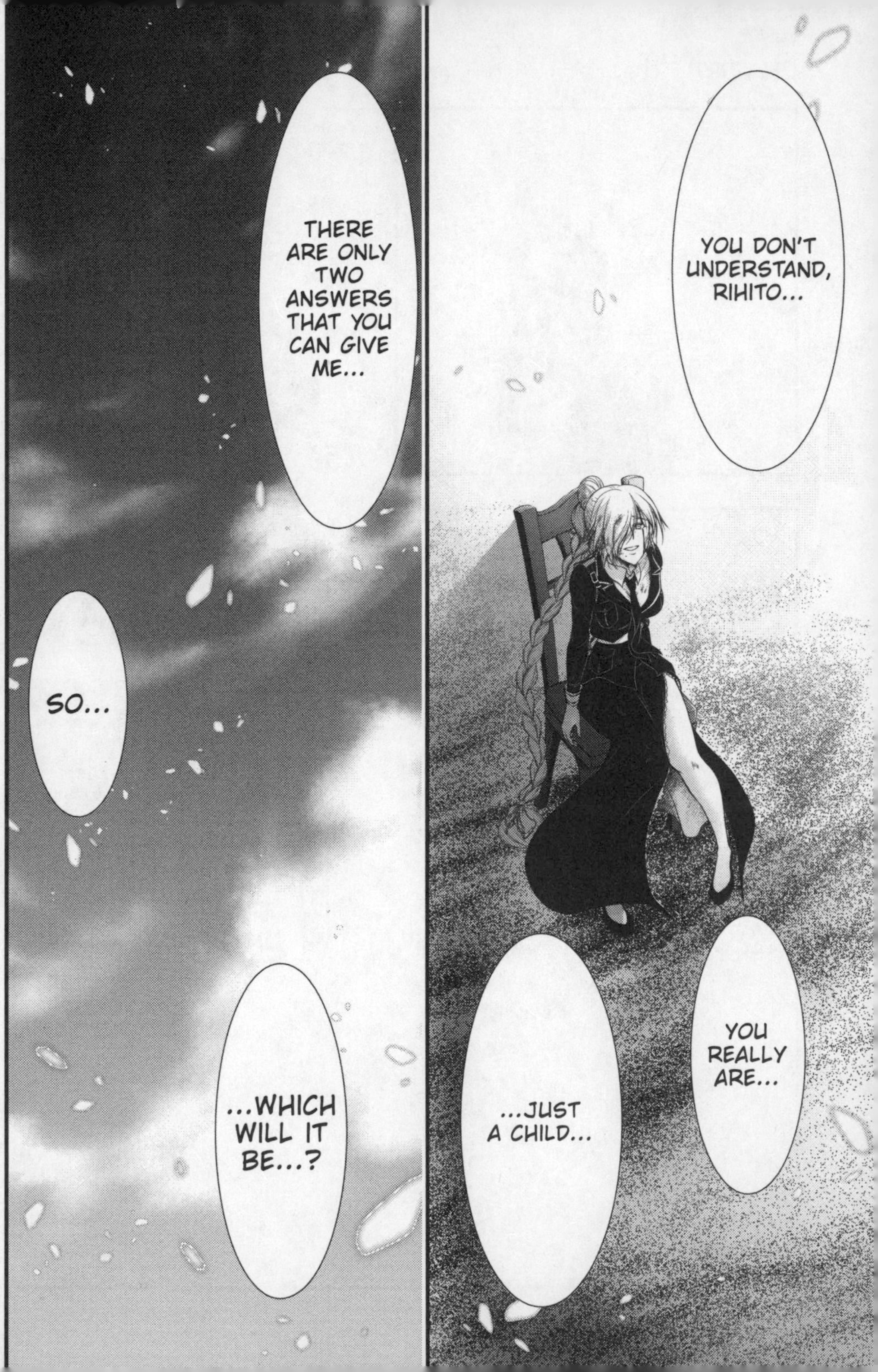
YOU DON'T UNDERSTAND, RIHITO...
YOU REALLY ARE...
...JUST A CHILD...
THERE ARE ONLY TWO ANSWERS THAT YOU CAN GIVE ME...
SO...
...WHICH WILL IT BE...?

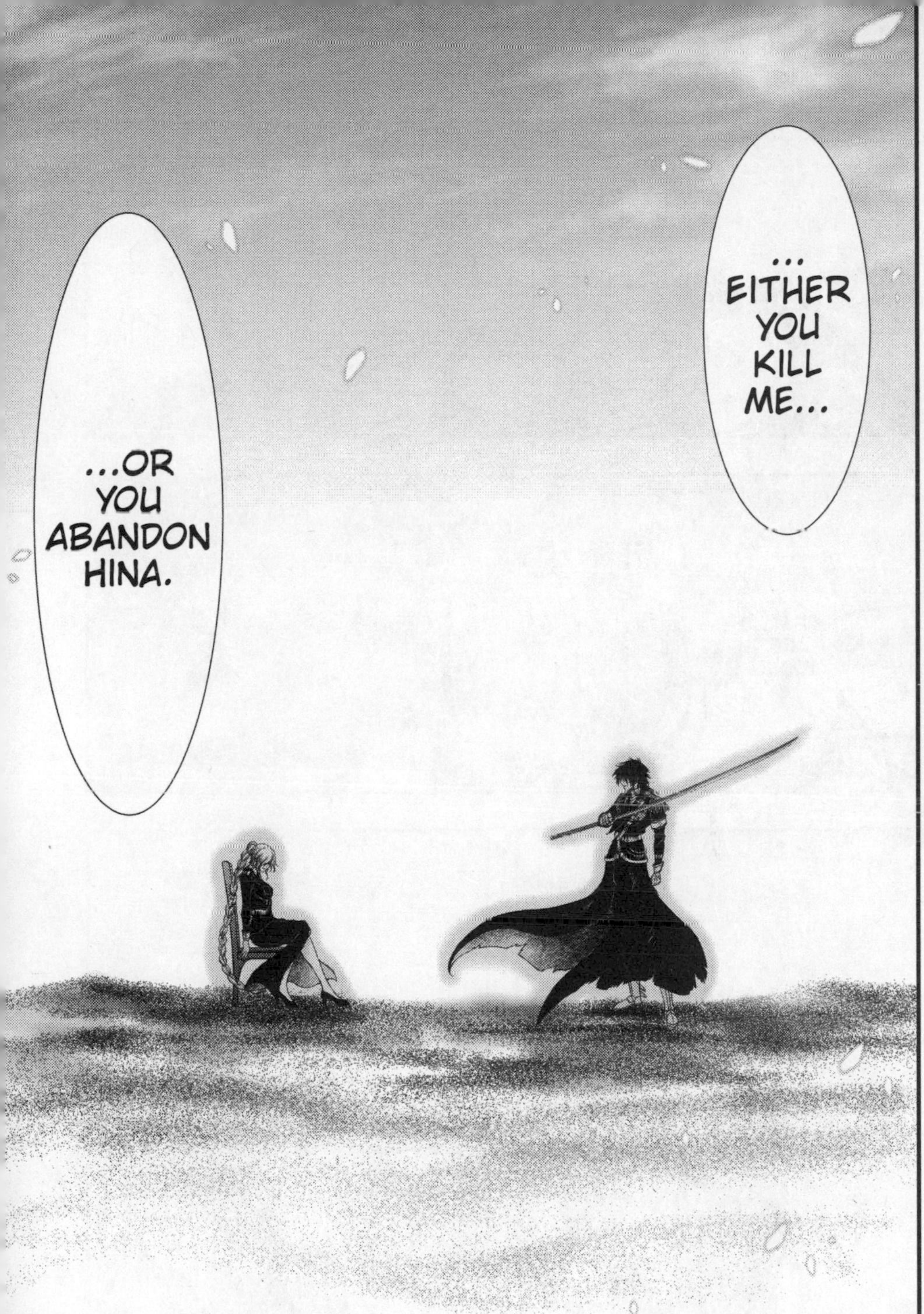
...EITHER YOU KILL ME...
...OR YOU ABANDON HINA.

CHAPTER 78: PATH TO SALVATION

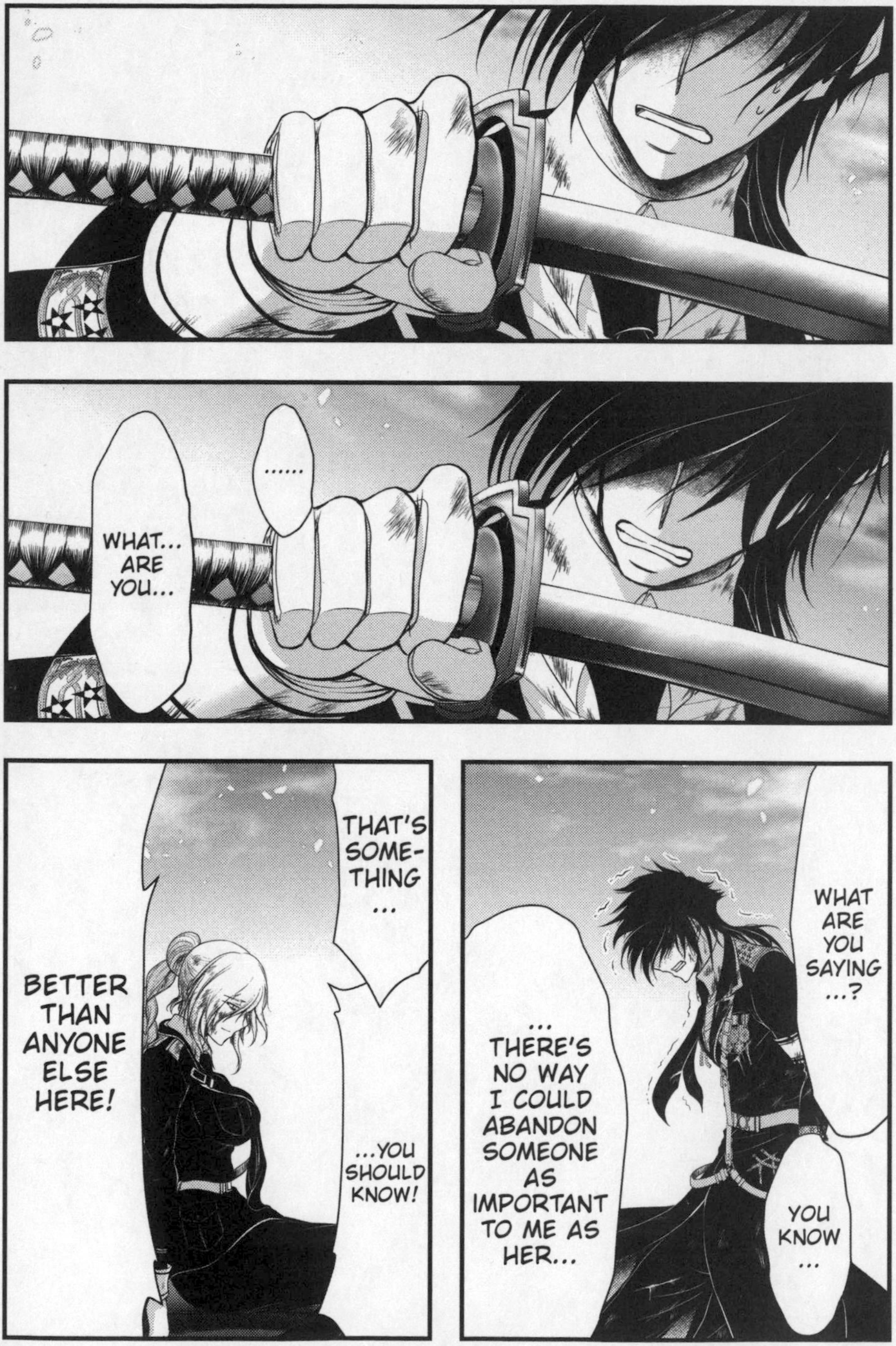

......
WHAT... ARE YOU...
WHAT ARE YOU SAYING ...?
YOU KNOW ...
... THERE'S NO WAY I COULD ABANDON SOMEONE AS IMPORTANT TO ME AS HER...
THAT'S SOME-THING ...
...YOU SHOULD KNOW!
BETTER THAN ANYONE ELSE HERE!

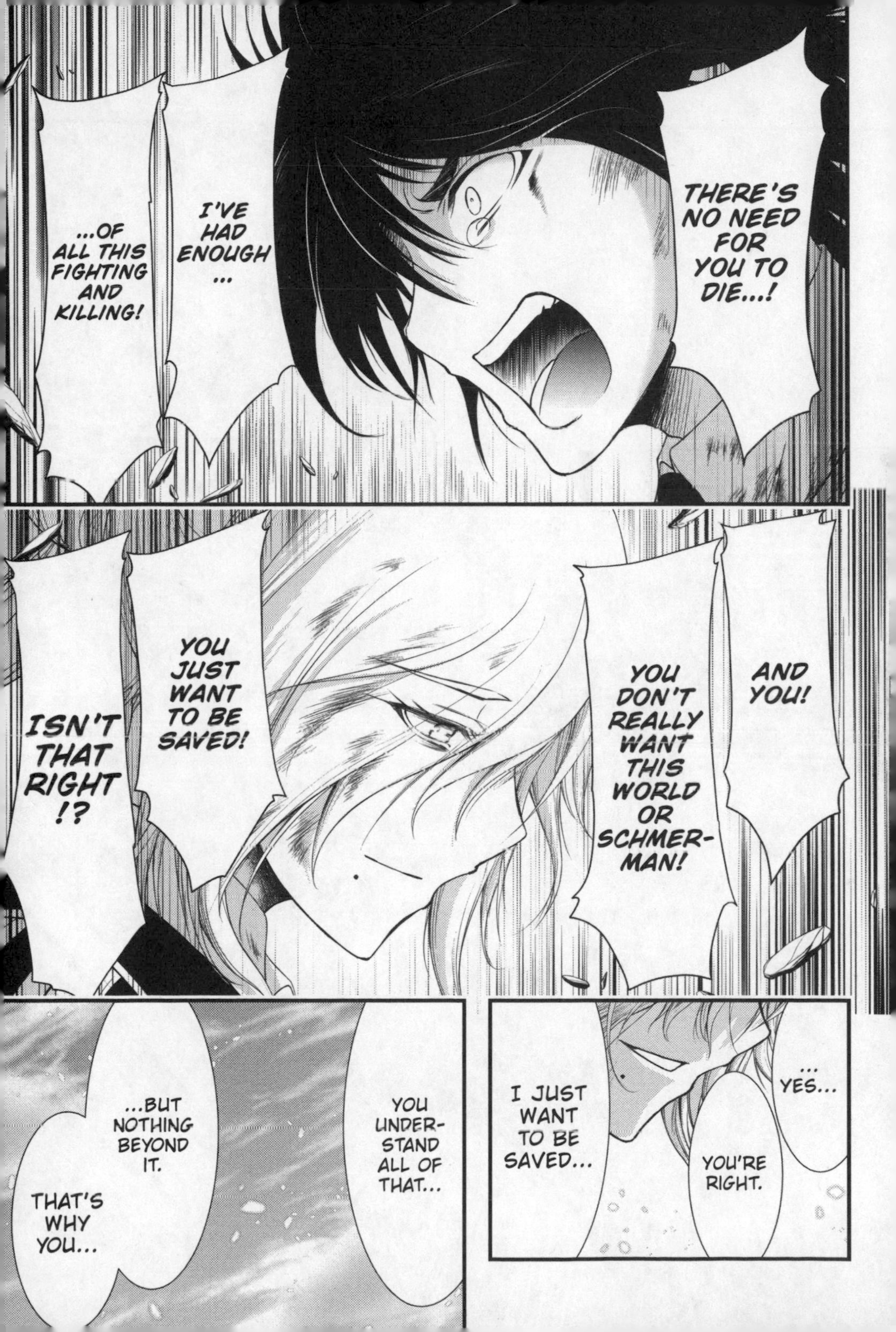
THERE'S NO NEED FOR YOU TO DIE...!
I'VE HAD ENOUGH...
...OF ALL THIS FIGHTING AND KILLING!
AND YOU!
YOU DON'T REALLY WANT THIS WORLD OR SCHMER-MAN!
YOU JUST WANT TO BE SAVED!
ISN'T THAT RIGHT!?
...YES...
YOU'RE RIGHT.
I JUST WANT TO BE SAVED...
YOU UNDER-STAND ALL OF THAT...
...BUT NOTHING BEYOND IT.
THAT'S WHY YOU...

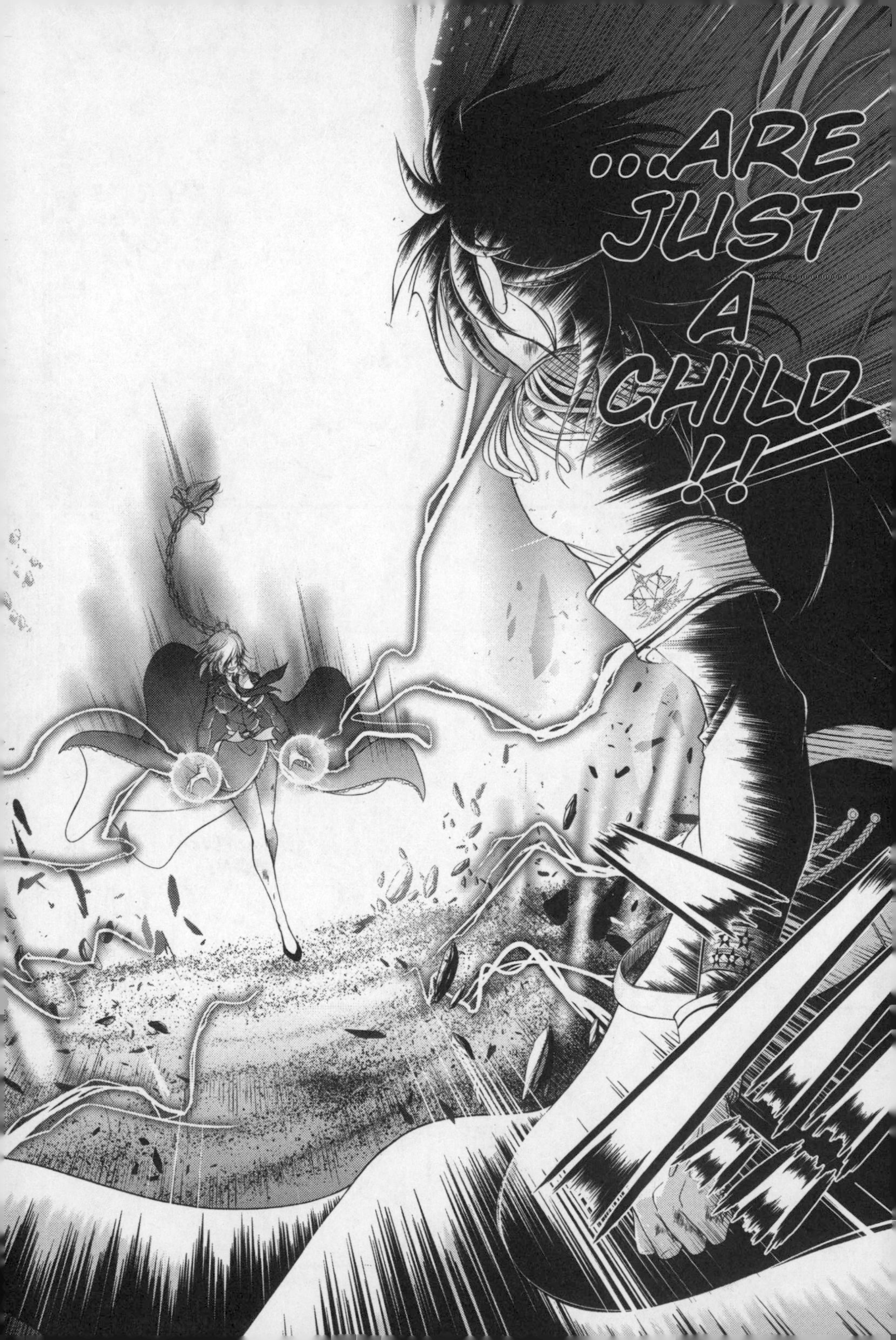
...ARE JUST A CHILD !!

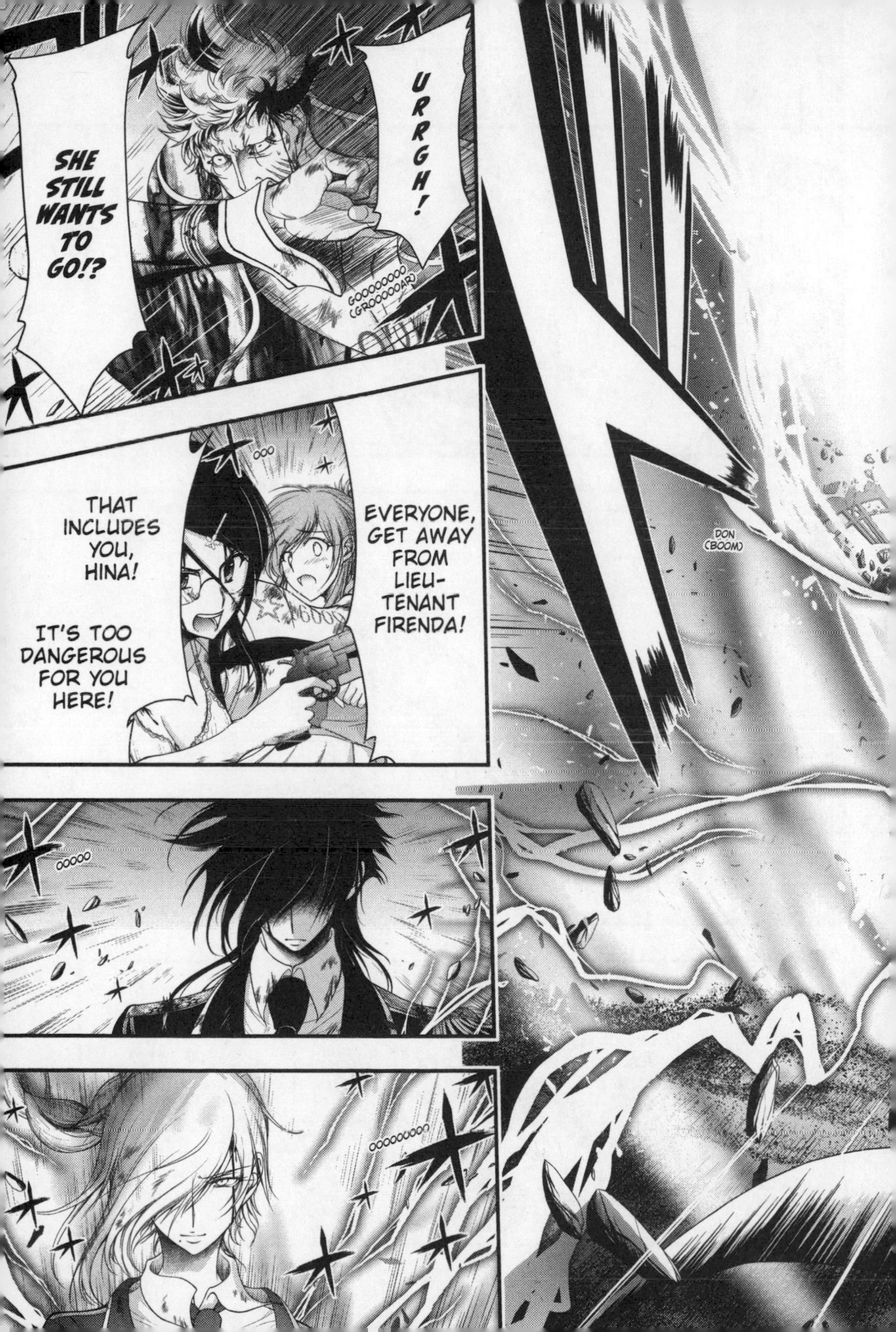
DON (BOOM)
URRGH!
GOOOOOOOOO (GROOOOOAR)
SHE STILL WANTS TO GO!?
EVERYONE, GET AWAY FROM LIEU-TENANT FIRENDA!
OOO
THAT INCLUDES YOU, HINA!
IT'S TOO DANGEROUS FOR YOU HERE!
OOOOO
OOOOOOOOO

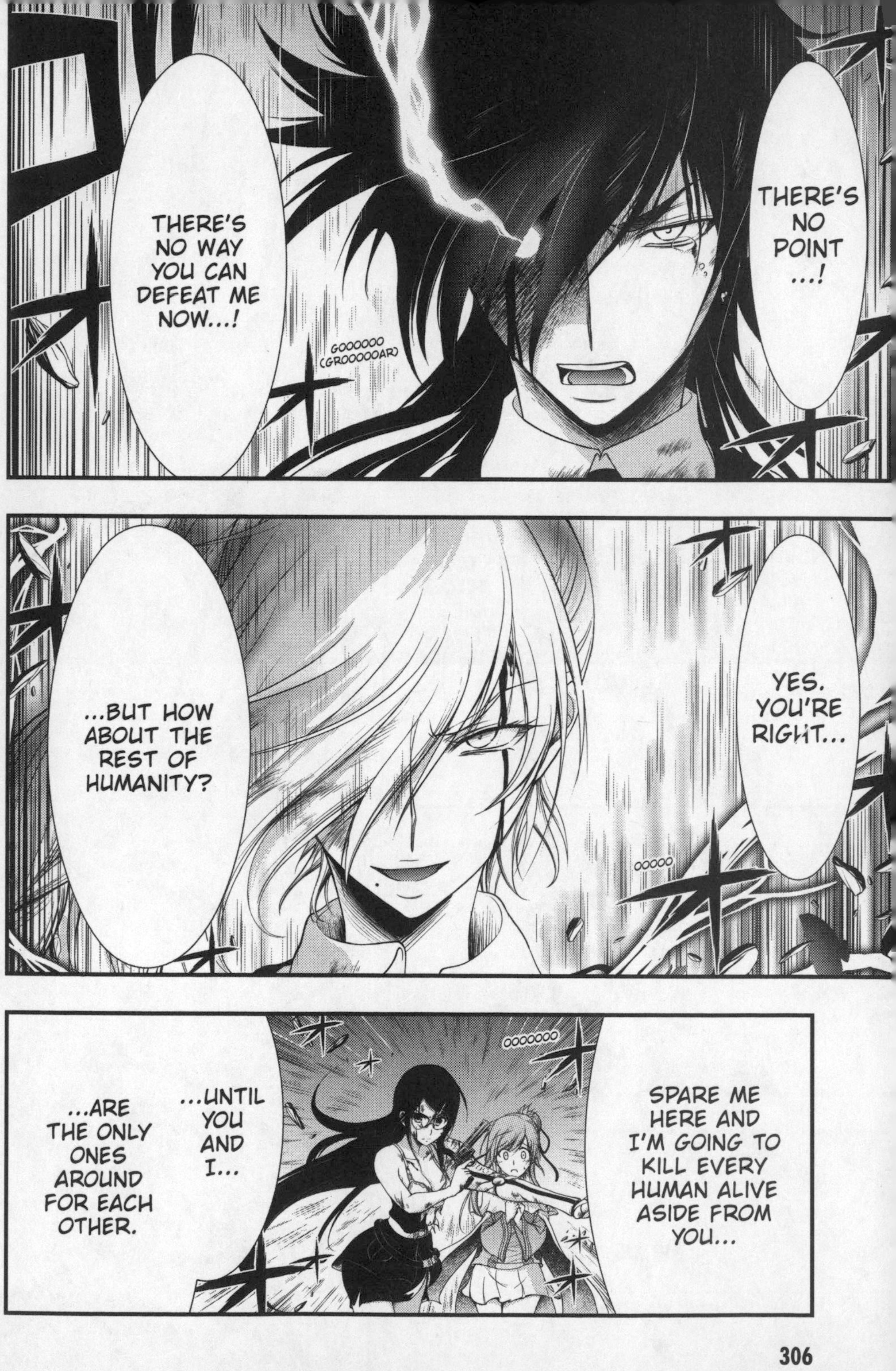
THERE'S NO POINT ...!
GOOOOOO (GROOOOOAR)
THERE'S NO WAY YOU CAN DEFEAT ME NOW...!
YES. YOU'RE RIGHT...
...BUT HOW ABOUT THE REST OF HUMANITY?
SPARE ME HERE AND I'M GOING TO KILL EVERY HUMAN ALIVE ASIDE FROM YOU...
...UNTIL YOU AND I...
...ARE THE ONLY ONES AROUND FOR EACH OTHER.

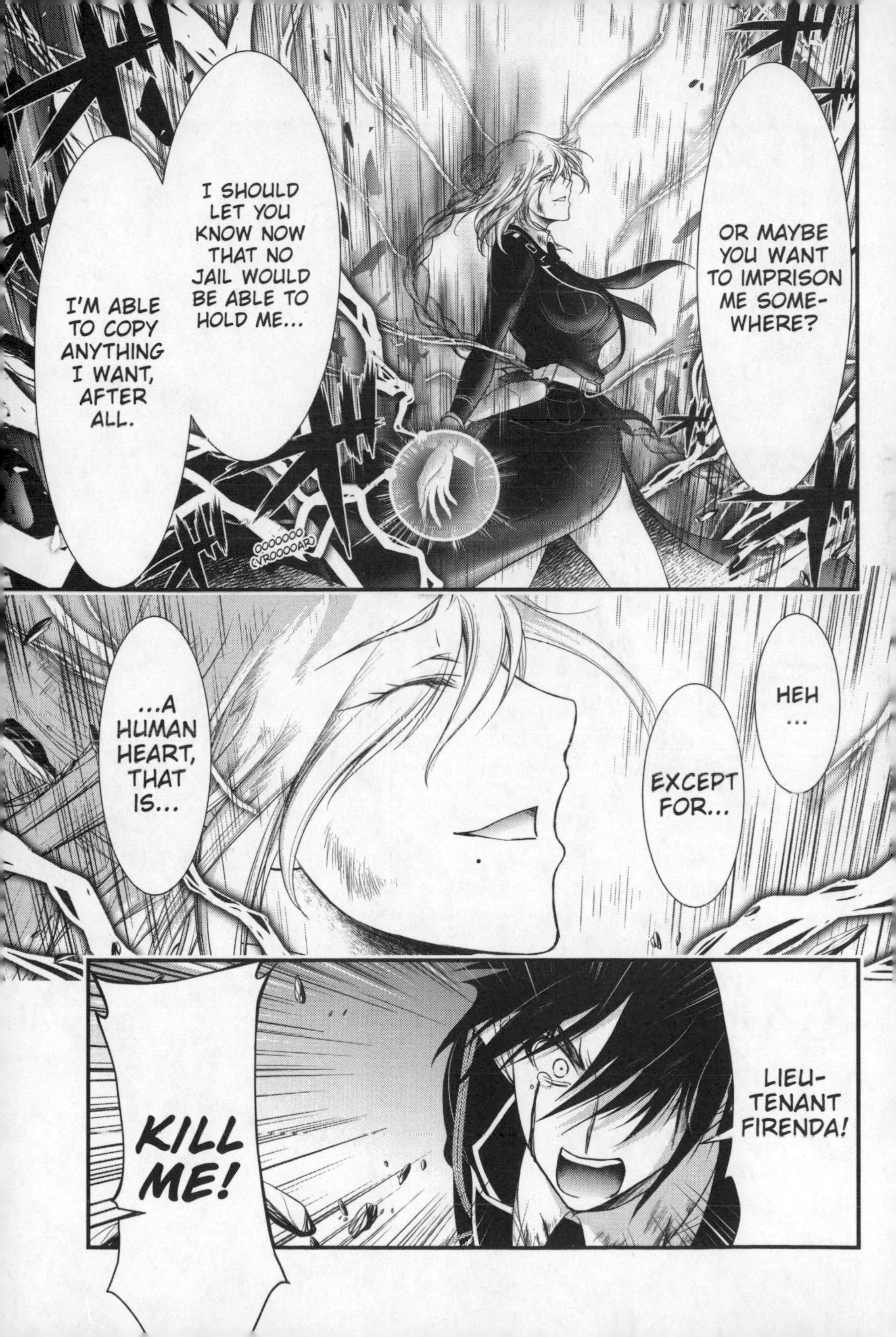
OR MAYBE YOU WANT TO IMPRISON ME SOME-WHERE?
I SHOULD LET YOU KNOW NOW THAT NO JAIL WOULD BE ABLE TO HOLD ME...
I'M ABLE TO COPY ANYTHING I WANT, AFTER ALL.
OOOOOOO (VROOOOAR)
HEH...
EXCEPT FOR...
...A HUMAN HEART, THAT IS...
LIEU-TENANT FIRENDA!
KILL ME!

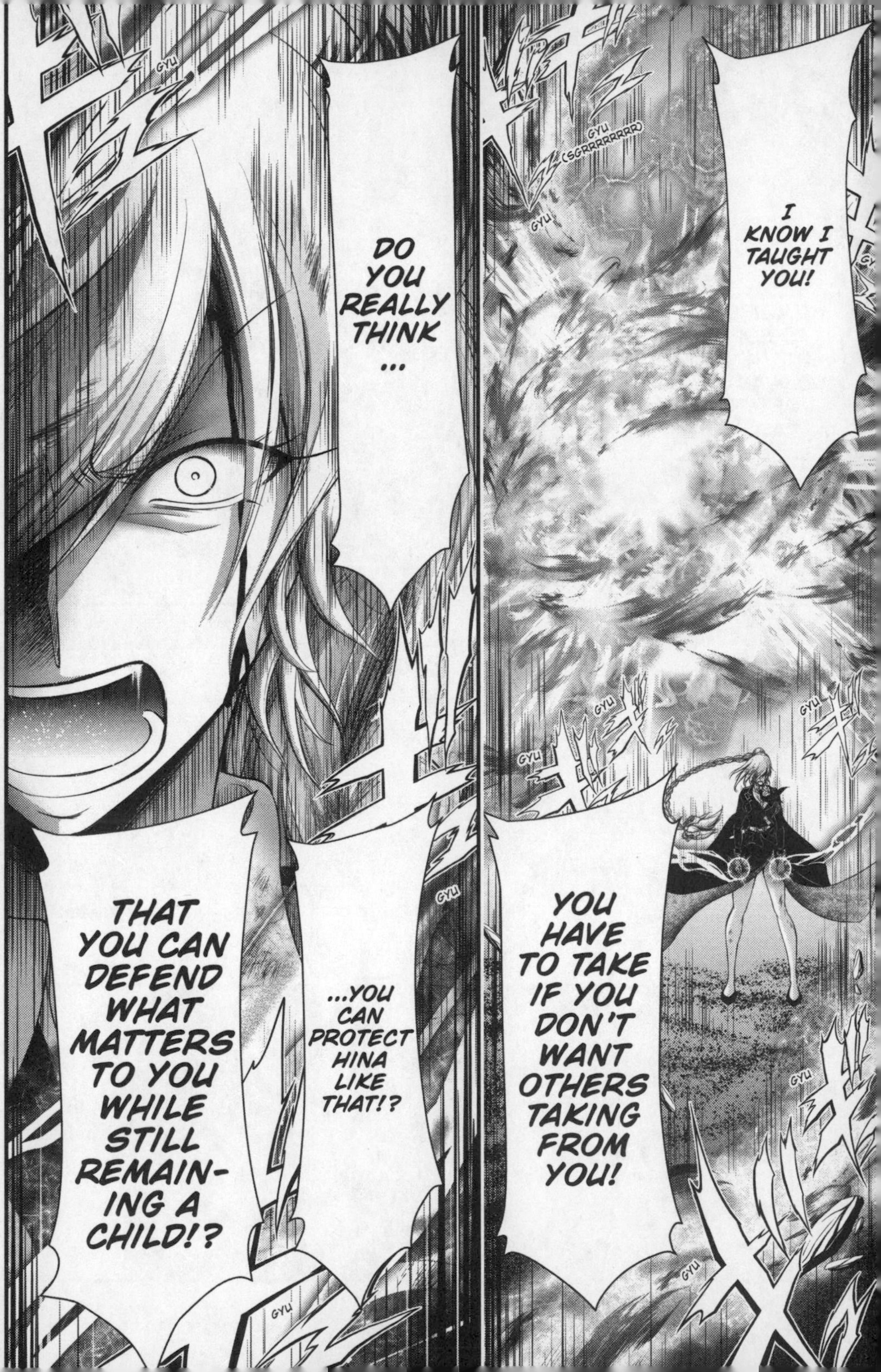
GYU
GYU (SGRRRRRRRR)
GYU
I KNOW I TAUGHT YOU!
GYU
GYU
GYU
YOU HAVE TO TAKE IF YOU DON'T WANT OTHERS TAKING FROM YOU!
GYU
GYU
GYU
DO YOU REALLY THINK...
GYU
...YOU CAN PROTECT HINA LIKE THAT!?
THAT YOU CAN DEFEND WHAT MATTERS TO YOU WHILE STILL REMAINING A CHILD!?
GYU

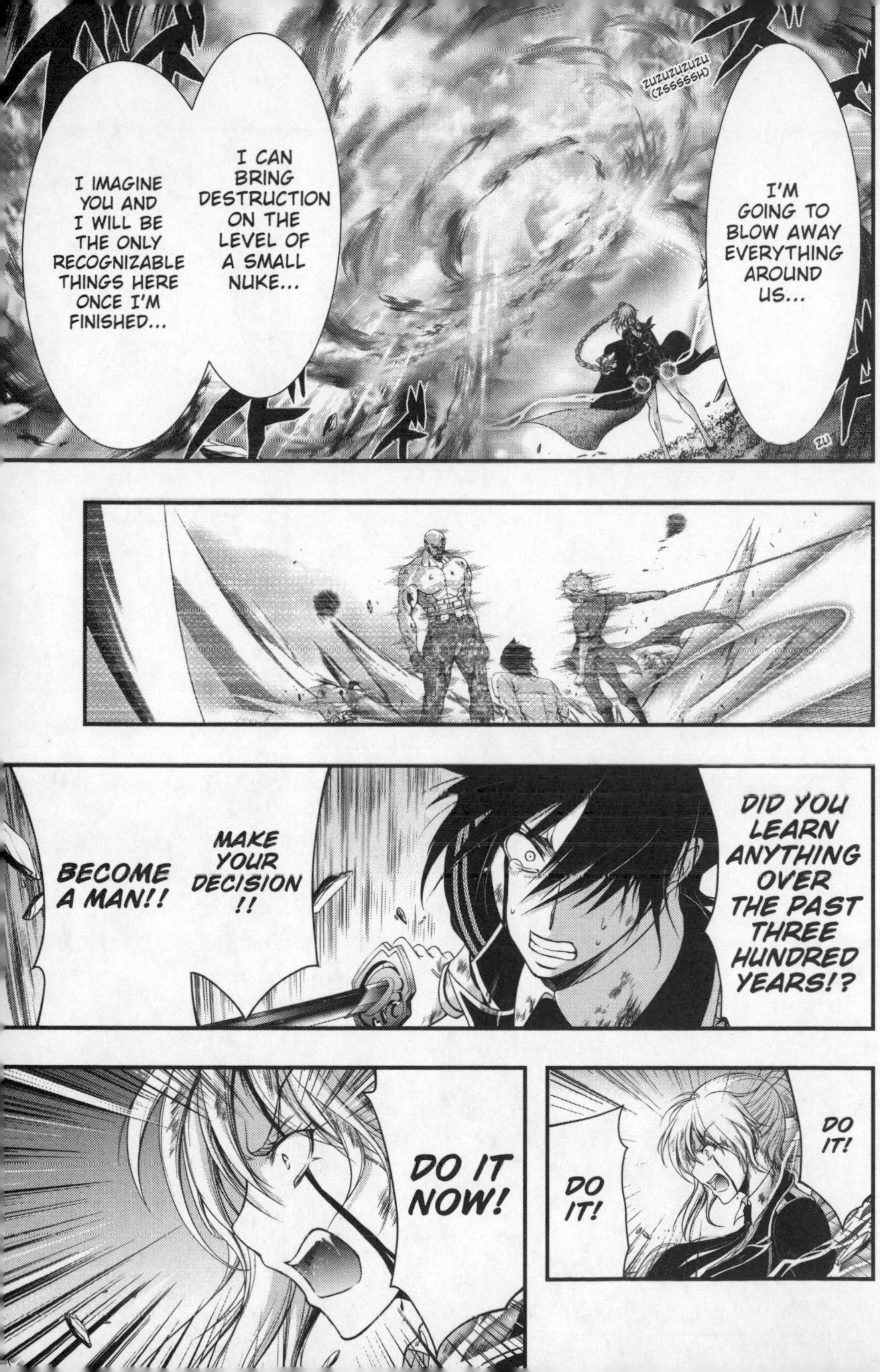
ZUZUZUZUZU (ZSSSSSSH)
I'M GOING TO BLOW AWAY EVERYTHING AROUND US...
ZU
I CAN BRING DESTRUCTION ON THE LEVEL OF A SMALL NUKE...
I IMAGINE YOU AND I WILL BE THE ONLY RECOGNIZABLE THINGS HERE ONCE I'M FINISHED...
DID YOU LEARN ANYTHING OVER THE PAST THREE HUNDRED YEARS!?
MAKE YOUR DECISION!!
BECOME A MAN!!
DO IT!
DO IT!
DO IT NOW!

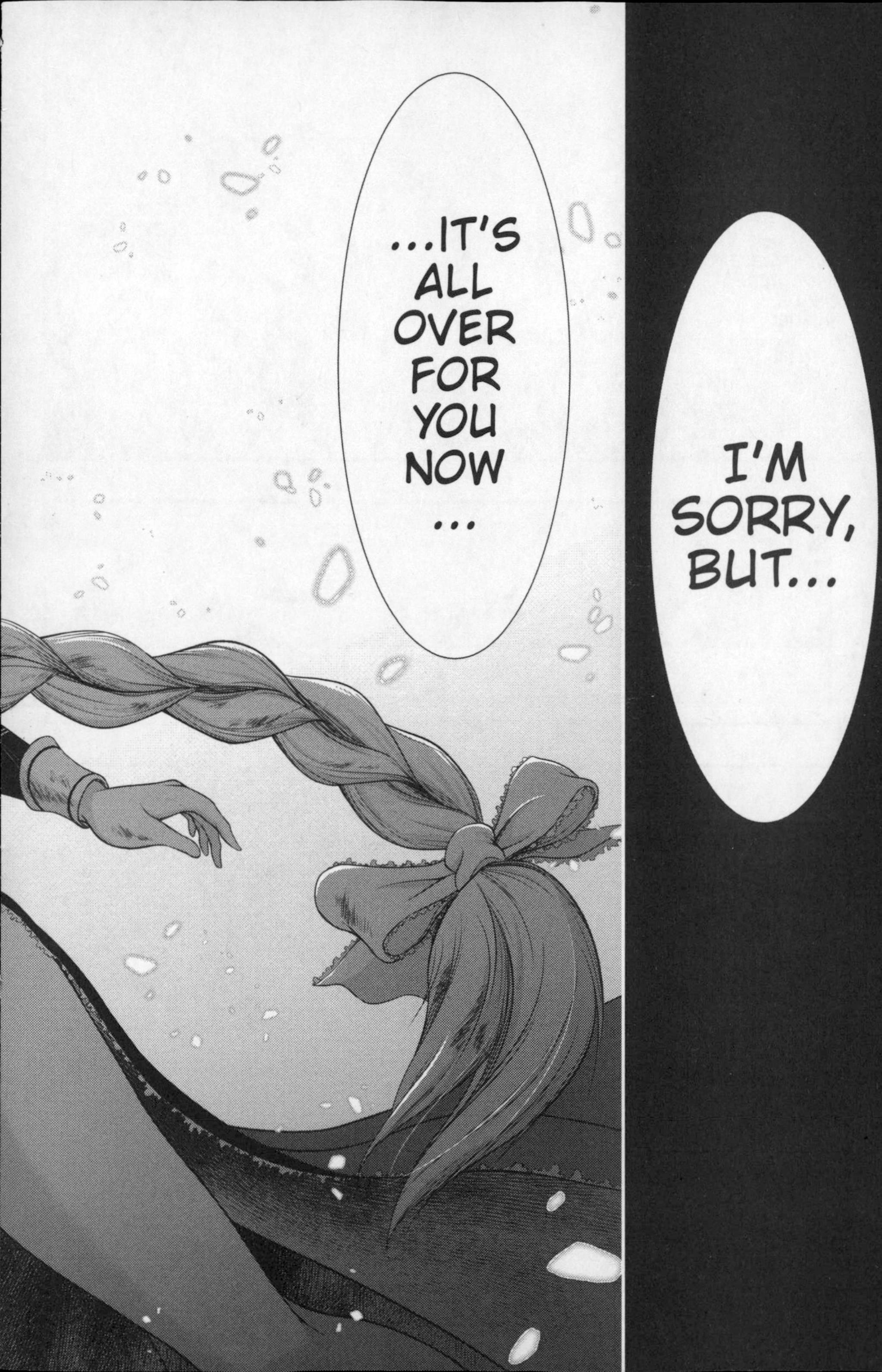
I'M SORRY, BUT...
...IT'S ALL OVER FOR YOU NOW...

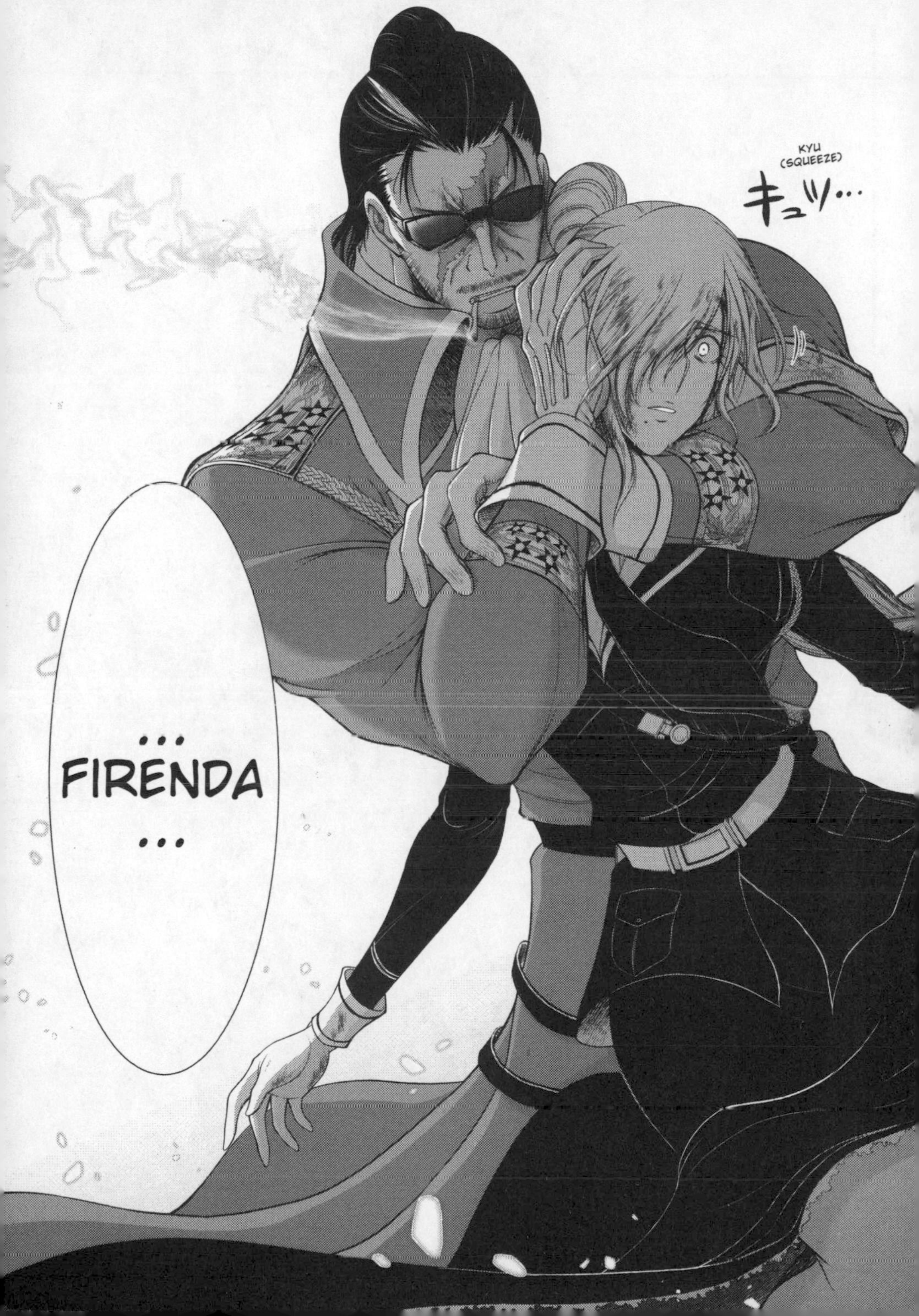
KYU (SQUEEZE)
キュッ…
...FIRENDA...

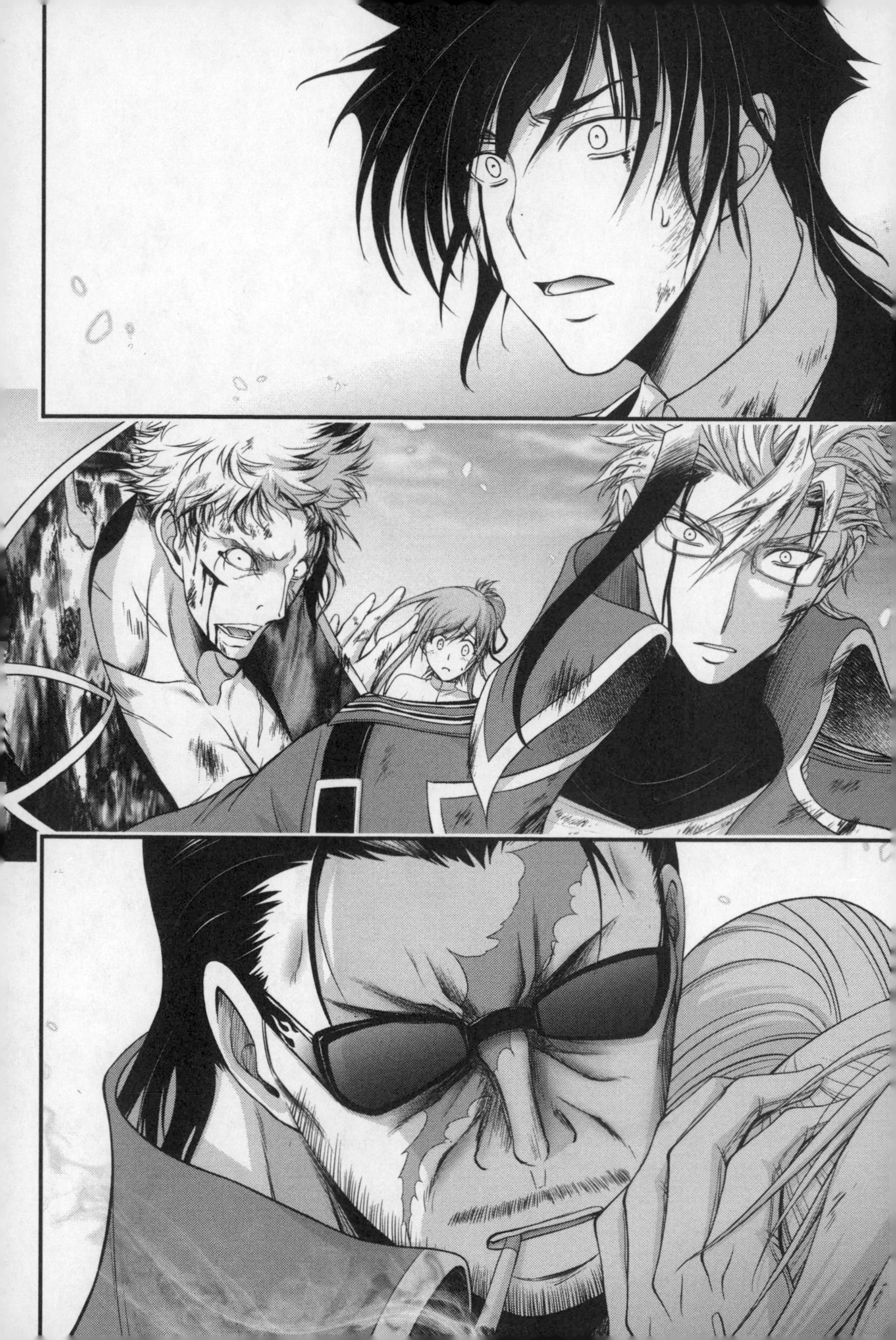

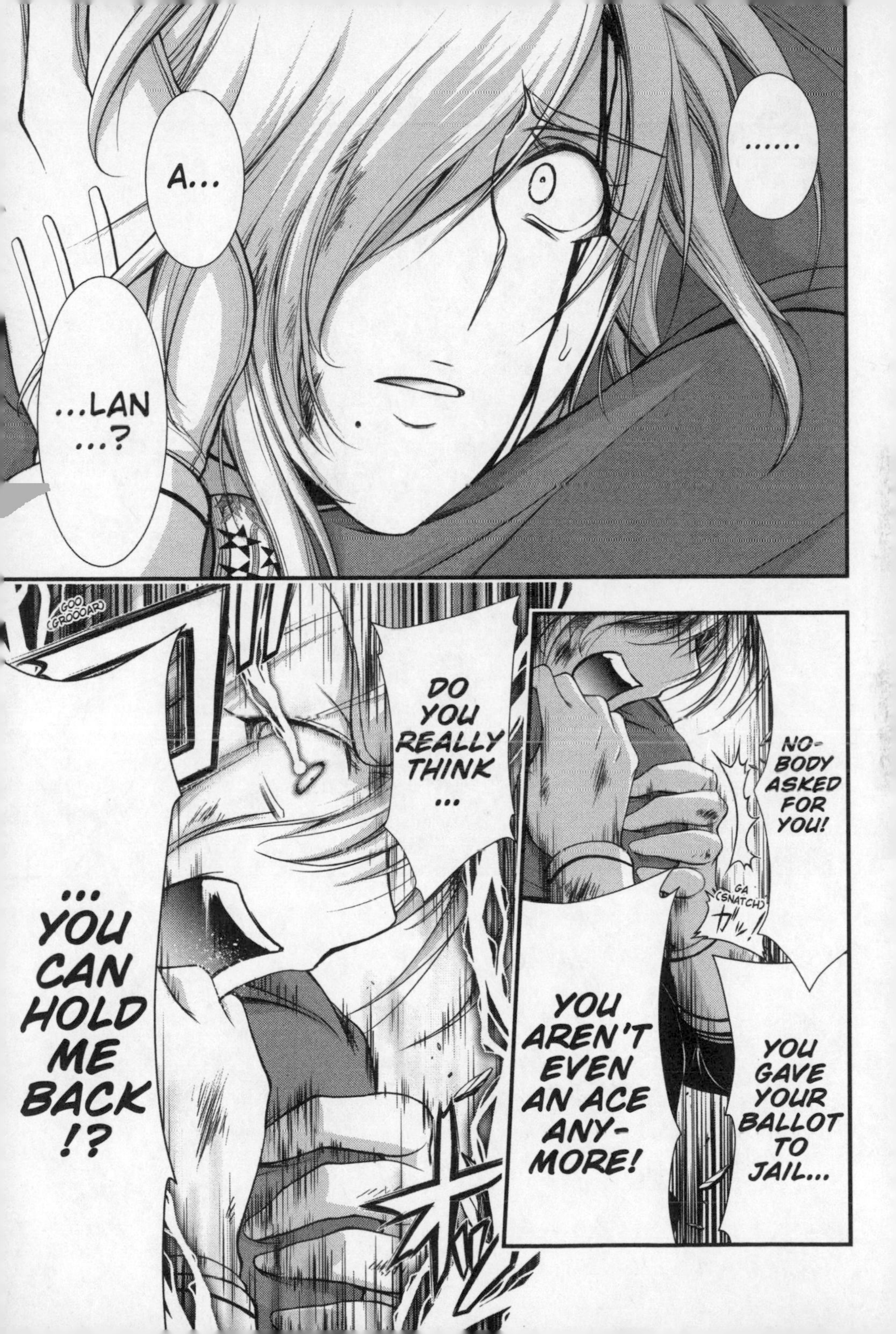
......
A...
...LAN ...?
NO-BODY ASKED FOR YOU!
GA (SNATCH)
YOU GAVE YOUR BALLOT TO JAIL...
YOU AREN'T EVEN AN ACE ANY-MORE!
GOO (GROOOAR)
DO YOU REALLY THINK...
...YOU CAN HOLD ME BACK!?

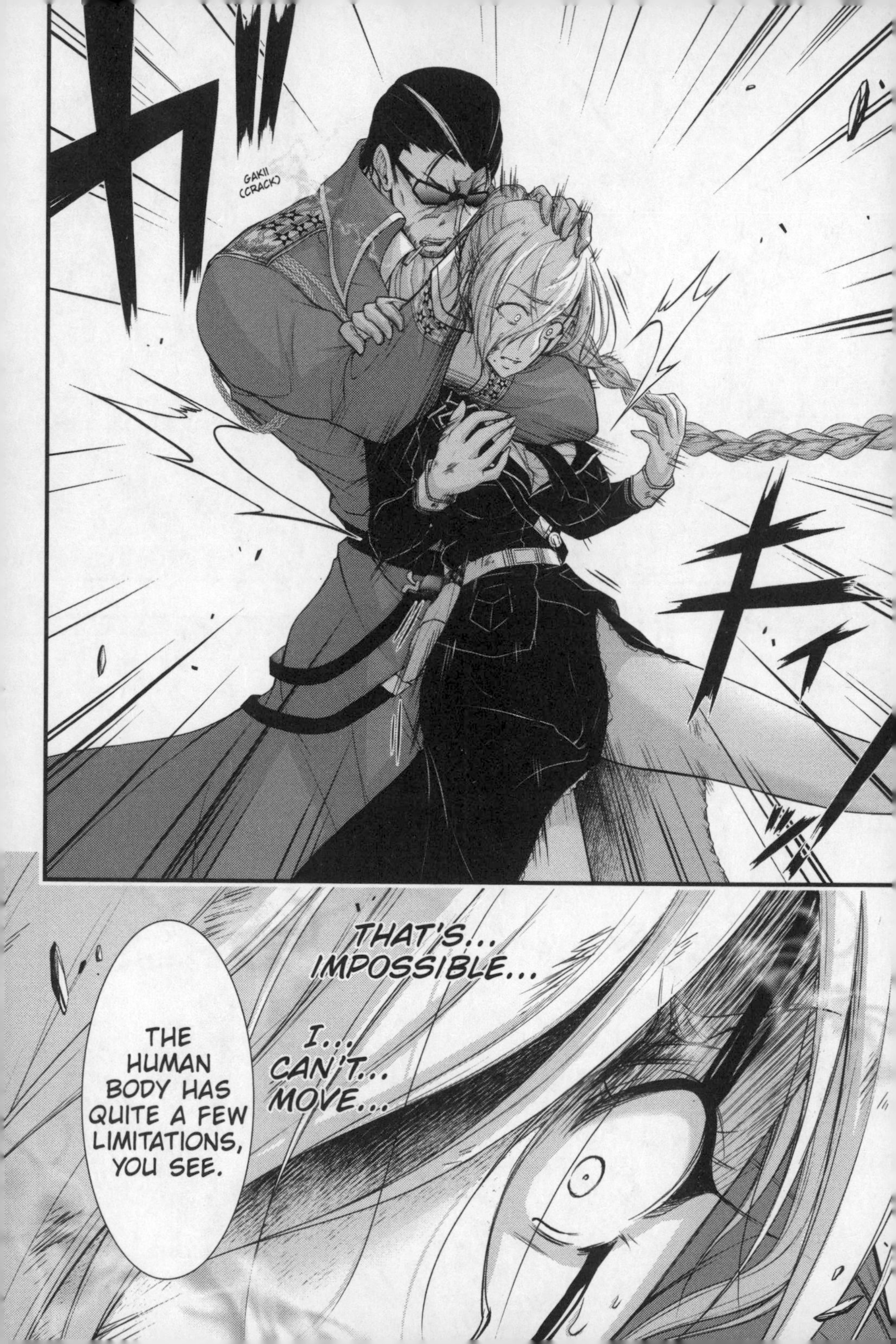
GAKII (CRACK)
THAT'S... IMPOSSIBLE...
I... CAN'T... MOVE...
THE HUMAN BODY HAS QUITE A FEW LIMITATIONS, YOU SEE.

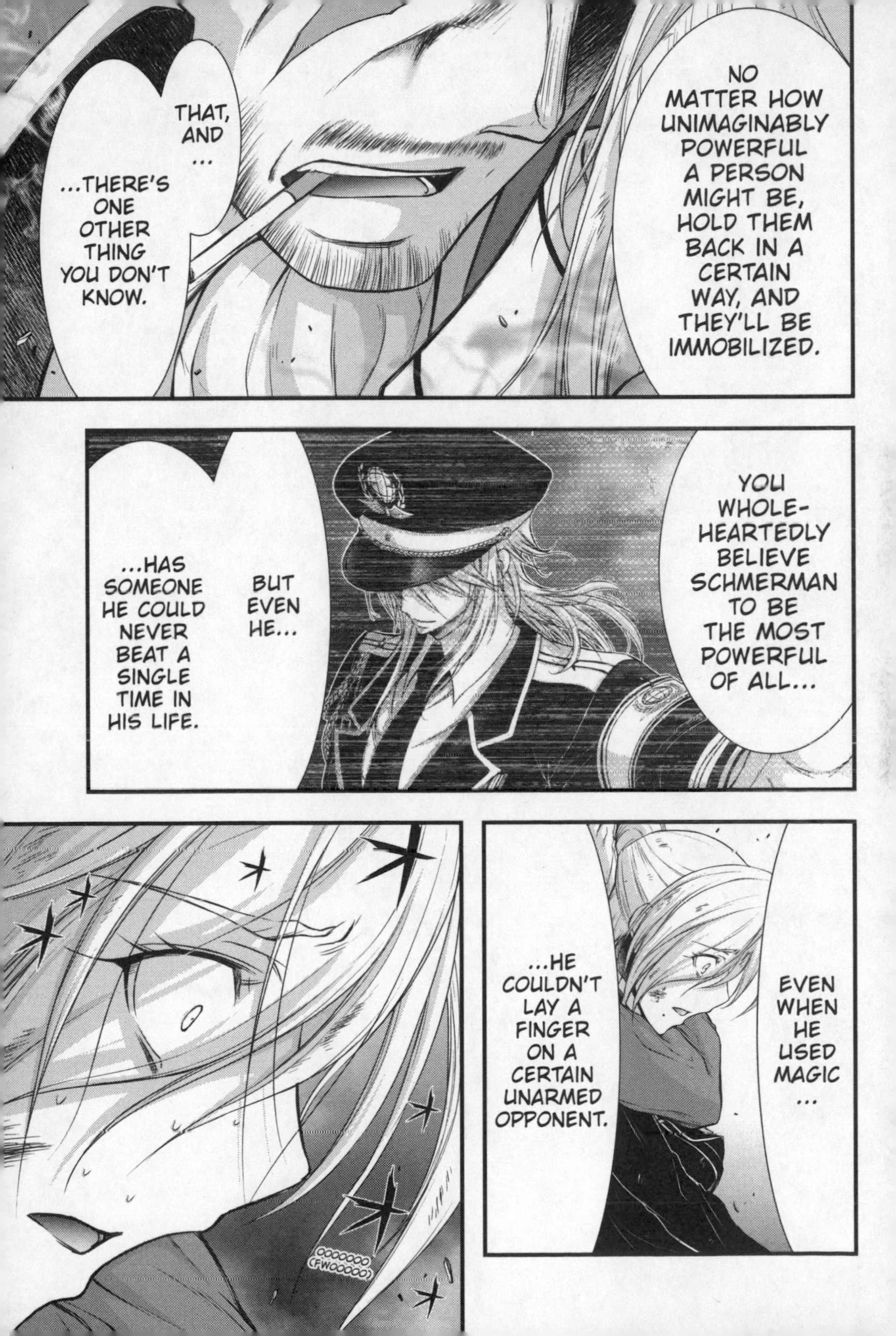
NO MATTER HOW UNIMAGINABLY POWERFUL A PERSON MIGHT BE, HOLD THEM BACK IN A CERTAIN WAY, AND THEY'LL BE IMMOBILIZED.
THAT, AND ...
...THERE'S ONE OTHER THING YOU DON'T KNOW.
YOU WHOLE-HEARTEDLY BELIEVE SCHMERMAN TO BE THE MOST POWERFUL OF ALL...
BUT EVEN HE...
...HAS SOMEONE HE COULD NEVER BEAT A SINGLE TIME IN HIS LIFE.
EVEN WHEN HE USED MAGIC ...
...HE COULDN'T LAY A FINGER ON A CERTAIN UNARMED OPPONENT.
OOOOOOO (FWOOOOOO)

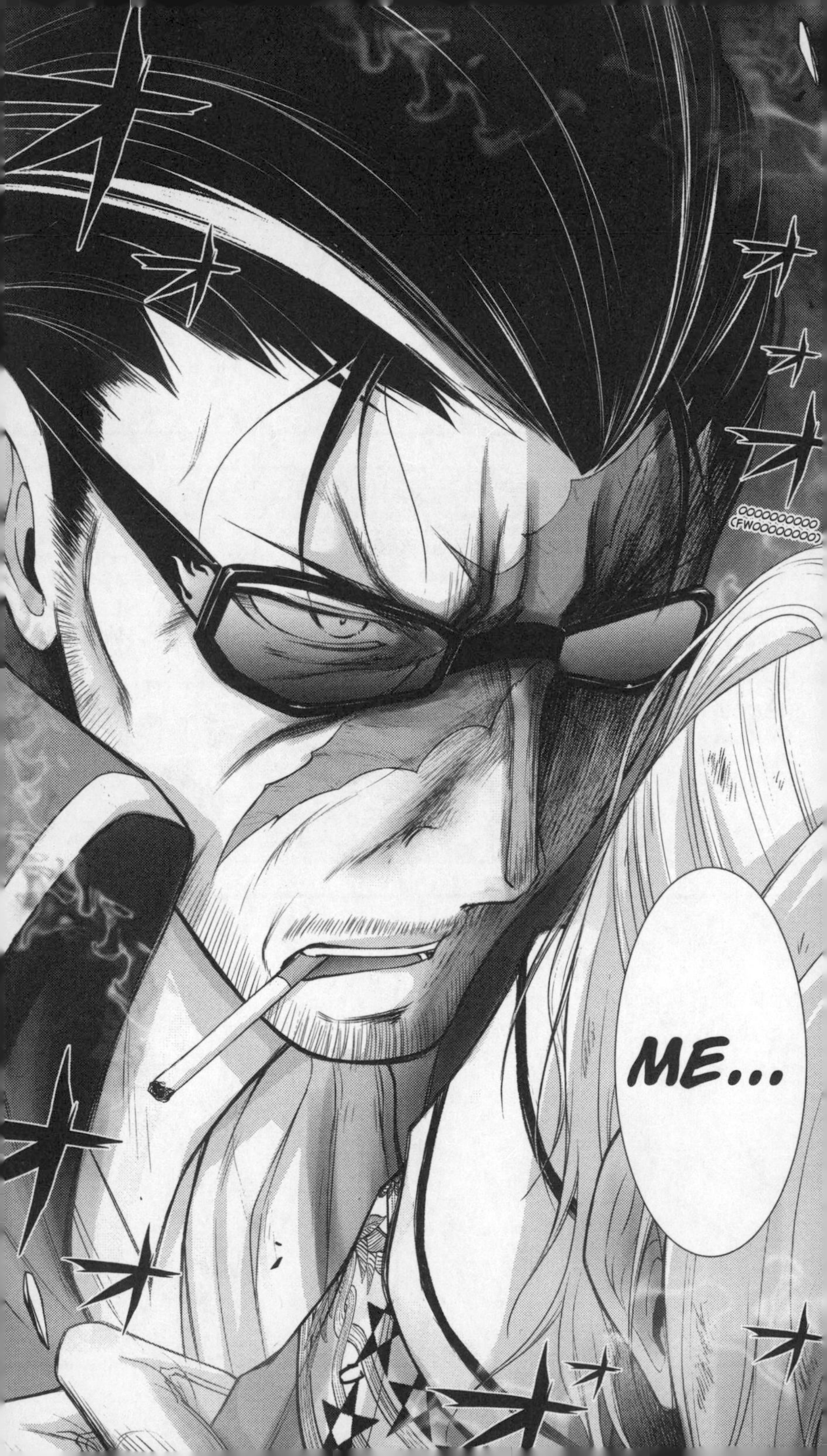
OOOOOOOOOO
(FWOOOOOOOOO)
ME...

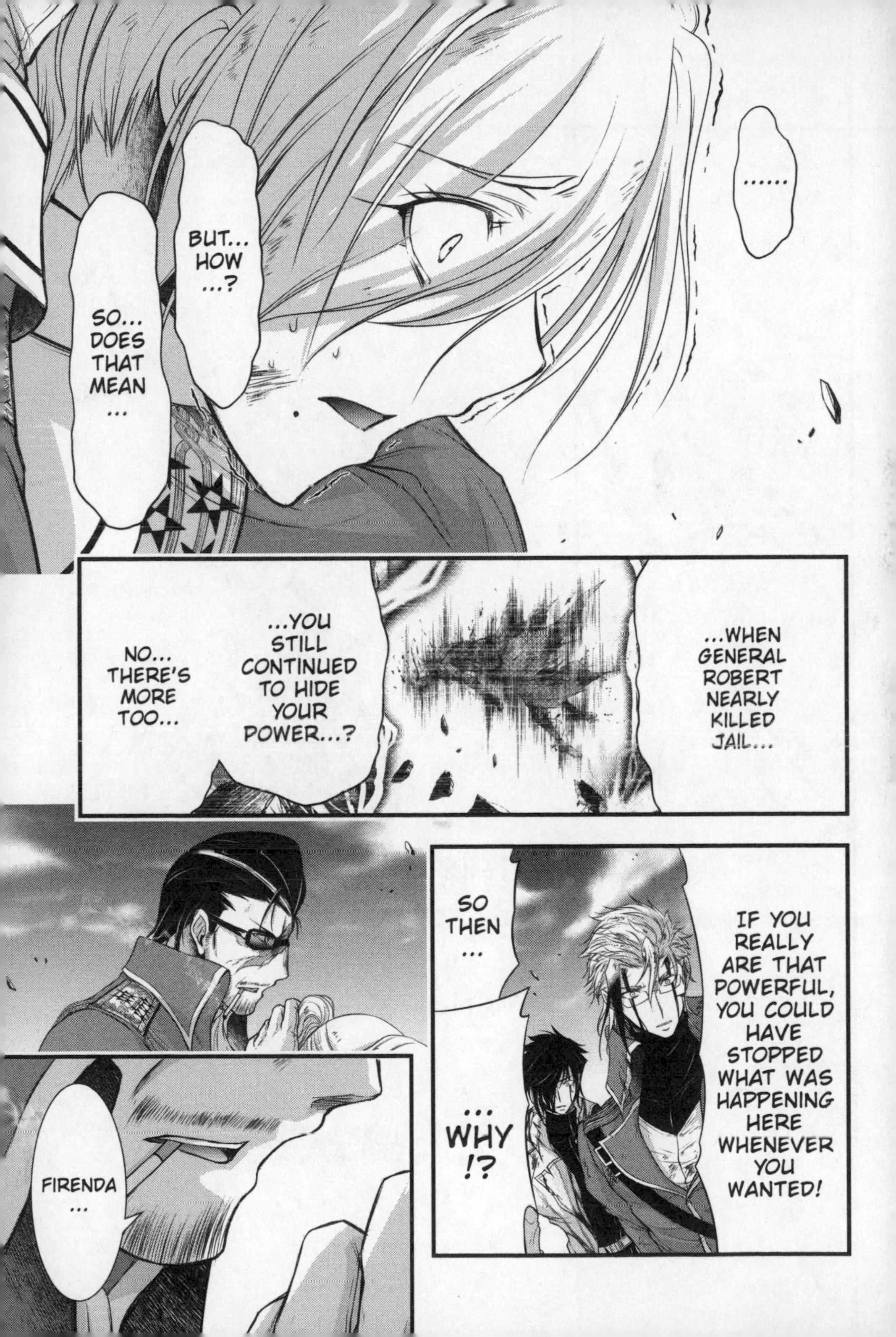
......
BUT... HOW ...?
SO... DOES THAT MEAN ...
...WHEN GENERAL ROBERT NEARLY KILLED JAIL...
...YOU STILL CONTINUED TO HIDE YOUR POWER...?
NO... THERE'S MORE TOO...
IF YOU REALLY ARE THAT POWERFUL, YOU COULD HAVE STOPPED WHAT WAS HAPPENING HERE WHENEVER YOU WANTED!
SO THEN ...
...WHY!?
FIRENDA ...

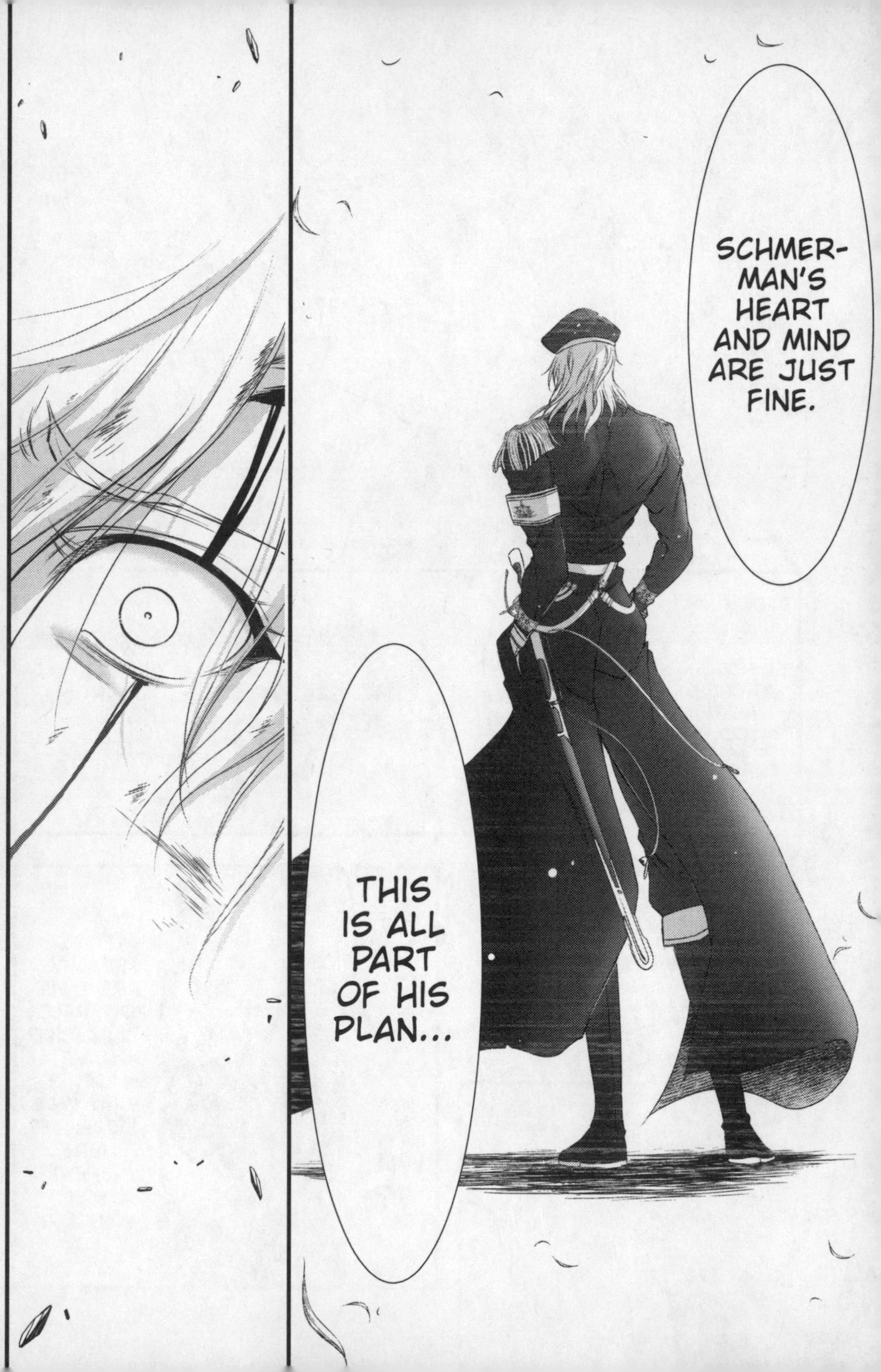
SCHMER-MAN'S HEART AND MIND ARE JUST FINE.
THIS IS ALL PART OF HIS PLAN...

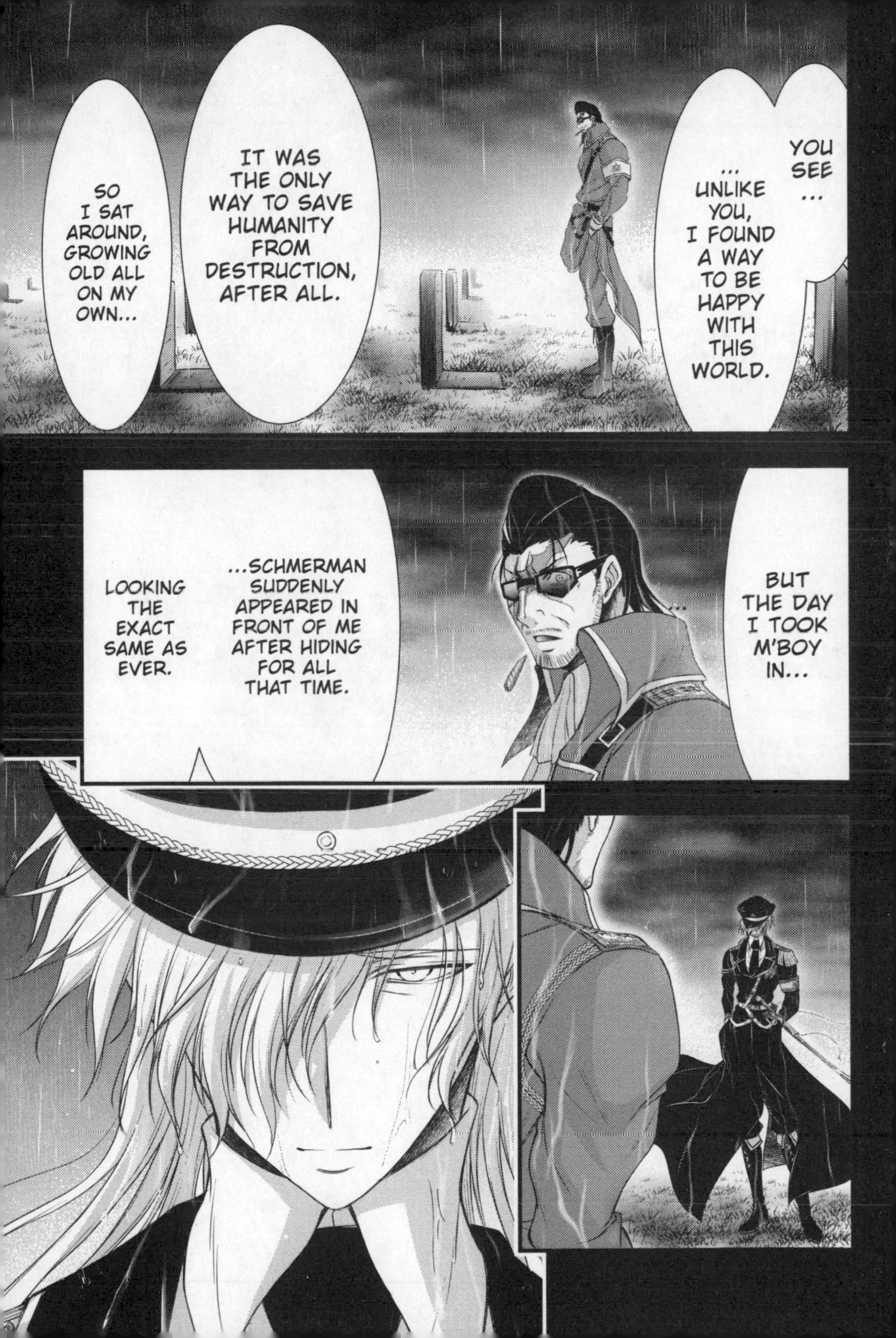
YOU SEE...
...UNLIKE YOU, I FOUND A WAY TO BE HAPPY WITH THIS WORLD.
IT WAS THE ONLY WAY TO SAVE HUMANITY FROM DESTRUCTION, AFTER ALL.
SO I SAT AROUND, GROWING OLD ALL ON MY OWN...
BUT THE DAY I TOOK M'BOY IN...
...
...SCHMERMAN SUDDENLY APPEARED IN FRONT OF ME AFTER HIDING FOR ALL THAT TIME.
LOOKING THE EXACT SAME AS EVER.

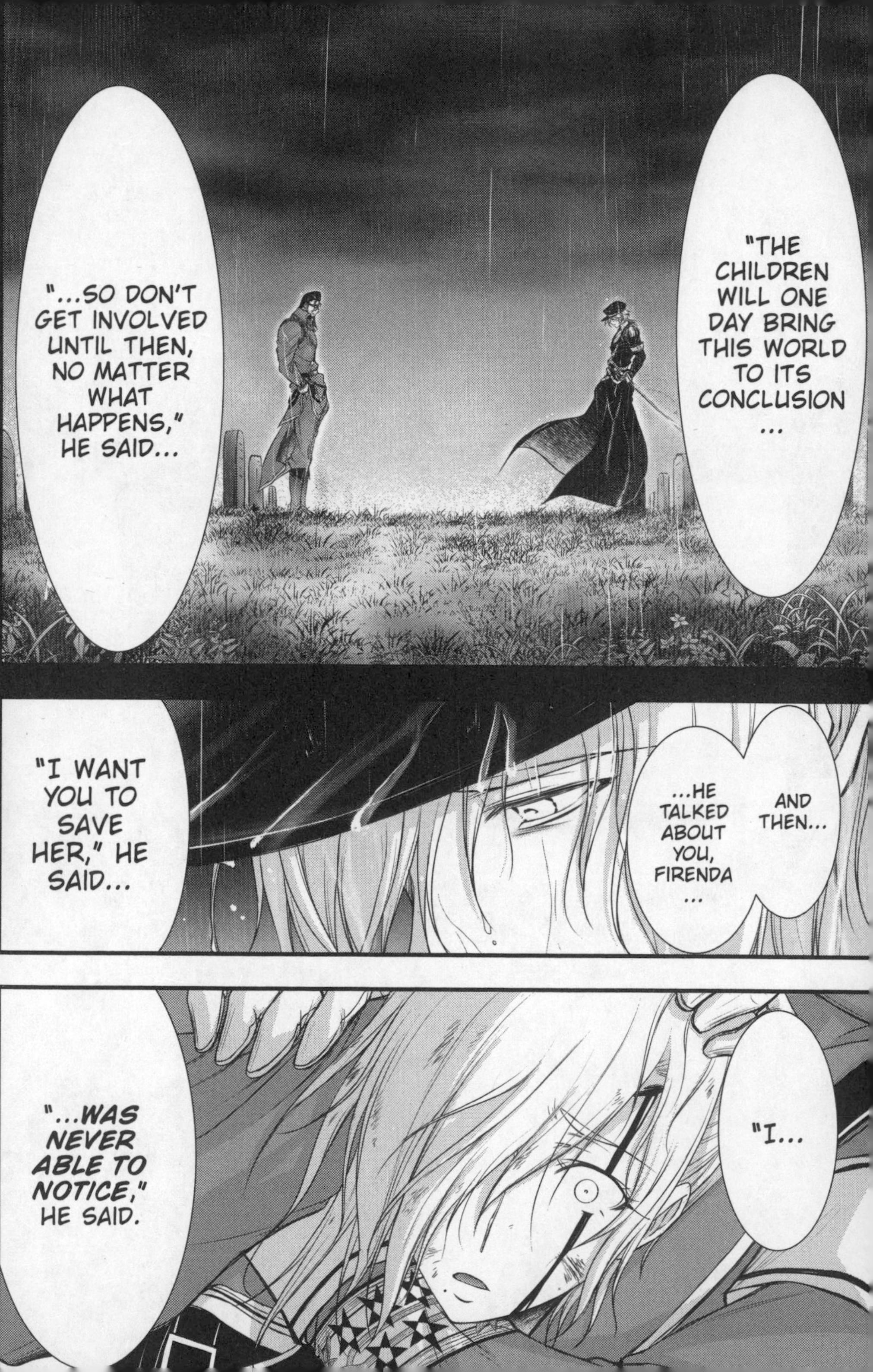
"THE CHILDREN WILL ONE DAY BRING THIS WORLD TO ITS CONCLUSION ...
"...SO DON'T GET INVOLVED UNTIL THEN, NO MATTER WHAT HAPPENS," HE SAID...
AND THEN...
...HE TALKED ABOUT YOU, FIRENDA ...
"I WANT YOU TO SAVE HER," HE SAID...
"I...
"...WAS NEVER ABLE TO NOTICE," HE SAID.

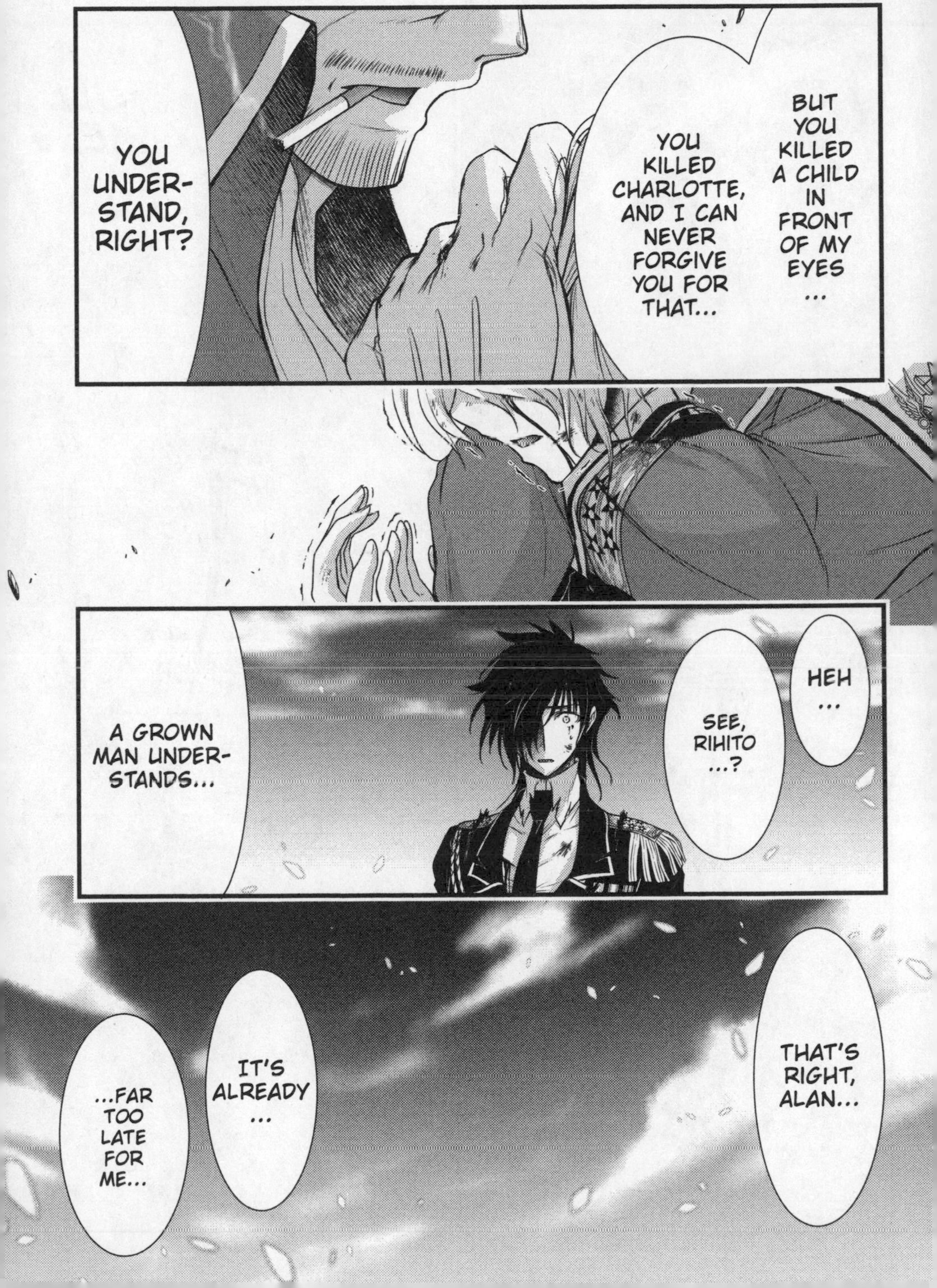
BUT YOU KILLED A CHILD IN FRONT OF MY EYES...
YOU KILLED CHARLOTTE, AND I CAN NEVER FORGIVE YOU FOR THAT...
YOU UNDER-STAND, RIGHT?
HEH...
SEE, RIHITO...?
A GROWN MAN UNDER-STANDS...
THAT'S RIGHT, ALAN...
IT'S ALREADY...
...FAR TOO LATE FOR ME...

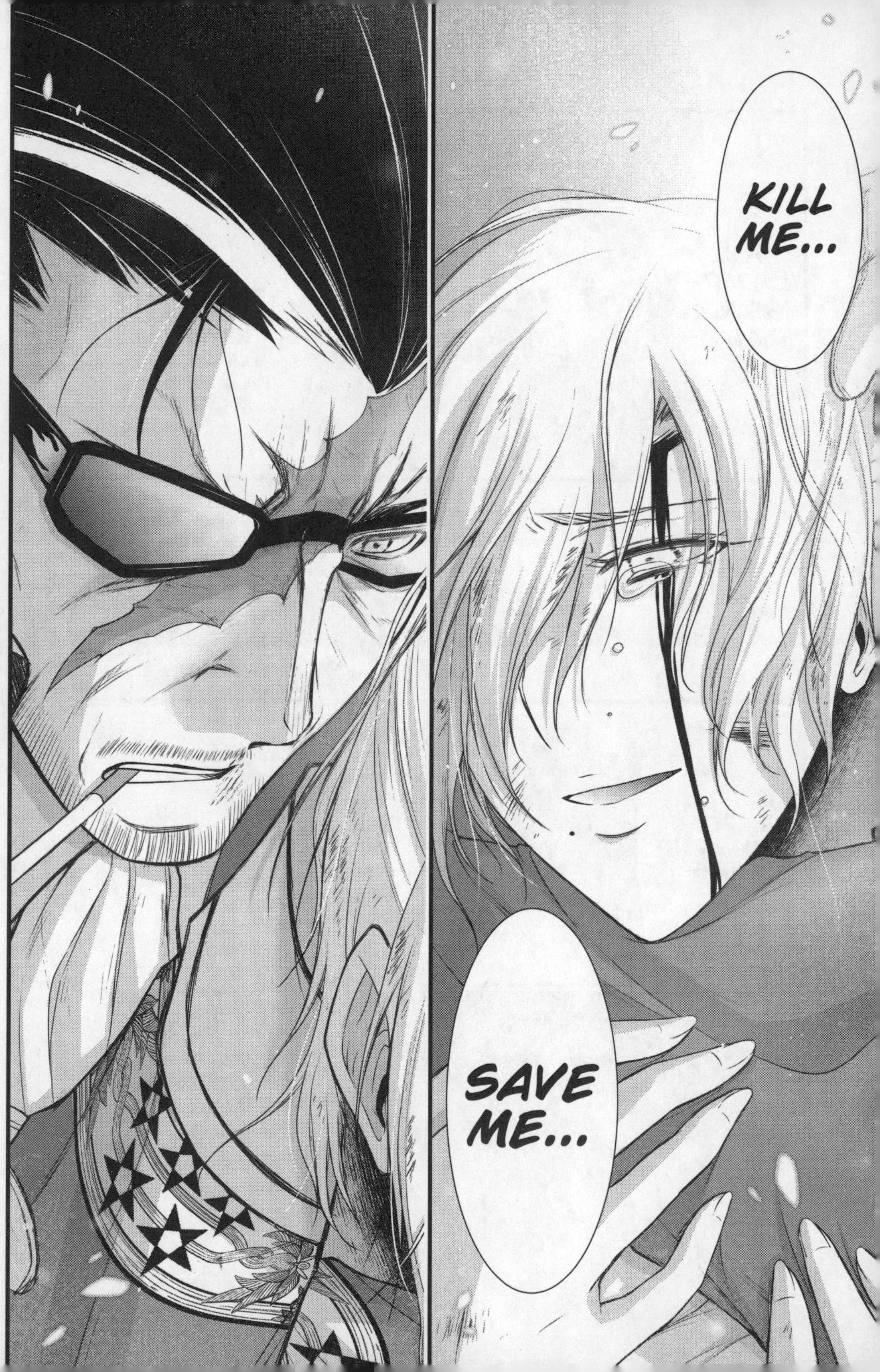
KILL ME...
SAVE ME...

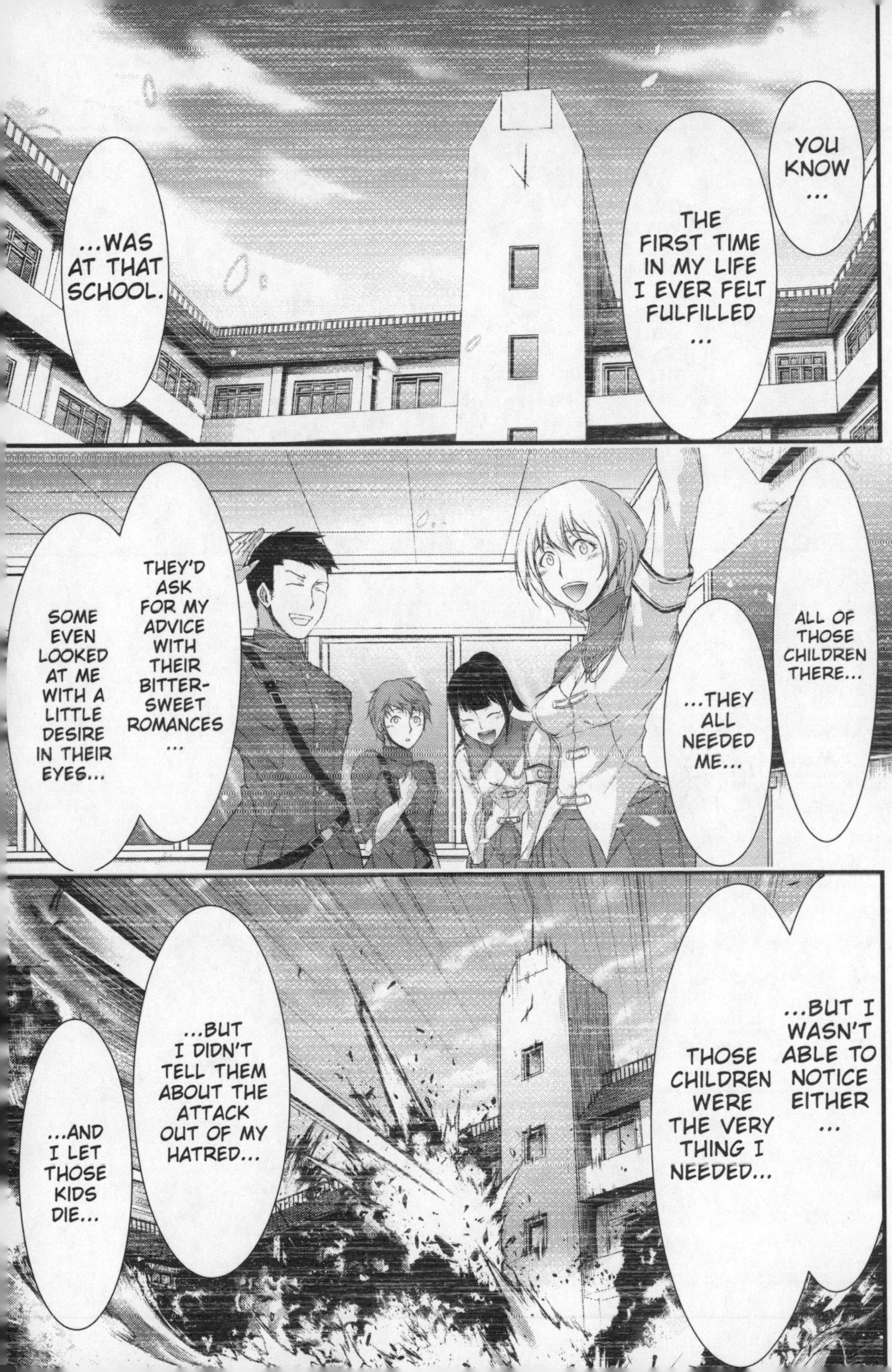

YOU KNOW...
THE FIRST TIME IN MY LIFE I EVER FELT FULFILLED...
...WAS AT THAT SCHOOL.
ALL OF THOSE CHILDREN THERE...
...THEY ALL NEEDED ME...
THEY'D ASK FOR MY ADVICE WITH THEIR BITTER-SWEET ROMANCES...
SOME EVEN LOOKED AT ME WITH A LITTLE DESIRE IN THEIR EYES...
...BUT I WASN'T ABLE TO NOTICE EITHER...
THOSE CHILDREN WERE THE VERY THING I NEEDED...
...BUT I DIDN'T TELL THEM ABOUT THE ATTACK OUT OF MY HATRED...
...AND I LET THOSE KIDS DIE...

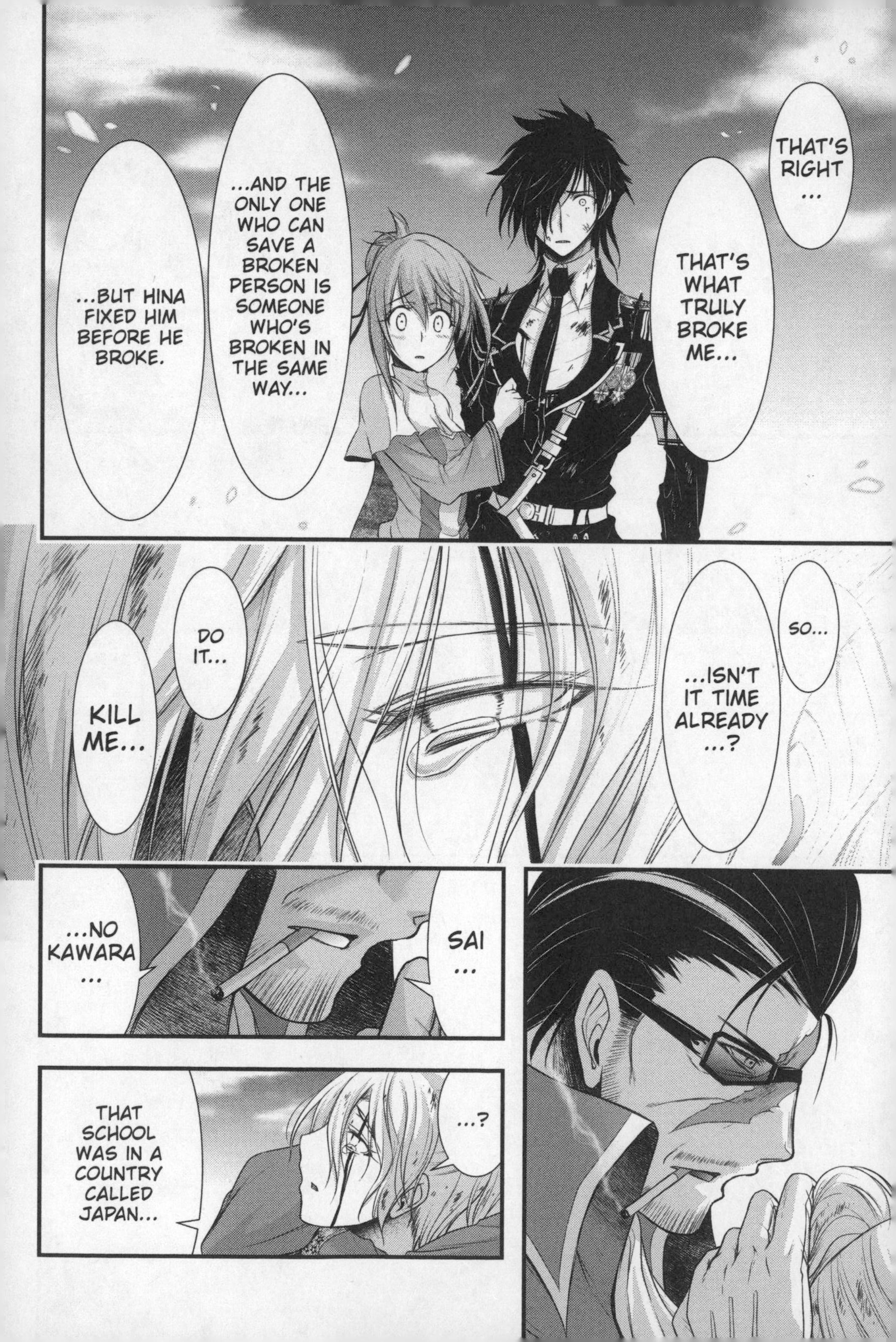
THAT'S RIGHT ...
THAT'S WHAT TRULY BROKE ME...
...AND THE ONLY ONE WHO CAN SAVE A BROKEN PERSON IS SOMEONE WHO'S BROKEN IN THE SAME WAY...
...BUT HINA FIXED HIM BEFORE HE BROKE.
SO...
...ISN'T IT TIME ALREADY ...?
DO IT...
KILL ME...
SAI ...
...NO KAWARA ...
...?
THAT SCHOOL WAS IN A COUNTRY CALLED JAPAN...

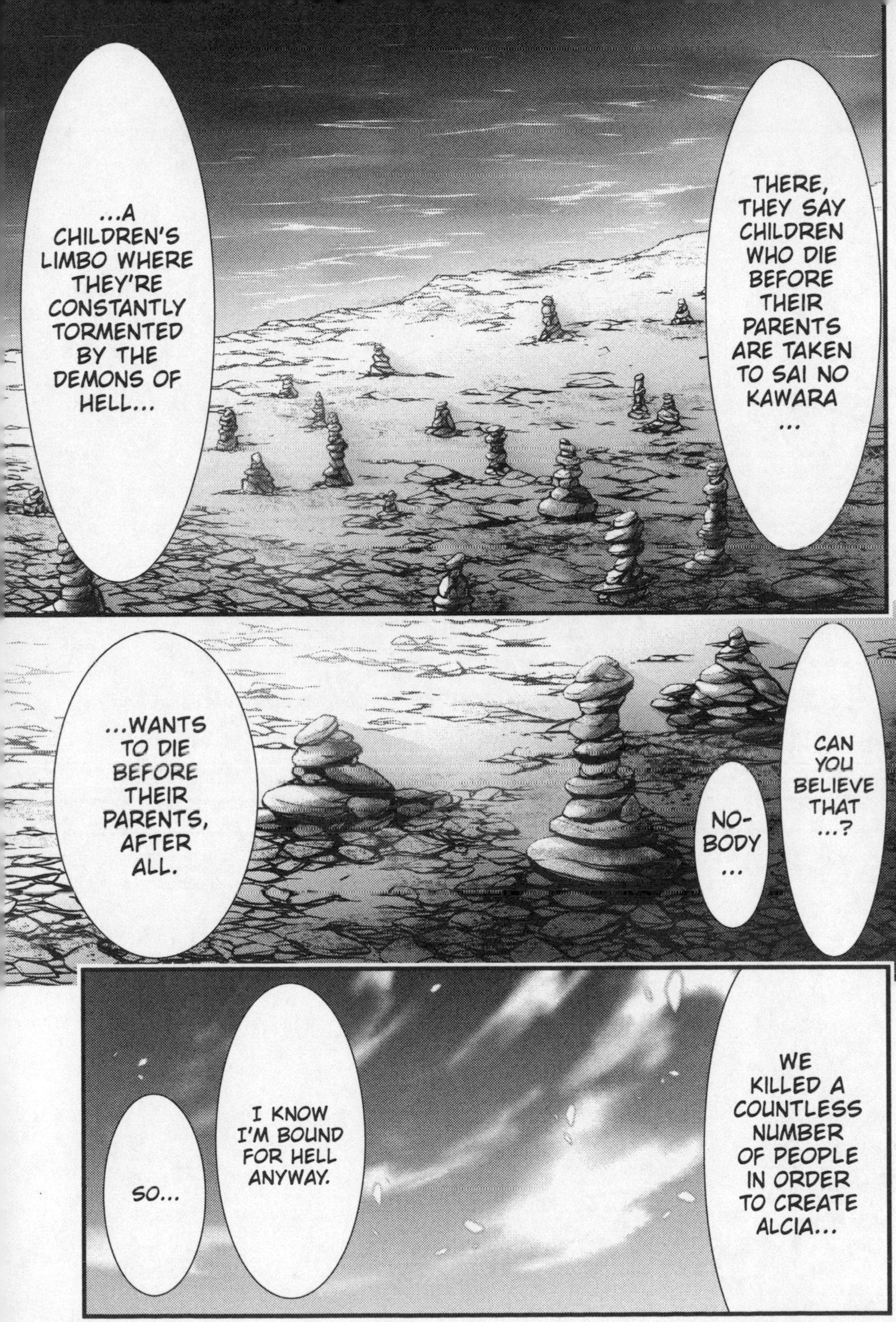
THERE, THEY SAY CHILDREN WHO DIE BEFORE THEIR PARENTS ARE TAKEN TO SAI NO KAWARA ...
...A CHILDREN'S LIMBO WHERE THEY'RE CONSTANTLY TORMENTED BY THE DEMONS OF HELL...
CAN YOU BELIEVE THAT ...?
NO-BODY ...
...WANTS TO DIE BEFORE THEIR PARENTS, AFTER ALL.
WE KILLED A COUNTLESS NUMBER OF PEOPLE IN ORDER TO CREATE ALCIA...
I KNOW I'M BOUND FOR HELL ANYWAY.
SO...

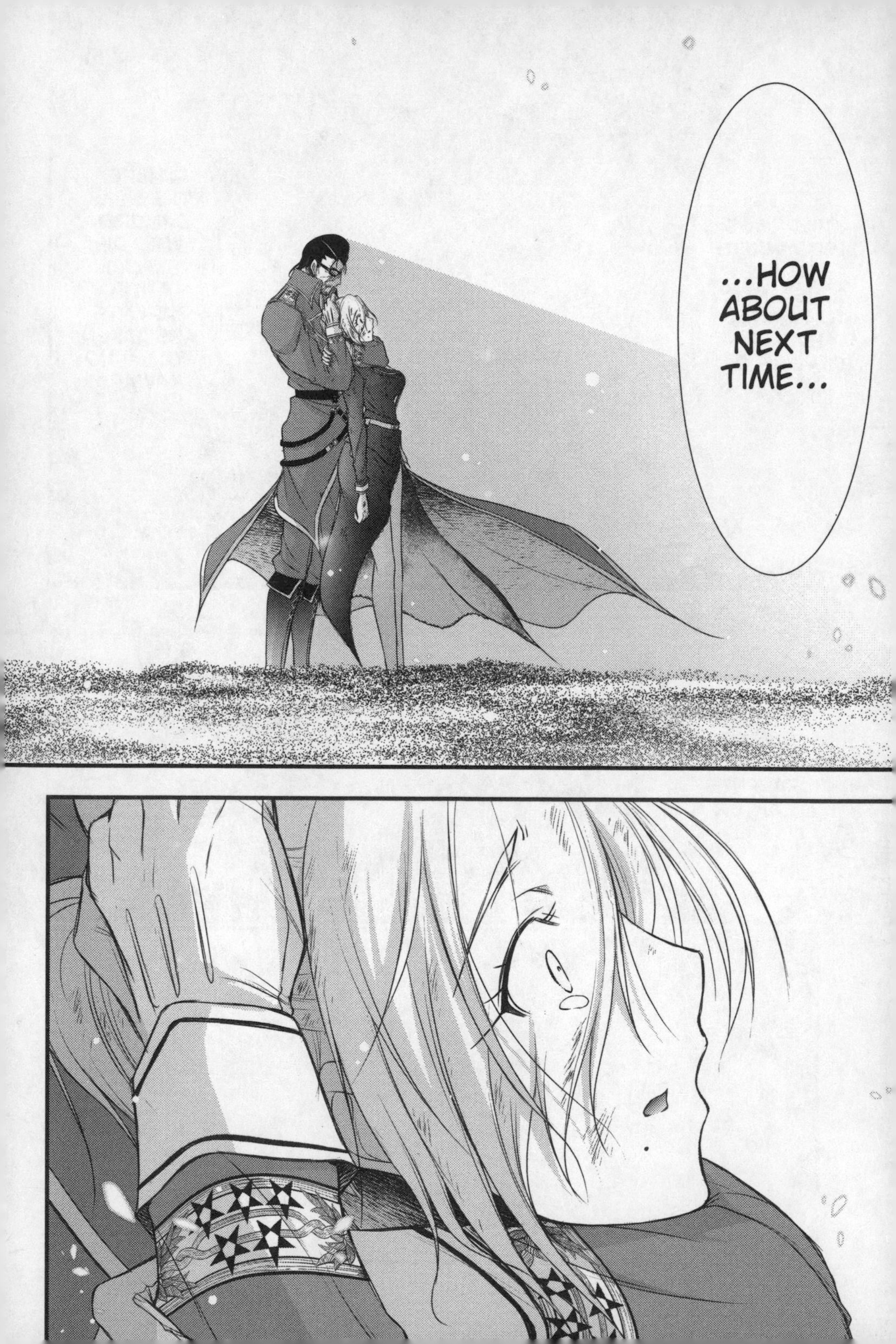
...HOW ABOUT NEXT TIME...

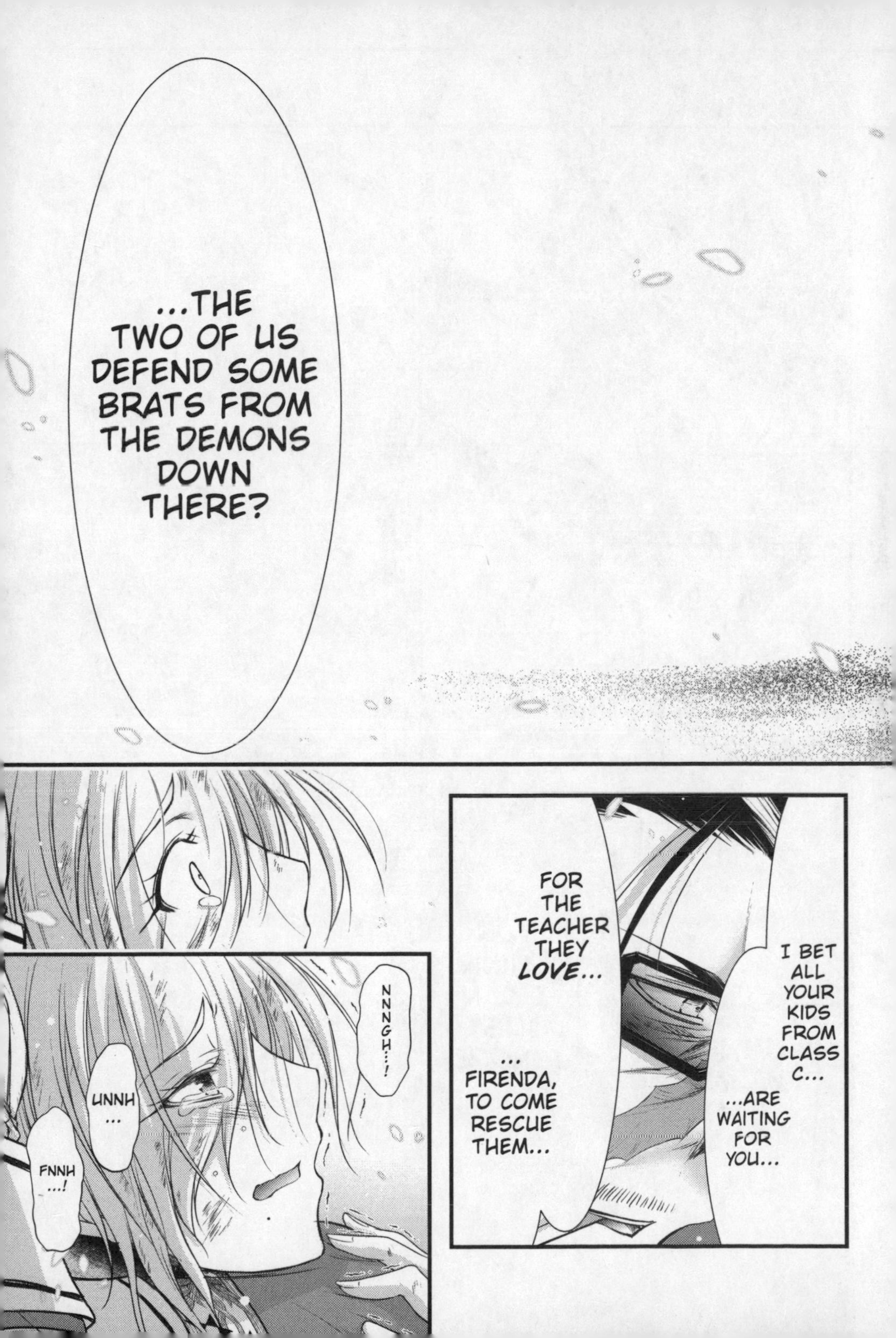
...THE TWO OF US DEFEND SOME BRATS FROM THE DEMONS DOWN THERE?
I BET ALL YOUR KIDS FROM CLASS C... ...ARE WAITING FOR YOU...
FOR THE TEACHER THEY *LOVE*... ...FIRENDA, TO COME RESCUE THEM...
NNNGH...!
UNNH...
FNNH...!

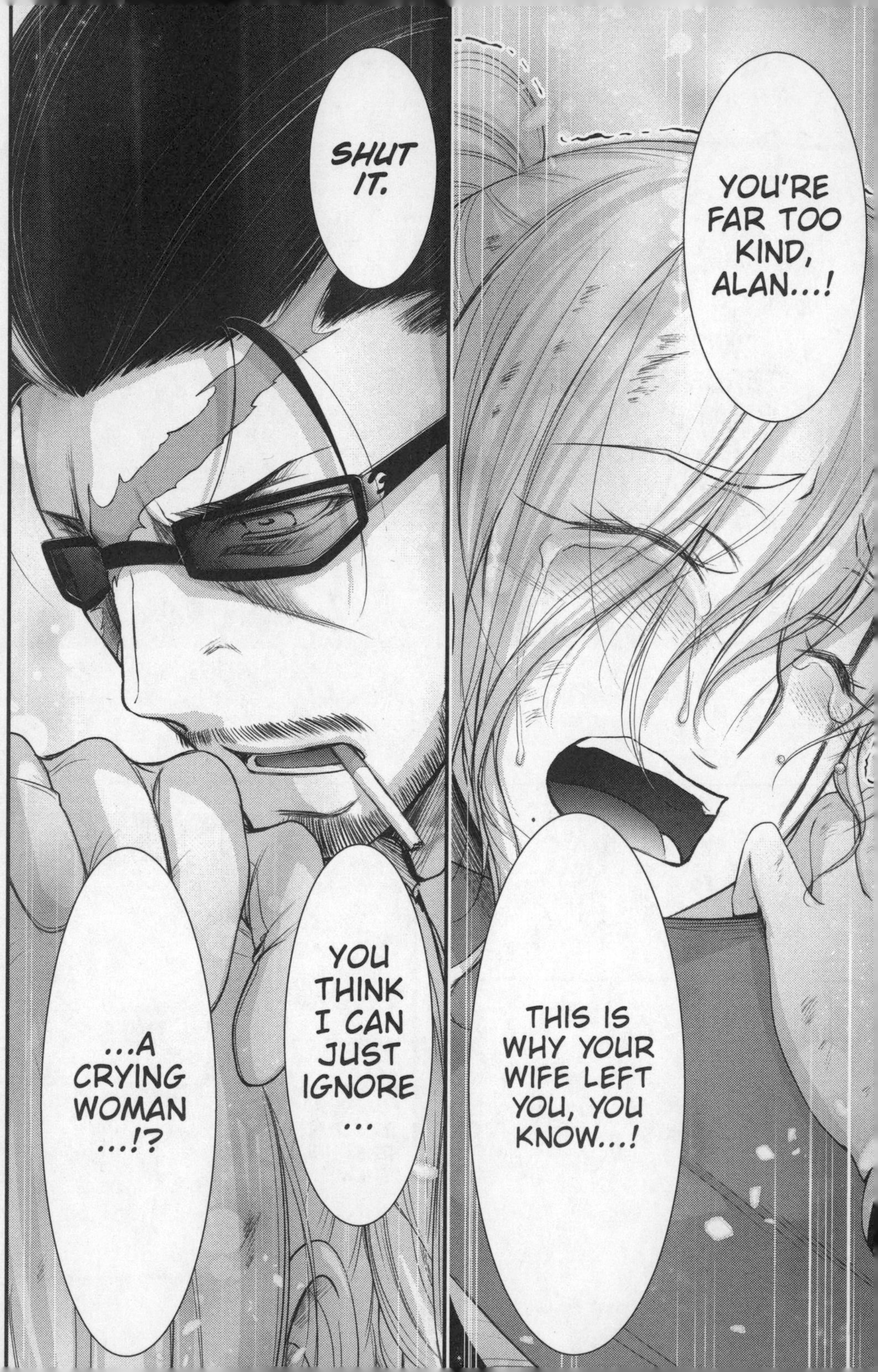
YOU'RE FAR TOO KIND, ALAN...!
THIS IS WHY YOUR WIFE LEFT YOU, YOU KNOW...!
SHUT IT.
YOU THINK I CAN JUST IGNORE...
...A CRYING WOMAN...!?

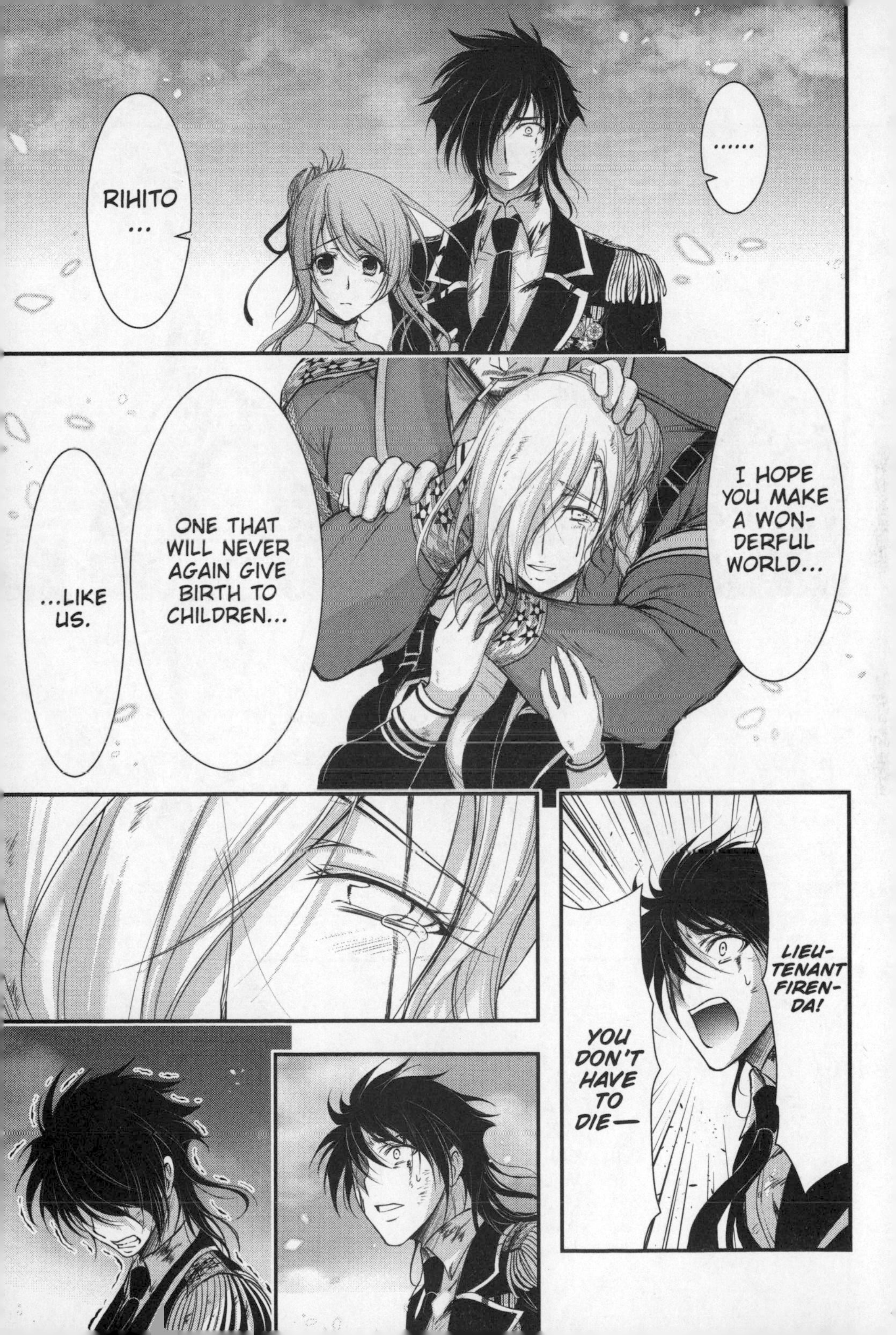
......
RIHITO ...
I HOPE YOU MAKE A WONDERFUL WORLD...
ONE THAT WILL NEVER AGAIN GIVE BIRTH TO CHILDREN...
...LIKE US.
LIEUTENANT FIRENDA!
YOU DON'T HAVE TO DIE—

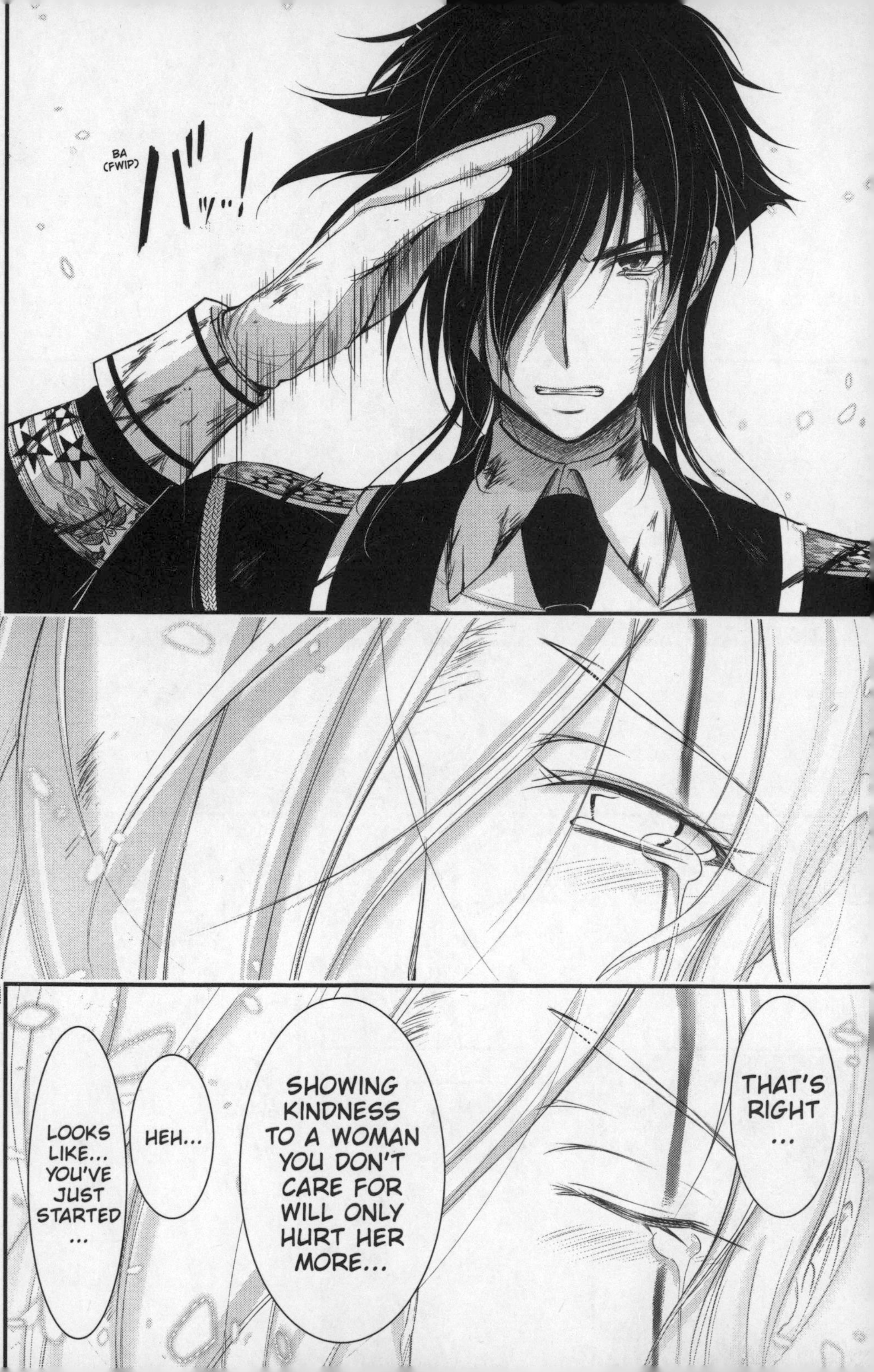
BA (FWIP)
バッ!
THAT'S RIGHT...
SHOWING KINDNESS TO A WOMAN YOU DON'T CARE FOR WILL ONLY HURT HER MORE...
HEH...
LOOKS LIKE... YOU'VE JUST STARTED...

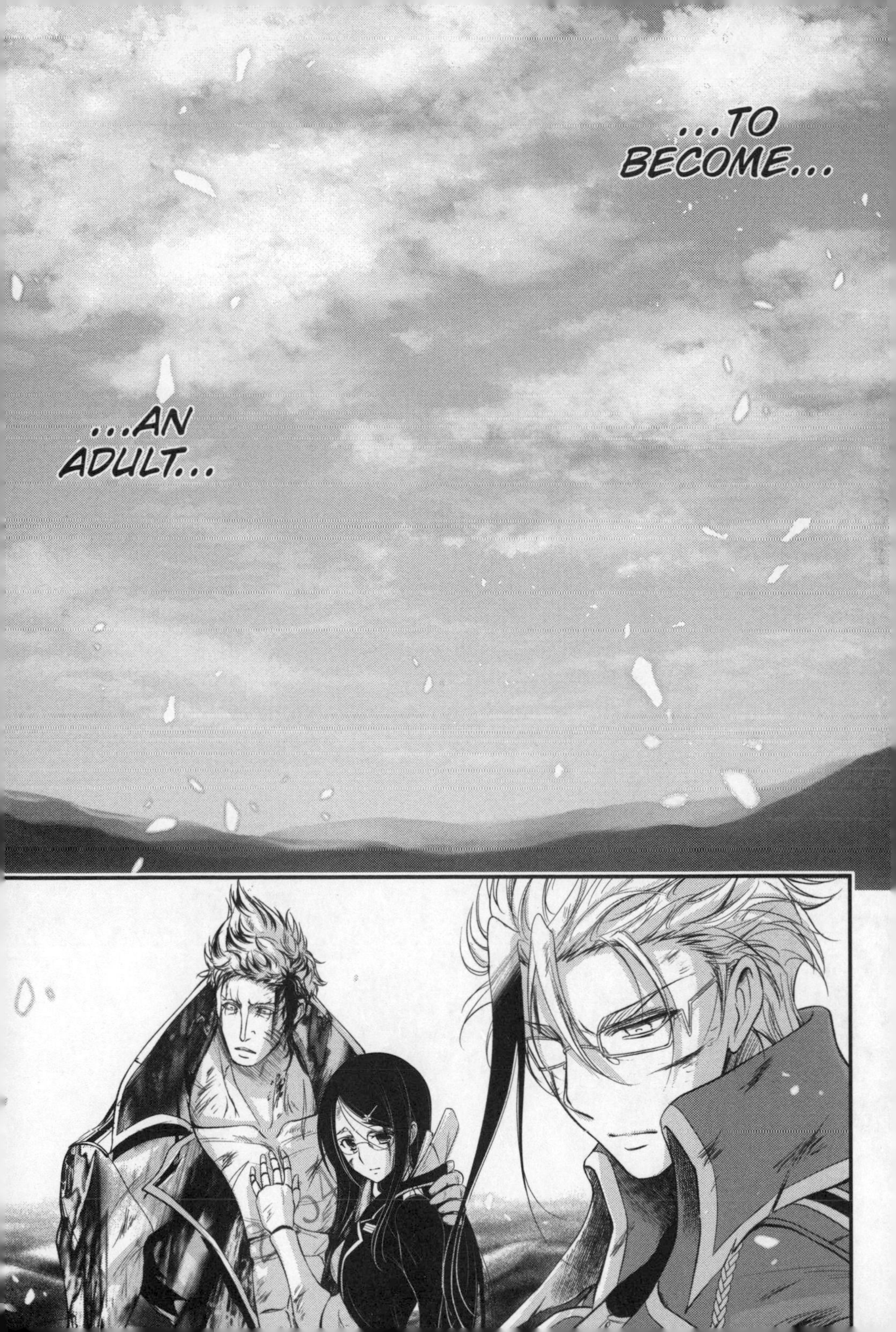
...TO BECOME...
...AN ADULT...

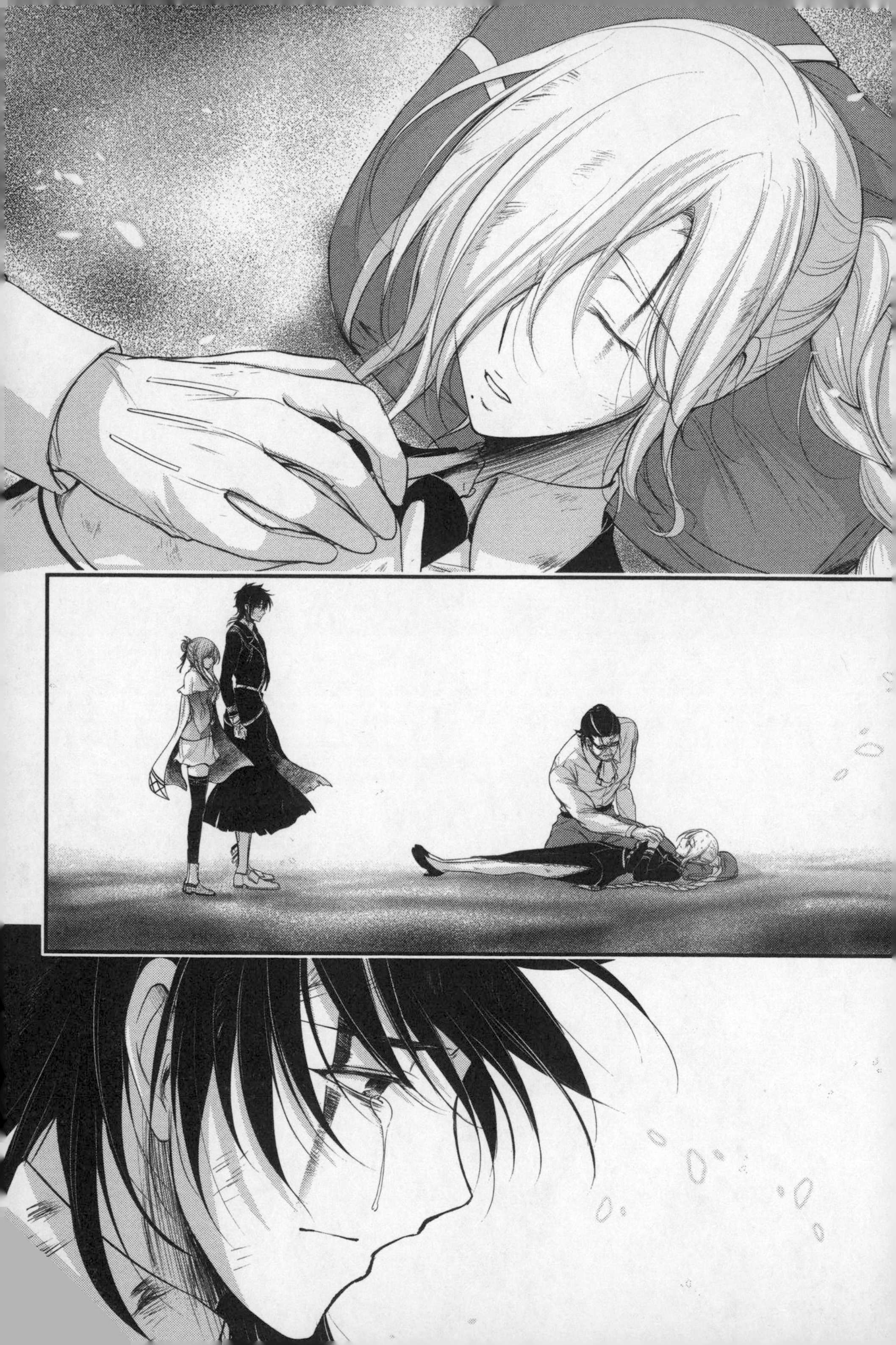

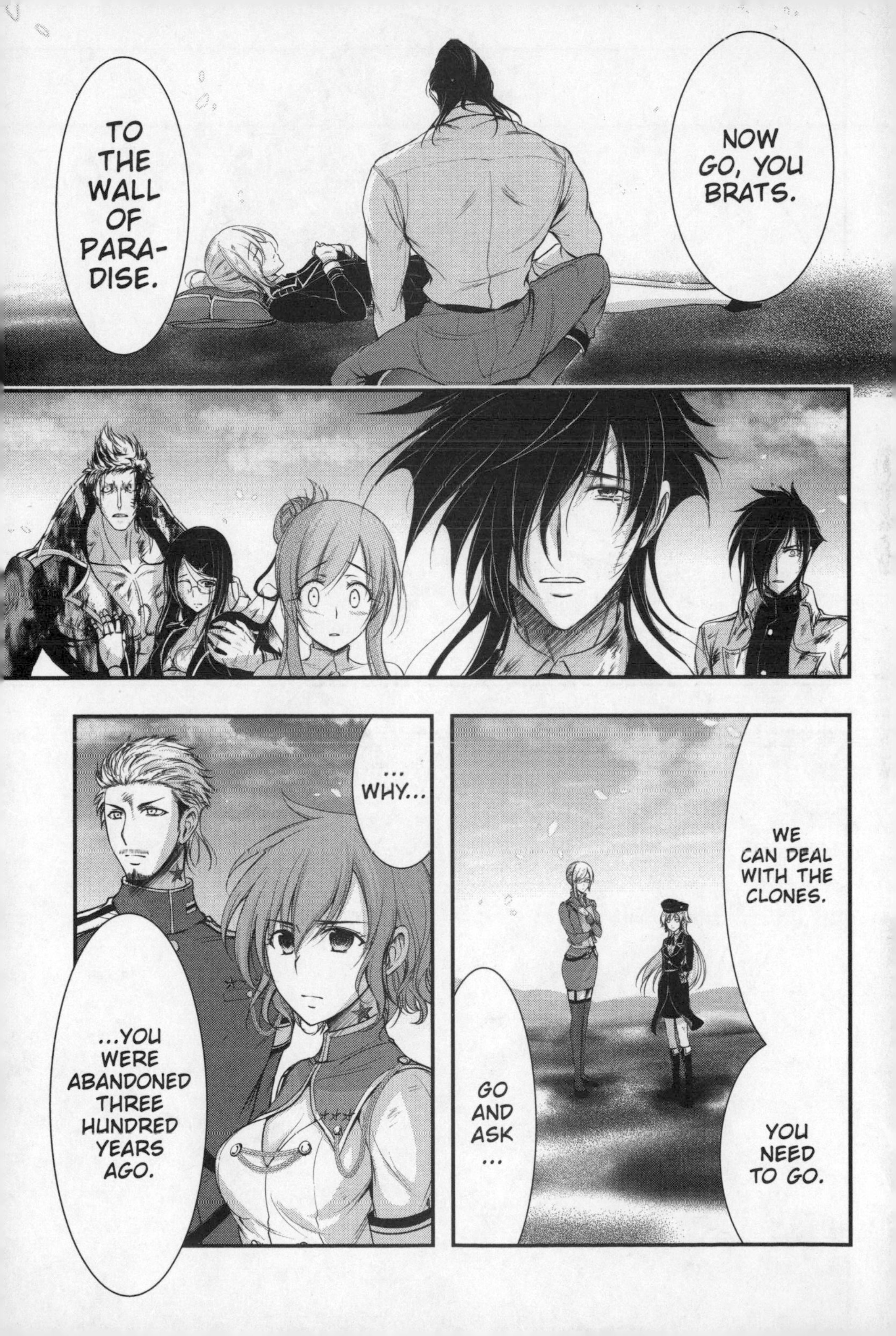
NOW GO, YOU BRATS.
TO THE WALL OF PARA-DISE.
WE CAN DEAL WITH THE CLONES.
YOU NEED TO GO.
GO AND ASK ...
... WHY...
...YOU WERE ABANDONED THREE HUNDRED YEARS AGO.

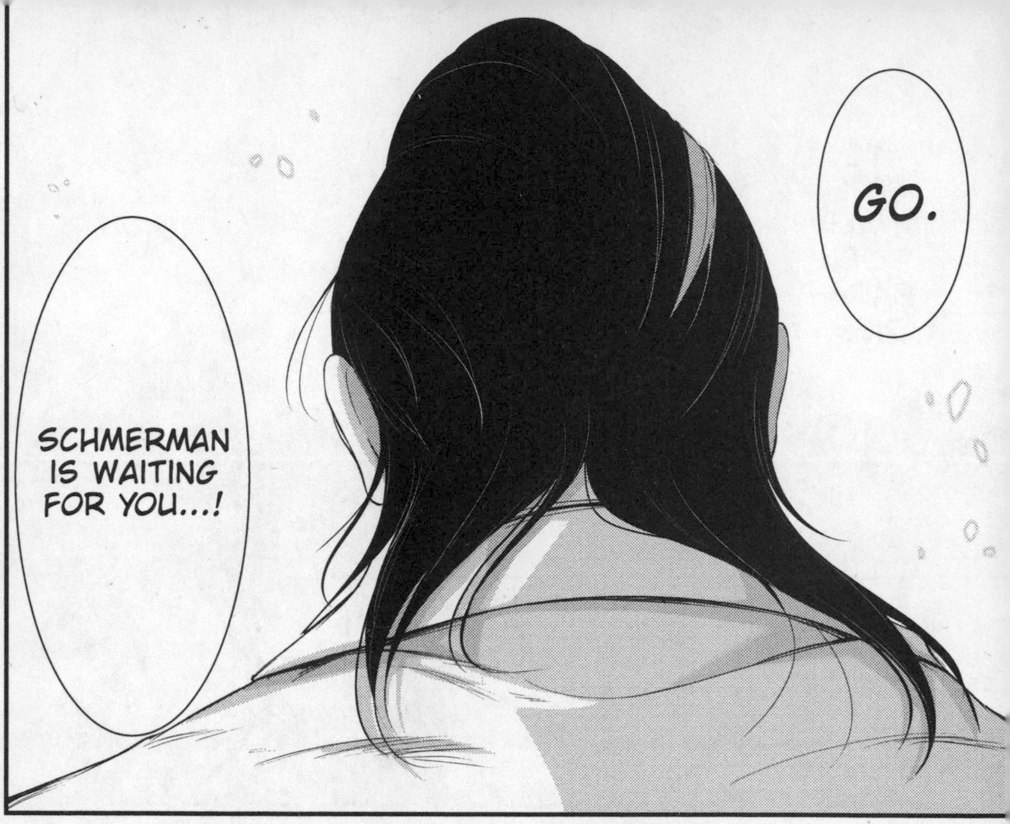
GO.
SCHMERMAN IS WAITING FOR YOU...!

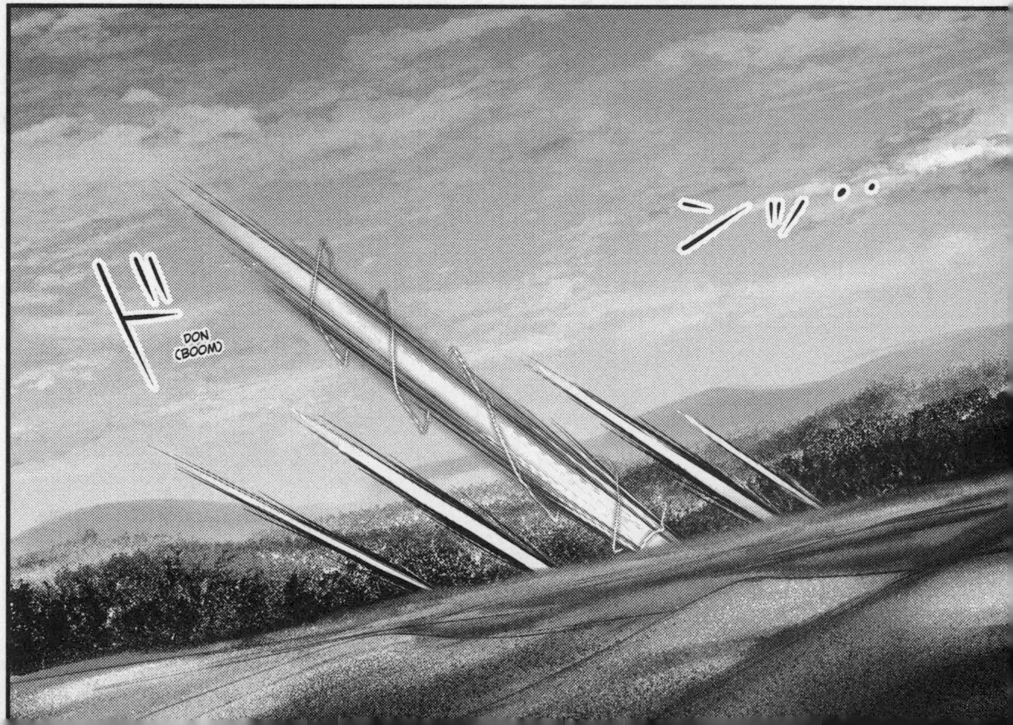
ド
DON (BOOM)
ンッ・・

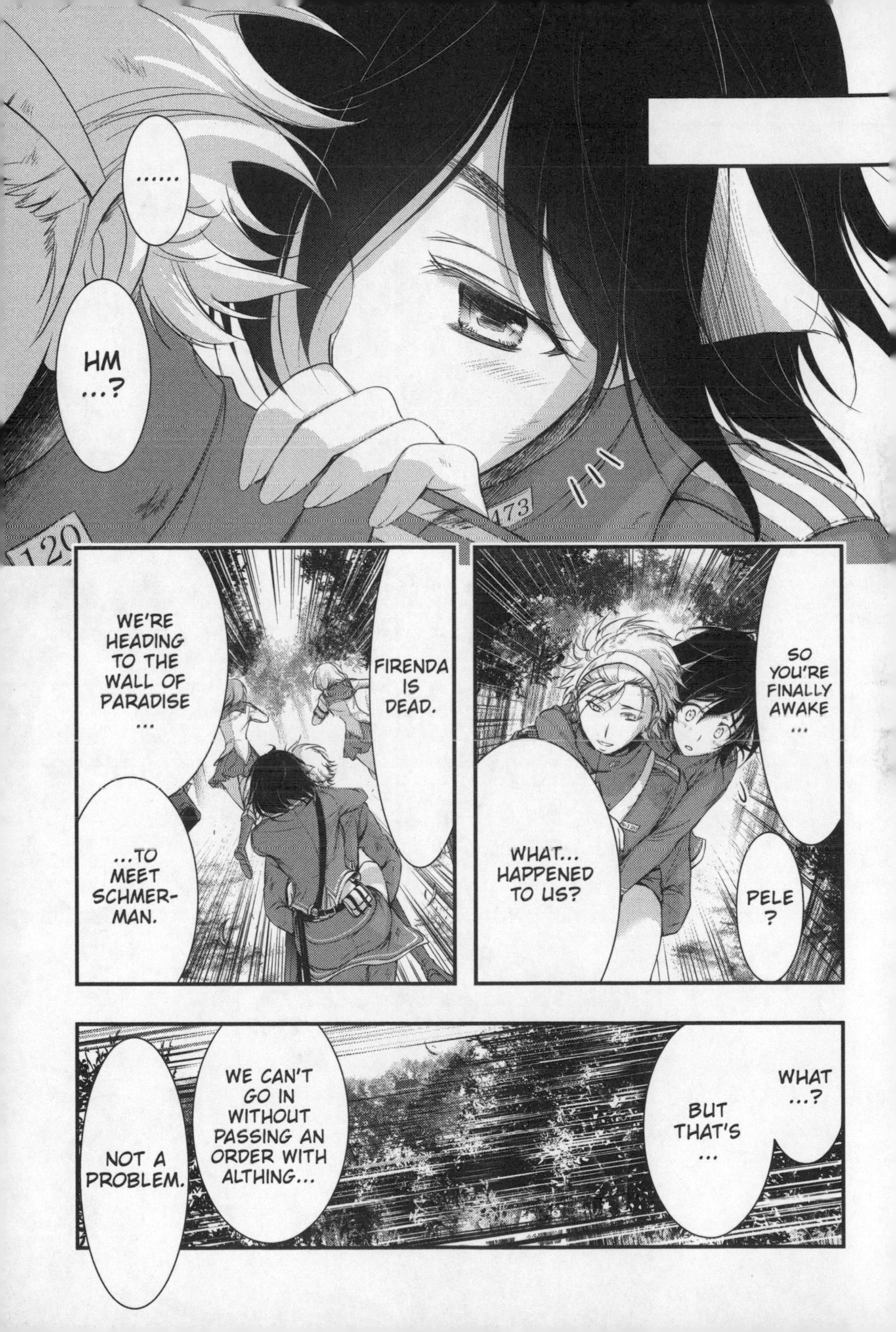
......
HM ...?
473
120
SO YOU'RE FINALLY AWAKE ...
PELE ?
WHAT... HAPPENED TO US?
FIRENDA IS DEAD.
WE'RE HEADING TO THE WALL OF PARADISE ...
...TO MEET SCHMERMAN.
WHAT ...?
BUT THAT'S ...
WE CAN'T GO IN WITHOUT PASSING AN ORDER WITH ALTHING...
NOT A PROBLEM.

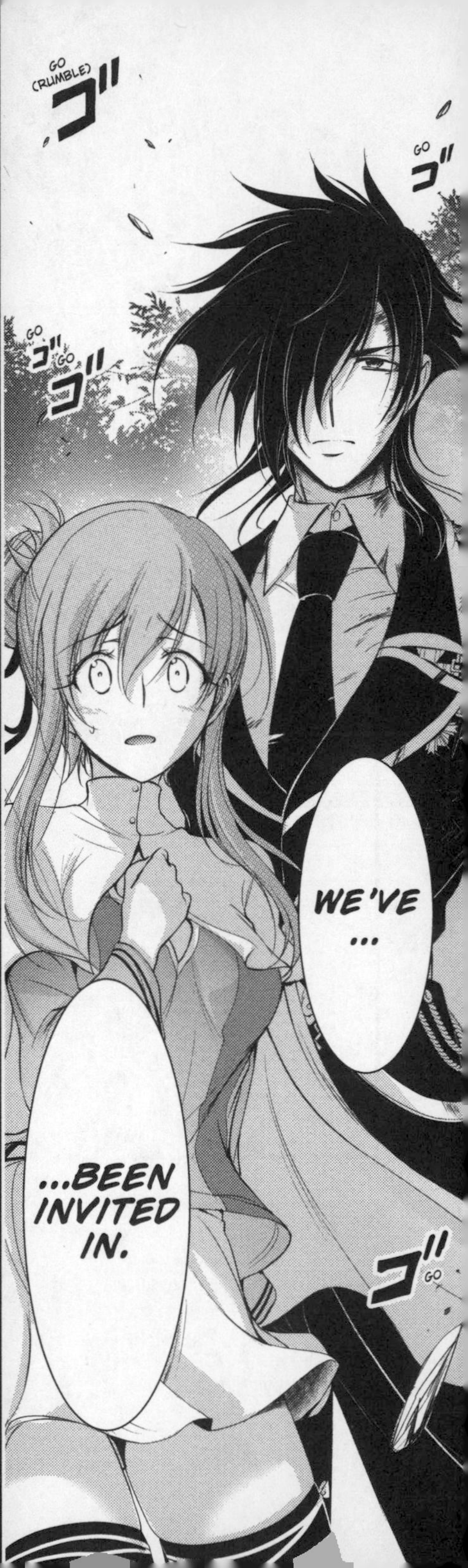
GO (RUMBLE)
ゴ
GO
ゴ
GO
ゴ
GO
ゴ
WE'VE ...
...BEEN INVITED IN.
ゴ
GO
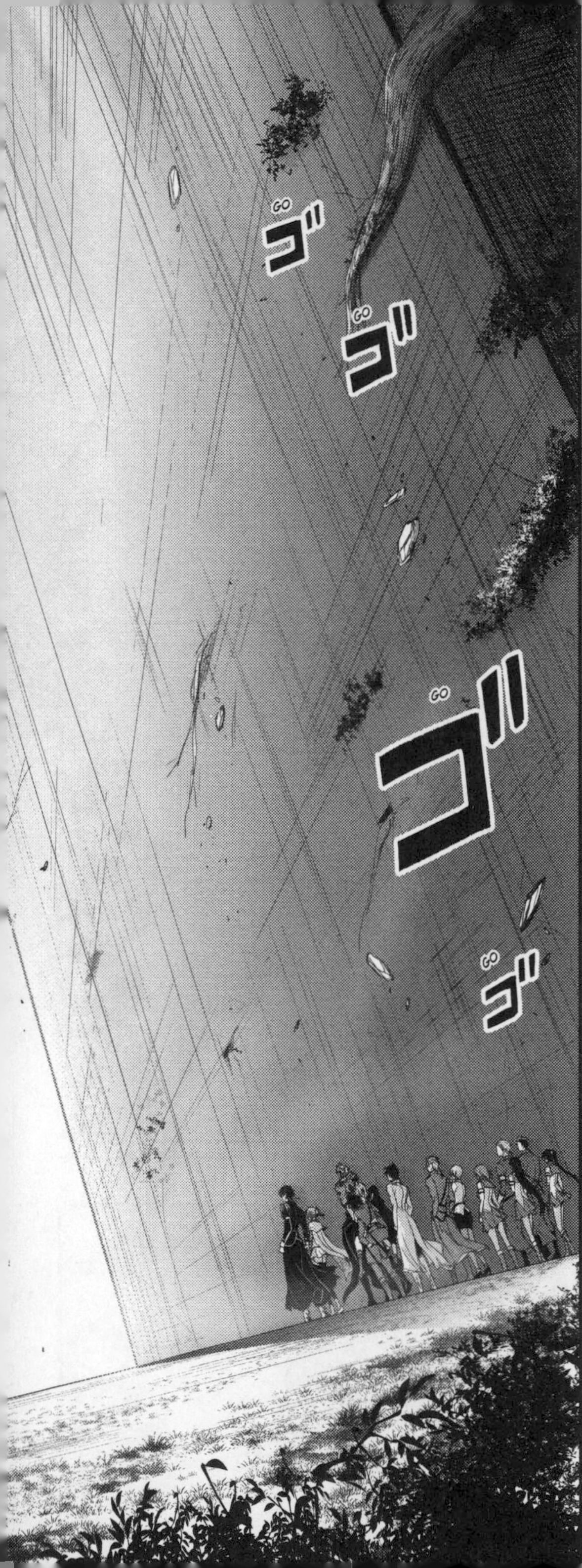
GO
ゴ
GO
ゴ
GO
ゴ
GO
ゴ

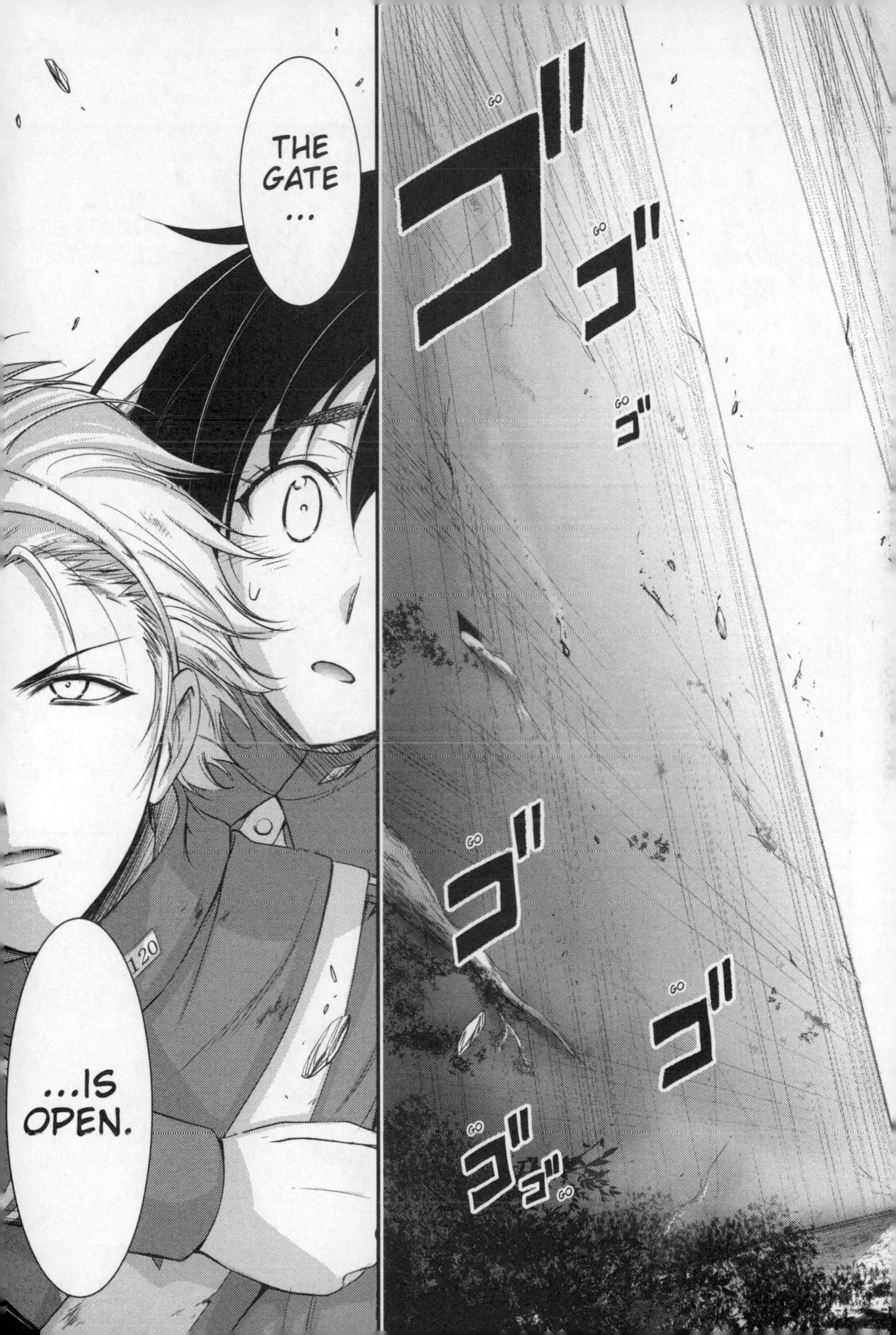
GO ゴ
GO ゴ
GO ゴ
GO ゴ
GO ゴ
GO ゴ GO ゴ
THE GATE ...
...IS OPEN.

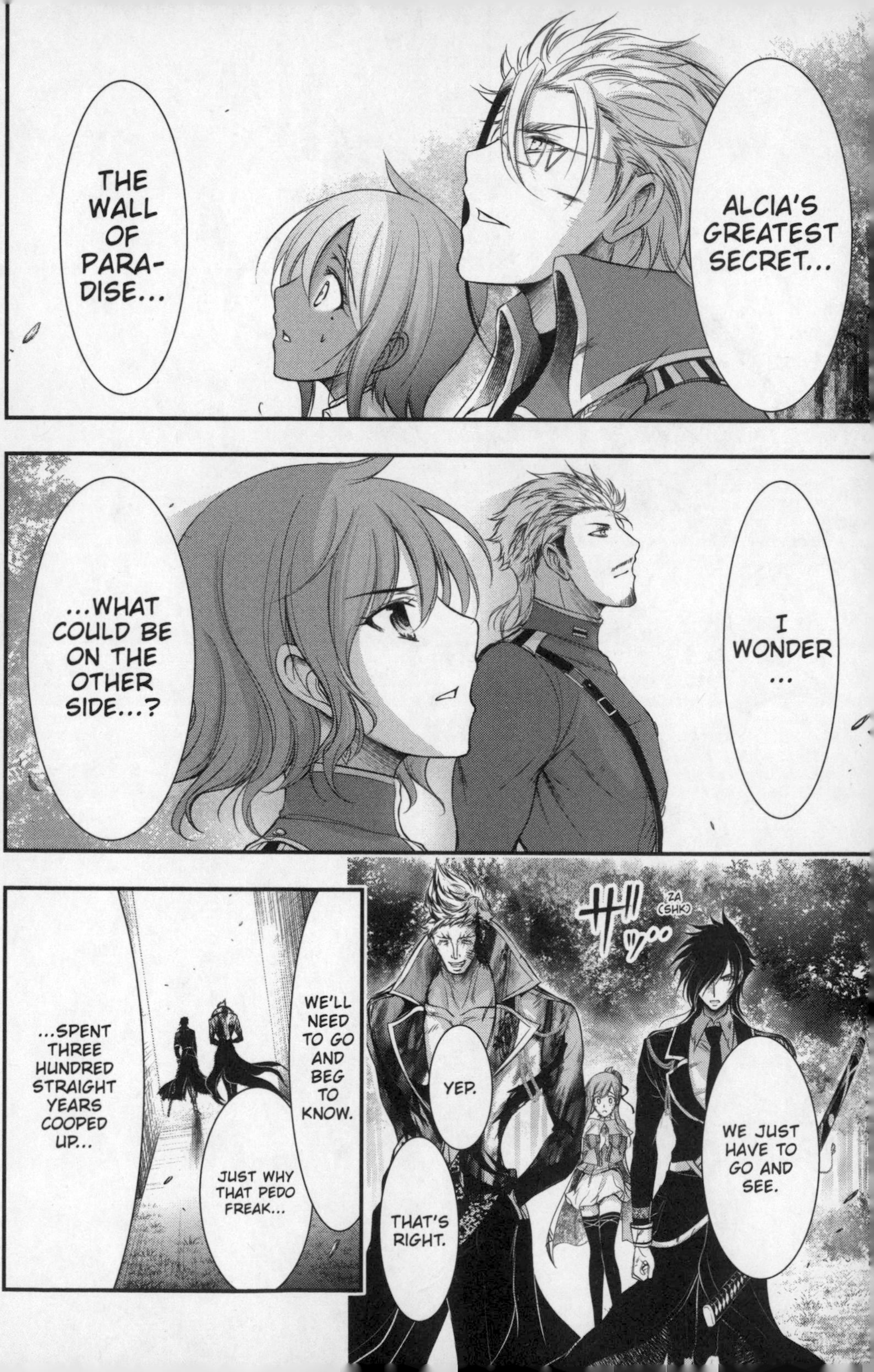
ALCIA'S GREATEST SECRET...
THE WALL OF PARA-DISE...
I WONDER...
...WHAT COULD BE ON THE OTHER SIDE...?
ZA (SHK)
WE JUST HAVE TO GO AND SEE.
YEP.
THAT'S RIGHT.
WE'LL NEED TO GO AND BEG TO KNOW.
JUST WHY THAT PEDO FREAK...
...SPENT THREE HUNDRED STRAIGHT YEARS COOPED UP...

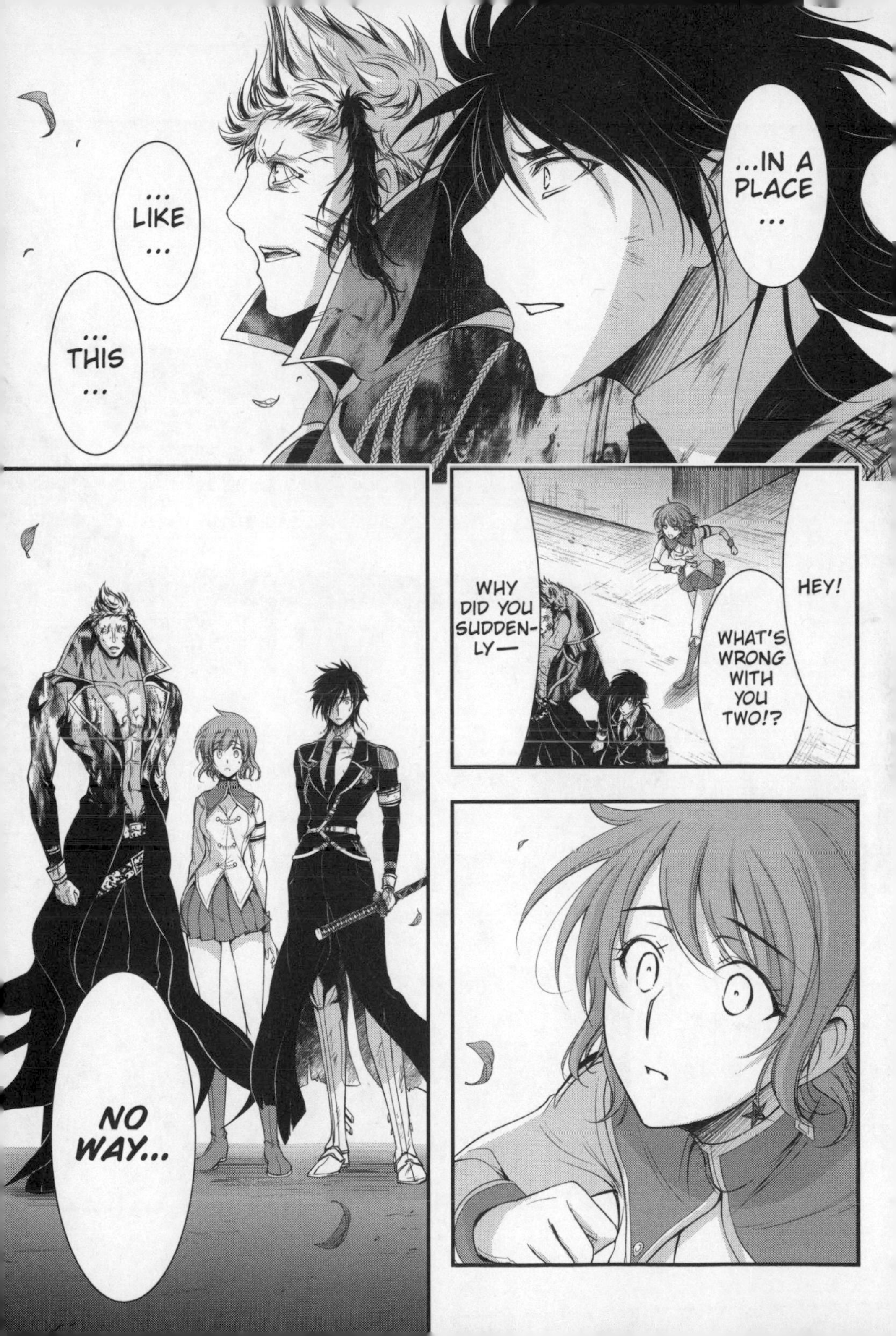

...IN A PLACE ...
... LIKE ...
... THIS ...
HEY!
WHAT'S WRONG WITH YOU TWO!?
WHY DID YOU SUDDEN-LY—
NO WAY...

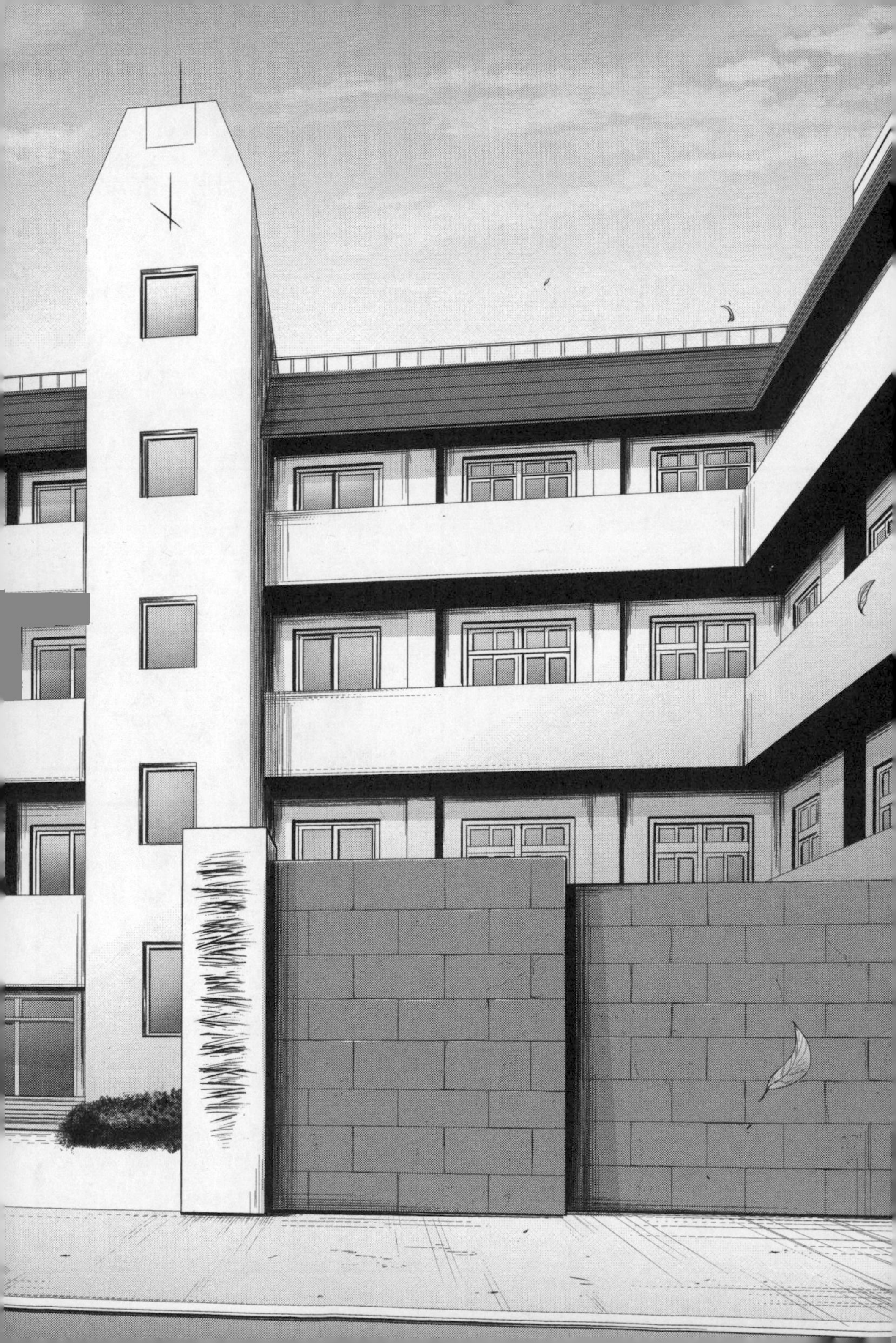

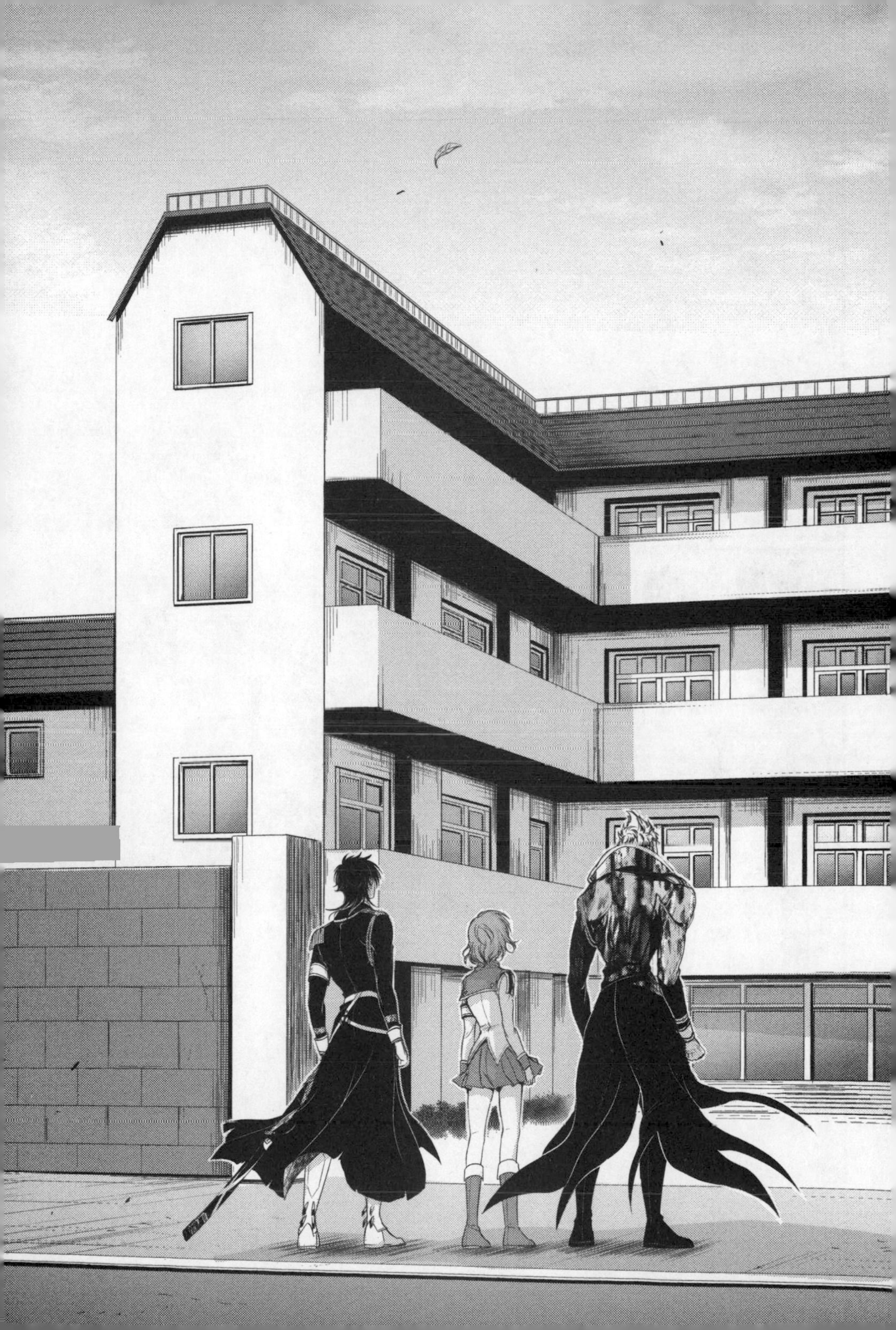

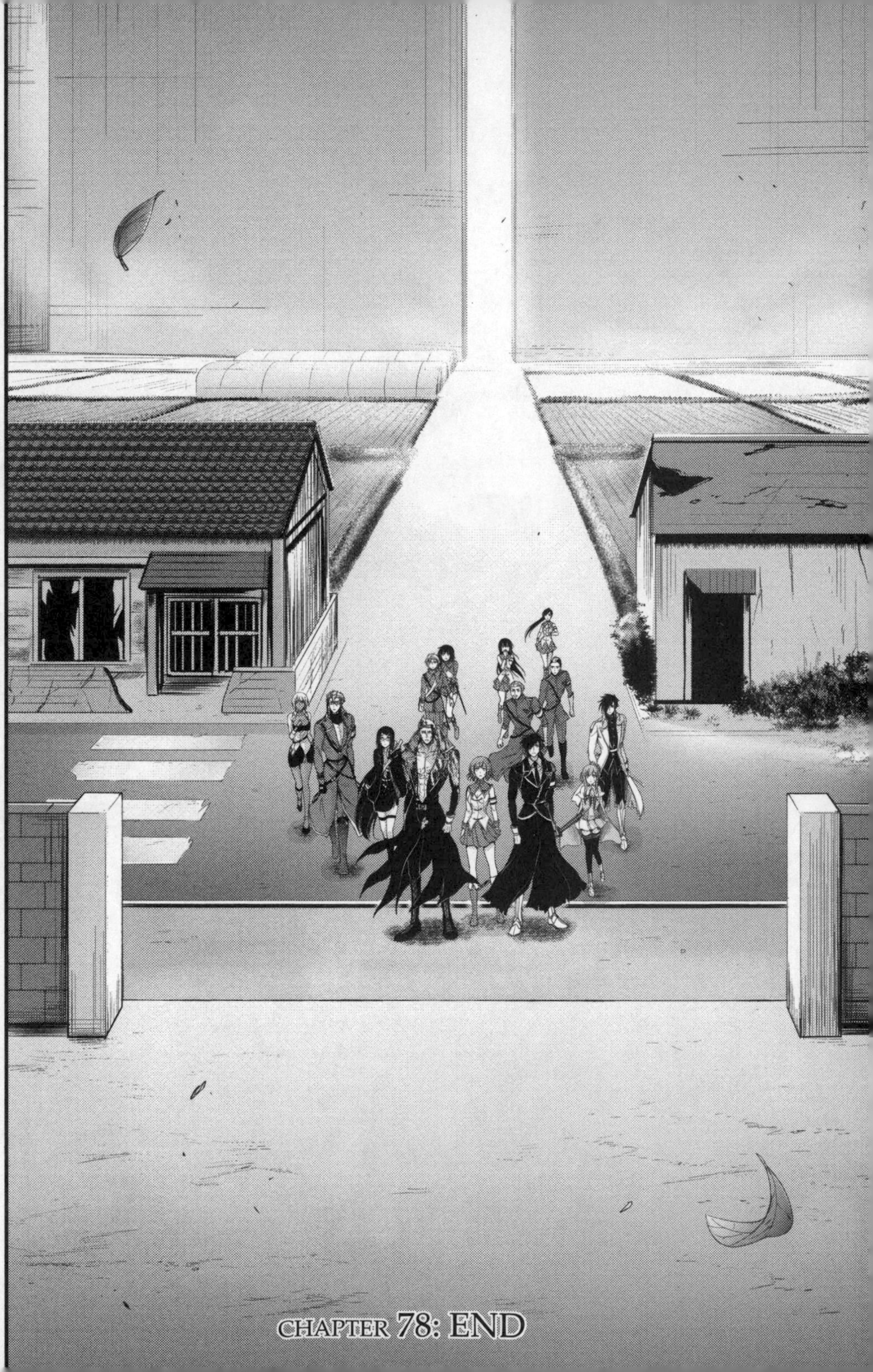
CHAPTER 78: END

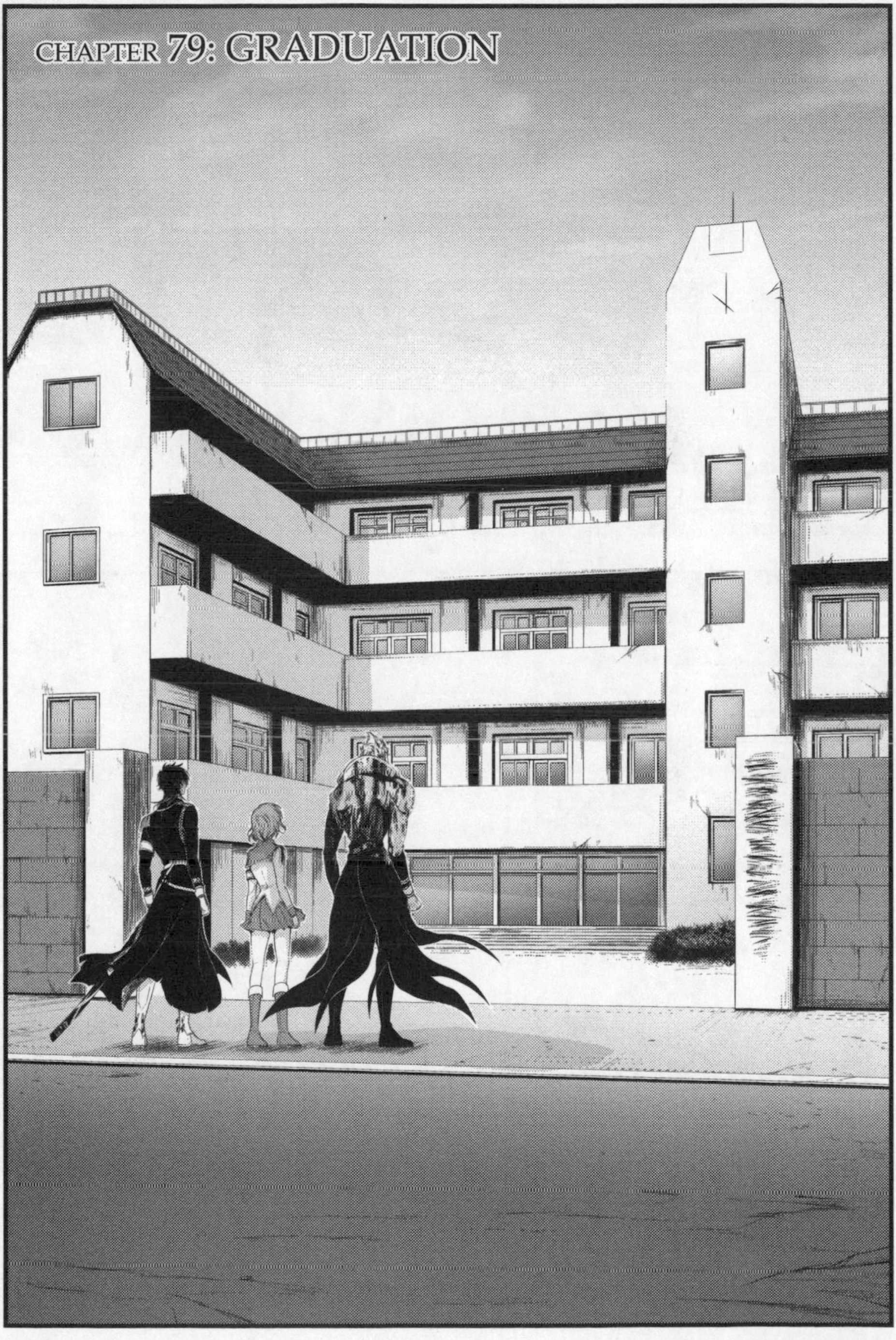
CHAPTER 79: GRADUATION

THIS...

......

THIS IS...

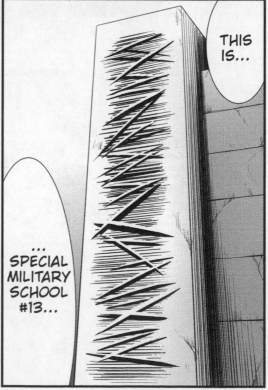

...SPECIAL MILITARY SCHOOL #13...

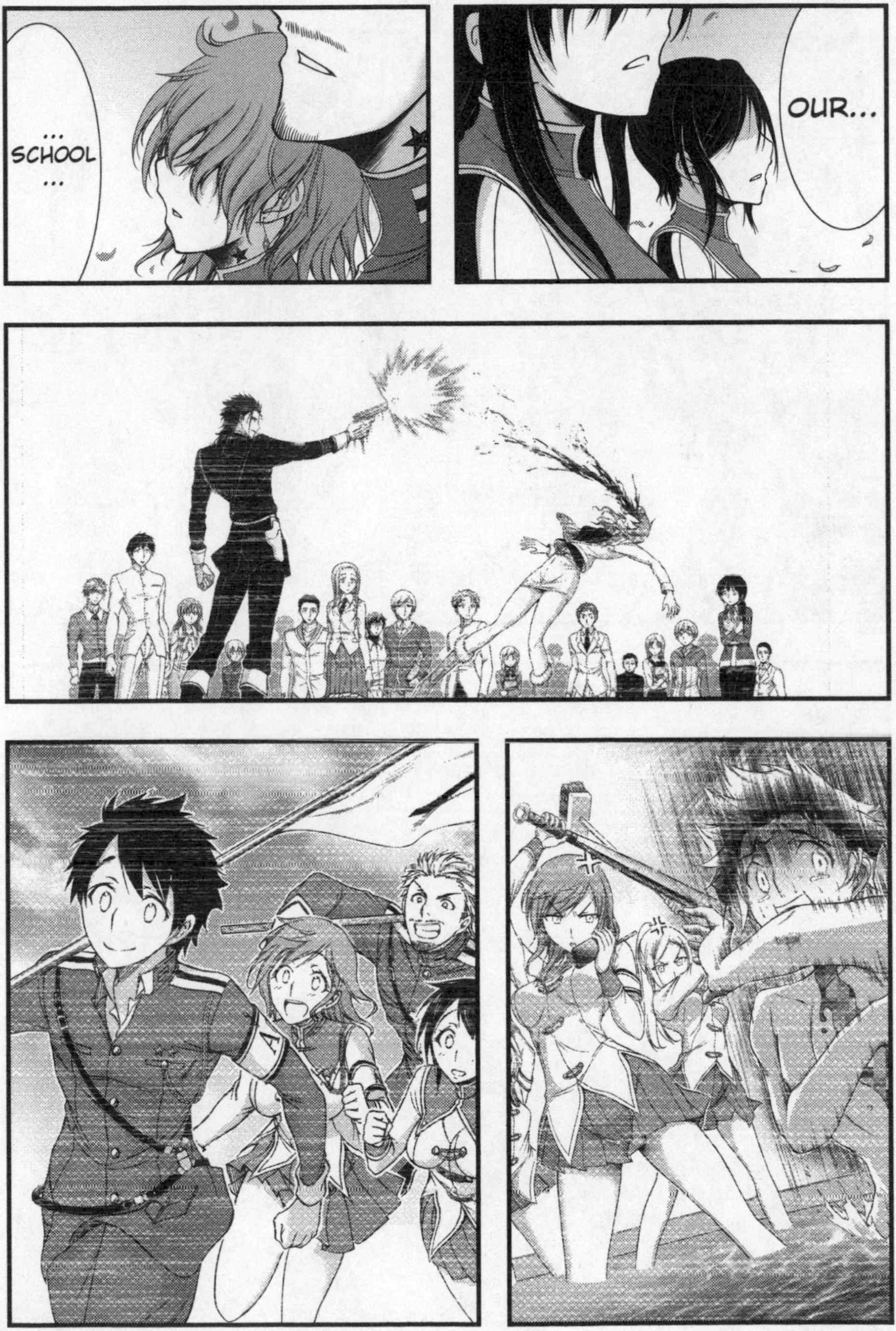
OUR...
... SCHOOL ...

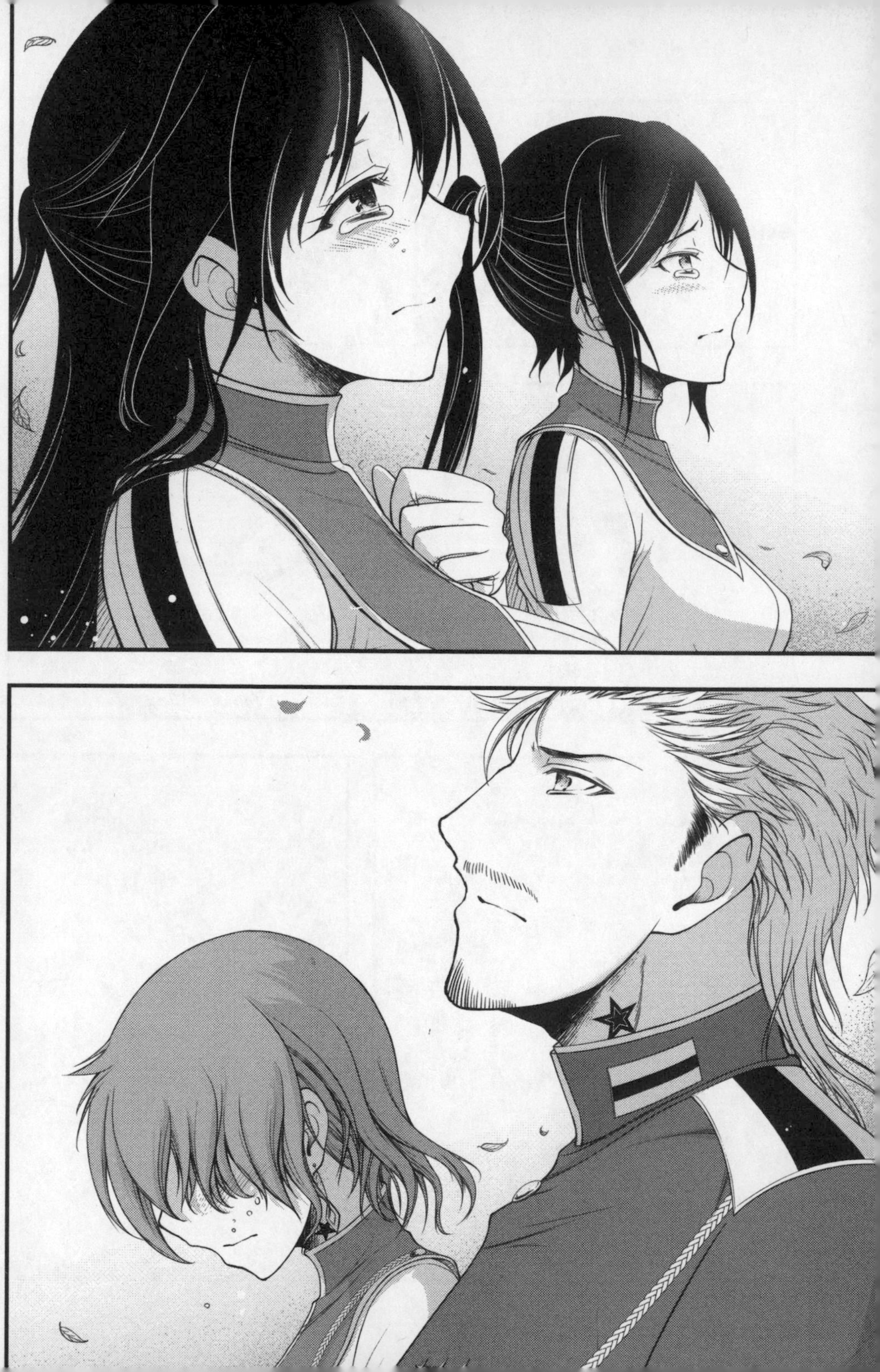

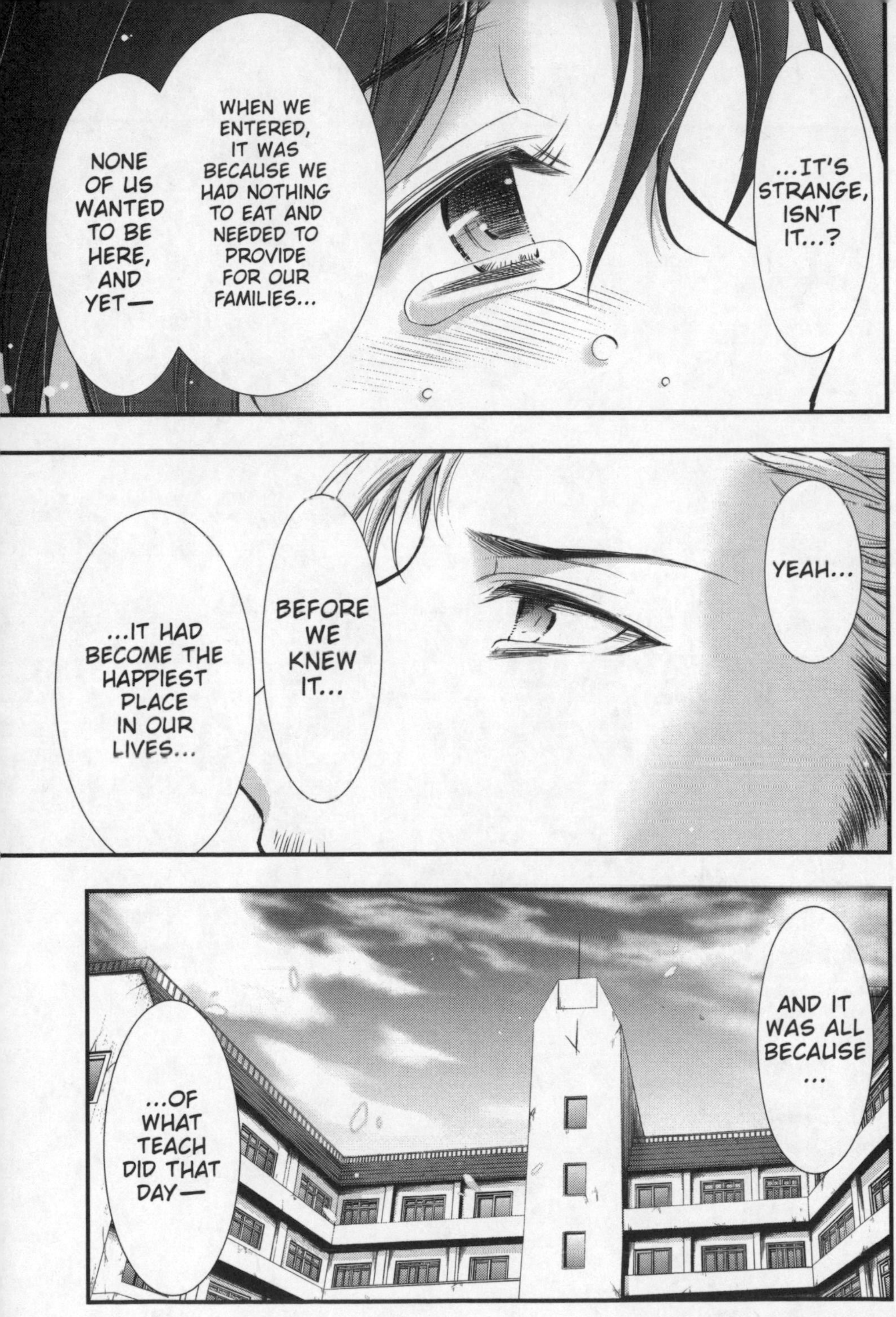
...IT'S STRANGE, ISN'T IT...?
WHEN WE ENTERED, IT WAS BECAUSE WE HAD NOTHING TO EAT AND NEEDED TO PROVIDE FOR OUR FAMILIES...
NONE OF US WANTED TO BE HERE, AND YET—
YEAH...
BEFORE WE KNEW IT...
...IT HAD BECOME THE HAPPIEST PLACE IN OUR LIVES...
AND IT WAS ALL BECAUSE...
...OF WHAT TEACH DID THAT DAY—

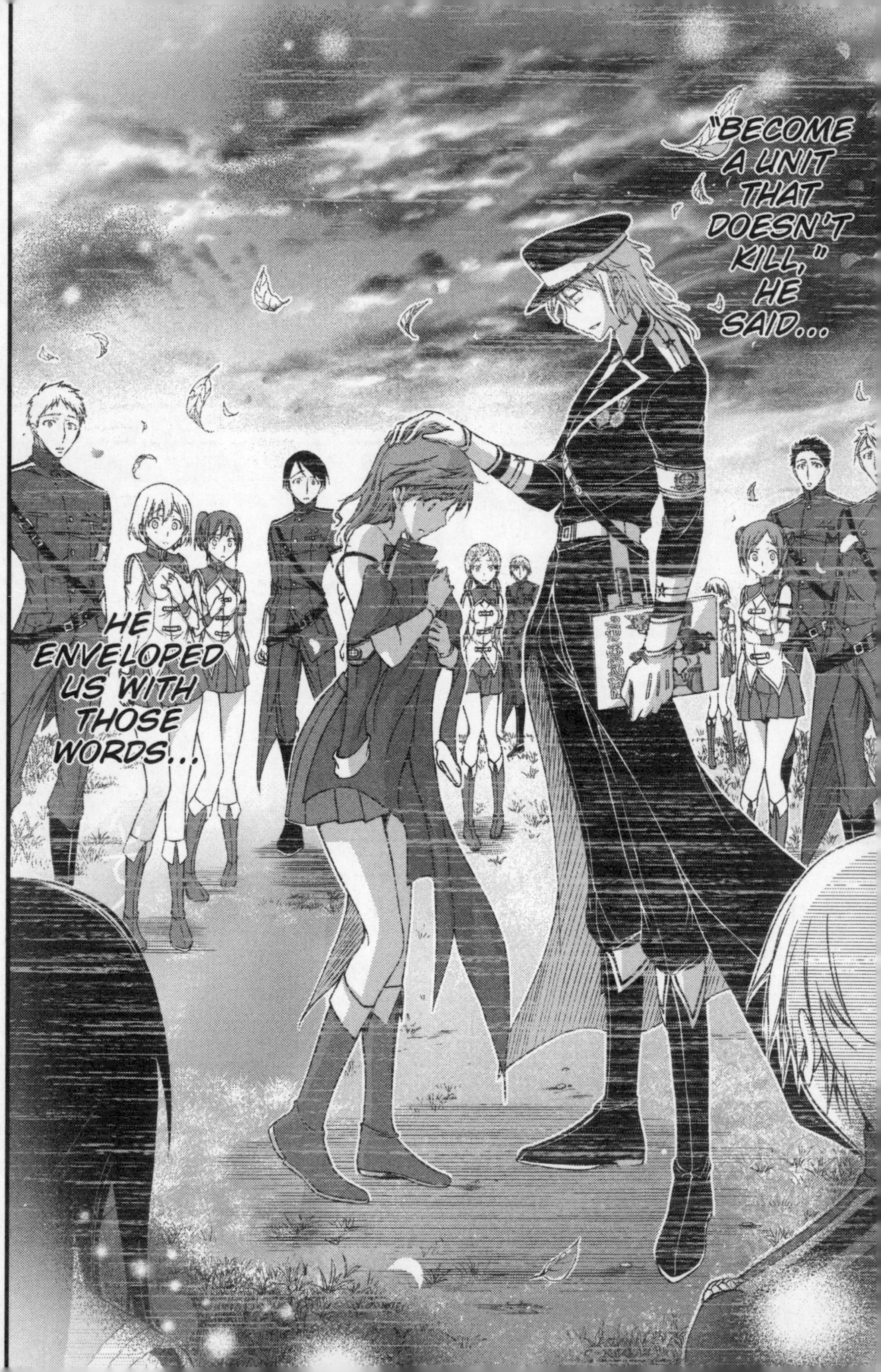
"BECOME A UNIT THAT DOESN'T KILL," HE SAID...
HE ENVELOPED US WITH THOSE WORDS...

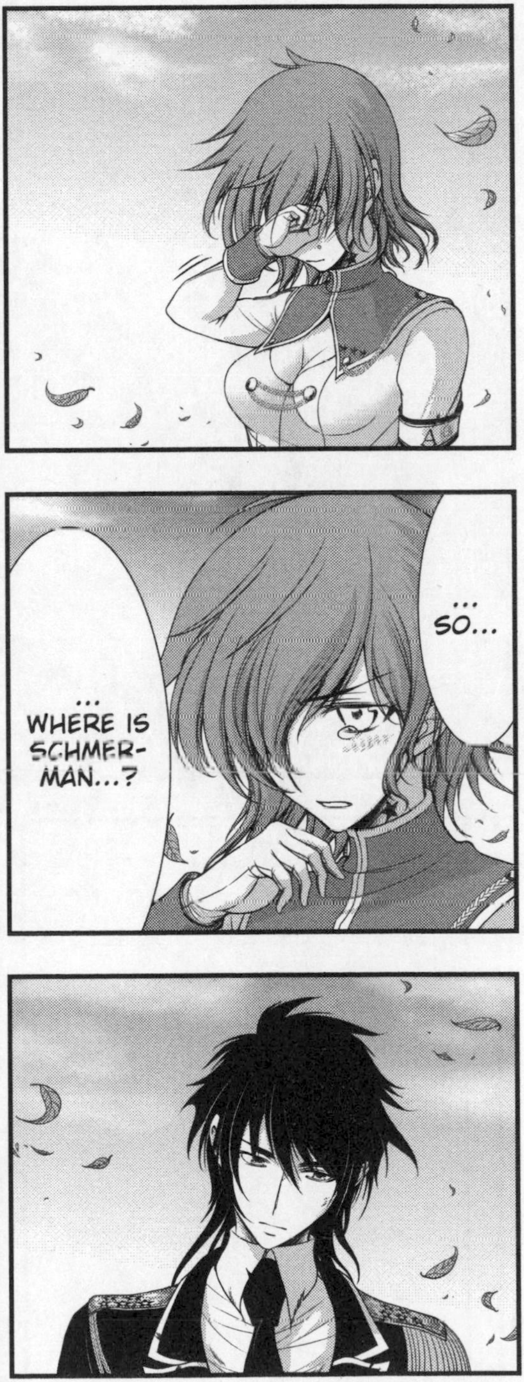
... SO...
... WHERE IS SCHMER-MAN...?
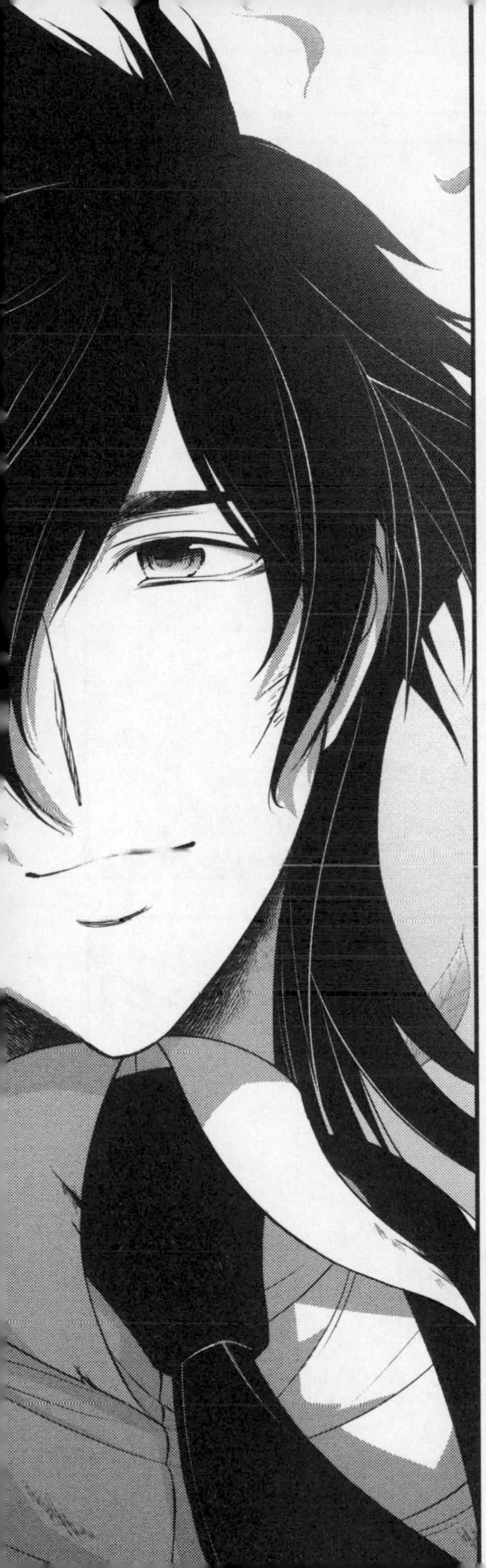

WHERE ELSE COULD HE BE?

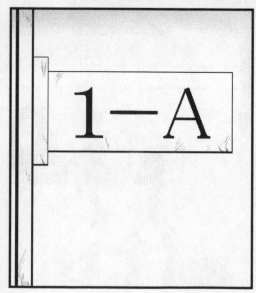

1－A

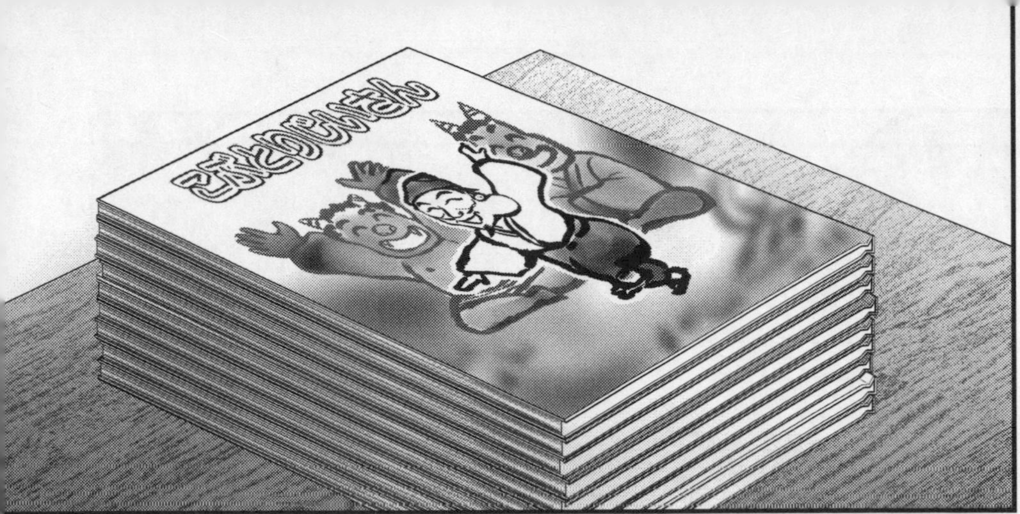

BOOK: THE MAN WITH THE LUMP

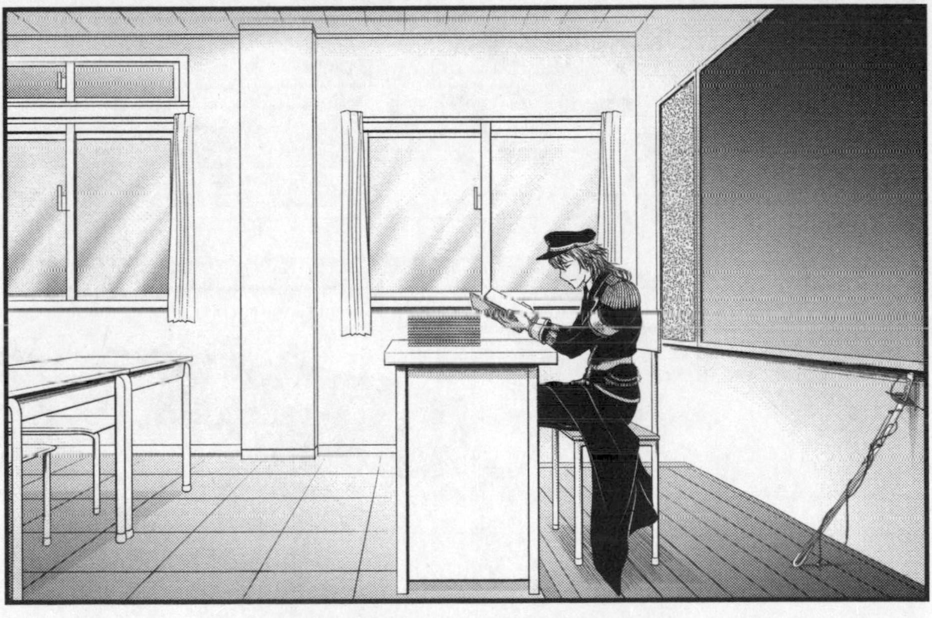

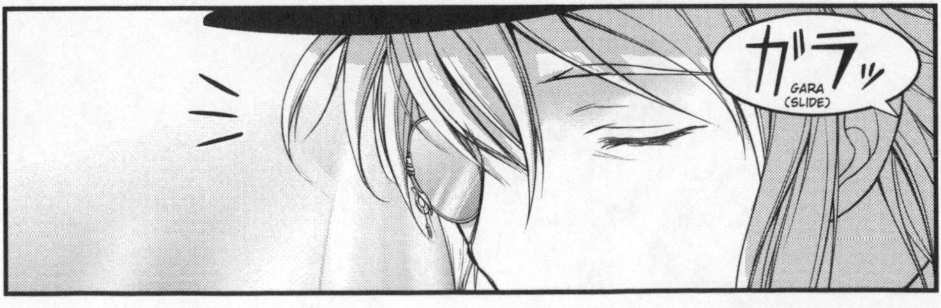
ガラッ
GARA (SLIDE)

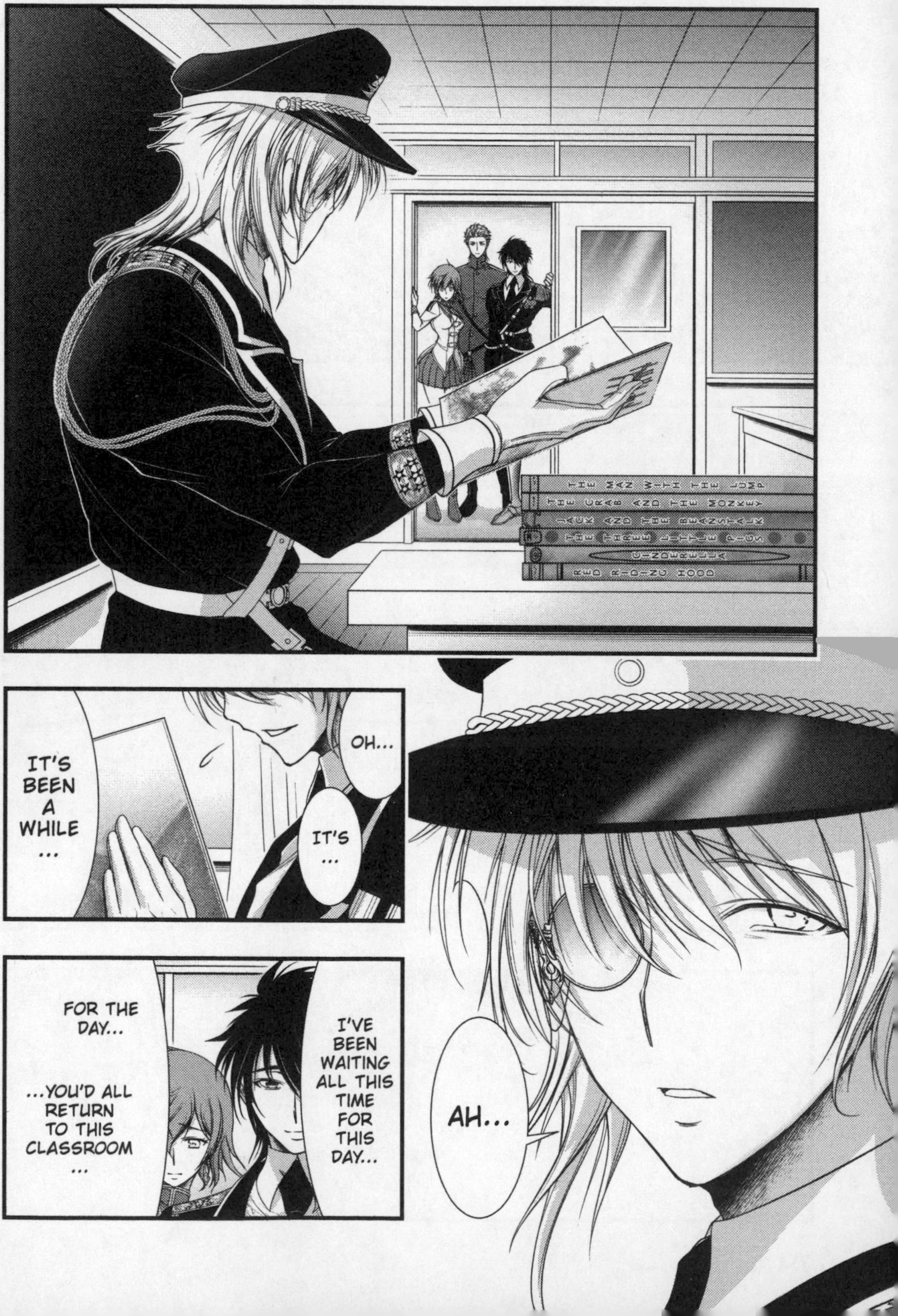
THE MAN WITH THE LUMP
THE CRAB AND THE MONKEY
JACK AND THE BEANSTALK
THE THREE LITTLE PIGS
CINDERELLA
RED RIDING HOOD
AH...
OH...
IT'S...
IT'S BEEN A WHILE...
I'VE BEEN WAITING ALL THIS TIME FOR THIS DAY...
FOR THE DAY...
...YOU'D ALL RETURN TO THIS CLASSROOM...

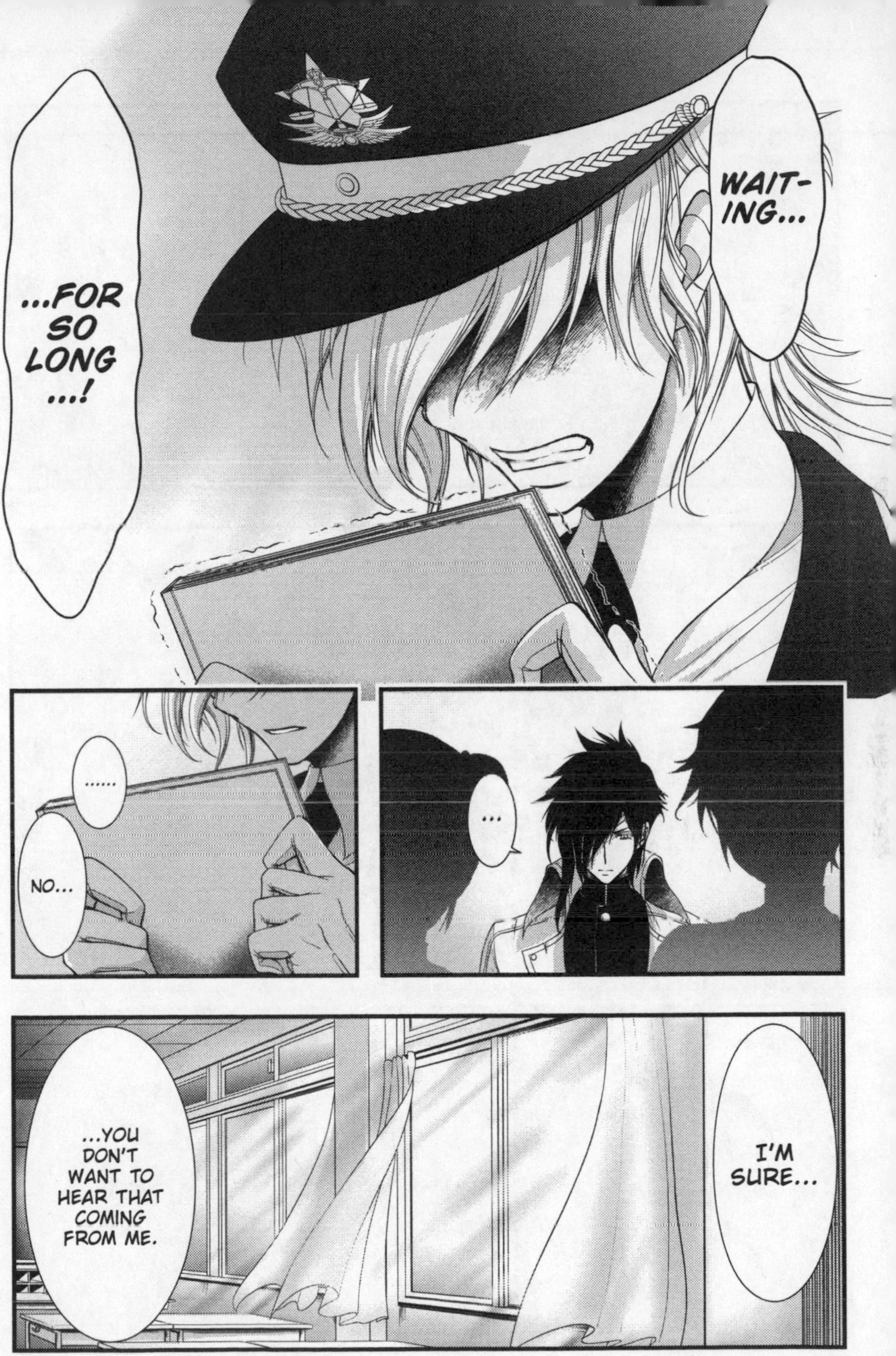
WAIT-ING...
...FOR SO LONG...!
...
......
NO...
I'M SURE...
...YOU DON'T WANT TO HEAR THAT COMING FROM ME.

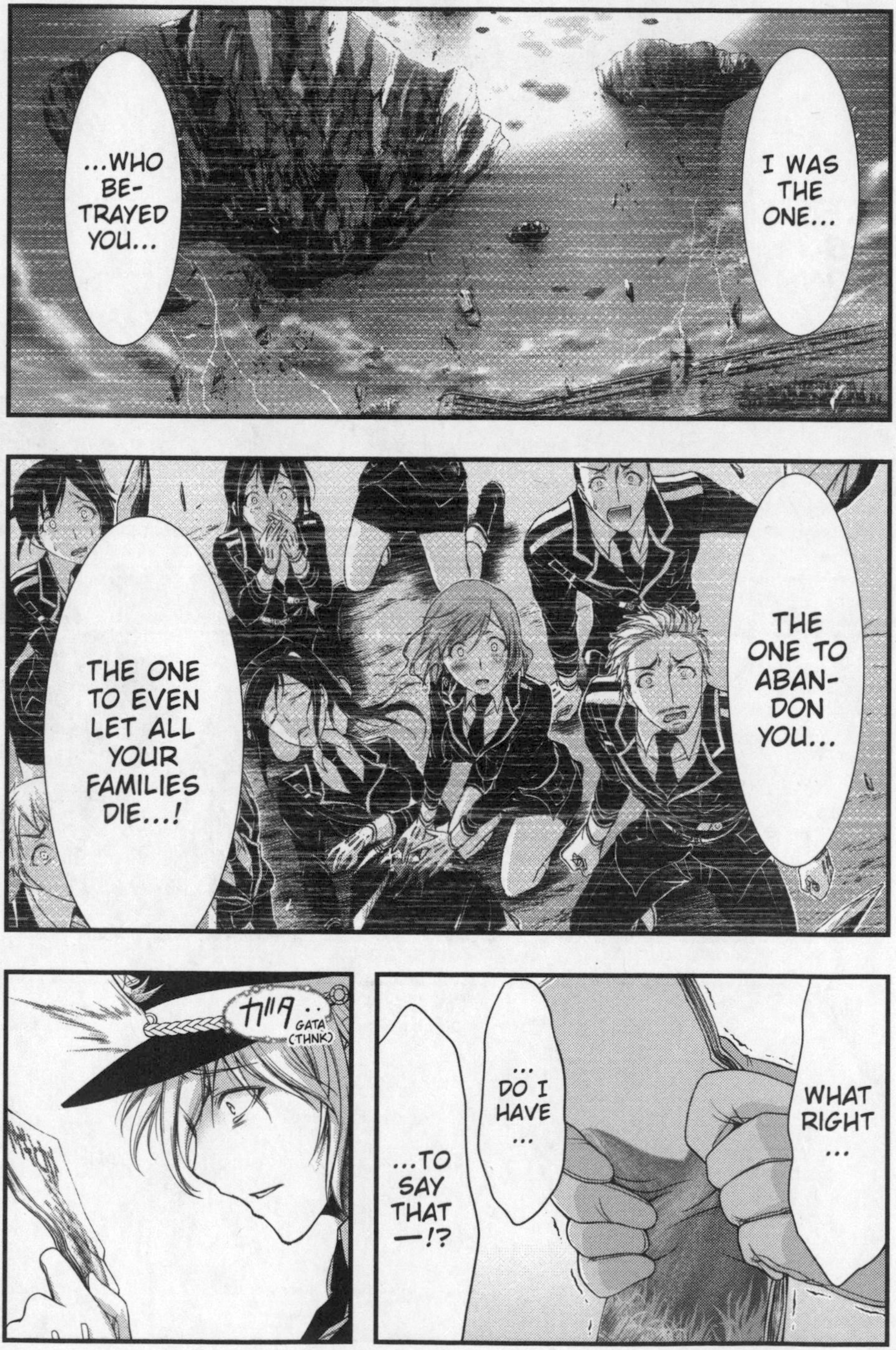
I WAS THE ONE...
...WHO BE-TRAYED YOU...
THE ONE TO ABAN-DON YOU...
THE ONE TO EVEN LET ALL YOUR FAMILIES DIE...!
WHAT RIGHT...
...DO I HAVE...
...TO SAY THAT—!?
カタ..
GATA (THNK)

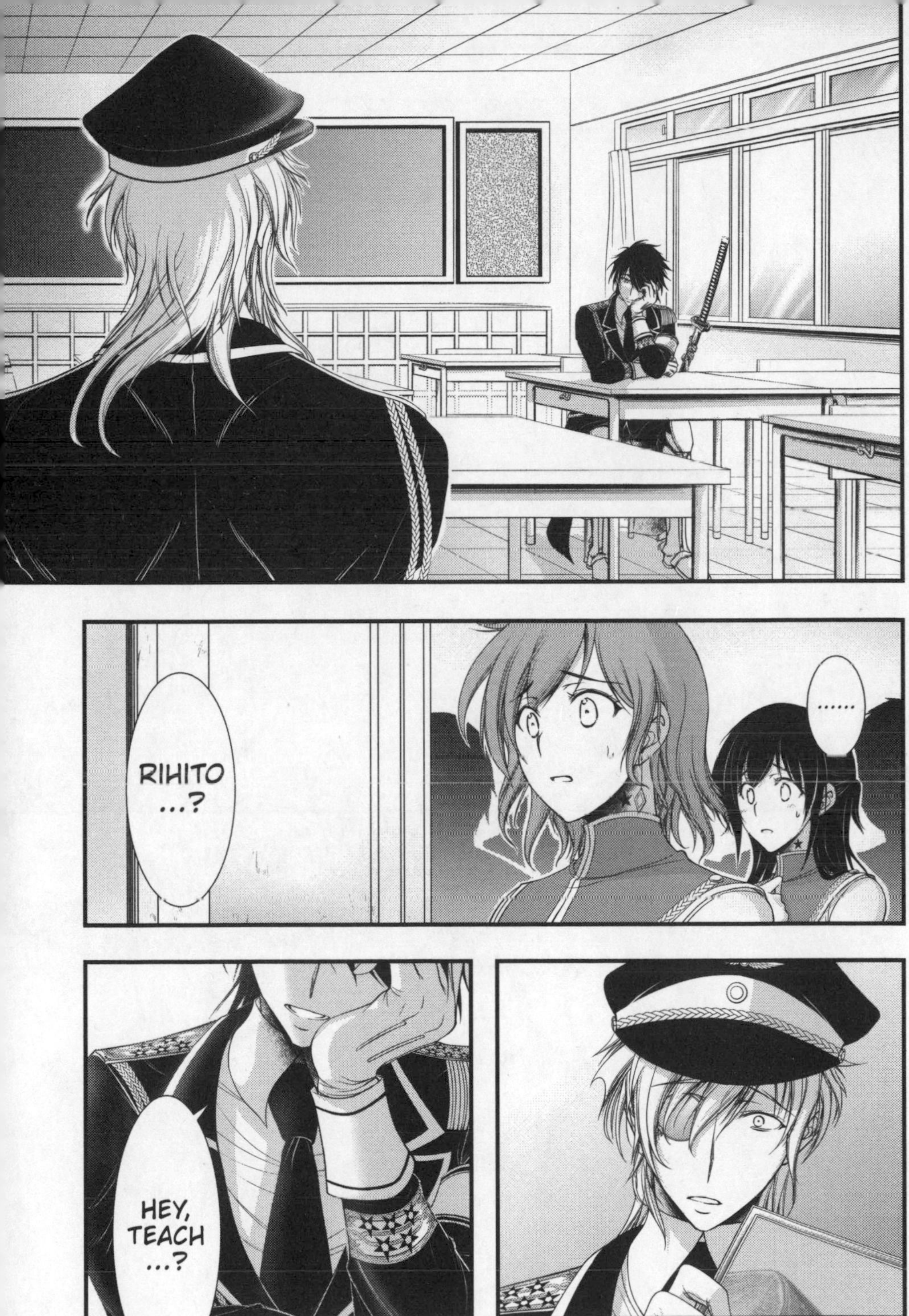
......
RIHITO ...?
HEY, TEACH ...?

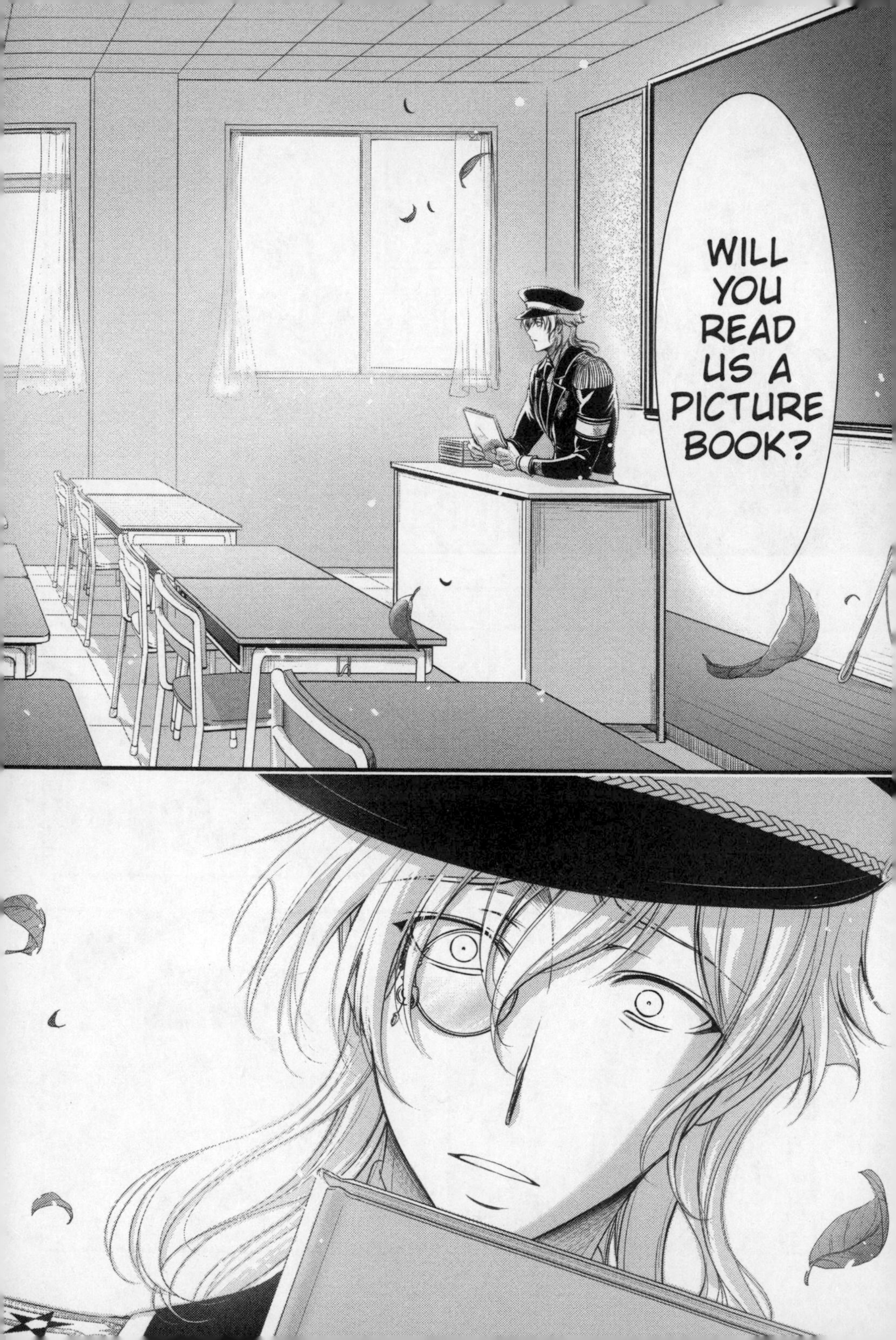
WILL YOU READ US A PICTURE BOOK?

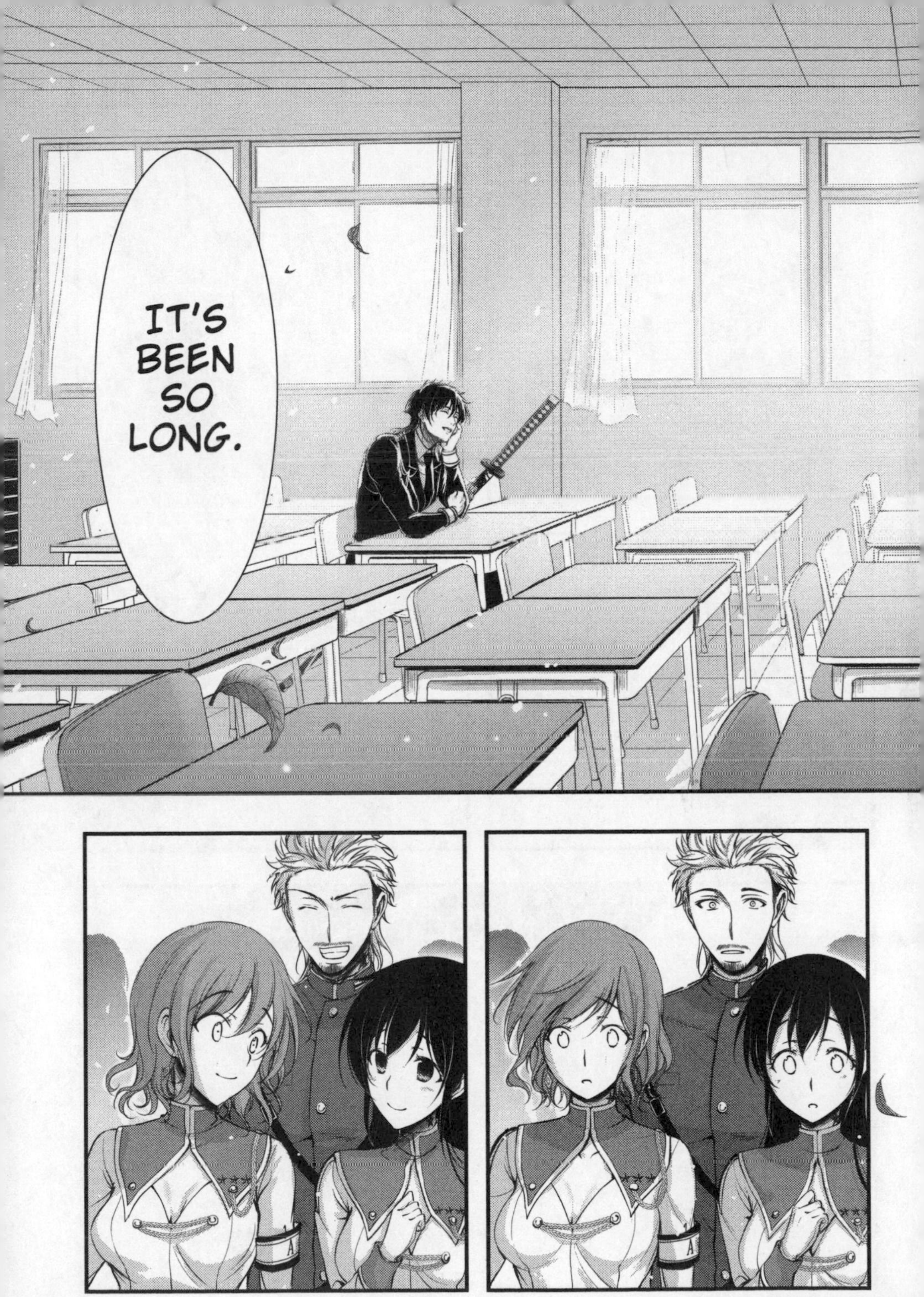
IT'S BEEN SO LONG.

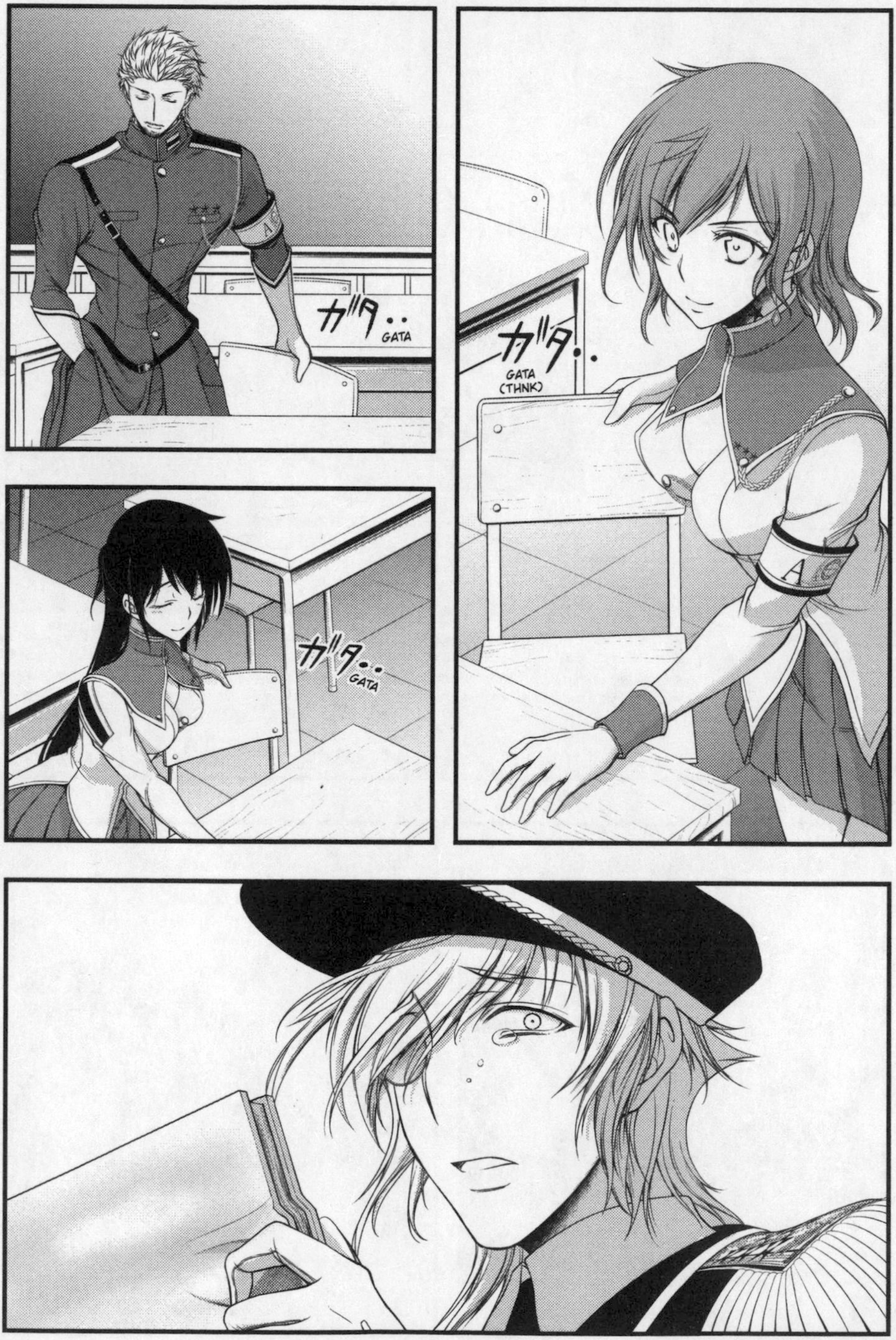
ガタ..
GATA
(THNK)
ガタ..
GATA
ガタ..
GATA

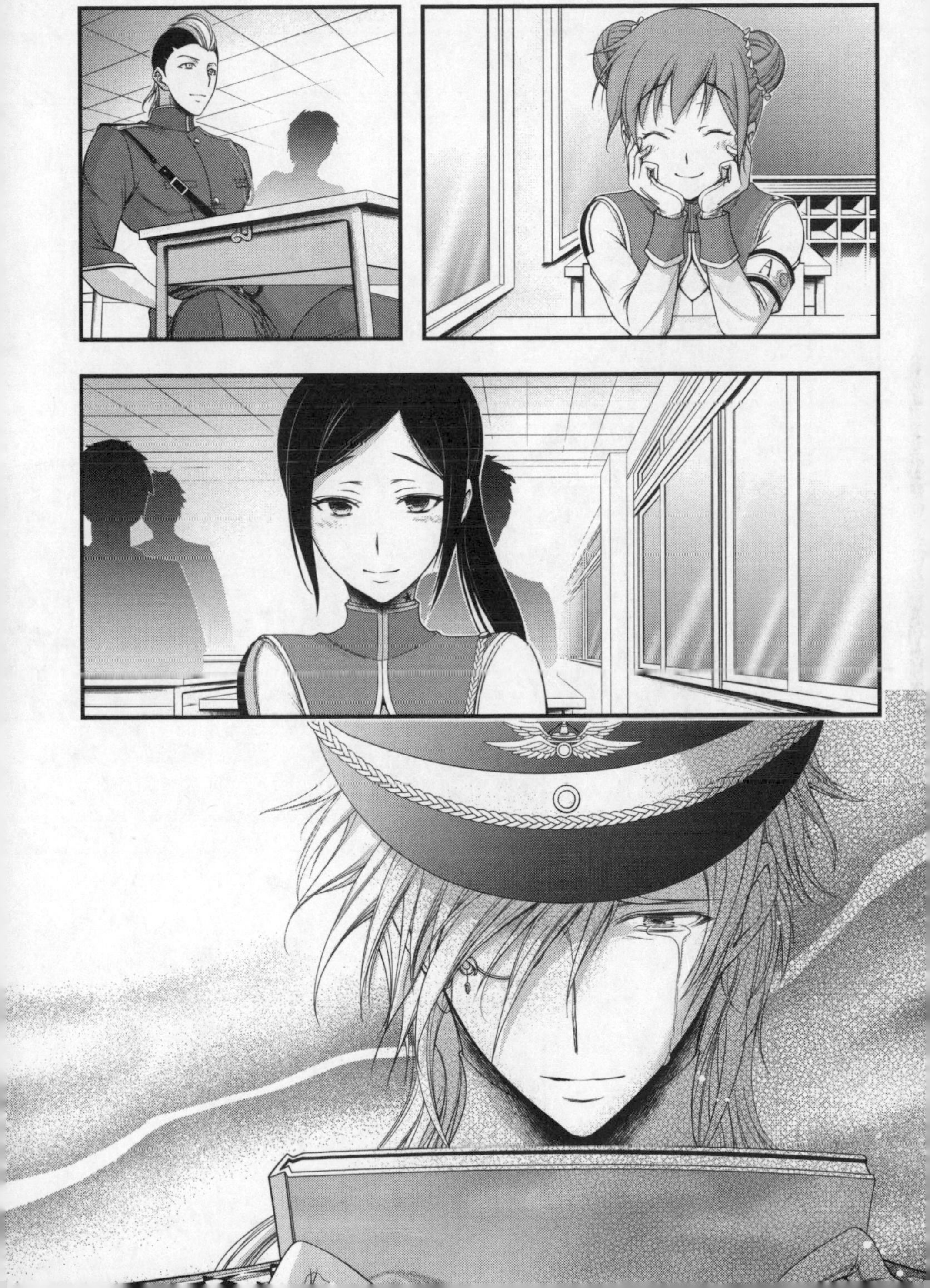

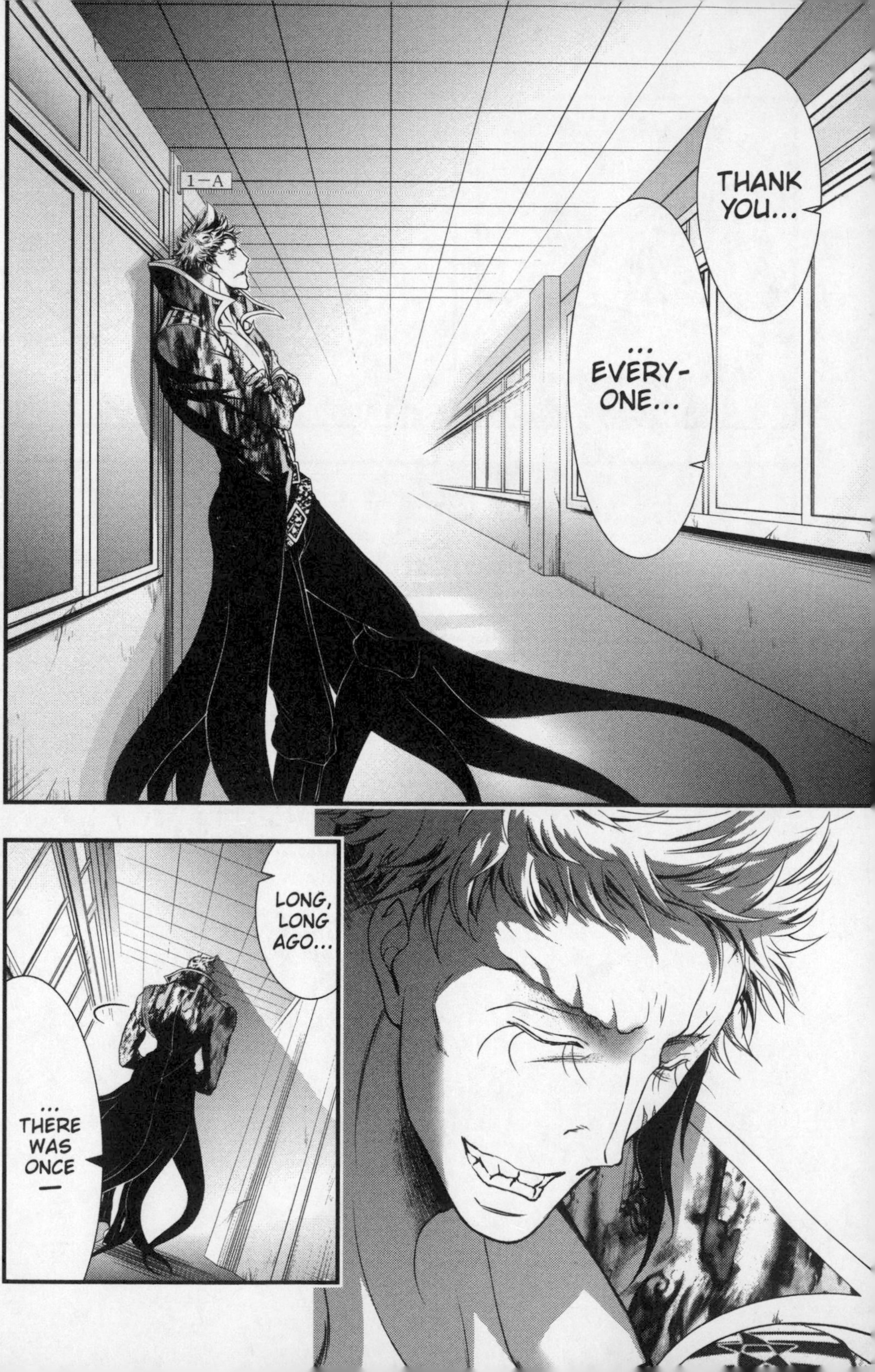
THANK YOU...
... EVERY-ONE...
1—A
LONG, LONG AGO...
... THERE WAS ONCE —

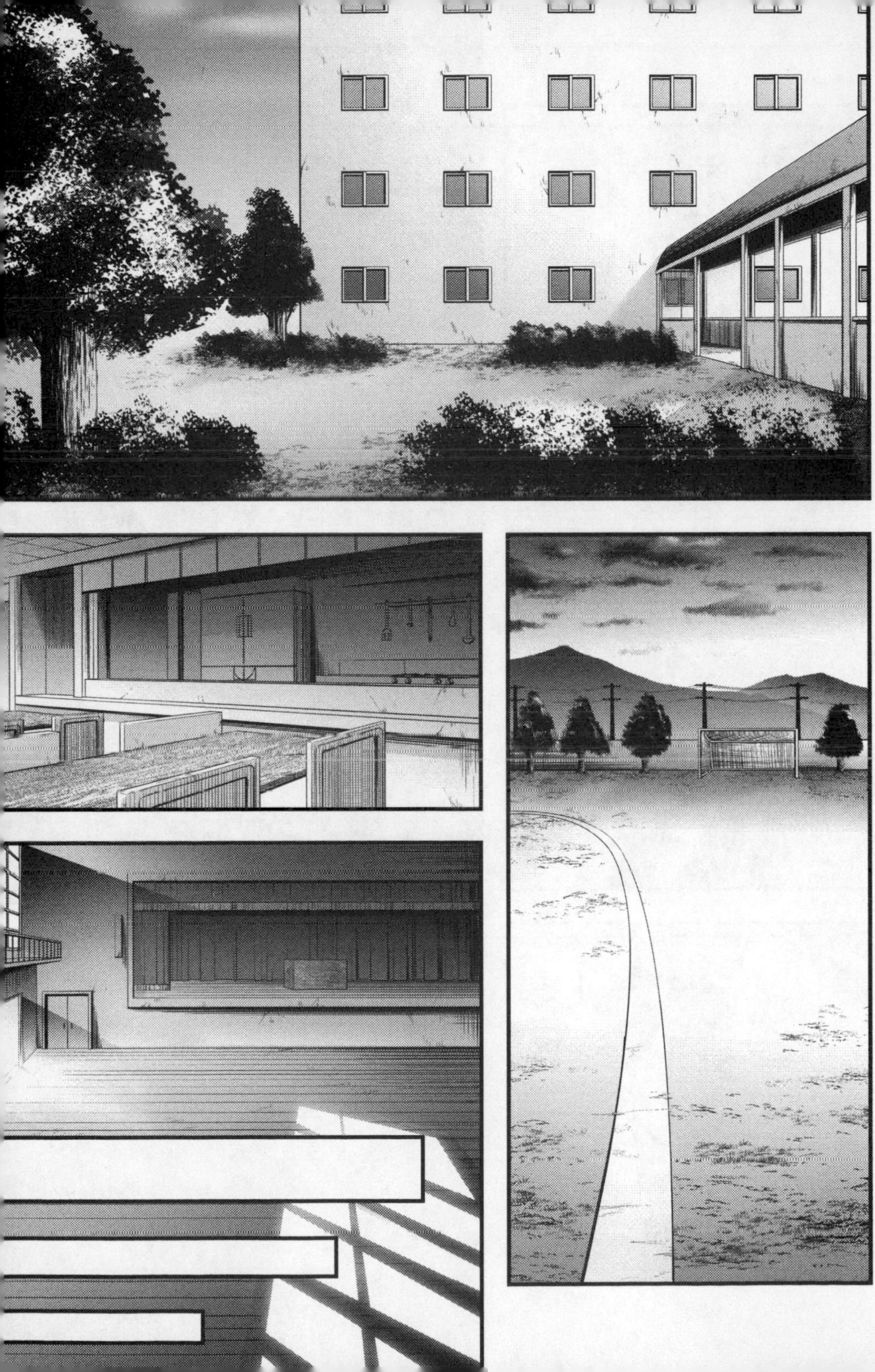

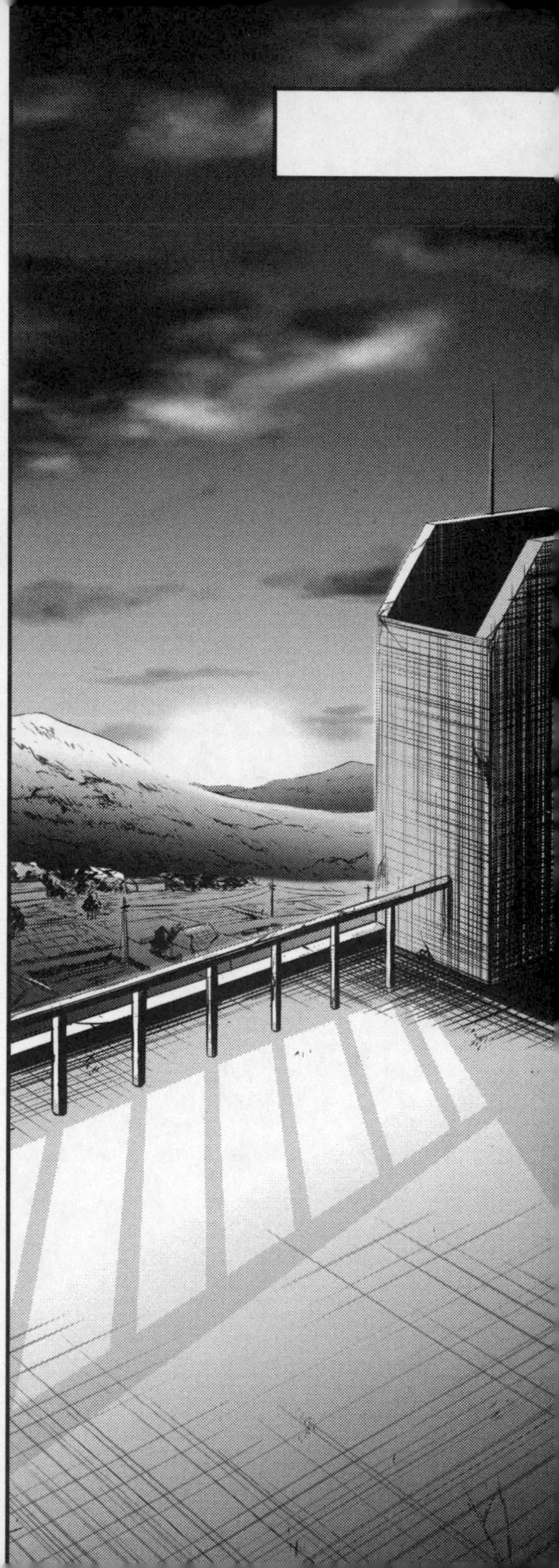

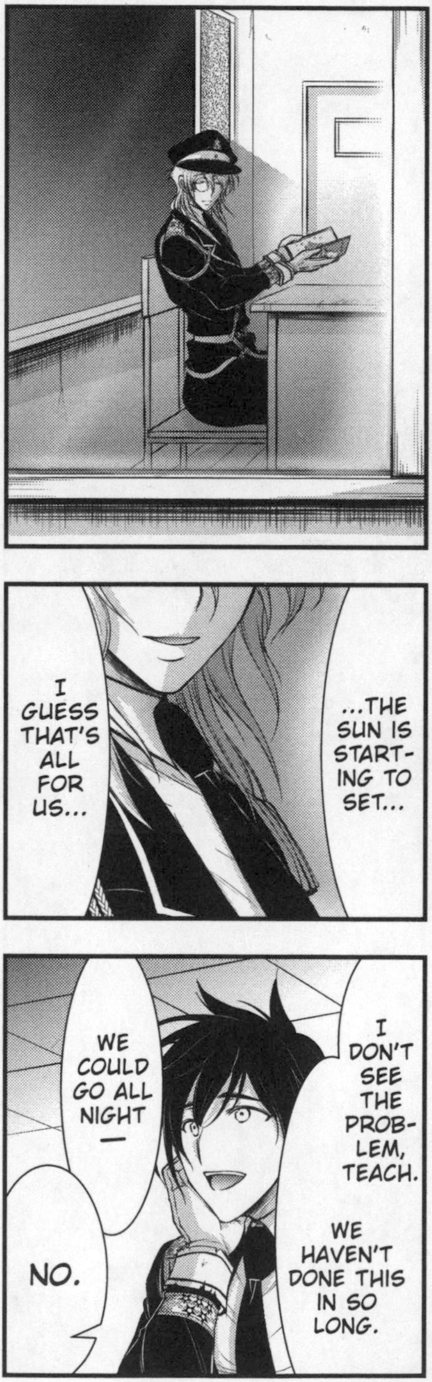
...THE SUN IS STARTING TO SET...
I GUESS THAT'S ALL FOR US...
I DON'T SEE THE PROBLEM, TEACH.
WE HAVEN'T DONE THIS IN SO LONG.
WE COULD GO ALL NIGHT—
NO.

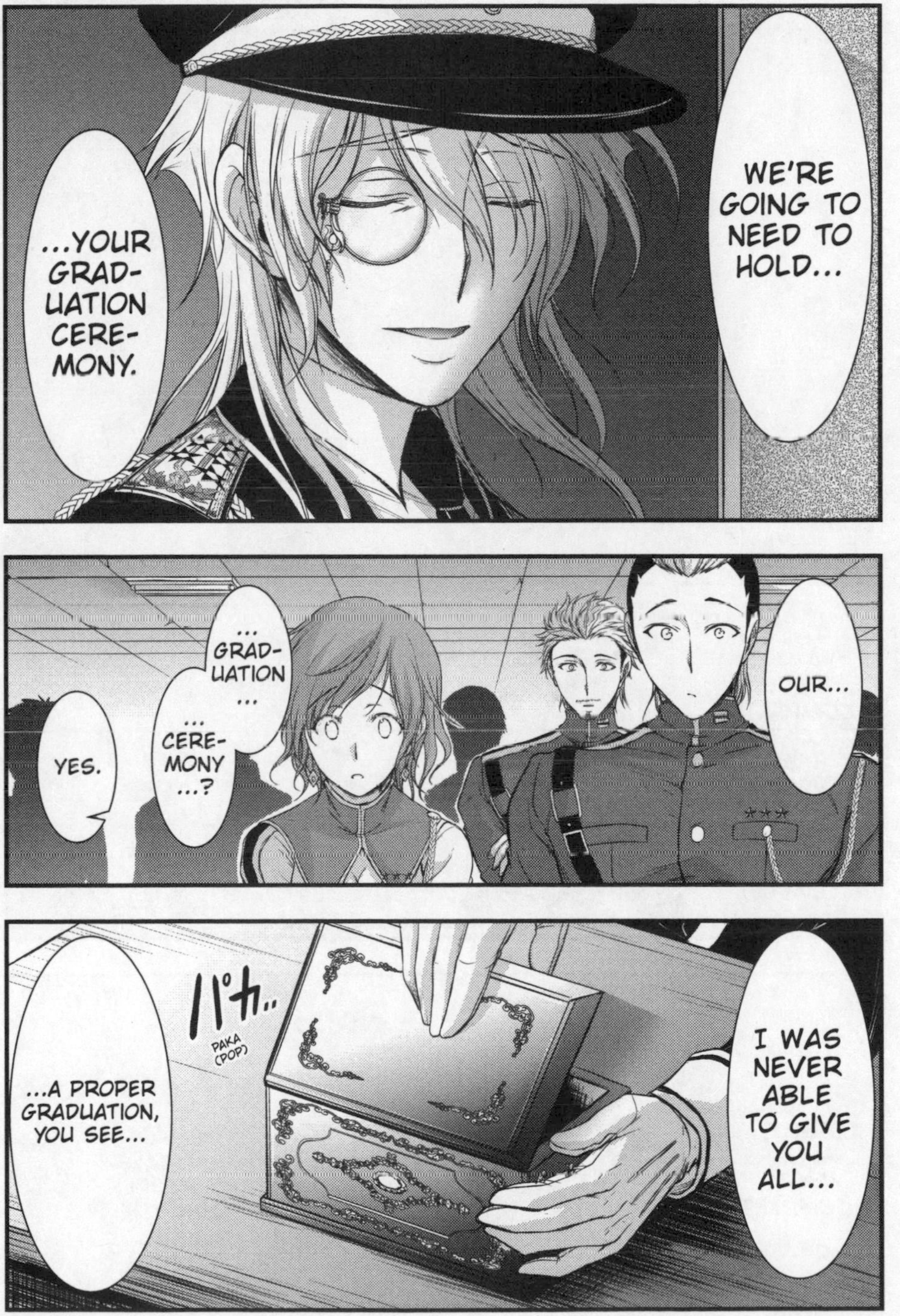
WE'RE GOING TO NEED TO HOLD...
...YOUR GRAD-UATION CERE-MONY.
OUR...
...GRAD-UATION...
...CERE-MONY...?
YES.
I WAS NEVER ABLE TO GIVE YOU ALL...
パカ..
PAKA (POP)
...A PROPER GRADUATION, YOU SEE...

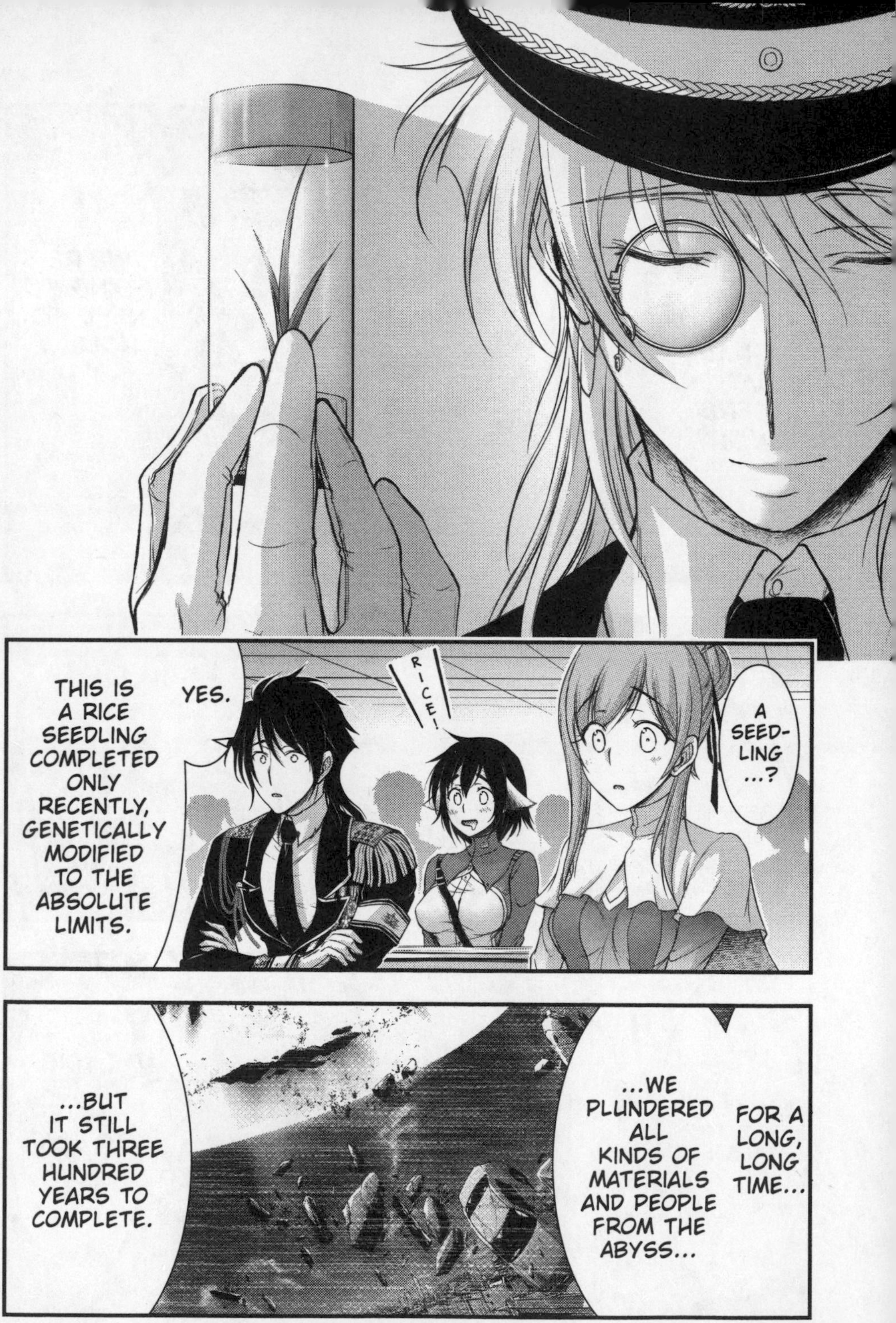
A SEED-LING...?
RICE!
YES.
THIS IS A RICE SEEDLING COMPLETED ONLY RECENTLY, GENETICALLY MODIFIED TO THE ABSOLUTE LIMITS.
FOR A LONG, LONG TIME...
...WE PLUNDERED ALL KINDS OF MATERIALS AND PEOPLE FROM THE ABYSS...
...BUT IT STILL TOOK THREE HUNDRED YEARS TO COMPLETE.

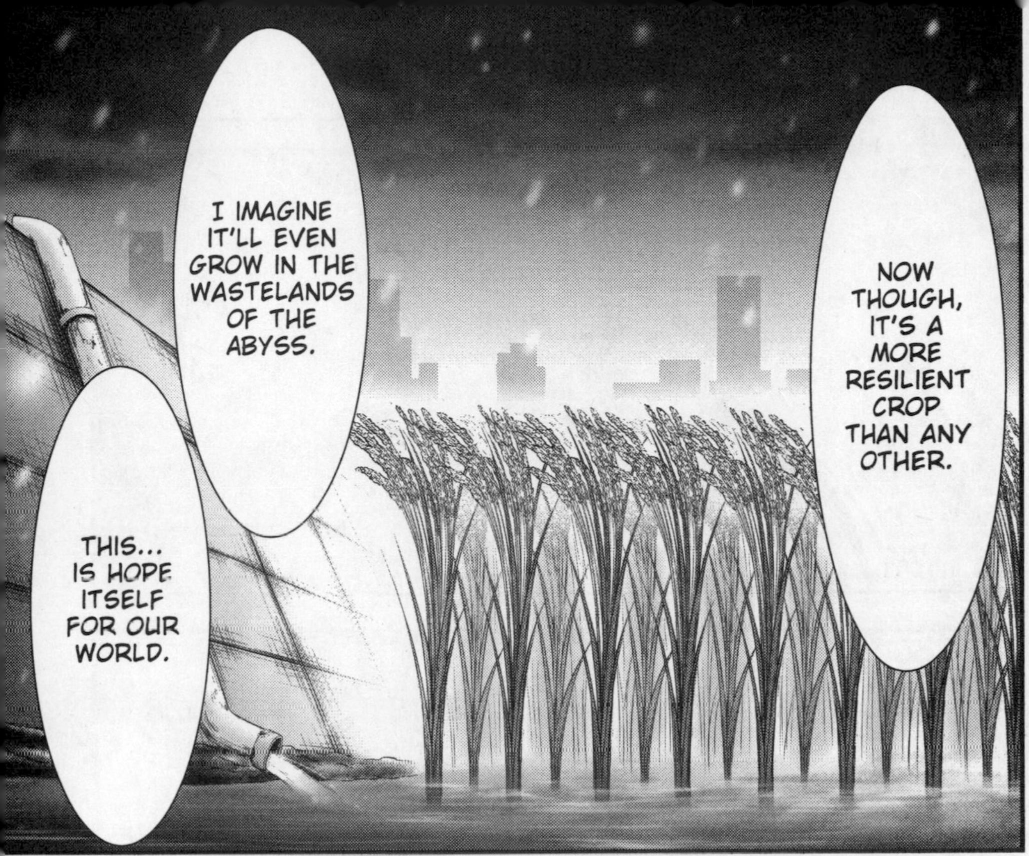
NOW THOUGH, IT'S A MORE RESILIENT CROP THAN ANY OTHER.
I IMAGINE IT'LL EVEN GROW IN THE WASTELANDS OF THE ABYSS.
THIS... IS HOPE ITSELF FOR OUR WORLD.
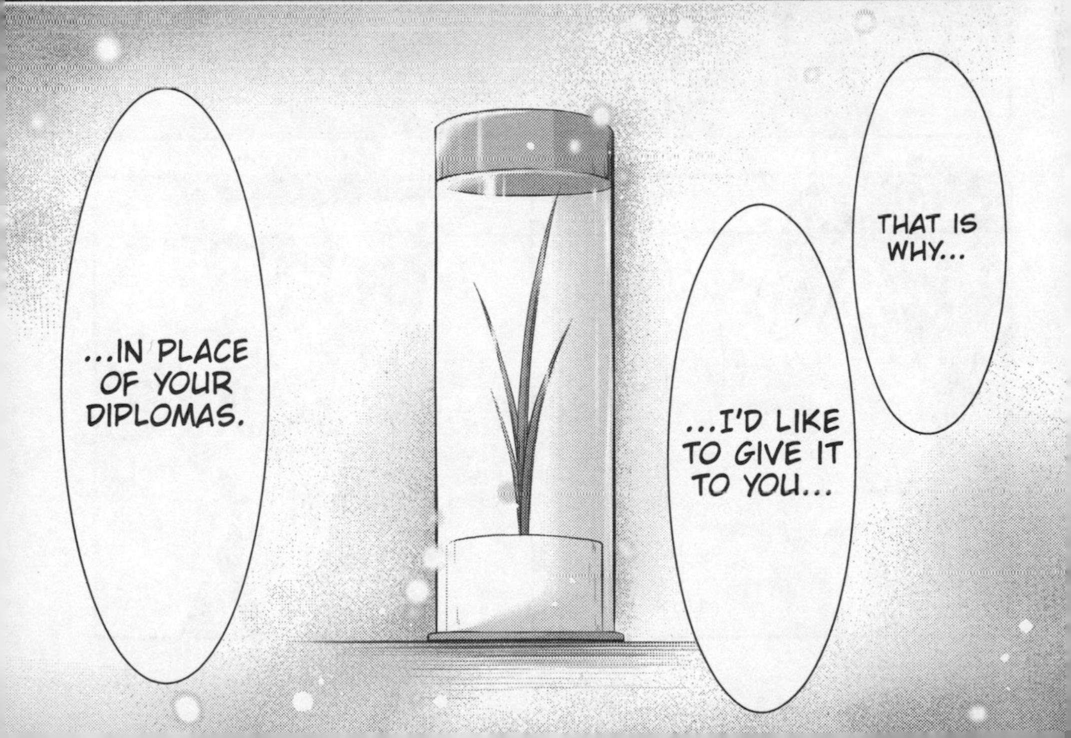
THAT IS WHY...
...I'D LIKE TO GIVE IT TO YOU...
...IN PLACE OF YOUR DIPLOMAS.

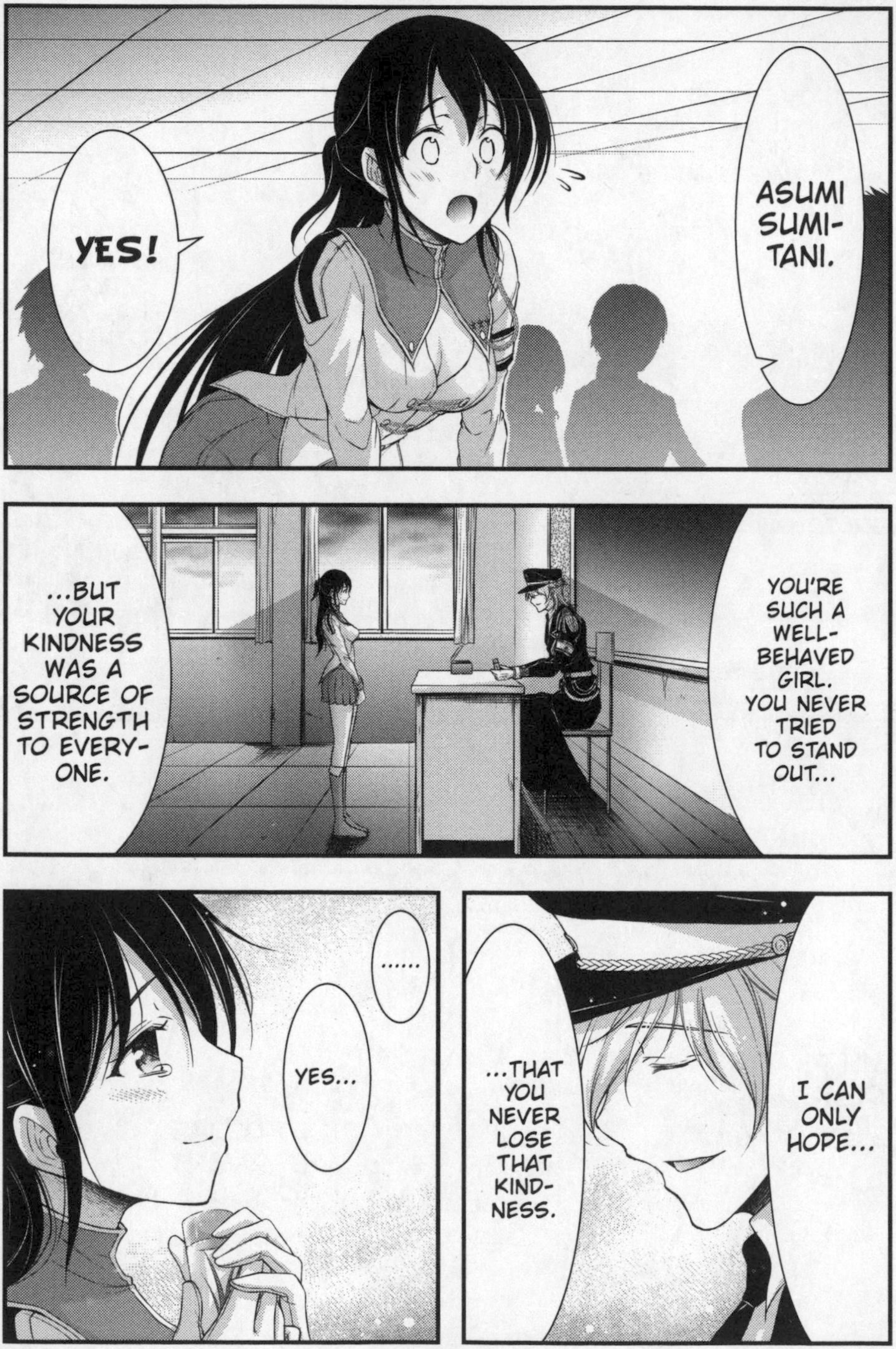
ASUMI SUMI-TANI.
YES!
YOU'RE SUCH A WELL-BEHAVED GIRL. YOU NEVER TRIED TO STAND OUT...
...BUT YOUR KINDNESS WAS A SOURCE OF STRENGTH TO EVERY-ONE.
I CAN ONLY HOPE...
...THAT YOU NEVER LOSE THAT KIND-NESS.
......
YES...

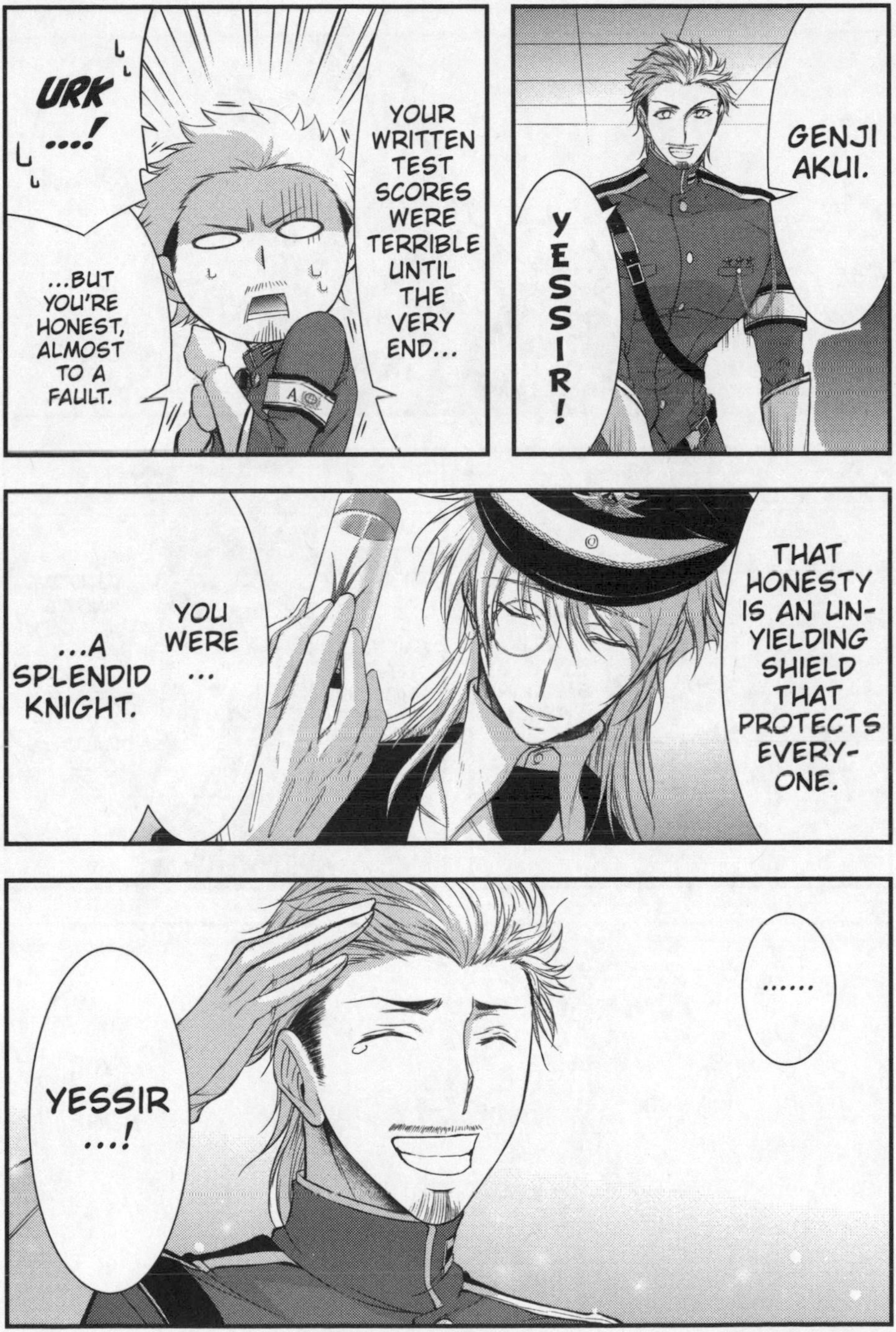
GENJI AKUI.
YESSIR!
YOUR WRITTEN TEST SCORES WERE TERRIBLE UNTIL THE VERY END...
URK ...!
...BUT YOU'RE HONEST, ALMOST TO A FAULT.
THAT HONESTY IS AN UNYIELDING SHIELD THAT PROTECTS EVERYONE.
YOU WERE ...
...A SPLENDID KNIGHT.
......
YESSIR ...!

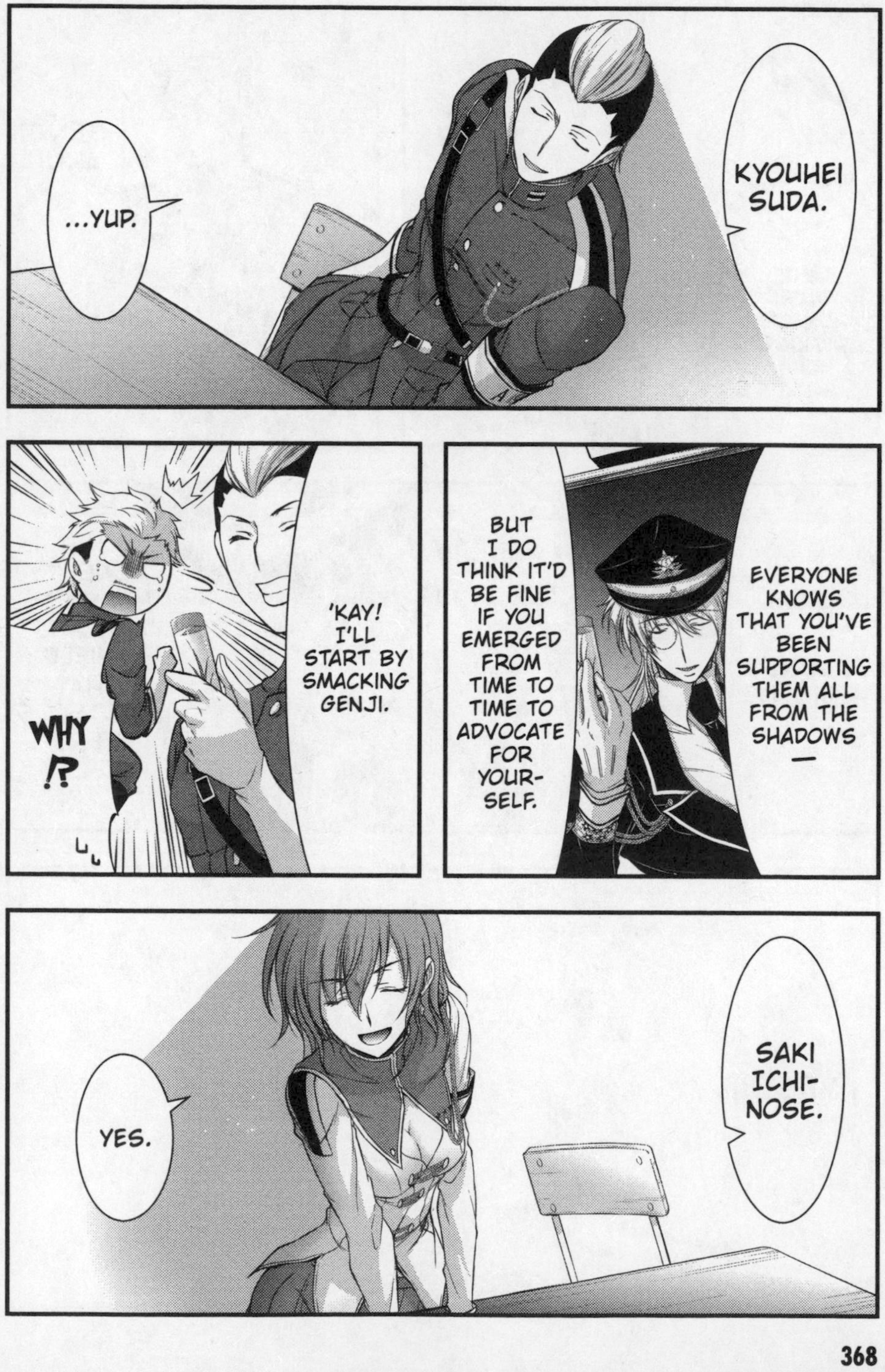
KYOUHEI SUDA.
...YUP.
EVERYONE KNOWS THAT YOU'VE BEEN SUPPORTING THEM ALL FROM THE SHADOWS—
BUT I DO THINK IT'D BE FINE IF YOU EMERGED FROM TIME TO TIME TO ADVOCATE FOR YOURSELF.
'KAY! I'LL START BY SMACKING GENJI.
WHY!?
SAKI ICHINOSE.
YES.

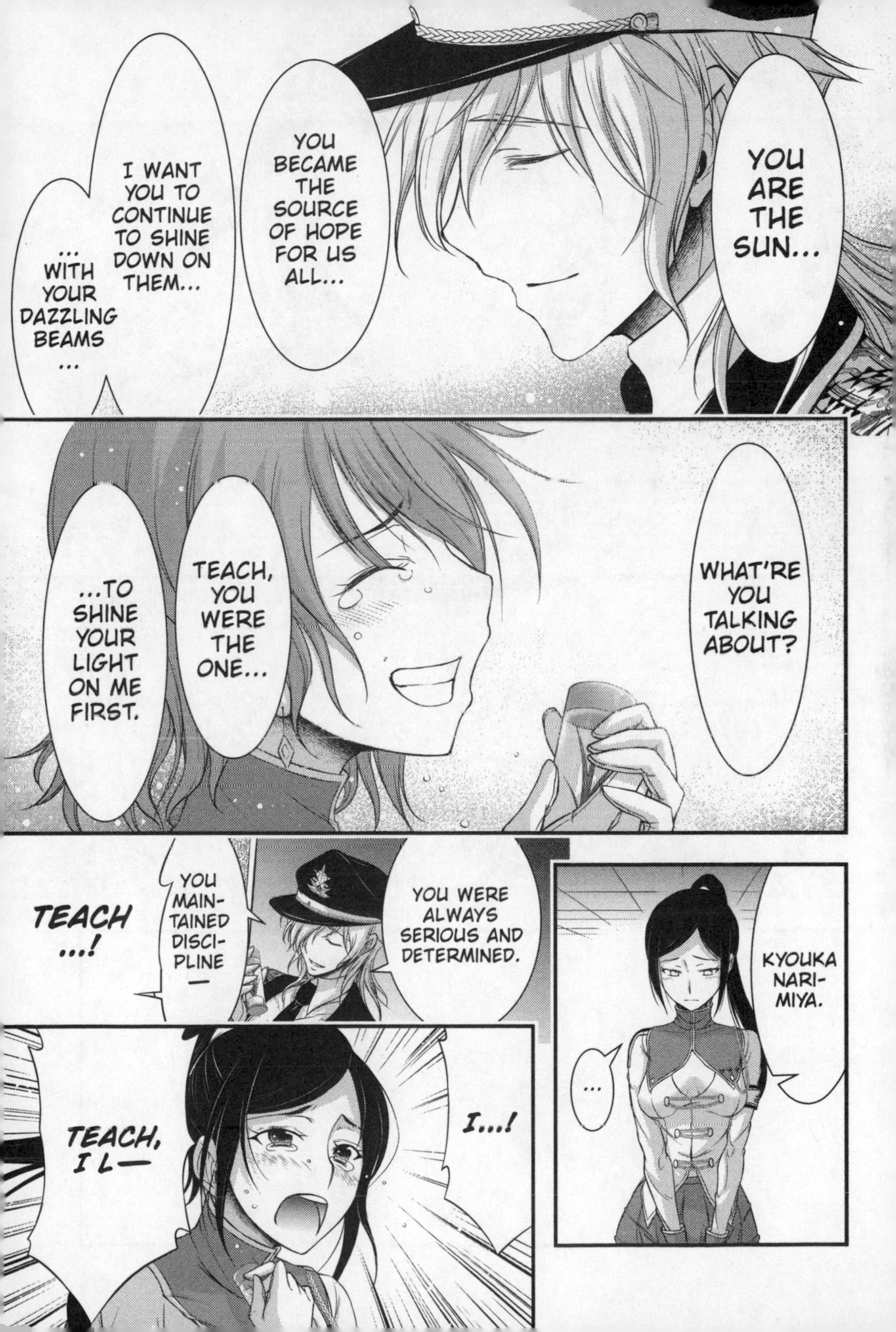
YOU ARE THE SUN...
YOU BECAME THE SOURCE OF HOPE FOR US ALL...
I WANT YOU TO CONTINUE TO SHINE DOWN ON THEM...
...WITH YOUR DAZZLING BEAMS...
WHAT'RE YOU TALKING ABOUT?
TEACH, YOU WERE THE ONE...
...TO SHINE YOUR LIGHT ON ME FIRST.
KYOUKA NARI-MIYA.
...
YOU WERE ALWAYS SERIOUS AND DETERMINED.
YOU MAIN-TAINED DISCI-PLINE—
TEACH...!
I...!
TEACH, I L—

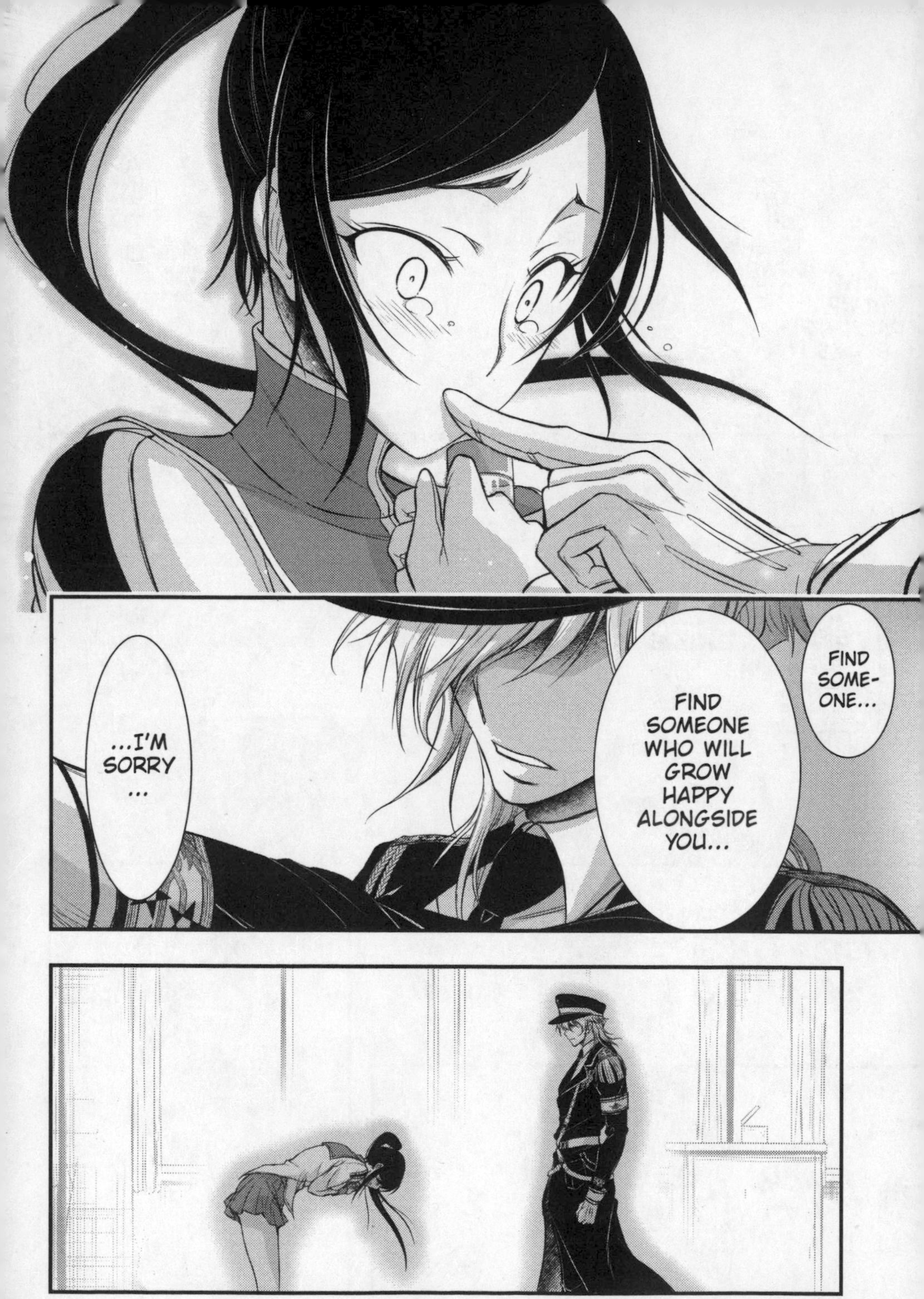
FIND SOME-ONE...
FIND SOMEONE WHO WILL GROW HAPPY ALONGSIDE YOU...
...I'M SORRY ...

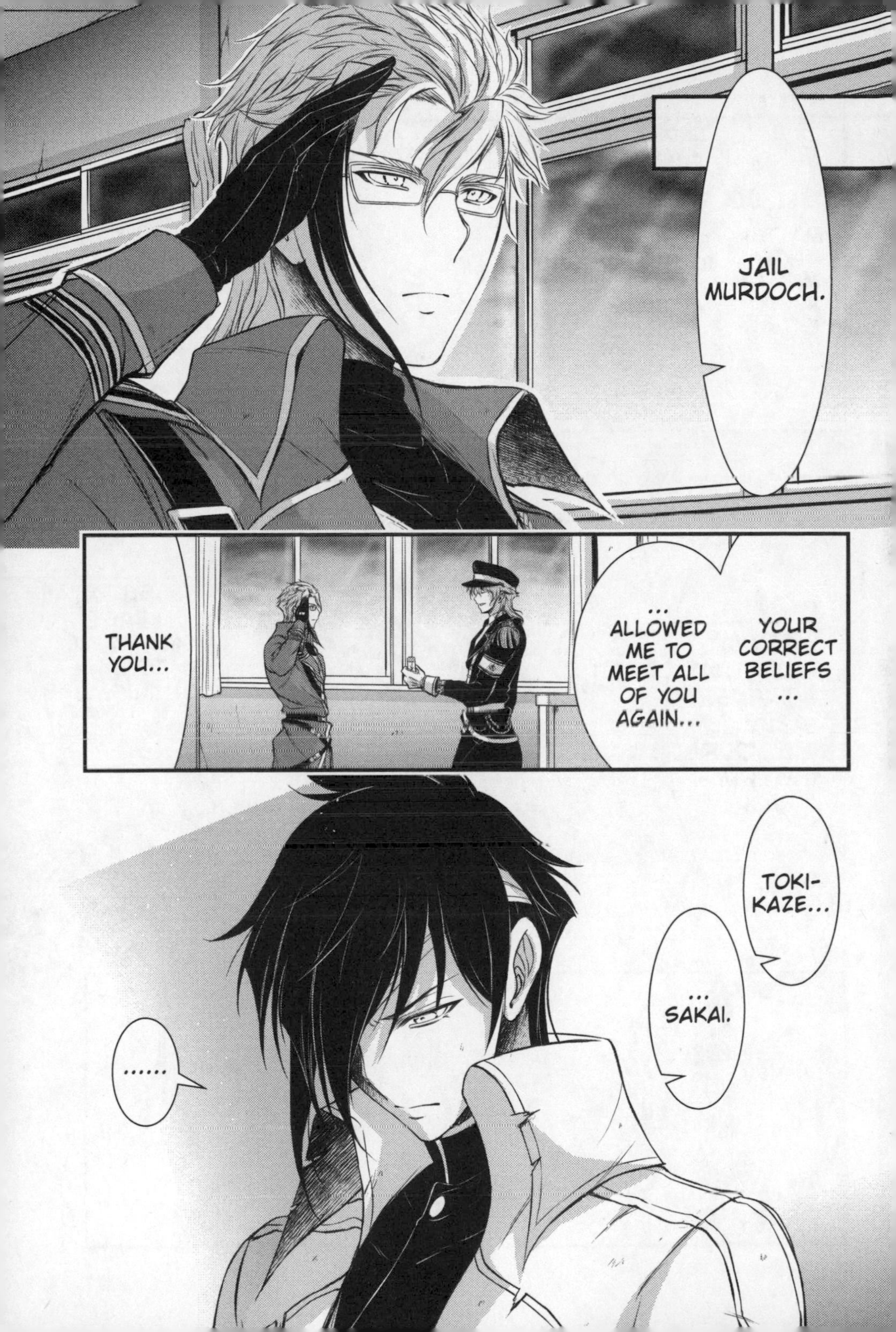
JAIL MURDOCH.
YOUR CORRECT BELIEFS ...
... ALLOWED ME TO MEET ALL OF YOU AGAIN...
THANK YOU...
TOKI-KAZE...
... SAKAI.
......

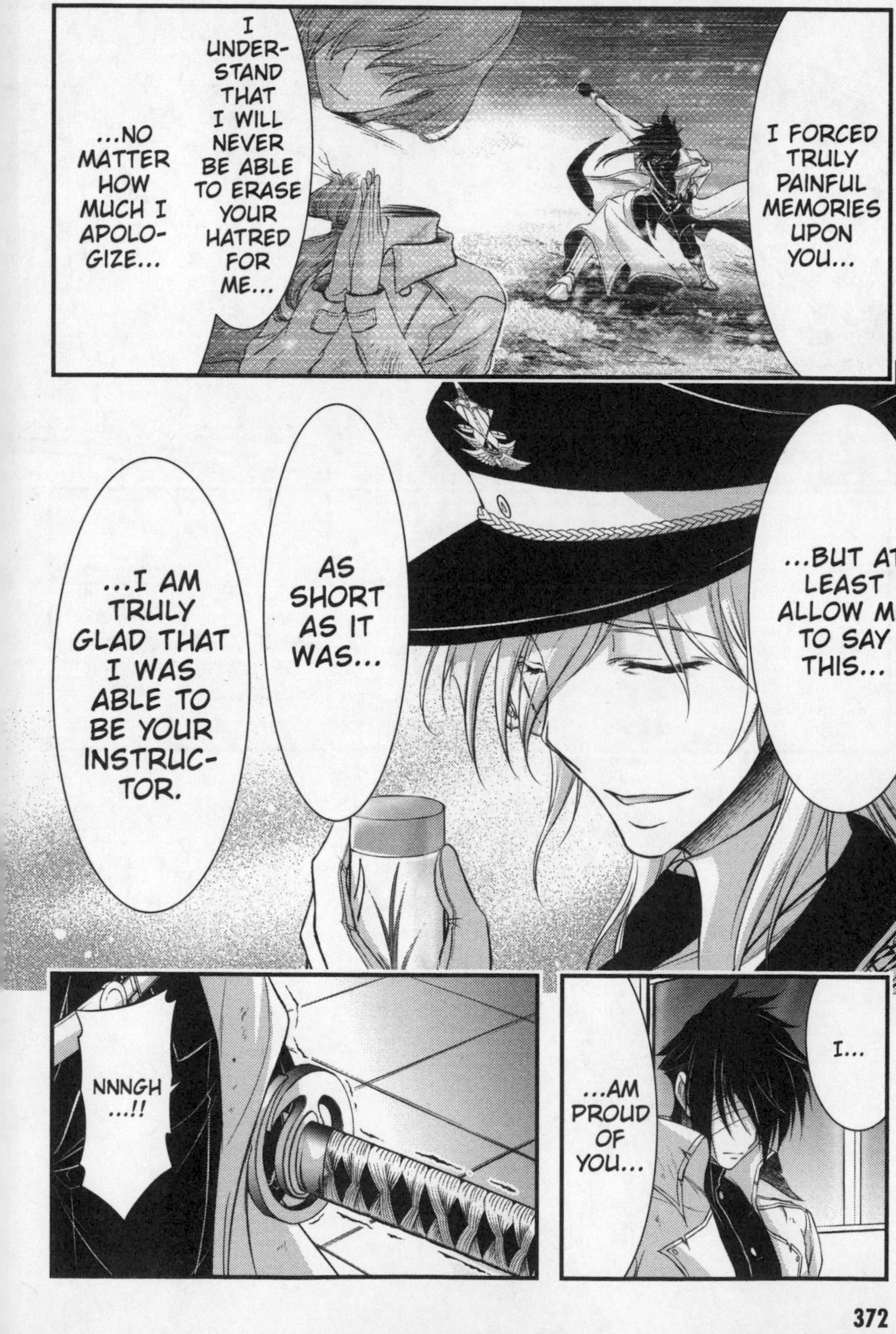
I FORCED TRULY PAINFUL MEMORIES UPON YOU...
I UNDER-STAND THAT I WILL NEVER BE ABLE TO ERASE YOUR HATRED FOR ME...
...NO MATTER HOW MUCH I APOLO-GIZE...
...BUT AT LEAST ALLOW ME TO SAY THIS...
AS SHORT AS IT WAS...
...I AM TRULY GLAD THAT I WAS ABLE TO BE YOUR INSTRUC-TOR.
I...
...AM PROUD OF YOU...
NNNGH ...!!

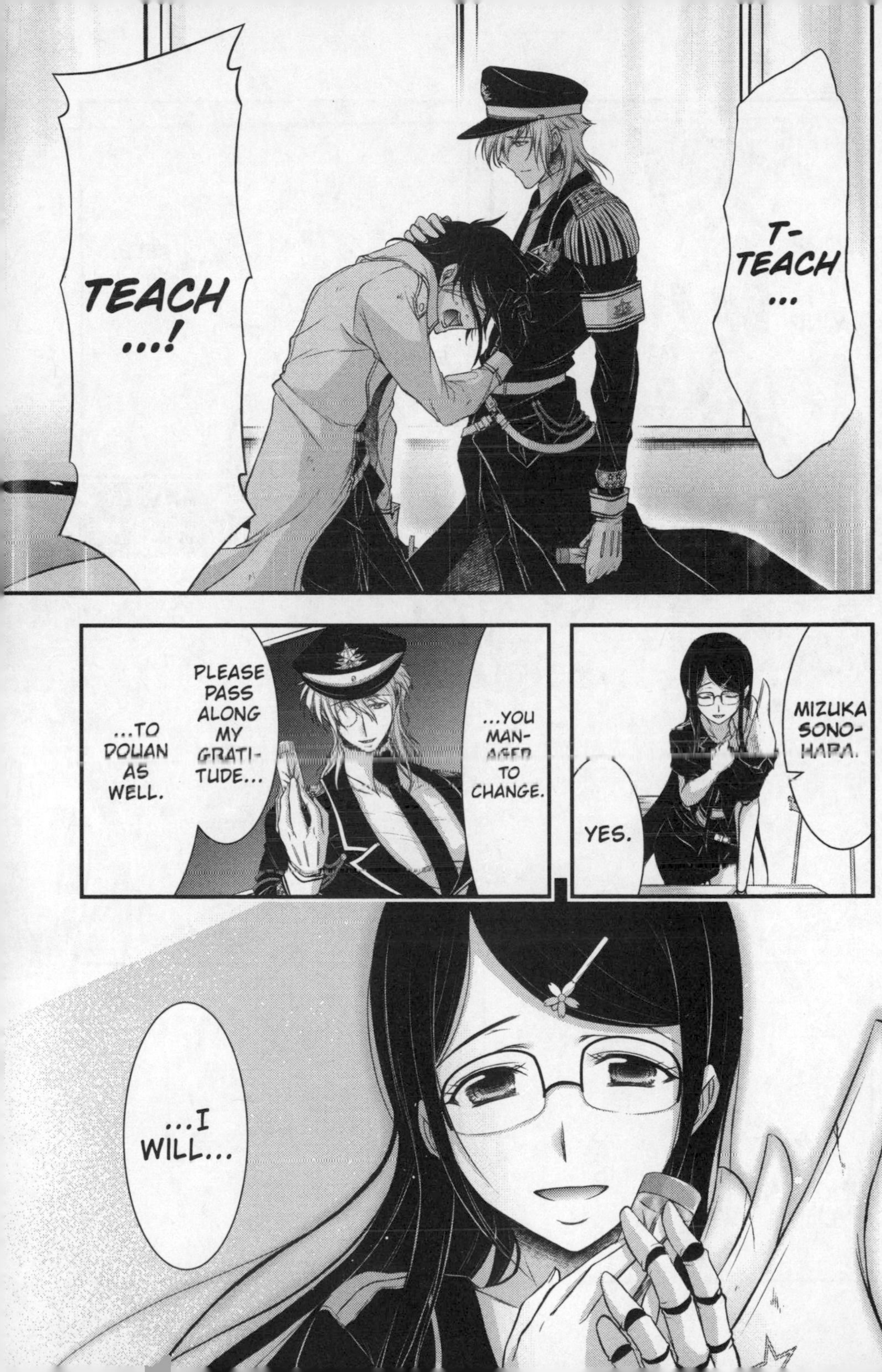
T-TEACH...
TEACH...!
MIZUKA SONOHARA.
YES.
...YOU MANAGED TO CHANGE.
PLEASE PASS ALONG MY GRATITUDE...
...TO DOUAN AS WELL.
...I WILL...

COME. READ MY MIND...

I'M SORRY, BUT... I HAVE ONE FINAL REQUEST FOR YOU.

PELE... POPOLO.

SUP.

YES...

I'M COUNTING ON YOU...

FOR REAL...?

BOSO (WHISPER)

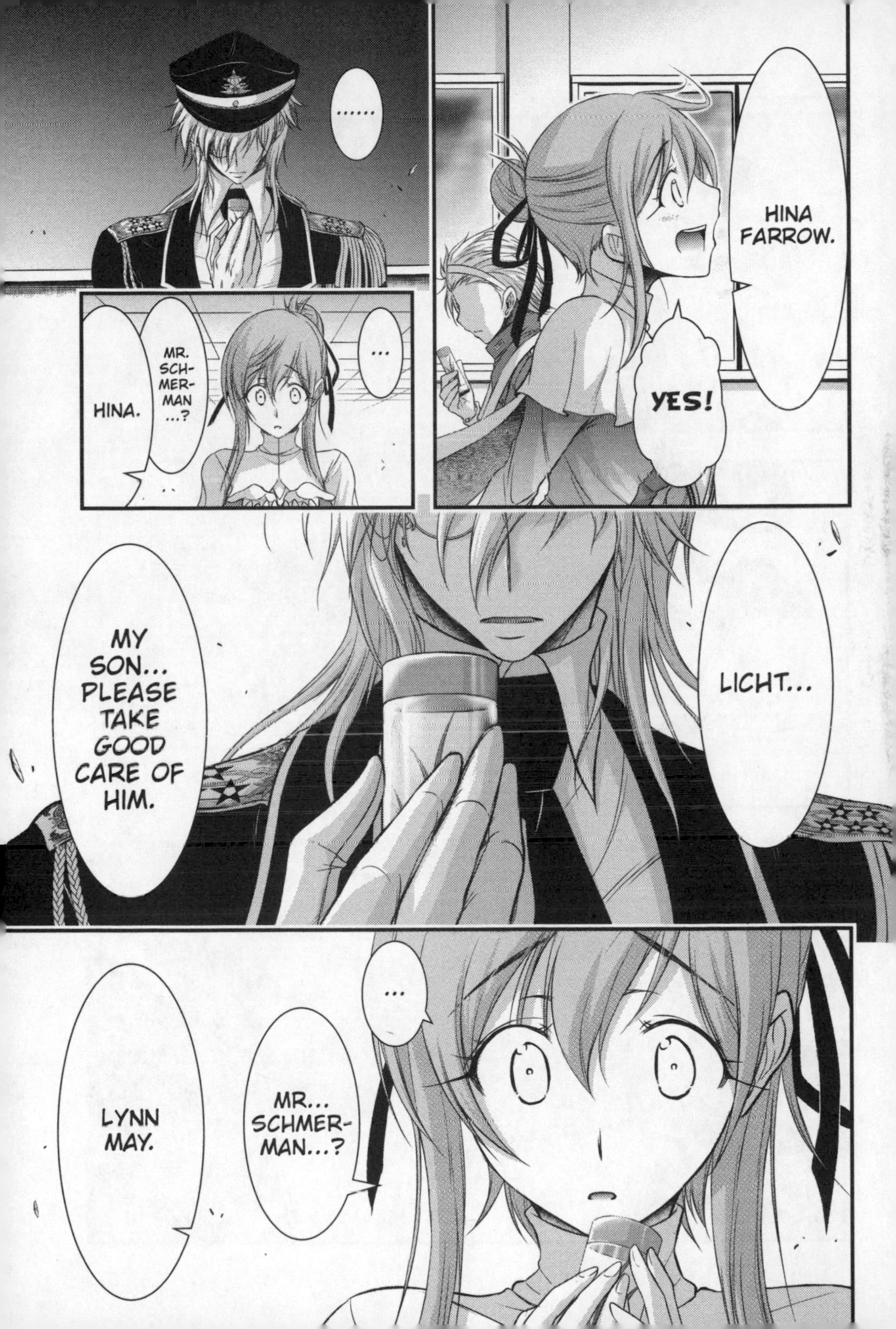
HINA FARROW.
YES!
......
...
MR. SCHMER-MAN...?
HINA.
LICHT...
MY SON... PLEASE TAKE GOOD CARE OF HIM.
...
MR... SCHMER-MAN...?
LYNN MAY.

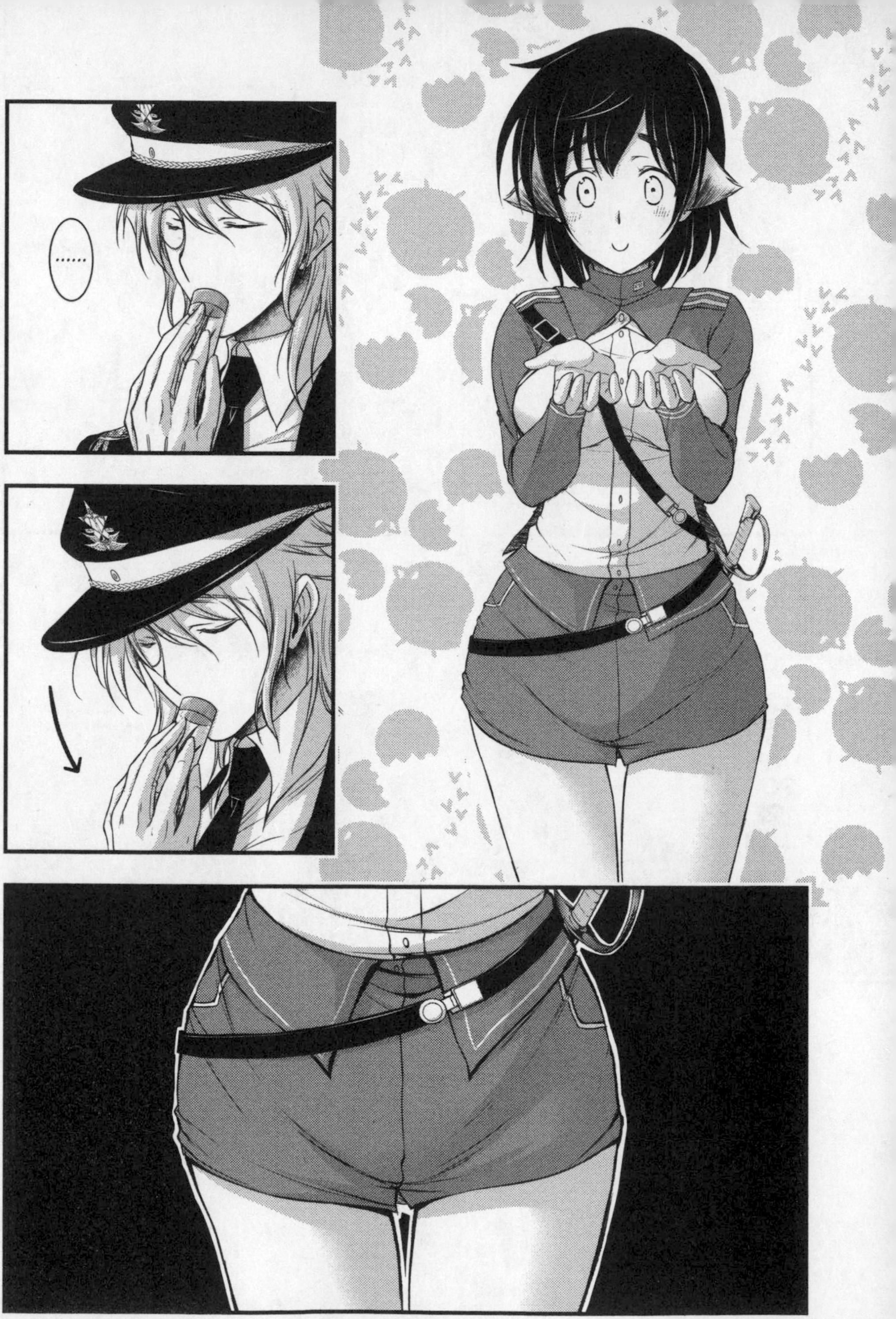
……

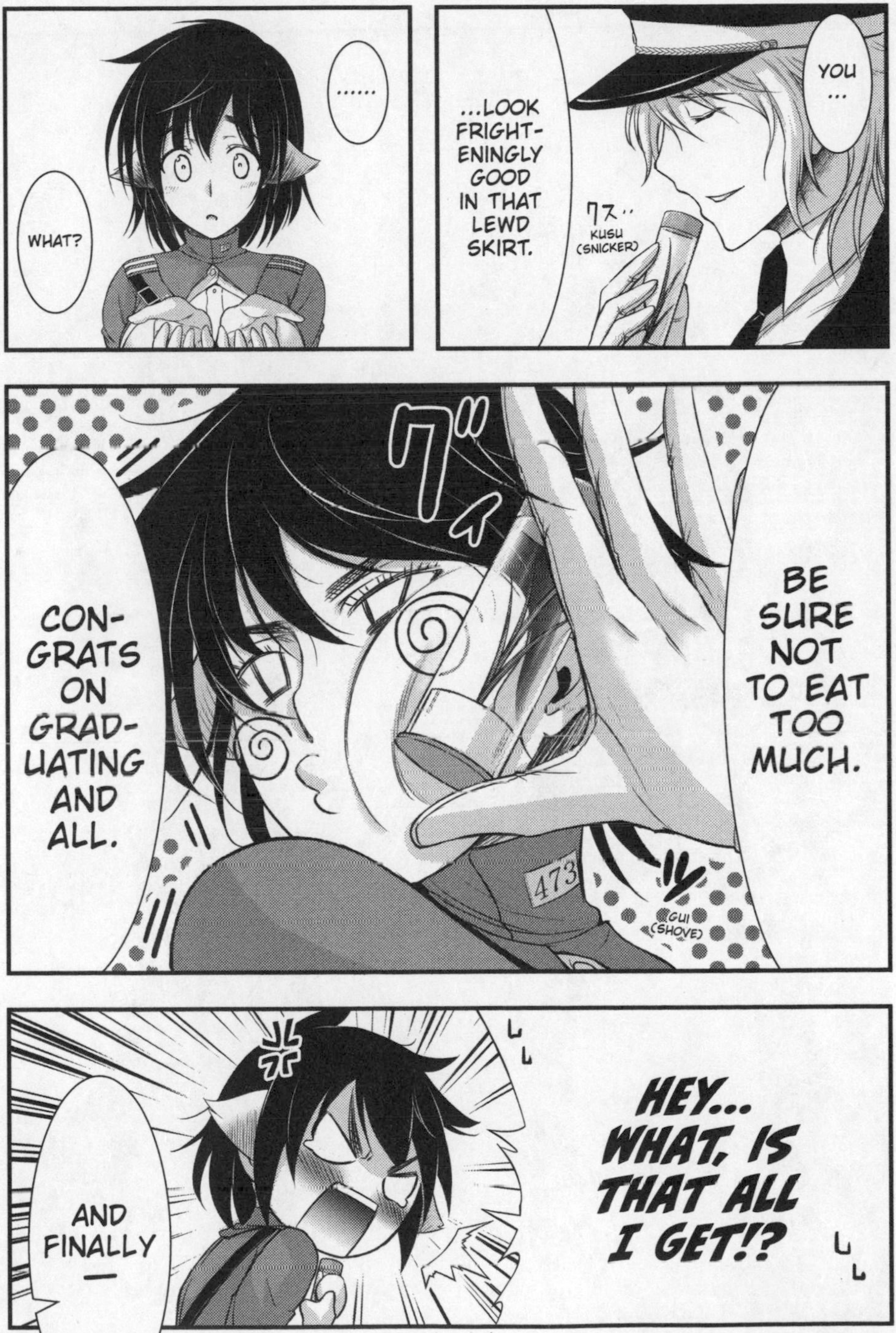
YOU ...
...LOOK FRIGHT-ENINGLY GOOD IN THAT LEWD SKIRT.
クス‥
KUSU (SNICKER)
......
WHAT?
BE SURE NOT TO EAT TOO MUCH.
CON-GRATS ON GRAD-UATING AND ALL.
473
GUI (SHOVE)
HEY... WHAT, IS THAT ALL I GET!?
AND FINALLY —

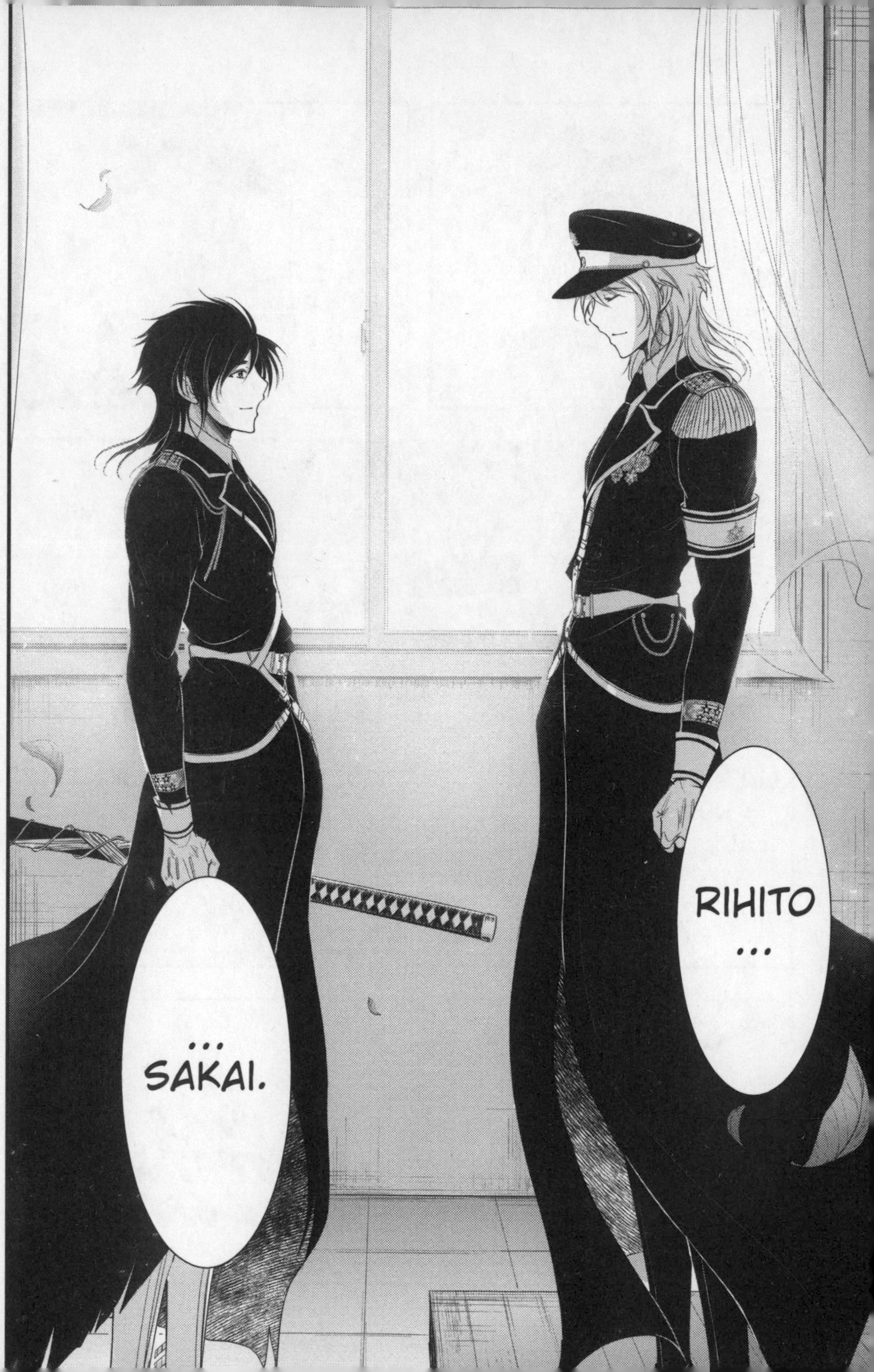
RIHITO ...
... SAKAI.

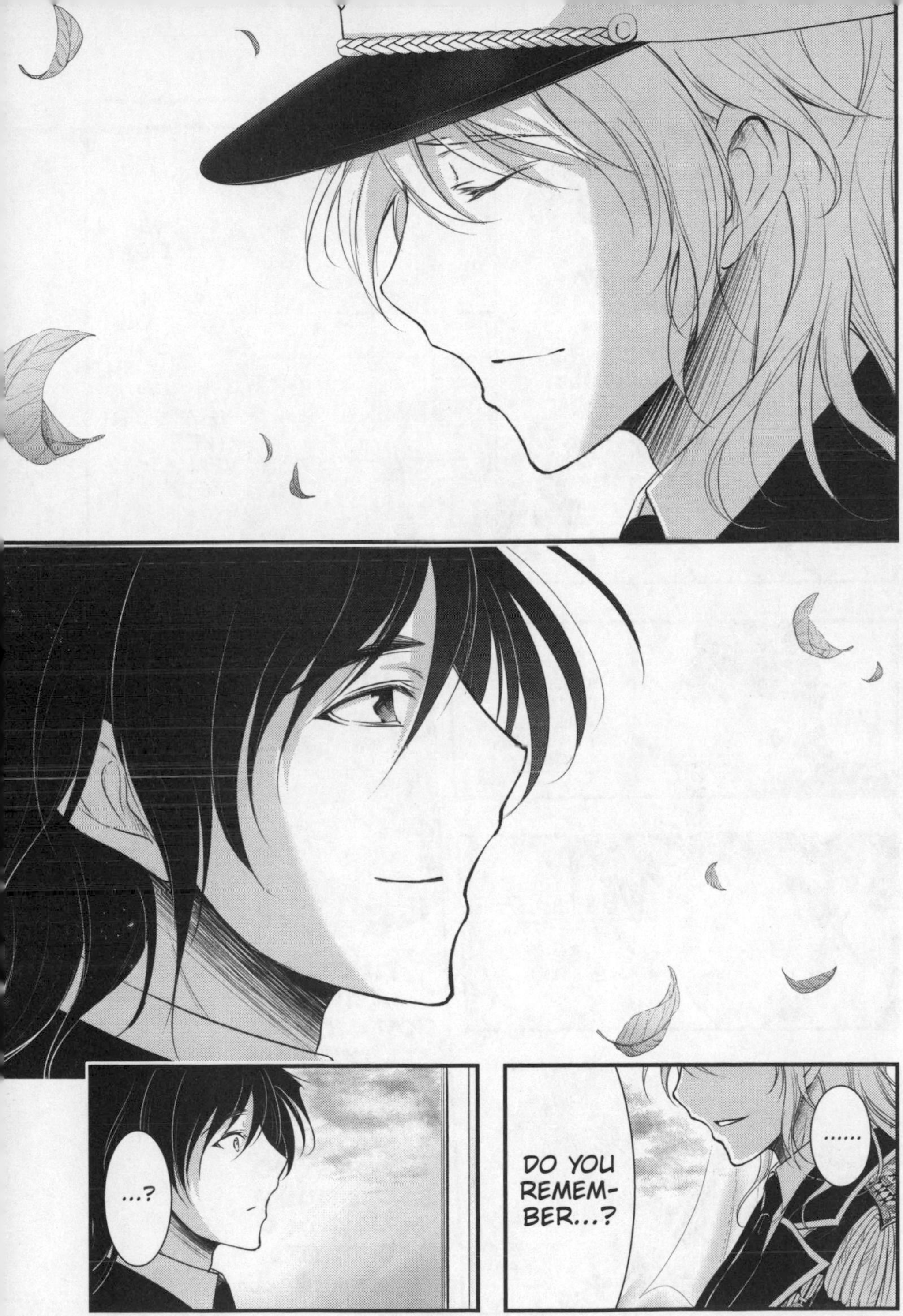
......
DO YOU REMEMBER...?
...?

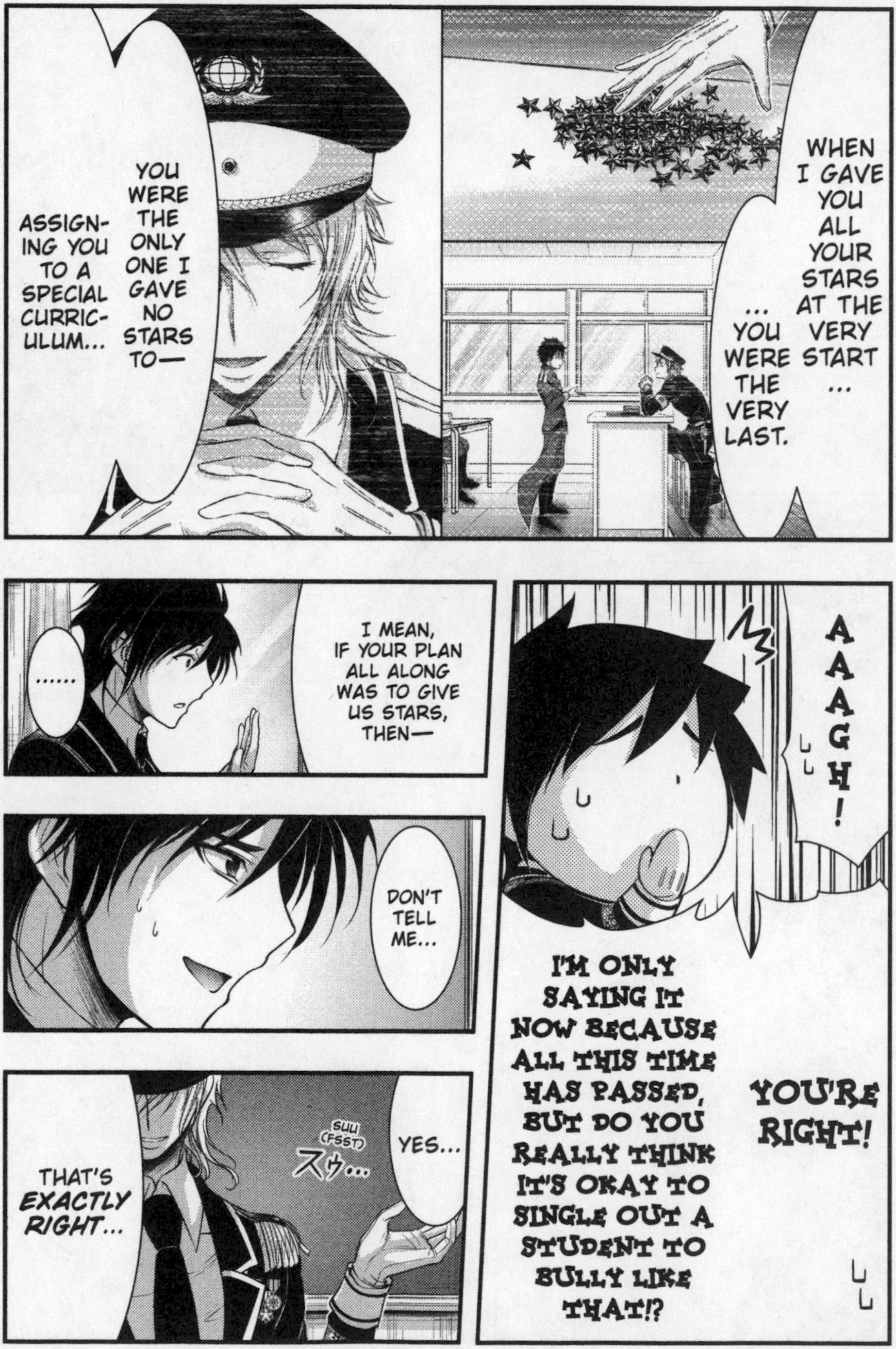
WHEN I GAVE YOU ALL YOUR STARS AT THE VERY START...
...YOU WERE THE VERY LAST.
YOU WERE THE ONLY ONE I GAVE NO STARS TO—
ASSIGNING YOU TO A SPECIAL CURRICULUM...
AAAAGH!
YOU'RE RIGHT!
I'M ONLY SAYING IT NOW BECAUSE ALL THIS TIME HAS PASSED, BUT DO YOU REALLY THINK IT'S OKAY TO SINGLE OUT A STUDENT TO BULLY LIKE THAT!?
I MEAN, IF YOUR PLAN ALL ALONG WAS TO GIVE US STARS, THEN—
......
DON'T TELL ME...
YES...
SUU (FSST)
スウ...
THAT'S EXACTLY RIGHT...

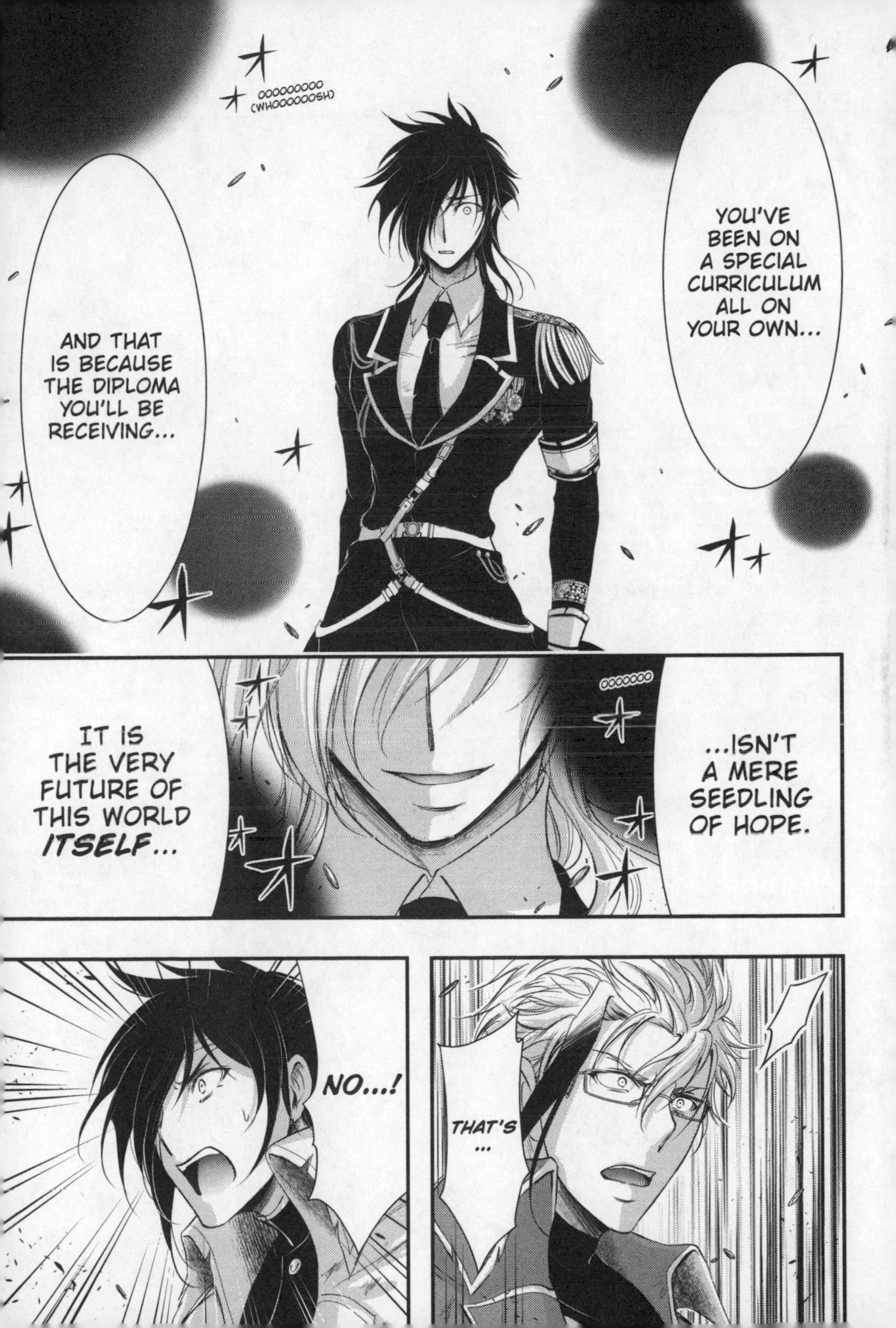
OOOOOOOOO
(WHOOOOOOSH)
YOU'VE BEEN ON A SPECIAL CURRICULUM ALL ON YOUR OWN...
AND THAT IS BECAUSE THE DIPLOMA YOU'LL BE RECEIVING...
OOOOOOO
...ISN'T A MERE SEEDLING OF HOPE.
IT IS THE VERY FUTURE OF THIS WORLD *ITSELF*...
THAT'S ...
NO...!

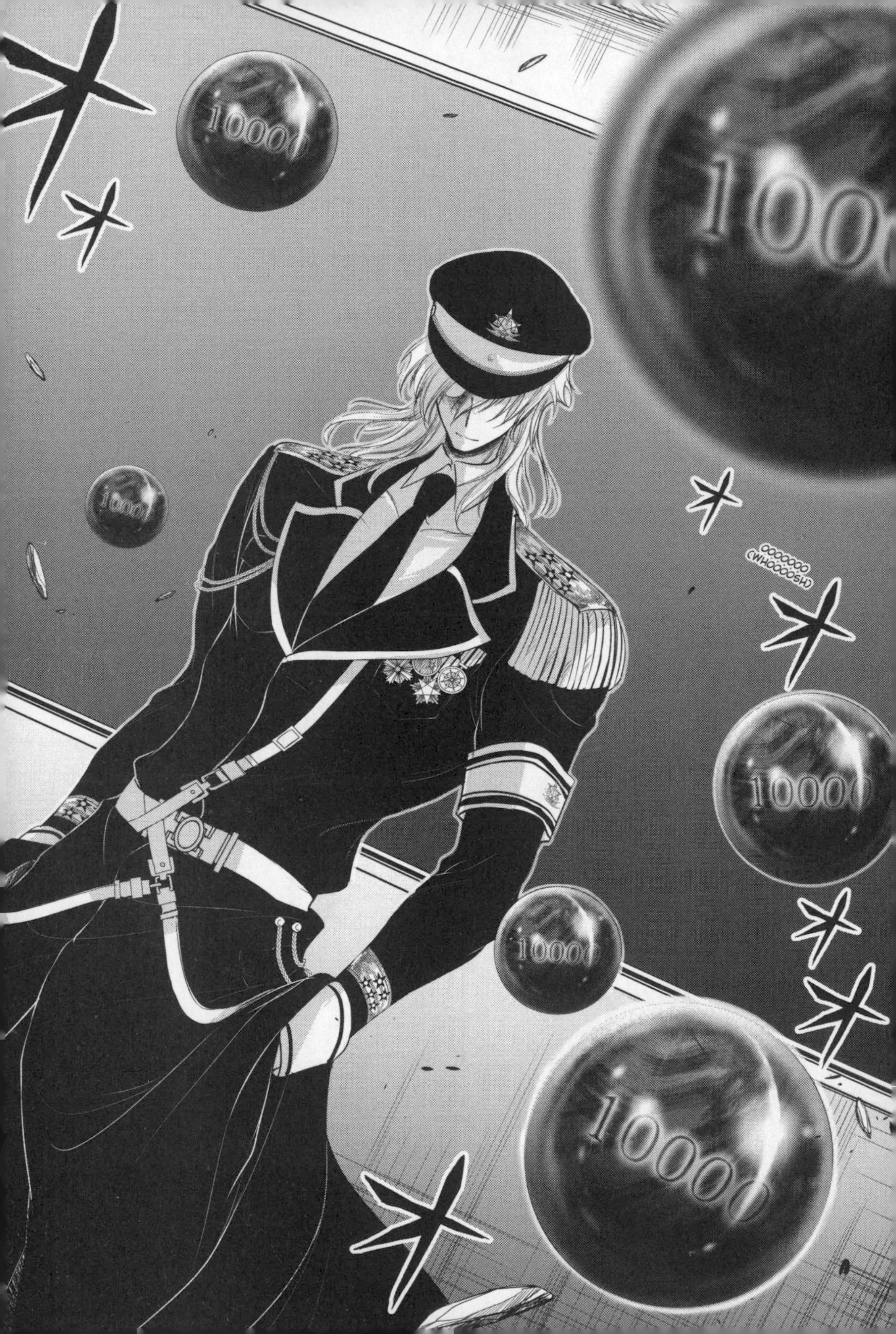
OOOOOOO
(WHOOOOSH)

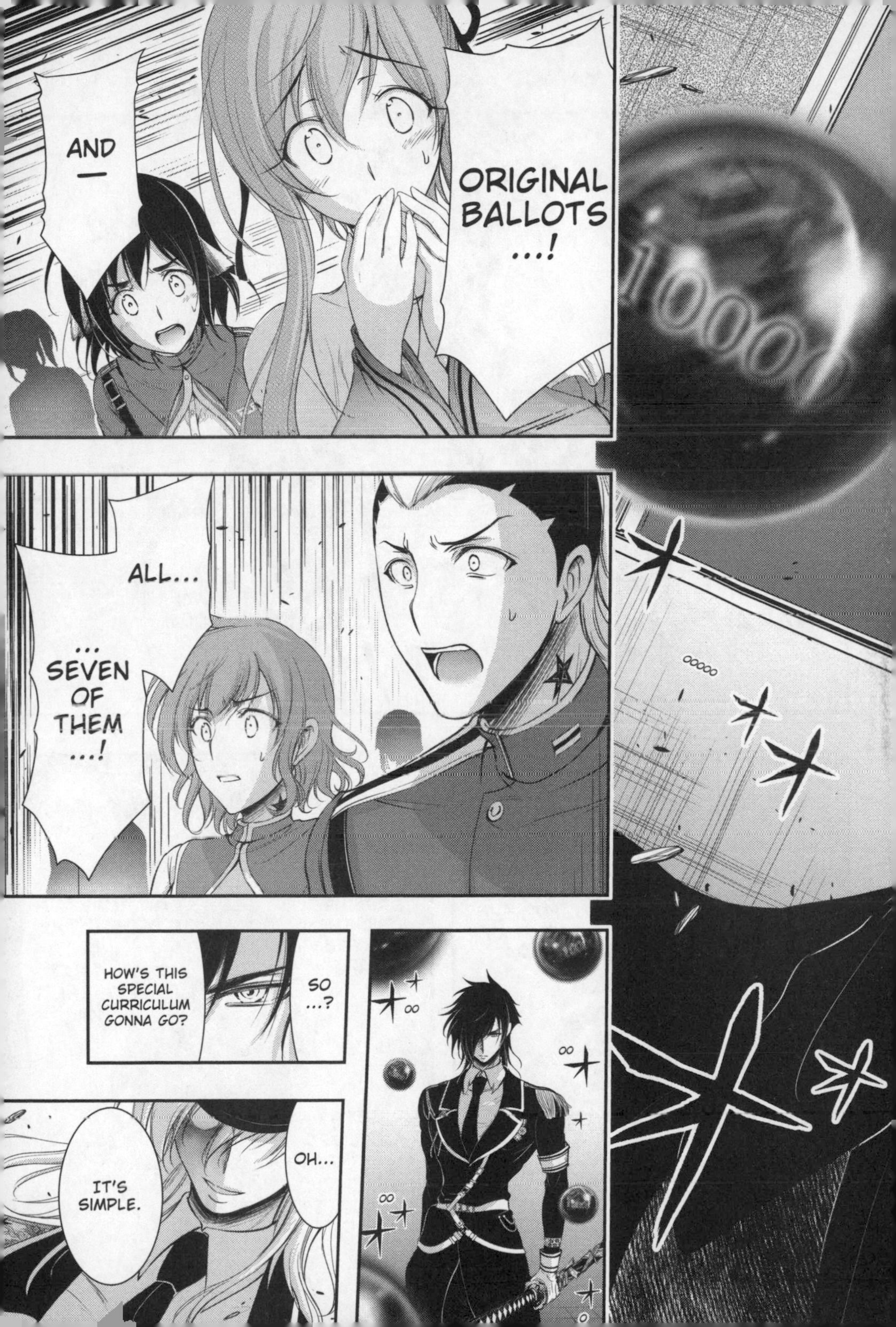
ORIGINAL BALLOTS ...!
AND —
ALL...
... SEVEN OF THEM ...!
SO ...?
HOW'S THIS SPECIAL CURRICULUM GONNA GO?
OH...
IT'S SIMPLE.

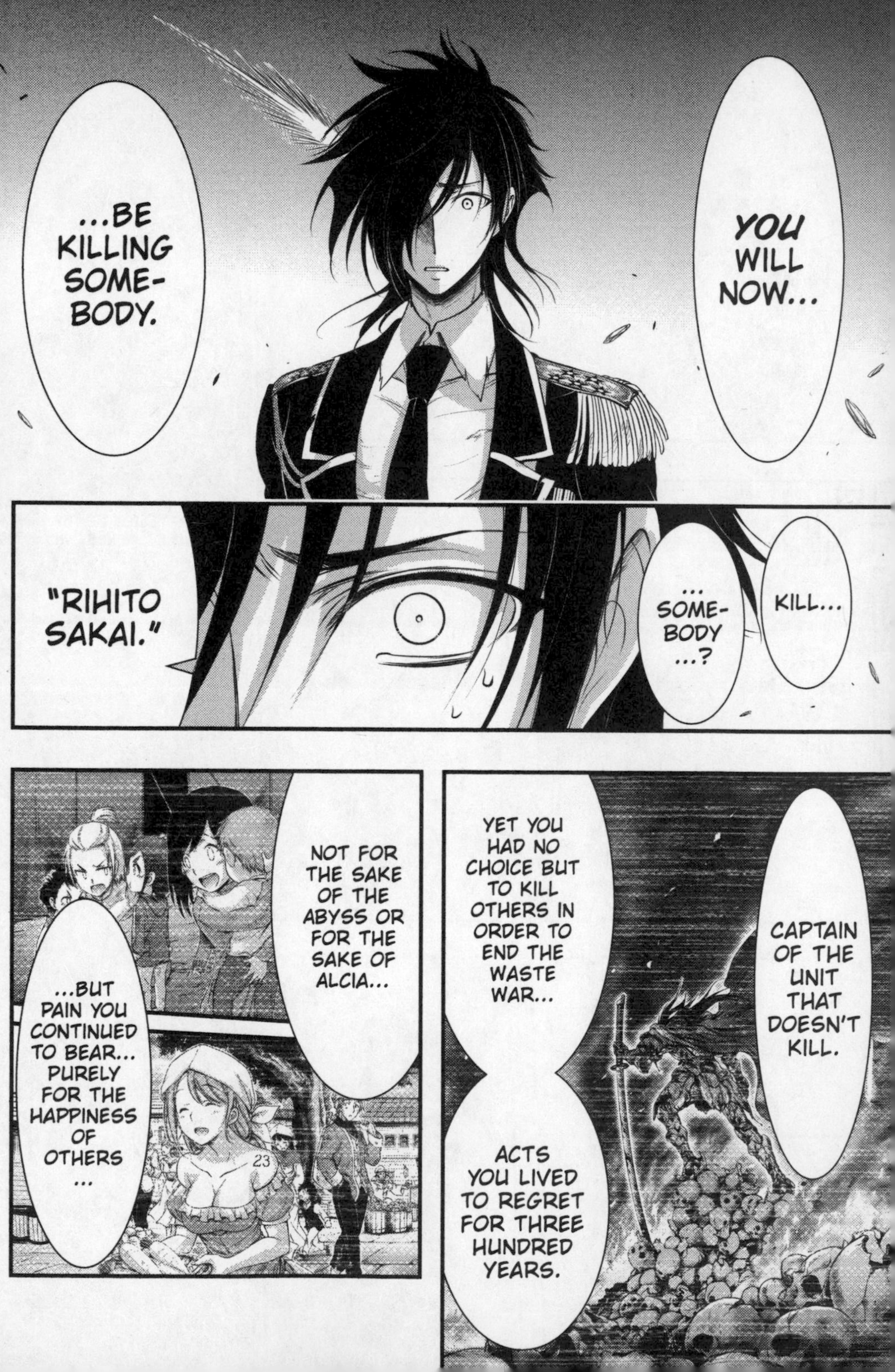
YOU WILL NOW...
...BE KILLING SOMEBODY.
KILL...
...SOMEBODY...?
"RIHITO SAKAI."
CAPTAIN OF THE UNIT THAT DOESN'T KILL.
YET YOU HAD NO CHOICE BUT TO KILL OTHERS IN ORDER TO END THE WASTE WAR...
ACTS YOU LIVED TO REGRET FOR THREE HUNDRED YEARS.
NOT FOR THE SAKE OF THE ABYSS OR FOR THE SAKE OF ALCIA...
...BUT PAIN YOU CONTINUED TO BEAR... PURELY FOR THE HAPPINESS OF OTHERS...

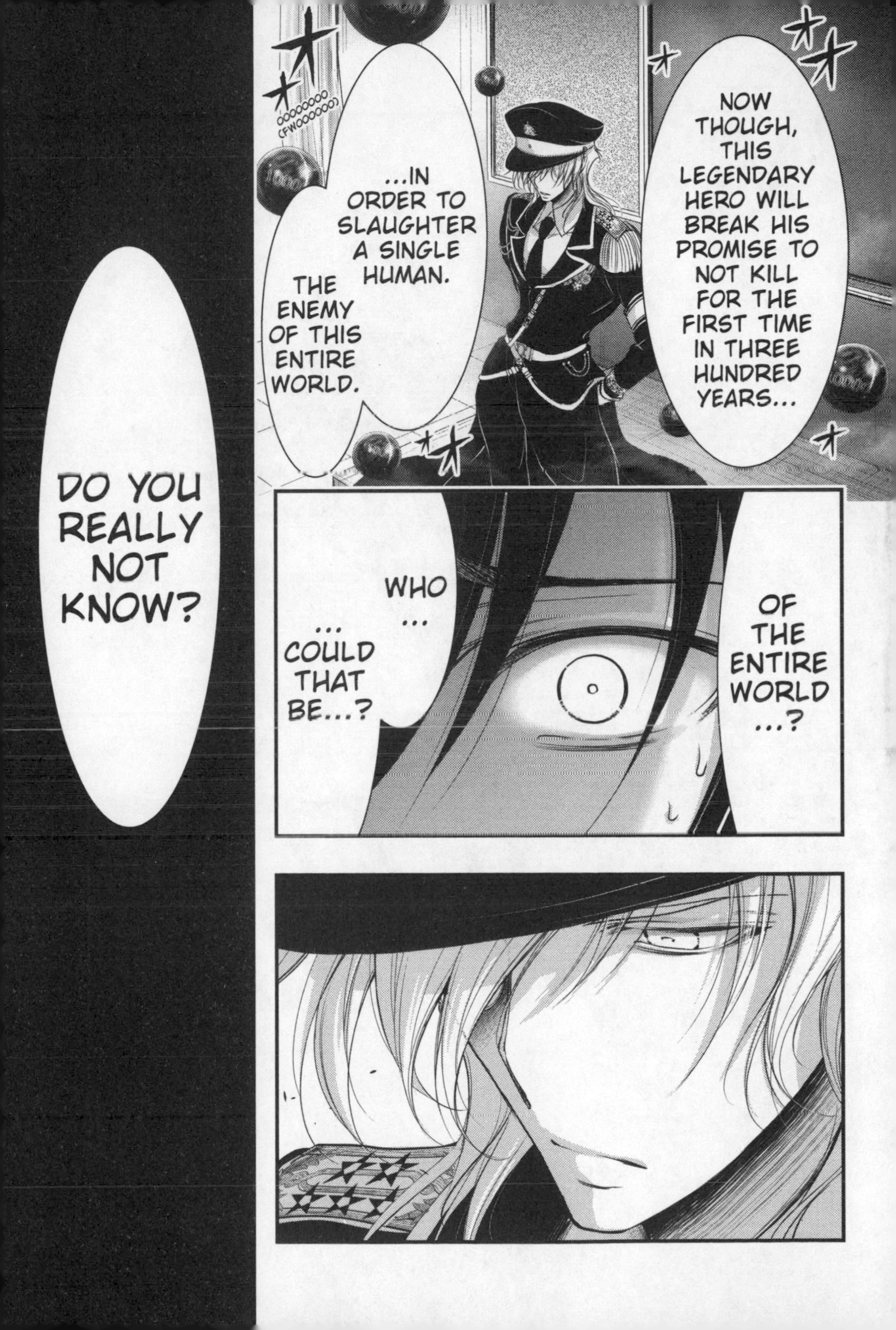
NOW THOUGH, THIS LEGENDARY HERO WILL BREAK HIS PROMISE TO NOT KILL FOR THE FIRST TIME IN THREE HUNDRED YEARS...
...IN ORDER TO SLAUGHTER A SINGLE HUMAN.
THE ENEMY OF THIS ENTIRE WORLD.
(FWOOOOOOO)
OF THE ENTIRE WORLD ...?
WHO ... ... COULD THAT BE...?
DO YOU REALLY NOT KNOW?

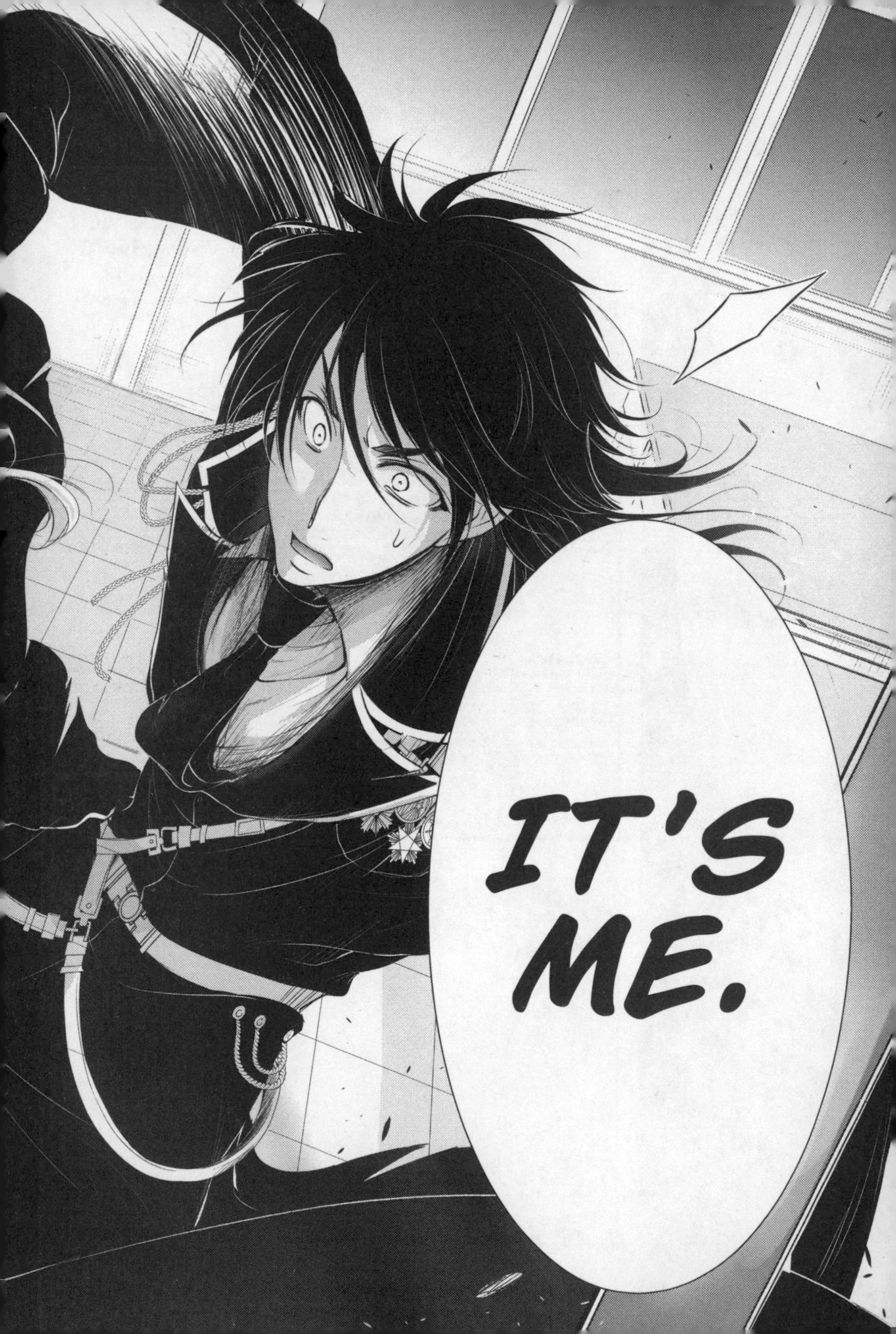
IT'S ME.

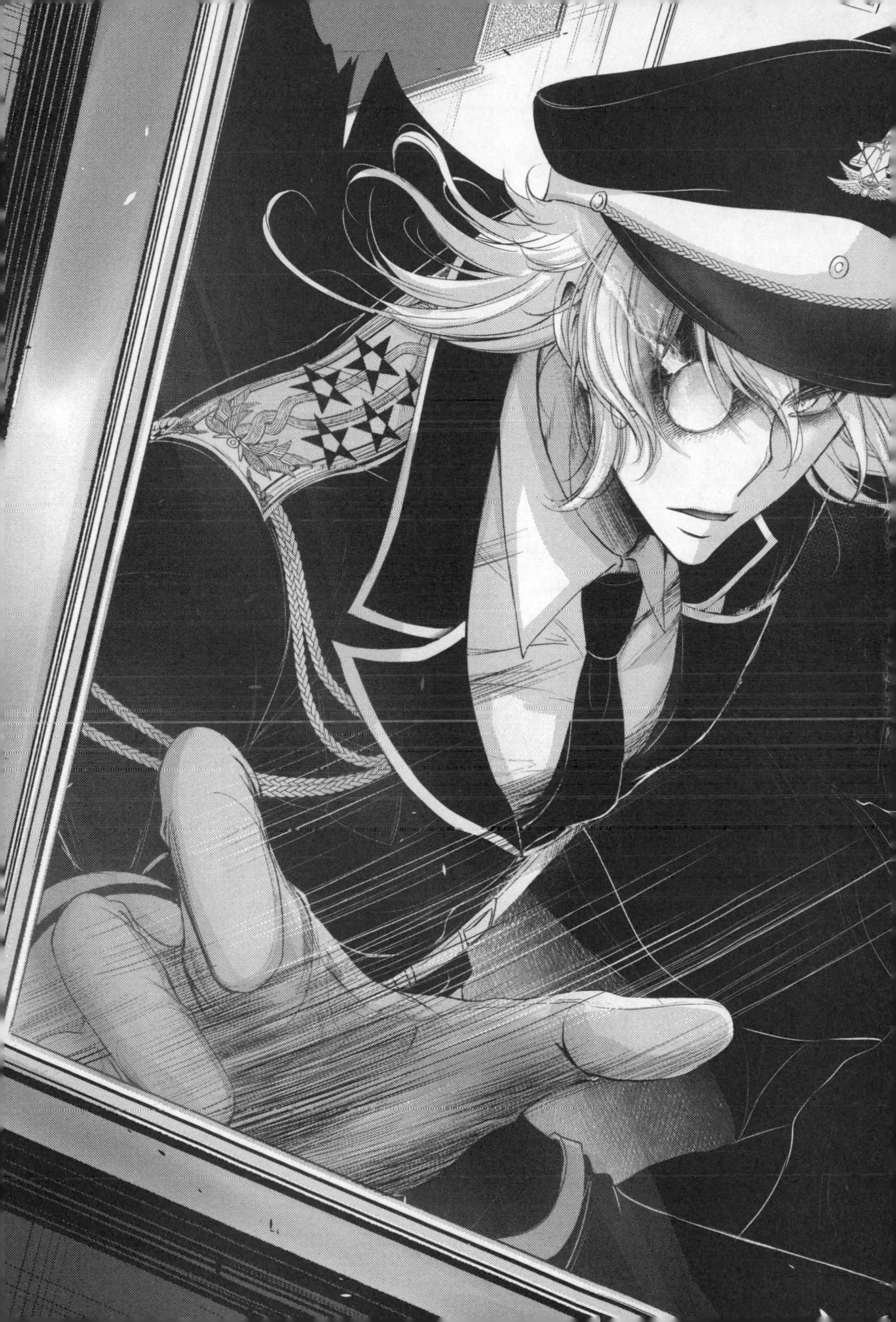

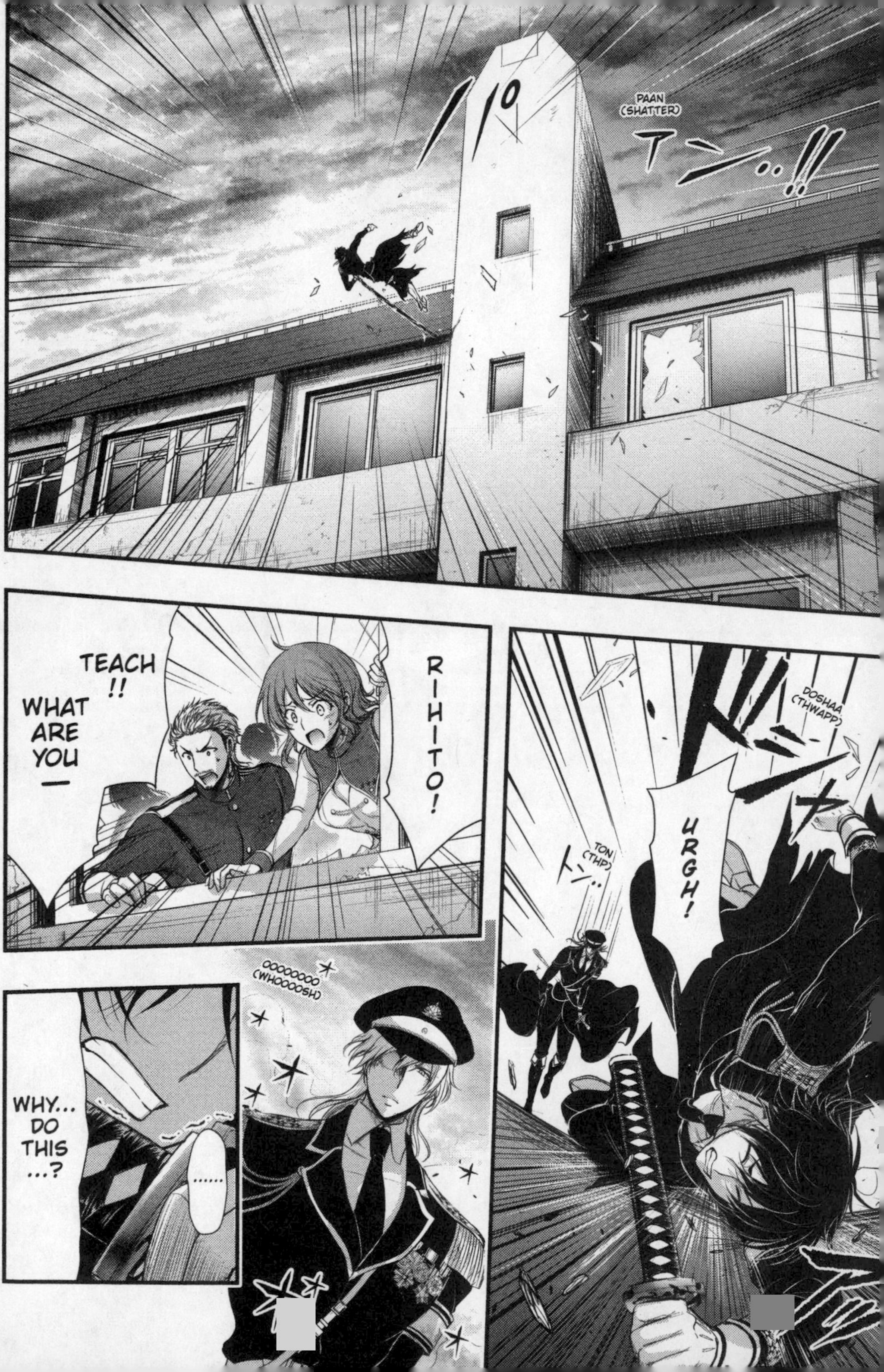
PAAN (SHATTER)
DOSHAA (THWAPP)
TON (THP)
URGH!
TEACH!!
WHAT ARE YOU—
RIHITO!
OOOOOOOO (WHOOOOSH)
WHY... DO THIS...?
......

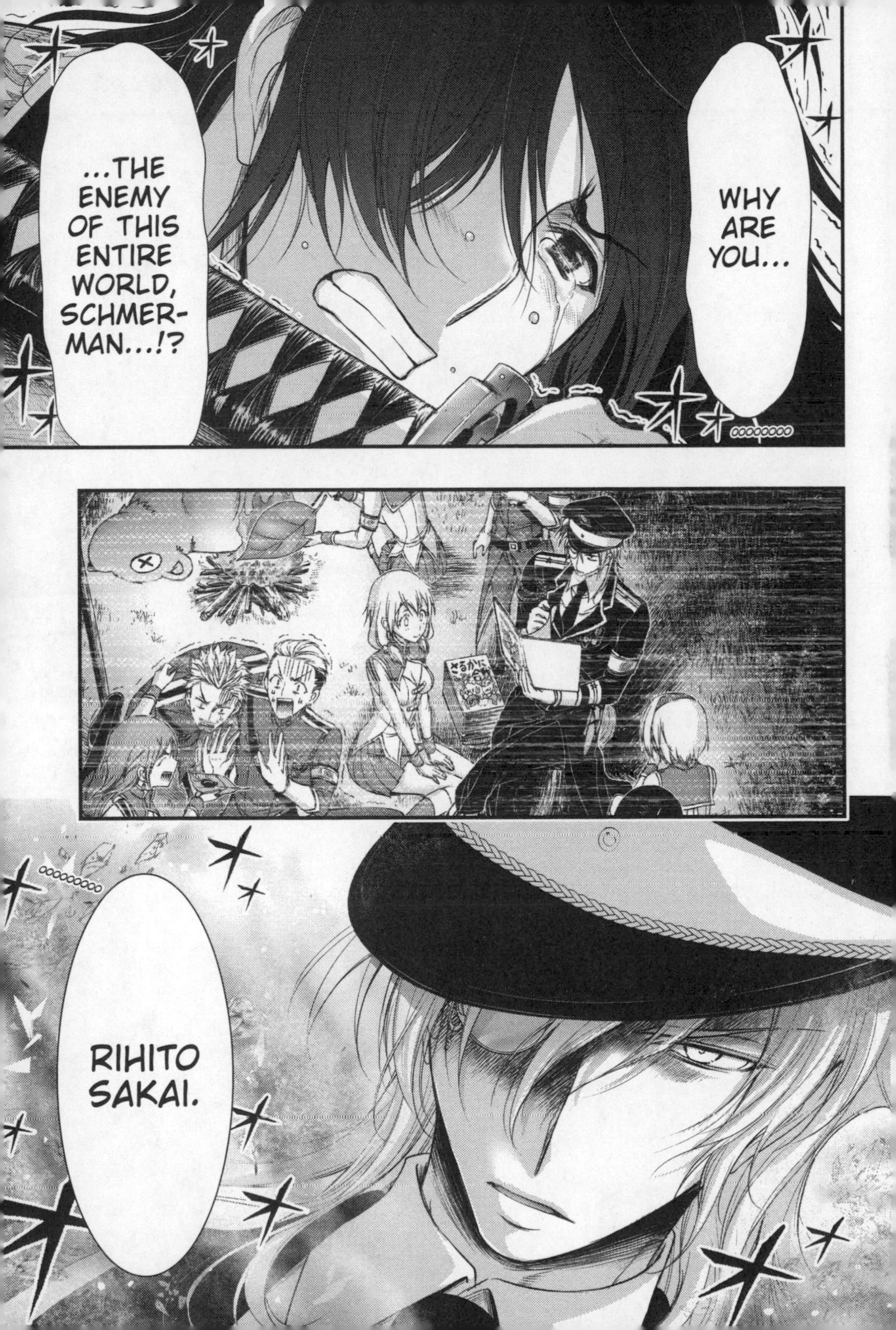
WHY ARE YOU...
...THE ENEMY OF THIS ENTIRE WORLD, SCHMER-MAN...!?
RIHITO SAKAI.

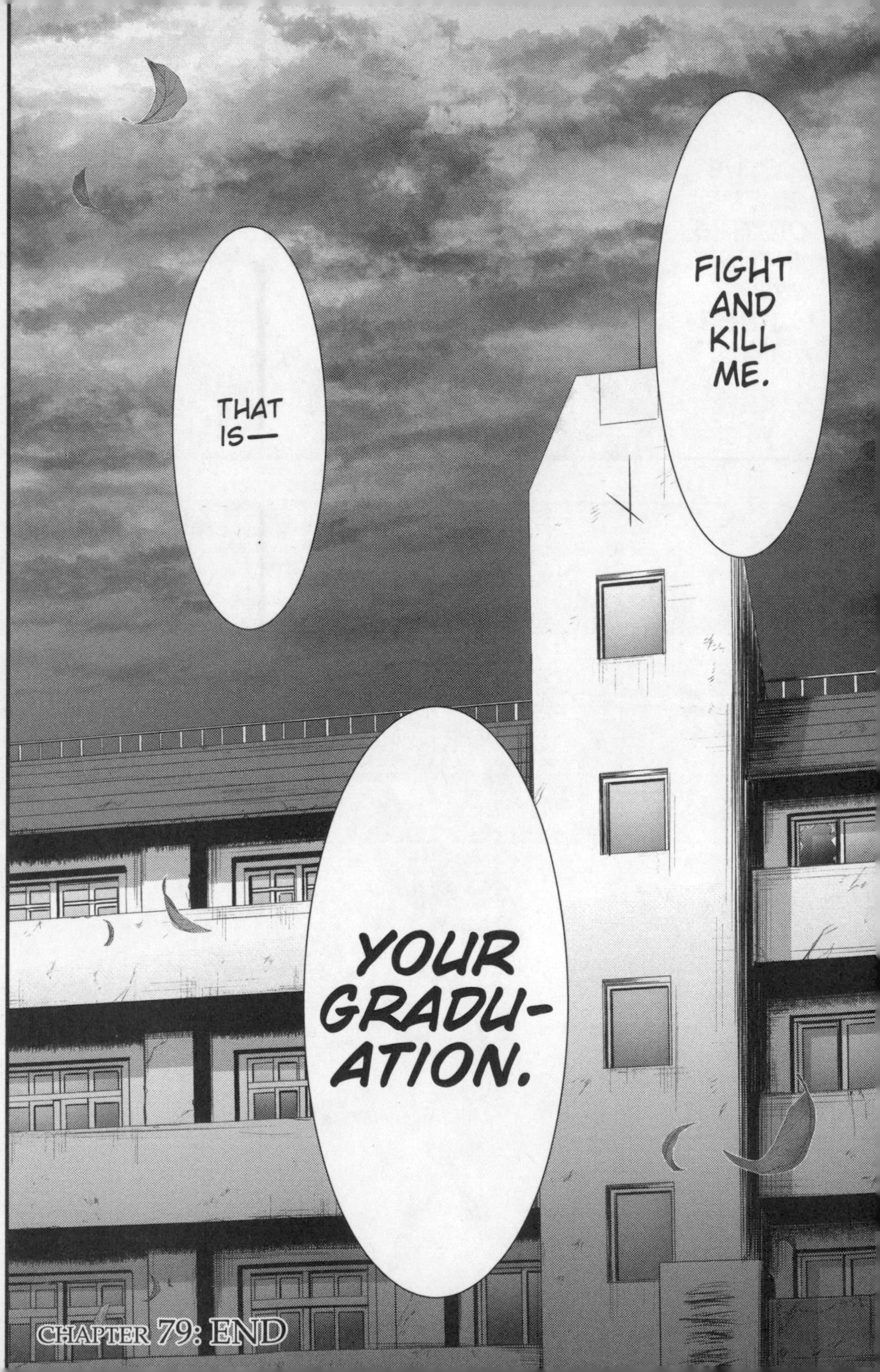
FIGHT AND KILL ME.
THAT IS—
YOUR GRADU-ATION.
CHAPTER 79: END

NEXT VOLUME PREVIEW

The
final
fight
to the
death.

Plunderer, Volume 11
Coming Soon!

SUU MINAZUKI

Vol.

10

Translation: Ko Ransom   Lettering: DK

PLUNDERER Volumes 19, 20
©Suu Minazuki 2021, 2022
First published in Japan in 2021, 2022 by KADOKAWA CORPORATION, Tokyo.
English translation rights arranged with KADOKAWA CORPORATION, Tokyo through TUTTLE-MORI AGENCY, INC., Tokyo.

English translation © 2022 by Yen Press, LLC

Yen Press
150 West 30th Street, 19th Floor
New York, NY 10001

Visit us at yenpress.com
facebook.com/yenpress
twitter.com/yenpress
yenpress.tumblr.com
instagram.com/yenpress

First Yen Press Edition: December 2022
Edited by Yen Press Editorial: Mark Gallucci, Thomas McAlister
Designed by Yen Press Design: Jane Sohn, Andy Swist

Yen Press is an imprint of Yen Press, LLC.
The Yen Press name and logo are trademarks of Yen Press, LLC.

Library of Congress Control Number: 2018964275

ISBNs: 978-1-9753-5119-9 (paperback)
       978-1-9753-5120-5 (ebook)

10 9 8 7 6 5 4 3 2 1

WOR

Printed in the United States of America